THE PAPERS OF
Andrew Johnson

Sponsored by
The University of Tennessee
The National Historical Publications and Records Commission
The National Endowment for the Humanities
The Tennessee Historical Commission

The New President: Andrew Johnson, May 1865
By John Wood Dodge
Courtesy Library of Congress

THE PAPERS OF
Andrew Johnson

Volume 8, May–August 1865

PAUL H. BERGERON
EDITOR

PATRICIA J. ANTHONY   RICHARD B. McCASLIN

PATRICIA P. CLARK   R. B. ROSENBURG

LeROY P. GRAF   MARION O. SMITH

THE EDITING STAFF

1989
THE UNIVERSITY OF TENNESSEE PRESS
KNOXVILLE

Library of Congress Cataloging-in-Publication Data
(Revised for vol. 8)

Johnson, Andrew, 1808–1875.
    The papers of Andrew Johnson.

    Vol. 8— edited by Paul H. Bergeron.
    Includes bibliographical references and index.
    Contents: v. 1. 1822–1851.—v. 2. 1852–1857.—
[etc]—v. 8. May–August 1865.
    1. Johnson, Andrew, 1808–1875—Archives. 2. Presi-
dents—United States—Archives. 3. United States—Politics and government—1849–1877. I. Graf, LeRoy P., ed.
II. Haskins, Ralph W., ed. III. Bergeron, Paul H.,
1938– . IV. Title.
E415.6.J65   1967   973.8′1′0924 [B]   67-25733

Library of Congress Cataloging-in-Publication Data
ISBN 0-87049-098-2 (v. 2)
[ISBN 0-87049-613-1 (v. 8)]

TO
Patricia P. Clark
In grateful appreciation
for nearly thirty years
of important service to the
Johnson Project

Contents

1865

Illustrations

Introduction

The frantic, loud knocks on Andrew Johnson's door at the Kirkwood House on the night of April 14, 1865 reverberated across the nation, north and south, and summoned him to the presidency. It was a sudden challenge for which he apparently had been preparing his entire political life, yet it was a challenge for which he seemed ill prepared, by reason of temperament, attitude and experience. As Johnson stumbled to respond to the pounding at his door that night of the Lincoln assassination, so he would stumble as he attempted to lead the nation through the demanding process of reconciliation and restoration.

Given the many obstacles that stood athwart the path of success, it is not easy to discern how Johnson could have succeeded. (Probably neither Lincoln nor his closest advisers had ever given thought to the remote likelihood that Johnson might be thrust into the presidency.) After all, he was both a life-long Democrat and a resident of a Confederate state. Moreover, Johnson was burdened by a narrow, harsh outlook on life and a kind of bullying attitude toward other persons—attributes rooted in his difficult youth. Of equal or more importance, however, Johnson had recently completed nearly three years as Lincoln's military governor of Tennessee, during which time he was the more or less undisputed "boss" of the state. Whatever earlier inclinations toward compromise and flexibility he might have possessed were lost or forgotten as he held sway in Tennessee.

Under normal circumstances a vice president could expect to have four years (or more) of training before aspiring to the presidency, but in Johnson's case he had only a scant six weeks. One could speculate whether Johnson might have developed special skills and abilities under Lincoln's tutelage over a span of some four years. But such was not to be; instead, the calamity of that April night brought an abrupt end to Johnson's apprenticeship.

Whereas hindsight judgment has provided much of the harsher assessment of Johnson's tenure as president, his contemporaries had high expectations for him in 1865 (despite the unfortunate vice-presidential swearing-in ceremony in March). Indeed the early weeks and months of his presidential administration were marked by success. Undeniably the greatest advantage which he enjoyed was that Congress was not in session and would not convene until December. Johnson was therefore virtually free to fashion his own reconstruction program without serious challenge from other political leaders; and in fact that is precisely what he did. These months constitute what one historian has aptly

labelled the time of executive hegemony.[1] Not troubled by Congressmen looking over his shoulder or attacking him in the halls of the national legislature, the new President set his hand to the task of restoring
his native South to the Union. Ironically it was similar to the challenge
he had dealt with, albeit on a much smaller scale, as he attempted—
without success—for nearly three years to bring Tennessee back into
the Union.

But before he could set in motion his own reconstruction agenda,
Johnson first had to act upon the demands of a victorious North which
insisted upon the arrest and imprisonment of the principal Confederate
leaders and the trial and execution of Lincoln's assassins. Not surprisingly then on May 1 and May 2 Johnson addressed these concerns in
an executive order and a presidential proclamation.[2] Shortly thereafter,
Jefferson Davis was captured in Georgia and transported to federal
prison. Concurrently the military trial of the accused Lincoln conspirators began; it concluded at the end of June with convictions of all eight
but with varying sentences for them. Johnson reviewed the recommendations of the military commission and upheld them, including the execution of Mary Surratt. He announced his support in an executive order
of July 5 and two days later four of the conspirators were hanged. Concerning the other four, Johnson modified his position slightly in an
executive order of July 15 in which he shifted the place of incarceration
to the military prison at Dry Tortugas, Florida.[3] With his actions on
the matters of the Confederate leaders and the Lincoln assassins he
virtually eliminated these issues as impediments to his governing.

There would be other obstacles, but for the moment Johnson charted
his course on restoration with a steady hand at the helm. It may be
accurately maintained that presidential reconstruction began on May
29, for on that day Johnson launched out into the churning seas of
postwar discord by offering the former Confederacy an Amnesty Proclamation and also an initial plan for provisional governments.[4]

The President's cabinet lent its unanimous support to his Amnesty
Proclamation. This document, although derivative of Lincoln's earlier
amnesty efforts and other influences, was distinctly Johnson's. The first
of four such proclamations that Johnson would eventually offer, it was
the most significant. Although pretending to extend pardons widely,
the proclamation in reality proscribed thousands of ex-Rebels, for it

1. James E. Sefton, *Andrew Johnson and the Uses of Constitutional Power* (Boston,
1980), 117.
2. Order for Military Trial of Presidential Assassins, May 1, 1865; Proclamation of
Rewards for Arrest of Sundry Confederates, May 2, 1865.
3. Order *re* Lincoln Assassins, July 5, 1865; Order Modifying July 5 Order, July
15, 1865, Richardson, *Messages*, 6:348.
4. Amnesty Proclamation, May 29, 1865; Proclamation Establishing Government
for North Carolina, May 29, 1865. Following Lincoln's lead, Johnson had accepted as
legitimate and valid the governments in Virginia, Tennessee, Arkansas, and Louisiana.

enumerated fourteen different categories that were exempt from general forgiveness. Persons falling under any of these exceptions had to seek special individual pardon from the President and take an oath of amnesty as well. As Johnson doubtless knew from the outset, the most important group would be those former Confederates who held $20,000 or more of property (the thirteenth exception). While it is impossible to comprehend the President's complex motives for the various exceptions that he outlined, other than his life-long resentment of the affluent, it is clear that he intended to make thousands of southerners, particularly wealthy ones, beg for absolution.

And thousands did, especially in the summer and fall months of 1865. Although requests for presidential pardons were theoretically to go first through the governors and then to the President, hundreds if not thousands went directly to Johnson. As for the others, most governors anxiously forwarded them to Johnson for action. In any event, his office was inundated with applications for amnesty, so much so that at times they clogged the channels of business and distracted Johnson from other pressing concerns. The claim by one historian that Johnson "merely performed the mechanical act of granting what was already decided by the Provisional Governor" will not withstand careful investigation. And neither will the assertion by another scholar that in the early months "very few pardons were actually granted."[5] In reality the White House did a land-office business in pardons in the months immediately following the issuance of the Amnesty Proclamation.

Examining the lists provided to Congress by the President's office, for example, we have computed the number of pardons granted in three of the states—Alabama, North Carolina, and Virginia. Our calculations reveal that *fifty-one percent* of the 5,291 pardons awarded in those states in 1865 took place in the months of June–August. Without further investigation, of course, it is not possible to know exactly how representative the experience of these three states might have been; yet the point remains, thousands of special pardons were issued by Johnson in the summer months. One has only to make a cursory survey of the Amnesty Papers to be impressed, if not overwhelmed, by the number of pardon applications that reached Washington during this critical period of presidential reconstruction.

The numbers escalated as the weeks went by, because former Confederates needed presidential pardon in order to regain political and property rights and privileges. As Johnson commenced establishing civilian governments across the South, the demand for persons to occupy the hundreds of vacant official posts increased correspondingly. Theoretically, at least, no one could hold a government job unless he

5. Michael Perman, *Reunion Without Compromise: The South and Reconstruction, 1865–1868* (Cambridge, 1973), 129; Eric L. McKitrick, *Andrew Johnson and Reconstruction* (Chicago, 1960), 145, 146.

had been already pardoned; thus the matters of amnesty and of provisional governments went hand in glove. Borrowing a page from Lincoln's notebook, Johnson devised the scheme of exerting executive prerogative to appoint provisional governors for those southern states that had no semblance of genuine government. He began with North Carolina on May 29, and then followed in June with five additional appointments, and concluded finally in mid-July with Florida.

As has been pointed out by scholars, these provisional governors were given impressive powers, which often exceeded those enjoyed by conventional governors. Concerning William W. Holden, a fellow North Carolinian asserted, "the Governor is in the full exercise of powers, not merely greater than known to any of his predecessors, but greater than ever were claimed for an English monarch since 1688."[6] Although admittedly an exaggeration, the observation nevertheless was not completely off target.

Johnson moved boldly on this second front, the naming of provisional governors, in hopes that they would in effect carry out the work of restoration for him. Because of his conservative, strict constructionist, states' rights views, this aspect of his reconstruction program is remarkable. He could justify it, of course, as a direct legacy of the war experience and also as the best and surest way to guarantee a republican form of government in all of the states of the South.

Through various means Johnson made known to these governors in particular and to the former Confederacy as a whole what he required of them for complete restoration. Despite some early tentativeness, the policy quickly evolved into three basic demands: the constitutional conventions must repeal the ordinances of secession, abolish slavery and ratify the Thirteenth Amendment, and repudiate all Confederate debts. As is well documented, the states responded with varying degrees of compliance. The President made one hesitant move toward black suffrage when in a letter to Governor Sharkey of Mississippi he suggested the possibility of limited voting rights. Sharkey dismissed the matter in a peremptory fashion, however, and Johnson regrettably but not surprisingly never bothered to pursue the matter again.[7] Mississippi was the only one of the seven states with provisional governors to hold a convention in the summer months; but when the later ones were held, Johnson failed to raise the question of suffrage. Thereby he drove a wedge between himself and Congressional leaders and handed to the Radicals the primary issue around which they eventually could and did rally.

In better moments during the summer Johnson could allow himself the luxury of a general satisfaction with the accomplishments of his

6. Swain to William A. Graham, July 4, 1865, as quoted in Perman, *Reunion*, 110.
7. Johnson to William L. Sharkey, Aug. 15, 1865; Sharkey to Johnson, Aug. 20, 1865.

governors. Yet as he sensed early on, the restoration process did not move as smoothly as he desired. In fact so disgruntled with his governors did he become by late August that he took the extraordinary step of issuing a warning to them in the form of a circular. The particular source of disappointment was the undeniable reality that his men were using their appointive prerogatives to fill a large number of offices with persons of questionable loyalty and were consequently ignoring "the true Union men."[8] The President's document naturally elicited a spate of replies which somewhat self-righteously protested against the charge, confessing only to occasional lapses. By the end of the summer Johnson could begin to wonder if his two-part strategy—pardons and provisional governments—was leading to the restoration for which he had hoped. The fall months would provide more clues and more discomfort.

Amidst the tribulations of being chief executive of a fragmented country, Johnson also had personal concerns in the summer months. Primary among them was his desire to have his family join him in Washington. The President sent and received a number of telegrams on this subject, although curiously there are no extant entreaties to his wife, Eliza. For a variety of reasons different relatives were not eager to leave Tennessee in the late spring and early summer months. Part of the reluctance may have been related to the fact that Johnson did not have suitable quarters for them until June 9, when he finally moved his residence into the White House. Ten days later the first installment of family arrived, including Eliza Johnson, Martha Patterson and children. The final group, however, did not reach Washington until early August; among them was the President's troubled and troublesome son, Robert. The presence of family brought some satisfaction and comfort to the harried Chief Executive, but he nevertheless suffered from two extensive periods of illness during the summer. Outings with family members and boat trips on the Potomac afforded enough relief from the burdens of office so that Johnson did not become incapacitated or distracted by them.

Unfortunately for those who wish to know more of Johnson the person, the documentary record in the summer of 1865 is very thin, much as it was for earlier periods. In fact, were it not for the existence of telegrams sent out from the presidential office, we would have virtually nothing from him. Johnson was not a man given to musings and introspections, at least insofar as written records indicate. Nor was he inclined to write letters, revealing or otherwise, to close friends. Nor was he likely to receive correspondence of a personal nature, except for tantalizing letters from certain female acquaintances, such as Rae Burr Batten, M. Elizabeth Young, and Mary A. White.[9] These documents

8. Circular to Provisional Governors, Aug. 22, 1865.

9. Batten to Johnson, May 26, 1865; Young to Johnson, June 12, 1865; White to Johnson, July 23, 1865.

add more than a dash or two of spice to an otherwise pedestrian personal correspondence file.

Whether wrestling with private concerns relating to family and friends or with public matters of restoration of the South, Johnson persevered in the summer months of 1865.[10] In fact, he seemed to establish himself as a solid chief executive who not only had an agenda but also intended to pursue it. No one judged him to be a weak leader in those early months; indeed he had a host of admirers across the nation, north and south, Democrat and Republican. By the end of August, it appeared that Johnson had reconstruction very much under control. A strong case may be made for the claim that the summer and fall months constituted Johnson's "finest hour."

Yet these weeks contained the seeds of conflict, if not destruction. As early as mid-May, for example, Thaddeus Stevens warned Johnson that Congress would likely look upon reconstruction "as a question for the Legislative power exclusively." He therefore urged the President to suspend any further executive efforts "untill the meeting of Congress."[11] But Johnson disregarded this and any other word of caution that came from various quarters, particularly from the vicinity of Radicals. Instead he pushed ahead, determined to bring the southern states back into the Union prior to the convening of Congress. But as historian James Sefton has observed: "What Johnson had proclaimed in May he must explain in December. . . ."[12] Thus the day of reckoning would come; yet in the summer months the President did not worry about future problems with Congress. Rather he took advantage of the relatively tranquil scene in Washington (most notably the absence of Congress) and deceived himself into believing that he could accomplish restoration almost by executive edict or fiat.

This one-time tailor from Greeneville, Tennessee, had reached a remarkable pinnacle: President of the United States successfully confronting the incredible challenge of putting the entire country back together again. In his private moments he could indulge in self congratulations for what he had already accomplished by the end of the summer. But his confident strides would subsequently yield to stumbling steps and his presidency would never be the same again.

ACKNOWLEDGMENTS

One of the most enjoyable prerogatives of the Editor is to acknowledge those institutions and individuals who, through their tangible support and encouragement, have made this volume possible.

10. The President was also troubled by personal threats made against him by certain angry Southerners. Given the volatile situation that prevailed in the aftermath of the Lincoln assassination, such letters and statements could not be dismissed lightly.
11. Stevens to Johnson, May 16, 1865.
12. Sefton, *Johnson and Constitutional Power*, 117.

Across the decades the National Historical Publications and Records Commission has lent financial aid to our Project. In addition, various individuals associated with that agency, particularly Frank Burke, Roger Bruns, Mary Giunta, and Sara Dunlap Jackson, have been enormously helpful to us in a wide variety of ways. Likewise the National Endowment for the Humanities has awarded grants that have enabled us to continue. Within that organization, Kathy Fuller and David Nichols have been of special assistance.

Since its inception, the Johnson Project has benefitted from financial contributions and other forms of support from the Tennessee Historical Commission. We are grateful to the executive director, Herbert L. Harper, for his continued interest in our endeavors.

Needless to say, the University of Tennessee, Knoxville has provided for us in many significant ways, not the least of which has been financial and spatial. Dean Lorman A. Ratner and Associate Dean Charles O. Jackson of the College of Liberal Arts have been instrumental in sustaining and promoting our cause. This was made even more evident when they spearheaded the move in 1987 to create the Tennessee Presidents Center, which brought together the Jackson, Polk, and Johnson projects. Along with this remarkable development came new, expanded, and quite suitable offices for all of the projects.

In addition, the staff and administrators of the John C. Hodges Library and of the Special Collections Department, headed by James B. Lloyd, have been crucial to our research efforts. Finally, we are extremely appreciative of our important relationship with the University's Development Office and with the University of Tennessee Press.

Throughout the nation many libraries, archives, and historical societies have provided copies of documents and other research assistance. Among the most important have been the Library of Congress and the National Archives. Much closer to home, the Lawson McGhee Library (Knox County Public Library) has been a vital research center for us. All of these institutions have demonstrated repeatedly the advantages of cooperation between repositories and scholars.

It should surprise no one to learn that numerous individuals have made special contributions to advancing the work of the Johnson Project in general and this volume in particular. We are grateful, for example, to our longtime benefactors, Margaret Johnson Patterson Bartlett and Ralph M. Phinney, both of Greeneville; their continuing support has not only materially aided us but it has also inspired us as well. Moreover, we express our gratitude to Hope Holdcamper, a retired member of the National Archives staff, who has devoted years to searching for Johnson documents in that institution.

I am indebted beyond calculation to the persons who constitute the staff of the Johnson Project. The "veterans," Patricia J. Anthony, Patricia P. Clark, LeRoy P. Graf, and Marion O. Smith, warmly welcomed me when I joined them in September 1987 as the new Editor. From that date to this moment, they have carried forth the work of this Project with their customary diligence and expertise and also with good will, as they have adapted to changes and new ways of doing things. Meanwhile our volunteer staff person, Ruth P. Graf, has contributed to our efficient functioning by undertaking many routine but necessary chores. Before his departure from the Johnson staff in the summer of 1987, Brooks D. Simpson assisted the work on this present volume in important ways. In 1988 we were fortunate to add two new persons to our staff: Richard B. McCaslin and Randall B. Rosenburg. They have taken on responsibilities and assignments that have enabled us to reach our goal of completing this volume and launching the next one. Each of these staff members has been indispensable; they have made my work both pleasant and rewarding. Together we have accomplished much.

I pause in conclusion to acknowledge friends and family who have believed in my decision to assume the Johnson editorship and have encouraged me as I have sought to meet the challenges of this new venture. Since they know to whom I am referring, I shall refrain from listing their names here. But my wife, Mary Lee, and our sons, Pierre, Andre, and Louis Paul, have supported me and loved me so much that I simply cannot omit their names. To them and to the unnamed friends, I express my profound appreciation and affection.

Paul H. Bergeron

Knoxville, Tennessee
January 1989

Editorial Method

With the advent of Johnson's presidency and the arrival of a new Editor, some changes have invariably been made in this volume.

The prospect of dealing with thousands of documents for the summer months of 1865 forced us to embrace a rather severe policy of selectivity. Believing that politics constituted the main focus and function of the Johnson presidency, we have chosen documents that best reflect this situation. Yet, even at that we have had to eliminate tens of hundreds of documents from inclusion in this volume. Our selection guidelines have disposed us to include virtually all personal correspondence between Johnson and his family and closest friends, primarily because there is so little extant during these early months of the presidency. Given Johnson's long and notable career in Tennessee politics, we have endeavored to include much of the exchange between him and state or local leaders.

Correspondence between the President and cabinet members and other close advisers has been another selected group of documents, except for routine letters or telegrams. Likewise prominent political leaders outside of Washington have been represented in our final published documents.

Among the calendared or summarized letters and documents appearing in this volume are all of the letters from designated observers of the South which were published in our special volume, *Advice After Appomattox: Letters to Andrew Johnson, 1865–1866.*

The nearly overwhelming amount of documents found in the Amnesty Papers has caused us much anguish. We have endeavored to identify and include samples of almost all of the fourteen different exceptions which Johnson listed in his proclamation. In addition, we have selected amnesty letters that are particularly interesting or involve some quite well known former Confederates.

Not surprisingly, in his early days as president Johnson had a number of dealings with the question of blacks in the South. We have been sensitive to this dimension of his presidency and have therefore striven to include as much on this issue as seemed important or of special interest. These various examples, while not comprehensive, should provide some understanding of how we have gone about the process of inclusion and exclusion of documents.

Having made exhaustive searches for Johnson material (most of which has been located in the National Archives and the Library of Congress) and having agonized over what to include and what to exclude, we next dealt with certain particularities of transcribing the documents. We have made certain deviations from or modifications of some practices followed in previous volumes.

We have decided, for example, that in a given document every sentence should begin with a capital letter, whether the writer provided one or not. Furthermore, the somewhat annoying dashes at the conclusion of sentences have been silently converted to either periods or question marks, as appropriate. In this volume we are indenting the first line of every paragraph in a document, whether the original was so rendered or not.

Other practices which we have followed include, for instance, bringing all interlineations in a document down to the line. The same is true of superscript contractions or abbreviations. Marginalia found in a document are added to the conclusion of the letter in the manner of a postscript. Extraneous dots or periods in a sentence and obvious slips of the pen are omitted silently from our final version. We employ square brackets whenever it is absolutely necessary to make an editorial insertion, such as to clarify a word or to provide certain information. When square brackets are found in the original document, however, we render them as angle brackets. Headings, inside addresses, salutations, and complimentary closings are standardized and consolidated. The date and provenance, for example, are placed in the upper right corner, regardless of their position in the original document. The inside address and salutation similarly are placed flush left. The closings are situated at flush right at the conclusion of the document. The spelling of words, no matter how unorthodox, is reproduced without alteration, unless there might be confusion in which case we have added a bracketed rendering or a *sic* to assist the reader.

We have made a valiant effort to identify all persons and to explain all references to special events or circumstances in any given document. But persons identified in earlier volumes (consult the Index) are provided with only brief mention here or else are passed over silently. We have attempted to indicate our defeats by noting whenever we have been unable to identify a particular person or to illuminate a mystifying reference to place or thing.

While conceding that modern printing technology compels us to alter some things in a nineteenth-century handwritten letter, we have striven to be faithful to the original document. In all respects we have adhered to the accepted canons of the historical editing profession.

SYMBOLS AND ABBREVIATIONS

REPOSITORY SYMBOLS

| A-Ar | Alabama Department of Archives and History, Montgomery |
| CSmH | Henry E. Huntington Library, San Marino, California |

DLC Library of Congress, Washington, D.C.
DNA National Archives, Washington, D.C.

RECORD GROUPS USED*

RG15 Records of the Veterans Administration
RG45 Naval Records Collection of the Office of Naval
    Records and Library
RG48 Records of the Office of the Secretary of the
    Interior
RG56 General Records of the Department of the
    Treasury
RG58 Records of the Internal Revenue Service
RG59 General Records of the Department of State
RG60 General Records of the Department of Justice
RG75 Records of the Bureau of Indian Affairs
RG94 Records of the Adjutant General's Office,
    1780s–1917
RG105 Records of the Bureau of Refugees, Freedmen,
    and Abandoned Lands
RG107 Records of the Office of the Secretary of War
RG108 Records of the Headquarters of the Army
RG109 War Department Collection of Confederate
    Records
RG123 Records of the United States Court of Claims
RG153 Records of the Office of the Judge Advocate
    General (Army)
RG204 Records of the Office of the Pardon Attorney
RG249 Records of the Commissary General of Prisoners
RG366 Records of Civil War Special Agencies of the
    Treasury Department
RG393 Records of United States Army Continental
    Commands, 1821–1920

*We have also used nearly twenty microfilm collections from the National Archives, all of which are parts of the various Record Groups listed here.

GU University of Georgia, Athens
IHi Illinois State Historical Society, Springfield
MHi Massachusetts Historical Society, Boston
MdBJ Johns Hopkins University, Baltimore, Maryland
Ms-Ar Mississippi Department of Archives and History, Jackson
NHi New-York Historical Society, New York
NN New York Public Library, New York
NNPM Pierpont Morgan Library, New York
NRU University of Rochester, Rochester, New York
Nc-Ar North Carolina Division of Archives and History, Raleigh

NcD   Duke University, Durham, North Carolina
PHarH   Pennsylvania Historical and Museum Commission,
          Harrisburg
RPB   Brown University, Providence, Rhode Island
Tx-Ar   Texas State Library, Archives Division, Austin
Vi   Virginia State Library, Richmond

MANUSCRIPTS

AL   Autograph Letter
ALcopy   Autograph Letter, copy by writer
ALS   Autograph Letter Signed
ALS copy   Autograph Letter Signed, copy by writer
ALS draft   Autograph Letter Signed, draft
Copy   Copy, not by writer
CopyS   Copy Signed
D   Document
DS   Document Signed
Draft   Draft Signed
ES   Endorsement Signed
L   Letter
LBcopy   Letter Book copy
LBcopyS   Letter Book copy, Signed
LS   Letter Signed
LS(X)   Letter Signed "X"
Mem   Memorial
PD   Printed Document
Pet   Petition
PL   Printed Letter
PLS   Printed Letter Signed
Tel   Telegram

ABBREVIATIONS

ACP   Appointment, Commission, and Personal Branch
Appl(s).   Application(s)
Appt(s).   Appointment(s)
Appt. Bk.   Appointment Book
Arty.   Artillery
Atty. Gen. Attorney General
Bde.   Brigade
Brig.   Brigadier
Bty.   Battery
Bvt.   Brevet
Cav.   Cavalry
Cld.   Colored
Co.   Company

Commr.	Commissioner
Corres.	Correspondence
CSR	Compiled Service Records
Enum.	Enumeration
fl.	flourishing
Inf.	Infantry
JP	Andrew Johnson Papers
Let. Bk.	Letter Book
Lgt.	Light
Pt(s).	Part(s)
Recd.	Received
Recomm.	Recommendation
Rgt.	Regiment
Ser.	Serial, Series
Supp(s).	Supplement(s)
TSLA	Tennessee State Library and Archives
U.S.C.T.	United States Colored Troops
Vols.	Volunteers

SHORT TITLES

BOOKS

Advice	Brooks D. Simpson, LeRoy P. Graf, and John Muldowny, eds., *Advice After Appomattox: Letters to Andrew Johnson, 1865–1866* (Knoxville, 1987).
Alexander, *Reconstruction*	Thomas B. Alexander, *Political Reconstruction in Tennessee* (Nashville, 1950).
American Annual Cyclopaedia	*American Annual Cyclopaedia and Register of Important Events* (42 vols. in 3 series, New York, 1862–1903).
Appleton's Cyclopaedia	James G. Wilson and John Fiske, eds., *Appleton's Cyclopaedia of American Biography* (6 vols., New York, 1887–89).
Basler, *Works of Lincoln*	Roy P. Basler, ed., *The Collected Works of Abraham Lincoln* (9 vols., New Brunswick, N.J., 1953–55).
BDAC	*Biographical Directory of the American Congress, 1774–1961* (Washington, D.C., 1961).

BDTA — Robert M. McBride and Dan M. Robison, comps., *Biographical Directory of the Tennessee General Assembly* (2 vols., Nashville, 1975–79).

Beale, *Welles Diary* — Howard K. Beale, ed., *Diary of Gideon Welles* (3 vols., New York, 1960).

Benedict, *Compromise of Principle* — Michael L. Benedict, *A Compromise of Principle: Congressional Republicans and Reconstruction, 1863–1869* (New York, 1974).

Boatner, *CWD* — Mark M. Boatner, III, *The Civil War Dictionary* (New York, 1959).

Bonadio, *North of Reconstruction* — Felice A. Bonadio, *North of Reconstruction: Ohio Politics, 1865–1870* (New York, 1970).

Brandt, *Burn New York* — Nat Brandt, *The Man Who Tried to Burn New York* (Syracuse, 1986).

DAB — Allen Johnson and Dumas Malone, eds., *Dictionary of American Biography* (20 vols., supps., and index, New York, 1928–   ).

Dyer, *Compendium* — Frederick H. Dyer, comp., *A Compendium of the War of the Rebellion* (Des Moines, Iowa, 1908).

Goodspeed's *Tennessee, East Tennessee, Fayette* [and other counties] — Goodspeed Publishing Company, *History of Tennessee, from the Earliest Time to the Present . . .* (Chicago, 1886–87).

Harris, *Presidential Reconstruction* — William C. Harris, *Presidential Reconstruction in Mississippi* (Baton Rouge, 1967).

Heitman, *Register* — Francis B. Heitman, *Historical Register and Dictionary of the United States Army, from Its Organization, September 29, 1789 to March 2, 1903* (2 vols., Washington, D.C., 1903).

Howard, *Black Liberation* — Victor B. Howard, *Black Liberation in Kentucky* (Lexington, Ky., 1983).

Johnson Papers — LeRoy P. Graf and Ralph W. Haskins, eds., *The Papers of Andrew*

Johnson (7 vols., Knoxville, 1967–   ).

Kibler, *Perry*

Lillian A. Kibler, *Benjamin F. Perry: South Carolina Unionist* (Durham, N.C., 1946).

Klement, *Dark Lanterns*

Frank L. Klement, *Dark Lanterns: Secret Political Societies, Conspiracies, and Treason Trials in the Civil War* (Baton Rouge, 1984).

McCrary, *Lincoln and Reconstruction*

Peyton McCrary, *Abraham Lincoln and Reconstruction: The Louisiana Experiment* (Princeton, 1978).

Men of Maryland and District of Columbia

The Biographical Cyclopedia of Representative Men of Maryland and District of Columbia (Baltimore, 1879).

NCAB

National Cyclopaedia of American Biography . . . (63 vols. and index, New York, 1893–1984 [I–XVIII, Ann Arbor, 1967]).

NUC

Library of Congress, *The National Union Catalog: Pre-1956 Imprints* (754 vols., London, 1968–   ).

OR

War of the Rebellion: A Compilation of the Official Records of the Union and Confederate Armies (70 vols. in 128, Washington, D.C., 1880–1901).

Parks, *Brown*

Joseph H. Parks, *Joseph E. Brown of Georgia* (Baton Rouge, 1977).

Powell, *Army List*

William H. Powell, *List of Officers of the Army of the United States from 1779 to 1900* (Detroit, 1967 [1900]).

Raper, *Holden*

Howard W. Raper, *William W. Holden: North Carolina's Political Enigma* (Chapel Hill, 1985).

Richardson, *Messages*

James D. Richardson, comp., *A Compilation of the Messages and Papers of the Presidents, 1789–1897* (10 vols., Washington, D.C., 1896–99).

TICW

Civil War Centennial Commission, *Tennesseans in the Civil War: A Military History of Confederate*

	and Union Units with Available Rosters of Personnel (2 pts., Nashville, 1964--65).
Tyler, *Va. Biography*	Lyon G. Tyler, ed., *Encyclopedia of Virginia Biography* (5 vols., New York, 1915).
U.S. Off. Reg.	*Register of the Officers and Agents, Civil, Military and Naval in the Service of the United States . . .* (Washington, D.C., 1851–).
Wakelyn, *BDC*	Jon L. Wakelyn, *Biographical Dictionary of the Confederacy* (Westport, Conn., 1977).
Warner, *Blue*	Ezra J. Warner, *Generals in Blue* (Baton Rouge, 1964).
Warner, *Gray*	Ezra J. Warner, *Generals in Gray* (Baton Rouge, 1959).
Warner and Yearns, *BRCC*	Ezra J. Warner and Wilfred Buck Yearns, *Biographical Register of the Confederate Congress* (Baton Rouge, 1975).
Webb and Carroll, *Handbook of Texas*	Walter Prescott Webb and H. Bailey Carroll, eds., *The Handbook of Texas* (2 vols., Austin, 1952).
White, *Messages of Govs.*	Robert H. White, *Messages of the Governors of Tennessee* (8 vols., Nashville, 1952–72).

JOURNALS

AR	*Alabama Review*
At Mon	*Atlantic Monthly*
AHR	*American Historical Review*
Con Vet	*Confederate Veteran*
CWH	*Civil War History*
CWTI	*Civil War Times Illustrated*
ETHS *Pubs.*	East Tennessee Historical Society's *Publications*
FHQ	*Florida Historical Quarterly*
GHQ	*Georgia Historical Quarterly*
Harper's	*Harper's Monthly Magazine*
InMH	*Indiana Magazine of History*
JMH	*Journal of Mississippi History*
JSH	*Journal of Southern History*
Lin Her	*Lincoln Herald*
LHQ	*Louisiana Historical Quarterly*
MdHM	*Maryland Historical Magazine*

NCHR	North Carolina Historical Review
PMHB	Pennsylvania Magazine of History and Biography
Records CHS	Records of the Columbia Historical Society
SCHM	South Carolina Historical Magazine
SWHQ	Southwestern Historical Quarterly
VMHB	Virginia Magazine of History and Biography
WVH	West Virginia History

Chronology

1808, December 29	Born at Raleigh, North Carolina
1812, January 4	Death of father Jacob Johnson
1826, September	Arrives in Greeneville, Tennessee
1827, May 17	Marries Eliza McCardle
1828, October 25	Birth of daughter Martha
1829–35	Alderman, then mayor
1830, February 19	Birth of son Charles
1832, May 8	Birth of daughter Mary
1834, February 22	Birth of son Robert
1835–37, 1839–41	State representative
1841–43	State senator
1843–53	Congressman, first district
1852, August 5	Birth of son Andrew, Jr.
1853–57	Governor
1857, October 8	Elected to Senate
1860, December 18–19	Senate Speech on Secession
1862, March 3	Appointed military governor of Tennessee
1863, April 4	Death of son Charles
1864, June 8	Nominated for Vice President
1864, November 8	Elected Vice President
1865, February 25	Leaves for Washington
1865, March 4	Inaugurated as Vice President
1865, April 15	Sworn in as President
1865, May 1	Order for Military Trial of Presidential Assassins
1865, May 2	Proclamation of Rewards for Arrest of Sundry Confederates
1865, May 4	Order re Closing for Lincoln Funeral
1865, May 9	Order Restoring Virginia
1865, May 24	Moves offices into the White House
1865, May 29	Amnesty Proclamation
	Proclamation Establishing Government for North Carolina
1865, June 9	Takes up residence in the White House
1865, June 19	Some family members arrive in Washington

THE PAPERS OF
Andrew Johnson

From Stephen M. Barbour [1]

Philad   May 1st 1865

President Johnson

Allow me for myself, and I think the whole working class of this country to express my joy at your views of government, but especially at what you think should really constitute the real aristocracy of the land. I greatly admire that part of your speech before the Vermont delegation [2] in which you said you would punish the wealthy traitor by confiscating his property and so deprive him of his only influential power.

We plebeins, the majority of the U.S. have great confidence in your ability and sympathy but above all your determination to do the greatest good for the greatest number, founding our belief upon the basis that you never can forget the fact that you were once one of us who toil.

There is even now I think many wealthy men in the North who would favor slavery for the sake of having capital controll labor but I trust in future the country will see that the most good will be accomplished by electing their presidents more from the people. We hope Mr Lincoln and you will furnish a precedent for all future presidents.

I feel proud of you as our President coming as you did from the ranks, and the enthusiasm that I feel must be my excuse for the presumption in thus addressing you.

I am no politician but an American through four generations in this glorious country. I have a position in a first class clothing house where I have a good chance of conversing with many different men every day and I tell you I do not leave a stone unturned in favor of our Government that my feeble abilities will allow for my whole heart is in the cause.

Yours Truely   Stephen M. Barbour
Philada.

ALS, DLC-JP.

1. Barbour (c1827–c1895), a Philadelphia resident, was variously listed as "salesman," "clerk," and "tailor." 1880 Census, Pa., Philadelphia, 170th Enum. Dist., 8; Philadelphia directories (1858–96).

2. In meeting with the group headed by Stoddard B. Colby on April 22, Johnson had assured them that the wealthy traitor "must pay the penalty" for his crime (though he made no specific reference to confiscation of property), while the "misguided thousands who have been deluded and deceived" would be offered "conciliation, forbearance and clemency." *Washington Evening Star*, April 22, 1865.

From John F.H. Claiborne [1]

Zama Plantation, near Ft. Pike,
Hancock Co. Miss, May 1 65.

To the President,
Sir:

Many of the people of this State are considering the means of resuming their place in the Union, and the proposition has been made to assemble a Convention next month.[2]

I am anxious to see my native State once more in her proper position, but I desire to harmonize our action, in all things, with the Executive policy. And, as yet, there has been no occasion for the development of your views. Nor are the people of Mississippi in the condition to discuss & determine, judiciously, the great questions that must come before such a Convention. But lately distracted by this unhappy rebellion, they do not yet sufficiently comprehend the force of events, and the duty of accepting them in perfect good faith. In a word, they are not just now capable of administering their own affairs, or of adopting a State government adapted to existing facts, and to new social organizations. My opinion is that, for 12 months to come, they would be better under the immediate eye of the Executive and controlled by military rule.

I beg you to pardon me for thus obtruding my opinion. Tho' wholly unknown to you, I have often, during a long connexion with the democratic press, had occasion to defend your views & eulogize your services.

It is my duty to add that, I have been, from the first, a Union man, & have had confidential relations with all the U.S. Generals here, since the arrival of Gen. Butler at Ship Island.[3]

I have the honor to be, With much respect
Your Friend & Sert, J F H Claiborne.

ALS, DLC-JP.

1. Claiborne (1809–1884) was a native Mississippi lawyer, state representative, and congressman. *BDAC*.

2. On April 18, unionist Armistead Burwell had called on Mississippians to elect delegates to a state convention to seek the state's restoration to the Union. Harris, *Presidential Reconstruction*, 15–16.

3. Union forces occupied Ship Island on December 3, 1861. The following February and March Gen. Benjamin F. Butler concentrated his troops there preparatory to the move against New Orleans. Boatner, *CWD*, 591.

From Charles B. Dungan

May 1, 1865, Philadelphia, Pa.; ALS, DNA-RG60, Office of Atty. Gen., Lets. Recd., President.

Inquires on behalf of himself and other "disinterestedly loyal" Philadelphians about procedures by which they may recover control of Deep River, Chatham County, N.C., coal and iron mines seized and used by the rebels. Makes similar query about recovery of stock rights in the Charleston, S.C., Gas Works and in the Stewart Gold Mining Company of North Carolina, in both cases confiscated and sold by the rebels. [Referred by the President to the attorney general "for consideration."]

From Thomas J. Durant[1]

Neworleans. 1 May, 1865.

To His Excellency, Andrew Johnson,
President of the United States.
Respected Sir,

As state organizations are essential to the action of the Government of the United States, the eventual object of the war for the suppression of the rebellion, must be to restore such as have been swept away.

If all the officers of the three Departments of Government in the state of Massachusets were to die, the President of the United States could not order an election in that state.

All the state officers here having become disqualified by treason, the President could not order an election here. He cannot through his Major Generals here generate civil power, for the Military is subordinate to the civil and cannot create it.

No power on earth can create a state Government but the people of the state. If Congress should unanimously declare the people of Utah to be a state, such they would not be, unless willing to make a state organization, for themselves.

When the entire machinery of a state Government has been broken up: "the powers of Government incapable of annihilation return to the people at large for their exercise." Under such circumstances no one man has any greater right than another to order an election, to fix the qualifications of voters, to hold an election or to vote. For the sake therefore of producing harmonious and uniform action, and as the soil of the state when occupied by the federal arms is held as conquered territory, Congress should pass an act enabling the inhabitants of each state at the proper time and after a sufficient term of probation to form a state constitution, to the end that they may be guaranteed a republican government under the provisions of the Constitution of the United States.

The system established in Louisiana by the military authority, and designed to extend to the whole of it, is neither in accordance with the requirements of the loyal citizens nor with those of the Government of the United States.

The Constitutional Convention ordered to be elected by the militry commander[2] exhibited traits which might have been expected would characterise an assembly hastily elected from one race alone, long accustomed to lord it over the other.

On page 71 of the Journal of the Convention, it appears that when the Report of the Committee on Emancipation was under debate, Mr Edmond Abell[3] a delegate from Neworleans offered the following as a proviso:

"Provided always that the Legislature shall never pass any act authorising free Negroes to vote, or to immigrate into this state under any pretence whatever."

The question was divided at the portion of the sentence ending with the words "to vote"; and this portion was adopted by a vote of Seventy five to fifteen.

This was the true mind of the Convention on the 19th May 1864. Yet on the 13th June the same convention adopted a clause empowering the legislature to extend the elective franchise to other persons meaning colored by a vote of forty eight to thirty two.[4] See Journal p. 130.

It is well understood that this change was produced by the corruption of official patronage as investigation would easily show.[5]

On page 128 of the Journal of the Convention, it will be found that when the question of the police force of Neworleans was under discussion Mr Thorpe,[6] a member from the city moved an amended "that no one shall be appointed on the police, who shall have been mustered into the rebel army," and this amendment was laid on the table—a fate equivalent to a defeat of a vote of fifty yeas to thirty one nays.

It must be borne in mind that the rebel conscription act was never in force in Neworleans, as the occupation of the city by the national forces prevented it, and every man who went into the rebel army from Neworleans was a volunteer.

A word As to the Legislature elected under the new constitution: a petition was presented from persons of african decent asking an extension of suffrage, but it was smotherd by referral to a committee which did not report.

In the House of Representatives, Mr Lewis[7] introduced a bill declaring that "any person now holding or who may hereafter hold a Commission in the so called confederate army and who, on or before the first day of May 1865, shall not have complied with the requirements of the President's proclamation of December 8, 1863, shall forever be debarred from the right of holding any office of profit or trust, whether state, parochial or municipal in the state of Louisiana." This bill was defeated on the 2end day of March 1865 by fifteen yeas to forty five nays. Not even so mild an approach as this to an imposition of disabilities on the rebel leaders could be secured. The speaker of the House[8] had borne a Commission in the armed rebel service.

Passing from the Representatives to the Constitu[t]ion we find that The electoral basis on which this Convention and Legislature were reared by the military architect was spurious.

The whole number of votes proclaimed by Mr Hahn, Governor, to have been polled on the question of the ratification of the Constitution was 6836 for and 1566 against, majority in the favor 4470. In the city of Neworleans, there were 4662 votes for, and 789 against the constitution; majority in favor 3873. Now the Register of voters of the city of Neworleans in a report made to Governor Wells on the 6th March 1865, declares that 4918 (pretended) voters were imperfectly registered and that of this number some 4000 have not been naturalized. This is sufficient to raise a presumption of nulluty against the whole movement.[9]

The administration of the so-called civil Governmt has exhibited enormous corruptions. The printing of the Convention cost one hundred and sixty thousand dollars, when competent Judges believe it could have been done for thirty thousand and yielded a profit. This vast sum was paid to the True Delta, a newspaper which is reputed to have been owned at the time by Michael Hahn then Governor, Alfred Shaw, Sheriff of the Parish of orleans, and Wm. R. Fish[10] clerk of the Second District (or probate court) of Neworleans, the two most lucrative offices in the south west, and both of them incumbents, at the same time members of the Convention.

There is not much more than one fourth of the territory of Louisiana even now under the control of the National army, and no taxes can be directly levied outside of the Parishes of Plaquemines and St Bernard, (below the city on the river) the city of Neworleans, and the Parish of Jefferson next above the city on the river.

The most important and influential of the offices in the gift of the so-called State Government are now being distributed to men who held commissions in the rebel army, who signed the ordinace of secession in January 1861, who took a leading part in the rebel movement; you can see them now as Judges, sheriffs, and important officers of the new state, and when the whole of the population now within the rebel districts of Louisiana shall have been brought to participate in this state government, and all the ammestied rebels come forward to vote what can the real friends of liberty and Union expect? They will be overwhelmed, and subjected to every species of indignity, unless they can receive the assistance of new voters.

I think that some such bill as Mr Ashley[11] of Ohio introduced into the House last session [12] should be passed with certain modifications the most prominent and indispensable of which should be the registration of the blacks as voters. They are ceretainly illiterate but they are loyal hearted, and this is the best guarantee of safety in the south you can have at present.

I remain with great respect
Your obdt. Servt Thomas J. Durant.

ALS, DLC-Carl Schurz Papers.

1. Durant (1817–1882), a New Orleans Democrat, had been a state senator, wealthy slaveholder, and a unionist. After the city was occupied he became involved in the movement to organize Louisiana as a free state, and served as district attorney general. After a "bitter controversy" with Gen. Nathaniel P. Banks he moved to Washington, D.C., where he practiced law. *DAB*; Joseph G. Tregle, Jr., "Thomas J. Durant, Utopian Socialism, and the Failure of Presidential Reconstruction in Louisiana," *JSH*, 45 (1979): 485–512.

2. On March 11, 1864, General Banks called for the election of delegates to a constitutional convention. The subsequent election was poorly attended and the constitution adopted by the delegates, who met from March 28 to July 23, 1864, was rescinded four years later. Joe Gray Taylor, *Louisiana Reconstructed, 1863–1877* (Baton Rouge, 1974), 42–52.

3. Edmund Abell (b.c1811), a New Orleans lawyer, became a district court judge after the war. 1850 Census, La., Orleans, City of New Orleans, 403; McCrary, *Lincoln and Reconstruction*, 250.

4. The convention adopted this clause on June 23 while Abell was momentarily absent from the floor. Ibid., 263.

5. Governor Michael Hahn and General Banks, "by unremitting efforts," secured the amendment. George Denison to Salmon P. Chase, Nov. 25, 1864, ibid.

6. Thomas B. Thorpe (1815–1878) had spent many years in Louisiana before moving to New York City (1853). During the war he was a colonel on Butler's staff and served as surveyor of the port of New Orleans. *DAB*; McCrary, *Lincoln and Reconstruction*, 246.

7. Probably Edward T. Lewis (1834–1927), a lawyer who rose from private to captain in the Confederate army. He subsequently served in the U.S. Congress and as a federal judge. *BDAC*.

8. Simeon Belden (c1830–fl1901), a lawyer who was chosen speaker October 4, 1864, and later served as state attorney general. 1860 Census, La., St. Martin, 94; Andrew B. Booth, comp., *Records of Louisiana Confederate Soldiers* (3 vols., Spartanburg, S.C., 1984 [1920]), 1: 157; *New Orleans Picayune*, Oct. 5, 11, 1864; New Orleans directories (1866–1901).

9. On May 3 Gov. J. Madison Wells ordered the resignation of Joseph Randall Terry (c1829–fl1870), a New Orleans druggist who had been appointed register of voters by Banks. Terry refused to resign, but was forcibly removed in early June. 1870 Census, La., Orleans, New Orleans, 3rd Ward, 108; Walter M. Lowrey, "The Political Career of James Madison Wells," *LHQ*, 31 (1948): 1025, 1030; McCrary, *Lincoln and Reconstruction*, 248, 310–11, 315. See also Letters from Cottman, July 20, 28, 1865.

10. Shaw (c1830–fl1886) and William R. Fish (c1836–fl1879) were both former schoolmasters. Shaw was sheriff until his forced ouster by Governor Wells in the spring of 1865. Fish, Hahn's former law partner, who edited the *True Delta* until July 5, 1865, later served as assistant postmaster. McCrary, *Lincoln and Reconstruction*, 219, 249, 310; New Orleans directories (1867–86); 1860 Census, La., Orleans, 3d Rep. Ward New Orleans, 254, 540; *New Orleans Picayune*, July 6, 1865. See also Letter from Wells, July 3, 1865.

11. James M. Ashley (1824–1896), Toledo druggist, was a Republican congressman (1859–69) and governor of Montana Territory (1869–70). *BDAC*.

12. Introduced December 15, 1864, the bill resembled the Wade-Davis bill but included clauses enfranchising all "loyal male citizens" (including blacks) and recognizing

the Louisiana government. The debate over the suffrage provision, however, led to the tabling of the bill, as amended, on February 21, 1865. McCrary, *Lincoln and Reconstruction*, 287–92.

From Henry S. Foote [1]

New York City May 1st 1865.

To the President:

The undersigned has the honor, most respectfully, to make known that (being yet under parol, and restricted in regard to his movements, so that he is not allowed, for the present, to go to any place South of this City) begs leave to state that, inasmuch as it is deemed advisable that he shall not return at once to his own residence in the City of Nashville, he may be permitted to go to the Pacific coast, where he has four daughters residing, 8 grandchildren, and an only sister. The War being evidently at an end, the undersigned hopes that this, his wish, will be gratified, as he is exceedingly solicitous to be restored once more to the society of his family and friends and to spend the evening of his days in quietude and repose. If your Excellency shall consent to my release from the obligations which at present rest upon me, I hope to be permitted, ere I go to the far West, to pay a short visit to an old and respected friend, Judge Swayne,[2] of Columbus, Ohio, & take leave there of my wife and children.[3] Wishing you, most sincerely and cordially, continued health, and a prosperous and glorious Administration of the public affairs committed to your management,[4]

I have the honor to be
Your friend & obedient servant, H. S. Foote

ALS, DNA-RG107, Lets. Recd., EB12 President 2988 (1865).

1. A former U.S. senator, Mississippi governor, and Confederate congressman from Tennessee, Foote had fled from the Confederacy to England in February 1865. Upon his return to the U.S. in April, he was ordered confined to New York City by Johnson. Foote's May 1 request was enclosed in a letter dated May 2 from Nevada Senator William Stewart, Foote's son-in-law. John E. Gonzales, "Henry Foote in Exile, 1865," *JMH*, 15 (1953): 90–97; Stewart to Johnson, May 2, 1865, Lets. Recd., EB12 President 2988 (1865), RG107, NA.

2. Noah H. Swayne (1804–1884) was a U.S. Supreme Court justice (1862–81). *DAB*.

3. Mrs. Foote and children returned to Nashville, from whence she wrote Johnson for "permission" for her husband to "remain unmolested," because he would "not ask to return into the Cotton States or into Tennessee; but will locate North." Rachel D. Foote to Johnson, May 22, 1865, Lets. Recd., EB12 President 1988 (1865), RG107, NA.

4. In response, Johnson ordered Foote to leave the country within forty-eight hours or be tried for treason. Refugeeing in Montreal, Foote, in a longer, more detailed supplication, again applied for presidential pardon on June 30. His exile ended in late August, when the President permitted him to return, on condition that he take the oath and give his parole of honor. Gonzales, "Foote in Exile," 97–98; Edwin M. Stanton to John A. Dix, May 5, 1865, Tels. Sent, Sec. of War, Vol. 31 (1865), RG107, NA; Foote to Johnson, June 30, 1865, Amnesty Papers (M1003, Roll 49), Tenn., Henry S. Foote, RG94, NA; Johnson to Foote, Aug. 26, 1865, Corres. A. Johnson, Misc. Col., Tenn. Historical Society, TSLA.

From John W. Forney [1]

Washington, D.C. May 1st 1865.

Dear Mr. President;

With all my care mistakes will occasionally happen as they do in the best families. This morning the article under the editorial head,[2] but not seen before it appeared in type, contains the expression that "the State governments were overthrown" by the rebellion. I have corrected it in the brief article which Mr. Forney[3] will hand to you, and from which you will see that I am square upon your platform, and shall continue to stand there until the bitter end. Whenever you desire to see me please let me know.

Your's Very truly J. W. Forney

Hon. Andrew Johnson

LS, DLC-JP.

1. Editor of the *Washington Chronicle* and secretary of the U.S. Senate.
2. The article, entitled "What Next?," stated that the surrender of Lee and Johnston left the "Southern people, for a time, without any regular government," because both the Confederate and "State governments are overthrown," thus leaving "no alternative but to fall back upon the military power, as a temporary expedient." *Washington Morning Chronicle*, May 1, 1865.
3. D. Carpenter Forney, John Forney's cousin and publisher of the *Chronicle*.

From Robert S. Northcott [1]

National Telegraph Office,
Clarksburg, West Virginia
May 1st 1865

To His Excellency Andrew Johnson, President U.S.

Respected Sir,

Enclosed, you will find a letter from some of the most influential citizens of Clarksburg, and West Virginia[2] in relation to traitors who previous to the war dwelt in these parts, but either left at the commencement of the rebellion or sometime during its progress and took up arms against the united States or accepted civil positions in the so-called Southern Confederacy.

The gentlemen whose names are appended to the letter addressed to your Excellency all possess high moral worth and have been indefatigable in their labors for the Union cause from the beginning of the struggle. T. W. Harrison,[3] whose name stands at the head of the list, is Judge of our Circuit Court. Among the other names are those of our members of the Legislature Clerks of Courts &c.

During the whole war the Federal Court has held its regular sessions in Clarksburg, and from time to time the Grand Jury has found bills for treason against the prominent rebels who left here at the beginning of the war; but as they have occasionally returned and have been permitted to roam at large, and the Federal Court thus far has taken but little cognizance of them, the loyal citizens deem it time that the said Court adopt more stringent measures. Especially have they become particularly alive to this matter since the recent rebel reverses have caused a greater influx of these traitors than at any former period. Knowing as I do the status of affairs in West Virginia, I should think it would be very appropriate to instruct Hon John J. Jackson,[4] Judge of the Federal Court and Col. Ben. Smith,[5] Prosecuting Attorney for the District of West Virginia to use the most stringent measures in prosecuting these traitors, many of whom were leading men and held high official position under Jeff. Davis and Gov. Letcher,[6] both in a military and civil capacity.

The class of rebels alluded to rendered themselves so obnoxious before leaving that I fear that in some instances the people will resort to Judge Lynch's Court[7] if they are permitted to return. In many communities vigilance committees have already been appointed for the purpose of ejecting these traitors, and if your Excellency can interpose some means of preventing their return here or of having them prosecuted immediately upon their return, it will add much to the future harmony of our State.

Pardon me for trespassing upon your valuable time, and be assured that I am actuated only by a desire to be of service to the loyal people of my adopted State who have suffered more during the rebellion than any other people, except loyal East Tennesseans.

Hoping to hear from you soon in regard to this and other matters concerning which I have recently written to you,[8]

> I remain with the highest considerations of
> Respect and Esteem Your Friend and Obt. Servt.
> R S. Northcott

P S. The Loyal citizens here are not anxious to punish rebels, but they want some legal means of getting rid of obnoxious ones.

> N.

ALS, DNA-RG60, Office of Atty. Gen., Lets. Recd., President.

1. Clarksburg, W. Va., newspaper editor.

2. Fourteen Harrison County citizens, who "have read with great satisfaction" Johnson's words that "treason is the highest crime," assure the President that his position "has our unqualified approbation." The "men who went from our midst breathing threatnings and death against us" are now returning. Some have been indicted for treason, but all have "been turned loose" by the U.S. Court and "not one has been prosecuted." The citizens ask the President to order the officers of the court "to cease bailing" and "to proceed to enforce the law against those *who may return* within its jurisdiction." Clarksburg citizens to Johnson, Apr. 26, 1865, Office of Atty. Gen., Lets. Recd., President, RG60, NA.

3. Thomas W. Harrison (1824–*fl*1890), native Clarksburg lawyer, had become the local circuit court judge two years earlier. 1860 Census, Va. [W. Va.], Harrison, Clarksburg, 2; George W. Atkinson and Alvaro F. Gibbens, *Prominent Men of West Virginia* (Wheeling, W. Va., 1890), 442.

4. Jackson, Jr. (1824–1907) was a long-time Federal judge for the District of West Virginia (1861–1905). Ibid., 168–69; *New York Times*, Sept. 3, 1907.

5. Benjamin H. Smith (1797–1887), wealthy Charleston lawyer, had been a legislator and U.S. district attorney. A postwar Democrat, he lost the 1866 West Virginia gubernatorial election. William S. Laidley, *History of Charleston and Kanawha County, West Virginia* (Chicago, 1911), 287, 949–50; Isaiah A. Woodward, "Arthur Ingraham Boreman: A Biography, Part I," *WVH*, 31 (1969): 262.

6. John Letcher, Confederate governor of Virginia.

7. Any extralegal trial or punishment, the term probably originating from the so-called tribunals conducted by Charles Lynch (1736–1796), a Virginia militia colonel, who took the law into his own hands in suppressing back-country Tory lawlessness during the revolutionary period. Mark M. Boatner, III, *Encyclopedia of the American Revolution* (New York, 1966), 665.

8. Northcott was awaiting a reply to his request to be appointed minister resident to Sardinia. Northcott to Johnson, Apr. 18, 1865, Johnson Papers, LC.

Order for Military Trial of Presidential Assassins

Executive Chamber
Washington City. May 1. 1865

Whereas the Attorney General[1] of the United States hath given his opinion:

That the persons implicated in the murder of the late President, Abraham Lincoln, and the attempted assassination of the Honorable William H. Seward, Secretary of State, and in an illegal conspiracy to assassinate other officers of the Federal Government at Washington City, and their aiders and abettors are subject to the jurisdiction of, and lawfully triable before a Military Commission.[2]

It is ordered—1st That the Assistant Adjutant General[3] detail nine competent military officers to serve as a commission for the trial of said parties, and that the Judge Advocate General[4] proceed to prefer charges against said parties for their alleged offences, and bring them to trial before said military commission; that said trial, or trials, be conducted by the said Judge Advocate General, and as Recorder thereof, in person, aided by such assistant, or Special Judge Advocates as he may designate, and that said trials be conducted with all diligence consistent with the ends of justice, the said Commission to sit without regard to hours.

2d That Brevet Major General Hartranft[5] be assigned to duty as Special Provost Marshal General for the purposes of said trial, and attendance upon said commission, and the execution of its mandates—

3d That the said commission establish such order, or rules of proceeding as may avoid unnecessary delay, and conduce to the ends of public justice.

Andrew Johnson

Copy, DNA-RG153, Unregistered Lets. Recd. *re* Lincoln Assassination Suspects (1864–65).

1. James Speed.

2. David E. Herold, G. A. Atzerodt, Lewis Payne, Michael O'Laughlin, Edward Spangler, Samuel Arnold, Mary E. Surratt, and Dr. Samuel A. Mudd were all tried by military court convening on May 9. See Letter from Joseph Holt, July 5, 1865.

3. Edward D. Townsend (1817–1893), a lieutenant colonel and member of Gen. Winfield Scott's staff in 1861, the next year became assistant adjutant general of the War Department, a position he held until his retirement in 1880. *DAB*. For the selection of commission members, see Special Orders 216, May 9, 1865, Richardson, *Messages*, 6: 336–37.

4. Joseph Holt.

5. John F. Hartranft (1830–1889), special provost marshal for the trial of the Lincoln conspirators, left the army in 1866. He became an active politician, including serving two terms as Pennsylvania governor. Warner, *Blue*.

From James Speed

May 1, 1865, Washington, D.C.; *House Ex. Docs.*, 39 Cong., 1 Sess., No. 99, pp. 3–8 (Ser. 1263).

In response to the President's April 21 request for an opinion "as to the proper construction and effect" of Lincoln's December 8, 1863, and March 26, 1864, amnesty proclamations, especially in relation to those who had taken the oath, the attorney general first sets forth "some of the obvious principles upon which the power to grant pardons and amnesty rests," with the goal of deducing "from those principles the limitations of that power." Asserting that the two proclamations "must be read together and regarded as one instrument," he declares, subject to subsequent court review, that those who have taken the oath "*voluntarily, with the purpose of restoring peace and establishing the national authority* . . . are entitled to all the benefits and rights so freely and benignly given by a magnanimous government." Considers Lincoln's propensity to be "as ready to pardon the unrepentant as the sincerely penitent offender," and announces that "the President had no power to make an open offer of pardon which could be relied upon as a protection for offences committed after notice of the offer." Cites the language of the first proclamation, addressed to "*all persons who have participated in the existing rebellion*," pointing out that these are "words referring to the past." Thus he sees need for another proclamation "covering the now past." Advises that "Persons who have been constantly engaged in rebellion should know distinctly what they are to do, when and how they are to do it, to free themselves from punishment, in whole or in part, or to reinstate themselves as before the rebellion. Such as have been affected merely by their treasonable associations should be absolutely forgiven. Appropriate conditions should be appended to the pardon of many. The grace and favor of the Government should now be large and generous." A second question raised by Johnson related to those who had not taken or offered to take the oath. Speed makes the point that the late proclamation was "a measure *to aid in the suppression* of the rebellion. . . . Now, one is desired *to aid in restoring* order and reorganizing society in the rebellious States." Sees the need to extend mercy "largely"; not to the great leaders and offenders, but "to the great mass of the misguided people." Properly used, the pardoning power can help "root out the spirit of rebellion, and bring society in those States into perfect accord with the wise and thoroughly tried principles of our government." Thus, he recommends that "another and a new offer of amnesty, adapted to the existing condition of things, should be proclaimed." [Although the attorney general's office dated this opinion May 8, the newspapers, as well as this *House* report, use the May 1 date.]

From Horace Maynard

Private & Unofficial

Nashville April 3 [May 2],[1] 1865

Dr. Sir,

Leaving Washington Thursday night, I arrived here, on time, Sunday night.

I called on Mr East, touching the subject of our conversation.[2] He made no decision other than to go to Washington during this week. He will probably arrive the last of this or the first of the next week.

The object of the dispatch calling me home was not misinterpreted by me. The election will occur on Thursday next.[3] Many changes, have taken place during my absence, unfavrable to me. The result I look upon as extremely doubtful. The probabilities are that Judge Patterson & either Mr. Fowler or Mr. Wisner will be elected. A few days will settle it.

I saw Mr. Graham yesterday, who says that Judge Catron is very low & cannot possibly last long.[4]

To-day elections were held for the following officers with the following results,

Public Printer	Mercer
Comptroller	Hutchen of Gibson Co
Librarian	Dr. Gattinger
Entry Takr Ocoee District	Thos. H. Calloway,[5]

A. J. Fletcher had previously been elected Secretary of State, & Dr. Stanford, Treasurer.[6]

I will write again after the election.

I am very Respectfully Your Obt. Servt.

Horace Maynard

His Excy Andrew Johnson President

ALS, DLC-JP.

1. Maynard obviously misdated this; the elections in the legislature to which he refers occurred on May 2.

2. Edward H. East, Tennessee secretary of state during Johnson's military governorship. Although the subject of the conversation is unknown, Johnson was eager to have East come to Washington. See Telegram to East, July 16, 1865.

3. The election of two U.S. senators was held Thursday, May 4, when the joint session of the Tennessee legislature chose David T. Patterson, Johnson's son-in-law, over Maynard, and Joseph S. Fowler over William H. Wisener. White, *Messages of Govs.*, 5: 441.

4. Daniel Graham was an old friend of U.S. Justice John Catron, who died May 30.

5. The Tennessee house and senate met in joint session to elect these officers. Samuel C. Mercer was designated public printer, Samuel W. Hatchett (not Hutchen) was named comptroller, Augustin Gattinger, librarian, and Calloway, register and entry taker for the Ocoee District. Hatchett (c1817–fl1880) was a Whig newspaper editor and Gibson County circuit court clerk (1860–62), before becoming state comptroller (1865–66). Gattinger (1825–1903), German-born botanist and physician, became U.S. surgeon at Cumberland Hospital in Nashville during the war and afterwards state librarian (1865–

71). Callaway (1812–1870), large Polk, Bradley, and Monroe County landowner, was president of the East Tennessee and Georgia Railroad (1852–53, 1865–70). *Tenn. House Journal, April–June, 1865*, pp. 106–9; 1860 Census, Tenn., Gibson, 7th Dist., 135; (1870), 4; (1880), 38th Enum. Dist., 21; Frederick Culp and Mrs. Robert E. Ross, *Gibson County Past and Present* (Trenton, Tenn., 1961), 84; Goodspeed's *Gibson*, 800; Charles A. Miller, *Official and Political Manual of the State of Tennessee* (Nashville, 1890), 172, 196; *Nashville Banner*, July 20, 1903; *NUC*; Penelope Johnson Allen, *Leaves from the Family Tree* (Easley, S.C., 1982), 24; Ernest L. Ross, comp., *Historical Cemetery Records of Bradley County, Tennessee* (2 vols., Cleveland, Tenn., 1973), 2: 74.

6. Andrew J. Fletcher and Robert L. Stanford.

From Robert J. Powell[1]

Private

Washington, D.C. 2nd May 1865.

Dear Sir:

As a personal friend, for I claim to have been such from our first acquaintance, nearly twenty years ago—permit me, very respectfully to suggest as follows:

In some parts of the North, you may not have been fully understood. Would it not have an influence for good—if you should show yourself to our soldiers and at least shake hands with the officers, when on their way to their Northern homes?

If you think it best so to do—the matter can be arranged and carried out in a quiet way—and not known to the public until it is accomplished.

With high respect Very truly Yours
R. J. Powell

To the President Andrew Johnson.

ALS, DLC-JP.
1. Powell (c1813–*fl*1883), a North Carolina native working in the Land Office in Washington, was named the state's agent in the capital. Later he was a clerk in the Pension and Post Office Departments. 1860 Census, D.C., 4th Ward, Washington, 83; Washington, D.C., directories (1858–83).

Proclamation of Rewards for Arrest of Sundry Confederates[1]

May 2, 1865

Whereas, it appears, from evidence in the Bureau of Military Justice, that the atrocious murder of the late President, Abraham Lincoln, and the attempted assassination of the Honorable William H. Seward, Secretary of State, were incited, concerted, and procured by and between Jefferson Davis, late of Richmond, Virginia, and Jacob Thompson, Clement C. Clay, Beverly Tucker, George N. Saunders,[2] William C. Cleary,[3] and other rebels and traitors against the Government of the United States, harbored in Canada:

Now, therefore, to the end that justice may be done, I, ANDREW
JOHNSON, President of the United States, do offer and promise for the
arrest of said persons, or either of them, within the limits of the United
States, so that they can be brought to trial, the following rewards:

One Hundred thousand dollars for the arrest of Jefferson Davis.

Twenty-five thousand dollars for the arrest of Clement C. Clay.

Twenty-five thousand dollars for the arrest of Jacob Thompson, late
of Mississippi.

Twenty-five thousand dollars for the arrest of George N. Saunders.

Twenty-five thousand dollars for the arrest of Beverly Tucker.

Ten thousand dollars for the arrest of William C. Cleary, late clerk of
Clement C. Clay.

The Provost Marshal General of the United States is directed to
cause a description of said persons, with notice of the above rewards, to
be published.

In testimony whereof, I have hereunto set my hand and caused the
Seal of the United States to be affixed.

Done at the city of Washington, this second day of May, in the year
of our Lord one thousand eight hundred and sixty-five, and of the Independence of the United States of America the eighty-ninth.[4]

ANDREW JOHNSON.

By the President:

W. Hunter, Acting Secretary of State.

PD, DLC-JP7A.

1. This proclamation, presented by Stanton, discussed and agreed upon by the cabi-
net on May 2, was supported by Judge Advocate General Holt, whose opinion was that
Davis and others were implicated in the conspiracy to assassinate Lincoln. Beale, *Welles
Diary*, 2: 299–300.

2. Former U.S. interior secretary Thompson, Confederate senator (and former U.S.
senator) Clay, and Tucker had been dispatched to Canada as commissioners to represent
Confederate interests, while Sanders appeared as a self-styled peace agent. Nathaniel
Beverly Tucker (1820–1890), who served as consul at Liverpool (1857–61), during
the war was a contractor of supplies for the Confederate army and as such traveled to
France and Canada. Remaining abroad until 1872, he returned to Washington, where he
wrote for newspapers. Ruth K. Nuermberger, *The Clays of Alabama* (Lexington, Ky.,
1958), 231–40; *DAB*.

3. William W. Cleary (1831–*fl*1887), Clay's private secretary and a native Kentucky
lawyer, worked in the War Department at Richmond. Remaining in Canada until 1869,
he returned to Kentucky and resumed law practice. William H. Perrin et al., *Kentucky:
A History of the State* (9 vols., Easley, S.C., 1979[1885–88]), 7: 768; *Nashville Times
and True Union*, May 10, 1865.

4. See Letter from George N. Sanders and Beverly Tucker, May 4, 1865.

From Gideon Welles

Navy Department, Washington, May 2, 1865

Sir,

I have the honor to return herewith the letter, referred by you to the
Department, from the Hon. Leonard Myers,[1] enclosing a petition for

the pardon of *Michael Mulhearn*, a private of the Marine Corps, now imprisoned in the Joliet State Penitentiary, Illinois, under the sentence of a Naval General Court Martial.[2]

In obedience to your directions a statement of the facts in the case of Mulhearn is endorsed on the petition.

More than one half of the punishment awarded by the Court having been remitted by the Acting Rear Admiral,[3] and the testimony being somewhat unfavorable to the character of the accused, the Department did not, at the time of reviewing the case, deem any further mitigation called for.[4]

> With great respect, Sir, your obedt. serv't, Gideon Welles
> Secretary of the Navy

The President.

LS, DNA-RG45, Subj. File N, Subsec. NO, Courts-Martial, Box 316, Michael Mulhearn.

1. Pennsylvania congressman.

2. Mulhearn (c1845–fl1874), a Philadelphia resident and marine since July 1862, had been convicted November 29, 1864, for "sleeping at his post" while guarding the navy yard at Mound City, Ill. His sentence of five years' imprisonment and loss of pay had already been reduced to two years' imprisonment. Subj. File N, Subsec. NO, Courts-Martial, Box 316, Michael Mulhearn, RG45, NA; Philadelphia directories (1870–74).

3. Samuel P. Lee (1812–1897), a naval officer from 1825 to 1873, had during the war commanded the North Atlantic and Mississippi squadrons. *DAB*.

4. Contrary to Welles's recommendation, Johnson discharged Mulhearn May 8, 1865, and he subsequently became a "maltster." Subj. File N, Subsec. NO, Courts-Martial, Box 316, Michael Mulhearn, RG45, NA; *Gopsill's Philadelphia Directory* (1874), 978.

From William G. Brownlow

Nashville Tenn May 3 1865

President Johnson.

In this days mail to you a letter.[1] Great Speculations going on at Knoxville among the leading copperheads. Gen Stoneman is arresting some of them & I hope will stand firmly up to them. There will be a storm there. Samuel A. Cunningham John Williams & Netherland[2] seem from the letter to be mixed up with it.

> W. G. Brownlow
> Gov

Tel, DLC-JP.

1. Brownlow included part of William Hunt's April 27th letter from Knoxville in which efforts by T.A.R. Nelson and John Williams to bring iron, cloth, salt, and tobacco from Virginia were discussed, in addition to the report that the arrest of Samuel A. Cunningham at Carter's Depot had been ordered by Gen. George Stoneman "for Acting *Spy* when we were at that place last fall fighting Vaughn." Brownlow added that "the very *old scratch* will be to pay in Knoxville." Brownlow to Johnson, May 3, 1865, Johnson Papers, LC.

2. Cunningham (1834–1905), who had married T.A.R. Nelson's daughter, Alice, was a farmer after the war. Both Williams and John Netherland were conservative unionists, the latter an unsuccessful gubernatorial candidate in 1859. Charles M. Bennett and

Loraine Bennett Rae, eds., *Washington County, Tennessee, Tombstone Inscriptions Plus Genealogical Notes* (3 vols., Nashville, 1977–79), 2: 13; 1880 Census, Tenn., Washington, 31st Enum. Dist., 6.

From Benjamin F. Butler

Lowell May 3d 1865

Hon Andrew Johnson
President of the United States.
Dear Sir.

Availing myself of your kindness in allowing me to make suggestions of such thoughts as may strike me relating to public affairs. I take leave to bring to your attention what doubtless may have been a subject of thought with yourself, the present condition of the people of the South in this regard. The surrender of their forces, and the stopping of the War, happening quite late in the season for planting, Southern men are doubtful what is to be the policy of the Government in regard to confiscation, and in regard to the parcelling out of the lands to the Freedmen and Refugee's. Such doubt we all know, tend to paralyse industry, but unless they plant in seed time, they cannot harvest, and in the present state of the Country, there must be almost starvation the coming winter, which will call for aid from the Government unless provided for.

I would therefore suggest that an Executive Proclamation in regard to Agriculture, like in its beneficent purposes that issued by the President in regard to trade,[1] be at once put forth, to reassure the people of the South upon this point, while the Government is maturing its policy as to the disposition of property in the South, and getting the necessary machinery to work. Seed time will not wait for that, therefore let it be stated to the South under your signature, that whatever may be final policy of the Government as to the disposition of the lands and property of the South, he who sows or plants, shall also reap and that his right in the product of the soil produced by his labor and care, shall appertain to him, whether loyal or disloyal, so far at least as the present season is concerned and let every man, white or black, in the South be exhorted to sow and plant everything that can be sown and planted, especially corn and bread-stuffs. To that might also be added the production of meat especially Bacon, the staple food of the South with the assurance that the Government will protect them in that production.

The necessity of immediate action upon this point, even while the Government is determining its policy, is my apology for troubling you with this note; and that it may meet your eye, I will enclose it to a friend[2] asking him to lay it before you.

With sentiments of the highest regard I am Very Respectfully
Your Obedient Servant Benj. F. Butler

Draft, DLC-Benjamin F. Butler Papers.

1. On April 29 Johnson had issued an Executive Order Removing Certain Restrictions on Trade in the South east of the Mississippi. He did not follow Butler's suggestion as to an order relating to agriculture. See *Johnson Papers*, 7: 669.

2. Butler had asked David K. Cartter, chief justice of the district court of Washington, D.C., to carry this letter personally to the President. Butler to D. K. Cartter, May 3, 1865, Mrs. Jessie (Ames) Marshall, ed., *Correspondence of Gen. Benjamin F. Butler . . .* (5 vols., Norwood, Mass., 1917), 5: 613–14.

From Peter C. Ellmaker [1]

Philada May 3. 1865

His Excellency Andw. Johnson
President of the U.S.
Sir,

Referring to the accompanying testimonials (some of which are addressed to your lamented predecessor) I desire to say that in the event of a vacancy, I wish to be considered an applicant for the position of marshal for the Eastern District of Pennsylvania. I will merely add that if appointed to that or any other position which I may be considered competent to fill I will endeavor to deserve your confidence and good opinion.[2]

I am Very Respy Yr Obt Servant
P C Ellmaker

ALS, DNA-RG60, Appt. Files for Judicial Districts, Pa., P. C. Ellmaker.

1. Ellmaker (c1814–c1890), a Philadelphia notary and colonel of two Pennsylvania regiments, was variously listed as a shoe and skate merchant, clerk, and accountant during the 1870s and 1880s. 1860 Census, Pa., Philadelphia, 10th Ward Philadelphia, 178; Philadelphia directories (1857–91); Frank H. Taylor, *Philadelphia in the Civil War 1861–1865* (Philadelphia, 1913), 18, 19, 133.

2. The marshalship of eastern Pennsylvania was given to Ellmaker, who held it throughout Johnson's administration. *U.S. Off. Reg.* (1865–67).

To Henry W. Halleck

Executive Mansion May 3d 1865

To Maj Gen. Halleck
Commanding Military Division James
Richmond Va

You have the authority to Exclude Spiritous Liquors from your command and will therefore exercise it if you deem it necessary to the maintenance of order and military discipline.[1]

Andrew Johnson President U.S.

Tel, DNA-RG107, Tels. Sent, President, Vol. 2 (1865).

1. See Letter from Edwin M. Stanton, June 14, 1865, both for complaints against Halleck's use of this authority and for the secretary's advice.

From James E. Hamilton [1]

New York May 3/65

Dear Sir

Do you want to break down the accursed Slave aristocracy? Let the negro *vote*. Do you want justice done to the loyal whites of the South? Let the *negro* vote. Do you want to educate the negro, & make him a man? *Let* him vote. He will not become either until he votes. Do you want traitors kept out of power? *Let the negro vote*. Do you want, under *all* circumstances, votes for "Liberty & Union?"[2] Let the negro vote. However ignorant he may be, his vote is *sure* for both. Do you want the fruits of this Ocean of blood & treasure to be enduring, & make *sure* the foundations of the Republic? Then let *loyal* men, *black* & white *vote*. The public mind is ripe for it. For Gods' sake, & mans', & your own *eternal* fame, have this in the organic law of *every* re-constructed State.

From a loyal southern refugee, who has lost two sons in the war, & all his property.

Yours truly James. E. Hamilton

To His Ex'y Andrew Johnson

ALS, DLC-JP.
1. Not identified.
2. A common phrase derived from Daniel Webster's reply to Robert Y. Hayne on the floor of the Senate in 1830: "Liberty and Union, now and forever, one and inseparable."

From Hannibal Hamlin

Bangor May 3 1865

My Dear Sir

As you suggested you would be pleased to hear from me, I am inclined to address you briefly.

My principle, if not my only object is to assure you truly in all you have said of the *crime* of *treason* and its *punishment*, you have the honest loyal public heart with you. We have no true men with us who are not delighted with your course. Adhere to your course, as I know you will, follow out your own instincts of right, and you will be sure to make your Administration cherished and respected by all good men; and you will thus give it a place in history second to none other. Rest assured the people will be with you, and will sustain you with willing hands and harts. Whatever timid or time serving men may say we the people believe treason is a crime to be punished, and that is the only *security* for the future.

I do not mistake the signs of the times. You will have the earnest

honest and cordial support of the country in sustaing you in your public
duties.

I have said these few words, in the hope that they may cheer you in
your arduous duties, as it can be but gratifieng to you to know what is
the sentiment of the people. It is truly flattering. All you could ask or
desire.

The fighting, I take it may be regarded as over. The accounts of traitors remain to be settled. That done as I am sure you will do it, and I
trust then you will have a time of peace and quiet, and the whole country will advance most rapidly in its course of unequalled prosperity.

                                                    Yours Truly H Hamlin
To the President of the United States.

ALS, DLC-JP.

Interview with Pennsylvania Delegation[1]

                                                        May 3, 1865

MR. CHAIRMAN AND GENTLEMEN   I can only reply in general
terms; perhaps as good a reply as I can make would be to refer to or
repeat what I have already said to other delegations who have come for
the purpose of encouraging and inspiring me with confidence on entering upon the discharge of duties so responsible—so perilous. All that I
could now say would be but a reiteration of sentiments already indicated. The words you have spoken are most fully and cordially accepted
and responded to by me. I, too, think the time has arrived when the
people of this nation should understand that treason is a crime. When
we turn to the catalogue of crime we find that most of those contained
in it are understood, but the crime of treason has neither been generally
understood nor generally appreciated, as I think it should be. And there
has been an effort since this rebellion commenced to make the impression that it was a mere political struggle, or, as I see it thrown out in
some of the papers, a struggle for ascendancy of certain principles from
the dawn of the government to the present time, and now settled by the
final triumph of the Federal arms. If this is to be a determined, settled
idea and opinion the government is at an end, for no question can arise
but they will make it a party issue, and then to whatever length they
carry it the party defeated will be only a party defeated, and no crime
attaches thereto. But, I say treason is a crime—the highest crime
known to the law—and the people ought to understand it and be
taught to know that unless it be so considered there can be no government. I do not say this to indicate a revengeful or improper spirit. It
is simply the enunciation of deliberate consideration and temperate
judgement. There are men who ought to suffer the penalties of their
treason; but there are also some who have been engaged in this rebel-

lion, who, while, technically speaking, are guilty of treason, yet are morally not. Thousands who have been drawn into it, involved by various influences—by conscription, by dread, by force of public opinion in the localities in which they lived—these are not so responsible as those who led, deceived and forced them. To the unconscious, deceived, conscripted—in short, to the great mass of the misled—I would say mercy, clemency, reconciliation, and the restoration of their government. To those who have deceived—to the conscious, influential traitor, who attempted to destroy the life of a nation, I would say "On you be inflicted the severest penalties of your crime." (Applause.) I fully understand how easy it is to get up an impression in regard to the exercise of mercy; and, if I know myself and my own heart, there is in it as great a disposition to mercy as can be manifested on the part of any other individual. But mercy without justice is a crime. In the exercise of mercy there should be deliberate consideration, and a profound understanding of the case; and I am not prepared to say but what it should often be transferred to a higher court—a court where mercy and justice can best be united. In responding to the remarks of your chairman in reference to free government and the discharge of my duties, I can only say again that my past public life must be taken as the guide to what my future will be. My course has been unmistakable and well defined. I know it is easy to cry out "demagogue;" but let that be as it may. If I have spent the toil of youth and the vigor of my life for the elevation of the great masses of the people, why it was a work of my choosing and I will bear the loss. And if it is demagogism to please the people—if it is demagogism to strive for their welfare and amelioration—then I am a demagogue. I was always proud when my duties were so discharged that the people were pleased. A great monopoly— the remark of your chairman brings me to it—existed: that of slavery; and upon it rested an aristocracy. It is the work of freemen to put down monopolies. You have seen the attempt made by the monopoly of slavery to put down the government. But the making of the attempt, thereby to control and destroy the Government, you have seen the government put down the monopoly and destroy the institution. (Applause.) Institutions of any kind must be subordinate to the government or the government cannot stand. I do not care whether it be North or South. A government based upon popular judgment must be paramount to all institutions that spring up under that government; and if, when they attempt to control the government, the government does not put them down, they will put it down. Hence the main portion of my efforts have been devoted to the opposition of them. Hence I have ever opposed aristocracy—opposed it in any shape. But there is a kind of aristocracy that has always, that always will, command my respect and approbation—the aristocracy of talent, the aristocracy of virtue, the aristocracy of merit, or an aristocracy resting upon worth, the aristocracy of labor, resting upon honest industry, developing the industrial resources of the country—this commands my respect and admiration—my support in life. In regard to my future course in connection with this rebellion, nothing that I can say would be worth listening to. If my past is not sufficient guarantee, I can only add that I have never knowingly deceived the people, and never have betrayed a friend—(applause)—and, God willing, never will. (Applause.) Accept my profound and sincere thanks for the encouragement you have given me, and believe me when I say that your encouragement, countenance and confidence are a great aid and a great spur to the performance of my duties. Once more I thank you for this manifestation of your regard and respect.[2]

New York Herald, May 4, 1865.

1. Former secretary of war Simon Cameron, chairman of a committee appointed at a Harrisburg meeting, had a personal interview with the President to present the resolutions adopted at the meeting. Congressman Thaddeus Stevens and other prominent Pennsylvanians, along with committee members, were in the audience. After a brief address by Cameron, the President responded.

2. The *National Intelligencer* of May 5, in its report of the Pennsylvanians' visit, trenchantly observed: "The President made a lengthy reply, in which, however, he suffered no more of his intentions to be revealed than he had made public through his speech to the Indiana and other delegations."

From Samuel McKee[1]

Mount Sterling Ky May 3rd 1865

Andrew Johnson President U S
Washington D C
Dr Sr

Permit me to Call your attention to the State of Affairs in Ky. A very large Rebel Element (Soldiers) is now being turned loose upon our State. It is wholy useless to attempt any defense for the policy attempted and partially carried out by those whoe have been Political Leaders in this State. She has been against the policy of this Goverment during the whole war & while she has, and always has had thousands of truly Loyal men, a majority of her People have always been either open enemies of the Government, or the friends & Sympathisers of those whose whole aim has been to break up and destroy the Union. And while they are Conquered, whiped and subjugated, so far as they have power through arms—they still hold that fiendish spirit of bitterness toward our Cause & those who through the whole struggle have been steadfast to the administration. 1200 Rebels have just been turned loose in our midst at this Town; & these same men, who have been for four years engaged in the wicked attempt to make a wreck of our Ship of State, who have carried murder plunder & devastation over our own State, and the State which gave them birth, some of them the vey men who with torch in hand fired this Town and laid a large portion of it including the County Buildings, in ashes; now walk our streets decked out in Confederate Uniforms with their Pistols belted around them, feasted and made more of by the majority of the People here; than any soldiers or Officers of the [Federal] army, who have for four years periled their lives in defending our Country from the attempts of these traitors, and in protecting the homes of these Secession Sympathisers *alias "Conservative Union men."* It is an insult to the Loyal men of Kentucky to permit such things. These professed Union men, are now as they have always been allied heart & soul, with the enemies of our Country. To day they hate the U S. Govermt as it has been, & I trust will continue to be administered, more thoroughly than the men who have been outspoken friends of Jeff Davis from the begining. They hate real Union men more thoroughly, than the Rebels themselves hate us. The whole concern will vote together in the Coming August Election for members of Congress and the State Legislature & Rebel Sympathising Citizens here openly boast that the Rebels have the power and will control the Elections in this State.[2] It is a sad state of things for a Union man to reflect upon. In the face of all these things—we hear all over the land—that these traitors must be pardoned & have all their rights as before. As an humble Citizen of the State of Kentucky—I have seen and felt the effects of this war—served my Country 20 months in the army—15 of the time in Rebel Prisons, and both as Citizen & Soldier have fought them from the begining to this day, in the field & on the Stump, and will continue so long as God gives me life to fight their nefarious cause & strive to render all who have engaged in it odious to all future generations. I protest against the Lenient policy that has been and is still pursued toward Kentucky traitors. Let these men be striped of their traitor garb, & their arms handed over to the Federal authorities. I cannot see why a Paroled Prisonr of war is allowed privileges here, that are denied him in other States.[3] Let the masses live—So long as they act honestly and behave themselves—but let them be subjects (not rulers at the ballot box, or elsewhere,) of the Loyal People. We must have federal aid here more stringent than it has been. Our state authorities are too weak—too soft and mild, to meet the designs of the Goverment, and the Loyal mired in the present important crisis. These are facts no fancies. Born and raised in this State I know this people, and I know their views; we have a strong Loyal Party in Kentucky—but the Federal authorities, must aid us in our efforts, or Kentucky will stand next August opposed to the great issues which tend not only to her own peace & happiness, but to [the] great end of freedom and prosperity for our whole land.

Very Respectfully Samuel McKee

ALS, DNA-RG60, Office of Atty. Gen., Lets. Recd., President.
    1. McKee (1833–1898), native Kentucky lawyer, served as captain, 14th Ky. Cav.,

USA, Republican congressman (1865–67), and pension agent at Louisville (1869–71). *BDAC*.

2. McKee's prediction proved accurate; despite the efforts of Kentucky governor Thomas E. Bramlette and Gen. John M. Palmer to bar ex-Confederates from the polls, Conservative forces prevailed, albeit narrowly, over the Republicans in the August 7, 1865, election. E. Merton Coulter, *The Civil War and Readjustment in Kentucky* (Chapel Hill, 1926), 280–82. See also Telegram to Palmer, August 1, 1865.

3. In an opinion on April 22, Attorney General Speed denied the right of Confederate officers to wear their uniforms—the "traitor's garb"—or of paroled officers and soldiers to return to their homes in loyal states, having "abandoned" them when they went South and joined the Confederate army. Palmer had been somewhat lenient in allowing these veterans to return to Kentucky, one of the "loyal" states. J. Hubley Ashton, ed., *Official Opinions of the Attorneys General* (42 vols., Washington, D.C., 1852–1974), 11 (1869): 204–9; *Philadelphia Press*, Apr. 27, 1865; Coulter, *Civil War Kentucky*, 273–74.

From Edwin M. Stanton

War Department Washington City,
May 3 1865

Mr President.

Evidence has this moment been received from Charleston showing Governor Aiken[1] to have been directly and actively engaged in the rebellion and a Stockholder in a blockade running company.

Please enter into no arrangements or give no promise to him until I can show you these proofs.[2]

Yours truly Edwin M. Stanton

ALS, DLC-JP.

1. William Aiken (1806–1887), wealthy Charleston rice planter, had been a legislator, governor, and congressman. Opposing secession, he nonetheless aided the southern cause by giving supplies and by subscribing to Confederate loans. *DAB*.

2. Arrested April 26, Aiken was taken to Washington, where Stanton "directed him to report to the President." Johnson "received him most cordially, and readily granted his request to be allowed parole, to report whenever he should be wanted." Aiken's interview with Johnson may have already occurred when Stanton's note was written, or, if not, the Executive may have chosen to ignore it. On August 28, 1865, Johnson pardoned Aiken. *Charleston Courier*, Apr. 28, May 16, June 1, 7, 1865; *House Ex. Docs.*, 39 Cong., 2 Sess., No. 31, p. 2 (Ser. 1289).

From Salmon P. Chase

May 4, 1865, Beaufort, N.C.; ALS, DLC-JP. See *Advice*, 17–19.

The chief justice makes his initial report on conditions in the postwar South. Having briefly stopped in Virginia, he counsels the early move of Governor Peirpoint to Richmond and wide distribution of the amended state constitution, as desirable steps in the restoration of civil government. Conversations with several North Carolinians reveal that while they find black suffrage "distasteful," and "would *prefer* to have the reorganization in their own hands & those of *their friends* . . . they would acquiesce in any mode of reorganization rather than see any more rebellion." He has reminded them "that no functionaries who derived their powers from rebels can be recognized in any way by the national government," and concludes, "You *can* do what you think right & do it *safely*. In my judgment the most decided & prompt action is safest."

From Joseph W. Etheridge[1]

Roanoke Island N.C.
May 4th 1865.

To his excellency Andrew Johnson
president of the United States.
Sir

I hope you will not consider it presumption in me for addressing you this epistle. I assure you it is the great interest I feel for my people who have been and are still loyal to the United States government, that prompts me to act in this matter.

There is an effort being made by the secession sympathizers and a number of the members of the rebbel legislature of N.C. who have come in our lines since the surrender of Lee & Johnson[2] to get Brig. Genl. I. N. Palmer[3] appointed Military Governer of this State. There are particians being circulated by this said class of men with Genl. Palmer's approveal asking the people to sign ther names requesting you to make this appointment. We who have made a sacrifice of our *Homes* and all that was near and dear to us—are opposed to this appointment, not from any ill feeling for we all respect Genl Palmer as a kind harted gentleman, but from these reasons.

1. Because Genl. Palmer has identified himself with the secessionist by being favorable to thems since he has been in N.C.

2 Because Genl. Palmer used his influance in New Berne at the last election in favor of Genl. George B McClellan a man who we Union men of the South did not look upon as our friend.

3 Because Genl. Palmer has expressed himself as being opposed to punishing those who have been guilty of treason—he has declaired that Jeff Davis should go unpunished.

4. Because Genl. Palmer is not competent to discharge the duties of such a position not having any experience in political affairs.

5 Because Genl. Palmer has advised and insisted upon Union men opperating with some of the most vile rebbel officers in the reorganization of the state government.

6 Because When the rebbel Col. John Whitford[4] surrendered his Regt. to Genl Palmer, He (Palmer) allowed Whitfords men to retain their arms, and since their return home some of them belonging to this regt. have threatened to shoot Union Men.

Mr President we who are acquainted with these facts think they are sufficient to ask you to give us a different man. We are now having peticians signed by those who have been & are still loyal, requesting you to appoint D. R. Goodloe, Esq.[5] formally of N.C. now a resident of Washington City, D.C.

Our Communication is so much interrupted that it will be some time before we can get every thing to work. As we have no boats at our command as the others have. We wish Mr Goodloe because we believe he will make these leading Rebbels *feel* that they have been guilty of treason—And allow those who have been driven from their Homes—imprisoned—and their property taken and appropriated for the benefit of the enfernal Rebelion to be used once more as independant Citizens of the U.S. Yes we wish to be permitted, when we choose to give three cheers for that old *Flag*, the *Stair Spangled Banner—and no one dare make me affraid.* Mr President I am willing the privates in the army should be allowed to return home quietly—but I never want one of the leaders to have any power over me again. For I would hang them—"by the Eternal." I have written just as I feel—and I hope you will pardon me for such *presumption.*

I remain Sir with much respect

Your Obt. Servt. J. W. Etheridge
formerly Capt. in N.C.W. Vols
now Agt. Treas. Dept

ALS, DLC-JP.

1. Etheridge (b. c1837), a fisherman, had been a first lieutenant, 1st N.C. Inf., USA, resigning February 21, 1863. Subsequently, he served the Republican party as a delegate-at-large in the 1872 election. 1860 Census, N.C., Carrituck, North Banks Dist., 112; *Official Army Register of the Volunteer Force of the United States Army for the Years 1861, '62, '63, '64, '65* (8 vols., Washington, D.C., 1865–67), 4: 1145; James A. Padgett, ed., "Reconstruction Letters from North Carolina: Part VI, Letters to William E. Chandler," *NCHR*, 19 (1942): 70.

2. Joseph E. Johnston (1807–1891), Confederate general. Warner, *Gray.*

3. Innis N. Palmer (1824–1900) held various commands in eastern North Carolina during the last half of the war. Warner, *Blue.*

4. John N. Whitford (b. c1837), Craven County merchant, had risen from captain of an artillery company to colonel, 67th N.C. Inf., CSA. Louis Manarin, comp., *North Carolina Troops, 1861–1865: A Roster* (10 vols., Raleigh, 1966–   ), 1: 138; 2: 84.

5. Daniel R. Goodloe, an antislavery leader and newspaper correspondent for the *New York Times*, did return to North Carolina but as U.S. marshal. *NCAB*, 10: 71.

Order re *Closing for Lincoln Funeral*

Executive Mansion Washington, May 4, 1865

This being the day of the funeral of the late President Abraham Lincoln at Springfield Illinois the Executive Office and the various Departments will be closed at 12N. today.

Andrew Johnson Prest U.S.

Official copy respectfully furnished to the Honorable Secretary of the Interior.[1]

W. A. Browning
Private Secretary

DS, DNA-RG48, Appts. Div., Misc. Lets. Recd.
    1. Browning sent official copies of this announcement to the secretaries of the several departments.

From George N. Sanders and Beverly Tucker [1]

Montreal May 4th 1865.

Andrew Johnson
President United States,
Sir,

Your proclamation[2] is a living, burning lie, known to be such, by yourself and all your surroundings, and all the hired perjurers in Christendom, shall not deter us from exhibiting to the civilized world, your hellish plot to murder *our* Christian President. We recognize in many of your distinguished Generals, men of honor, and we do not beleive that their association, even with you, has so brutalized them, as to prevent their doing justice to a public enemy under such grave charges.

Be this, as it may, we challenge you to select any nine of the twenty five Generals we now name to form a Court Martial for our trial, to be convened at the United States Fort at Rouse's Point, or any other place, that you will not have the power to incite the Mob to destroy us *en route*.

Generals Scott, Grant, Sherman, Meade, Rosecrans, Howard, Burnside, Hancock, Hooker, Scofield, Wright, Dix, Cadwallader, Emory, Blair, Pleasanton, Logan, Steele, Peck, Hatch, Franklin, Rodman, Alexander, Carr, Reynolds, Meagher.[3]

The money that you have so prodigally offered to have the unoffending neutrality of a neighboring state violated, by the unwarrantable Seizure of our persons, to be paid over, to defray our professional and other expenses of the trial, to the lawyers that we shall designate, and who are in no wise, to be prejudiced by appearing in our defense. Our witnesses to have the fullest protection, and upon our acquittal of the Charges preferred against us in your proclamation, we are to be permitted to return under safe escort.

In conclusion, we say, we have no acquaintance whatever, with Mr. Booth,[4] or any of those alleged to have been engaged with him. We have *never seen*, or had any knowledge, in any wise, of *him* or *them*, and *he has never written us a note*, or *sought an interview with us*.

Geo. N. Sanders
Beverly Tucker [5]

ALS (Sanders), DLC-JP.
    1. Confederate agents in Canada.
    2. See Proclamation of Rewards for Arrest of Sundry Confederates, May 2, 1865.
    3. Winfield Scott, Ulysses S. Grant, William T. Sherman, George G. Meade, William S. Rosecrans, Oliver O. Howard, Ambrose E. Burnside, Winfield S. Hancock, Joseph Hooker, John M. Schofield, Horatio G. Wright, John A. Dix, George Cadwalader, Wil-

liam H. Emory, Frank P. Blair, Alfred Pleasanton, John A. Logan, Frederick Steele, John J. Peck, John P. Hatch, William B. Franklin, Isaac P. Rodman, A. J., B. S., or B. Alexander, Eugene A. or Joseph B. Carr, Joseph J. Reynolds, Thomas F. Meagher.

4. John Wilkes Booth.

5. On the same day Tucker asked Johnson for a copy of the evidence, reported to be in the Bureau of Military Justice, that he was among those who "incited, concerted and procured" the assassination of Lincoln and attempted assassination of Seward. "If furnished a copy of such evidence," he pledged himself "to disprove it." Tucker to Johnson, May 4, 1865, Johnson Papers, LC.

From Nehemiah D. Sperry

May 4, 1865, New Haven, Conn.; ALS, DLC-JP.

New Haven postmaster recommends for a position in Johnson's cabinet Montgomery Blair, one of the "most efficient workers in the Union cause," who sacrificed his position as Postmaster General in Lincoln's cabinet "in order to promote party harmony, and to conciliate certain elements of discord."

From George M. Swan[1]

Norwalk, Warren Co., Iowa,
May 4, 1865.

Honored Sir:

Permit a stranger to furnish some evidence of the heart-felt regard entertained by the People, even in remote rural districts, for your welfare and happiness.

Fearing I may trespass upon your time, I close with assurances that the People will sustain you, with all their might.[2]

Your obt. servant, Geo. M. Swan.

ALS, DLC-JP.

1. Swan (b. c1813) was a native Connecticut farmer, who moved to Iowa by way of Ohio, where he had lived for more than ten years. 1860 Census, Iowa, Warren, Lynn Twp., 157.

2. Though brief, Swan's letter is typical of the many messages of support from rank and file citizens, which descended upon the new President.

From Benjamin H. Brewster[1]

706 Walnut Street Philadelphia
May 5 1865

Mr. President

Many persons here who think and act with me, have again and again asked me to write and express to you in a short way the views they hold in common with you as to the policy to be taken towards the leaders of this recent rebellion. It was my intention to have gone to see you in person with the gentlemen who were headed by Genl. Cameron & Mr. Stevens; but my professional affairs detained me. The answer given by you[2] to the remarks made by their leader, are so satisfactory to the large body of old Democrats with whom I have acted that they have again applied to me and asked me to say that you have reflected their wishes and that they believe you have defined the real sentiments of the larger part of the loyal men in Pennsylvania. I should rather say of nearly all of the loyal men in this State. In you they recognize an old Democrat and like you 70,000 such men in Penna: have gone out from their old party associates & given new life and vigor to the Republican ranks. Without their help the Goverment would have been frustrated in all of its attempts to enforce the law & probably the rebellion would have been triumphant. While the War lasted they made no struggle for party honor's or promotions. It is well they did not as it would have impeached the sincerity of their action. Now the War is over [and?] a Democrat of like temper holds the authority, they hope that they will not be fused into the mass of Republicans, loose their identity and be subject to the command & discipline of old Whig & Republican leaders or driven to the necessity of again acting with a party—their old party—polluted by lawless sympathy with traitors & their bad deeds. To you we all look for that protection which must come from you or we will be laid aside and sacrifised to an organization of which we are but an accidental part and with which we are not permitted to have connection unless it shall be as subordinates and inferiors.

I am Sir Truly Your Friend
Benjamin Harris Brewster

To His Excellency Andrew Johnson
The President of the United States
Washington City D C

ALS, DLC-JP.
1. Brewster (1816–1888) was a native New Jersey lawyer, who became Pennsylvania's attorney general (1867–69) and later U.S attorney general (1881–85). *NCAB*, 4: 253.
2. See Interview with Pennsylvania Delegation, May 3, 1865.

From R. L. Brooks

May 5, 1865, New Orleans, La.; ALS, DLC-JP.

Understanding that Governor Wells is about to go to Washington seeking appointment as military governor, this Illinois-born teacher, who was conscripted into the Confederate army and who, as a member of the Free State Legislature of Louisiana, has been supportive of Wells—"I am personally his friend"—asks that if such an appointment is made, it not be Wells, who "has betrayed the party that elected him." Speaking on behalf of the "poor men of this State," he urges that if they are to have a military governor, he be "one who is of undoubted loyalty, who is opposed to *Treason* in all its forms; one who has *no sympathy* for rebels or rebel sympathizers." Reports in some detail the evidence, principally seen in Wells's appointments, for considering him as "nothing more than a pliant tool in the hands of a few who constitute a nucleus of the old secession party in this State." Assures Johnson that Louisiana did not secede "by the popular voice, but was tricked into it by the aristocratic leaders of the State." Does not want again to "fall into the hands of these unscrupulus men to be at some future day again tricked into rebellion."

From James Dixon [1]

Hartford, May 5, 1865

My Dear Sir,

Since my return from Washington I have been highly gratified to witness the almost universal disposition to support your administration. It seems to be a restoration of the "Era of good feeling." Never since my earliest acquaintance with public affairs, has so warm and generous a disposition been manifested towards any President. It is impossible not to perceive that your old Democratic associates feel a revival of their ancient regard for you. It would not surprise me at all, if you should find them among the warmest of your supporters. A very significant fact occurred yesterday in our Legislature. I mean the *unanimous* ratification of the Amendment to the Constitution of the United States abolishing slavery. The entire Democracy voted in the affirmative. From this it is easy to see that they do not mean hereafter to be trammelled by slavery—or to allow it to remain a party issue.

I rejoice that you have before you so bright a prospect. Your agreeable duty is to restore the Government to its former position, and to bind together in friendly relations the alienated sections of the Country. If you succeed as I have no doubt you will, a grateful people will reward you with renewed honors.

I shall not venture to say one word by way of advice—but this I hope you will pardon me for saying—that should you call new members into your cabinet, your best friends here hope for the appointment of *Montgomery Blair* to the head of a Department. I know Mr Blair well. He is a wise, firm, capable, honest man. You can trust him in any emergency. I hope he will be placed in some position where his abilities may benefit the Nation as well as yourself.

With the highest respect & esteem, I remain
Your faithful friend, & obt. Svt. James Dixon
To his Excellency Andrew Johnson
President of the United States

ALS, DLC-JP.
1. Dixon (1814–1873), a native Connecticut lawyer, was a state legislator, congressman, and U.S. senator (1857–69). *DAB*; *BDAC*.

From Anson Herrick

[May] 5, 1865, New York, N.Y.; ALS, DNA-RG56, Appts., Internal Revenue Service, Assessor, N.Y., 9th Dist., Hugh M. Herrick.

The editor of the *New York Atlas* and former congressman, who had become "the subject of considerable party abuse" and had "sacrificed" his position in the Democratic party by advocating and voting for the antislavery amendment while in Congress, asks Johnson to appoint his brother Hugh assessor of internal revenue for the 9th New York District. Lincoln had nominated him too late for action before Congress adjourned in March and had subsequently been thwarted in his efforts to commission Herrick. [Although the President referred this letter to the secretary of the treasury, the incumbent was not replaced.]

To David T. Patterson

Washn. May 5. 1865.

Hon David T. Patterson
Nashville, Tenn.

I desire the family to come as soon as arrangements can be made here. Mrs Lincoln is expected to leave in a few days.[1] The package sent contained articles for Mary and Martha's children.

Andrew Johnson.

Tel, DNA-RG107, Tels. Sent, President, Vol. 2 (1865).
    1. Mrs. Lincoln moved out of the Executive Mansion in late May. A short time later Johnson moved his office into the White House, but he did not take up residence there until early June. Although some members of his family arrived in Washington on June 19, they lived at the Soldiers' Home during most of the summer. *New York World*, May 23, 26, 1865.

From Jacob Srite [1]

LaFayette Ga May 5th 1865

Dear Friend

If you recollect me a fiew years since I lived in Sullavan county Tenn and was a friend and admirer of yours and have continued to be so. I am truly glad that you have succeeded so well in this wicked Rebellion. At one time I was fearfull that you and Brownlow was in great danger. The union men have suffered verry much here on account of their being true to the united states. I have been with you in sentiment & feeling all the time. The time will soon arrive when you will want some men in this state for Federal officers who have been well tried and whoes notions accord with your own. Permit me to present to you the name of Lawson Black[2] of Walker county Georgia for judge of the united states court for the district of Georgia. He is a good lawyer and a man of firmness and decession, of good character and has been a true & firm supporter of the union all the time, and will make you just such an officer as you aught to have in this state. For which I refer you to aney union man who knows him. I am in good health and remain yours Truly

                                                                Jacob Srite

ALS, DNA-RG60, Appt. Files for Judicial Dists., Ga., Lawson Black.
    1. Srite (1793–1885), Tennessee-born farmer, had moved his family to Georgia in 1853. 1860 Census, Ga., Walker, Lafayette, 678; James A. Sartain, *History of Walker County, Georgia* (Carrollton, Ga., 1972[1932]), 537.
    2. Black (b. *c*1805), a former state legislator and neighbor of Srite, did not receive the judgeship. Ibid., 300; 1860 Census, Ga., Walker, Lafayette, 677.

From James M. Thompson

May 5, 1865, Fairfax Seminary Hospital, Va.; ALS, DLC-JP.

A contract physician from Pennsylvania urges "the advantages and propriety of appointing Frederick Douglas (or some other black American citizen of executive ability), the military governor of South Carolina," seeing "the poetic justic as well as the punishment of that traitor state in such a consumation." Moreover, it would attract free blacks from the free states and Canada to South Carolina and "thus add materially to the civilization and enlightenment of the native population of the state!"

From J. Madison Wells

                                State of Louisiana, Executive Department,
                                        New Orleans, May 5th 1865
Sir

    About half past one o'clock this P.M. Several officers, among whom was Samuel M. Quincy[1] 73d United States Colored Infantry arrived at the Mayoralty of this City and presented themselves at the room of Mayor Kennedy[2] with whom I was engaged on business. Col Crosby[3] of Gen'l Banks Staff Said that Col Quincy had come by order of the commanding Gen'l to take charge of the City of New Orleans as the Acting Mayor, and presented an order to that effect, which I enclose for your information.

    I immediately protested as Governor of the State against the extraordinary proceeding, Characterizing it as a flagrant abuse of Military power, contrary to the well understood wishes of the National Government and calculated to create wide spread dissatisfaction and distrust.

    Mayor Kennedy accepted the office only at my earnest Solicitation and Since he has Charge of it, the happiest evidences of confidence in Civil government and local administration have been given. The blow however is not aimed at him, but at Civil government in Louisiana and

I feel if this act of Gen'l Banks is Sanctioned by you Mr President and he is retained in power here, there is no necessity whatever for keeping up a shadow of civil authority when the Substance is destroyed.

The Steamer for New York will leave in the morning and I have not therefore time to explain at greater length, the peculiar difficulties now created by Gen'l Banks.[4]

I have the honor to be &c J Madison Wells
Governor of Louisiana

Andrew Johnston
President of the U States

LS, DLC-JP.

1. Quincy (1833–1887), a native Massachusetts lawyer and colonel of the 73d USCI, had been ordered on May 5, 1865, to become the acting mayor of New Orleans. After leaving the military, he resumed law practice in Boston. Heitman, *Register*, 1: 811; *OR*, Ser. 1, Vol. 48, Pt. 2: 320; *NUC*; Boston directories (1870–80); McCrary, *Lincoln and Reconstruction*, 311.

2. Hugh Kennedy was subsequently reinstated as mayor. See Letter from Wells, July 3, 1865.

3. New Yorker John S. Crosby (1839–1914) served as a staff officer under Banks and his successor, Philip H. Sheridan. Subsequently, he was American consul to Florence and territorial governor of Montana. Powell, *Army List*, 264; *DAB*.

4. Wells carried a letter of introduction from U.S. Marshal Cuthbert Bullitt, who characterized Wells as "as thorough a unionist, as we have in the country," and concluded: "If there is any man in the state that is calculated to harmonize & bring back all parties into line it is Governor Wells." Bullitt to Johnson, May 5, 1865, Johnson Papers, LC. See Letter from Wells and Others, May 26, 1865, regarding the special commission which investigated Louisiana affairs.

From Andrew Cunningham

May 6, 1865, Charleston, W. Va.; ALS, DNA-RG60, Office of Atty. Gen., Lets. Recd., President.

A Virginia-born plasterer seeks the removal of Benjamin H. Smith as district attorney for the Federal Court of the District of West Virginia on the ground that "no prosecution for treason,—or for confiscation of property, will be prosecuted to conviction" by him because he is not a Union man, despite his protestations. Cites a variety of evidence of Smith's sympathy and support for treason and traitors: he knows of the treason of his own son and of many others, yet does nothing; he has many times vouched for captured traitors; he has sent money from the sale of confiscated property to those at war with the U.S. government; he has appointed disloyal persons to county offices; he has "never at any time given one argument or word of encouragement to the really loyal people of this County"; both his mother-in-law and his blacks attest to his secessionist sentiments, one of the latter saying that Smith is a Union man outdoors and along the streets, "but in de house—he's good secesh as any uv um." Charges that all the prominent legal men of the Kanawha Valley in 1861 "espoused the insergents cause, either openly or covertly," explaining that they arranged to have part of the family "go for the Union" and part for the Confederacy so as to protect the family property by assigning it to those members on the victorious side. Smith was a party to such a "compromise with the iniquity of treason." [Johnson referred the matter to the attorney general; Smith was not replaced.]

From William M. Fishback

Carrollton Ills May 6th 1865

Hon A. Johnson
President—Sir:

You will probably remember my name as the Senator elect from Ark.[1]

Having noticed in your proclamation removing the restrictions upon trade in certain Rebellious States that Ark. is omitted, I take the liberty of calling your attention to certain considerations which I could hope would induce you to open to unrestricted trade all that portion of Ark. lying north of the Arkansas River and including the post of Ft. Smith.

As you will remember the State of Ark. has never seceded by a vote of her people and the convention, after voting down the ordinance, finally voted for secession only at the point of the bayonett.[2] This should entitle them to favorable consideration at least.

In the city of Ft Smith and the northwestern portion of the State where the loyalty has always approached unanimity (being a mountainous region composed mostly of East Tennesseeans) the Armies of the Union remote from any base of supplies were compelled for a long time to subsist on the people consuming their all before the River rose so that supplies could be furnished from elsewhere. Since the rise of the River the trade regulations have still kept back supplies and thus those who have not been compelled to emigrate are left in an absolutely suffering condition.

The River will be down in a few weeks so that no more provisions can be carried up. Hence the need of immediate relief and Hence this appeal for which under the circumstances I may be pardoned.[3]

Very respectfully Your ob'dt Servt
W. M. Fishback

ALS, DNA-RG56, Misc. Div., Claims for Cotton and Captured and Abandoned Property.

1. Though the Senate failed to seat both Arkansas senators in the fall of 1864, Fishback proved the more objectionable, having offered in the secession convention the resolution to resist all Federal coercion "to the last extremity." Michael B. Dougan, *Confederate Arkansas* (University, Ala., 1976), 51.

2. A secession convention had assembled in Little Rock in March 1861, but Conservatives led by Fishback prevented passage of an ordinance in favor of disunion. The delegates did authorize a referendum on the issue to be held August 5, 1861, but Lincoln's call for volunteers and the seizure of Fort Smith impelled the reassembly of the convention, which almost unanimously endorsed secession as an accomplished fact. Ibid., 56–64, 68; Ralph A. Wooster, *The Secession Conventions of the South* (Princeton, 1962), 157, 161–65.

3. Johnson on May 14 referred the letter to General Grant "for his opinion as to the propriety of complying with the request." In returning Fishback's communication, Grant indicated that the request "with great propriety [could] be complied with," so long as it

did not include the part of the state south of the Arkansas River. A final endorsement from the treasury secretary's office read: "Keep this in view—but the Secy thinks no action just now."

From Benjamin B. French

Office of the Commissioner of Public Buildings,
Capitol of the United States,
Washington City, May 6, 1865

Andrew Johnson President of the U.S.

Dear Sir,

In compliance with your request at our personal interview a few days since I report to you the names of all those persons employed at the Presidential Mansion who receive their appointment from, and are paid by me, as Commissioner, viz.

J[ohn]. R[K]. Vernon Night Watchman	$720 per ann.	
Jas. Kelly " "	720	"
Edward Burke Door Keeper	720	"
Alphonso Dunn Assist. Do	720	"
Thos. H. Cross (cold.) Fireman	720	"

A section of the Civil Appropriation act of March 3d, 1857, Vol. 11, p. 228, authorizes the President to employ, in his official household, one private secretary, salary $2,500, one steward, salary $1,200, one messenger, salary $900 (now, with the per centage, $1,000)

The secretary to sign land patents, and other clerks necessary to carry on the business of the President's Office, and usually one messenger, and sometimes I believe two, have been detailed from the Interior Department in conformity with the desire of the President.[1]

The person now performing the duty of Messenger, appointed by President Lincoln, & now absent, having accompanied the remains to Springfield, is Thomas Pendell.[2]

Since the adjournment of Congress a quantity of china and glass ware for the House was purchased by Mrs. Lincoln, the bill for which has been presented to me for approval since the President's death, approved by Mrs. Lincoln. I did not think proper to approve it, not having been consulted relative to the purchase. I have examined, carefully, the glass & china & find it all in the house, and it will be necessary for your use, there being but little other. The bill amounts, I think, to between 2 & 3 thousand dollars.[3] I understand the gentleman who furnished it, Mr. Kerr[4] of Phila. who is a most respectable man, offers to take it back, but, before suffering this to be done, I have thought it proper to call your attention to the subject, & follow any direction you may give.

My opinion is that it had better be kept, & Mr. Kerr be assured that his bill will be paid when the appropriation for furnishing the House has been passed by Congress.

I was told yesterday, at the house, which I visit daily, that Mrs. Lincoln had fixed upon Monday after next as the time of leaving. Mr. Stackpole[5] thinks she will not be able to leave earlier than the 20th.

As soon as she leaves it is my purpose to have all the mourning in the East Room removed & sold at public auction, the avails of which will be devoted to the payment of the bills for the funeral expenses.

Any instructions you may give me will be faithfully carried out.

With high respect Your friend & Obt. Servt. B. B. French
Com. of P.B.

ALS, DLC-JP.

1. Edward D. Neill, followed by Frank Cowan, son of Pennsylvania congressman Edgar, were detailed to Johnson's official household from the Interior Department to sign patents. According to William H. Crook, Johnson had six clerks detailed to him from the departments. Basler, *Works of Lincoln*, 8: 552; Frank Cowan, *Andrew Johnson, President of the United States: Reminiscences of His Private Life and Character* (Greensburgh, Pa., 1894); Margarita S. Gerry, ed., *Through Five Administrations: Reminiscences of Colonel William H. Crook* (New York, 1910), 85.

2. Pendel (1824–*fl*1902) was messenger and doorkeeper at the White House from 1864 to 1902. Thomas F. Pendel, *Thirty-Six Years in the White House* (Washington, D.C., 1902), 9–11, 38, 168; Washington, D.C., directories (1858–64).

3. Mrs. Lincoln, ordering china in January for a state function on the 14th, had also purchased a set for her personal use. The bill for the White House china was still unpaid in October 1865, when Mrs. Lincoln, settling her personal account with the retailer, James K. Kerr, wrote to him. In addition to a sarcastic comment about the Johnsons' lack of knowledge about setting a table, Mrs. Lincoln informed Kerr that it was up to French and Congress to settle with him for the White House china. Justin G. and Linda L. Turner, *Mary Todd Lincoln* (New York, 1972), 198, 262, 276.

4. James K. Kerr (*c*1823–*fl*1892), a lawyer long engaged with his brothers in the china and glassware import business on Philadelphia's Chestnut Street, was subsequently a U.S. appraiser. 1850 Census, Pa., Venango, Borough of Franklin, 291; Philadelphia directories (1865–81).

5. Thomas Stackpole (*c*1825–*c*1872) was a White House watchman (*c*1858–65), before becoming captain of a steamboat. 1860 Census, D.C., Washington, 1st Ward, 203; *U.S. Off. Reg.* (1863), 118; Washington, D.C. directories (1858–78).

From Lewis M. Jacobs[1]

Shelbyville Mo May 6th 1865

Dear Andrew Johnson

It has bin a long time since I seen you being as you fill the station you do. It brought old times back to me. I am in moderate health at present, hoping this will find you the same. Andy what did I tell you years ago that if you lived long you would be president and you would lay back and laugh at me. Well Andy how are you getting along these trying times? I live at the same place that I first moved at when I left old green. It is in shelby Conty shelbyville missouri. I Just live one half mile west from the Courthouse. I have worked tolerably hard andy since I have bin here. I live on a farm. I do not know whether you knew or knot that I had lost the sight of my left eye. I am loozing the use of my hands. They are so stiff I can scarcely write. The season is very late here this spring. The farmers have not planted any corn here yet. This is very good country out here. We have had a long and tedious war. I do wish as you have it now in your power to prolong or stop this war and shedding of blood I do sincerely hope and wish you would stop this war. My wife sends her compliments to you and lady and says she would like very much to see both of you. She often speeks of you. Give my love to your lady and reserve a portion for yourself. I would like very much to see you. If you deem this letter worthy of and answer you will gladden my heart very much. I will expect to hear from you soon.[2] When you write please write and give me all the knews. Your and &

Lewis M Jacobs

ALS, DLC-JP.
1. Jacobs (b. c1799), a Virginia-born farmer who had lived in Greene County, Tenn., during the 1830s, had moved to Missouri about 1840. 1850 Census, Mo., Shelby, 94th Dist., 435.
2. According to the endorsement, this letter was "Answered." The reply has not been found.

To Robert Johnson

Executive Office Wash'n May 6, 1865

Colonel Robert Johnson,
Greenville, East Tennessee

In all my telegrams and letters I stated expressly that I desired the whole family to come to Washington which of course included you, and when here I hope you will comply with all you have stated in your letter.[1] Mary and the children had better come.[2]

Andrew Johnson

Tel, DNA-RG107, Tels. Sent, President, Vol. 2 (1865).
1. Although Robert's letter has not been found, it may be presumed to have reassured his father that he would in the future refrain from excessive drinking and would responsibly discharge any duties assigned to him.
2. See Telegram to Robert Johnson, May 9, 1865.

From Egbert G. Leigh

May 6, 1865, Petersburg, Va.; ALS, DNA-RG60, Appt. Files for Judicial Dists., Va., Egbert G. Leigh.

A reluctant Confederate—"When my state went out of the Union, and not until, I went out with and joined my destinies to hers"—asks appointment as marshal of the Eastern District of Virginia, though "the individuals of distinction to whom I might refer [for testimonials] would I am aware under existing circumstances be no political recommendation." Before the war he was "elected by the people almost unanimously" clerk of several county courts, but neither bore arms nor functioned in office under the Confederate government. [Leigh did not obtain the appointment.]

From Horace Maynard

Private and official.

Nashville May 6, 1865

Dr. Sir,

The election has resulted as I predicted in my last, by the choice of Patterson & Fowler. I being now relieved from public duty, shall report to Mrs. Maynard at Knoxville & go to the practice of law.[1]

I called to-day at your house & found your family well, except Mrs. Johnson in her usual ill-health.

I fear little will be done by the Legislature towards disfranchising rebels. The old fear is still upon too many.[2]

I am very Respectfully
Your Obt. Sevt. Horace Maynard

His Excy Andrew Johnson, President

ALS, DLC-JP.

1. His retirement was short-lived; elected to Congress in August 1865, he served from July 1866 to March 1875.

2. The bill to disfranchise Confederates was being heatedly debated in legislative committees, with Conservative Unionists in the house attempting to modify the Radicals' more extreme franchise measure. As it turned out, Maynard's fear was misplaced, for the legislature denied rebel voting rights. White, *Messages of Govs.*, 5: 429–32; Alexander, *Reconstruction*, 73–75.

From John Overton[1]

Nashville May 6th/65

His Excellency Andrew Johnson
President
Dr. Sir

I came to Memphis Tenn, (near which point in Tennessee I was staying at the time) on the first of Feby last—immediately offered to subscribe to the Amnesty oath both before the Clerk of the Federal Court and Provost Marshal and was told at both places that Genl. Dana[2] then Comg there had issued an order prohibiting any one who had never[sic] borne arms against the Government or was connected with the Rebel Government in any way as agent, from taking said Oath. A few days thereafter I took the oath of Allegiance[3] and started home. At Louisville, that being then the best way, was detained getting a pass. The Federal Court being in session & feeling it to be my duty as well as privilege to take the Amnesty oath at the first point when I could, I went before the clerk of that court & did so, the original of which was sent to Washington. I took it in good faith and so help me God I intend hereafter to be governed by it—did not take it at Louisville under any apprehension that I would not be allowed to take it at

Nashville or with any intention of treating the Comg Genl here disre-spectfully.[4] All of which Miss Maxwell[5] my Sister in Louis[ville] can more fully explain.

I respectfully ask to be restored to my rights which have been denied me except by the Federal Court releasing property here from confiscation.[6]

Very Respectfully Yr Obt Sert Jno. Overton

ALS, DLC-JP.

1. Overton, having fled behind southern lines during the war, had attempted to re-turn home in March, at which time John M. Lea had interceded with Johnson on his behalf. See Letter from Lea, March 20, 1865, *Johnson Papers*, 7: 526–28.

2. Napoleon J. T. Dana.

3. The terms "oath of allegiance" (the pre-amnesty oath for military paroles and non-combatants) and "amnesty oath" were used interchangeably. According to Dorris, Over-ton took the amnesty oath in Louisville. Jonathan T. Dorris, *Pardon and Amnesty Under Lincoln and Johnson* (Chapel Hill, 1953), 236.

4. Gen. George H. Thomas, wishing to control administering the oath in Tennessee, confronted Overton, apparently reproved him sharply, and charged that he took the oath in Kentucky because he "feared he would be unsuccessful if he applied to me" and that he was trying to save his property. *OR*, Ser. 2, Vol. 8: 319, 336, 501, 513.

5. Mary E. Maxwell (1829–*fl*1900) was Overton's sister-in-law. Jeannette T. Ack-len, comp., *Tennessee Records* (2 vols., Baltimore, 1967[1933]), 2: 218; 1900 Census, Tenn., Davidson, 123rd Enum. Dist., 13A.

6. Overton was pardoned the following August 19. Amnesty Papers (M1003, Roll 50), Tenn., John Overton, RG94, NA.

To George H. Thomas

Washington May 6th 1865.

Geo. H. Thomas Maj. Genl. U.S.A.

Citizens of Tennessee inform me that passes are still required from Louisville to Nashville. Could they not be dispensed with?[1]

Andrew Johnson Presdt. U.S.

Tel, DNA-RG393, Dept. of Cumberland, Tels. Recd., Vol. 71.

1. Thomas replied the same day that "orders have been given no longer to require passes of persons wishing to come to Nashville from Louisville." Johnson Papers, LC.

From Joseph E. Brown[1]

Macon Ga May 7th 1865

His Excy Andrew Johnson
President of U S

The complete collapse in the currency and the great destitution of provisions among the poor, makes it absolutely necessary that the Leg-islature meet to supply this deficiency and with a view to the restoration of peace and order by accepting the result which the fortunes of war have imposed upon us.

I have called the Legislature to meet 22d inst. Gen Wilson informs me that he cannot permit the assemblage without instructions from the gov't at Washington.[2] Does he reflect the views of the Government or will you order that no force be used to prevent the meeting of the Legislature?[3]

Jos E Brown
Govr. of Georgia

Approved & will be sent
J H Wilson B M Genl

Tel, DNA-RG107, Tels. Recd., President, Vol. 4 (1865–66).

1. Brown (1821–1894), governor of Georgia since 1857, briefly aligned with the Republican party during Reconstruction; he subsequently served as chief justice of the state supreme court and as U.S. senator. *DAB.*

2. Gen. James H. Wilson believed that the call for a special session violated the terms of the parole which he had issued to Brown on May 5. Parks, *Brown,* 325–28. See Letter from Brown, May 20, 1865.

3. On the evening of May 7, Secretary of War Stanton, following Johnson's instructions, angrily retorted to General Wilson that the collapse of the Georgia economy had been caused by "the treason, insurrection, and rebellion . . . incited and carried on for the last four years by Mr. Brown and his confederate rebels and traitors." Furthermore, by convening the legislature without the President's permission, Brown had "perpetrated a fresh crime" that would be "dealt with accordingly." An hour later, Stanton ordered that Brown be arrested and transported to Washington. Moreover, on May 14, Gen. Quincy A. Gillmore, of the Department of the South, forbade the Georgia legislature to convene. Stanton to Wilson, May 7, 1865, Tels. Sent, Sec. of War (M473, Roll 89), RG107, NA; Stanton to Johnson, May 7, 1865, Misc. Lets. and Papers (1804–67), RG107, NA; *OR,* Ser. 1, Vol. 47, Pt. 3: 498–99, 505–06; Derrell C. Roberts, *Joseph E. Brown and the Politics of Reconstruction* (Tuscaloosa, 1973), 26–28; Alan Conway, *The Reconstruction of Georgia* (Minneapolis, 1966), 19; Parks, *Brown,* 325–29.

From Salmon P. Chase

May 7, 1865, Beaufort Harbor, N.C.; ALS, DLC-JP. See *Advice,* 19–21.

Having conferred with Gen. William T. Sherman on the administration's disavowal of his convention with Gen. Joseph E. Johnston, Chase reports that the nettled general fails "to take into account the great changes produced by the conversion of slaves into free citizens; which alone are sufficient to make honorable reorganization through rebel authorities impossible." Concluding from conversations at New Bern and Beaufort that "All agree that slavery is at an end," but "All seem embarrassed about first steps" to political reorganization, the chief justice encourages Johnson to issue "an order for the enrollment of all loyal citizens without regard to complexion, with a view to reorganization." Urges the President to make a short address promising support in the restoration of state governments if done by conventions of "loyal citizens" without regard to color.

The President and some early advisers
Courtesy Tennessee State Library and Archives

From Daniel Christie[1]

New Orleans May 7/65

To his Excellency, Andrew Johnson,
President of the United States.
Honored Sir.

Louisiana is the *key* to the Rebellious States. She is deserving of a *higher order* of free state men more determined and resolute in favour of the U.S. Govt. Such should be selected to fill the offices in the gift and control of the Government. God help us Loyal men in Louisiana, from the Judge on the Bench of the U.S. Court[2] to the lowest there is *leaning* to traitors, Copperheads, and *infidels* to our govt. We are retrograding in Louisiana. "Wells" is appointing Traitors and Signers of the act of Secession to office. The Loyal men have not a Newspaper to defend them and would have been wholly ruined had not Genl. Banks returned in time to thwart their infamous designs. Oh "for a Parson Brownlow[3] in Louisiana or were it possible for an Andrew Johnson incog." that either might view the machinations of the enemy—more shrewd than those of the arch traitor *Slidell*[4] and equally subversive of the interest of our government. Since Genl. Banks absence we have gone back in the power of traitors in proof of which I cite—the evidence conveyed in the Louisiana *act* of *secession* and Governor Wells has given Commissions to such men ["]*knowingly*"   Chas. Bienvenu
A Veret—
Andrew McCollum[5]

More he has done, equally infamous. If required, I will furnish *proof*.
Your Friend D Christie.

["]Wells" Copperhead Mayor, has been removed by Genl. Banks. This morning I learn that ["]wells" has left for Washington. God grant that for the sake of *truth* and *freedom* and *loyalty* in Louisiana, he may be there defeated.

C—

ALS, DLC-JP.
     1. Christie (d. *c*1870), a carpenter, had been active in the 1864 gubernatorial campaign. New Orleans directories (1859–70); McCrary, *Lincoln and Reconstruction*, 267–68; Ted Tunnell, *Crucible of Reconstruction: War, Radicalism and Race in Louisiana, 1862–1877* (Baton Rouge, 1984), 224.
     2. U.S. district court judge Edward H. Durell (1810–1887), a lawyer who emigrated to New Orleans before the war, presided over the 1864 constitutional convention and, contrary to Christie's assertion, could usually be found on the Radical side of the fence. Ibid.; *DAB*.
     3. William G. Brownlow, governor of Tennessee.
     4. John Slidell, former U.S. senator and Confederate diplomat.
     5. Charles Bienvenu (*c*1824–*fl*1873), a New Orleans attorney, state legislator, and former superintendent of the mint, who replaced Alfred Shaw as sheriff of Orleans parish. Both Adolph Verret (b. *c*1819) and Andrew McCollam (*c*1811–1873) were wealthy planters. All three men had been members of the secession convention, the first two

voting against, and the last in favor of, the secession ordinance. *Official Journal . ... of the Convention of . . . Louisiana* (New Orleans, 1861), 3–4; New Orleans directories (1850–73); J. Carlyle Sitterson, "The McCollams: A Planter Family of the Old and New South," *JSH*, 6 (1940): 347–65; 1860 Census, La., Terrebonne, 12th Ward, 13; 3rd Ward, 96; (1870), Orleans, 7th Ward, New Orleans, 133.

To Henry W. Halleck

Executive Office, Washington City
May 7, 1865.

Major General Halleck, Richmond, Va.

I observe in your order of the third instant to Major General Ord,[1] you authorize him to administer the Amnesty oath to all persons in the civil or military service of the late rebel government without regard to their rank or employment.

I have to request a modification of said order to the effect that, instead of the Amnesty oath, such an oath of allegiance substantially as is prescribed by Act of Congress of August 6, 1861, shall be administered. The Amnesty oath of December 8th 1863[2] will only be administered to those who apply for and are entitled to its benefits.

Andrew Johnson President U.S.

Tel, DNA-RG107, Tels. Sent, President, Vol. 2 (1865).

1. Edward O. C. Ord, commander of the Department of Virginia. In his May 3 order, Halleck had stated that all persons "in the civil or military service of the late rebel government" could take the amnesty oath. Those excluded could "make application for pardon and restoration of civil rights," and such persons who "voluntarily come forward" to take the oath "will be evidence of their intention to resume the status of loyal citizens and constitute a claim for executive clemency." *OR*, Ser. 1, Vol. 46, Pt. 3: 1077.

2. The August 6, 1861, "Act Requiring an Oath of Allegiance . . . to be administered to certain Persons in the Civil Service of the United States," was essentially a loyalty oath, a traditional pledge of affirmation, whereas the amnesty oath of December 8, 1863, was a commitment pledge of loyalty henceforth and included an expression of agreement in the abolition of slavery. Harold M. Hyman, *Era of the Oath* (Philadelphia, 1954), 157, 173.

To James W. Scully

Executive Office, May 7th 1865

Colonel J. W. Scully
Commanding 10th Tennessee Infantry
Greeneville, East Tennessee.

I hope the mustering officer will find time very soon to muster the men out of service.[1] If not, we will try and find some body who will. Steps will be taken to have the Regiment paid off without delay.

I desire Mrs Stover and children to return to Nashville immediately.[2]

Andrew Johnson

Tel, DNA-RG107, Tels. Sent, President, Vol. 2 (1865).

1. The plight of Scully's unionist troops, stationed in an unfriendly neighborhood as the war drew to a close, is delineated in Letter from James W. Scully, May 14, 1865.

2. Johnson's second daughter, Mary, and her children had returned home to East Tennessee. *Johnson Papers*, 7: 597.

From Alabama Citizens

May 8, 1865, Montgomery, Ala.; Pet, DLC-JP.

Signed by seventy-three prominent Alabamians, this petition calls upon the President, in view of his "recent enunciation at Washington of the principle that the states which attempted to secede and permanently sever their connection with the Union are to remain states still, and are not to be lost in Territorial or other divisions," to "permit" the governor to convene the legislature for the purpose of calling a convention to restore the state to her political relations with the United States. If this course is not consistent with Johnson's views, then they ask that one of their prominent men be appointed military governor with authority to call such a convention. They pledge their, and the people of Alabama's, cooperation in the work "To forever put at an end the doctrine of secession—to restore our state to her former relations to the Union, under the Constitution and laws thereof—to enable her to resume the 'respiration of her life breath' in the Union." [A second version, endorsed by a minority of the steering committee at Montgomery, omitted reference to a military governor and to abjuring the doctrine of secession.]

From Alexander R. Boteler

May 8, 1865, Richmond, Va.; Copy, Vi-Executive Papers, Gov. Francis H. Peirpoint, 64–1738.

Having "voluntarily renewed my vow of allegiance to the Govt of the United States," a former Virginia congressman—a Bell supporter who had "labored . . . unremittingly . . . to preserve the Union & to avert from our homes the horrors of civil war"—asks for presidential pardon. Explains that when Virginia, "*contrary* to all my expectations, efforts & desires" seceded and called on "her sons to stand by & defend her from Northern invasion," he could not refuse "to share her fate—for I had been taught to love Virginia better than I loved my life." After serving in the first Confederate congress, he refused several other offices. "But being exiled from my family—*deprived* of *all my property*—my once happy home a *smoking heap of ruins* and being besides, *liable to conscription* for service in the reserves," he accepted appointment as colonel of cavalry, serving on a military court for the Army of Western Virginia until paroled following capture at Appomattox Court House. [Although submitting a second petition on July 8, 1865, he was not pardoned until August 20, 1866.]

From Lewis D. Campbell[1]

Hamilton, O. May 8th 1865.

My Dear Sir—

In compliance with your own suggestion and my promise when we parted at Washington a few days since, I write hastily to express frankly my ideas in regard to the general line of policy by which your official action should be governed, with the understanding that you will only read when you have leisure, and give them just such weight, and no more, as, in your better judgment, they may deserve.

It is fortunate indeed that in your off-hand speeches to various delegations, you referred to your *past history* as furnishing a more reliable guaranty for your future conduct than any promises now made. And I especially liked the announcement of your determination not to decide important questions until they should be legitimately presented for your official action. *Stick to that.* A judge, who, on the bench would take up cases on the docket out of their regular order, and decide grave questions of law not at all involved in the cases in hearing, or who would give judgment in cases not reached or heard, would soon make himself an object of ridicule among sensible men. There are men about Washington and elsewhere, who for sinister purposes, will press you to take ground upon abstract theories; and if once you begin to yield you will soon be pressed for an opinion on "vegetable diet"—the "Maine liquor law" "Woman's rights" &c, &c. I beg of you stick to your idea of giving opinions on important questions only as your official action becomes necessary. There is no practical wisdom in arraying opposition prematurely by taking sides on all the various abstract *isms* and *ills* to which the human intellect is heir.

Your views expressed in regard to the proper treatment of Rebels meets with a hearty concurrence among the people. Your proposed discrimination between the *intelligent leaders* and the *cajoled masses*, is well taken and just. The whole country indorses it.

Our relations with England and France are interesting, and perhaps delicate, as there is prevalent in the country a pretty strong *war spirit*, which will probably be enhanced when our soldiers are disbanded and return home. I would avoid a foreign war and resort to it only when our National honor requires it. The country needs repose and the recuperative influences of peace. If diplomacy should fail in bringing England to a proper redress of the wrongs she has allowed to be inflicted on us during the rebellion, it will be then time enough to call her to account after our fighting men shall have had a little rest, and the whole nation shall have been re-united and prepared with "a good ready!"

If *Juarez*[2] with the *floating* strength he may receive from this and other countries fails to eject Maximillian in a reasonable time, and re-establish the Mexican Republic, then we may with more propriety than now, serve notice on the French Emperor to withdraw his bayonets. In prosecuting the "Monroe Doctrine" we should be cautious not to violate our American principle of *"non intervention.["]* If the people of Mexico of *their own voluntary free will and without force* see fit to change their form of government from a Republic to a Monarchy, I do not see how we could consistently interfere; but if they are compelled at the point of the French and Austrian bayonet to do this, it will, at the proper time, become a high duty we owe to our historic record and to the integrity of our policy long since enunciated, and on all proper occasions re-iterated, to interfere, even though war ensue.

Among other questions in our domestic policy there is one which is beginning to assume much significance—that of *negro suffrage*. This is being every where pressed by those who style themselves *radicals*—a class who sometimes in the grand march of human progress, are inclined to get "*ahead of the music!*" Of course you will be called on to take sides. I regard that question as one belonging exclusively to the States and not to the Federal Government. Congress has declared what an *alien* shall do in order to become a *citizen*; but it has never undertaken to decide who shall be entitled to vote—not even for Federal officers. Illinois and other states allows an alien to vote on a residence of six months: Ohio requires him to naturalize under the act of Congress and reside twelve months in the State. Massachusetts allows the African to vote: Indiana excludes him. I mention these instances to show that the qualifications of the voter is a subject over which the States and not the Federal Government have always heretofore exercised jurisdiction. And as you have very properly assumed the ground that *a State once in the Union cannot go out*, and that the rebellion has only been a gigantic *mob* that temporarily impeded the operations of the Federal government, I cannot see with what consistency you can now interpose Federal Executive authority to settle the right of suffrage in a state. If as President you can settle that question for the State of Tennessee or Louisiana, why may you not also settle it for Ohio and Pennsylvania and relieve the people of its embarrassments. You have already many embarrassments and my advice to you is to *let this question alone. Leave it where it has always been—with the States.*

Your determination to make no sudden change in the Cabinet, until at least the funeral ceremonies of our late lamented President were over, was also wise, and meets universal approval. The proprieties of life and a respect for public opinion required this. But, whenever, in your judgment, the shocked sensibilities of the people are calmed, it may be a grave question whether you should not re-organize to some extent. On this subject I expressed my opinion pretty freely when at Washington. If you live you are to administer the government for four years. If your administration fails, the *odium* will fall on you; and if (with the present Cabinet continued) it is successful the credit will go to the men whom Mr. Lincoln called into power. The naked question presented is whether the administration is to be marked in American history as *yours*, or as a *mere continuation of Mr. Lincoln's*—whether you are to open books for business *on your own account*, or merely to act as "administrator with the will annexed" of your predecessor. Your friends will expect you to *carry on business on your own account.*

I was fully advised of the hot haste of certain parties to get Mr Seward out, even when it was uncertain whether he would live from day to day. On this subject I expressed my views fully to you—perhaps with too much of indignation. I will now only add that all grades of loyal men in this region—radicals and conservatives—believe that Mr. S. is "the right man in the right place" during the existence of our present complications with Foreign powers, and his removal would cause much regret. Public opinion seems to settle down upon Mr. McCullogh[*sic*] as the proper person for the Treasy Dept. But if the residue of the Cabinet were replaced, I think the country would generally approve of it. Mr. Stanton (whether justly or not) has become very unpopular both in and out of the Army and a new man in his place would perhaps give satisfaction and produce harmony. I have but little acquaintance with the residue of the Cabinet excepting Mr. Dennison. He is a very pleasant gentleman and being an Ohioan I would not if I could utter a word in disparagement of him. If it be your purpose to re-organize the Cabinet at all, I think it would be well to do it before long.

But I have already bored you enough for one occasion and I will close. You must find an excuse, my dear Sir, for the freedom with which I write in the fact that I feel an indescribeable interest in your success. After you visited Ohio in 1861, and went with me to address the people in the Scioto, Muskingum and Miami Valleys, I spoke of you to our prominent men as a suitable person to fill the place you now occupy by act of Providence. At my instance our paper published in this city raised your name for the Presidency under its editorial head as early as 1861. After I returned from Tennessee in 1862 I initiated the movement to have the Ohio & Indiana Legislatures invite you to these states. And when recently the uncharitable assaults were made on you by the *sensational* press on the occasion of the inauguration, and the *howl* became almost universal, I was abused and cursed for my activity in your behalf by canting hypocrites. For these reasons, as well as for the sake of our Common Country I do most sincerely desire that your Administration may be one that will redound to the prosperity and true glory of the American Republic and to the honor of yourself and friends. And if I can at any time by word or deed aid you in your great work or relieve you of any burthen it will afford me great pleasure to do so.

In haste Very truly Your &c

Lewis D. Campbell

His Excellency Andrew Johnson
Washington, D.C.

ALS, DLC-JP.

1. A Johnson friend and confidant.

2. Benito Juarez (1806–1872) was governor of his home state and chief justice of the supreme court, among other positions, before becoming president of Mexico in 1858. He organized a successful resistance movement when the French occupied Mexico in 1862 and installed Ferdinand Maximilian as emperor. After French expulsion in 1867, Juarez served five years as president. *Encyclopedia Americana.*

From Salmon P. Chase

May 8, 1865, Wilmington, N.C.; ALS, DLC-JP. See *Advice*, 21–22.

Reiterating that conversations with southerners reinforce "the opinions I have already expressed on the subject of reorganization," he suggests several procedures for "the enrollment of loyal citizens" and urges the President to relax restrictions on trade in states like North Carolina, where the war is no longer active, to facilitate economic rehabilitation.

From William S. Cheatham[1]

Nashville Tenn May 8th 1865

Hon Andrew Johnson
President of U S

A petition is being gotten up in this city requesting you not to withdraw trade restrictions from Tennessee and to allow no one any privilege who is not known to be undoubtedly loyal to the Government signed by the most prominent union men.

Do not withdraw the restrictions for the present.

W R[*sic*] Cheatham

Tel, DNA-RG107, Tels. Recd., President, Vol. 4 (1865–66).
1. Nashville liquor dealer.

From Disabled Union Soldiers

May 8, 1865, Washington, D.C.; ALS, DNA-RG107, Lets. Recd., EB10 President 1135 (1865).

Wishing their "*Stumps*" to speak for them, twenty-nine signers protest that they have been "suddenly deprived" of their jobs as watchmen in the assistant quartermaster's department, "relieved by *able-bodied enlisted* men." Pointing out that "we were, four years ago, able to earn a living honorably" and were "still able to do the duty we have been doing," they ask "*What are we to do? What can you do for us?*" [Upon referring the matter to Stanton's attention, Johnson was reminded that the quartermaster's department, under orders to reduce expenses, had "the duty . . . to discharge all hired persons whose places can be filled by details of Soldiers necessarily retained in the Service."]

From David W. Kurtz

May 8, 1865, Hartford City, Ind.; ALS, DNA-RG60, Office of Atty. Gen., Lets. Recd., President.

Men "who escaped to Canada—to evade serving their Country—are now returning, and as defiant as men can be, some openly applauding the miscreant who assassinated your illustrious predecessor . . . [they] openly revile the Government, and still claim protection, from it." Pointing out that in this part of the country "Union men are largely in the minority," the assistant assessor of Internal Revenue (Indiana) asks whether "men who purposely evaded the military authorities" are to be "allowed the privelege of the elective franchise." Requests that Johnson "issue a proclamation . . . forbidding all persons that ever served in the Rebel Army, or left their homes, or places of abode, for the purpose of evading any Draft, from exercising the elective franchise, or holding any office whatever, for a period of time."

From William J. Leonard

May 8, 1865, Salisbury, Md.; ALS, DNA-RG56, Appts., Customs Service, Naval Officer, Philadelphia, William J. Leonard.

Longtime Johnson supporter and former colonel in Maryland regiment seeks nomination as naval officer of the Port of Baltimore. Praising Johnson for his actions and designating him *"The Man"* to fill his current role, Leonard reminds him that in the June 1864 National Convention, he was the only Maryland delegate to vote for admitting the Tennessee, Arkansas, and Louisiana delegations, and one of two to vote for Johnson as vice-presidential candidate. Had the Tennessee delegation not been admitted to the convention, Johnson probably would not have been elected. Leonard "never regarded any of the seceded states as out of the Union, but their Federal powers in a state of abeyance."

From Halsey F. Cooper

May 9, 1865, Memphis, Tenn.; ALS, DNA-RG108, Lets. Recd. *re* Military Discipline.

U.S. assessor recommends that Gen. A. L. Chetlain, stationed at Memphis for the past two years and respected for his "straightforward Military and gentlemanly bearing," succeed Gen. C. C. Washburn as commander of the district of West Tennessee. "The only objection likely to be made against Genl Chetlain is that he is a Genl of black soldiers, but this objection will be raised only by Secesh Sympathizers and *peculiar* Union men." [Gen. John E. Smith succeeded Washburn on May 29, 1865.]

From William H. Doherty [1]

Newbern, May 9th 1865.

To His Excellency Andrew Johnson,
President of the United States;

The Memorial of Captain W. H. Doherty, of Newbern, N.C., Assist. Quarter Master of Vols., formerly associated, during five years, with the late Hon. Horace Mann,[2] as Senior Professor in Antioch College, Ohio, & late President of Graham College, N.C.,

Respectfully sheweth; That, having been a Citizen of North Carolina for many years, & well acquainted with the sentiments, feelings & deep rooted prejudices of the people of the South, Captain Doherty thinks it his duty, as a man of education & loyalty, to offer to the supreme Authority of our Country, the following suggestions, as to the most efficient mode of settling disputed questions, maintaining the just authority of the Federal Government, securing the Country against all future attempts at rebellion, and re-constructing society in these Southern States, where its very basis has been shaken & disintegrated by the radical, but most righteous and necessary measure of abolishing Negro Slavery.

The following measures are, in his opinion, *absolutely essential to the public good*; & as such he humbly, but very earnestly, recommends them to the consideration of Our respected & esteemed Chief Magistrate.

1st That this State should have a Military Governor, & be ruled by Martial Law, for, at least, two or three years, to come.

2nd That a special U.S. Court should be appointed to examine into the condition of all those vast Estates, subject to confiscation by law— & the continuance of which under their present Rebel proprietors would be, in the highest degree dangerous to the peace & well being of the State.

3d That there will be *immediately instituted* a public sale of these confiscated estates, in lots of not more than one hundred acres each, to individual & actual settlers, bound to reside upon their lands, to cultivate them, build houses & dwell in them. That these lots will be sold at a moderate rate, & ten years time at least of credit given to make payment.

4 That all the purchase Money obtained from such sales will be applied to the payment of the National debt & other expenses of the Federal Government.

5 That a system of Free Schools, both for Whites & Blacks, be established, & supported by Government, and that a man of high education & experience be placed in authority over them, as Inspector & Superintendent, to appoint & pay the teachers, &c.

6th That equal civil rights be at once accorded to the colored people, who are settled & industrious.

7th Every expression of Rebel sentiment to be suppressed, promptly and no Rebel sympathizer to be eligible to any place of honor or profit under the Government of the State.

8th All the present Judges to be dismissed, as having been more or less in sympathy with Rebels,—also all the officers of the State University, & all other public Institutions, & their places filled with loyal men.

9th Every proper exertion to be made to advance the education of the poorer classes, & to encourage the industry of the Colored people & poor whites.

Respectfully Submitted, W. H. Doherty.

ALS, DLC-JP.
1. Doherty (c1810–1890) had resigned in December 1860 as principal and language teacher of Graham College, Alamance County, in order to head an academy at New Bern.

After Federal occupation he established free schools for white children and was appointed
school inspector by Gen. John J. Peck. Captain and aide-de-camp of volunteers during
the last year of the war, he subsequently was the Freedmen's Bureau agent at Elizabeth
City and an applicant for various consulships. 1860 Census, N.C., Alamance, Graham,
7; Heitman, *Register*, 1: 377; Lets. of Appl. and Recomm., 1861–69 (M650, Roll 15),
W. H. Doherty, RG59, NA.

2. Mann (1796–1859) became secretary of the Massachusetts state board of education in the 1830s. Later he was a congressman (1849–53) and president of Antioch.
DAB.

From Jesse Gillmore

May 9, 1865, Philadelphia, Pa.; ALS, DLC-JP.

Ten-year resident of Texas, obliged to leave his home in Gonzales County in
1863, because he had "opposed the damnable scheme of secession" and was
"unwilling my children should grow up inculcated with that vile doctrine,"
endorses Judge Isaiah A. Paschal for an unspecified appointment. The judge
is "an able Lawyer and exceedingly popular with the people of Western Texas,"
who "battled gloriously for the union and so did his noble wife." Cites Samuel
A. Maverick as one of the "blood thirsty vigilence men of Texas" who threatened Judge Paschal and hanged and shot "many hundred unfortunate union
men."

To William W. Holden[1]

Executive Office Washington May 9, 1865

W. W. Holden
Editor Raleigh Standard, Raleigh, N. C.

Can you come to Washington immediately?[2] I wish to confer with
you in reference to North Carolina affairs. The military authorities will
pass W. W. Holden and such other person as he may indicate[3] to Washington and return on Government Transports and over Military Railroads, and furnish transportation and subsistence. General Schofield[4]
will please afford every facility to Mr. Holden in said visit.

Andrew Johnson.

Tel, DNA-RG107, Tels. Sent, President, Vol. 2 (1865).
1. Soon to be appointed provisional governor of North Carolina.
2. Holden accepted Johnson's invitation three days later and arrived on May 18. *OR*,
Ser. 1, Vol. 47, Pt. 3: 486; Raper, *Holden*, 60.
3. William Mason, Robert P. Dick, John H. P. Russ, John C. Williams, and W. R.
Richardson accompanied Holden. Ibid.
4. John M. Schofield, commander of the Department of North Carolina.

To Robert Johnson

Washington City, May 9, 1865.

Robt. Johnson
Greeneville, Tenn.

I want your sister and children to be ready at the earliest moment practicable.[1] My health is tolerable.

Andrew Johnson.

Tel, DNA-RG107, Tels. Sent, President, Vol. 2 (1865).
1. Robert responded by telegraph the same day: "Frank is with me. Mrs. Mary could not come. If you deem it necessary I remain here & bring her with me." Robert Johnson to Johnson, Johnson Papers, LC.

From "Loyal Citizens" of New Orleans

May 9, 1865, New Orleans, La.; Copy, DLC-Nathaniel P. Banks Papers.

New Orleans businessmen, expressing "entire confidence" in Johnson, "are content with and wish to be Governed by the Military Authority" until "a legal, fair and general election by qualified citizens" is held. They endorse General Banks as having been "eminently successful in administrating the affairs of this department" and assure Johnson that "laborers for a reasonable compensation" will be available and thus will not "be an obstacle to the future success of the Planter." They request the President to lift commercial restrictions to foster economic recovery.

Order Restoring Virginia

May 9, 1865, Washington, D.C.; PD, DLC-JP7A.

Declaring null and void "all acts and proceedings of the political, military, and civil organizations" in Virginia since April 17, 1861, the order announces that all persons claiming to act under the authority of Jefferson Davis, John Letcher, or William Smith were in rebellion against the United States "and shall be dealt with accordingly." Serially, each head of a federal department, from state through interior, is directed to make necessary appointments, put into effect the laws relating to his department, and repossess such property as belongs to the United States. Further, Governor Francis H. Peirpoint "will be aided by the Federal Government . . . in the lawful measures which he may take for the extension and administration of the State government throughout the geographical limits of said State."

Resolution from the Tennessee Legislature

May 9, 1865, [Nashville]; D, DLC-JP.

Invoking Article 4, Section 4, of the Constitution ("the guarantee clause"), the legislature asks federal aid to suppress "armed bands of Guerrillas," citing both the absence of "young and middle aged loyal men" still in the U.S. Army and fiscal stringencies to explain the state's inability to take measures to restore order and peace.

From George Whipple[1]

Washington D.C. March [May] 9. 1865[2]

His Excellency President Johnson.

Sir—

In accordance with your suggestion, I waited on the Sec. of War, in relation to the Freedmens Bureau; and beg leave to report his earnest assurance that no man can *feel* more than he does the importance of the early, immediate establishment of that Bureau.

He assures me that he is only waiting authorization from you, to proceed immediately. Will you permit me, in behalf of the friends of the Freedman, to solicit your early attention to this matter, and an order for its establishment.[3]

Very respectfully, Your Obt. Servt. Geo. Whipple
Cor. sec. A. M. A.

ALS, DNA-RG105, Records of the Commr., Lets. Recd. from Executive Mansion.

1. Whipple (1805–1876), Congregational minister and Oberlin professor, was for thirty years corresponding secretary of the American Missionary Association. *New York Times*, Oct. 8, 1876.

2. Although clearly "March," this communication must have been sent and received in May. Johnson was not President in March. Furthermore, the act of March 3, authorizing the Freedmen's Bureau as a temporary agency of the War Department, provided for the President's appointment of a commissioner. Since Lincoln had not made such an appointment, friends of the freedmen now looked to Johnson for action. Donald G. Neiman, *To Set the Law in Motion: The Freedmen's Bureau and the Legal Rights of Blacks, 1865–1868* (Millwood, N.Y., 1979), xiv.

3. No response to Whipple has been found. However, on May 12 the War Department issued General Orders No. 91, which, "by direction of the President," assigned Gen. Oliver O. Howard as commissioner of the Freedmen's Bureau—further substantiation of May's being the correct month of this letter. *OR*, Ser. 3, Vol. 5: 19.

From John M. Frazier[1]

Legislature of Maryland,
House of Delegates.
Balt. May 10, 1865

To His Excellency, President Johnson.

Dear Sir:

I sincerely hope that my friend Marshal Bonifant[2] will be continued in the position he now holds. He is a gentleman of high standing in this State, and possesses a great deal of influence with our people. He has always been loyal and true, and I am persuaded that four fifths of the Union men of Maryland, earnestly desire his retention in office. May we not indulge the hope that our wishes, in this respect, will be gratified. Such a result would strengthen the Union party in this State.

Very respectfully Your Obdt. Servant—
Jno. M. Frazier

P.S. I cannot refrain from stating that Wm. Clayton,[3] who is spoken of for the position, is the most obnoxious man to the great body of the people, that is to be found within the entire limits of the State.

J.M.F.

ALS, DNA-RG60, Appt. Files for Judicial Dists., Md., Washington Bonifant.

1. Frazier (1828–1870) was a lawyer and legislator. *The National Union Catalog of Manuscript Collections 1969: Index 1967–69* (Washington, D.C., 1970), 482; Baltimore directories (1864–70).

2. Washington Bonifant (b. *c*1814), a Montgomery County, Md., farmer, was appointed marshal by Lincoln in 1861 and was retained in office by Johnson. 1850 Census, Md., Montgomery, 5th or Berry's Dist., 715; *U.S. Off. Reg.* (1861–67).

3. Not further identified.

From Joshua Hill[1]

Madison, Ga. May 10, 1865.

His Excellency Andrew Johnson,
President of the U.S.
Sir,

I take the liberty of addressing you on a subject of pressing importance to the people of Georgia—and to the Southern people generally. It is one that demands a speedy solution. I am prompted by no other motive than a desire to see tranquility restored to a distracted land, and society relieved of the terrible evils of War. I am no sectionalist, and have never been a separatist in thought, act or deed. I have never given a vote or taken an oath recognizing any other nationality than that of the United States. I say this much in indication of my principles.

Since the occupancy of the principal cities of this State, it has become a question of deep and absorbing interest to the people—to ascertain clearly the exact policy of the government respecting the slave population of the State. The disposition of these people is of great consequence no matter when nor where it may occur, but its importance is greatest in the rural districts and is magnified by the season for growing crops of grain. The general policy of the government is known to embrace emancipation, but the time and mode of retiring the institution are not so well understood. The greatly impaired means of the farmers for the cultivation of their lands, renders it certain that the crop of provisions the present year can not be a full one. The existing supply is far from being sufficient for the wants of the Country. We are in the midst of the crop growing season, and to be even partially successful must have regular labor for the next two months. Anything that occasions a shock to the labor system of the country at this critical period of the year, must seriously diminish the amount of production. Regarding it in either an economical or philanthropic light, it seems inexpedient to make a serious innovation upon the established system at this particular juncture. A single weeks interruption occurring now will be productive of evil results. All men accustomed to a system of servitude—must require time to accomodate their actions to the novel condition of freedom. It is not to be expected that they can immediately comprehend their altered estate, its requirements and responsibilities. Hence the importance of selecting for the change of their relations, a period of comparative inactivity and relaxation on the plantations. In the impoverished condition of this and other states—it is not improbable—that the national government may be appealed to, for aid to maintain the lives of some of its people. As far as is consistent with the policy of the government, such a consequence should be avoided.

So far as I am informed of the details and practical working of the new labor system introduced by Genl. Banks, in Louisiana²—I think well of it. I can not see wherein its leading features could be improved. At this precise time, however, the substitution of that system, would necessarily interrupt the labor and industry of the Country. A more opportune period will soon present itself.

The necessity of adopting a new system of police regulations in the State—to conform to the change that is anticipated is quite apparent. I trust that the representatives of the people will soon be permitted to show their wisdom in devising some regulations suited to the public wants. I will not further trespass on your Excellency's time. You are familiar with the wants of this unhappy section. I rely upon your wisdom and benevolence—to provide a remedy or antidote for the evils likely to flow from too sudden and violent a change in our labor system.

It affords me great satisfaction to be able to state—that from a general intercourse with the people of different parts of the State—the great mass weary of the wretched and causeless war, in which they have lost and suffered so much, are prepared to accept the restoration of the authority of the Union, and to yield a cheerful obedience to the constitution and the laws. Firmness, coupled with a mild exercise of authority—will soon erdicate the lingering spirit of discontent wherever it may exist. Earnestly hoping that your Excellency may be successful in your efforts at pacification—and in restoring the lost prosperity of the deluded people—and reviving their ancient attachment, to the government over which you have been called to preside—I am sir, with high regard,

your Excellency's obedient servant,
Joshua Hill.

P.S. This letter is written at Augusta—but from habit dated at my residence. I am at this point endeavoring to make myself useful—to both country and people. You may rest assured, that the ultraists of this State, have abandoned all idea of further following the fortunes of Mr. Davis, or the phantom of Southern independence. I trust you may remember me, as one of the Representatives of Ga. at the time of her secession—who condemned the movement—standing alone—amongst her public men—in the National Councils.

ALS, DLC-JP.

1. Hill (1812–1891), a lawyer, Know-Nothing congressman, and bitter opponent of secession, ran against Governor Joseph E. Brown in the election of 1863. He was a peace movement initiator a year later; subsequently he was a U.S. senator (1869–73). *DAB*.

2. In late January and early February 1864, General Banks had issued orders to create a labor system based on the "necessity of toil." Blacks not employed in towns were required to work on plantations. They could choose their master but were bound for a year. They were to be paid, according to ability, up to ten dollars a month; or, if mutually agreeable, they could sharecrop. Fred H. Harrington, *Fighting Politician: Major General N. P. Banks* (Philadelphia, 1948), 104–5.

From North Carolina Blacks [1]

Newbern, May 10, 1865.

To His Excellency Andrew Johnson, President of the United States:—

We, the undersigned, your petitioners, are colored men of the State of North Carolina, of the age of twenty-one years and upwards; and we humbly come to you with our request, and yet in great confidence, because you are occupying a place so recently filled by a man who had proved himself indeed our friend, and it must be that some of his great and good spirit lingers to bless his successor; and then we are assured that you are a man who gives kind attention to all petitioners, and never turns a deaf ear to any one because he may be in poor or humble circumstances. In many respects we are poor and greatly despised by our fellow men; but we are rich in the possession of the liberty brought us and our wives and our little ones by your noble predecessor, secured to us by the armies of the United States and promised to be permanent by that victorious flag which now flies in triumph in every State of the Union. We accept this great boon of freedom with truly thankful hearts; and shall try by our lives to prove our worthiness. We always loved the old flag, and we have stood by it, and tried to help those who upheld it through all this rebellion; and now that it has brought us liberty, we love it more than ever, and in all future time we and our sons will be ready to defend it by our blood; and we may be permitted to say that such blood as that shed at Fort Wagner and Port Hudson is not altogether unworthy of such service. Some of us are soldiers, and have had the privilege of fighting for our country in this war. Since we have become freemen, and been permitted the honor of being soldiers, we begin to feel that we are men, and are anxious to show our countrymen that we can and will fit ourselves for the creditable discharge of the duties of citizenship. We want the privilege of voting. It seems to us that men who are willing on the field of danger to carry the muskets of republics, in the days of peace ought to be permitted to carry its ballots;

and certainly we cannot understand the justice of denying the elective franchise to men who have been fighting for the country, while it is freely given to men who have just returned from four years fighting against it. As you were once a citizen of North Carolina, we need not remind you that up to the year 1835 free colored men voted in this State, and never, as we have heard, with any detriment to its interests. What we desire is that, preliminary to elections in the returning States, you would order the enrolment of all loyal men, without regard to color. But the whole question we humbly submit to your better judgment—and we submit it with full belief in your impartial integrity, and in the fond hope that the mantle of our murdered friend and father may have fallen upon your shoulders. May God bless and ever protect you and our beloved country from all assassins shall be the constant prayer of your faithful friends and humble petitioners.

New York Herald, May 19, 1865.
    1. According to the report in the *Herald*, this petition was widely circulated in North Carolina for the "purpose of encouraging emigration to the South and restoring the lost dignity to labor." *New York Herald*, May 19, 1865.

From Aaron F. Perry

[ca. May 10, 1865, Cincinnati, Ohio]; LS, DNA-RG94, Lets. Recd. (Main Ser.), File P-1038-1865, Richard T. Semmes.

Averring that although Richard T. Semmes, nephew of Confederate Admiral Raphael Semmes, was "technically and legally connected with" the Chicago conspiracy of November 1864, Perry insists that because the youth was "without a knowledge . . . of the unlawful and treasonable purposes of its [the Sons of Liberty] managers," and "*his purposes were not criminal*," he should be pardoned. Semmes is now in the penitentiary at Columbus, Ohio, under a three-year sentence; yet the "Members of the Court who tried him . . . united in recommending a remission of his sentence." [With the judge advocate's approval, Johnson, on May 15, remitted "So much of the sentence in the within case as imposes imprisonment."]

From Richard Yates [1]

Jacksonville Ills May 10. 1865

His Excellency President A. Johnson
Dear Sir

    The friends of Geo. W. Chamberlain[2] Esq of Galesburg Ills design applying for his appointment as Secretary of Montana. I have known Mr. Chamberlain for many years as a Lawyer of acknowledged ability, a Gentleman of the strictest integrity, of great moral worth and in every respect well qualified for the position. He has been a most able faithful and effective co-worker in the Union cause from the beginning. I sincerely hope he may be appointed and will feel that you have done me a *personal* favor if you will do so.[3]

Very Respectfully Richd. Yates

ALS, DNA-RG60, Appt. Files for Judicial Dists., Mont. Terr., George W. Chamberlain.
    1. Former governor of Illinois now serving in the U.S. Senate.
    2. Chamberlain (b. *c*1832) was a Vermont native. 1860 Census, Ill., Knox, Galesburg, 399.
    3. Johnson received a terse missive from Chamberlain on June 2 which said simply: "I thought of asking an office from you: but seeing the crowd boring you for that purpose I'll be damned if I'll do it." In response, Johnson appointed him U.S. district attorney for Montana Territory on June 4. The order for appointment was subsequently revoked "as there was no vacancy," but in September he was appointed U.S. attorney for Colorado Territory. Chamberlain to Johnson, June 2, 1865, Appt. Files for Judicial Dists., Mont. Terr., George W. Chamberlain, RG60, NA; *U.S. Off. Reg.* (1865–67).

From Christopher C. Andrews
Private

Hd. Qrs. 2d Div. 13th A.C.
Selma Ala. May 11 '65

Hon. Andrew Johnson
President U. States

Dear Sir: I have been in command here two weeks, but am now ordered down the river with my division.

I enclose a paper containing proceedings of a large and respectable public meeting.[1] Some of the men you will perhaps know. Mr. Grey[2] was formerly member of Congress from Kentucky. Judge Byrd[3] is one of the most influential citizens of this part of Alabama.

The people are glad to have peace on almost any terms. But they prefer gradual emancipation. They feel great anxiety as to their future condition in consequence of the supposed extinction of slavery. You will readily appreciate the state of feeling on that account.

A few who were originally union men embrace the change of fortune with enthusiasm. And indeed the most come back into the Union gracefully.

It would be of great advantage if the terms on which they can come back could be soon made known to them.

There is a good feeling between the citizens and the soldiers. It has done our cause great good by having the people of the South see and converse with our brave frank and generous common soldiers. It causes a reaction.

Hoping you are in good health I remain

With great respect your friend C. C. Andrews
Brig. Genl Comdg

ALS, DLC-JP.

1. According to the clerk's endorsement, a recent issue of the *Selma Federal Union*, "containing report of a public meeting calling a Session of the General Assembly &c," was attached.

2. Benjamin E. Grey (c1809–1875) had been a Kentucky lawyer and office holder before moving to Selma about 1856. *BDAC*; Amnesty Papers (M1003, Roll 4), Ala., Benjamin Edward Grey, RG94, NA; Pauline Jones Gandrud, comp., *Marriage, Death and Legal Notices from Early Alabama Newspapers, 1819–1893* (Easley, S.C., 1981), 128.

3. William M. Byrd (1819–1874) was a legislator, Confederate chancellor of the middle division, and associate justice of the supreme court (1865–68). Thomas M. Owen, *History of Alabama and Dictionary of Alabama Biography* (4 vols., Chicago, 1921), 3: 277.

From David Davis and David McDonald

May 11, 1865, Indianapolis, Ind.; LS, DNA-RG153, Court-Martial Records, NN-3409.

Davis of the United States Supreme Court and McDonald of the Federal District Court in Indiana, while not calling into question the guilt of Dr. William A. Bowles, Lambdin P. Milligan, and Stephen Horsey in conspiring against the United States, do question the wisdom of executing them until after the Supreme Court has had a chance to rule on the jurisdiction of such cases. If these executions go forward "now, and if hereafter the authority of the Military tribunal, on whose sentence the execution is had, should be judicially denied, a stain on the national character would be consequence." Furthermore, there are those for whom the conviction and sentence by military commission would be revolting but who would doubtless "very generally acquiesce" if the judgment came through the civil courts. In addition to the legal question, the jurists fear the "effect upon the public mind" if these men become "political martyrs."

From Oliver P. Morton [1]

State of Indiana Executive Department.
Indianapolis, May 11th 1865.

Hon. Andrew Johnson,
President of the United States.
Private and confidential.
Dear Sir.

Bowles, Milligan, and Horsey [2] are by the published Orders of Major General Hovey, [3] to be executed in this city on the 19th instant. That these men are guilty of the crimes charged against them and whereof they have been convicted there is no doubt. To grant them a pardon would in my judgement be most unfortunate, or to let the cases pass by, as if under advisement or involved in doubt, would be scarcely less detrimental. They have already reposed too long. But after looking over the whole ground and consulting many of the soundest friends of the Government, I have come to the conclusion that the demands of public justice, and public interest, would be quite as well subserved by commuting their punishment to imprisonment for life, in some Fortress or place outside of and distant from the State. This would not be a pardon, but only a change of punishment. It would recognize to the fullest extent the jurisdiction of the Court that tried them; the guilt of the parties; and the right and power of the government to punish. As the man, the destruction of whose life and official power was specially aimed at by the conspiracy of which these men are guilty, I trust it will not be considered unbecoming, or improper for me, to present their cases for your consideration, and I do it, earnestly urging the commutation as above suggested, sincerely beleiving such a course would be better for the present and for the future.

Had the death penalty been inflicted shortly after their conviction, and while the country was still in great peril I should have uttered no word against it, but after the cases were allowed to linger until a great and happy change has taken place in our National circumstances, I beleive the change in the mode of punishment which I have suggested will meet with general acquiescence on the part of those who are most determined in their opinions, that it is necessary to punish treason as a crime, and make it odious.[4]

I am Very Truly Your Friend O. P. Morton
Governor of Indiana

LS, DLC-JP.

1. Morton, who had earlier advocated harsh punishment for Indiana copperheads, and used their arrests and trial to help win his reelection as governor, here reverses his stance. Klement, *Dark Lanterns*, 184–85.

2. William A. Bowles (c1798–1873), a doctor and postmaster at French Lick Springs, Lambdin P. Milligan (1812–1899), a lawyer, and Stephen Horsey (b. c1822), a farmer, were arrested in the fall of 1864, tried by a military commission, and sentenced to be hanged, for conspiring against the United States and inciting insurrection by setting up lodges of the Knights of the Golden Circle, the Order of American Knights, and the Sons of Liberty. 1860 Census, Ind., Orange, French Lick Twp., 153; Martin, Halbert Twp., 153; *U.S. Off. Reg.* (1855–61); Florence L. Grayston, "Lambdin P. Milligan—A Knight of the Golden Circle," *InMH*, 43 (1947): 381–91; Klement, *Dark Lanterns*, 174–85.

3. Alvin P. Hovey (1821–1891), Indiana lawyer, after meritorious service at Shiloh and in the Vicksburg and Atlanta campaigns, was breveted major general and appointed commander of the District of Indiana. Warner, *Blue*.

4. See Letter from Stanton, May 30, 1865.

Reply to Delegation of Black Ministers [1]

May 11, 1865

In responding to what you have said on this occasion as the representative and organ of those colored men who stand about you, I presume it is hardly necessary for me to inform them as to what my course has been in reference to their condition. I imagine there is not a colored man within the reach of information but has to some extent been informed upon, and placed in possession of, a knowledge of the course I have pursued in the past in reference to their present condition.

Now I shall talk to them plainly. They know I have been born and raised in a slave State; that I have owned slaves, raised slaves, but I never sold one.

They know, I presume, that my slaves have been made free, and that there is a difference in the responsibility that persons have taken in reference to emancipation when living in or out of slave States. It is very easy for a man who lives beyond the borders to talk about the condition of colored men, when in fact they know little about it. They know they have some friends who feel as cordially toward them, and who live beyond the Southern lines. They know, too, there are men there who, though they have been masters, yet feel as deep an interest in and regard for them, and would do as much for their elevation and amelioration, as those who live anywhere else.

I feel it would be unnecessary for me to state what I have done in this great cause of emancipation. I have stood in their midst, met their taunts and jeers, and risked all in the shape of property, life, and limb—not that I would claim anything to myself in establishing, sustaining, and carrying out the great principle that man could not own property in man. I was the first that stood in a slave community and announced the great fact that the slaves of Tennessee were free upon the same principle as those were who assumed to own them.[2]

I know it is easy to talk and proclaim sentiments upon paper, but it is one thing to have theories and another to reduce them to practice; and I must say here, what I have no doubt is permanently fixed in your minds, and the impression deep, that there is one thing you ought to teach, and they should understand, that in a transition state, passing from bond to free, when the tyrant's rod has been bent and the yoke broken, we find too many—it is best to talk plain—there are, I say, too many in this transition state, passing from bondage to freedom, who feel as if they should have nothing to do, and fall back upon the Government for support; too many incline to become loafers and depend upon the Government to take care of them. They seem to think that with freedom every thing they need is to come like manna from heaven.

Now, I want to impress this upon your minds, that freedom simply means liberty to work and enjoy the product of your own hands. This is the correct definition of freedom, in the most extensive sense of the term.

There is another thing; and I have been surprised that people beyond the lines have not pressed upon you this important idea. It is easy in Congress and from the pulpit North and South to talk about polygamy, and Brigham Young, and debauchery of various kinds,[3] but there is also one great fact, that four millions of people lived in open and notorious concubinage. The time has come when you must correct this thing. You know what I say is true, and you must do something to correct it by example as well as by words and professions.

It is not necessary for me to give you any assurance of what my future course will be in reference to your condition. Now, when the ordeal is passed, there can be no reason to think that I shall turn back in the great cause in which I have sacrificed much, and perilled all.

I can give you no assurance worth more than my course heretofore, and I shall continue to do all that I can for the elevation and amelioration of your condition; and I trust in God the time may soon come when you shall be gathered together, in a clime and country suited to you, should it be found that the two races cannot get along together.

I trust God will continue to conduct us till the great end shall be accomplished, and the work reach its great consummation.

Accept my thanks for this manifestation of your respect and regard.

Washington Morning Chronicle, May 12, 1865.

1. Following a request from the Reverend Edmund Turney, Johnson met with, and received the resolutions of, a delegation from the National Theological Institute for Colored Ministers. The Institute members, "most of them from various sections of the South" and all "even while yet in a state of slavery, highly esteemed among their own people as *preachers*, and *leaders* in religious matters," would soon be returning south. At the interview Turney spoke for the delegation. Turney to Johnson, May 8, 1865, Johnson Papers, LC.

2. See "The Moses of the Colored Men" Speech, October 24, 1864, *Johnson Papers*, 7: 251.

3. In 1847 Young (1801–1877), the second president of the Mormon Church, led the church to Utah, where he remained as its head and at the same time served as that territory's first governor. In 1856 the Republican platform had declared that it was the "imperative duty of Congress to prohibit in the Territories those twin relics of barbarism—Polygamy, and Slavery." *DAB*; William E. Gienapp, *The Origins of the Republican Party, 1852–1856* (New York, 1987), 335.

From John A. Winslow

May 11, 1865, Roxbury, Mass.; ALS, DNA-RG60, Office of Atty. Gen., Lets. Recd., President.

Native North Carolinian, now commanding the USS *Kearsarge*, seeks Johnson's aid in recovering the estate of his late father, Edward Winslow of Charleston, S.C., a strong Union man who left no will, but wrote a memorandum stipulating that his house servants should not be sold and that his estate should go to his son. By order of the South Carolina courts—there being no relative in the state—the entire estate, including the slaves, was sold during the war, with payment in Confederate bank notes and bonds, now considered worthless. Having suffered the abuse of those who called him an "abolitionist," owing to his refusal to "join the rebels," and having lost the sight of one eye in a service-related injury, Winslow asks that he be reimbursed, either by South Carolina or by the Federal government, from seized Confederate property. [Winslow's letter was referred by the President to the attorney general's office.]

From Salmon P. Chase

May 12, 1865, Charleston, S.C.; ALS, DLC-JP. See *Advice*, 23–26.

Southerners may be divided into three classes: conservatives, who oppose black suffrage; "acquiescents," who want peace and will accept any measures proposed by Johnson ("this is the largest class"); and "progressives," who favor black citizenship and suffrage. Transmits the views of Bartholomew F. Moore, a prominent conservative lawyer, outlining a minimal policy of reorganization, based on white control of legislature, courts, and constitutional convention. Contrasts Moore's conservatism with the progressive views of CSA Col. John A. Baker, who is willing "to take an active part in the regeneration of North Carolina on the basis of universal suffrage." Describes his interview with a delegation of blacks who inquired about voting rights and lands. Conversations with both whites and blacks persuade Chase "that there is no course open . . . except to give suffrage to all." If the President will "follow out the great principles you have so often announced," Americans "will be as little willing to spare Andrew Johnson from their *service* as to spare Andrew Jackson."

From William D. Kelley [1]
Private

Philada May 12th 1865

Dear Sir

In our last conversation I advised you of the general support the proposition to extend the right of suffrage to American citizens of African descent was recieving through our newspaper press, and mentioned the facility with which Col Forney could bring his pen to support it.

You will percieve by the marked passage in the enclosed slip[2] that he has committed the *Press* to the proposition. We have now but one loyal paper that is not out spoken in its advocacy of the measure—the North American.

Yours very truly Wm. D Kelley

His Excellency Presdt Johnson

ALS, DLC-JP.
1. "Pig-Iron" Kelley (1814–1890), native Philadelphia lawyer, was a longtime Republican congressman (1861–90). *BDAC*.
2. The "slip" from the *Press* apparently has been lost. However, in a May 11 "Letter from 'Occasional,' " Forney wrote, "But you are afraid of negro suffrage? Well, were not hundreds of thousands afraid of negro soldiers in 1861 . . . ? Why not, then, wait before you rush into a passion over the dangers and excesses of allowing the black man to vote?" *Philadelphia Press*, May 12, 1865.

From Henry S. Lane

May 12, 1865, Crawfordsville, Ind.; LS, DNA-RG153, Court-Martial Records, NN-3409.

As a senator from Indiana, he had signed a petition to the President demanding that the sentences of the military court that had tried William A. Bowles and others be carried out. Now that the "rebellion is . . . substantially at an end" and the "public peace is no longer threatened," he asks that their sentences be commuted to "imprisonment for life or for a definite period." "All the ends of public justice might be secured" in this way, while at the same time "deluded followers" of these "great criminals" could not "regard them rather in the light of Martyrs than traitors."

From Sam Milligan

Knoxville Tennessee May 12, 1865

Hon. Andrew Johnson,
President of the United States:

Sir: I have Seen and conversed with the Hon. Horace Maynard since the Senatorial election. He is, of course, somewhat disappointed at his defeat; but he speaks unkindly of no one, and is as zealous in the Union cause as ever. The spirit he manifests is truly commendable, and I would be gratified to see him rewarded for his past services.

Mr Maynard, like many others who have passed through the fires of this war, has no estate to sustain him in defeat; and I am assured, he would be grateful for any honorable and remunerative position in the service of the United States Government. I need not say that his habits of life, experience, and intelligence, eminently qualify him for almost any position within your gift. I believe him to be truly loyal, and heartily earnest in the great work of restoring the authority of the National Government in every State of the Union.

I would not venture to suggest the position to which he ought to be assigned, but I feel satisfied a Diplomatic Appointment, would not only be satisfactory but altogether acceptable to him.

I have written this letter not to complicate your many annoyances, but in the earnest hope you will find it both to the interest of the Government, as well as in accordance with your sense of duty, to provide for him some honorable and remunerative position.

I am with great respect
Your obt. Sert. Sam Milligan

ALS, DLC-JP.

From Henry Winter Davis [1]

Baltimore, Md 13 May, 65

His Excellency Andrew Johnson
Sir

It is not my habit to give advice unasked.

But I cannot refrain from expressing to you my conviction that the trial of the persons charged with the conspiracy against President Lincoln & Secretary Seward by Military Commission will prove disastrous to yourself your administration & your supporters who may attempt to apologize for it.[2]

It is in the very teeth of the express prohibition of the constitution; & not less in conflict with all our American usages & feelings respecting criminal proceedings; & if it be *necessary* to *secure conviction*, that confesses the *legal* innocence of the accused.

I assure you Sir in all the circle of my acquaintance I have found *not one* person who does not deplore this form of trial.

The damage it threatens to do the Republic may possibly be averted, but rest assured it will be at the cost of the ruin of your administration.

The only safety is to stop *now*, deliver the accused to the *law* & let the Courts of the United States Satisfy the people that the prisoners are either guilty or innocent in law: for the people want justice and vengeance.

I pray you to pardon this freedom of expression & accept my assurances that they are dictated solely by my desire to see your administration powerful enough to execute the great work which is before it—which this false step at the threshhold threatens to embarrass.

Very resply yr obedient Servt
Henry Winter Davis

ALS, DLC-JP.
1. Maryland congressman (1855–61, 1863–65) and coauthor of the Wade-Davis Reconstruction Bill.
2. On April 28 Attorney General Speed had advised Johnson that the conspirators should be tried by a military court; therefore, on May 6 Johnson named the members of the court. At a cabinet meeting three days later, Welles and McCulloch regretted the President's action, but Stanton "was emphatic" in support of such a trial. Thomas R. Turner, *Beware the People Weeping: Public Opinion and the Assassination of Abraham Lincoln* (Baton Rouge, 1982), 138–51; see also Order for Military Trial of Presidential Assassins, May 1, 1865.

From William W. Holden

Raleigh NC May 13 1865.

His Excy President Johnson

I have been unavoidably detained but will reach Washington by thursday evening next. The condition of affairs in this state is cheering. A large majority of the people are delighted on immediate emancipation and are ready for civil Government as soon as it can be conveniently established. Gen Schofield the Dept Commander is acting with wisdom and firmness and giving satisfaction to the true men.[1] With high respect

W. W. Holden

Tel, DLC-JP.
1. Gen. John M. Schofield telegraphed Johnson to report that former Governor David L. Swain and prominent lawyers Bartholomew F. Moore and William Eaton, Jr., wished to confer with the President: "I suppose they represent some shade of political opinion different from that of Mr Holden and his friends who are going to Washington but I understand they all agree on the main question of Union and Freedom." Schofield to Johnson, May 13, 1865, Johnson Papers, LC; William C. Harris, *William Woods Holden: Firebrand of North Carolina Politics* (Baton Rouge, 1987), 162.

From Carl Schurz[1]

Bethlehem Pa. May 13th 1865.

Hon. Andrew Johnson,
President of the United States.
Dear Sir,

Permit me to avail myself of the privilege you gave me, to write to you whenever I had anything worthy of consideration to suggest.

A few days ago I found it stated in the papers that the trial of the conspirators was to be conducted in secret. I did not believe it until I now see it confirmed. I do not hesitate to say that this measure strikes me as very unfortunate and I am not surprised to find it quite generally disapproved. Yesterday I returned from Philadelphia where I had spent two days, and I can assure you that among the firmest supporters of the Administration I did not hear a single voice in favor of it. I admit, I do not know what objects are intended to be gained by secrecy. I take it for granted that they are of no futile character. But if it is important that the accused should be convicted and sentenced and that, perhaps with a view to farther developments, the testimony as it appears should be kept from some conspirators still at large, it is of vastly greater importance that the trial should be absolutely fair, not only in spirit but also in appearance.

When the Government charged, before the whole world, the chiefs of the rebellion with having instigated the assassination of Mr. Lincoln, it took upon itself the grave obligation to show that this charge was based upon evidence sufficient to bear it out. I am confident you would not have ventured upon this step had you not such evidence in your possession. But the Government is bound to lay it before the world in a manner which will command the respect even of the incredulous. You will admit that a Military Commission is an anomaly in the judicial system of this Republic; still I will not question here its propriety in times of extraordinary dangers. At all events, to submit this case to a Military Commission; a case involving in so pointed a manner the credit of the government, was perhaps the utmost stretch of power upon which the government could venture without laying itself open to the imputation of unfair play. But an order to have such a case tried by a Military Court behind closed doors, thus establishing a Secret Tribunal, can hardly fail to damage the cause of the government most seriously in the opinion of mankind. The presumption will be that evidence was to be elicited by a Court made up for the purpose, by means not fit to be divulged; and evidence brought forth under such circumstances will certainly lose in weight what it may gain in completeness.

I repeat, I am far from supposing that the Government is unable to make good its charge; but even if it should fail to do so and admit its failure in the broad daylight of an open Court, it would stand in a better attitude before the world than if it succeeded in establishing its charge only by the unseen transactions of a Secret Tribunal appointed for the occasion. This is the most important State-trial this country ever had. The whole civilized world will scrutinize its proceedings with the utmost interest, and it will go far to determine the opinion of mankind as to the character of our government and institutions.

I am well aware that some of the public papers which are indulging in strong language about this matter, have for some time been confessedly hostile to Mr. Stanton and avail themselves of this opportunity to give color to their attacks. I may assure you that I do not belong to that class. I greatly esteem him for the eminent services he has rendered and even for his disregard of popularity, and I should deeply regret to see the honors he has won, curtailed by so vulnerable an act. But still more have I at heart the character of this government and the success of your Administration; you may count me among its most zealous supporters and among your sincerest friends. But because I am sincere I cannot refrain from laying before you my apprehensions as to the consequences of this measure, and from testifying to the unequivocal disapprobation it has already met with among those whose opinions we are in the habit of respecting. It is still time to throw open the doors of the court-room, and I would entreat you not to hesitate.[2]

Pardon me for this frank and unreserved expression of my views. I considered it the duty of a loyal man and the office of a friend.

Very truly yours C. Schurz

LS, DLC-JP.
    1. Union general and emerging Radical Republican.
    2. Schurz's wishes were realized—probably before Johnson read his letter. Although the trial commenced in secrecy, on May 14 it was opened to the press. *New York Times*, May 15, 1865.

From John Austin Stevens, Jr.

May 13, 1865, New York, N.Y.; ALS, DLC-JP.

Secretary Stevens transmits resolutions from a May 4 meeting of the New York Chamber of Commerce. After expressing gratification over suppression of the rebellion and the "total extinction of slavery," the resolutions recommend "magnanimity and clemency" during the restoration of the South; hail the recent presidential order to relieve all those residing in the former Confederate states "from unnecessary commercial restrictions," inasmuch as commercial intercourse "will prove to be the most powerful agency which can henceforth be employed, for restoring peace and prosperity to all portions of our common country"; and praise Johnson's recent address "stigmatizing treason as 'the greatest crime known to the law.'"

From Richard Yates

May 13, 1865, Jacksonville, Ill.; ALS, DLC-JP.

Illinois governor, calling attention to memorials presented to Lincoln before his death recommending Jesse K. Dubois of Illinois for secretary of the interior, explains that the late President, after indicating that the recommendation "was a powerful one" and that "his long friendship for Col Dubois made it very unpleasant for him to pass him over," nevertheless felt obliged to name Senator James Harlan because a representative of the "Methodist Church, which had been so unanimously loyal," had urged the appointment. Desiring again to sponsor Dubois for a cabinet post, "in the event that in your own good judgement any changes should be made," Yates reminds Johnson that Illinois is the fourth largest state and has "contributed her full share in the suppression of the rebellion."

From Edgar Conkling

May 14, 1865, Cincinnati, Ohio; ALS, DNA-RG153, Court-Martial Records, NN-3409.

An Ohio businessman, who refused to sign a petition requesting clemency for the "three rebels now condemned to be hung at Indianapolis," writes to express his reservations concerning clemency. Such a policy "will seriously impair public confidence in your Administration for many reasons," just as it had for "*good* Abraham Lincoln," whose mercy had encouraged treason and corruption. "Let us see your promises fulfilled, in hanging Jeff Davis & his Cabinet & leaders, including Lee, and such like." "Our bleeding and suffering country demands that past leniency find its grave with the good man they assassinated."

From "Pro Patria et Preside"

14th May/65.

Andrew Johnson
President United States

By your infamous bribe,[1] the hirelings of your government have captured President Davis. He is in your power; in no idle spirit of threatening I say to you Chief Magistrate of the United States, beware of how you exercise that power.

Mr Davis is in no way responsible for the death of your predecessor: nor is *he* responsible for what you call the Rebellion. His part in it has been the *servant* of the *people*, of whom I am one. He was made so by their will, and that will would today uphold him if untrammeled by your horde of bayonets. It *has* upheld him to the death of the noblest and bravest men the world ever saw. The few remaining would still give their lives for the cause which *he* has so nobly and conscientiously sustained, and many (*I* for one) would give their lives for his, and *I will if his is taken*. You dare not hang that man! Do so, and YOUR LIFE SHALL

BE THE FORFEIT. Gaurded at every step as your craven life is, *it will not always be* so. There will come the time when you think, even the *spirit* of our people is crushed and exterminated, as are our *rights*, and you have nothing to fear from a rebellion so dead and buried. For that time I will watch and wait, WITH A RESOLVE AS FIRM & FIXED AS THE HEAV-ENS—to avenge my President and my country, with my life as the sacrifice. From this purpose your hanging of the alleged "conspirators" and a hundred times their number will not intimidate or turn me.

Pro Patria et Preside[2]

ALS, DNA-RG153, Lets. Recd. by Col. H. L. Burnett (Apr.–Aug., 1865).

1. A reference to the Proclamation of May 2, in which $100,000 was offered for Jefferson Davis' capture and lesser amounts for Clement C. Clay, Jacob Thompson, George N. Sanders, and Beverley Tucker. Davis was captured May 10. See Proclamation of Rewards for Arrest of Sundry Confederates, May 2, 1865.

2. The anonymous devotee of "country and president" conveyed his warning not merely by threatening words but also visually by a menacing arm with dagger drawn above his Latin sobriquet.

From James W. Scully

Camp near Greeneville, Tenn.
May, 14th 1865

Dear Sir:

I received your dispatch on the 8th inst.[1] and answered it by telegraph on same date.[2] About the time I received it, Robert & Frank arrived from Carter, and Frank told me that Mrs. Stover had made up her mind to stay at home all summer, as she was now fixed very comfortably. I stated so to you in my dispatch.

Mrs. Stover arrived here last night accompanied by Mr. Murray Stover.[3] I showed her your telegram, but she is undecided about what she had best do. She says that she is in no danger whatever at home, as the robbers do not molest her although they have robbed her neighbours. She goes back again on monday as she only came down with Mr. Stover, who is desirious of renewing his allegiance to the United States. He left for Knoxville this morning. I gave him a letter to Genl. Stoneman.

The Mustering Officer has paid no attention to us as yet, although I have an order from Genl. Thomas dated May 5th Authorizing Capt. Hargrave,[4] Div. Mus. Offr. to muster the men out as fast as their terms expired.

I am averse to making complaints, and would not do so under ordinary circumstances, but knowing the interest you feel in this Regiment,[5] and that it is my duty to see that they get at least *Justice* while I am with it, I cannot refrain from telling you that we have been pretty badly treated since you left us. I have only about one hundred men now in Camp. Two companies are herding Broken-down stock; Two companies are guarding bridges; Two Companies are on guard in town under the command of a 2nd. Lieut of the 1st Ohio Heavy Arty.[6] and who is so obnoxious to the people that they are about sending you a petition to have him removed. All the other Regts. of the Brigade are laying in camp doing only the common routine of duty.

Upward of two thirds of the men are desirious of joining the new state Militia, and have repeatedly asked that I request you to have an order issued to muster-out the whole Regiment at the same time, as by that means they could go to their homes already organized. If such an order could be issued, consistent with the interests of *all the states* I think it would benefit the State of Tennessee in particular, as well as the men of this Regiment.

Genl. Tillson has resigned, and is gone north, and Col. Hawley,[7] 1' O.H. Arty. is in command of the Division, pro. tem. It is expected that Genl. Gillem[8] is to be placed in command.

I am pretty sure that I will be mustered out with the first three companies, and for the sake of the remaining Officers and men I would request that they be ordered to some place where they will not be harassed by their *personal* enemies, and the enemies of the *State of Tennessee.*

As an instance of the manner in which they do business: Lieut. Lynn[9] was for some trivial offence, placed in arrest by the aforementioned 2nd. Lieut. Wood, "By order of Genl Tillson"—(who is now on his way home having left here five days ago) and after having considered the matter and found the arrest was illegal, he got Col. Hawley to order *Lt. Lynn to Bull's Gap with 30. of my men* to relieve a company of some other Regiment stationed there.

Lynn was arrested for saying that a Genl. could not command a Division that was a thousand miles away from him.

I hope sir, you will excuse this apparently selfish letter, and allow me to remain,

Your devoted J. W. Scully

ALS, DLC-JP.

1. See Telegram to Scully, May 7, 1865.
2. Not found.
3. Probably Mary's brother-in-law, Samuel M. Stover (b. *c*1824), a native Tennessee farmer. 1860 Census, Tenn., Carter, 1st Div., 31.
4. Possibly William P. Hargrave (*c*1832–1897) of the 91st Ind. Inf., who was discharged in July, 1865. *Off. Army Reg.: Vols.*, 6: 148; Pension Records, Martha O. Hargrave, RG15, NA.
5. The 10th Tenn. Infantry had been Johnson's original "Governor's Guard," formed in 1862.
6. Probably Thomas D. Wood (1839–1909), who had enlisted as a sergeant in Co. H, 2nd Ohio Heavy Arty. and had risen to 2nd lieutenant. A provost marshal on Gen. Davis Tillson's staff, he would a month later be promoted to 1st lieutenant, Co. K of the same regiment. Pension Records, Louisa Wood, RG15, NA; *OR*, Ser. 1, Vol. 49, Pt. 2: 21–22; CSR, RG94, NA.
7. Davis Tillson, Commander of the District of East Tennessee, and Chauncey G.

Hawley (c1828–1903), who after the war was postmaster at Gerard, Kansas (c1875–81). Pension Records, Chauncey G. Hawley, RG15, NA; *U.S. Off. Reg.* (1875–81).

8. Alvan C. Gillem was commanding a cavalry division, District of East Tennessee but did not succeed Davis Tillson. Boatner, *CWD*, 343; Warner, *Blue*.

9. Austin O. Lynn (b. c1842), lieutenant in Co. G, 10th Tenn. Inf., before transferring to Co. K, 8th Tenn. Cav. (July 1865), briefly ran a Nashville woodyard following the war. CSR, RG94, NA; *King's Nashville Directory* (1869), 171.

From Atlanta Refugees

May 15, 1865, Cincinnati, Ohio; ALS, DNA-RG105, Records of the Commr., Lets. Recd. (M752, Roll 16).

Ten families, faced in September 1864 with General Sherman's order "requiring 'all persons' to leave the city with choice to go 'north or South,' are now, in the prospect of peace and protection, anxious to return to their homes." Lacking means to return by rail, they ask Johnson to authorize rail transportation to their homes. [Two weeks later the President directed Stanton to "give the orders necessary to carry the Petitioners' request into effect."]

To Samuel D. Baldwin [1]

Executive Office Washn. May 15, 1865.

Rev W.[*sic*] D. Baldwin Nashville Tenn

I have just been informed that the McKendree Church has not been turned over according to the decision made under the direction of the President. If not done let me know why.[2]

Andrew Johnson

Tel, DNA-RG107, Tels. Sent, President, Vol. 2 (1865).

1. Minister of Nashville's McKendree Methodist Church prior to Federal occupation. For Decision in McKendree Church Case, January 23, 1865, see *Johnson Papers*, 7: 426–27.

2. See Letter from Baldwin, June 5; Telegram to Matthew Simpson, August 10; Letter from Matthew Simpson, August 16; Letter from Allen A. Gee, August 23, 1865.

From William Dils

May 15, 1865, Parkersburg, W. Va.; ALS, DNA-RG107, Lets. Recd., EB10 President 1319 (1865).

As secretary of an April 22 public meeting, Dils calls upon the President to enforce General Orders No. 73, which reflects the opinion of Attorney General Speed that, when General Grant gave permission to the men of Lee's army who had "abandoned their homes in the loyal states . . . to return to their homes," it was not "understood as a permission to return to any part of the Loyal states." Thus, those former residents of the Parkersburg area who went "off to the Rebel Army not forgetting generally to clean their Loyal neighbors of Horses and such other necessaries as they wanted" and who subsequently made "raid after raid . . . till there is scarcely a good horse in our county" should not now be permitted to "have homes amongst us and . . . be treated as gentlemen."

From Henry S. Foote

May 15, 1865, Montreal, Canada; *Montreal Gazette*, May 18, 1865.

In a lengthy public letter to the President the recently exiled southerner describes somewhat sarcastically the circumstances surrounding his banishment and offers at any time to return to face a jury trial "upon any charges which it may be deemed proper to prefer against me." Reminds Johnson of serving together in Congress and, while never intimate or holding "familiar intercourse either socially or politically," they shared "much similitude in our general political opinions, and in our votes upon the floor of Congress," including opposition to secession. Alludes to his efforts in the Confederate congress "to prevent the establishment of a military despotism—to suppress corruption, to bring to punishment the atrocious abuses of entrusted power, and to bring about as early as possible an honourable peace," culminating in his one-man, unauthorized peace mission to the North proposing return of the southern states to the Union committed to a plan of gradual emancipation. "It has been my fate to have been grossly misjudged and misrepresented by men of extreme views, both in the North and in the South." Protesting his love of country and earnest desire for "the prosperity and happiness of the great Republic," he leaves it to Johnson "to decide whether you are justified in keeping me in exile."

From Brice M. Moore

May 15, 1865, Columbus, Miss.; ALS, DNA-RG56, Appts., Customs Service, Appraiser, Mobile, Brice M. Moore.

Former Tennessean, while asking for "Some lucretive office where I can Sustain my family," urges Johnson, whom he knew in Tennessee, "at once to inaugerate Steps to restore confidence in and affection for the government. This cannot be done by confiscation and Sevire measures indiscriminately upon the people." After four years of war, "the passions of the people are much inflamed and nothing Should be done to add to the irritation."

From Newton A. Patterson[1]

Kingston Roane Co E Tenn.
May 15th 1865

Hon Andrew Johnson
Dear Sir

I have just returned from the campaign in Upper E. Tenn. & N.C.; and, whilst in Jonesborough, learned a fact to which the attention of the authorities should be called. "Ben Green"[2]—son of Duff Green— for the last year or two has had charge of the Nail Factory near Jonesbor'o. Some time during the moths of Jan. or Feb, last, he (Ben Green) came from Richmond to Jonesbor'o and offered to bet any amount of money—gold or Confederate—that Lincoln would be assassinated by or before the 4th of March. I am satisfied that he had knowledge of the conspiracy. I refer to "Wm. Boyd"[3] a good loyal man of Jonesborough, who can give the names of witnesses &c. Green is likily now at some point where he can be reached.

Your Ob't Servant N. A. Patterson
(Late of Subsistence Dept 4th Div. Army of Cumb.)

ALS, DNA-RG153, Lets. Recd. by Col. H. L. Burnett (Apr.–Aug., 1865).

1. Patterson (1827–1910), a Kingston newspaperman, lawyer, and postmaster, was a circuit judge after the war before editing the *Cleveland Commercial Republican* and later moving to Johnson City, Tenn. Bennett and Rae, *Washington County*, 1: 2; Goodspeed's *East Tennessee*, 803, 822, 824; *Nashville Union and American*, Dec. 11, 1868; Roy G. Lillard, ed., *The History of Bradley County* (Cleveland, Tenn., 1976), 223, 224.

2. Benjamin E. Green, a Dalton, Ga., resident, had late in the war been superintendent of his father's iron works in Bumpass Cove, Washington County, Tenn. Later he was an organized labor activist and Greenback Party supporter. Fletcher M. Green, "Ben E. Green and Greenbackism in Georgia," *GHQ*, 30 (1946): 1–4; Paul M. Fink, "The Bumpass Cove Mines and Embreeville," ETHS *Pubs.*, 16 (1944): 48–57. For Green, see *Johnson Papers*, 2: 15n.

3. Probably William R. Boyd (b. c1832), a cabinet maker. 1860 Census, Tenn., Washington, Jonesboro Dist., 131.

From William Tanner[1]

East Liberty Allen Co Ind.
May 15th 1865

Mr President Dear Sir

Will you please to listen to one humble in life. Our late Beloved President lost his life by presumeing to mutch upon the goodness of the people. Dont do that yourself. There is men here my neighbors who say if they could they would pop you over as soon as they could find a chance and enough is said in my hearing daily to hang (acording to law) some of my near neighbors and if i was not a poor man and near 70 years old i would come to washington and report them to you and the Executive officers. I mention no names now but my dear friend I say friend for you love my Country and hence i love you as a Ruler for your Patriotism do not let your goodness of heart permit the dager or pistle to End your career in life while in the hand of a traitor. To give you the grounds of my fears persons here tell me they new Mr Lincoln would not live untill June and Expected the Tyrant would ben killed long ago. Put Justice to the verry line and dont let Mercy mouve it back one haire at least for a while untill those Knights of the golden Circle are scattered or Properly Punished. If you want to know who i am ask our honored Suprem Judge S P Chace[2] if he knew me as the 9 street Blacksmith in Cincinanati Ohio. My hand trembles to mutch to write with heard Laybor but i felt it a duty and if you have time to read do so and you may rest assured you are adressed by one whos Patriotism never was questioned in the treying times through which our Country has passed.

I am verry Respectfully your obedient servant
William Tanner

My adress is East Liberty Allen Co Ind.

I could specify Charges in this that would shurely criminate some by Law. But perhaps i have said Enough to you for the presant.

Wm. Tanner

ALS, DLC-JP.

1. In the early 1840s a William Tanner was listed as a Cincinnati blacksmith at "Walnut bet. Mercer and Allison," and at mid-century the same name appeared as a carpenter. Cincinnati directories (1842, 1850).

2. Salmon P. Chase.

From Three Alabama Unionists

May 15, 1865, Nashville, Tenn.; ALS (James Q. Smith), NcD-Andrew Johnson Papers.

Governor Lewis E. Parsons, Joseph C. Bradley, and James Q. Smith recommend John Hardy for U.S. marshal. As a former newspaper editor and Alabama loyalist, who "long before the rebellion battled with Yancey and his precipitating Cotton Confederacy men," Hardy "is now indicted in four counties . . . for his Strictures on Yancey & Co—and his opposition to the disunion of the States and establishment of a Confederacy." He "knows the traitors well, what they have Said & done and where to find them." [Hardy was appointed the following February 23.]

From Jacob Ziegler [1]
Confidential

Harrisburg May 15th/65

Prest. Johnson.

As you yourself say, I come from the ranks of the people. I want no office at your hands or at the hands of any other public officer. As American citizen I desire to say, in the Spirit of that loyalty which preseves the American union in its integrity, that some thing must be done not for your personal benefit, but for the union in your person as its chief head. I will be a delegate in the democratic June Convention of this state. And I intend to offer a resolution [2] appointing a committee composed of twenty six persons, a member from each Congressional District to wait upon you and inform you, that the Great Conservative Democratic party of the State of Pennsylvania are willing to give your administration a united and energetic support based upon the assertion which you made to all those *Volunteer Committees* who waited upon you, that "*Your passed course on all questions, shall be an indication of your future.*" [3] The time has come when a representative man at the head of our government, shall bring things back to the palmy days of Andrew Jackson—and you are the man. Whether God intended this or not by removing our beloved President is not for me to say. This I will say however, that a man of the people is now at the head of the nation and if he behaves himself well, we are safe. We of course you do not know. I am too humble to be recognized by the powers at Washington, but I am among the people and while I write for no object but your good and the welfare of the poor masses who are to be governed by you, let me say beware of the many sharkes who flatter but for spoils. The democracy of this state *must and shall go for Andy Johnson.*

Thousands of men are with me. I was for ma[n]y years clerke of the House of Reps in this state and therefore you may know I write understandingly. We are determined on this course and will carry it through. When at home I live in Butler Penna. Bear this in mind. It is not the offspring of office, but the fledgling of good old democratic times.

Truly J. Ziegler

ALS, DLC-JP.
   1. Ziegler (b. c1813), native Pennsylvania attorney, had been prewar clerk of the state house of representatives. 1850 Census, Pa., Butler, Butler, 93; *Boyd's Business Directory of . . . Dauphin . . . Pennsylvania* (1860), 79.
   2. Ziegler attended the Democratic state convention which met in August, not June. Although no resolution such as that proposed here was passed, one solidly supporting Johnson's reconstruction policy did win the convention's endorsement. *Philadelphia Bulletin*, Aug. 25, 1865; *American Annual Cyclopaedia* (1865), 693–94.
   3. For examples of this reiterated assurance, see Response to District of Columbia Ministers, April 17; Remarks to Illinois Delegation, April 18; and Response to Massachusetts Delegation, April 20, 1865, *Johnson Papers,* 7: 576, 584, 598.

From Ira A. Batterton[1]
Private

Vicksburg, Miss., May 16, 1865.

His Excellency Andrew Johnson,
Prest. U.S. Washington, D.C.
Dear Prest.

May it please your excellency to receive a letter from me! I trust the circumstances which surround me will be sufficient apology for addressing you. Having served as a soldier in the U.S., on the capture of this city, I was discharged and began the publication of "The Vicksburg Daily Herald" one year ago. Then I fought the rebels in arms against our Flag; but now they are completely conquered in this state. The Sword can no longer be used; Reason—common sense must now be employed. As a public journalist, I must deal with question and the policy which the Government intends pursuing. I wish to do so understandingly. The military have done their part.

What course and how shall we proceed to resume civil government in this state in accordance with, and in harmony to, the laws of the United States?

No armed force against the Government now exists in the state of Mississippi. The Military arm of the Government is Supreme. This stated. The Governor, Charles Clarke,[2] (elected under rebel rule) has ordered the State Legislature to convene on the 18th inst to call a convention of the people to repeal the Secession Ordinance, etc. the military acquiescing. (Conventions of the people of this state have always been called by the Legislature of the State.) Now, can there be any objection to the convention so called on account of the political status of the authority calling it? Can there [be] any legality attached to Legislation of that Legislature? They are very willing to come forward now, but nevertheless they are rebels and traitors and as such are exceedingly objectionable. I am opposed to them.

The state of Miss. was never out of the Union. What then is the necessity of a convention to repeal the Secession Ordinance? The laws of the State have been suspended in their operation during the rebellion so far as the United States is concerned. The legislation of state officers during that time so far as relating to the socalled Confederacy, is null and void. Now, Sir, will his excellency indicate the best way to resume the civil functions of the State Government?

There is a convention (informal,) called to meet in this city on the 5th of June, which is to take into consideration the propriety of calling into existance a Convention (formal) of the people to amend the State constitution abolishing slavery at once. This informal convention convenes upon the recommendation of Judge A. Burwell[3] in an address to the people of the state issued in April (18th) long before the present status of affairs came about. This convention originates with the people and none but men of well known loyalty will be its members. This is, I think, the best policy—one to which there can be no objections. The action of such a convention will settle the status of Slavery and Secession forever, which must be done properly in order that the great victories our national arms have achieved may not be in vain—blot them from existence. Judge Burwell's proposed Convention is in no way connected with the present Governor or legislature. I favor it in preference to the other on account of its loyalty—a most important consideration. I would be pleased to have a letter from you on the subject—for the sake of securing *unity* of action.[4]

I have the honor to be, Sir, Your most Obdt Servt.

Ira A. Batterton Editor
Daily Herald Vicksburg Miss

ALS, DLC-JP.

1. Batterton (c1838–1865), associated with the *Bloomington Pantagraph* (Ill.) before arriving in Vicksburg, became in December 1864 a partner in a "general Grocery and Plantation Supply business." Later appointed state printer by Governor Sharkey, he died in a shooting accident two months after writing this letter. 1860 Census, Ill., McLean, Lawn Dale Twp., 21; *Vicksburg Herald*, Dec. 14, 1864; *Chicago Tribune*, July 17, 1865; *Louisville Journal*, July 27, 1865.

2. Clark (1811–1877), a lawyer, had been a Confederate brigadier before becoming governor in 1863. Wakelyn, *BDC*.

3. Armistead Burwell (c1811–1878), Vicksburg lawyer. A staunch unionist, refugeeing during the war in St. Louis, he had urged Lincoln to adopt a moderate plan of reconstruction. In April 1865 he attempted to call an independent convention, asking each county to send delegates to Jackson on June 5 for a meeting, which Johnson did

not permit. 1860 Census, Miss., Warren, Vicksburg, 43; Burwell to Lincoln, August 28, 1863, Lincoln Papers, LC; St. Louis directories (1864–67); Harris, *Presidential Reconstruction*, 15–16; *NUC*; Cong. Case File 118, Priscilla W. Burwell, RG123, NA.

4. Batterton, writing the next day that Clark had convened the legislature, urged that it "should not be permitted," but the "military here are slow to act." Batterton to Johnson, May 17, 1865, Johnson Papers, LC.

From Horace Maynard
Unofficial.

Knoxville May 16, 1865.

Dr. Sir.

The Federal Court met here yesterday. The military authorities had suspended the taking of the Amnesty oath. The Judge's[1] attention was called to it. He delivered an opinion to the effect that the Amnesty Proclamation was a part of the law of the land, as much as an act of Congress, & as such was to be administered by the courts of the country that military orders could have no effect & were inoperative upon the officers of his court—the Proclamation having emanated from the President in his capacity of Civil Magistrate and of Military Commander. Upon this decision there was a rush upon the Commissioner to take the oath, & I suppose he has administered it to over a multitude in the last two days.

Some policy ought to be determined upon. As things are going the Law & the Government are brought into disrepute & loyalty does not command a premium. It is to be regretted that we are deprived of the services of our Circuit Judge,[2] whose health I learn is fast declining.

A conflict is likely to arise between the Court & the Treasury Department, touching the occupation of Thos. C. Lyon's[3] farm. Mr. Henry the Treasury Agent,[4] under Mr. Browlow, leased the place to an old union man.[5] The court, without hearing him, ordered him turned out. The Treasury Agent called upon the military to protect the tenant. The Judge gave this in charge to the Grand Jury, as a violation of the statute against resisting legal process. His manner was very excited, showing much feeling. The Agent, I am confident acted in good faith & ought to be protected from annoyance.

Many rebels are returning, soldiers & citizens, desiring their constitutional rights.

I am very Respectfully Your obt. Servt.
Horace Maynard

His Excy. The President.

ALS, DLC-JP.
1. Connally F. Trigg, U.S. District Court.
2. Supreme Court Justice John Catron, who had held U.S. District Court in Nashville in April, died on May 30. Supreme Court justices frequently served and were members of district and circuit courts; at this time there were no separate U.S. circuit courts.
3. Lyon (1810–1864), a Confederate sympathizer, had owned with his brothers a

500-acre farm five miles west of Knoxville at Lyons Bend, along the Tennessee River. Goodspeed's *Tennessee*, 403; *Knoxville Whig and Rebel Ventilator*, Mar. 1, 1865.

4. John R. Henry (1801–1869) was a treasury agent in 1863. He was subsequently a commissioner of the Freedmen's Bureau and briefly Tennessee state treasurer. *Knoxville Whig*, May 26, 1869.

5. The "old union man" was Joseph Mullins, to whom the farm was leased in October 1864. Trigg ordered Mullins ousted and the property turned over to a lawyer for the Lyon heirs. *Knoxville Whig and Rebel Ventilator*, Mar. 1, 1865.

From James G.D. Pettyjohn

May 16, 1865, Washington, D.C.; ALS, DNA-RG56, Appts., Internal Revenue Service, Assessor, Ill., 11th Dist., J.G.D. Pettyjohn.

Having earlier applied for appointment as a revenue agent with a supporting endorsement from the late President, he is now asking to be named assessor in the 11th Illinois collection district, in order to be able to increase the government's revenue from that "Copper" district. Points out that the 12th and 13th districts now produce far more revenue than does the 11th, a reflection, he believes, of the present assessor, described as "an honorable and clever man but . . . a very poor and inefficient officer." [Pettyjohn received the appointment on August 5.]

From Benjamin Severson [1]

Washington May 16, 1865

To His Excellncy Andrew Johnson
President of the United States.
Sir.

As President you are by Act of Congress charged with the care of the Capitol Buildings. I therefore beg leave to bring to your notice a most glaring fraud that has been perpetrated within the last few days by T. W. Walters [2] giving a contract for the iron work of the Congressional Library extension, amounting to some one hundred and sixty thousand dollars, to Fowler & Co [3] of New York, without notice of the same having been given for 60 days in the public news papers as is required by Acts of Congress. See statutes at large vol. 10 page 93. Which act was passed particularly to stop the frauds practiced in the letting of contracts on the Capitol and patent Office Buildings, by the same parties.

I would refer you to the late report of the joint Committees of Congress, No 128, [4] which will show my position as a contractor for such iron work, as my calculations have been acted on in Congress. Yet I, with other competent citizens are not allowed to know of proposed letting of contracts and the nation is thus wronged by illegal acts.

Knowing well sir that you will never allow such shameful frauds to be practiced, I, a loyal citizen respectfully ask of you to send this matter to Mr Harlan the Secretary of the Interior, or to some other such authority for investigation, where it will appear on proof that this contract, and former ones by the same parties, were obtained by means of paying a heavy percentage besides other sums of money to T. W. Walters.[5] It is such acts which has made the capitol works to cost double their value, and should be stopped some time *now*. For in this case there is no time so fit as the present, before the work shall be commenced.

Very respectfully Your Obt. Servt.

B. Severson

ALS, DNA-RG48, Patents and Misc. Div., Lets. Recd.

1. Severson (*fl*1881), civil engineer and architect, during the war had been watchman at the census bureau and inspector of the Washington aqueduct. Washington, D.C., directories (1863–81).

2. Thomas U. Walter, the Capitol architect.

3. William Fowler & Co. were builders, located at 1319 Broadway, New York City. Charles Fowler was the contractor for the Library of Congress enlargement. *Trow's New York City Directory* (1865), 305; Ihna T. Frary, *They Built the Capitol* (Richmond, 1940), 196.

4. The previous December, Severson had contracted to alter and raise the roofs and ceilings in Senate and House chambers at respective bids of $136,085.25 and $146,006.55. *Senate Reports*, 38 Cong., 2 Sess., No. 128, pp. 26–27 (Ser. 1211).

5. Walter resigned ten days after Severson's letter, inasmuch as James Harlan had cancelled the architect's contract with Fowler, because of the failure to advertise for bids. Frary, *Capitol*, 196.

From Thaddeus Stevens

Caledonia Iron Works May 16, 1865

His Excellency Andrew Johnson,

Sir

I hope I may be excused for putting briefly on paper what I intended to say to you only. Reconstruction is a very delicate question. The last Congress, (I expect the present) looked upon it as a question for the Legislative power exclusively. While I think we shall agree with you almost unanimously as to the main objects you have in view I fear we may differ as to the manner of effecting them. How the executive can remoddle the States in the *union* is past my comprehension. I see how he can govern them through military governors untill they are reorganized. The forcing [of] governor Peerpoit,[1] done by a thousand votes on the million inhabitants of Virginia as *their* governor and call it a republican form of government may provoke a smile, but can hardly satisfy the judgt. of a thinking people. Had you made him a military govr. it were easily understood.

My only object now is to suggest the propriety of suspending further "reconstruction" untill the meeting of Congress. Better call an extra Session, than to allow many to think that the executive was approaching usurpation.

We shall have enough to combat in military trials in the midst of civil courts. Do not I pray you burden us further.

With great respect Your obt Servt
Thaddeus Stevens

The President

ALS, DLC-JP.

1. Francis H. Peirpoint, who in 1881 changed the spelling of his name and is better known as Pierpont, had during the war been elected governor of loyal Virginia and was recognized as governor in Johnson's order reestablishing federal authority in the state. See Order Restoring Virginia, May 9, 1865.

From George W. Tabor and S. S. Case[1]

Chattanooga Tenn. May 16, 1865

President Johnson
Dear Sir

As the Rebellion is virtually at a close and orders have been already issued for retrenchment in all branches of the service, there is no point in our opinion where it is more needed than here. Millions of dollars have already been expended at this place and the works are still progressing. Of course a few contractors & shoulder-strapped gentry would be glad to have the works spun out to the last possible moment— but we hope your Excellency will bear in mind that the people will hereafter have to foot up all these bills. And it unfortunately falls upon those least able to bear it. We pray you therefore, that you suspend all public works at this point, and discharge all artizans and soldiers not needed to guard the forts.[2]

Yours Rspfy Geo. W. Taber[sic]
S. S. Case

Hundreds would sign the above here if necessary.

L, DNA-RG107, Lets. Recd., EB10 President 1262 (1865).

1. Possibly the George W. Tabor (b. c1842), a corporal, Co. D, 1st Mtd. Inf., USA, who enrolled at Jamestown, and who had been a Crossville, Tennessee, farmer in 1860. Case is unidentified. TICW, 2: 590; 1860 Census, Tenn., Cumberland, 6th Dist., 54.

2. Stanton, to whom Johnson referred the letter, sought a report from the chief engineer, Gen. Richard Delafield, who assured the secretary that there were "no grounds whatever to sustain the statements of Mr. Taber and others." Delafield to Stanton, May 31, 1865, Lets. Recd., EB10 President 1262 (1865), RG107, NA.

From Salmon P. Chase

May 17, 1865, Hilton Head, S.C.; ALS, DLC-JP. See Advice, 26–34.

Discussions with prominent Charlestonians have convinced the chief justice of "the utter absence of all *purpose* if not of all disposition to offer any further resistance to the authority of the Union," and yet there is "a strong desire to retain if possible the political ascendancy in their several states." Stressing that blacks "attach very great importance to the right of voting," Chase recounts his visits, along with the Reverend Richard Fuller, to the Sea Islands and Beaufort, where both men addressed the crowds. During an excursion to Savannah, he observed the similarities there with Charleston attitudes, except for "a greater desire to be protected against" disloyalism "by the extension of suffrage to the colored citizens." Congratulates Johnson on the capture of Jeff Davis, which "makes it impossible for insurrection to revive, & leaves to you only the task of restoring peace by reorganization." Encloses his own ten-point plan of reconstruction, including his recommendations for military officers to fill various posts; concludes that "the restoration of national relations through the reorganization of the state governments . . . taxes nerve & brain."

From John Hogan

May 17, 1865, St. Louis, Mo.; ALS, DLC-JP.

Democratic congressman-elect, thanking Johnson for a political favor, commends him for recent actions—releasing "prisoners, who refused exchange," and "orders encourageing trade," thereby "removeing obstacles to Union & harmony." Envisions "new party arrangements for the future." Observes that "in all this region the old Democratic masses, hope much from your position, and whether old party names are miscontinued or not I think they will rally to your Standard."

From Robert W. Latham [1]

National Bank of Virginia,
Richmond, May 17. 1865

To His Excellency Andrew Johnson
President of the United States
My Dear Sir

Please read the enclosed, it is written by a Northern man,[2] who knows you, and loves you, and who is one of the most comprehensive men in this Nation.

There is nothing that he could do, to advance your personal interest, and produce the greatest good to the whole Country, that he would not do with prompness, and pleasure.

No stone will be left unturned, by him, or myself, to place you upon the highest pinicle of the mount of Fame, with no competitor by your side, not even Washington, or Lincoln.

Your sincere friend R. W. Latham

ALS, DNA-RG94, Amnesty Papers, Jefferson Davis, Pets. to A. Johnson.

1. Latham (b. c1811), Washington, D.C., banker and Wall Street broker, in the early 1870s was "Financial agent of Jay Cooke & Co." 1860 Census, N.Y., Kings, 2nd Dist., Brooklyn, 6th Ward, 26; Washington, D.C., directories (1850–55; 1871–74); Brooklyn directories (1857–67); *Nashville Union and American*, Jan. 4, 1871.

2. Enclosed was a clipping of a letter from Aaron Bang to the editors of the *Richmond Republic*, dated May 1, 1865, condemning the prospect of hanging Jefferson Davis and declaring that "the almost entire feeling of the North is against any further effusion of blood."

Resolutions from Paducah, Kentucky, Mass Meeting

May 17, 1865, Paducah, Ky.; Tel, DNA-RG107, Tels. Recd., President, Vol. 4 (1865–66).

A May 16 meeting of "at least 2,500" loyal Paducah citizens (James J. Husband, chairman; J. N. Beadles, secretary) unanimously approved resolutions denouncing those who secured Gen. Solomon Meredith's removal as commander of that district, expressing their "gratitude to Genl Meredith for his vigorous policy and successful Efforts in Enforcing . . . the wise and magnanimous policy of our National Government for the suppression of the rebellion," and imploring the President—"a worthy successor" to the late chief magistrate—to reinstate Meredith "until he shall have finished his noble work."

From George L. Stearns [1]

Boston May 17th 1865

To Andrew Johnson President of the U.S.
Washington
Sir

The conversations we had during my sojourn in Tennessee on the policy to be pursued towards the Rebel states must be my apology for intruding this letter on you at the present time.

It is well known that you are a Democrat, opposed to aristocratic men and measures under all the potean forms in which they deceive and delude the world. As such I wish to call your attention to the danger our country is in from the Southern aristocrats and their allies the late Democratic Party.

Federal Whig and Republican are local and transient party names, which appear and disappear as the occasion calls for them. The Democratic Party is permanent and extends its ramnifications as far as civilization has opened the eyes of mankind to the blessings of free government therefore the name is a valuable acquisition, potent for evil as we have already seen when used by unscrupulous politicians, more potent for good when a leader shall be found who will conscientiously employ it as the exponent of a free and impartial Government in which all men without distinction of Race or Color shall be equal before the law.

A Revolution not surpassed in magnitude and importance by any in history has placed you over this great people. To day you occupy a position more potent for good or evil, than any man on the face of the earth, and the lovers and supporters of free institutions everywhere now look anxiously for the fulfillment of that promise which your previous life has pledged you to redeem. Born of the people, nurtured in adversity, educated under influences that usually make men devotes of wealth and power, you have always been true to the instincts of a noble nature and adhered to Democratic Principle.

The question that the toiling millions of the world ask to day is, will Andrew Johnson President of the United States, be true to the Democratic principle of Government, or will he like all his predecessors ally himself with Capital and continue the war against labor.

We have been accustomed to call this rebellion a southern war against the Union, a slaveholders war against Liberty, and truly it was that and much more. It was the deadly strife of the aristocratic Principle against the Democratic, of the Capital of the country, against its Labor, of Ignorance against Education, of Barbarism against Civilization, of Crime against Justice, of Heathenism against Christianity. Born at the south, the natural offspring of Aristocratic Institutions, it had so far seduced the North, that it was questionable whether, the people of the Free states would sustain or overthrow the regularly constituted government. Fortunately for our country, and the world, the First Gun fired at Sumpter, decided that question, and to day after a fierce struggle for four eventful years the rebellion is crushed, its leaders are outcasts and fugitives, and the south lies desolate, a horrible sacrifice to the insatiate ambition of a Class of unprincipled men. The most remarkable fact of this stupendous contest is that, the people of the North and their rulers did not understand the nature of the contest, or foresee the inevitable result of it, and consequently carried on the war in the interest of capital, until forced by the severity of the contest to call the labor of the South as well as the North to its aid. Even when success had at last crowned its efforts, and by the aid of its new allies it had crushed the rebel armies, the instinct of capital was so strong in the Govt. that it proceeded in haste to ally itself with rebel Capital to the exclusion of that labor which had insured the Victory from any share in the Government. Fortunately southern hate, averted that catastrophe.

The death of Abraham Lincoln your predecessor assassinated by the same power that sought to overthrow the Govt. opened the eyes of our people, to the danger of such an alliance. With the rule of the late President the Whig or aristocratic Principle passed away, and the country already accepts Democratic Principles as enunciated by a Democratic President.

Thus is the Revolution complete, and under your rule we have for the first time the government of the United States allied to the labor of the country, being administered for the good of the people, and not in the interests of a faction.

Are you ready to accept the great responsibility that rests on you, and perfect this most noble form of Government, by carrying out the principles *enunciated* by our fathers in the Declaration of Independence, but which *they* failed to *establish*? This is the auspicious moment, when a declaration of your determination to be true in all respects to the principles of Republican Govt. will strengthen the new-born zeal of our people, and make your future course prosperous and happy.

I most earnestly entreat you to lose no time in giving assurance to the country, that in the future as in the past, recognizing all men as equal in the sight of God, you will use your utmost endeavor to make them so before the Law, that, so far as the great power with which the people have clothed you, will suffice for that purpose, you will secure to all men without distinction of Race or Color, equal rights, and privileges, and in the many changes of existing institutions which the present condition of the country requires you will steadily bear in mind that the wellfare of the people and not that of a Class is to be secured.

The proper solution of the many questions that will arise when those of immediate interest are disposed of will only be attained by our adherance to the principles of Democratic Govt. If Principle is our guide, the settlement will be easy and natural, insuring peace and prosperity for our country to the latest generation. But if, disregarding the warnings of the past, we are tempted to sacrifice Justice on the alter of expediency, we shall again renew the war, reopen the bleeding wounds of our Country, and must bear the reproach of having shed oceans of blood in vain. For the Democratic principle of Government is permanent, and however perverted to base ends by unprincipled men always avenges itself. Such has been the history of Europe in the past ages and the future has the same lesson in store for us if we disregard the warnings of the past.

Respectfully George L. Stearns

ALS, DLC-JP.
1. Former recruiting commissioner for black troops, stationed in Nashville in the fall of 1863.

From John C. Underwood[1]

[Alexandria, Va.],[2] May 17, 1865

His Excellency President Johnson
Sir

Senator Wilson[3] has just informed me of the new amnesty Proclamation[4] which delights me. I desire to say how ever that to us in Virginia it is very important that contractors who have supplied the rebel Army & made fortunes by investing in real estate are a most pernicious class & should not be permitted longer to take the oath of amnesty.

Your obt Servt—John C. Underwood

ALS, DLC-JP.
1. Underwood (1808–1873), native New Yorker who became a lawyer in Clarke County, Virginia, returned to New York in 1856 because of the public reaction to his antislavery sentiments. Appointed U.S. district judge for Virginia in 1864, he was an advocate of harsh measures against ex-Confederates, in favor of trying Robert E. Lee for treason and refusing bail to Jefferson Davis. *DAB*; Tyler, *Va. Biography*, 3: 291–92.

2. Underwood's home, the seat of the court of eastern Virginia.
3. Massachusetts senator Henry Wilson.
4. Johnson's May 29 proclamation had been discussed by the cabinet as early as May 9. Beale, *Welles Diary*, 2: 301.

From Catherine Campbell[1]

Hamilton Ohio May 18th 1865

My Dear Friend.

Now that delegations are through their calls upon you will you deem me intrusive for writing a short letter? Whilst I deeply regret the manner by which you was called to your new position, yet I am rejoiced to see *you* occupy that proud position. The expressions of confidence are gratifying but are useless—no true American could for a moment doubt your ability for the place.

I hope your ambition will not tempt you to overwork yourself. You need rest. I am disappointed in not seeing you as you promised.

I wanted to go with Father but was not able to stand the trip. I have been trying to induce him to go on to see the "Review"[2] but he can not leave his farm—so I must wait for another war.

I enclose pictures of Grace.[3] They make her look older than she is but are the best our place can afford.

Wishing you perfect success always,
I am still your Little Kate.

ALS, DLC-JP.
1. Daughter of Johnson's friend, Lewis D. Campbell.
2. On May 23 and 24 there was a "Grand Review" in Washington of Meade's and Sherman's armies. Margaret Leech, *Reveille in Washington, 1860–1865* (New York, 1941), 414–17.
3. Catherine's younger sister.

From James M. Edmunds[1]

General Land Office, May 18, 1865.

To the President:

I have the honor to acknowledge the receipt of the note of Mr O. M. Horton[2] of Buffalo N.Y. with accompanying Newspaper extract, of which the following is a copy:

A person who for two years was Purser of the Rebel Pirate Alabama has been appointed to a clerkship in the Land Office at Washington, with a fat salary![3]

In reply I have to state that such a man is employed in this office, and has been for some months. His admission here was under the following circumstances:

On his first appearance in this office he presented to me an Order of which the following is a copy:

Department of the Interior, Washington, Oct 18, 1864.
Sir: The secretary of the Interior requests that you will cause the bearer,
Mr J. Edwards Davies, to be examined, with a view to his appointment to a
first class clerkship in your office.

Very respectfully, Your Obt Servant,
(signed)——Geo. C. Whiting,
Act'g Ch'f Clerk.

To Hon J. M. Edmunds,
Comr. Gen. Land Office.

In the course of the examination by a board of three members which
followed the receipt of this Order, I drew from Davies the history of his
career since the breaking out of this Rebellion, and among other things,
the fact that he had been employed as Purser of the Alabama, for about
two years. I expressed to him plainly and fully my repugnance to the
employment of any man with such antecedents, and stated that I should
present these objections to the Head of the Department, which I immediately proceeded to do. My objections to the appointment were
frankly stated to the Secretary of the Interior on the same day, and the
Secretary replied substantially as follows:

That Mr Davies had deserted the Alabama at a critical time, and
proceeded at once to our Minister at London, Mr Adams,[4] and given
much detailed and important information, in consideration of which Mr
Adams had promised to make some provision by which he could procure a livelihood for himself and family. This promise Mr Adams had
asked Secretary Seward to redeem. Mr Seward did not feel safe in putting such a man into the State Department and had made an earnest
request of the Secretary of the Interior to aid him in redeeming the
promise of Mr Adams, which he had promised Mr Seward he would
do: that under the circumstances he would be compelled to give Mr
Davies a place, notwithstanding my objections, and his own feeling
which he freely confessed coincided with mine. The Secretary however
withdrew the order for his examination as a regular appointee, and gave
an order for his temporary employment as follows:

Department of the Interior,
Washington, D.C. Oct 20, 1864.

Hon Commissioner of the Gen. Land Office.
Sir: You are hereby authorized to give clerical employment to Mr J. Edwards Davies until further orders.

I am Sir, Very respectfully, Your Obt Sev't.
(Signed)——J. P. Usher, Secretary.

As I do not wish to trouble you with the details of the severe lesson
which I gave Mr Davies, or the preliminary examination, I submit the
case upon this brief statement of the facts, simply adding that I placed
Mr Davies under the Eye and Control of a vigilant employee of the
Office where his course has been daily and hourly watched, and that he
has been a faithful and efficient clerk since he has been here.

If there is anything wrong in the employment of Mr Davies, it rests primarily with Hon Charles F. Adams, our Minister to England, and Mr Secretary Seward, and finally with the late Honorable Secretary of the Interior, whose order I could not disobey.

I return herewith the note of Mr Horton addressed to the President.

I am, with great respect,

Your obedient Servant, J M Edmunds
Commissioner.

LS, DNA-RG48, Appts. Div., Misc. Lets. Recd.

1. Commissioner of the General Land Office (1861–66).

2. Cornelius M. Horton (c1820–fl1901) was a Buffalo hardware merchant. Buffalo directories (1861–1901); 1870 Census, N.Y., Erie, Buffalo, 10th Ward, 194.

3. James E. Davies, who boarded at 435 Fourth Street while working as a patent office clerk earlier in 1865, was no longer employed by that office or the Land Office by September. Horton's note had observed: "It sounds bad in *Loyal Ears*." *U.S. Off. Reg.* (1865); Horton to Johnson, May 12, 1865, Appts. Div., Misc. Lets. Recd., RG48, NA.

4. Charles Francis Adams.

From Jonathan Light[1]

Greeneville Tennessee May 18th 1865

President Johnson
Dear Sir—

I am now occupying your little house on the street, where you had your Library.[2] Your books were moved out and were taken care of, and I moved in the house, and I am shure that I saved it more than one time from going into ashes. I have made some garden, and would like to remain there at least until Fall. I will be responsible for good care of the property, no part of it shall be abused, and just what you say I will pay in rent. I am a poor man as you very well know, and there is not another house in Town that I could get, if you were to require me to leave the one I am in, and being a shoe & boot maker by trade it suits me much better to live in Town. On receipt of this Letter you will please write me and let me know the Terms and I will comply with them.[3]

yours respectfully Jonathan Light

ALS, DLC-JP.

1. Light (b. c1815) was a native Tennessee shoemaker. 1860 Census, Tenn., Greene, 10th Dist., 85.

2. A small building on Main Street, near the residence, which had served as Johnson's prewar office. Ernest A. Connally, "The Andrew Johnson Homestead at Greeneville, Tennessee," ETHS *Pubs.*, 29 (1957): 137.

3. A notation, "Ansd May 29/65," gives no clue to Johnson's decision in this matter.

From Lyttleton F. Morgan[1]

Balto. May 18th 1865

Mr. President
My dear Sir

On leaving you the other day you did me the honor to say you would be glad to hear from me and my brethren who were associated with me in the visit we paid,[2] derived so much pleasure from it, that several of them have urged me to write you of the fact. I wish you could have heard the report made to the Preachers Meeting. Mr. Brown, Mr. Furlong, Mr. Gibson[3] & myself were all called upon to speak. Mr. Sewell[4] was not present. Mr. Brown especially, (The gentleman who wept & responded while you spoke to us) made a most eloquent & enthusiastic speech, & the body that sent us to you with the expression of their sentiments towards you, were gratified beyond measure at the report we made. Since I had the engineering of the whole affair the result was particularly agreeable to me. I covet for you the good opinion, not only of my friends, but of all your country men.

Now, a word on another matter. Through a card I published in one of the papers of this city,[5] vindicating you against certain slanders which I heard coming from ministers of the Gospel in their pulpits, it has become known that I claim a personal acquaintance with you. This has given rise to application after application for letters to you, by those who seek office, and by those who wish to retain the office they hold. I determined at once not to annoy you, so have refused all; but I have written two letters which I know it to be the purpose of the parties to get before you, *anxious*, like drowning men catch at straws. One is addressed to one of the Police Com: of Balto, stating my impressions of Mr. Francis S Corkran,[6] a member of the Society of friends, and a man of such unspotted reputation that his retention of his office, while it might *disappoint* somebody, would *offend* nobody. The other is addressed to the Secretary of the U S Treasury, Mr. McCulloch, in behalf of my friend, Mr. Jno. F Meredith,[7] a Member of the M. E Church, in which I took the liberty of referring the Hon Secy to you for a knowledge of me. These gentlemen, with several others equally worthy, were appointed at a time when they suffered scorn for their devotion to the government. These two letters are as near as I have come to boring you in the matter of appointments to office; and if possible to resist both friends & strangers, I will get no nearer to a direct application. I am not willing to subject my regard for you to the *possibility* of decline, through any failure I might make; nor am I willing to furnish you any ground to suspect that my professions of it has a selfish object. I have written a much longer letter, I know, than is proper to a man who is

occupied with so many, & such high duties, as yourself. But it seemed
to me when I saw you that your being President, changed neither your
appearance nor manner toward your old

Sincere friend L. F. Morgan

ALS, DLC-JP.
    1. Morgan (1813–1895) was pastor of Baltimore's Charles Street Methodist Epis-
copal Church. *NUC*; Baltimore directories (1864–81).
    2. The delegation, headed by Morgan, met with Johnson ten days earlier. *Washington
Morning Chronicle*, May 9, 1865.
    3. Either B. Peyton Brown (b. *c*1825), Virginia-born Washington minister, or
J. Wesley Brown (1837–1900), Baltimore native, who left the Methodist church to
become an Episcopal deacon in 1866, and Henry Furlong (1797–1874), a Baltimore-
born Methodist minister. Alexander E. Gibson (*fl*1874) was pastor of Broadway Methodist Church. 1870 Census, D.C., Washington, 4th Ward, 377; *NUC*; *NCAB*, 8: 300;
Men of Maryland and District of Columbia, 505; *Woods' Baltimore City Directory* (1865–
66), 615.
    4. Thomas Sewell was a Methodist minister. Ibid. (1864), 582.
    5. Not found.
    6. Corkran (b. *c*1814) had been in charge of locating vessels to be sunk in southern
harbors, in order to close those ports. He did not retain his position as naval officer of the
Port of Baltimore. 1850 Census, Md., Baltimore, 16th Ward, 121; Baltimore directories
(1856–65); *Official Records of the Union and Confederate Navies in the War of the Rebellion* (30 vols., Washington, D.C., 1894–1927), 6: 17, 50; *U.S. Off. Reg.* (1861–65).
    7. Meredith (*c*1812–*fl*1883), Maryland native and Baltimore house painter, became
custom house appraiser general under Lincoln, a post he continued to hold during the
Johnson administration. 1850 Census, Md., Baltimore, 4th Ward, 42; *U.S. Off. Reg.*
(1865–69); Baltimore directories (1867–83).

From E. A. Thomas [1]

Union May 18th/65

Dear President
Sir
    I do feel unworthy to write to you, but because the trouble We have
out North here, with the copperheds, I can not live without letting you
know about it. They rejoice in Lincoln's death & you know that they
would like to see your downfall & they talk hard aganest the Government, but they talk verry soft words about old *Jeff* & Lee & *Mc*lelan &
all of the traitors & leading rebells of the cursed South. Now Mr President are such men fit to live with us at the north. We have tared &
fethered som of them & if they are not carfull I am afraid som of them
will be hung. Now Mr President are such men fit to bee at liberty? I
think they ought to have som punishment or put in prison or confisicate
there property, & now Mr President I wish if there could bee som bill
or act passed to som affect to punish those copperheds or Southern
Simpthisers. I am willing to do all in my power to asist to put them
down So the very name of *C.h* will Sink to oblivion.
    I feel verry glad that you are eusing the rebells rough. They deserve
it. I hope you will get old Jeff & all of which you have offered such big
rewards, & hang all of them 500 *ft* high & all of the rebells officers &

Slave holders. N.B. If I could leve I would go & try to aketch some of them that you offer rewards for. I wouldent want better funn.

Well Dear President I must close those few lines. Hoping that the Lord will keep you from all harm & give you Wisdom & Bless you, is my furvant prayer.

Yours with much Respect
Your Unworthy Servant E. A. Thomas

ALS, DNA-RG94, Amnesty Papers, Jefferson Davis, Pets. to A. Johnson.

1. Although every midwestern state from Michigan to Iowa had a village named Union, the writer may have been Elias A. Thomas (b. c1815), a McHenry County, Ill., farmer, who lived some fifty-five miles northwest of Chicago, the scene of recent Copperhead plots. 1860 Census, Ill., McHenry, Algonquin, 40.

To George H. Thomas

Executive Office Washington May 18 1865

To Maj Gen. Geo. H. Thomas
Comdg Dept Cumberland Nashville Tenn.:

I should be gratified to see you in Washington as soon as convenient for the purpose of conferring with you in relation to civil and military affairs within your command.[1]

Andrew Johnson
President U. S.

Tel, DNA-RG107, Tels. Sent, President, Vol. 2 (1865).

1. Thomas responded two days later: "Will start for Washington on tuesday next which is the very earliest time I can leave here cosistent with my duties." Johnson Papers, LC.

From William G. Brownlow

Nashville May 19, 1865.

Prest Johnson

The Senate is all right. I have no hope of the House.[1] It will do nothing that strikes a rebel down. I beleive they will allow all rebels to vote and if so we are to be run over, the State Controlled by rebels. City full of returned rebels, many of them insolent & defiant Cursing you & I & others by name. They will Elect rebels & Copperheads to Congress from Middle & West Tennessee & if so I hope Congress will reject them. What are we to do? Put forth some-thing from Washn.

W G Brownlow

Tel, DLC-JP.

1. Although unionists had majorities in both houses of the Tennessee legislature, conservatives were stronger in the house and dominated the judiciary committee, where a franchise bill was under consideration. White, *Messages of Govs.*, 5: 430–32; Alexander, *Reconstruction*, 73–75.

Comments on the Restoration of Georgia[1]

[May 19, 1865][2]

President Johnson expressed himself very kindly toward the masses of our people, who he believed had never been at heart the enemies of the government, but that they had been overreached by the cunning of artful and unscrupulous leaders.

The chief obstacle he thought to the restoration of good feeling would be in prompt recognition of the fact that slavery was dead forever and ever. That fact cordially admitted, the remaining difficulties might be easily removed. He was indisposed to continue the military Government in Georgia beyond the period when the civil administration might be safely resumed. At present he considered the civil offices of the State of every grade as vacant, and all the actions and doings of their occupants from the commencement of the rebellion as null and void.

The President thought if the people of Georgia really desired a loyal civil Government organized in Georgia that there would be some spontaneous movement in their primary assemblies.

Mr. D.[3] also says that President Johnson would prefer appointing a military Governor from the State if a suitable one can be found. Otherwise he shall be compelled to select from some other State.

Savannah Herald, June 5, 1865.

1. James L. Dunning, Alexander N. Wilson, and William Markham, all citizens of Atlanta, had an interview with the President "touching the condition of affairs in Georgia." Upon their return, Dunning "authorized" the editor of the Augusta Chronicle and Sentinel "to mention some facts in connection with that interview." National Intelligencer, June 19, 1865; Savannah Herald, June 5, 1865.

2. The newspaper accounts omit the date of the interview, but Dunning later recalled that it had taken place on this day. See Letter from Dunning, July 2, 1865.

3. Dunning (c1814–1874), Connecticut-born Atlanta machinist and partner in an iron foundry before the war, became an agent for the Freedmen's Bureau and eventually Atlanta's postmaster (1869–74). Cassville Standard, Feb. 26, 1852; Franklin M. Garrett, Atlanta and Environs (2 vols., Athens, Ga., 1982[1954]), 1: 628, 705, 803, 893, 908.

From Henry P. Fessenden[1]

70 Wall St., New York,
May 19. 1865.—

Hon. Andrew Johnson
President of the United States
Sir

A recent occurrence in my practice as a conveyancer induces me to take the liberty of laying before you the suggestion that in your forthcoming proclamation of amnesty you reserve the right to revoke it as to any persons included in its terms who may relapse into rebellion or treasonable practices. The most careful of us sometimes forgets to insert a power of revocation in his family settlements; and is almost always sorry for it afterwards. Such a clause may not be usual in a proclamation of amnesty, but the circumstances of our national case are unusual; and there is going to be need of something of the sort with the gentry with whom you have to deal.[2]

With great respect Your obedient servant
H. P. Fessenden.

ALS, DLC-JP.
    1. Fessenden (c1820–fl1867) was a native New York lawyer. 1860 Census, N.J., Essex, Orange, 1st Ward, 63; New York City directories (1865–68).
    2. Johnson did not heed this admonition.

From William T. Sherman

Head-Quarters Military Division of the Mississippi,
Camp near Alexandria May 19 1865.

To his Excellency President Johnson
Dear Sir.

    I am just arrived. I have travelled a part of the way with each of my four Corps and this is the day all should halt within four miles of Alexandria. I have also this moment received orders for a Review on Wednesday next.[1] This will keep me busy, and I write this as an excuse for not hastening up to pay you my cordial & personal respect. As the Case now presents itself it seems to me more appropriate to await your pleasure, and to appear at the head of my troops, but if there be any matter on which you desire to see me personally, I will hasten up to see you.[2] I have marched from Richmond slowly on purpose to spare the men, and by reason of the very hot weather, but I can assure you all are in good order and condition for parade, Review or fighting.

With sincere respect Your friend & Servant,
W. T. Sherman Maj Genl.

ALS, DLC-JP.
    1. The "Grand Review" of May 23 and 24.
    2. Sherman met Johnson the next day and later recalled that the President was "extremely cordial" to him, denying foreknowledge of Stanton's publication of correspondence condemning Sherman's April 18 agreement with Confederate Gen. Joseph E. Johnston. William T. Sherman, *Memoirs of General William T. Sherman* (2 vols., New York, 1875), 2: 375.

From Joseph E. Brown

Carroll Prison May 20th 1865

His Excellency Andrew Johnson President &c. &c.
Sir

    In accordance with a suggestion of the Secretary of War I reduce to writing the substance of my conversation with you this afternoon at

The Grand Review, May 23, 1865
Courtesy National Archives

your office in reference to the objects of my late Proclamation convening the legislature of my state after the surrender of Gnl Lee's army.[1]

The agreement which was made between Genl Sherman & Genl
Johnston at the commencement of the armistice had reached Georgia,
by which it was understood that the states were to be recognized in
their soverignty, and that the present state Govermnts were not to be
disturbed. In connection with this report it was also published and
believed that Gov Vance of North Carolina had been invited with the
sanction of the Govermnt at Washngton to return to the Capital and
resume the exercise of the functions of his office and to convence the
legislature of his state.[2]

The state of Georgia had by its legislature appropriated $8,000,000,
in currency for the relief of the poor and the soldier's families who were
destitute. The collapse in the currency had rendered this appropriation
entirely unavailable, while the sufferings for provisions were such that
it was matter of great importance that relief be afforded as early as
possible.

All the other fiscal operations of the state government were stopped
for want of funds, and we were threatened with great suffering, and
with anarchy, if some provisions were not made speedily.

I was fully satisfied when Genl Lee's army surrendered that we had
no further prospect of a successful prosecution of the War and I considered it criminal to continue to shed blood in a struggle that could not
be maintained with any reasonable hope of success.

In this state of things I confered with several of the most distinguished Gentlemen who had been known as Sympathisers with the
United States govermnt, and who had been called union men by our
people, as well as with other Gentlemen of distinction, and they all
without a single exception urged the propriety of convening the legislature at as early a day as possible to take such action as might be
necessary to put the state back into harmonious relations with the Govermnt of the United States without unnecessary delay, and to relieve
the distress of the poor and provide such currency as would keep the
state Govermt in motion till other arrangmts could be made, or till the
United States currency should obtain circulation.

In making the call I had no intention of advising further resistance
or of doing any act that could delay or hinder a restoration of peace and
order by a return of the state to the Union, nor did I understand or
believe that the course proposed would be objectionable to the Governmt. I knew it had the power to dictate its own terms, and that the
people of the South had no ability to resist its will. The issues which
had divided the two sections had not found a peaceful solution in the
Forum of reason. They had finally been submitted to the arbitrament
of arms and after a long and arduous struggle, in which each had been
taught to respect the gallantry of the other, the decision had been made

in favor of the *ideas* of the Northen people, whose superior numbers and resources had given them the victory. This I considered a settlemnt of the questions involved in favor of the policy of the Govermt of the United States, and I considered it the duty of our people to accept it as such, and do all in their power to restore prosperity and repose to the whole Country.

As the call made by me for the session of the legislature was construed as an additional act of hostility and was assigned as the immediate cause of my arrest, I have felt it due to candor, and a duty to myself and your Excellency to submit this statemnt of facts for your consideration and action. Frankness requirs that I state further that I was an original secessionist, and an ardent and I trust an honest believer in the correctness of the doctrins of that school of statesmen. But when the decision was made against that right by the most powerful tribunal known among nations—the sword—I felt and still feel that it is the duty of the people of the South to yield, and accept it as the law of their conduct in future, and do all they can in the new state of things to repair the losses sustand by the war.

The facts in relation to my parole have already been submitted to your consideration. And I will not repeat them here.

I am Very respectfully Your obdt Servt.

Joseph E. Brown

ALS, DNA-RG94, Lets. Recd. (Main Ser.), File W-1131-1865, Joseph E. Brown.

1. Arrested on May 9, Brown had finally arrived in Washington under "close custody" on May 20. Earlier that morning he had submitted a letter through the provost marshal general, requesting an opportunity to "explain verbally" to the President the circumstances of his alleged parole violation. Johnson granted Brown an interview at 3:30 that afternoon, but shortly afterwards Brown was confined to the Old Capitol prison annex where he drafted this account. Brown to Johnson with Endorsement, May 20, 1865, Lets. Recd. (Main Ser.), File W-1131-1865, Joseph E. Brown, RG94, NA; Parks, *Brown*, 329–30; Roberts, *Brown and Politics*, 29–30; Leech, *Reveille*, 148.

2. On May 13 Confederate Governor Zebulon B. Vance had been arrested in Statesville and then transported to Washington, where he was placed in prison on May 20 with Brown. Frontis W. Johnston, ed., *The Papers of Zebulon Baird Vance, 1843–1862* (Raleigh, 1963), 1: lxxiii; Roberts, *Brown and Politics*, 29.

From Sherrard Clemens[1]

Willard's, May 20, 1865.

His Excellency Andrew Johnson
President U.S.
Sir:

I presume you are aware, that, while I reside in West Virginia, I married in Louisiana, and have two plantations in Madison Parish. Since the rebellion broke out, I have been there, and at Vicksburg, under Federal protection several months each year.

From these circumstances, I am enabled to assure you, that, many of the non-combatants were compelled to retire, from the Parishes of Carroll, Tensas and Madison, to the interior, and to the northern part of Texas. I have letters and information, which enables me to state that, many of these people are now anxious to take the oath of allegiance and return to their homes.

In a conference with Gen Grant, this morning, he intimated, that no Federal force, would at present, be sent, to Northern Louisiana, indeed, for the time being the country, is well nigh depopulated.

What I have to ask in connection with this matter, is, that, under government sanction, (but at my own expense) I be permitted to proceed in a gun boat, up Red River, or under an armed escort, from Gaines or Goodrich's landing, or De Soto, to Shreveport La, to hold out to the people from the river counties, who have taken refuge there, the policy of the government, as already announced;—the hopeless condition to which the rebellion is reduced;—the attitude in which, they will stand to Federal authority, by persistent resistance, after the capture of Davis, Stephens, and the surrender of Lee and Johns[t]on, leaving them, without even the semblance of a *de facto* government; and generally, addressing them by every consideration which, bears, upon their future.

I have a father in law, and two brothers in law, among these people. The former is over 60 years of age. They and their families are in great distress. They have never been in the army, as far as I know. My father in law, I am positive never has been.

Besides, accomplishing a mission of mercy to them, I believe, I can accomplish a great local good for my country, by inducing those people to submit to your authority, and thus spare the further effusion of blood, in that afflicted region.

Be pleased, to submit this application to General Grant, who is perfectly familiar with the localities.

I shall await till Wednesday next your answer to this application. It may be addressed, Care of Willards Hotel.[2]

I have the honor to be, Most Respectfully Yours
(Signed)[3] Sherrard Clemens.

ALS, DNA-RG108, Lets. Recd. *re* Military Discipline.
1. Clemens (1820–1881), an attorney of Wheeling, W. Va., was a Democratic congressman (1852–53, 1857–61) and a unionist during the secession crisis. *BDAC*.
2. Reuben D. Mussey, for the President, referred this request to General Grant; ultimately Clemens received the authority. See Letter from Clemens, July 17, 1865.
3. Because the letter appears to be in Clemens' hand, there is no reason for this notation to have been affixed.

From Edgar Conkling[1]

National Union Association,
Cincinnati, O. May 20 1865

His Excellency Andrew Johnson
President of the U S
Dr Sir

Now that the leaders of the rebellion will be tried for treason & assassination & other enormities, please allow me to suggest the importance of proving against them the fact that they employed Genl. Geo B McClellan & others, from the beginning to fight their battles on free soil.[2] I have reason to think there is abundant evidence among the public archives with different departments at Washington to prove it, which as I think, from a mistaken policy, has been smothered. I have written months since to Mr. Lincoln,[3] Stanton, Holt, Whiting,[4] & Committee on Conduct of the War. What I had learned could be proven against McClellan. When in Washington in Feby, I delivered to Committee on C of war a document which fully explains my views.

You will certainly find out that a part of the programme to succeed, was to keep in our employ their representatives like McClellan, and some others, that seemed to adhere to him & his fatal policy so strongly. McClellan was a Member of the Golden Circle. Made so by Yancy here in Oct 1860.[5] I think can be proven here by different ones. If the Govt. will provide the means to ascertain as my document to Committee on Conduct of the War suggests. Put Col Baker[6] after it. I[n] getting at this fact, other facts will leak out, showing the different plans to be adopted for success. There can be no good reason for the Govt. longer suppressing the facts, it has long had. The development of Conspiracy will be imperfect without this part of the programme. A very general feeling exists that much is smothered up by the Govt. fearing that the enemy keeping McClellan so long employed in the face of evidence against his Competency & loyalty will reflect on its efficiency & wisdom. When I am applied to for information, I will give it leading to important facts. The day will come when private parties in N York will develop it in a history showing what the Govt. might have done in discharging its duty in this department of the history of the rebellion.

This Chapter cannot be, will not be smothered. I want to see it done by the Govt. It is due the people it should do so. It is the most important Chapter to be written. A number of times an army was well nigh lost by treason on the field, as well as in the Navy. Treason solves many mysterious losses of battles & vessels.

Shall we have it ventilated?[7]

I am very Respy Yr Obdt Servt.
Edgar Conkling

ALS, DNA-RG107, Lets. Recd., EB10 President 1324 (1865).

1. Cincinnati resident Conkling (*c*1811–*fl*1869) before the war had been a lead manufacturer, railroad and "Exploring and Mining Company" agent. More recently he had been head of the subcommittee on halls, speakers, etc., of the local National Union Association, and a special agent of the Relief Commission of Ohio. 1860 Census, Ohio, Hamilton, Columbia Twp., 56; Cincinnati directories (1849–69); Conkling to Johnson, Sept. 20, 1864, Johnson Papers, LC; Conkling to Lincoln, Jan. 29, 1865, Lincoln Papers, LC.

2. A reference to McClellan, Fitz-John Porter, Don Carlos Buell, and other Union generals of Democratic sympathies.

3. See Edgar Conkling to Lincoln, Sept. 28, Oct. 20, 24, 1864, Lincoln Papers, LC.

4. William Whiting, solicitor of the War Department.

5. Republican senator Benjamin F. Wade had publicly stated in 1862 that William L. Yancey, former U.S. senator and ardent Alabama secessionist, had initiated McClellan into the Knights of the Golden Circle. This accusation resurfaced during the presidential campaign of 1864. Klement, *Dark Lanterns*, 22, 32.

6. Lafayette C. Baker (1826–1868) was a Union spy before becoming a detective and special provost marshal of the War Department. Dismissed by Johnson for "maintaining an espionage system at the White House," he was later a star witness against the President during the impeachment trial. *DAB*; Warner, *Blue*.

7. Mussey, by order of the President, referred this to Stanton.

From James R. Hood[1]

Nashville May 20 1865.

His Excy Andrew Johnson

The Legislature is about passing a bill authorizing the raising of troops in each Division of the State to be mustered into its service mounted equipped subsisted & paid by it.[2] It is urged as a military necessity. If passed it will utterly bankrupt our people. May I not say to our fellow citizens that the Govt. will keep a sufficient force in the State to clean out all the organized bands of robbers. With an assurance of this kind from you the bill can be defeated and at least five (5) millions per annum saved to the people. Please answer immediately by Telegraph.[3]

Job N [James R.] Hood[4]
Chairman Com on finance

Tel, DLC-JP.

1. Hood, *Chattanooga Gazette* editor, was a conservative unionist in the lower house of the legislature.

2. Although the senate had adopted a bill to amend the militia law, the house, reconsidering after passage on second reading, rejected the legislation on June 2. *Tenn. Senate Journal, April–June, 1865*, pp. 54, 58, 61; *Tenn. House Journal, April–June, 1865*, pp. 186, 230, 260.

3. Johnson replied the next day: "General Thomas will furnish whatever number of Troops is necessary to the defense of the state. Confer with him on the subject. The enrollment and organization of the militia should be carried out so that they can be called upon if actually needed." Tels. Sent, President, Vol. 2 (1865), RG107, NA.

4. The telegrapher garbled Hood's name.

From John W. Leftwich

May 20, 1865, Memphis, Tenn.; ALS, DLC-JP.

Largely in debt to citizens of Ohio and Kentucky at the beginning of the rebellion, this merchant and staunch unionist had at that time adequate resources
in sugar and molasses to pay his debts, but during the war these commodities
were seized by the Confederates. With his debts "still unpaid" and being "unable to pay them though anxious to do so," he proposes that since "the Govt
has collected large amounts as rents from the property of rebels and rebel sympathisers in Memphis . . . that a sufficiency of this rebel rent fund be paid to
me or my creditors to compensate me for the loss of my property."

From Richard Yates

Jacksonville Ills
May 20. 1865

His Excellency President Andrew Johnson
Dear Sir

Hon. D. L. Philips[1] U.S. Marshal for Southern Dist. of Ills and one
of the Editors of the Ills State Journal at Springfield is a most competent man for the place—has discharged its duties well and ought to be
retained. He has rendered our cause much service—canvassed the State
last fall with great ability—is an able speaker and one of the most effective political tacticians in the U. States. He is also a gentleman of integrity and high standing and most extensively acquainted throughout the
State and at the same time a thorough going, energetic business man.
I think beyond doubt he is the man for the place and ought to be
retained.[2]

Very Respectfully Richd. Yates

ALS, DNA-RG60, Appt. Files for Judicial Dists., Ill., D. L. Phillips.
1. David L. Phillips (1823–1880), a partner in a land agency, had been marshal since
1861. With his appointment expiring July 22, Phillips wrote Johnson on May 23. Former Governor Yates had also written a week earlier, as had Senator Trumbull, recommending Phillips' reappointment. NUC; Appt. Files for Judicial Dists., Ill., D. L. Phillips, RG60, NA.
2. He was reappointed July 12, 1865, by direction of the President, and confirmed
by the Senate in January 1866. Recess Appts., 5: n.p., Ser. 6B, Johnson Papers, LC.

From Salmon P. Chase

May 21, 1865, Fernandina, Fla.; ALS, DLC-JP. See Advice, 34–36.

Transmits Gen. Milton S. Littlefield's order establishing "Mitchelville," a self-
governed black town at Hilton Head, and claims that blacks there have already
demonstrated their ability to govern themselves. Everywhere blacks are organizing Union Leagues: "They form a power which no wise statesman will disregard." Pointing out that both blacks and whites participated in municipal

elections at Fernandina, he contrasts this with former U.S. Senator David Yulee's opposition to black suffrage. "It is curious to observe, how little" Yulee and others "seem to realize that any change in personal or political relations has been wrought by the war."

From J. George Harris [1]

Key West, Florida May 21, 1865

My Dear Sir—

I suppose you are fully informed with reference to matters in Florida through official channels. Nevertheless permit a word from an old personal and political friend.

A friend just from Tallehassee informs me that the late acting Rebel Governor [2] has proposed to Gen. McCook [3] to wheel the State back into the Union line just as she stands with her rebel officers and crew.

I know this is not a part of your policy. My own belief is that the great mass of the people in Florida are determined to come directly and quickly back *in any form that you may prescribe*, but it does not appear that they are desirous of coming with the present State government.

A judicious provisional government might complete a new and most acceptable Constitution and organise a new State Government with loyal and unsuspected men—and it may all be done in a very short time.

I believe a provisional Governor from one of the Middle States would meet with no difficulties in harmonizing the masses and cordially uniting them in support of your administration. Mallory and Yulee deceived them most grossly, they say—and it is my belief they are anxious to come back into full fellowship on your just and generous terms. [4]

Very truly Your Friend J. Geo. Harris.

Andrew Johnson
President of United States

ALS, DLC-JP.

1. Sometime editor of the *Nashville Union* and since 1845 a navy disbursing officer.

2. Abraham K. Allison (b. *c*1813), lawyer and president of the state senate when Confederate governor John Milton committed suicide, became governor on April 1, 1865. After the fall of the Confederacy, he attempted to reorganize the state until his proclamations were nullified by Federal military authorities, who declared martial law on May 19. Allison, along with Stephen R. Mallory and David Yulee, was arrested and imprisoned. John E. Johns, *Florida During the Civil War* (Gainesville, Fla., 1963), 19, 205, 210; Ralph A. Wooster, "The Florida Secession Convention," *FHQ*, 37 (1958): 383.

3. Edward M. McCook (1833–1909) became a brigadier in 1864, serving in Tennessee, Georgia, Alabama, and Florida. Resigning in 1866, he was later minister to Hawaii and governor of the Colorado Territory. Warner, *Blue*; Jerrell H. Shofner, *Nor Is It Over Yet: Florida in the Era of Reconstruction* (Gainesville, Fla., 1974), 17, 36.

4. The next day, in a letter marked "Unofficial & Private," Harris reported that "the people in this part of the State are canvassing the question of a State Convention to form a new Constitution," and that a petition was being sent to Johnson recommending Harris as military governor, a position "entirely unsolicited by me." The petition, signed by a U.S. district judge, a U.S. district attorney, the collector of customs, and the clerk of the

circuit and district courts—all citizens of Key West—suggested that "reconstruction may be speedily and effectually accomplished" by placing the state under a military governor. Harris to Johnson, May 22, 1865; Thomas J. Boynton and others to Johnson, May 23, 1865, Johnson Papers, LC.

To George Bancroft[1]

Executive Mansion, Washington,
May 22, 1865.

My dear Sir,

I am in receipt of your note of the 19th. ins't,[2] and in reply have to say, that it will afford me great pleasure to meet you at any time you may find convenient, during your stay in the City.

I shall be particularly glad to confer with you, and have the benefit of any suggestions you may think proper to make, with the view of promoting the public interests.

Yours Truly, Andrew Johnson

Hon Geo: Bancroft. New York City.

LS, MHi-George Bancroft Papers.
    1. The historian diplomat who provided the language in which Johnson's policies and ideas were expressed in the first annual message.
    2. Bancroft's of the 19th has not been found.

From Horace H. Harrison and Adrian V.S. Lindsley

May 22, 1865, Nashville, Tenn.; ALS (Harrison), DNA-RG58, Direct Tax Commission for Tenn., Records Relating to Personnel Actions (1864–66).

Declaring that "There is no matter connected with the operations of the internal affairs of the government requiring more care and fairness than the collection of direct taxes from the people," they ask Johnson to replace the present direct tax commissioners (two from out of state and a Tennessean who "does not enjoy the confidence of the people") with three men from Tennessee. "We want fair minded honest men who know our people and will make friends for the government instead of making the people feel that they are unduly oppressed." The favorable reaction to the appointment of Joseph R. Dillin as supervising agent of the Treasury Department "illustrates the propriety of the course we suggest." [Johnson removed the incumbent Tennessean (John B. Rodgers) in August, replacing him and one of the northerners (Delano T. Smith), who resigned in June, with Tennesseans Absalom A. Kyle and Edward P. Cone. Meanwhile, Elisha P. Ferry from Illinois was retained until 1867.]

From Robert H. Milroy

May 22, 1865, Tullahoma, Tenn.; ALS, DLC-JP.

Having found his one-year tour of "comparative inactive duty" at Tullahoma "most most irksom," Major General Milroy, wishing to perform some active duty before leaving the service, desires a post on the border of Mexico or, should that prove unavailable, the military governorship of Alabama: "I think I understand your policy of mercy to the misguided masses & Justice to the leaders who misled them. I feel very sure that if I could be sent there in that capacity, with an adequate military force, and some discretionary powers, I could bring Ala. in all right with the machinery of civil Govt. in good working order in a short time."

From Nashville Chamber of Commerce

[May 22, 1865][1]

To His Excellency Andrew Johnson
President of the United States—
Sir:

We the undersigned citizens and Merchants of the City of Nashville desire respectfully to submit to your Excellency that we have reason to believe that strenuous efforts are being made by the Mercantile community of Louisville to the end that the Fourth U.S. Army Corps now stationed in the vicinity of this city be removed to Louisville, there to receive the pay, due its members by the Government.

We would respectfully represent that such action would be detrimental to the interest of our city and State, and *unjust* and oppressive upon our Mercantile community, from the fact that large amounts of money, estimated at hundreds of thousands of dollars, are now, and have been some time, owing to us for supplies furnished by us for the use and subsistance of said corps. Your Memorialists therefore pray your intercession that the Fourth Army Corps be allowed to remain here, if not incompatible with the interest of the Government, until the indebtedness due it by the Government is liquidated.

We further pray, that this petition may meet with your approval and receive your early consideration.[2]

W. W. Totten
Vice President Chamber of Commerce
In behalf of the Mchts of Nashville
A A Breast Secty Chamb Commerce
M. N. Parmele Vice President
in behalf of the Merchants[3]

Pet, DNA-RG108, Lets. Recd. *re* Military Discipline.

1. Received on this date.

2. Johnson, through his secretary, Reuben D. Mussey, forwarded the petition to General Grant.

3. William W. Totten, Arthur A. Breast, and Myron N. Parmele. Totten (*fl*1883) and Parmele (*c*1811–*c*1872) were grocers, while Breast (*c*1840–1887) was a longtime hardware merchant before becoming successively a coal and an insurance agent. Nashville directories (1865–83); *Nashville American*, Nov. 11, 1887; 1870 Census, Tenn., Davidson, 17th Dist., 71.

To New York City Merchants

Washington City May 22. 1865.

Messrs A. A. Low Esq, Phelps, Dodge &C, Hoyt Brothers, J. S. Schultz & others [1]

Gentlemen:

I am in receipt of your very complimentary note dated New York May 17, 1865, wherein you request my acceptance of a coach, span of horses, harness, etc, as a token of your high appreciation of my public course. [2]

While I fully appreciate the purity of your motives in thus generously tendering me such substantial evidence of your regard, I am compelled solely from the convictions of duty I have ever held in reference to the acceptance of presents by those occupying high official positions, to decline the offerings of kind and loyal friends.

The retention of the parchment conveying your sentiments, and the autographs of those who were pleased to unite in this manifestation of regard, is a favor I would ask, and I assure you, gentlemen, I shall regard it as the highest mark of respect from any portion of my fellow citizens.

Trusting that I shall continue to merit your confidence and esteem in the discharge of the high and important duties upon which I have but just entered, & with best wishes for your health &c individually [3]

I am, gentlemen, Yours truly,

Andrew Johnson

LS, CSmH-Misc. 8214.

1. Abiel A. Low and Phelps, Dodge & Co. were importers; Joseph B., Oliver, and William Hoyt traded in leather, and Jackson S. Schultz in hides. *Trow's New York City Directory* (1865), 427, 537, 699, 788.

2. Signed by 31 New York City citizens and merchants, the letter expressed "their high appreciation of his fidelity to the country—as a statesman well approved, by word and deed, in all the various offices to which he has been called" and indicated that the coach and horses were already in transit via the Camden and Amboy Railroad. New York Citizens to Johnson, May 17, 1865, *Washington Morning Chronicle*, May 26, 1865.

3. The merchants, "disappointed, indeed, that their proffered gift is declined," and willing to submit "their own motives to the public tribunal," released the correspondence to the press, admitting to "feeling gratified that the President of the United States is governed by such lofty views of duty." From this highly publicized refusal, Johnson gained much popular and journalistic approval. Ibid.

From J. Madison Wells

Washington D.C. May 22nd 1865

Sir

I notice that Capt. Hoyt [1] the predecessor of Dr Hu Kennedy in the Mayoralty of New Orleans has arrived in Washington and I understand is one of a number of Eastern Missionaries who altho wholly unidentified by residence or property with Louisiana consider our domestic affairs as perculiarly within their Supervission and control. Capt Hoyt will no doubt call upon you, President, to make fresh representations of his own and others immaculacy and in expectation of this I beg most respectfully to place before you the following statement that the pay legal and proper of Mayor is five thousand dollars per Annum.

Capt Hoyt as mayor paid himself for Services as follows viz

Salary as fixed by Law	$5000 00
Charges for Carriage hire	2600 00
Secret Police (put in his own pocket[)]	4240 00
	$11840.00

Capt Hoyt also occupies a building for which he pay neither rent or other expense of that kind and where he was supplied at public cost with fuel and lights and perhaps also servants and board at cost equalent in value to three thousands dollars per Annum.

He also derives a forced contribution of five thousand dollars from gamblers under pretence that it is for Sanitary Commission, which proper enquiry established was not the case. I would also avail myself of this occasion to mention that this gentleman had placed the name of a brother of Gen Banks[2] upon the pay roll of the City Controller for one hundred and twenty five dollars per month which said Banks continued for months to draw although he lived forty miles from New Orleans never rendering any services for the pay and while he was drawing it was conducting in some way or other two or three confiscated plantations in the Parish of Plaquemines in part ownership with a registered enemy. I[n] conclusion I affirm all above facts to be true and undeniable and I further declare with equal positiveness that any Mayor of New Orleans acting as Capt Hoyt did could steal short almost without possibility of detection or exposure fifty seventy five or one hundred thousand dollars per Annum.

I have the honor to be President—
faithfully and greatfully Yours
J Madison Wells

His Excellency Andrew Johnson
President United States

ALS, DLC-JP.

1. Stephen Hoyt (b. c1808), Massachusetts native, Mexican War veteran, and municipal official in St. Louis, was a captain when General Banks appointed him mayor of New Orleans in 1864; Wells removed him the following March. 1850 Census, Mo., St. Louis, St. Louis, 3rd Ward, 822; Heitman, *Register*, 1: 550; Melvin G. Holli and Peter d'A. Jones, eds., *Biographical Dictionary of American Mayors, 1820–1980* (Westport, Conn., 1981), 173; McCrary, *Lincoln and Reconstruction*, 308.

2. Probably Gardner Banks (c1830–1871), an officer in the 16th Mass. Inf., who resigned in September 1863 and settled permanently in New Orleans. In August 1864, General Banks asked his brother to visit several parishes "to ascertain and report their

condition and their relations with each other." He was subsequently manager of a sugar refinery and custom house gauger of distilled spirits. *New York Times*, July 13, 1871; *Off. Army Reg.: Vols.*, 1: 169; *OR*, Ser. 1, Vol. 41, Pt. 2: 869–70; New Orleans directories (1867–71).

From Salmon P. Chase

May 23, 1865, Key West, Fla.; ALS, DLC-JP. See *Advice*, 36–38.

Comments on Key West, a place "of little political importance." Uneasy with the current operation of the pardon policy, he suggests that Johnson establish commissions to attest to the loyalty of ex-rebels before extending pardons. Expressing reservations about the actions of several generals concerning the restoration process, the chief justice urges the President to make sure that the officers he assigns are "in full sympathy with your own views."

From Thomas Fitzgerald

May 23, 1865, Philadelphia, Pa.; ALS, DLC-JP.

Sending the proof of an article to appear in the *Philadelphia Item* on May 23, the paper's publisher writes that "the canvass for the next Presidency has commenced already hereabouts. The friends of Judge Chase are beginning to move." Philadelphia's "young Democrats . . . are very anxious to make a demonstration of some kind in your favor; but they are deterred by the old heads, who urge them not to commit themselves."

From Robert H. Holbrook

May 23, 1865, Somersworth, N.H.; LS, DNA-RG45, Subj. File N, Subsec. NO, Courts-Martial, Box 312, Hiram Holbrook.

Requests clemency for his youngest son, Hiram, who at age seventeen "enlisted as a landsman" in the U.S. Navy in March 1864 and was found guilty of sleeping at his post on board the USS *Agawam* by a general court martial in October 1864, pleading that he had fallen asleep "from sheer exhaustion" after being "in action all day." Holbrook closes by noting that his family has contributed much to the war effort: his oldest son, William, was honorably discharged, his second son died "in the service" at Hilton Head, and "he himself volunteered without bounty and was rejected on medical examination." [On June 12, the President remitted the remainder of the sentence.]

From A. D. Jones[1]

May 23rd/.65 Chester Hill O.

Your Majestys Excellency
Most Excellent Sir
    Hear the Pleadings & Beseeching of a Humble Youth for His oppressed & Degraded race.
Mr. President Sir
    Having Searched Every page of History Relative to the Degradation

of my Beloved Race. The Elevation of us as a People Scattered amongst the Whites as we are is I believe a matter of impossibility.

Now for the Sake of the Elevation of a race of people Disfranchise us in every State Except a few of the Southern States & then concentrate Us there. I trust to the Powers that Be that this Subject may be agitated. Concentration & give us a representation in congress is my Hope. I am Entreating not Dictating.

I would be thankful a thousand times to You Excellency if you would condescend to give an Humble Youth You Honors oppinion of this Disfranchising & concentrating Of Representation Scheme.

Please give me your opinion.

Your Most Humble Subject
A D Jones

Hon Andrew Jonhson
My P.O. Address Chester Hill Morgan Co O.

ALS, DLC-JP.
   1. Not identified.

From William G. Brownlow

Nashville Tenn May 24th 1865

His Excellency Andrew Johnson
President of U.S.

Gen Thomas advises me to telegraph you that Trigg is again administering the amnesty oath at Knoxville.[1] He takes his own way in everything.

W C Kain[2] is in New York. Have him arrested at once.[3]

W G Brownlow

Tel, DNA-RG107, Tels. Recd., President, Vol. 4 (1865–66).
   1. Three days later the President sought to reassure the governor: "In two days will be published an Amnesty Proclamation which excepts from Pardon and Amnesty certain classes of persons not excepted by Mr. Lincoln's proclamation." Johnson to Brownlow, May 27, 1865, Tels. Sent, President, Vol. 2 (1865), RG107, NA.
   2. William Claiborne Kain (1824–1894), Knoxville lawyer and sometime editor, was captain of Kain's Lgt. Arty., CSA (1862), provost marshal at Bristol, and commandant of Wytheville (1864) during the war. Charged with complicity in the murder or "military execution" of three Greene County unionists early in the war, he was the subject of a series of telegrams between Brownlow and the President. Captured June 1 in Hartford, Conn., Kain was returned to Knoxville, where after a long imprisonment he was ultimately released and resumed his law practice. *Obituary Record of Graduates of Yale College* (New Haven, 1900), 295; *TICW*, 1: 133–34; *Knoxville Whig and Rebel Ventilator*, July 5, 1865.
   3. The following day Johnson wired Gen. John Dix to arrest and confine Kain "and report Execution of order to me." Tels. Sent, President, Vol. 2 (1865), RG107, NA.

From Oliver P. Morton

State of Indiana Executive Department.
Indianapolis, May 24th, 1865.

To His Excellency The President.

Dear Sir.

This letter will introduce to you the Hon. John U. Pettit,[1] Speaker of the present House of Representatives of this State. He is a man of high intelligence and character, and can express to you very fully my sentiments and those of many of our prominent citizens in regard to the execution of Bowles and Milligan. I desire again most earnestly to urge the commutation of their punishment to imprisonment for life, and to protest against their execution. I hope you will give him an interview and hear his statement.

Very Respectfully Yours, O. P. Morton
Governor of Indiana

LS, DNA-RG153, Court-Martial Records, NN-3409.
1. Pettit (1820–1881), a Wabash lawyer, had before the war been a consul in Brazil and a three-term Republican congressman. *BDAC*.

From E. James Purdy

May 24, 1865, New Albany, Ind.; ALS, DNA-RG94, ACP Branch, File P-890-CB-1865, E. James Purdy.

Holding his appointment as a hospital chaplain as a consequence of nomination by President Lincoln and now about to be mustered out, Purdy asks a regular appointment with assignment to a military post in the South. Refusing to acquiesce in August 1861 to "peremptory orders to pray for the Prest. of the 'Confederate States'" in his "fine parish at the South," he was compelled to resign, was arrested, and escaped to Kentucky only through the help of Bishop Leonidas Polk. Recognizes that he "who prefered the subjugation, or even the extermination of the South, to disunion" cannot expect a call from a southern church, yet he wants to return south.

From Alexander Ramsey

May 24, 1865, Washington, D.C.; ALS, DNA-RG94, ACP Branch, File F-231-CB-1864, James L. Fisk.

The senator from Minnesota, pointing out that there are many discharged soldiers and citizen employees of the government who are seeking in vain for employment, urges that Capt. James L. Fisk, who has for three years been "organizing and conducting Emigration," be retained in the army and "detailed to resume Superintendance of Emigration from the northwest to the Gold bearing Mountain Territories." According to Secretary Stanton there are "no moneys on hand for Emigration purposes," but Ramsey has learned of at least $8,000 in unexpended money in "the Old Emigration fund." He feels "that it is not only Expedient but almost absolutely obligatory upon the Government to tender its aid and encouragement at this time." [Unbeknownst to the senator, Fisk had two days earlier tendered his resignation; he nonetheless led a wagon train of emigrants to Idaho the following year.]

From Abbie W. Johnson

May 25, 1865, North Brookfield, Mass.; ALS, DNA-RG105, Records of the Commr., Lets. Recd. (M752, Roll 116).

"A humble Farmers Daughter in Old New England" concludes from Johnson's response to an unidentified committee that, in elevating the condition of the freedmen, he would use his influence to help with their education and "would protect those self denying Women who leave their northern homes to teach and elevate the oppressed." Detailing the woes consequent upon the war—"Many a *Vacant Chair*" in northern homes, the "hear[t]s hardened" by war experiences, the "vacant look" of "those who come back from those *horrid Slave-pens*"—a war caused by southerners, she declares: "We call loudly for *Justice*. We believe in *Retributive Justice*. We ask it." But the purpose of her letter is "to urge the Appropriation of a *large sum* of *money* to send out more *Teachers* to the *Freedmen*," inasmuch as "200 are now waiting with satisfactory recommendations to the Committee of Associations in New York alone."

From David M. Key

May 25, 1865, Paterson, N.J.; ALS, DNA-RG94, Amnesty Papers (M1003, Roll 50), Tenn., David M. Key.

A Chattanoogan and Johnson friend, "not an original secessionist," but one who felt "bound by the action of my state," assures Johnson that while stationed with Confederate troops in East Tennessee, he "always respected the feelings, persons and property of the Union citizens" and "often labored, and sometimes with effect, for the release of those who were arrested." Captured and paroled at Vicksburg, he resigned his commission and, because his "health is completely shattered," has had no connection with military or civil service since. Uncertain what has happened to his Chattanooga property after having taken his family north because of his health and because of his desire to escape "the annoyance and turmoil of all armies," he wants to return and resume the practice of law. Protesting his loyalty to the federal government and eagerness "that entire harmony should be restored," he wishes to know "what sort of penalties or disabilities I may labor under." [Johnson's June 14 endorsement directs the attorney general to "issue the pardon as requested."]

From Rae Burr Batten [1]
(*Private*[)]

Philada May 26th/65

To His Excellency, Andrew Johnson
Valued Friend

Believing you have not received my letters to you, I once again attempt to write you. Will you write if only a few lines, saying *you are well*, and *I am not forgotten.* Cicile was married to a young lawyer, Helen is Still disengaged![2] They *send love.*

Loved friend, may I ask of you the favour to remember my husband A. N. Batten, also brother J. E. Burr,[3] if possible. I would be pleased if Doctor could obtain some position whare he could receive a neat income. He is *reliable* and *competent* having a good education would be able to fill any position, you might favour him with honorably & with credit to himself.

Joshua has a large and interesting family, and is not only *competent* but as well, worthy, your favour. If you can possibly do anything for either Doctor, or brother Joshua, write me, dear friend, Will you?[4]

I would appreciate a few lines from you if only writing me you were well & whare is Robert? All join me in sending best wishes to you all. Write soon and—

Remember Your Friend Truly Mrs Rae Batten
811 Race St

Remember Rae's request to favour A. N. Batten and J. E. Burr, will you?

811 Race St.

Love from all.
Take Care of *Your Health.*[5]

Rae

ALS, DLC-JP.

1. Longtime friend of the Johnson family.

2. Batten's orphaned nieces, Cecelia (whose husband remains unidentified) and Helen Morton.

3. Dr. A. Nelson Batten; Joshua Earl Burr (*c*1825–*fl*1888) was a New Jersey-born tailor. 1860 Census, Pa., Philadelphia, 13th Ward, 310; Philadelphia directories (1863–88).

4. Less than two months later, not having received a response to her request, Batten wrote again. By mid-September 1865, her brother had been appointed a measurer in the Philadelphia customhouse, a position he held until 1868. Mrs. Batten's husband, however, failed to obtain an appointment. Rae Batten to Johnson, July 19, 1865; William B. Thomas to Johnson, Sept. 11, 1865; Burr to Johnson, Nov. 4, 1865, Johnson Papers, LC; *U.S. Off. Reg.* (1865–67).

5. In a letter to William A. Browning, Johnson's secretary, Mrs. Batten also inquired as to the whereabouts of Eliza and the rest of the family and whether the President had received her letter. Batten to Browning, May 26, 1865, Johnson Papers, LC.

From S. S. Fairfield[1]

Grenada Missi May 26th 1865

President Johnson
Sir

Deeming it the duty of all good and loyal citizens to do every thing in their power to ameliorate and remedy the present state of things, and supposing that the government will gladly receive any and all information in regard to political affairs in this state at the present time, I, in behalf of the loyal men of this neighborhood, propose to make known to you our feelings and opinions in regard to the momentous questions relating to our social and political existence. Our first and all absorbing want is a government. Mississippi to day is in abject ruin, morally, politically and especially *financially*. As far as we understand the loyal sentiment of the state, it is to hold a convention to reorganize the state government and place ourselves in harmony with the general government at once, and in good faith. In fact a convention has been called to meet at Vicksburg on the 5th of June next. But we apprehend great difficulties in holding this convention. The first ground of apprehension is that the rebel influence will intrude itself upon such convention and render its labors fruitless. While the rebel cause was to them hopeful, they would have spurned such a convention and never sought to enter it. But now it is otherwise, their cause is broken and lost forever and they are determined to strike for the next best thing they can. They say "that they had a clear casus belli, that they were acknowledged as belligerents, that they fought gloriously in a good cause, that they are not traitors but defeated patriots and merit the sympathy and respect of the world." With these sophisms they will attempt to go to the people and rule them as they were wont to do. You are well aware sir, what chicanery the old slave aristocracy will resort to, to retain some thing of their ancient dominion, and if permitted to have their own way the contest between them and union men will not be doubtful. Our second ground of apprehension is that financial matters will be greatly in the way of holding such a convention as would be desirable at the present time. As a general thing union men in the state are men of moderate means, and they have been totally prostrated during the rebellion. They have not absolutely got the means to go to the convention and pay they own expenses. Some might do it. We think it would be folly for the convention to issue state paper for the state credits are looked upon with loathing and contempt now. It is true the state issues during the rebellion will doubless be regarded as a nullity, but the people have lost large amounts of state and confederate funds of late and they are very suspicious. We hope our apprehensions will be groundless. We hope the convention at Vicksburg will be fully attended by loyal citizens and accomplish all that is desirabl, but even should this be the case we dont see how the ordinances of the convention will be enforced with out some superior power. And in view of the whole state of facts we suggest to your consideration the propriety of appointing some good man military governor of the state with sufficient power and with such rules and regulations as to compel the secession rebels to go home and attend to their domestic affairs until they learn to be good citizens and cease their treasonable designs. Perhaps no state in the union has been as badly ruled by as rascally a set of politicians as the state of Mississippi. And it so happened that the whole *ruling* party together with the whig party

that was always kept out of power, but generally being large slaveholders, went over en masse into the rebellion, hence that portion of the
citizen that are to be depended upon for hea[l]thy reconstruction are
inexperienced and unaccustomed to exercise the functions of government and consequently poorly prepared to meet the adverse circumstances of the present crisis, if the rebels are not restrained. We think
reconstruction would take place much more satisfactorily to the friends
of the union and good government if the state were placed in the hand
of some firm but good man until such time as the loyal citizenry are
fully prepared to take charge of and control affairs in the state in spite
of opposition. These suggestions are made for what they are worth
without any ulterior object in view but the welfare of the state. We
suggest the name of John W. Wood Esq.[2] as a suitable person to fill the
office of military Governor of the state. He is a man of fine abilities,
great firmness, and was elected to the convention that took the state
out of the union, as union man. He maintained his integrity during that
convention and cast the only vote that was cast against secession. He
was compelled to leave the state on account of his sentiments and now
resides in the City of Memphis Tenn.

Your Ob't servant S. S. Fairfield

ALS, DLC-JP.
1. Fairfield (b. *c*1825) was a Connecticut-born school teacher-lawyer of Grenada.
1860 Census, Miss., Yalobusha, S.W. Beat, Oakland P.O., 89.
2. Wood (*c*1821–1878), lawyer of Attala County, as a delegate to the state convention of 1861 had refused to sign the ordinance of secession. Subsequently he moved to
Memphis. 1860 Census, Miss., Attala, Kosciusko Twp. 14, Range 7, p. 1; *NUC*; *Memphis Appeal*, Aug. 14, 1878.

From Loyal Citizens of Georgia

May 26, 1865, [Ringgold ,Ga.]; LS, DLC-JP.

Thirty-six north Georgia unionists met at Ringgold on May 25 to begin "steps
towards placing the State of Georgia in her proper position as a member of the
Union" only to have their meeting disrupted by "Those who had been favorable
to the rebellion." Asserting that except for those parts "within military lines,"
the state is "in a state of anarchy," they believe that "it is indispensable that we
have a Military Governor" and recommend the appointment of Col. Timothy
R. Stanley, former commander of the post at Chattanooga, a man in whom "we
all have the fullest confidence."

From Stephen Miller

May 26, 1865, St. Paul, Minn.; ALS, DNA-RG59, Misc. Lets., 1789–1906
(M179, Roll 224).

The governor of Minnesota reports that for three years "the frontiers of this
State, and of Iowa, have been devastated by the Dakota or Sioux Indians" who
"are supplied with arms and ammunition by British traders, and when pursued

by the Federal forces . . . take refuge in her Majestys conterminous Possessions." He calls upon Johnson to approach the British government to get either "a sufficient body of British troops to be posted along the line, or secure permission to the U. States forces to pursue the hostile bands wherever they may take refuge."

From William M. Smith

Memphis May 26th 1865

To His Excellency, The President.

I have already signed an application for the appointment of John L. Williamson Esqr. to the office of U.S. District Atto for West Tenn; but feeling a very great interest in the matter, I write again.

Mr. Williamson is a Tennessean, loyal to the core, talented and energetic. He heartily endorses the policy of the government, and is giving it his earnest support. He is also earnestly supporting the present state government. Now it is absolutely necessary that we have such a man in the office named. His appointment will strengthen the friends of the government. He, until recently resided in Gibson County, and is well known in West Tennessee, and thoroughly identified in interest with its people. This fact alone, it seems to me, should give him prominence. But then, as before stated, he has all other qualifications.

You will pardon me, for urging this appointment; for I assure you, Sir, I regard it of great importance that it shall be made. *The appointee should not be in the least tinctured with disaffection*; and Mr. Williamson certainly is not.[1]

Respectfully Wm. M. Smith

To the President of The United States.

ALS, DNA-RG60, Appt. Files for Judicial Dists., Tenn., John L. Williamson.
    1. Williamson received the appointment. *U.S. Off. Reg.* (1865), 29.

From J. Madison Wells and Others

Willard's Washington, May 26th 1865.

Sir,

Permit us to submit with most deferential respect for your consideration, the following suggestions in regard to certain offices in Louisiana, the incumbents of which can from their official influence seriously retard or efficiently promote a satisfactory reorganization of the State government.

At present we only know two officers in Federal employment of any importance who can be relied upon implicitly to sustain faithfully your administration there.

They are Cuthbert Bullitt,[1] Marshal of the Eastern District of Louisiana, and Wells,[2] Naval Officer of Customs.

G. S. Denison,[3] Collector of the Port, is a relative and appointee of Mr. Chase, Chief Justice, and never resided in Louisiana before his appointment.

The Surveyor of the Port[4] is from Boston, Massachusetts, where his family reside and who have never been in Louisiana.

The two Deputy Collectors[5] are both strangers to Louisiana.

The Superintending Special Agent of the Treasy. Dept. B. F. Flanders[6] was appointed by Mr Chase and is a devoted champion of the principles & aspirations of that gentleman. He is the irresponsible custodian of *twenty millions of dollars worth of property*, nominally sequestered or held for confiscation.

It is stated that Denison, the Collector, and Flanders, Special Agent, were both superseded by the late President. They still hold their respective places however. Next in political importance to the Collector of the Port & the Special Agent of the Treasury Dept:, is the Assessor of Internal Revenue.[7] This officer and his sub-assessors exercise influence in every Parish or County, and even with the State officials opposed to him, he could seriously hinder, if so inclined, the adoption of wise & beneficent regulations for the good of the people.

With a proper understanding between the State & City governments and the federal officers already enumerated, the policy or principles the national government desires to see put in practical & successful operation in Louisiana will encounter no serious opposition. That the machinery may move smoothly and effectively it is only necessary that the State authorities are deemed worthy of the confidence of the National Executive and that the Federal employees, chief & subordinate, are made to understand that they are to support, not thwart, their administrative endeavors.

The Assessor & Sub-Assessors derive their commissions or appointments directly & respectively from the President; but in reality the Assessor exercises the appointing power, almost exclusively, of his Assistants.

It is almost superfluous for us to represent the unpopularity, if not injustice, of filling the most important places in Louisiana with persons from the Eastern States, who are neither identified with us by feeling, family ties, residence or ownership of property. As a rule, they are insolent, over-bearing and rapacious, and as to the manner in which they have discharged the trusts entrusted to them in Louisiana, we would confidently refer you to the records of the Special Commission of which Major Genl. W. F. Smith was President, and James T. Brady, of New York, was legal adviser.[8]

Our determination is to set to work immediately on our return to Louisiana to push forward the work of State reorganisation in accordance with the views & ideas you have expressed to us, and to labor diligently & faithfully to strengthen at home and abroad that confidence

& respect for your administration your kind, frank & friendly assistance & assurances given us have inspired.

Strangers to each other, we do not make professions of devotion which the early future too often in this world dissipates, and which very frequently are made to cover mere mercenary designs; but we do challenge supervision of our conduct and comparison with the officials of every other State, so far as an honest & manly support of yourself & your administration is concerned. Should our advice or assistance be at any time deemed serviceable, we shall be ready and happy to give either or both, and will always esteem it a pride and an honor to be consulted by so worthy and exalted a representative of the political principles we profess as the present President of the United States.[9]

With the profoundest respect, we have the honor to subscribe ourselves, President,

Your obdt. servts: J Madison Wells
Hu. Kennedy
Thos. Cottman

Andrew Johnson President of the United States & & &

ALS (Hugh Kennedy), DLC-Hugh McCulloch Papers.

1. Bullitt (1810–1906), a wealthy "gentleman of leisure" and Hugh Kennedy's brother-in-law, divided his time between Louisville and New Orleans. Fleeing north at the outset of the war, he returned after Union occupation and served as collector of customs (1863) before his current post. *Louisville Courier-Journal*, Aug. 5, 1906; Basler, *Works of Lincoln*, 5: 346; 8: 242; McCrary, *Lincoln and Reconstruction*, 208; Tregle, "Thomas Durant and Reconstruction," 498–99.

2. Thomas M. (b. 1836), son of J. Madison Wells, had led Union guerrillas, attended the 1864 state constitutional convention, and was elected to, but not seated in, Congress. Lowrey, "Wells," 1000; McCrary, *Lincoln and Reconstruction*, 59.

3. George S. Denison (1833–1866), Vermont native and San Antonio, Texas, resident before the war, had strongly opposed secession. Fleeing north, he returned as special treasury agent and acting collector of customs in New Orleans soon after its occupation, remaining until June, 1865. Ibid., 97; James A. Padgett, ed., "Some Letters of George Stanton Denison, 1854–1866," *LHQ*, 23 (1940): 1132–1240; Tregle, "Thomas Durant and Reconstruction," 495.

4. Either James (*fl*1871), an engineer, or James F. Tucker (b. *c*1838), a railroad agent, who were postwar residents of New Orleans. The James Tucker, who in March 1864 was General N. P. Banks's secretary, was probably the surveyor. 1870 Census, La., Orleans, New Orleans, 1st Ward, 73; Appts., Customs Service, Surveyor, New Orleans, A. T. Stone, RG56, NA; McCrary, *Lincoln and Reconstruction*, 242.

5. The federal registers list only one deputy collector; therefore Wells was probably referring to Robert H. McMillan (b. *c*1814) and his replacement, Sidney A. Stockdale (b. *c*1835), natives, respectively, of New York and Illinois. McMillan was later a customs house clerk. 1870 Census, La., Orleans, New Orleans, 2nd Ward, 51, 78; *U.S. Off. Reg.* (1863–67); New Orleans directories (1866–71).

6. New Hampshire-born Benjamin F. Flanders (1816–1896), a New Orleans resident since 1843, was, after the Union occupation, city treasurer, captain of Co. C, 5th La. Inf., USA, congressman (1862–63), and special agent of the Treasury Department (*c*1863–66). Briefly governor by appointment of General Sheridan, he was subsequently mayor (1867–68) and assistant U.S. treasurer (1873–82). *BDAC*; Joseph G. Dawson, III, *Army Generals and Reconstruction in Louisiana, 1862–1877* (Baton Rouge, 1982), 54.

7. Either William H. Higgins (b. *c*1827), appointed by Lincoln, or Edmund Murphy, whose appointment was the "first" signed by Johnson, but was not confirmed by

the Senate. *U.S. Off. Reg.* (1863–65); 1860 Census, La., Orleans, New Orleans, 1st Rep. Ward, 247; Murphy to Johnson, Oct. 1866, Mar. 5, 1867, Appt. Files for Judicial Dists., La., Edmund Murphy, RG60, NA.

8. William F. Smith (1824–1903), who had served primarily in Virginia and Tennessee, and James T. Brady, a prominent New York attorney and friend of Secretary Stanton, conducted an investigation of internal affairs in Louisiana from April 9 to 26, 1865. The commission uncovered "a vast scheme" of fraud and corruption involving treasury agents, army provost marshals, and civilian officials under the Hahn regime. Following the submission of the Smith-Brady report, Johnson ordered on May 17 the reorganization of the Department of the Gulf, relieving General Banks from command. Warner, *Blue*; Benjamin P. Thomas and Harold M. Hyman, *Stanton: The Life and Times of Lincoln's Secretary of War* (New York, 1962), 461; Lowrey, "Wells," 1032; McCrary, *Lincoln and Reconstruction*, 312; *OR*, Ser. 1, Vol. 48, Pt. 2: 475–76; *New Orleans Picayune*, April 12, May 13, 25, 26, 31, June 4, 1865; *Little Rock Arkansas State Gazette*, May 29, 1865.

9. Johnson's endorsement of May 27 reads: "Respectfully referred to the Hon. Secretary of the Treasury, whose attention is especially directed to the within statement in reference to Treasury appointments in Louisiana."

From Joseph A. Wright[1]

30 Meridian St Indianapolis, Indiana

Private   May 26th 1865

Hon Andrew Johnson
President of the United States.
My Dear Friend,

I have been in this city two days, with our people who are here in large numbers from different portions of our state attending the Courts. There is not much excitement about the Bowles & Mulligan cases, a great number of the loyal men are for their execution, some, how ever are for the commutation of their sentence to Imprisonment for life, using this argument "As the question of the Jurisdiction of the Court before whom they were tried from this state is taken up to the Supreme Court, and will not be decided before next December at Washington, they suppose the Executive will not suffer their execution to take place until that question is decided.["] Whatever your action may be in this matter it will be approved. And I quote the language of one of the best men in the state (who has known you for years in Tennessee) "I will stand by *whatever* Andy does in this matter, for he will do what he *believes to be right*."

I will see you before you decide the Post Master appointment of this place. There are some things of importance you should be made acquainted with before the appointment is made.[2]

There is a general manifestation of confidence in your Administration, and no people were ever more determined to stand by an Executive, than the masses of the people of Indiana. Whenever they speak of you the remark is this, "We *expect* from President Johnson *firmness* & *decision* in *all his acts*."

You know my friend, how badly I felt over your refusal to accept the

Carriage & Horses &c.[3] I confess however the whole of the press of the West are sustaining you by Editorials.

Accept assurances of my high regard while I remain

yours most truly, and respectfully; Joseph A. Wright

ALS, DLC-JP.

1. Former Indiana governor, more recently senator, and close political ally of Johnson.

2. Alexander H. Conner, postmaster since May 1861, was retained until October 1866. *U.S. Off. Reg.* (1861–67).

3. For Johnson's refusal to accept a span of horses and new carriage, see Letter to New York Merchants, May 22, 1865.

From William G. Brownlow

Nashville Tenn May 27 1865.

President—

In a conversation with Gen Thomas he said he was willing to turn over the road[1] from Knoxville up to the state line if the War Dept concur. It can be easily turned over to the president & directors or to a receiver as may be most lawful and expedient.

W G Brownlow

Tel, DLC-JP.

1. The East Tennessee and Virginia Railroad. See Letter from John R. Branner, May 29, 1865.

To William G. Brownlow

Executive Mansion Washn. May 27. 1865.

His Excellency Governor. W. G. Brownlow
Nashville Tenn.

Steps are being taken to turn over all the Rail-roads to the several Companies that organize and present unquestionably loyal Presidents and Directors.[1] It would be best for the Companies to organize immediately, and give evidence of loyalty. It will be better for them to take charge than for the state to appoint Receivers. In other words, the Companies will make the most efficient and judicious receivers and will pay the interest on the bonds issued by the state much sooner. The roads will be turned over to the Companies together with any surplus material such as Engines, rolling stock, &c owned by the Government, upon the most advantageous terms. General Thomas is expected here soon and will be advised of the policy of the Government in regard to the subject of Railroads.[2]

Andrew Johnson.

Tel, DNA-RG107, Tels. Sent, President, Vol. 2 (1865).

1. According to Michael Burns, president of the Nashville and Chattanooga Railroad, in testimony to an 1867 House committee investigating southern roads, when Johnson became President he tried to "lessen the expenses of the government" by turning roads

over to their owners as soon as possible. *House Reports*, 39 Cong., 2 Sess., No. 34, "Affairs of Southern Railroads," p. 304 (Ser. 1306).

2. More than two months later the secretary of war's order of August 8, 1865, directed Thomas to turn railroads over to the owners. Ibid., 83.

From Benjamin F. McDonough[1]

Sabine Pass Texas May 27th 1865

His Excellency Andrew Johnson
President U S
Dear Sir

You will perhaps recognise in the signature attached to this letter an old friend and relative.

I am the son of James McDonough (Brother to your Decesd. Mother) of Bledsoe County Tenn. My Father now resides in Georgia.[2] The last time I had the pleasure of seeing [you] was in Pikeville Tenn. 9th May 1840, in great contest for the Presidency between Van Buren & Harrison since which time a great many changes have taken place. I have married and removed to Texas some years ago. When the war commenced I was appointed to the office of Collector of Customs for the Port of Sabine Texas, which office I have held until the re establishment of the U S Authority in this District.

I have nothing to conceal having acted my part as I believed properly & honestly and have nothing more to add except that as the war seems to have terminated and finally it appears to be the General wish to settle down once more in amicable relations &c.

The gift of the Collectorship of the Port of Galveston Texas in your hands in rememberance of times now past and our former friendship &c you will confer a favor by appointing me to the office of Collector of Customs for the Port of Galveston Texas. If my application is granted it [will] be remembered with pleasure. If not I shall not harbor an ill feeling or even feel disapointed.

I can give the best refferences as to my General Character. I refer immediately to Honl L D Evans[3] who is now in Washington and was formerly a member to Congress from this State who has known me for years in Henderson Texas.

Your Brother Wm. P Johnson who as you know married my Sister[4] is residing in Columbia Texas. Family all quite well. I will not further tresspass upon your time &c with a long letter well knowing how much you are occupied with public business &c.

Hoping soon to have a favorable reply I remain

very respectfully yours B F McDonough

address B F McDonough
Sabine Pass Texas

ALS, DNA-RG56, Appts., Customs Service, Assessor, Galveston, B. F. McDonough.

1. Ten days later, McDonough (1819–1888), "fearing the original should by accident be mislaid," forwarded another copy of this May 27th letter. Although not pardoned until August 11, he was appointed assessor at Galveston in July 1865. McDonough to Johnson, June 6, 1865, Appts., Customs Service, Assessor, Galveston, B. F. McDonough, RG56, NA; Amnesty Papers (M1003, Roll 54), Tex., B. F. McDonough, RG94, NA; *Washington Morning Chronicle*, July 19, 1865; genealogical data from James F. McDonough, Knoxville, 1979.

2. James McDonough (1794–1868), born in Raleigh, N.C., had migrated to Bledsoe County, Tenn., with his father. Living for a time in Indiana, by mid-century he was a Randolph County, Ala., resident. Ibid.

3. Lemuel D. Evans (1810–1877), a staunch unionist, later became collector of internal revenue (1867), a justice of the state supreme court (1870–73), and U.S. marshal for the eastern district of Texas (1875–77). Several months later, in a letter of recommendation for McDonough, Evans specified three positions—marshal of the Eastern District, mail agent for the state, or assessor of internal revenue, 1st Dist.—as being possibilities for McDonough's talents. *BDAC*; Evans to Johnson, Aug. 16, 1865, Andrew Johnson Papers, New York Historical Society.

4. President Johnson's brother married Sarah Giddings McDonough (1816–1882), a Sequatchie Valley, Tenn., native, February 23, 1832. Genealogical data from James F. McDonough.

From Joseph Noxon [1]

New York May 27/65

Andrew Johnson Prest.

You say you believe in democratic government, or *consent* of loyal people. Yet you *dare not* avow with practical effect the right of the colord man to vote. Are you honest?

You profess to protect loyal men & to punish traitors; yet you *refuse* the franchise to loyal colord people, the *only* means effectual for their protection or advancement. Are you honest?

You know rebels disappointed will wreak revenge on loyal blacks, & yet you refuse the franchise for their protection.

You say you have no right to grant it. You know in the first elections to be held to reorganize a seceded state *you* have the *power*, the *right*, & the *duty* to say who shall vote. Otherwise rebels will re-elect rebels, as witness Virginia.[2]

You know by *prompt* & vigorous action *now*, the question of negro suffrage can be *settled* & *accepted* by the people as an *accomplished fact*. Why not settle it & take it *out* of political controversy?

Do you believe the *loyal* Union partys' success essential to the peace & prosperity of this country? Then dont refuse 850,000 *loyal votes* that are *always sure* for liberty & the Republic.

I am deprived of all I have by Rebels. I was formerly a resident of Tennessee but the rebs drove me from home. I was a scout for the Union army & lived in the mountains 11 months. I have some right that you hear me.

Yours truly Joseph Noxon

ALS, DLC-JP.
  1. Not identified.
  2. See, for example, Letter from Committee of Richmond Blacks, June 10, 1865.

From William B. Scott and Son [1]

Nashville Tennessee May 27th 1865

His Excellency Andrew Johnson

Sir. We have Sent you A few numbers of our paper "The Colered Tennessean," knowing you to be A freind of our "*race*" and A lover of Tennessee! We hope that you As Chief Magistrate of the U.S. will sanction our course, for we are laboring for to enlighten our race to A Sense of their duty. And though we have not the Intellectual powers that is required, we have the will and ambition to understand and appreciate the gloraus priveledges that we now enjoy.

We are Your most Obedent Servants.

Wm. B. Scott and Son

Eds

To His Excellency President, U.S.

ALS, DLC-JP.
  1. In 1847 William B. Scott (c1821–1884), North Carolina native and free black, moved to Blount County, Tenn., where he was a saddler before the war. William B. Scott, Jr. (c1846–*fl*1880) as a very young lad worked in a Knoxville printing shop and then with his father started *The Colored Tennessean* in early 1865 in Nashville. Moving the press to Maryville, they later changed the name to the *Maryville Republican*. 1860 Census, Tenn., Blount, 2nd Dist., 80; (1880), Maryville, 194th Enum. Dist., 31; *Chattanooga Times*, Apr. 11, 1884; Inez Burns, *History of Blount County, Tennessee* (Nashville, 1957), 227; Alrutheus A. Taylor, *The Negro in Tennessee, 1865–1880* (Washington, D.C., 1941), 155, 260.

From Kiah B. Sewall [1]

Mobile, 27 May 1865.

To Andrew Johnson,
President of the United States.

The loyal citizens of Mobile propose to hold a public meeting to express their views in regard to a reorganization of civil government for the state, and a renewal of their relations with the Government of the United States. They believe there is now no legal state government. That the organization calling itself the State of Alabama, which has been in arms against the United States for the last four years, is not the State of Alabama of 1860, one of the United States, but a mere usurpation based solely on the ordinances of secession and the new constitution founded thereon, and is, therefore, without lawful authority and wholly null and void.

That this usurpation was not, as generally supposed, the act of the people of Alabama, either by origination, or confirmation, inasmuch as it was entirely the work of an illegal convention, illegally called by the Governor of the State, for an illegal purpose, and was never authorised by, or submitted to, the popular vote.

That a majority of the people of Alabama are loyal and anxious to get back to the legal civil rule, and to renew their relations with the Federal Government, subject to the constitution and laws of the United States as they now exist, including a prohibition of involuntary servitude.

That this can be done only by an amendment of the state constitution of 1860, or the formation of a new one, through the action of a convention elected by the loyal citizens, and not by, or through any officers, organizations, or agencies of the rebellion whatsoever.

That the people of Alabama are, by reason of this Usurpation, without the legal means of setting the wheels of Government in motion, being wholly disorganized, and having no State officers, either executive, legislative judicial, or ministerial.

That whenever a disposition, on the part of the people to reorganize a state government upon the basis above indicated shall be sufficiently manifest, the aid of the Military power of the United States will be requisite to enable the loyal citizens of the State, to elect delegates to a convention, which aid may be afforded either through the agency of a Military Governor, or that of the General commanding the Department.

That in the absence of congressional Legislation there seems to be no other starting point than the military power; and it is believed, there can and will be no objection to its use, so far as may be necessary, on the part of the people of the State.

These views will, it is believed, be adopted by the majority of the people, and they are here presented to you in advance, in order that you may know that they exist, and because there is reason to believe that other views have been urged upon your consideration.

Some persons have addressed you from this city, who, although till the late surrender, active and bitter participants in the rebellion, and exceedingly valiant in their persecutions of union men, have now the audacity and shamelessness of assuming to be the only true exponents of Union Sentiments and the indispensable leaders in all union movements. They are careful in the use of terms professing to desire a "restoration to former relations"—but meaning a re union with slavery as it was before.[2]

If the Government will promptly discountenance such insinuating attempts, and on the contrary sustain the views of reorganization above substantially set forth—Alabama will soon be in the full exercise of all her functions, state and Federal, on a foundation of peace and prosperity never before enjoyed.

Praying for your health and safety, and a wise administration of public affairs,[3]

I have the honor to be with great respect
Your Obt. Servant K. B. Sewall

ALS, DLC-JP.

1. Sewall (c1807–1865), native Maine lawyer and unionist, had lived in New York and St. Louis before migrating to Mobile about 1840. *American Annual Cyclopaedia* (1865), 646.

2. Sewall appears to be referring to a May 23 petition from 106 Mobile citizens, which was forwarded by Gen. Gordon Granger with a quite different evaluation. According to Granger, the "temper and spirit of these people, as far as Union sentiments are concerned, far exceed anything of the kind I have witnessed since this war commenced." The views of these men of "standing, influence, and in all respects representative men . . . are a true reflection of the sentiments of the citizens of Mobile and the State of Alabama." Mobile Citizens to Johnson, May 23, 1865; Granger to Johnson, May 29, 1865, Johnson Papers, LC; *New York Herald*, June 15, 1865.

3. A week later, concerned that General Granger had advised the calling of the old legislature, Sewall again aired his opinions to Secretary of State Seward. Sewall to Seward, June 2, 1865, Johnson Papers, LC.

From J. Madison Wells and Hugh Kennedy

May 27, 1865, Washington, D.C.; ALS (Kennedy), DLC-JP.

Recent spring flooding of the Mississippi River, "causing wide-spread distress and suffering, and exciting general apprehension of famine & pestilence on the subsidence of the floods," leads the Louisiana governor and New Orleans mayor to beseech "the generous interposition of the Executive" in ordering military authorities to make available for public use surplus stores and farm animals. Such action "would enable the people to renew intercourse with the interior, to feed the hungry, clothe the naked and cultivate the soil," thus "renewing in a more enduring manner these powerful moral ligaments which attach a people indissolubly to the institutions & government of their country." Meanwhile, at the beginning of May, in New Orleans "twenty two thousand persons were drawing rations daily from the Federal commissariat; and eight thousand suits at law were instituted . . . against small (city) property holders" for taxes for which they were in arrears. [See Letter from Wells, July 5, 1865.]

From James B. Bingham [1]

Memphis, Tenn., May 28 1865.

His Excellency Andrew Johnson,
President of the United States:

Dear Sir: As I indicated when I parted with you in washington, I now address you a few lines in reference to matters around Memphis.

As you have not yet acted in reference to the Postmastership of this city, may I not ask, on behalf of Mr. Loague,[2] that if there is no prospect of *immediate* action, he may be placed in Carlton's[3] place in office of collector and Surveyor of Customs. Mr. Carlton was appointed through the *Chase* influence, has never been connected with our Union movements, was not recommended by Union men for the position, and has used his office for his personal aggrandisement and to the injury of the service. Mr. Tomeny,[4] special Agent of the Treasury Department, before Mr. Lincoln's manager, Gen. Orme,[5] came here, preferred charges against Carlton for exacting fees in excess of what the law allowed, and the charge was proved, but there was so much corruption in the Custom House that he was white-washed and has been retained. As Depository of the Government, I learn that a heavy draft was made upon him for funds a few weeks ago, but the Express Agent had to wait till a cotton speculator, named Parkman,[6] who was in Red River, near Shreveport, could be sent for and the money raised, and even after the delay, only a part of the money was returned in currency, and the remainder by a draft on New York! Carlton made a bad failure here before the war, and is considered as unsafe in money affairs. Mr. Chase was informed by Mr. Tomeny that Carlton was not a man to be trusted, but Chase's friends—particularly Yeatman and Mellen[7]—managed to keep him in position. As the government may make out to get its money by timely action in his case—as Carlton is not, and never has been one of *your friends*—as all agree that he ought to be and will be removed, I write to ask that Mr. Loague, who has presented such a numerously signed petition and recommendation for Postmaster, may be placed at once in Carlton's place in the Custom House in Memphis. Loague is honest, capable, and faithful—is identified with your policy in Tennessee when it involved opposition to stand up for you,—is a hearty well-wisher, and will use his influence in your favor, and I hope you will, without delay, place him either in the Post Office, to which he was recommended, or the Custom House in Carlton's place. I can assure you that either position will be acceptable to him. He is now tax collector under the city government, but the fact that he took position for Emancipation, and has been recommended by the Union men of this city for that Postmaster, is so prejudicial to his standing as a candidate, in the estimation of the men who have just returned from the south, that he would stand but little chance for re-election. In Memphis, at the present time, there are about *three* rebels to *one* Union man, and it is as much as we can expect to be allowed to remain in the State. I tell you the fact, that I am now on my good behavior to the returned rebels, and have to shape my course not as I would, but as it may be *expedient.* I hope you will act in Loague's case with the least avoidable delay.[8] I understand that Gen. Orme has tendered his resignation to take effect on the 1st of July. He is reputed to have made lots of money.[9] If you would send a good man down here you could make it pay perhaps $50.000 to the government to examine into his case! A man named Bolling[10] has been appointed under Orme who was Assistant Sequestration Commissioner under the rebel government in this city— a man who gave Union men owning property here, or holding it for absent Union men, much trouble in Secession times. Orme has appointed him, and the government has confirmed it, when it is known that he is not, and never has been a Union man in sympathy or action. But enough for one time.[11]

Yours, truly, J. B. Bingham

P.S. A proposition to endorse the national government, and your administration, was voted down in committee which last week reported resolutions for a meeting at Somerville.[12] John R. Mosby[13] was its leading spirit, and Fayette county is the only one in which no election was held in March a year ago. Other meetings have pursued the same say-nothing policy.

ALS, DNA-RG56, Appts., Customs Service, Surveyor, Memphis, John Loague.

1. Memphis editor and frequent Johnson correspondent.

2. John Loague (1829–1899), Irish-born banker and lawyer, who arrived in Memphis in 1860, was appointed surveyor of customs (1865), and served subsequently as county court clerk, mayor, and legislator. *BDTA*, 2: 537.

3. George N. Carlton (b. *c*1820), an importer and dealer in hardware and household goods and furniture, was a delegate to the Memphis Union convention and a member of the Memphis Board of Trade; in 1863 he became surveyor of customs. Memphis directories (1859–66); Byron and Barbara Sistler, trs., *1860 Census, Tennessee* (5 vols., Nashville, 1981–82), 1: 314; Robert F. Futrell, "Federal Trade with the Confederate States, 1861–1865" (Ph.D. dissertation, Vanderbilt University, 1950), 283, 290; Ernest W. Hooper, "Memphis, Tennessee: Federal Occupation and Reconstruction, 1862–70" (Ph.D. dissertation, University of North Carolina, Chapel Hill, 1957), 69.

4. James M. Tomeny, former assistant special agent of the treasury.

5. William W. Orme, supervising special agent and former law partner of Leonard Swett, was a friend and adviser of Lincoln who had taken a personal interest in Orme's appointment. Ludwell H. Johnson, "Northern Profit and Profiteers: The Cotton Rings of 1864–1865," *CWH*, 12 (1966): 114.

6. Edward Parkman (b. *c*1822), a tobacconist and partner of Parkman, Brooks, and Co., Memphis, was profiting in the cotton trade. It was probably no coincidence that a onetime partner was assistant secretary of the treasury George Harrington, Chase's close friend. Johnson, "Northern Profit," 103–4; 1860 Census, Tenn., Weakley, Dresden, 164; Memphis directories (1865–66); see also Telegram to Alvin Hawkins, July 16, 1865.

7. Thomas H. Yeatman, former assistant special agent, now a "cotton attorney"; William P. Mellen, general agent of the first special agency of the treasury.

8. Loague was appointed surveyor after the President forwarded his letter to Secretary McCulloch on June 24, along with a note, penned by military secretary Reuben D. Mussey, to the effect that Johnson regarded "Mr. *John Loague* of Memphis as a suitable person for the Surveyor of the Port of Memphis." Mussey to McCulloch, June 24, 1865, Appts., Customs Service, Surveyor, Memphis, John Loague, RG56, NA; *U.S. Off. Reg.* (1865), 117.

9. Orme's office had been indiscriminately issuing permits to Leonard Swett for cotton shipments. When Secretary McCulloch found out, he warned Orme "to stop frauds and abuses and fully protect the interests of the government." There is no indication that Orme was profiting personally, but his resignation shortly thereafter implies some complicity. Johnson, "Northern Profit," 114.

10. Probably Bernard Bowling (*c*1834–*fl*1881), an "Ass't Special Agent and Deputy," who remained in Memphis to become, after a brief association with the grocery business, a cotton broker. 1880 Census, Tenn., Shelby, Memphis, 136th Enum. Dist., 33; *Memphis Bulletin*, May 17, 1865; Memphis directories (1865–81).

11. Bingham later thanked Johnson for Loague's appointment, after a petition he called "*a fraud*" had been presented in Carlton's favor. Bingham to Johnson, July 13, 1865, Johnson Papers, LC.

12. The absence of any reference to Johnson or his administration in the report of the

resolutions adopted at the Fayette County meeting on May 20 would appear to sustain
Bingham's observation. *Memphis Bulletin*, May 23, 1865.

13. Probably Joseph R. Mosby (*c*1819–*c*1879), a planter and railroad promoter,
who had served one term in the legislature. *BDTA*, 1: 536.

From John A. Dix[1]

New York 28, May 1865.

My dear Sir:

Allow me to express my sincere thanks to you for setting an example,
which the country very much needed, in declining the offering of the
N.Y. merchants.[2] I am sure they were actuated by no unworthy motives; and for that very reason your suggestions were the more valuable.

There is a subject, on which I desire to say a few words. I have found
in quarters entitled to great respect what I cannot but regard as a morbid tenderness towards the principal men, who have brought upon the
country multiplied evils of the rebellion. I certainly would not counsel
a vindictive or a too-extended retribution for the national wrongs. But
I do think the plainest considerations of justice and duty demand that
a few of the authors of the rebellion should be tried & executed for
treason. The community should be made to understand, in a way not
to be mistaken, that no set of men can be permitted to disturb the good
order of society with impunity—or, in other words, that rebellion leads
to the gallows. I believe such an example due to our own tranquillity &
to the cause of stable government throughout the world. No consideration short of this would have induced me to make these suggestions to
you, and I am sure you will deem the motive sufficient to excuse them.

I am, Dear Sir, Very truly yours,

John A. Dix.

His Excellency A. Johnson.

ALS, DLC-JP.

1. Former U.S. senator and prominent New York Republican, now major general
commanding at New York.

2. See Letter to New York City Merchants, May 22, 1865.

From John Martin[1]

Memphis May 28th 1865

Hon Andrew Johnson President
Washinton
Dear Sir

Under other circumstances I would offer you my congratulations on
your elevation to the high position you occupy, but will only say, the
whole country—the South especially is fortunate in having a man

of your ability and Statesmanship at the head of the Government at this time.

My object in writing, is simply to make a few Suggestions about the *negro*. Since I left Dandridge East Ten. in 1840, I have had a great deal to do with negroes and Planters and think I understand the character of both the White and back races in the South.

The War has liberated the negro. This was necessarily the consequence of the rebellion. The Southern people, so far as my observation goes, are Satisfied to let the negro go; What are we to do with him? "That is the question." And that is the question that you as a Patriotic Statesman must decide. First then, the policy would be good to remove all the negro troops from the Southern States as soon as practicable. They could be placed on the frontiers and in the Northern Garrisons where there presence would afford no cause of irritation; You can readily understand why the white troops will be the best for the Southern garrisons; Now as to the disposition of the great mass, of the negroes of the South in their ignorant and helpless condition. Something must be done and something ought to be done at the earliest moment. Freedom to them, without some organised, and if you please for the present compulsory system of labour simply means starvation; this is no boone. Further on many plantations, particularly in districts contiguous to where the Federal armies have occupied there are only old and young negroes who cannot work. How are they to be supported? I already know of instances where Planters have sent waggon loads of such into Memphis and put them in the Streets.[2] For such cases I could suggest no remedy; but in cases where there is enough efficient labor, the negroes ought to be compelled *for a while at least* to stay at home, and the Planters *forced* to treat them well and compensate them for their labour. How to work in this way in the face of our constitutions, State rights &c I cannot say, but there exists the necessity that something should be done, to save both the White & Black race in the South, I had almost said, from annihilation. Can your great mind suggest and apply the remedy to the existing state of things? I could write you at length, but know that a suggestion is all that is necessary for you to comprehend the situation.

Your Friend & obt St. John Martin

ALS, DNA-RG107, Lets. Recd., EB12 President 1956 (1865).

1. Martin (c1815–fl1870), Memphis lawyer and sometime Arkansas planter, had been a city alderman and was elected to the legislature in 1861. After testifying before the House committee investigating the Memphis riots in 1866, he moved to Paducah, Ky., where he edited a newspaper. *House Reports*, 39 Cong., 1 Sess., No. 101, "Memphis Riots," pp. 136–39 (Ser. 1274); *BDTA*, 2: 605; 1870 Census, Ky., McCracken, Subdiv. No. 112, p. 18.

2. Freedmen crowded into Memphis during and after the war, increasing the black population at least fivefold between 1860 and 1865. Most settled near the Federal troops stationed at Fort Pickering in south Memphis. George C. Rable, *But There Was No Peace: The Role of Violence in the Politics of Reconstruction* (Athens, Ga., 1984), 34.

From John H. Reagan

May 28, 1865, Fort Warren, Mass.; Copy, Tx-Ar, John H. Reagan Papers.

In solitary confinement at Fort Warren, the Confederacy's former postmaster general writes to plead "the cause of humanity and of our country's future," suggesting in this lengthy letter that "a humane and merciful policy on the part of the government" would be "more conducive to the public good, for the present and future, than a harsh, relentless, and vindictive policy." He outlines the logic of secession—that the Union was a voluntary compact of sovereign states, that the federal government had no power to interfere with slavery, and that, after John Brown's raid and the formation of the Republican party, the South chose secession as "the last and only remedy left for their security"—and concludes that the war "was not brought on by particular men but by great causes which involved all the people alike, and that it was intended only to separate the States concerned from a government supposed to be hostile to them, and to establish for them a government friendly to their interests." Since individuals were not responsible for the war, Johnson should support a course extending a general amnesty and thereby win "a victory greater than was ever won by arms, by securing the triumph of reason over passion, substituting peace for war, restoring to the country friendship instead of hatred, and substituting repose and happiness for the strife and sorrow which now covers the land, and so entitle yourself to all the gratitude and honors your country can bestow." [He was paroled by a special proclamation on October 11, 1865.]

From James O. Shackelford[1]

Clarksville May 28 1865

His Excelency Andrew Johnson
Dear Sir

Knowing the great interest you feel in all matters relative to our state, I take the Liberty of writing you. Since I saw you I entered on the duties of my office and I have Laboured to restore the supremacy of the Laws and so far my labours have been crowned with success. I have met with much opposition from the Slaveholding Aristocracy, but that is silenced though not Dead. My District is now quiet. I can travel th[r]ough most of the counties with out an escort. I am gratified at the feeling manifested by the returning soldiers. They seem perfectly satisfied much more so than the citizens at Home. If the troops were removed a Different feeling might Develop itself. There was for a time a strong feeling to assert the right to the negro, and if the troops were removed Difficulties might arrise. I held the criminal Court here last week for Judge Frazer,[2] and I endeavoured to impress on the people the condition of the negro and their Duty as citizens towards them. Our county is not yet fully organized. We will complete the organization this week, but I much fear the action of the present legislature will defeat the restoration of law in Middle & West Tennessee. The oath required for office holders[3] is such that few men in the middle or western Divisions can take it. In this County it will be impossible to fill the offices and it cannot be Done in any county in my District except perhaps Smith. In Dickson Stewart & Humphreys it will be impossible to find men who can take the oath required. The consequence is that the courts will have no officers to execute the Law. We will have no magistrates to conduct the County business and we will have no constables to preserve order. The consequence will be anarchy will overspread the land unless you interpose. I am satisfied such is the tendency of affairs. The members of the legislature seem to be influenced rather by feelings of Hostility towards the masses than broad and statesmen like views.[4] Unless the feelings manifested can be checked God knows what will be our condition. Brownlow seems to be more a partizan and sectarian Leader, than the Governor of the proud State of Tennessee. I have been frequently at Nashville and endeavoured to assist in affairs, but I fear to not much purpose. The elective Franchise ought to be restricted. That may perchance be done. As for my self I can take the oath required but few men in my District can. I am gratified to see you will be sustained by all true friends of the union. I have never Doubted of your success. I am gratified to see you are going to have Davis tried by the U S Court. If found guilty of participating in Lincons Death he ought to be Hung and richly Deserves Death for his treason. If convicted of treason I hope you will consider of the policy of Death. I say this as a friend wishing posterity to place you right. I hope to be in your city During the summer. Pardon this letter. I wished to give you truly the condition of matters in Tensee.

Respectfully yours J O Shackelford

ALS, DLC-JP.

1. Clarksville lawyer, recently appointed state supreme court justice by Governor Brownlow.

2. Thomas N. Frazier (1810–1887), former clerk and master at Pikeville, had been appointed by Johnson judge of the criminal court for Davidson, Rutherford, and Montgomery counties (1864–67, 1870–78). W. Woodford Clayton, *History of Davidson County, Tennessee* (Philadelphia, 1880), 459–60; *Roane County Republican*, October 3, 1887.

3. Probably the prospective test oath, included in the franchise act passed June 5, which was prescribed for elective officials and candidates for office. Alexander, *Reconstruction*, 75.

4. Shackelford, a more conservative unionist, was obviously concerned about the radical reconstruction proposals being aired in the present session of the legislature and the acrimonious debates over the franchise bills. Ibid., 73–75; White, *Messages of Govs.*, 5: 427–32.

Amnesty Proclamation

May 29, 1865

Whereas the President of the United States, on the 8th day of December, A.D. eighteen hundred and sixty-three, and on the 26th day of March, A.D. eighteen hundred and sixty-four, did, with the object to suppress the existing rebellion, to induce all persons to return to their loyalty, and to restore the authority of the United States, issue proclamations offering amnesty and pardon to certain persons who had directly or by implication participated in the said rebellion; and whereas many persons who had so engaged in said rebellion have, since the issuance of said proclamations, failed or neglected to take the benefits offered thereby; and whereas many persons who have been justly deprived of all claim to amnesty and pardon thereunder, by reason of their participation directly or by implication in said rebellion, and continued hostility to the government of the United States since the date of said proclamation, now desire to apply for and obtain amnesty and pardon:

To the end, therefore, that the authority of the government of the United States may be restored, and that peace, order, and freedom may be established, I, ANDREW JOHNSON, President of the United States, do proclaim and declare that I hereby grant to all persons who have, directly or indirectly, participated in the existing rebellion, except as hereinafter excepted, amnesty and pardon, with restoration of all rights of property, except as to slaves, and except in cases where legal proceedings, under the laws of the United States providing for the confiscation of property of persons engaged in rebellion, have been instituted; but upon the condition, nevertheless, that every such person shall take and subscribe the following oath, (or affirmation,) and thenceforward keep and maintain said oath inviolate; and which oath shall be registered for permanent preservation, and shall be of the tenor and effect following, to wit:

I, _____ _____, do solemnly swear, (or affirm,) in presence of Almighty God, that I will henceforth faithfully support, protect, and defend the Constitution of the United States, and the union of the States thereunder; and that I will, in like manner, abide by, and faithfully support all laws and proclamations which have been made during the existing rebellion with reference to the emancipation of slaves. So help me God.

The following classes of persons are excepted from the benefits of this proclamation: 1st, all who are or shall have been pretended civil or diplomatic officers or otherwise domestic or foreign agents of the pretended Confederate government; 2d, all who left judicial stations under the United States to aid the rebellion; 3d, all who shall have been military or naval officers of said pretended Confederate government above the rank of colonel in the army or lieutenant in the navy; 4th, all who left seats in the Congress of the United States to aid the rebellion; 5th, all who resigned or tendered resignations of their commissions in the army or navy of the United States to evade duty in resisting the rebellion; 6th, all who have engaged in any way in treating otherwise than lawfully as prisoners of war persons found in the United States service, as officers, soldiers, seamen, or in other capacities; 7th, all persons who have been, or are absentees from the United States for the purpose of aiding the rebellion; 8th, all military and naval officers in the rebel service, who were educated by the government in the Military Academy at West Point or the United States Naval Academy; 9th, all persons who held the pretended offices of governors of States in insurrection against the United States; 10th, all persons who left their homes within the jurisdiction and protection of the United States, and passed beyond the Federal military lines into the pretended Confederate States for the purpose of aiding the rebellion; 11th, all persons who have been engaged in the destruction of the commerce of the United States upon the high seas, and all persons who have made raids into the United States from Canada, or been engaged in destroying the commerce of the United States upon the lakes and rivers that separate the British Provinces from the United States; 12th, all persons who, at the time when they seek to obtain the benefits hereof by taking the oath herein prescribed, are in military, naval, or civil confinement, or custody, or under bonds of the civil, military, or naval authorities, or agents of the United States as prisoners of war, or persons detained for offences of any kind, either before or after conviction; 13th, all persons who have voluntarily participated in said rebellion, and the estimated value of whose taxable property is over twenty thousand dollars; 14th, all persons who have taken the oath of amnesty as prescribed in the President's proclamation of December 8th, A.D. 1863, or an oath of allegiance to the government of the United States since the date of said proclamation, and who have not thenceforward kept and maintained the same inviolate.

Provided, That special application may be made to the President for pardon by any person belonging to the excepted classes; and such clemency will be liberally extended as may be consistent with the facts of the case and the peace and dignity of the United States.

The Secretary of State will establish rules and regulations for administering and recording the said amnesty oath, so as to insure its benefit to the people, and guard the government against fraud.[1]

In testimony whereof, I have hereunto set my hand, and caused the seal of the United States to be affixed.

Done at the City of Washington, the twenty-ninth day of May, in the year of our Lord one thousand eight hundred and sixty-five, and of the Independence of the United States the eighty-ninth.

⟨L.S.⟩   ANDREW JOHNSON.
By the President:
WILLIAM H. SEWARD, *Secretary of State.*

PD, DLC-JP7A.
    1. The oath could be subscribed "before any commissioned officer, civil, military, or naval, in the service of the United States, or any civil or military officer of a loyal State or Territory, who, by the laws thereof, may be qualified for administering oaths." A certified copy was to be given to the applicant and the original sent to the Department of State, where a register would be kept and from which "certificates will be issued of such re-

cords." State Department Circular, May 29, 1865, Misc. Div., Claims for Cotton and Captured and Abandoned Property, RG56, NA.

From James V. Boughner[1]

Morgantown, W. Virga May 29. 1865.

His Excellency, Andrew Johnston,
President, U. States,

Sir: Allow me to state that, heretofore it seems to have been a fixed rule, for four years past, in relation to federal appointments in West Virginia, to make selections from those who had supported Mr Bell or Mr Lincoln in 1860, whilst a large majority of the Union voters supported either Mr Douglass or Mr Breckenridge, in this and adjoining counties. No endorsement, if the proposed appointee has ever been a democrat, has received any attention or credence. Permit me to call attention to the recent appointments of assessor and collector of Int. Revenue in this district as a case in point.[2]

In defiance of the request of the member of Congress[3] from the district, and the desire of a large majority of the supporters of the administration, a small clyque secured the appt. of these offices, as they have for four years of all other federal appts. I would like to see a reconsideration of the appts. just made for the 3d[sic] Cong. district.

Very Respectfully, Your obt servant
Jas. V. Boughner.

ALS, DNA-RG56, Appts., Internal Revenue Service, Collector, W. Va., 2nd Dist., James V. Boughner.

1. Boughner (1812–1882) served as pension agent in Morgantown on the eve of the war. "An enthusiastic Democrat" who supported the war, he was appointed collector by Johnson in June, though he was no longer in the post in 1867. Atkinson and Gibbens, *Prominent Men*, 671.

2. The second district assessor at this time was probably Thomas R. Carskadon, and the collector was Samuel R. Dawson (since January 1865). *U.S. Off. Reg.* (1865), 55; *Journal of the Executive Proceedings of the Senate of the United States of America* (90 vols., Washington, D.C., 1828–1948), 14: 13, 84.

3. William G. Brown (1800–1884), an antebellum Virginia state legislator and congressman, returned to Congress in 1861 as a unionist and continued to serve after the admission of West Virginia as a state. *BDAC*.

From John R. Branner[1]

Nashville May 29 1865

His Excellency Andrew Johnson President
Washington
Dear Sir

Allow me to say that I am here trying to make Some arrangements about our E T & Va RRd. I have Seen Genl Thomas and made a

statement of facts about our road and he informs me he has recco-
mended to the Sect of War that our road be delivered over to the stockholders. The goverment have recalled all the Construction Corps from
our road and are now only running it to Jonesboro Ten. The two
bridges over Holston at Union and Watauga at Carters are both down
and no arrangements to rebuild them and I am verry anxious that the
company should have the road so they can rebuild them before winter
unless the goverment will put them up. I will organise our board of
Directors and Elect officers to control its affairs which shall be men of
knowledge and undoubted loyalty. I would be much pleased if the goverment would complete the bridges on our road before it is returned to
the stockholders. All the bridges on our road that has been rebuilt are
only temporary and will have to be rebuilt over again. I hope you will
see that we have Justice done to us and that all our Rolling stock machine shops and supplies are returned to us or the same amt that we
delivered over to Genl Burnsides when he came to Knoxville as our
road delivered everything she could when the Union army entered E
Tennessee.[2]

                                    Yours Respectfully Jno R Branner

ALS, DLC-JP.
    1. President of the East Tennessee and Virginia Railroad.
    2. On June 10 Johnson replied: "You will please confer with General Thomas at
Nashville who will make arrangements in reference to turning your Road over to the
Company." East Tennessee Railroad stockholders elected new directors on July 12, who,
with those appointed by Governor Brownlow, chose a president. General Thomas relin-
quished the railroad to them on August 28, 1865. Johnson to Branner, June 10, 1865,
Tels. Sent, President, Vol. 2 (1865), RG107, NA; *House Reports*, 39 Cong., 2 Sess.,
No. 34, "Affairs of Southern Railroads," pp. 542–43 (Ser. 1306).

From Sexton Emley [1]

                                    Huntington [Indiana], May 29th 65
Mr Johnson President
    Sir the friends of Mr Milligen have got out Petitions and geting sing-
ers, and the Petitions will be persented to your honor, asking your
honor to change the sentens. I want to inform you that they is verry
few union men singing the Petitions a round here. The union men
think Mr Milligen is guilty of treasion and aut be hung. The Friends
of Mr Milligen have sent men to Witley County and Wells County and
to Fort Wayne in Allen County to get singers. They is some boys singing the Petition. The petition that will go from Huntington I dont
belive that one fourth of the singers live in the County. It is the wish of
the union men his scentens will not be chang.

                                    your Friend Sexton Emley

ALS, DNA-RG153, Court-Martial Records, NN-3409.
    1. Emley (b. c1829) was a New Jersey-born farmer. 1860 Census, Ind., Huntington,
Clear Creek Twp., 56.

From James R. Gilmore[1]

Office of the Tribune,
New York, May 29th 1865

My dear Sir,

In the "*Tribune*" of this morning, I notice the Indictment against Jeff. Davis.[2] I am not a lawyer, but those here who are lawyers fear that the Gov't will have difficulty in connecting Mr. Davis with the attack on Washington. Perhaps I can aid it in that particular. If I can, as a loyal man, I am ready to do it.

On the 16th, 17th, & 18th, of July, 1864, in company with Col. Jaquess[3] of Ills. I was in Richmond. On the evening of the 17th, we had a two hours interview with Messrs Davis & Benjamin.[4] In the course of that interview, Mr Davis several times alluded to the intended attack on Washn by "Genls" Breckenridge and Early,[5] expressing the opinion that it would succeed, etc. Saying, in short, enough to prove that the whole plan was his. In the "Atlantic Monthly" for Sep. 1864,[6] I gave some of the conversation which occurred in that interview, but by no means the whole. In fact I said only enough to bring out what Mr. Lincoln though necessary to bring out: (He read the proof of the article) namely, that Davis would negotiate only on the basis of So. Independence. About that, in that article, I quote Mr. Davis as saying, "We are not exactly shut up in Richmond. If your papers tell the truth, it is your capital that is in danger—not ours." But, Mr. D. said a vast deal more (in a boastful way) on that subject—enough in brief, to show that, he, himself, had planned the attack.

Further. I was at Camp Douglas in Nov. 1864, and there met Lt. Col. Maurice Langhorne[7] of the 31st. Arkansas, who, in Aug /64, was sent by Sedden[8] and Davis to Thompson (Jacob)[9] with despatches. The substance of what he said to me, is embodied in the enclosed extract from proofsheets of an article on the "Chicago Conspiracy" which will appear in the "Atlantic Monthly" for July[10]—(about 20 dys hence). I think Col. Langhorne would be an important witness to show Davis's connection with the whole Canada iniquity; which, as you will see from the extract I enclose, contemplated assassination, and every other diabolical instrumentality.

I write you about this, because I do not know who else to address. If I can be of any service, command me. I knew Mr. Lincoln well, and loved him, and he trusted me. His allowing us to go to Richmond at the time I did, is proof of that. I would gladly do anything in my power to avenge his death, and *serve the cause of justice*; therefore, I write you this. My residence is Cambridge Mass. where a summons will at any-time reach me.[11]

Yours very resp'y, James R. Gilmore.
("Edmund Kirke")

His Excellency The President.

ALS, DNA-RG60, Office of Atty. Gen., Lets. Recd., President.

1. Gilmore (1822–1903) engaged in a New York City shipping business until commencing a literary career. In July 1864, with Lincoln's approval, he had visited Richmond on an unofficial peace mission. *NCAB*, 10: 249; *DAB*.

2. The indictment, dated May 26, 1865, charged that Davis had incited the army on June 15, 1864, at Henrico County, Va., to march on Washington, "to levy and carry on war against the United States of America," and that on July 12 the army did attack Fort Stevens, D.C., reportedly killing and wounding "a large number" of U.S. troops. *New York Tribune*, May 29, 1865.

3. James F. Jaquess (1819–1898), minister and college president, commanded the 73rd Ill. Inf. Unsuccessful in his first mission in the South as a mediator, he had made a second, and more serious, attempt in 1864, accompanied by Gilmore. After the war he worked for the Freedmen's Bureau in Kentucky and cultivated cotton in Arkansas and Mississippi. *DAB*; Joseph McJames to Johnson, Sept. 14, 1865; Jaquess to McJames, Sept. 8, 1865, Records of the Commr., Lets. from Executive Mansion, RG105, NA.

4. Judah P. Benjamin, Confederate secretary of state.

5. John C. Breckinridge and Jubal Early. The latter (1816–1894) commanded the foray against Washington and unsuccessfully defended the Shenandoah Valley during 1864–65. In self-exile for a time in Mexico after the South's defeat, he subsequently practiced law in Lynchburg, Va. Warner, *Gray*.

6. Gilmore, "Our Visit to Richmond," *At Mon*, 14 (Sept. 1864): 372–83. Jaquess and the Richmond trip are also described in Gilmore's *Down in Tennessee* (New York, 1864), Chapters 19–20: 233–82.

7. In his testimony at the Chicago Conspiracy trial, Langhorne claimed to have been a Kentucky resident before practicing law in Crittenden County, Arkansas, and becoming a sergeant in a Louisiana battery. *House Ex. Docs.*, 39 Cong., 2 Sess., No. 50, pp. 76–91 (Ser. 1290).

8. James A. Seddon (1815–1880), a Richmond lawyer, served as Confederate secretary of war (Nov. 1862-Feb. 1865). Wakelyn, *BDC*.

9. A former congressman and secretary of the interior in Buchanan's administration, Thompson was one of three commissioners in Canada responsible for coordinating covert activities for the Confederacy. He supervised several "ill–conceived" and unsuccessful exploits, including attempts to free prisoners of war from Johnson's Island and to burn New York. Brandt, *Burn New York*, 66, 67–68, 139–40.

10. Gilmore, "The Chicago Conspiracy," *At Mon*, 16 (July, 1865): 108–20.

11. Referred to the attorney general, who sent Gilmore's letter to Judge Advocate Holt for his disposition. J. Hubley Ashton to Joseph Holt, June 5, 1865, Office of the Atty. Gen., Lets. Sent, Vol. D (M699, Roll 9), RG60, NA.

From Edwin D. Morgan [1]

New York May 29, 1865

Dear President

The country is impressed with the importance of punishing Jefferson Davis legally and promptly. Grave doubts exist whether this can be accomplished by a trial for treason at Common Law, and whether such a trial, with the able counsel that will be employed, and their revival of the Doctrine of State Sovereignty as a Constitutional defense of Davis, would not tend to demoralize the public mind and weaken our position. Even should he be convicted, the case would be carried up, in all probability. The Daily News in this city and some English papers, insist that the treason was committed (before Davis made war) by the state of Mississippi, that in obeying the orders of that state he obeyed his sovereign &c &c, that having recognized him as a Belligerent the United States, cannot now charge him with treason. But as a Belligerent Davis has committed crimes about the atrocity of which, there can be no question, and for which he deserves death. Such as the massacre of the blacks at Fort Pillow & elsewhere,[2] the murder of our prisoners by slow starvation and cruel treatment,[3] the attempt to burn N York[4] and to introduce yellow fever in northern cities.[5] His complicity with the assassination plots &c &c these are crimes in violation of the laws of war to be tried by court martial. I submit whether Davis may not be tried on those last mentioned and meet his just doom with the approval of the world.[6]

I am Dear President with the highest respect
Yours very truly E. D. Morgan

The President of the United States

ALS, DNA-RG60, Office of Atty. Gen., Misc. Papers re Imprisonment and Trial of Jefferson Davis.

1. Former New York war governor, now U.S. senator.

2. On April 12, 1864, Gen. Nathan B. Forrest's command overran the Union garrison (composed primarily of black troops) defending Fort Pillow, Tenn. Approximately one-third of the white Federals present were killed, and almost two-thirds of the blacks, many of them as they tried to surrender. John Cimprich, *Slavery's End in Tennessee, 1861–1865* (University, Ala., 1985), 92–97.

3. A reference to the treatment of Union prisoners at Andersonville Prison, Ga.

4. On November 25, 1864, six Confederate agents from Canada had attempted unsuccessfully to burn fifteen establishments in New York's main business district using Greek Fire—a mixture of phosphorous in a bisulfide of carbon that ignited when exposed to air. One of the raiders, Robert Cobb Kennedy, subsequently became the last Confederate soldier executed by the Federals during the Civil War. Brandt, *Burn New York*, 77, 101, 111, 119–20, 129, 227–31. See Letter from John W. Headley, July 18, 1865.

5. Luke P. Blackburn (1816–1887), a physician who served in several voluntary positions for the Confederate army, allegedly proposed to Confederate agents in Canada that yellow fever be introduced with bales of infected clothing. He was tried and acquitted by a Canadian court for charges stemming from this allegation. Years later, he returned to his native Kentucky and was elected governor. *DAB*; Nancy D. Baird, *Luke Pryor Blackburn: Physician, Governor, Reformer* (Lexington, Ky., 1979), 20–21, 24–35.

6. This letter, "As to the mode of trial & punishment of Jefferson Davis," was sent to the attorney general, "for consideration."

From J. Durbin Parkinson

May 29, 1865, New York, N.Y.; ALS, DLC-JP.

Because military commanders had branded the action as "premature," an English native, who has taught in southern academies for fifteen years and who was chairman of the meeting, belatedly forwards resolutions adopted by Florida unionists at Fort Myers on October 15, 1864. Following a lengthy, vivid description of the treatment of Florida unionists during the war—"The Conscript officers tracked us with bloodhounds, shot us in the swamps like wild beasts, and when they had decoyed Refugee soldiers by a flag of truce gave no quarter"—he begs Johnson "not to allow such offenders as these to live in the secure enjoyment of their ill gotten gains, but visit them with deserved punishment." Make large fertile plantations available "for sale in small lots." The attached resolutions ask confiscation of secessionists' property, colonization of "such of the colored race as wish to farm . . . in townships confined to themselves," trial and punishment of those forcing Union men into the rebel army, strict disfranchisement of rebel civil and military officers and of unionist oppressors, death to all guerrilla bands, establishment of a school system "such as at present exists in the Northern and Western States," adequate compensation for unionist wartime losses, etc.

Proclamation Establishing Government for North Carolina [1]

May 29, 1865

WHEREAS the 4th section of the 4th article of the Constitution of the United States declares that the United States shall guarantee to every State in the Union a republican form of government, and shall protect each of them against invasion and domestic violence; and whereas the President of the United States is, by the Constitution, made Commander-in-chief of the army and navy, as well as chief civil executive officer of the United States, and is bound by solemn oath faithfully to execute the office of President of the United States, and to take care that the laws be faithfully executed; and whereas the rebellion, which has been waged by a portion of the people of the United States against the properly constituted authorities of the government thereof, in the most violent and revolting form, but whose organized and armed forces have now been almost entirely overcome, has, in its revolutionary progress, deprived the people of the State of North Carolina of all civil government; and whereas it becomes necessary and proper to carry out and enforce the obligations of the United States to the people of North Carolina, in securing them in the enjoyment of a republican form of government:

Now, THEREFORE, in obedience to the high and solemn duties imposed upon me by the Constitution of the United States, and for the purpose of enabling the loyal people of said State to organize a State government, whereby justice may be established, domestic tranquillity insured, and loyal citizens protected in all their rights of life, liberty, and property, I, ANDREW JOHNSON, President of the United States, and commander-in-chief of the army and navy of the United States, do hereby appoint WILLIAM W. HOLDEN provisional governor of the State of North Carolina, whose duty it shall be, at the earliest practicable period, to prescribe such rules and regulations as may be necessary and proper for convening a convention, composed of delegates to be chosen by that portion of the people of said State who are loyal to the United States, and no others, for the purpose of altering or amending the constitution thereof; and with authority to exercise, within the limits of said State, all the powers necessary and proper to enable such loyal people of the State of North Carolina to restore said State to its constitutional relations to the Federal government, and to present such a republican form of State government as will entitle the State to the guarantee of the United States therefor, and its people to protection by the United States against invasion, insurrection, and domestic violence; *provided* that, in any election that may be hereafter held for choosing delegates to any State convention as aforesaid, no person shall be qualified as an elector, or shall be eligible as a member of such convention, unless he shall have previously taken and subscribed the oath of amnesty, as set forth in the President's proclamation of May 29, A.D. 1865, and is a voter qualified as prescribed by the constitution and laws of the State of North Carolina in force immediately before the 20th day of May, A.D. 1861, the date of the so-called ordinance of secession; and the said convention, when convened, or the legislature that may be thereafter assembled, will prescribe the qualification of electors, and the eligibility of persons to hold office under the constitution and laws of the State, a power the people of the several States composing the Federal Union have rightfully exercised from the origin of the government to the present time.

And I do hereby direct—

First. That the military commander of the department, and all officers and persons in the military and naval service, aid and assist the said Provisional Governor in carrying into effect this proclamation, and they are enjoined to abstain from, in any way, hindering, impeding, or discouraging the loyal people from the organization of a State government as herein authorized.

Second. That the Secretary of State proceed to put in force all laws of the United States, the administration whereof belongs to the State Department, applicable to the geographical limits aforesaid.

Third. That the Secretary of the Treasury proceed to nominate for appointment assessors of taxes, and collectors of customs and internal revenue, and such other officers of the Treasury Department as are authorized by law, and put in execution the revenue laws of the United States within the geographical limits aforesaid. In making appointments, the preference shall be given to qualified loyal persons residing within the districts where their respective duties are to be performed. But if suitable residents of the districts shall not be found, then persons residing in other States or districts shall be appointed.

Fourth. That the Postmaster General proceed to establish post offices and post routes, and put into execution the postal laws of the United States within the said State, giving to loyal residents the preference of appointment; but if suitable residents are not found, then to appoint agents, &c., from other States.

Fifth. That the district judge for the judicial district in which North Carolina is included proceed to hold courts within said State, in accordance with the provisions of the act of Congress. The Attorney General will instruct the proper officers to libel, and bring to judgment, confiscation, and sale, property subject to confiscation, and enforce the administration of justice within said State in all matters within the cognizance and jurisdiction of the Federal courts.

Sixth. That the Secretary of the Navy take possession of all public property belonging to the Navy Department within said geographical limits, and put in operation all acts of Congress in relation to naval affairs having application to the said State.

Seventh. That the Secretary of the Interior put in force the laws relating to the Interior Department applicable to the geographical limits aforesaid.

In testimony whereof, I have hereunto set my hand and caused the seal of the United States to be affixed.

Done at the city of Washington this twenty-ninth day of May, in the year of our Lord one thousand eight hundred and sixty-five, and of the Independence of the United States the eighty-ninth.

ANDREW JOHNSON.

[SEAL]
BY THE PRESIDENT:
WILLIAM H. SEWARD, *Secretary of State.*

PD, DLC-JP7A.
1. Similar proclamations were issued for Mississippi on June 13, Georgia and Texas on June 17, Alabama on June 21, South Carolina on June 30, and Florida on July 13. Richardson, *Messages*, 314–16, 318–31.

From Lorenzo Sherwood

May 29, 1865, New York, N.Y.; ALS, DLC-JP.

Former Texas lawyer and legislator, feeling that the only basis of peace is to have the South's unionists in charge politically, is concerned that "If the Military force is disbanded, and it is left to the civil authorities to close out the balance of work to be done . . . we are very far from a desirable peace." Fearing a resurgence of the slaveholders' power, he queries whether anyone can say that a "tittle of the spirit that raised our troubles is eradicated" and points to the "'knock-kneed logic'" of the *Tribune,* whose suggestion of "treating with equality and popular clemency those domestic enemies of the Union" is going to the extreme "of putting infidelity on a par with fidelity, treason on an equal footing with loyalty." Refers to "the cold-blooded, deliberate, life-long, and ingrained determination of Slave holders to maintain and perpetuate Slavery."

Speech to Washington Sunday School Union [1]

May 29, 1865

The President said, if he understood the design of the exhibition, it was intended, in part, to show how many children are collected together in good schools. This was their annual celebration, and they had come by what was generally known as the Executive Mansion in order, he supposed, to manifest their regard for the Chief Executive Officer of the nation. And this respect was offered now to one who knew well how to appreciate the condition of poor or obscure children. He had always opposed the idea of treating persons beyond their due, and what they justly merited, and he would lay that down as a general proposition in his address to the little boys and girls who had done him the honor to call upon him. He was opposed to deifying or canonizing anything that is mortal but there should always be a just and proper respect and appreciation of true merit, whether it belongs to the Christian, the statesman, or the philanthropist. This was the foundation of his creed, if he had any: that all things should be done with the approval of Him who controls the events and destinies of the world. To these children—he might say his little sons and daughters—he would say he desired them to appreciate the difference between merit and demerit, and he would address his remarks to those who were in better, as well as to those who were in humbler circumstances. To those who had superior advantages he would say, do not become foolish and silly because your parents can afford to dress you a little better, or to educate you better. They should feel and know that their parents and teachers cannot of themselves educate them. No one ever would be educated unless he educated himself. Whether you have superior advantages or not, you must educate yourselves. Parents, teachers, and advantages given are simply the means placed in your hands, from which you must mould and shape your own course through life. But never feel that you are superior to your more humble companions and comrades. Instead of trying to humble them and make their condition lower, your pride should be to elevate them to the standard you occupy. Sometimes one may come in rags, and begrimed with dirt; but beneath the rags and the dirt a jewel may be found as bright as any yet discovered, and the humble individual may develop that which would prove as bright an adornment as the jewels of any crowned head. All should understand this, and that even those who have no means can at least make an effort to be good and great. In this matter he (the speaker) was an agrarian—such an agrarian as would elevate and estimate all in proportion to their virtue and merit. Intrinsic merit should be the base upon which all should stand. He would pull none down, but would elevate all—level upwards, not level downwards. His notion had always been that the great mass of the American people could be elevated. If all will be elevated, we may become the greatest and most exalted nation on the earth.

My little daughters and sons, (said the speaker) give me your attention while I say, honestly and truly, that if I could inform you of something, and put that into immediate effect, which would tend to the elevation of you all, I would be prouder of it than to be President forty times. ⟨Applause.⟩ Here is the Executive Mansion, and yonder is the Capitol of a great nation, and you look to those who make and execute the laws as persons sublime and grand. But just think for a moment. You are the crop behind us. All those buildings, and all of this Government, will one day pass under your control and become your property, and you will have to put in force and control the principles of government, of religion, and humanity. And let all boys consider—every mother's son of them—<laughter.> that each one is born a candidate for the Presidency. <Laughter and applause.> Why not, then, commence at once to educate yourselves for the Presidency? And he would say to the little girls, that while they could not be Presidents, they are born candidates for the wives of Presidents. <Laughter.> While each little boy may feel he is a candidate for the Presidency, each little girl may feel she is a candidate for a President's wife; and each should commence at once to qualify himself and herself morally, intellectually, and socially for such high positions. While upon this subject, he would say that teachers occupy most responsible positions. It is the teacher who fashions, to a great degree, the mind of the child, and, consequently, the great importance of having good teachers, especially for the very young, in order to instill into their minds the foundation of a good education.

With regard to religion, the speaker said the time had come when the first inquiry should be whether one is a good man or a good woman. If they are good it matters little to what sect or church they belong. There can be no greatness without goodness, and all should remember with Pope, that

> Honor and fame from no condition rise;
> Act well your part—there all the honor lies.[2]

Under institutions such as ours, he who performs his part well, performs all his obligations, will sooner or later be properly estimated and rewarded by his friends, his neighbors, and the nation.

In looking upon the children, and upon the grown persons, too, the speaker said he could not but think of the heavy task and responsibility devolving upon those who rear children, and especially upon the mothers. The speaker then eloquently referred to the ancient Roman mothers, who ever took pride in infusing proper ideas into the minds of those who afterwards became distinguished in life. So, with them, each mother of to-day should feel that her children are her greatest jewels. They should be reared with a view to future usefulness; for much depends upon how they are educated in youth. The daughters should be raised to fit them for the high and exalted duties of wives and mothers. And much in this world depends upon woman. Her mind properly prepared and cultivated, she has an almost omnipotent power. Drop, then, into the minds of your daughters germs that will expand and grow, and fit them to occupy any position to which they may be called in life.

When we look at these boys and girls—at the banners which they carry—at the flags, with stripes and stars upon them, which they bear aloft; when we look upon the brave men and gallant officers around us, and remember what they have been contending for—we feel that we can best preserve this Government if we rear up our people properly, and make this, as we can, the most intelligent portion of God's habitable globe. The stars and stripes is not an unmeaning symbol when we look back through the din of battle and see what it has cost to perpetuate this Government; and should we not, then, use every effort to bring up properly these children, whose cause has been sustained by strong arms on the field of battle? It was but the other day, when the stern voices of our commanders were heard upon the field of battle, and when men were bravely rushing to death, that the Goddess of Liberty made a glorious flight and in thunder tones proclaimed victory. Victory *has* perched upon our standard, and the speaker said he trusted the children's little song of victory would be heard far up above; and that the angels, standing upon the battlements of Heaven, would take up the tune and make a response.

Then, my little sons and little daughters, (said the President, talking as a father to his children,) let me say to you, educate yourselves, be industrious and persevering; store your minds with all that is good, put all things worthy of preservation in your brain, and your intellects will expand and grow. And, in conclusion, I say again, may your little song of victory be heard in heaven. God bless you.[3]

National Intelligencer, May 30, 1865.

1. The twenty-fifth anniversary of the Washington Sunday School Union was celebrated with a parade of over 5,000 children and 700 teachers. As they assembled in front of the White House, Johnson, who was not yet occupying the residence, addressed them. *National Intelligencer*, May 30, 1865.

2. Either a newspaper misprint or a Johnson misquote of the beginning of Alexander Pope's couplet from *An Essay on Man*, IV, line 193: "Honour and shame from no condition rise."

3. The appreciative crowd, eager to shake the President's hand, detained him so that he "held a sort of impromptu levee" in the carriageway. *National Intelligencer*, May 30, 1865.

From Citizens of Chatham County, Georgia

[May 30, 1865], Chatham County, Ga.; Pet, DLC-JP.

"Being without civil government, and but partially protected by Military rule, and thus exposed to repeated depredations & violence from bands of lawless men, whites & blacks," the petitioners ask presidential protection, the reestablishment of "civil government with all its security & prosperity," and the appointment of a "military Governor over the State . . . imbued with wisdom, moderation & justice to administer its affairs . . . until the State shall have been fully restored."

From Thomas J. Foster [1]

Courtland Ala May 30 1865

His Excellency, Andrew Johnson
President of the United States
Washington, District Columbia
Dr Sir:

As a member of the late Confederate Congress I respectfully propose with your indulgence to submit a full, frank and candid statement in relation to the part taken by myself in the late unfortunate difficulty between the United States and the seceding States; and also, my Status upon the Union question previous to the secession of the State of Alabama of which State I am now, and have been for many years a citizen.

My devotion to the Union during the anxious and stormy period which preceded the election of Mr Lincoln was well known throughout North Alabama. Upon all occasions and in every circle both public and private I denounced the plans and purposes of the secession faction headed by Yancy Rhett & Co. asserted that it was their policy to divide and disrupt the Democratic Party for the purpose of dissolving the Union; denied their wild and impracticable dogma of *peaceable secession*, and predicted that if it should be in their power to carry their purposes they would plunge the country into a horrible and bloody war, and ourselves and posterity into the dark interminable chaos of anarchy and civil tumult: I believed and asserted that the safest and surest redress for the assumed grievances of the South was within the Union and under the Constitution; and that, to throw aside this panoply, besides other untold evils, would inevitably cost us the sacrifice of our domestic institution of Slavery.

In corroboration of these statements you will please allow me to advert to a conversation which occurred between your Excellency and myself sometime in the Fall of 1860 at the St Cloud Hotel in the city of Nashville. We were lodging in the same room and upon my return from a walk in the city about 11 Oclock in the morning, I found you engaged in writing at a table in the room: Being fatigued with the loss of rest the previous night I laid down upon the bed to rest and after a few moments of serious reflection I called to you in a familiar manner saying "Governor Johnson! You remind me of a ferryman rowing his boat one way, and looking another." "How so" you asked; I replied "You are now engaged in canvassing the State for Breckenridge whose nomination has been brought about by the Yancy faction for the sole and only purpose of electing Lincoln and giving them an opportunity of breaking up the Union, and I well know you to be no Disunionist." You replied that I "spoke truly when I said (you) were no Disunionist," and after a confidential and somewhat lengthy conversation I declared to you that so great were my fears and apprehensions of the designs of the Secession Party and the probable result, that I had solemnly made up my mind, to abandon the Whig Party, with which I had ever acted, and support Mr Douglass for the Presidency: believing his election, to be the only mode of preserving the Union.

I am thus particular in endeavouring to refresh your recollection of this conversation in order that your Excellency may comprehend and appreciate the above statements, and the zeal with which I supported the cause of the Union.

After the Presidential election, which (as I had predicted) resulted in the election of Mr Lincoln, the secessionists became violent and clamorous, conventions were called throughout the South, and the whole enginery of intrigue and agitation was put in motion to arouse the violent passions of the Southern People. I immediately took an active part in getting up opposition meetings and upon various occasions introduced resolutions denouncing Secession and urging the people to stand firm and true to the Union. At Moulton Ala sometime in November, I went so far as to propose, and aid in passage a resolution, instructing our County Delegates to the State Convention at Montgomery to resign their seats in the event the Convention should pass the Ordinance of Secession, and refuse to refer the same to the people of the state for their ratification or rejection.

I thus continued my unabated opposition to secession up to the 11th of January 1861, when the State of Alabama in solemn convention assembled, at Montgomery passed the fatal Ordinance of Secession. I did not believe the action of this Convention represented the wishes and convictions of the People of the state; but where was the remedy? The convention in consequence of its peculiar organization had persistently, I may say contumaceously given a numerical majority against the proposition to submit the ordinance to the popular vote: The only means of resistance were by counter conventions or in other words by revolution and resistance to the authority and power of the state as indicated by and through the Convention. This was to men of similar convictions with myself a dilemma of the most distressing and embarrassing character. Whilst I was not of that class of political thinkers known heretofore as "states rights men," I, in common with the more conservative minds of the country, believed that allegiance to the State, was of paramount obligation to that by which we were bound as citizens to the general Government: The state being a political organization preexistent and therefore paramount; the more immediate, and therefore the more potent; and that it was through and by the action of sovreign states that the United States Government derived its existence, and through the states that the allegiance of citizens to the Federal Government originated. Acting upon these convictions I saw no other course for myself but to bow to the mandates of state authority and acquiesce in the altered relations established by the actions of the state convention.

After the formation of the Government styled the Confederate States, I was chosen by the conservative men of my District, and elected a member of the Permanent Congress, which position I held and occupied until its last adjournment. Whilst holding this position I supported the interests of the state of Alabama as I believed with an honest fidelity, invariably opposing all measures which I conceived to be violent or oppressive or in the least tending to overthrow or compromise the rights of the People. For example: the policy adopted by the Confederate Congress of raising troops by general conscription, I opposed most earnestly, and vehemently; and denounced it as unjust and oppressive, particulary so: since the war was of a partisan character, upon the issues of which, citizens were most probably divided, and the result of the policy, was to force men into the ranks, to fight against the convictions of their own minds. Certain provisions of the Conscript Laws allowing men of wealth to employ substitutes; or slaveholders upon certain conditions to obtain exemption from military duty, I persistently opposed; believing as I did, these classes to have been chiefly instrumental in bringing about the war and that they of all others should have been forced into the ranks. I mention these things, (apparently *foreign* to the subject of this communication) in order that, the entire record may appear of my actions and conduct in the great and terrible struggle through which we have just passed. I have placed it before you fairly and candidly feeling conscious of the rectitude of my intentions, and deemed it proper to address your Excellency upon this subject for the reason that it is or may become your duty within the functions of your august office to inquire into the actions and conduct of all parties implicated in the recent difficulties.

I desire to make my peace with the Government and if required will cheerfully take any obligations to obey the Laws and authority of the United States.

I further most respectfully ask the privilege of remaining quietly at home, unmolested by military arrests, subject, (I shall expect, of course) to any civil process which may be instituted against me by the Government.[2]

> I have the honor to remain Most Respectfully
> Your obt Servt Thomas J. Foster

ALS, DNA-RG94, Amnesty Papers (M1003, Roll 4), Ala., Thomas J. Foster.

1. Foster (1809–1887), wealthy manufacturer and planter, headed a Confederate regiment before becoming a congressman. After the war he moved to Kentucky. Warner and Yearns, *BRCC*.

2. Foster's pardon was issued October 6, 1865. Amnesty Papers (M1003, Roll 4), Ala., Thomas J. Foster, RG94, NA.

From John J. Giers[1]

Decatur Ala. May 30th 1865

To his Excellency Andrew Johnson
President of the U. States
Sir!

I have the honor to inform you that the *original* and *unwavering* Union people, *and those only*, of Northern Alabama are now holding meetings in their different counties, and that I shall present their petitions to your Excellency as soon as ever possible.[2] Since the *entire* collapse of the Confederacy, the rebels have suddenly faced about, and making up in activity and shrewdness what they want in loyalty, they no doubt hope to regain by the ballotbox, what they have lost by the cartridge box.

A delegation headed by Jos: Bradley[3] and others just from Montgomery, reached Huntsville a few days ago, and they are now on their way to Washington City with certain "*overtures*" from Gov: Watts[4] and other rebels, that will no doubt greatly amuse you. I am requested to state to you most respectfully that the loyal people of Alabama do not recognize Gov: Watts' authority to act in this matter. I have nothing personal against any of these gentlemen, but I know that they are the representatives of the old Slave Aristocracy, who would again rule us if they could.

I would here state that the small landed proprietors and men of moderate means, who have been forced by conscription and circumstances which they could not control, to give in their adhesion to the Confederate Government have in my opinion returned to a *sincere loyalty* and can be trusted in the reestablishment of this Government, as many have convinced me that they are inimical to the party which the gentlemen above refered to represent. This has particular reference to the Counties on the South side of the river, the mountain Counties I mean, where the people are far more loyal than on the north side of the river. I shall be in Washington very shortly and hope to have the honor of an interview with you.

> I remain with great respect Your very obedt. Servt
>
> J. J. Giers

P.S.

Jos: Bradley was the Conf. Tax Collector for the State of Alabama. He organized a company called the *"Bradley Rebels."* Although his home and family were at Huntsville, he has never been within the Federal lines until Genl Wilson[5] placed him into them.

Judge D. C. Humphreys[6] who fought in the Rebel army, and tried to raise a Brigade under L. P. Walker[7] for the Confederate Service.

Nick: Davis,[8] a member of the Alabama Convention who voted for Secession to make it unanimous, and afterwards a member of the Rebel Congress.

Genl S. W. Houston,[9] formerly U.S. Senator, who spoke all over North Alabama in 1862, and used his influence generally to crush the Union feeling amongst the loyal people.

ALS, DLC-JP.

1. Giers (1815–1880), who had resided in the South for thirty years, had served as liaison between Alabama unionists and General Grant during the winter of 1864–65 in an effort to obtain a separate peace for the state. Later a clerk in the 6th auditor's office at Washington, he attended the Philadelphia unionist convention in 1866. In June 1865 Gen. Robert S. Granger introduced Giers to Johnson as a unionist, a frequent correspondent to Nashville newspapers, who "can give you as correct an account of affairs in this District as any other person." Tombstone inscription, Valhermoso Springs Cemetery, Morgan County, Ala.; *U.S. Off. Reg.* (1873–79); Walter L. Fleming, *Civil War and Reconstruction in Alabama* (New York, 1905), 146–47; *Nashville Press and Times*, Sept. 13, 1866; Granger to Johnson, June 12, 1865, Johnson Papers, LC.

2. On May 14, 1865, Giers had forwarded a copy of a resolution calling for a restoration convention adopted at a "Mass Union Meeting" at Somerville in Morgan County on May 13. He reported then that North Alabama was loyal, "but if the army were removed to-day, no Union man would be safe in the counties farther south, nor in many parts of the country farther North." Johnson Papers, LC.

3. Having reached Nashville, Bradley, on behalf of himself and another delegate "enroute to see you on subject of civil offices of Alabama," wired Johnson on the same day, asking "assistance in way of transportation . . . for our party of four." Bradley to Johnson, May 30, 1865, Johnson Papers, LC. See Reception of Alabama Delegates, June 5, 1865.

4. Thomas H. Watts (1819–1892) was Confederate attorney general before becoming Alabama's governor in December 1863. Wakelyn, *BDC*.

5. Gen. James H. Wilson.

6. David C. Humphreys.

7. Leroy P. Walker, first secretary of war in Davis' cabinet.

8. Nicholas Davis (1825–1875) had been a state legislator and solicitor at Huntsville. A unionist delegate to the secession convention, he acquiesced in its decision and was briefly a Confederate congressman and military officer. Warner and Yearns, *BRCC*.

9. Giers was mistaken about Houston in several respects. His given name was George S., and his prewar service was in the House of Representatives, rather than the Senate. William Garrett, *Reminiscences of Public Men in Alabama* (Spartanburg, S.C., 1975 [1872]), 324.

From Richard H. Northrop

May 30, 1865, New York, N.Y.; ALS, DLC-JP.

Concord, N.C., unionist, conscripted into the Confederate army in December 1864, suggests that the commandant of U.S. forces in North Carolina, "if possessed of ordinary executive ability," would be "more acceptible to the people as temporary ruler, than one chosen from themselves"; he could call a constitutional convention, supervise the elections, establish voter qualifications, and "prevent parties not purged of their treason from voting or becoming delegates." Also recommends that Confederate confiscation records dealing with "the estates of loyal men" and the estates themselves be seized "to prevent waste until they can be handed over to the rightful owners," while the estates of "disloyal men" should be leased for cultivation "until disposed of by the General Government."

From "A Plebian"

May 30, 1865, New York, N.Y.; ALS, DLC-JP.

Having previously urged that Preston King and Hannibal Hamlin "be called to some position near you at Washington," and having since learned that King has received an appointment, the correspondent now writes "a word for the other Statesman. You recently said that you never forsook your friends. Mr. Lincoln said the last day or two of his life that he *had not done right* by Mr. Hamlin. He should have invited him to a seat in his Cabinet." Reminds Johnson that it was Hamlin who expressed "so much willingness to bear whatever blame is charged" for the vice-president's intemperance during his swearing-in on March 4, 1865. [Appointed collector of customs at Boston in August 1865, Hamlin resigned a year later in protest over Johnson's Reconstruction policies.]

From Ainsworth R. Spofford

May 30, 1865, Washington, D.C.; LBcopy, DLC-U.S. Library of Congress Papers, Let. Bk., June 12, 1862-Dec. 22, 1865.

Librarian of Congress suggests that the portraits of six former U.S. presidents, painted by George P.A. Healy under an Act of Congress approved on March 3, 1857, be placed in the Executive Mansion for safekeeping while the outer rooms of the Library of Congress are demolished to prepare for its enlargement; "no other safe repository in the Capitol occurs to me for their reception."

To Edwin M. Stanton

Tuesday May 30 1865

Hon E. M. Stanton Secretary of War
Sir:

Will you please send a dispatch this night to General Hovey at Indianapolis informing him that I have commuted the sentences in the cases of Horsey Bowles and Milligan to imprisonment at hard labor for life in such Penitentiary as you may designate? [1]

I wish you would send the dispatch in cipher and direct General Hovey to keep the fact of the Commutation quiet until the day fixed for the execution. [2]

To prevent any mistake I wish you would have General Hovey report by telegraph the receipt of the Order and would also send an official copy of the Telegram by the first mail.

Very Truly Yours Andrew Johnson

LS, DNA-RG153, Court-Martial Records, NN-3409.

1. Following Governor Morton's plea, Johnson on May 16 had commuted Stephen Horsey's sentence to life in prison at hard labor and postponed the execution of William A. Bowles and Lambdin P. Milligan until June 2. Johnson to A. P. Hovey, May 16, 1865, Tels. Sent, President, Vol. 2 (1865), RG107, NA.

2. The Secretary of War immediately conveyed this subsequent decision, admonishing Hovey to keep the order "secret until the day of execution." Stanton selected the penitentiary at Columbus, Ohio, as the prisoners' place of incarceration. The following year the U.S. Supreme Court, in *Ex Parte Milligan*, ruled that all three should be released, because civilians could not be tried by military commissions in areas where the civil courts were open. Stanton to Hovey, May 30, 1865, Tels. Sent, Sec. of War (M473, Roll 89), RG107, NA.

From Jeremiah D. Tucker [1]

Columbus Ga May 30th 1865

Mr Andrew Johnson
President of the United State

Will you please excuse the liberty I take of addressing you as follows. I hope I am doing no wrong for certainly nothing can be farther from my intentions. The only motive that moves me to do what I am about to do is simply that after several days of calm reflection I am more convinced that it is my duty. To do my duty faithfully is my highest aim. That I have done it through life is, the highest mede of praise that I crave to have engraven on my tomb Stone. Being a soldier that was willing to fight for the existence & perpetuity of the Union while war lasted & threatened its overthrow I have now a great anxiety for its future welfare & honor & happiness. But I must come at the subject for which I commenced this letter even at the risk of being held to the indictment of insubordination. But I have too much confidence in your goodness to entertain serious fears. I speak but what I and all my fellow Soldiers believe when I say that negro's are killed daily by No's by their former & would be masters. I speak what I know when I say they are most brutally & barbarously punished in this city by the same masters or police & this with the full knowledge of the post commandant.

The masters say they had rather kill them than see them free. The negros say that they never were treated So in life as since we garrisoned the place.

After relating one little incident that I personally know of I will trouble you no more. One day last week a black woman accosted me as follows. Have you seen a colored girl of 14 in your qrs? I told her that I had not. She then told me that her little girl had left her master on acct of ill treatment & she had been sent to find her & bring her home. That if she did not bring the child home that night she should receive 100 lashes on her bare back. Taking a white Lady with me who believed in the divinity of slavery & one that would testify to the good character of the blacks they having worked for her & who from acquaintance with the master Mr Edward Croff[2] could testify concerning his character also I went to Post Head qrs to see if a note could not be elicited forbidding the master to punish the disappointed fear stricken mother. But my only satisfaction not withstanding the entreaties of the white Lady was I have no orders or authority to interfere with any local matters nor could he be prevailed upon to assume any. I said to myself it is high time you had & the mother went home & I have no doubt rec'd her promised 100 lashes for though I esteem the rebel portion of this country professional liars I think they keep all such promises. You are commander in chief of the army & navy. You can issue any orders you choose & they will sometimes be obeyed. You can see that they are published & that will be a great deal.[3]

> Very truly yours with some fear
> from Your Obt Servt J. D Tucker
> Co E 17 Ind. Vet Vols 1st Brig 2d Divs M D M.

ALS, DNA-RG105, Records of the Commr., Lets. Recd. (M752, Roll 18).
    1. Tucker (b. c1826), an Indiana farmer, was a recently drafted one-year private who would be mustered out August 8, 1865. CSR, RG94, NA.
    2. Edward Croft (b. c1816) was a Columbus merchant. U.S. Census, 1860, Ga., Muscogee, Columbus, 174.
    3. The President referred this letter to the Freedmen's Bureau.

From Clara Barton[1]

Washington D.C. May 31st 1865.
His Excellency President of the United States
Sir:

May I venture to enclose for perusal the within circular[2] in the hope that it may to a certain extent explain the object of the work in which I am engaged. The undertaking having at its first inception received the cordial and written sanction of our late beloved President, I would most respectfully ask for it the favor of his honored successor.

The work is indeed a large one; but I have a settled confidence that I shall be able to accomplish it. The fate of the unfortunate men failing to appear under the search which I shall institute is likely to remain forever unrevealed.

My rolls are now ready for the press; but their size exceeds the capacity of any private establishment in this city, no printer in Washingtn. having forms of sufficient size, or a sufficient number of capitals to print so many names.

It will be both inconvenient and expensive to go with my rolls to some distant city each time they are to be revised. In view of this fact I am constrained to ask our Honored President, when he shall approve my work, as I must believe he will, to direct that the printing may be done at the U.S. Government Printing Office.

I may be permitted to say in this connection that the enclosed printed circular appealing for pecuniary aid did not originate in any suggestion of mine, but in the solicitude of personal friends, and that thus far in whatever I may have done I have received no assistance either from the Government or from individuals. A time may come when it will be necessary for me to appeal directly to the American People for help, and in that event, such appeal will be made with infinitly greater confidence and effect, if my undertaking shall receive the approval and patronage of your Excellency.[3]

I have the honor to be, Sir Most respectfully
Your obedient servant Clara Barton

L, DLC-Clara Barton Papers.
1. Barton (1821–1912), Massachusetts native who during the Civil War conducted a private campaign to secure supplies to relieve the suffering of the wounded. *DAB*.
2. That the circular is missing from the Johnson Papers is explained by Johnson's June 3 endorsement in forwarding it to the superintendent of public printing: "Let this printing be done as speedily as possible consistently with the public interest." The publication consisted of the names of missing Union soldiers, compiled by Barton with the hope of finding information on as many of the missing as possible. For this project the War Department established an office in Annapolis for Barton, appointing her "General Correspondent for the Friends of Paroled Prisoners." William E. Barton, *The Life of Clara Barton* (2 vols., New York, 1969[1922]), 1: 304–9.
3. Recommendations from General Grant and others were also attached.

From George W. Bridges [1]

Washington City May 31 1865

For Gods Sake appoint a Sober man Military Govr. of Texas instead of A. J. Hamilton;[2] better known as drunken Jack Hamilton. The appointment of drunken "Dave Nelson"[3] of our State as Govr. could not be recd. with more disgust by the people.

Truly Your friend
Geo W. Bridges

To Andrew Johnson President of U.S.

ALS, DLC-JP.
1. Athens, Tenn., unionist and former congressman.
2. Andrew Jackson Hamilton, who became provisional governor (June 17, 1865). His penchant for the bottle was a well-established fact. John L. Waller, *Colossal Hamilton of Texas* (El Paso, 1968), 12, 98.

3. A reference to T.A.R. Nelson's son, David M., with whom Bridges had served in the 10th Tenn. Cav. *TICW*, 1: 344.

From William G. Brownlow

Nashville May 31 1865.

Prest Johnson

We would be glad you would not turn over this McKendree Church.[1] Let them institute suit and the loyal church north will meet the issue in Court where they want it. We all hope that you may give Maynard the place of Catron.[2]

W G Brownlow

Tel, DLC-JP.

1. For Johnson's January 23, 1865, order *re* restoration of the McKendree Church and subsequent action, see *Johnson Papers*, 7: 426–27, 483–84.

2. John Catron, U.S. Supreme Court justice, had just died, but Horace Maynard was not appointed.

From John Conness

May 31, 1865, New York, N.Y.; ALS, DNA-RG59, Lets. of Appl. and Recomm., 1861–69 (M650, Roll 6). W. H. Wallace.

A California senator, about to return to the west coast, regrets not having had "the pleasure of a final interview." Damning a governor sent to Idaho from the East [Caleb Lyon, a sometime New York congressman], and urging the appointment of William H. Wallace, a former territorial governor of both Idaho and Washington, he observes: "As a matter of wisdom and justice Eastern men should never be sent to organize society in the West. From among the brave and enterprising men who go out to build Empire in the wilds of our country, should the men be selected who are to Govern, and organize; to lead and direct. . . . Mr. Lincoln fully realized this, but his too kindly heart would yield to the pressure for place and this salutary rule would be violated." [Johnson appointed David W. Ballard, an Oregon Republican, to succeed Lyon on April 10, 1866.]

To John A. Dix

Washington, D.C. May 31st 1865.

To Maj Genl. Dix
New York City

I learn that John A Fisher President of the Bank of Tennessee is in New York on his way to Europe with stolen treasure.[1] I wish him arrested.

Call on George S. Jenkins[2] at Pomeroy and Sons[3] 312 Broadway for information.

Report receipt and execution of this Order.[4]

Andrew Johnson
Prest. U.S.

Tel, DNA-RG107, Tels. Sent, President, Vol. 2 (1865).

1. Fisher's arrest was ordered on May 15 along with the order to seize the bank's assets, then stored in Augusta, Ga. The funds were captured, but Fisher, expected in Augusta on the 16th, escaped. *OR*, Ser. 1, Vol. 49, Pt. 2: 741, 789, 799.

2. Jenkins (b. *c*1818), native West Virginian, was formerly a dry goods merchant in Cincinnati. Jenkins had alerted Johnson to Fisher's presence in New York, where he was "in all probability making arrangements to leave the Country with a large amount of ill goten gains justly belonging to the state of Tennessee." He offered to "smoke out" Fisher if he could be compensated for his expenses. 1860 Census, Ohio, Hamilton, Cincinnati, 3rd Ward, 52; Jenkins to Johnson, May 29, 1865, Johnson Papers, LC; Cincinnati directories (1849–67); New York City directories (1862–63).

3. George V. Pomeroy and his sons George V., Jr., and Edward G. were New York merchants. *Trow's New York City Directory* (1865), 706.

4. On the same day Dix responded: "Telegram relative to the arrest of John A. Fisher . . . received and will be acted upon." Tels. Recd., President, Vol. 4 (1865–66), RG107, NA.

From Henry Flanders [1]

Philadelphia, May 31, '65.

Sir.

A Democrat, and a supporter of the war for the Union, I venture to express to you the satisfaction I feel at the policy indicated by your Proclamation with regard to North Carolina. It shows that the rebellion alone is to be struck down and that the states themselves are to be preserved. It shows too that in working out the problem of their resuscitation and restoration to the Union the intelligent votes of white freemen are to be relied on and not the ignorant suffrages of emancipated slaves.

As I read the constitution it nowhere by express grant or necessary implication gives to the general government in any of its branches the power to determine who shall exercise the elective franchise within the limits of a state. That is a power which belongs to the several states themselves. And that the relations of a state to the Union have been pro tempore suspended by the pressure of rebellion or insurrection does not operate to deprive her of this power; and much less to vest it in the general government.

The disposition you have made of this question is satisfactory, I am sure, to the conservative men of all parties, and will tend to make the people unanimous in support of your administration. The small band of professional agitators, who like Wendell Phillips [2] are in favor of Negro suffrage and repudiation of the public debt, will be satisfied with nothing, especially if it is reasonable and constitutional. But the application of the political principles that have governed your life hitherto to the present state of affairs will result in giving to the country an era of good feeling such as prevailed in the time of Mr Monroe. Sincerely wishing your Administration so happy a consummation, I am, Sir,

Very Respectfully Your Obt. Servt.

Henry Flanders.

To the Honorable Andrew Johnson,
President of the United States

ALS, DLC-JP.
  1. Flanders (c1825–1911), Philadelphia admiralty lawyer, was later a compiler of
the massive *Statutes at Large of Pennsylvania* (1896–1911). *DAB*; *NUC*.
  2. Phillips (1811–1884), lecturer, reformer, and one of the nation's most radical abolitionists, after 1865 supported black rights, prohibition, penal reform, and women's
suffrage. *DAB*.

From David Gordon and Edward B. Grayson

May 31, 1865, Washington, D.C.; ALS (Grayson), DLC-JP.

"For many years citizens" of Mississippi with "large and extensive relations and
connections" there, they "respectfully suggest that the great end to be attained"
is the selection of a provisional governor of "a character and standing as to
loyalty and fidelity satisfactory to yourself and such as will make him acceptable
to an unfortunate and distracted people." They propose "*Col Luke* Lea, now
and for many years a citizen of Missi., but formerly of East Tennessee, as one
eminently fit for this appointment."

Interview with John A. Logan[1]

May 31, 1865

General Logan commenced by congratulating the President upon
the conservative policy which he had initiated, and which was already
productive of such excellent results. He said that the era of war was
necessarily closed, and that of reason and conciliation opened; and that
it was essential to peace that the passions of both sections should now
be allayed by kindly and considerate, yet firm, action on the part of the
Executive, and he looked upon the President's as such.

President Johnson replied that he desired to have the seceded States
return back to their former condition as quickly as possible. Slavery
had been the cause of the war. That cause was now, most happily,
removed, and consequently he desired to see the Union restored as it
was previously to the war, or, as the President laughingly remarked, as
our Democratic friends used to say, "the Constitution as it is, the Union
as it was," always saving and excepting slavery, that had been abolished. The war had decided that, and forever.

A gentleman present spoke of negro suffrage, and suggested that in
reconstructing the Union, it would be necessary to disfranchise some
leading rebels, and enfranchise others (meaning loyal colored people),
or that the case of the Virginia Legislature reassembling would be
repeated over again. The gentleman is a strong advocate of negro
suffrage.

The President replied that the case of the Virginia Legislature was
easily disposed of; that it had no power as a legislative body, and that it

could do nothing anyhow. With regard to the extension of suffrage, the sentiment of the country at present appeared to tend towards a restriction rather than an extension of the right of suffrage generally.

General Logan seconded the views of the President on the above, and then said that it might not be politic to give the rebels the right of suffrage immediately. He thought that it might be found advisable at first to hold them in a sort of pupilage by military force. As soon as they could be trusted, then give them the same power they possessed before. The General also remarked that the wheel of reconstruction was a large and ponderous one, and that many who would take their stand upon it would be ground to powder. He had been fighting for four years to save the Union. He now proposed that those who desired to reconstruct it might go in and see what they could do. For his part he felt inclined to be rather a looker-on than an active participant in the contest which would naturally grow out of it.

The President said: "General, there is no such thing as reconstruction. These States have not gone out of the Union, therefore reconstruction is unnecessary. I do not mean to treat them as inchoate States, but merely as existing under a temporary suspension of their government, provided always they elect loyal men. The doctrine of coercion to preserve a State in the Union has been vindicated by the people. It is the province of the Executive to see that the will of the people is carried out in the rehabilitation of these rebellious States, once more under the authority as well as the protection of the Union."

General Logan responded "That's so."

The President then passed on to the question of the public debt. He said that the finances of the country were in a hopeful condition; that probably it was possible to resume specie payments immediately, were it not for the commercial distress it would create throughout the country generally. As to the public debt of the country, he was in favor of paying it to the last dollar, and would never countenance any man, party, sect, or measure that even hinted at repudiation in any form. The debt was incurred to save the country. It was a legacy of the war bequeathed to us for good or evil. It was not possible to shirk it. On the other hand the great question would be to make it, if possible, an instrument of good, not evil, to the public generally.

Washington Morning Chronicle, July 1, 1865.

1. While in Washington General Logan called upon the President to pay his respects. He subsequently reported the interview to a correspondent of the *Chicago Republican*.

From Robert Johnson

Nashville Tenn May 31st 1865

Dear Father.

Judge Patterson[1] arrived here Monday 29th inst. in pretty good health. He will leave for Greeneville on Friday next.

We will leave for Washington about the 14th June. Will Telegraph you the precise time, before we Start.

Yesterday, Col Blackburn,[2] brought to the city, as a prisoner, the notorious *Champ Ferguson.*[3] He was captured at his home on the Calf Killer, in White County. He is now in the Military prison, and I understand will be tried by the Military, for his numerous crimes. Blackburn Says that the War Department ought now to order his muster on his respective commissions, as Lieut Colonel and Colonel of the 4th Mounted Infantry Owing to Some cause he has never been mustered.

A great many returned rebels in the city—as a general thing the mass are behaving themselves very well—but there are Some exceptions—especially when they get to drinking. Several have been arrested and confined in the Military prison. In East Tennessee, they are having Some trouble. The Union men will not permit the leaders, and others that persecuted their families to live in that Section. A few have already been killed—and others badly beaten—but things are getting more quite up there, and I think will Settle down in a short time. Emmerson Keller,[4] was killed a short time Since in his own yard. He was a very bad man. James Jones[5] (Son of George) Bob McFarland, Bill Stuart, Ed Harris and John Crawford[6] of Jonesborough, have been here, by invitation of the Military authorities. They have all returned—but I doubt whether they go home, or if they do how long they will remain there.

Six hundred thousand Dollars of the Bank of Tennessee, Books, Archives &c of the State, and Dunlap, Ray and Battle,[7] arrived here Monday evening from Georgia.

I enclose application for Special pardon for Wm. D. McNish,[8] formerly Postmaster of Nashville. You know the man and the case, and I will make no remarks. I hesitated at first about enclosing it, but concluded I would. Bob Armstrong[9] wishes me to call your attention to a letter he wrote you a short time Since, asking the release of his Cousin Capt R. H. Isbell,[10] 1st Reg't Ala Infantry, who was captured at Port Hudson, and now held as a prisoner of war at Fort Delaware. Armstrong says that he was a good Union man.

Andrew Johnson, Jr,[11] was elected on Monday by the Legislature, *Keeper* of the *Penitentiary.*

We are all in very good health. I will have everything ready to take to Washington. The Books and papers have been packed Some time—and in good Order.

I will write you again in a few days.[12]

Your Son Robert Johnson

ALS, DLC-JP.

1. David T. Patterson.
2. Joseph H. Blackburn.
3. Champ Ferguson, Confederate guerrilla.
4. Possibly William E. Keller (b. c1819), a Greene County farmer. 1860 Census, Tenn., Greene, 7th Dist., 228.
5. Tennessee-born James C. Jones (b. c1828) was a Greeneville merchant, whose father was one of Johnson's earliest acquaintances. Ibid., 10th Dist., 91.
6. Robert McFarland, Robert's former law partner and now a Jefferson County attorney; possibly W. G. Stuart (b. c1825), prewar constable; and John H. Crawford (b.c1814), circuit court clerk for Washington County. Harris has not been found. Ibid., 82; ibid., Washington, Jonesboro, 155.
7. James T. Dunlap, J. E. R. Ray, and Joel A. Battle. Dunlap (1812–1879) was a prewar state representative and senator before serving as state comptroller (1857–62). Battle (1811–1872) served as state treasurer under Governor Harris. Later he was a hotel owner and superintendent of the state prison (1872). Ray was secretary of state on the eve of the war. BDTA, 1: 217.
8. William D. McNish, Nashville's Confederate postmaster, was pardoned on August 19, 1865. House Ex. Docs., 39 Cong., 2 Sess., No. 116, p. 46 (Ser. 1293).
9. Robert H. Armstrong, wealthy Knoxvillian and former legislator.
10. Robert H. Isbell (b.c1834), captain, Co. D, 1st Ala. Inf., CSA, was among thirteen prisoners of war ordered released by the President on June 19. Orders and Endorsements, 1846–70 (M444, Roll 9), RG107, NA; 1850 Census, Ala., Talledega, Talledega Dist., 781; Edward Y. McMorries, History of the First Alabama Volunteer Infantry, C.S.A. (Montgomery, 1904), 33.
11. Johnson's nephew retained the keeper's office only a year.
12. A penciled notation, possibly by one of the President's secretaries, reads: "Opened by mistake. Private to the President."

From Benjamin P. Loyall

May 31, 1865, Norfolk, Va.; Copy, DLC-JP.

Virginian and former navy lieutenant, having returned to the U.S. in September 1861, following a three-year cruise, only to face imprisonment and exchange as a prisoner of war after refusing to take the oath of allegiance to the U.S., because it "would have bound me to join in the war . . . against my home, my family and the State of Virginia," now seeks presidential clemency and a restoration of his "rights and privileges" as a citizen, inasmuch as he is excluded from Johnson's recent amnesty proclamation, as a consequence of service as an officer in the Confederate Navy. [This letter was forwarded to Johnson through Francis P. Blair.]

From Oliver P. Morton

Indianapolis, May 31st 1865

His Excellency Andrew Johnson
President U.S. Washington.
Sir:

I have the honor to state that quite a number of Union refugees from Georgia came to Indiana under orders made by Gen'l. Sherman after the taking of Atlanta. There are perhaps one hundred such families now in this State.[1] Many of them desire to return to their homes in the South but have not the means to procure transportation. Some of them were the owners of valuable real estate at and near Atlanta when they were sent North. I think it is highly important that such of these families as are of undoubted loyalty should be aided to return to their homes. I am informed that Gen'l. Thomas is furnishing transportation to all such from Nashville south. I respectfully request that provision may be made for furnishing transportation from here to Nashville for all persons of the class above designated who shall establish their loyalty to the satisfaction of some officer who may be designated to hear their applications.[2] In a political point of view it would seem to be important that such persons should be enabled to return to their homes to assist in the re-organization of society and government.[3]

I have the honor to be Very Respectfully
Your Obedient Servant   O. P. Morton
Governor of Indiana

LS, DNA-RG105, Records of the Commr., Lets. Recd. (M752, Roll 15).

1. Two weeks later Morton wired O. O. Howard: "Their are now here one hundred and fifty (150) Refugees, sixty seven (67) adults eighty four (84) children waiting for transportation to their homes. . . . They are entirely destitute." Morton to Howard, June 16, 1865, Records of the Commr., Lets. Recd. (M752, Roll 16), RG105, NA. See Letter from Atlanta Refugees, May 15, 1865.

2. Johnson forwarded Morton's letter to Stanton, who in turn sent it on to Howard, who advised the governor: "If you will send me lists of such *Refugees*, as are mentioned in your letter, I will send through you *transportation* for the same . . . to their homes. Those who are able to pay their way, should not be embraced in such lists." Howard to Morton, June 8, 1865, Records of the Commr., Lets. Sent (M742, Roll 1), RG105, NA.

3. By mid-July Howard was having second thoughts about the wisdom of assisting unionist refugees to return south, suggesting to Morton that in view of reports from "the section of country to which most of those for whom transportation has been requested belong, their sufferings will be still greater there, as a great scarcity of food exists and the inhabitants are nearly all depending on the Government or benevolent associations for their food." By remaining in Indiana "they can probably earn their own living and if not be more easily and cheaply supported by the charity of the citizens." Howard to Morton, July 21, 1865, ibid.

Order re *Closing Federal Offices*

Executive Office Washington, D.C.,
May 31, 1865.

Tomorrow the First of June being the day appointed for Special Humiliation and Prayer in consequence of the Assassination of Abraham Lincoln late President of the United States, the Executive Office and the various Departments will be closed during the day.

signed Andrew Johnson
President U.S.

Official copy respectfully furnished by direction of the President to the Hon. Sec. of State

R. D. Mussey Military Sec.

Copy, DNA-RG59, Misc. Lets., 1789–1906 (M179, Roll 224).

From David T. Patterson

Nashville, May 31st 1865

To the President

I am informed by reliable authority that there is a large quantity of cotton in the vicinity of Montgomery Ala. I think it would be advisable to establish a cotton agency at that place.

Maj John Blevins[1] will leave for Washington to day and is very anxious to get the appointment of purchasing agent at Montgomery. I believe Maj Blevins will make an efficient officer, and in addition to this, if the appointment is conferred on Maj Blevins it will give loyal East Tennesseans an opportunity to make in a legitimate way, something out [of] the purchase of cotton, a privilege heretofore enjoyed exclusively by Northern men.

If entirely consistent with the public interests, I hope an agency will be established at Montgomery Ala. and the appointment of agent conferred on Maj Blevins.

Respectfully David T. Patterson

ALS, DLC-JP2.

1. Blevins, from Hawkins County, Tenn., was a landowner in and U.S. marshal of northern Mississippi (1866–69) before becoming a Tennessee legislator. *BDTA*, 2: 70–71; *U.S. Off. Reg.* (1865–69); Appt. Bk., 4: 193, Ser. 6B, Johnson Papers, LC.

From William B. Reese, Jr.

[May 31, 1865], Knox County, Tenn.; LS, DLC-JP.

East Tennessee native, former officer in the Confederate service, desirous of renewing his allegiance to the Union but excluded from Johnson's amnesty proclamation "by reason of being under Bond to appear before Federal Court at Knoxville E. Tenn: to answer a charge of treason," wishes "to invoke the Executive Clemency in my behalf." Assures that "The Executive Pardon will not be abused by me. I mean to make a good citizen. I shall endeavor to make the sincerity of my repentance manifest by my future good Conduct." [Recommended by both Brownlow and William Heiskell, Reese was pardoned on June 12, 1865.]

From "a Southern man"

Saint Louis May 31 1865

Andrew Johnson
Dear Sir

I am a Southern man, born & raised in the South, have fought with the south, suffered with the South & ruined with the South, & like other Southern men, although divested of resource & power with which to prosecute the war because we have surrendered all Still the same spirit which animated our breasts in the beginning still burns within us, & cannot be crushed, and Sir I write to warn you of danger. You now have it in your power to conciliate the Southern people if you will. On the other hand you may exasperate them until forbearance will cease to be a virtue, & *revenge revenge revenge* takes deep root in their hearts. When Genl. Lee the patriot the Soldier & the high toned Gentleman Surrendered to Genl. Grant, he did it on condition that he nor his men were to be molested by the U S authorities, and yet the wires bring inteligence that he has been arrested.[1] Is this the way the U S G keeps her faith & Sir by the Same Source the news reaches us that the patriot the Soldier & the Statesman Mr J Davis is both incarcerated & in Irons. This will be Sir a disgrace to you & your administration throughout all time & I think it possible eternity too.

For Sir Mr Davis & Genl. Lee though prominent men in the Confederacy, were no more to blame for the revolution we have Just passed through, than I was, & I am nothing more than a plain unpretending Citizen never having held an office either civil or military in my life, but Sir the people had been anraged by Northn fanatics (& saw that the Govmt at washington winked at it so that they were exasperated) & ripe for revolution, & these Leaders as you are pleased to call them could not have prevented the war if they had been disposed to do so, indeed the Southern people could not. It was the infernal abolitionist that brough it on & they alone are responsible, & therefore Sir *beware*. I am Sir no mad man. I am no assassin. I want peace. I do not thirst for the blood of any, but Sir *I swear* by all that is honorable beneath the Skies that if any of our *Great Captains* are made to suffer any severe penalty, that *I will be one* of a *host* that will neither rest day or night until your life pays the penalty of such a monstrous crime. You may keep your guards around you & you may escape even through the term of your administration, but Sooner or later what I now Say will be put into execution. This is no idle threat but words of soberness & truth & uttered by one who will dare to do though it may cost his life in two minutes. Therefore I say *beware* decision firmness.

AL, DLC-JP.

1. While Lee was never arrested, U.S. district judge John C. Underwood had empaneled a grand jury at Norfolk, Va., to charge Lee and other prominent Confederates with treason. Dorris, *Pardon and Amnesty*, 120. See also Letter from Robert E. Lee, June 13, 1865.

Memorial from South Carolina Citizens [1]

[Charleston, S.C., June 1865] [2]

To His Excellency Andrew Johnson
President of the United States of America.

The Undersigned, who have taken the oath of Allegiance, long residents of Charleston and other Sections of the State of South Carolina, and Citizens of the United States of America

Most respectfully memorialize your Excellency to obtain the restoration of civil government in this State.

The great civil war, which moistened our land with blood, ruined our people, and desolated our homes, is at an end. In good faith We have renewed our fidelity to the Constitution to the United States. There is no reserved intention to embarrass the Authorities: or sullen disposition to oppose the Government. The determination is universal, to be in spirit and in truth Loyal: and to do all that become citizens, whose interests are in the Union of the States, to promote the prosperity of their Country. The deprivation of civil government oppresses the energies of the people, creates distrust, diminishes if it does not wholly destroy commercial transactions, and inflicts on the Community lawless speculation, in the place of an invigorating legitimate commerce. Your Memorialists can, however effect nothing, without the aid of your Excellency's authority which they solicit.

The State has ever continued a part of the great Integral, the Union, the People are disorganized. The appointment of a Provisional Governor, with powers to reorganize the State Government, would lead to an early restoration of civil government; and confer on the People of this State the blessings of peace.

Your Memorialists therefore pray that some Citizen of this State, be appointed Provisional Governor of the State of South Carolina. [3]

Mem, DLC-JP.

1. A total of 311 signatures are to be found on the three copies of this memorial, which were posted at the office of the *Charleston Courier*, at John Russell's on King Street, and at Samuel G. Courtenay's on Broad. Johnson Papers, LC; *Charleston Courier*, June 10, 1865.

2. Although undated, the petition was published in the *Charleston Courier* on June

10 and delivered to Johnson eleven days later. See Interview with South Carolina Delegation, June 24, 1865.

3. Johnson received many similar memorials from South Carolina in the summer of 1865. See petitions from Orangeburg, June 12; South Carolina Citizens, June 17; Richland District and Columbia District, June 20; South Carolina Districts and South Carolina Business Committee, June 29; Union District, July 3; Spartanburg District, July 5; Barnwell District, July 11; and Kershaw District, July 12, Johnson Papers, LC; *Charleston Courier*, June 20, 1865; John L. Bell, Jr., "Andrew Johnson, National Politics, and Presidential Reconstruction in South Carolina," *SCHM*, 82 (1981): 358–59. See also Letters from William W. Boyce, June 23, July 5, 1865.

From James Mitchell

June 1865, Washington, D.C.; LS, DNA-RG59, Misc. Lets., 1789–1906 (M179, Roll 381).

Indiana clergyman, African colonization activist, and agent of emigration for the Interior Department, submits a lengthy brief "On Emigration and Colonization" of "persons of African descent." Asserting that "The policy of gradually separating the White and Negro races of this Republic has long been cherished by the best men in this country," he urges Johnson not only to follow Lincoln's policy, but also to see that "the office of Emigration and Colonization of persons of African descent, be made to comprehend all matters relating to the suppression of the African Slave Trade, as well as emigration" and that it be made a civil office, thus prepared to outlast the Freedmen's Bureau, "wisely limited by law to one year from this date." There follows an extended history of the intermittent Federal support for the African colonization movement until President Lincoln, in the Emancipation Proclamation of September 22, 1862, "fixed it firmly in the policy of our land." As far back as July 1862, Congress had empowered the President to make provision for colonization; the proviso in the emancipation document was merely a step "in the solemn exercise of this trust." Mitchell maintains that this is "the permanent foundation of all national colonization policies," binding on those southerners who return to their allegiance and "vesting certain rights in the negro population of the South."

From Marshall T. Polk

June 1865, Bolivar, Tenn.; ALS, DNA-RG94, Amnesty Papers (M1003, Roll 50), Tenn., Marshall T. Polk.

President Polk's nephew seeks pardon under the 8th exception to Johnson's Amnesty Proclamation. Graduating from West Point in 1852, he served as a subaltern officer for four years before resigning to become a private citizen. Never a secessionist, he nevertheless believed it was his "duty to side with my section & stay with the people among whom my lot was cast" and enlisted as a lieutenant colonel in the Confederate army. Now a cripple—"having lost a limb in the battle at Shiloh"—and having lost his property and stock as well, he believes he has suffered enough. [Polk apparently did not receive an individual pardon.]

From Daniel C. Trewhitt and Others [1]

[Chattanooga, June 1865] [2]

To his Excellency Andrew Johnson
President of the United States.

We beg leave to bring to your notice the following facts, with reference to the Military occupation of the property of Loyal Citizens of Chattanooga in the County of Hamilton State of Tennessee.

We most respectfully represent, that the residences of loyal citizens has been occupied by the military from the time the Federal forces took the place to the present time. In some instances citizens have [been] put in possession of private property, and held in possession in exclusion to the loyal owner. No rents have been paid for the property so occupied, and when application has been made to the authorities here, the papers are returned with the indorsement, that the Government will pay no rents for any property occupied by the military in Chattanooga at present or in the future. In many instances houses have been pulled down by command of some officer, the materials destroyed or used as suited the convenience of the parties, and the rights of the owner totally disregarded. A large quantity of property has been set apart for permanent occupation by the Government, and we are told that the houses of loyal men are to be permanently held and used by the Government without Compensation.

We wish also to bring to your attention the fact that private property is assigned by the military to private citizens, without regard to the owner, and the property is thus held in exclusion to the owner.

We most respectfully, yet earnestly ask that such property as is actually necessary for permanent use by the Government be condemned and paid for, and that the rents for past occupation be paid for, and also that damage done to property be also paid, and we also ask that all property of every kind not needed for public use be given up to the owner free from Military Control.

We most respectfully represent also that owners of property are not permitted to build on their property within one mile of the outer lines around the place, thus effectually prohibiting all improvement in the place except by permission of the military which is granted alone to favorites, and prevents those who have been turned out of their houses from erecting a shelter for their wives and children.

All these things have been patiently borne by our people, and we would not now make this application, if we were not impelled by dire necessity, and the unnecessary hardship and suffering caused thereby.

Private persons, strangers, are quartered in the residences of loyal citizens without their consent, and against their will, and in one instance a loyal man has verry recently been imprisoned for attemting to hold his own house, with the order of the Post Q. M. authorizing him to do so, the Same Q. M. being the party who imprisoned the citizen.[3]

Property once held by the Government and no longer needed is turned over on condition the property is rented to the favorite of the Post Q. M. If his favorite is not acceptable to the owner, the property is still held by the Post Q. M. and the owner thereby deprived of the use of his house, or any hope of ever obtaining pay for rents. Houses of rebels have been returned to them, while the houses of Union men are with held. These facts are presented to you as the Executive of the nation, so that the proper steps may be taken to relieve this community from such gross abuses. This appeal and memorial is made to you, under necessity for relief, and comes from those who are the personal & Political friends of the administration.[4]

Respectfully your obt serts.

D. C. Trewhitt.

R. Henderson T. R. Stanley

A.G.W. Puckett G. W. Rider

LS, DLC-JP.

1. Along with Trewhitt, the letter was signed by Richard Henderson (1815–1878), a lawyer soon to become mayor; Col. Timothy R. Stanley (d. 1874), a former commandant of the post at Chattanooga and now a resident; A.G.W. Puckett (d. 1887), county judge; and George W. Rider (c1817–fl1870), recent county sheriff. Trewhitt, a unionist, served as chancellor, second division (1864–70), appointed by Military Governor Johnson. Zella Armstrong, *The History of Hamilton County and Chattanooga, Tennessee* (2 vols., Chattanooga, 1940), 2: 53, 62, 199, 201; Heitman, *Register*, 1: 915; *Chattanooga Times*, Aug. 21, 1887; 1860 Census, Tenn., Hamilton, 14th Dist., 96; (1870), 3rd Ward Chattanooga, 12; Miller, *Political Manual*, 185.

2. The writers of the letter provided no provenance or date. There is no question that the letter was written in Chattanooga, given the internal evidence of the document. With regard to the date, however, much remains uncertain. The Library of Congress has assigned August 15, 1865 as the probable date; but we suggest instead that the Trewhitt letter was written in early June 1865. We base our claim upon internal evidence found in two letters that were apparently enclosed with the Trewhitt letter when it eventually reached President Johnson in Washington. The two letters, both of which are found in the Johnson Papers, LC, are: Timothy R. Stanley and Richard Henderson to Capt. J. H. James, June 8, 1865, and E. W. Wood to A.G.W. Puckett, June 7, 1865. The opening sentence of the Stanley and Henderson letter reads: "Since writing the enclosed to the President, a new matter of aggravation has occurred which we desire briefly to notice." From that point, the letter proceeds to provide details about the incident of Robert Anderson. Likewise the Wood letter offers information about the Anderson case. It is our speculation that all of the letters were forwarded to Capt. James in Nashville, who at some later date sent them on to Johnson. As noted below, Johnson on July 20 made an endorsement on the Stanley and Henderson letter.

3. The reference here is evidently to Robert Anderson, who was arrested and imprisoned by Capt. Charles H. Deane, an action which caused Anderson to be exiled outside the lines. Anderson's attorneys, Stanley, Henderson, and Puckett, appealed the treatment of their client. Wood to Puckett, June 7, 1865, and Stanley and Henderson to James, June 8, 1865, Johnson Papers, LC.

4. On July 20 Johnson endorsed the Stanley and Henderson letter: "Respectfully referred to Bvt. Maj Genl. A. C. Gillem Comdg District of East Tennessee. From the statement here it appears that great injustice has been done. General Gillem will have this case investigated thoroughly and see that justice is done and report action to me." In

a brief report, dated August 19, 1865, Gillem dealt with the Anderson case and related concerns and indicated that Anderson's property had been restored to him and that a general statement had been issued to military authorities there requiring them to vacate all property belonging to loyal citizens, insofar as "it can be done without serious detriment to the public service." In an addendum to his report, Gillem indicated that both Capt. Deane and Gen. Charles H. Grosvenor "have been relieved from duty in this district." There is an additional endorsement on the Gillem document, dated September 5, 1865, and from the Executive Mansion, which claims that the document or documents have been referred to Gen. George Thomas. It appears, however, that this endorsement has been stricken out. The Gillem report is found in the Johnson Papers, LC.

From Richard T. Allison

June 1, 1865, Richmond, Va.; ALS, DLC-JP.

Chief Justice Roger Taney's son-in-law, a navy paymaster until May 1861, and subsequently paymaster of the Confederate Marine Corps until war's end, has taken the amnesty oath and requests that all the benefits of the President's Proclamation of May 29, 1865, be extended to him. [Although Frank P. Blair urged the President to "pardon a folly that had not the malice of treason mixed with it & which shed no blood," Allison was not pardoned until February 6, 1867.]

From Charles Green

June 1, 1865, Savannah, Ga.; ALS, DNA-RG94, Amnesty Papers (M1003, Roll 19), Ga., Charles Green.

Savannah commission merchant, a British subject, having approached Lincoln in March, now attaches oath and seeks amnesty because his business is stopped until he is pardoned. "It was not, Sir, because of personal antipathy to the North that I gave my sympathy to this people in their struggle," but "my affinities had been made with them. My children were borne of them; I went with the current." [By special order of July 29, the President approved Green's pardon.]

From George E. Pickett[1]

Richmond Va. June 1st 1865

To His Excellency Andrew Johnson
President of the United States
Sir:

I have the honor to state that your amnesty proclamation of the 29th day of May 1865, has just been read. I find myself among the classes of persons excepted from the benefits of the proclamation, under exceptions, third, fifth, and eighth. Having held the rank of Major General in the C.S. Army, resigning my position as Captain U S Army, and being a graduate of West Point, I write making a special application.

At the commencement of our domestic troubles I was stationed on the disputed Island San Juan,[2] occupying it conjointly with the British forces, and did not leave 'till my resignation had been sent in, and I

[was] properly relieved by the commanding Officer of the Department of the Pacific, and leave granted me to proceed to my home, and then only through the conscientious duty (as I conceived) to my mother state—Virginia. Had *she* not have seceeded, *I* should not have been in the Confederate Army, as no one was more attached to the old service, nor ever stood by, and fought for it, with more fidelity, nor could any one have been sadder, and more loth to leave it than I, who from my youth had been so devoted to it; and I now am, and have been since the surrender of Genl. Lee (to whose army I belonged) willing, and ready to renew my allegiance as a loyal citizen, to the United States Government, and have advised and counseled all men belonging to my division to return to their homes, and the peaceful pursuits of life—to take the oath of allegiance—and observe with scrupulous truth its stipulations, and to faithfully obey the laws of their country. My wish as expressed is a *sincere* one; and this communication addressed with a hope that the liberality spoken of in the amnesty proclamation may be extended to cover my case.[3]

> I have the honor to be Sir Very Respectfully
> Your Obt Sert, G E Pickett
> Maj Genl C.S.A.

Address care Andrew Johnston[4] Esq
Atty at Law Richmond Va.

LS, DNA-RG94, Amnesty Papers (M1003, Roll 67), Va., George E. Pickett.
    1. Pickett (1825–1875) was a Confederate colonel, brigadier and major general with Lee's army. After the war he was an insurance agent at Norfolk. Warner, *Gray*.
    2. The subject of a boundary dispute between the U.S. and Canada, the San Juan Islands are located in Puget Sound and are now a part of Washington State. *Encyclopedia Americana* (1984 ed.).
    3. There is no evidence that Pickett received an individual pardon. On June 19, 1865, Secretary Stanton reported that the general was under investigation for ordering the execution of at least eighteen Confederate deserters who had joined the Federal army in North Carolina and been captured in 1864. Pickett was not tried for his actions; as General Grant wrote in his endorsement of the former Confederate's application, the terms of surrender "protects them against punishment for acts lawful for any other belligerent." Presumably, Pickett eventually was pardoned under the general amnesties of 1868. *House Ex. Docs.*, 39 Cong., 2 Sess., No. 11, pp. 1–9 (Ser. 1288).
    4. Andrew Johnston (c1817–1873), Richmond lawyer for thirty years, came to Washington and personally presented Pickett's letter to the President. *Richmond Dispatch*, Feb. 21, 1873; James G. Randall, ed., *The Diary of Orville Hickman Browning* (2 vols., Springfield, Ill., 1925–33), 2: 32.

From "A Southerner for life"[1]

Canada 1 June/65

The President U.S. AM
Sir.

If you attempt to do anything unbecoming the justice of the free Country over which you rule to Either Jeff Davis or General Lee I swear that your life as well as others will be the penalty We of Canada

will Exact. I will shoot you and others & will not *run* as my poor friend
Booth did. This is *true*. It is a shame after taking their parole you arrest
them for Treason—disgrace to the trust that they should not act honorably. Be just—be merciful—& your reward will be hereafter.

A Southerner for life

ALS, DNA-RG153, Lets. Recd. by Col. H. L. Burnett (Apr.–Aug., 1865).

1. The President received a number of warnings and threatening letters, the latter
mostly anonymous, which were forwarded to Col. H. L. Burnett, judge advocate of the
Northern Department in Cincinnati, who was assigned to investigate the "murder of
President Lincoln, and the attempted assassination of Mr. Seward." Special Order No.
180, Apr. 22, 1865, RG94, NA.

From Daniel B. Turner [1]

Huntsville, Ala: June 1st 1865.

His Excellency, Andrew Johnson,
President of U.S.
Sir:

I understand L. P. Walker [2] of this place is an applicant for pardon
from participation in the late rebellion. I have known him from boyhood, & have for more than ten years last past, resided in the same
community with him. It is true that in the early stages of the rebellion,
he was a very active & zealous supporter of it. But early in 1862, he
resigned all employment civil or military in its service, and from thence
to the present, has been a recognised advocate of peace, and of a restoration of Alabama to her Federal relations. In the fall of 1862, and the
winter of 1863, when the persecution and proscription of Union men
was most violent here, he was their friend and supporter, and to his
efforts only are they indebted for their exemption from military despotism. When citizens were arrested by the military, for disloyalty, as it
was termed, he would present their arrests to the State Courts, and
secure their release, and when indicted for treason, he defended them.
By this course he incurred the censure of the disunionists, and was
subjected to the bitterest assaults from them. When the rebellion began,
a man of large fortune, it has in a great measure been swept away by
the accidents and consequences of war.

Under all the circumstances, his pardon, would be gratifying to the
great mass of the Union men of Alabama, and permit me to say, an
especial gratification to me personally. May I ask this from you, also, as
a *personal favor*. [3]

Very Respectfully D. B. Turner

ALS Draft, A-Ar, Leroy Pope Walker Papers.

1. Turner was a commission merchant.

2. Leroy P. Walker had retired in 1862 to Huntsville, where for two years he defended unionists victimized by local Confederates. From June 1864 to war's end, he was
judge of the military court of north Alabama. William C. Harris, *Leroy Pope Walker:
Confederate Secretary of War* (Tuscaloosa, 1962), 120–23.

3. The President ordered Walker pardoned, September 28, 1865. *House Ex. Docs.*, 40 Cong., 2 Sess., No. 16, p. 37 (Ser. 1330).

From Levi S. White[1]

Oak Hill, Virginia June 1 1865

To His Excellency—
Andrew Johnson—President of the U.S—
Dear Sir—

I respectfully beg leave to set forth; That being a citizen of Baltimore, I am among the tenth (10th) class of *excepted* persons, embraced in your Excellency's recent Amnesty Proclamation, by "having left my home within the jurisdiction of the U.S. &c."

During the period of the Rebellion I have been engaged in procuring supplies within the Federal Lines, and transporting the same to Richmond, some of which were for the use of the "so-called Confederate Government."

I thus candidly admit this my connection with the Rebellion, because I believe the spirit of your Excellency's Proclamation requires *candor* and *frankness*, and to do otherwise, at this time, on my part would be hypocritical.

I beg leave to state however that the above embraces *all* acts of mine during the rebellion for which I could be held accountable to the U.S. Government.

I now respectfully request the extension to me of the privileges of your Proclamation, and should your Excellency think proper to bestow your *Amnesty* upon my past acts, I will pledge myself to *strictly* and *faithfully* perform its obligations to the best of my ability.

Hoping you will give this your *kind* and *prompt* attention—

I remain Dear Sir—Very Respectfully Yrs.

Levi S. White

I take the liberty of referring to
Saml. Hindes Esq[2] Police Commissioner of Balto—
James Young Esq[3] Prest, First Branch City Council Balto—

ALS, DNA-RG94, Amnesty Papers (M1003, Roll 30), Md., Levi S. White.
1. White (c1823–fl1901), a Baltimore editor-turned-commission merchant, was subsequently president of an insurance company. Johnson granted his pardon on June 15. 1860 Census, Md., Baltimore, 6th Ward, 90; Baltimore directories (1860–1901); *House Ex. Docs.*, 39 Cong., 2 Sess., No. 116, p. 5 (Ser. 1293).
2. Hindes (c1808–c1872) was a hatter. Baltimore directories (1860–72); 1860 Census, Md., Baltimore, 5th Ward, 119.
3. Young (c1810–fl1891) was a master printer. Ibid., 6th Ward, 247.

From Rufus K. Williams[1]

Louisville Ky June 1, 1865

His Excellency Andrew Johnson
President U S
Sir

The vote taken yesterday in our Legislature shows a gain of from 14 to 16, since the February recess, for the Constitutional Amendment.[2]

There have been many important changes in the State since your Inauguration, and our friends are sanguine of success in the Coming August election.

Chief Justice Bullett of our Appellate Court was yesterday addressed out of office by our Legislature.[3]

Your proclamations of 29th Inst have given great satisfaction to the loyal masses and members of the Legislature, and have released them from a sort of indifinite and indescribable apprehension that the loyal masses might be left under the domination of that insolent class of slave propagandist which has ruled the South with an iron rod for four years. The decision of Attorney General Speed and its affirmance by the President and Cabinett that rebels can have no home in the loyal States and have no legal rights there, by virtue of Lees Capitulation to Lt Genl Grant, meets with universal approval from loyal men.

In the Legislative Caucus held eveng of 30th ulto, your administration was fully endorsed, they fully determined no longer to engage in the political folly of drawing a distinction between the Government and its Administration, trying to uphold the one whilst the other was permitted to be denounced and made odious, without a defence.

I reviewed the propositions and their effects upon the loyal masses of the Shearman-Johnson agreement[4] and the unanswerable reasons for its prompt and efficient rejection by you and the Cabinett and your action was vociferously chee[re]d, and Secty Stanton fully justified whilst Genl Shearmans conduct was not approved. I desired that specific resolution of approval of its rejection should be adopted, but sensible true men thought the general resolutions sufficiently embraced it, and as Genl Shearman was to be our Military Commander it would be unwise and detrimental to our people for their representatives to incur his displeasure.

The disloyal Democracy and discontented slaveocrats, calling themselves Union men, had a convention at Frankfort 24th ulto[5] and resolved that the Shearman-Johnson agreement was entirely constitutional and right and the only means of preserving the rights and republicism of the States, and that the military must be subservient to the Civil power, without qualification.

I was appealed to in Cincinnatti to know if I would not return to the old Democratic party, on the basis of this agreement and with Genl Shearman as the Standard bearer.

The indications are that this is to be the next political issue with us.

The reccommendations of Hon L. Anderson, W. H. Randall, G. Clay. Smith, Geo. H. Yeaman, B. J. Clay[6] members of the last Congress, and of the Administration members of both branches of our Legislature, and of other prominent members of our party, also the letter of U.S. Senators Fowler and Patterson of Tennessee, are on file, with Atty Genl Speed, for my promotion to the Federal Bench. Permit me to ask the favor of your examining the flattering terms these gentlemen have seen proper to use.

I had learned to revere you as a Democratic Statesman, previous to the unfortunate Charleston Convention, being myself a Delegate for the state at large in it. I saw you on the floor of the Senate on my return and in a private conversation you denounced the secession therefrom and agreed with my own action.

I next saw you late in August 1861, when you rendered me and the Union men of my section, a peculiar service, by going with and introducing me to President Lincoln and advocating a measure greatly to our advantage.[7] You may have forgotten these things, but they made a deep impression on my mind and attached me to you personally.

I was chairman of the Ky Delegation to the late Baltimore Convention,[8] and although the Ky delegation complimented Genl Russeau[9] with its vote, yet it almost immediately, and before the ballot had progressed far, and the first of all changed its vote for you unanimously save Dr Breckenridge.[10] I mention these things to show that you have a personal as well as political popularity in Ky.

Whilst qualification, integrity, and patriotism are all essential in appointments to such an officer, yet Sir, I fully recognize the fact that no President since Washington has had such a complicated, confused, discordant mass of materials from which to bring order and harmony, and whilst I recognize in you the great elements, morally and intellectually, adequate to this emergency, yet I know you will need the cordial support of every department and officer of the Government, and that it is due yourself, your people and their government that you surround yourself with your political and personal friends who will work cordially and harmoniously with you, and whether in or out of official relations with you, I shall feel it both a pleasure and duty to sustain your administration, and hope you will win renown.

Respectfully R. K. Williams

ALS, DLC-JP.

1. Williams (b. c1816), a lawyer and prewar Democrat, was circuit court judge on the eve of the war and a Union delegate to the border state convention in 1861. Elected judge of the Kentucky court of appeals in 1862, he served until 1870. *NCAB*, 12: 102–3; 1860 Census, Ky., Graves, Mayfield, 272.

2. Although debating the 13th Amendment since December 1864, the legislature failed at this and ensuing sessions to bring it to a vote. Howard, *Black Liberation*, 76–90.

3. Joshua F. Bullitt (1821–1897), Danville lawyer who served on the court of appeals, was chief justice when arrested in 1864 and jailed under suspicion of being a Confederate sympathizer. After his release in January 1865, he fled to Canada, and on May 29, on charges of "absence from office and non-residence in the state," was formally removed from office. Four years later he was exonerated by the legislature. *NCAB*, 13: 19–20; *Louisville Journal*, June 1, 1865.

4. The initial agreement arrived at between Generals William T. Sherman and Joseph E. Johnston at Durham Station, N.C., for the surrender of the latter's army on April 18, 1865.

5. In response to a National Union rally in Frankfort on May 23, a Conservative assembly the next day not only endorsed the Sherman-Johnston agreement but also declared themselves opposed to amending the Constitution to allow the federal government to emancipate slaves in any state. *Cincinnati Enquirer*, May 30, 1865.

6. Larz Anderson, Cincinnati; William H. Randall, Richmond; Green Clay Smith, Covington; George H. Yeaman, Owensboro; Brutus J. Clay. Randall (1812–1881) was a member of Congress (1863–67) and district judge, 15th circuit (1870–80); Smith (1826–1895) served in Congress (1863–66) and as governor of Montana Territory (1866–69); Yeaman (1829–1908) was elected as a unionist to Congress (1862–65); Clay (1808–1878), planter and stockraiser, served in Congress (1863–65). *BDAC*.

7. Williams probably refers to Johnson's sponsorship of a bill which would arm and equip loyalists in border states like Kentucky and Tennessee, and after its passage, to his unremitting efforts for its implementation. See Bill Appropriating Arms to Loyal Citizens, July 20, 1861; Letter to Abraham Lincoln, August 6, 1861, *Johnson Papers*, 4: 592–93, 670–71.

8. The National Union Convention which nominated the Lincoln-Johnson ticket.

9. Gen. Lovell H. Rousseau.

10. Robert J. Breckinridge, Sr.

From Perry E. Brocchus

June 2, 1865, Baltimore, Md.; ALS, DLC-JP.

Confident that Johnson desires to use Alabama's "best men" while bringing the state back into the Union, the former editor of the *Florence Gazette* suggests George S. Houston, member of Congress until he resigned in 1861 to "cast his lot" with his state, but who, the writer is convinced, now considers secession "a heresy, & that the South had . . . committed an error in adopting it as a remedy for avowed wrongs." Avers: "There is no man in north Ala. who better understands the temper of the people of that section of the state than he, or whose counsel would have more weight with them, & I have no doubt that he might be of material service to you in preparing Alabama to resume her status of loyalty to the Federal government." [Houston was elected to the U.S. Senate in 1865 but was not seated.]

From Schuyler Colfax

June 2, 1865, Denver, Colo.; ALS, DNA-RG60, Appt. Files for Judicial Dists., Colo., Moses Hallett.

Indiana Congressman, late speaker of the House, during a westward tour, reporting on territorial conditions, notes the absence of a U.S. judge in the Colorado Territory, where conflicting mining claims are accumulating, and recommends appointing Moses Hallett and Samuel H. Elbert to judgeships and Capt. Uriah B. Holloway to succeed the latter as secretary of the territory. Compliments the performance of Governor John Evans, although he "may be criticised by that portion of the Republicans who, on arguments as to draft, taxation

&c, united with the Anti Admn. party last fall in voting down the State movement, of which Gov Evans, at Mr. Lincoln's desire, was an earnest advocate."
[Hallett was appointed attorney general, then chief justice of Colorado Territory, and Holloway became marshal. Elbert received no subsequent appointment from Johnson after resigning as territorial secretary in June 1866.]

From Richard D. Goodwin[1]

No 104 West 49th Street
New York June 2d 1865

Mr. Johnson

I have always been an advocate for human liberty but I believe the
negro should not be permitted to vote for ten years to come in order to
avoid another revulsion. I can explain to you my reasons for saying so.

I hope you will put them on probation whilst the white population
are becoming educated up to the justice of equal rights to all humanity.[2]

Most truly Yours R. D. Goodwin

ALS, DLC-JP.

1. Goodwin (c1817–fl1875), New York City broker, moved to the St. Louis area,
where he became a practicing physician. New York City directories (1855–66); 1870
Census, Mo., St. Louis, Central Twp., 185; St. Louis directories (1870–75).

2. Two weeks later Goodwin advised Johnson of his election to the "Practical Aid
Association of New York," an organization devoted to finding employment for veterans.
Goodwin to Johnson, June 17, 1865, Johnson Papers, LC.

From Duff Green

Washington 2nd June 1865

To the President of the United States

As in the opinion of the attorney General I am not embraced in your
amnesty proclamation because the value of my taxable property may be
estimated at more than twenty thousand dollars and therefore I should
apply for a special pardon I respectfully do so annexing the requisite oath.[1]

The only difficulty in making this application is the construction
which may be placed upon the proscribed Oath. To so much as requires
me to support the constitution of the United States and the union of
the States thereunder I have no objection. So also if by the support of
the "laws and proclamations which have been made during the existing
rebellion with reference to the emancipation of slaves" it be meant that
I will give such support as it is the duty of all loyal citizens to give to
the laws and authorised acts of the government, reserving the lawful
rights of a loyal citizen to think, to speak, publish and act in relation
thereto as it is the privilege and duty of such citizens to think, speak
publish and act, I give my assent and with this understanding and intent have taken the Oath.[2]

As to Emancipation I am not now and was not a slave owner when the laws and proclamations to which the Oath refers were made. I would not advise nor is it my desire to change the status of the emancipated slave further than it can be done by providing funds to give him constant and profitable employment and fair wages for his labor. I annex the Oath.[3]

Very respectfully
Duff Green

ALS copy, DLC-Duff Green Papers.
1. Other drafts of Green's amnesty application, dated May 31 and June 2, are found in Duff Green Papers, Southern Historical Collection, University of North Carolina.
2. At this point the writer deleted from another version reference to his "well known" opinions on "the institution of Slavery, and the rights of the States," as well as the assertion that "I was opposed to and exerted what influence I had to prevent disunion, believing the movement, altho unwise and inexpedient was the result of the organization of the antislavery party as a northern sectional political[sic]." Green to Johnson, June 2, 1865, Green Papers, Southern Historical Collection.
3. Green was pardoned July 29, 1865, under the 13th exception of Johnson's May 29 proclamation.

From George E. Spencer

June 2, 1865, Huntsville, Ala.; ALS, DLC-JP.

Colonel of the 1st Ala. Cav., USA, stationed in Huntsville, in forwarding a petition from his regiment for the appointment of William H. Smith, a unionist, as provisional governor, requests that "the appointment of any other person be staid until the *real*, Union people of the state can be heard." Warns Johnson that "several delegations of former politicians working in the interests of the rich and rebels and at heart hating both the Gov't and yourself, with the deadliest hatred, have gone to visit you."

From Milton H. Cook

June 3, 1865, Cincinnati, Ohio; ALS, DNA-RG60, Office of Atty. Gen., Lets. Recd., President.

Planing mill owner and builder, wanting to recoup a debt of nearly $60,000 from prewar, mainly Louisiana, purchasers, seeks help in collecting from Charles D. Stewart, who is located west of the Mississippi River in Point Coupee Parish and who owes him about $25,000. Inquires whether "his property is of that class that the Government intends Confiscateing, and if so what would be my best course in order to get Something for my worke?" ["Ans by circular letter June 9, 1865."]

From John W. Gorham[1]

Clarksville Tenn. June 3rd 1865
Honl. Andrew Johnson President U.S.
Dr. Sr

I percieve that I was not mistaken last winter when we were in a private conversation at the Capitol when I said to you your old Enemies would pounce upon you the first opportunity. I also remember well one remark you maid to me, and that was Gorham, I am for a *white* Mans Government in America. I thought then that that would be the issue between you and the radicals so soon as the war was over. The Question of Loyalty was then union but its now Negro Sufferage regardless of all State and Federal Constitutions, but thank Heaven you have taken the wright course and the White People will sustain you. Your time honored doctering of the Constitution the union and the Law, in other words the True Democratic Principles will yet Prevail despite all of its enemies. The People of this Country was frightened when they first learned that you was the President, but those of us that knew you best and had bin your life long Political Friends assured them that you would not addopt the Radical but the Constitutional Polacy in which I see that I was not mistaken. You know that I am under promise to help carry out your Pollacy. I ment what I said and am now ready to enter uppon any dooty you may assighn me in this or any other Country. Say whare what and when and I am ready. I am out of Business, broken up by the War, tho not insolvent. My son[2] has got Home safe and sound, and I am ready to work for you during your Presidential Term, but give me [illegible] that I can make some money at for I assure you that times are hard with me. My kind regards to your son, *Bob* and tell him not to let you forget to give me some good appointment and that too verry son.

As ever your Friend Truly
Jno W. Gorham

P.S Over

Of the *Nownothings* of this county who seemed to fear most that yours would be the most Bloody reighn in american History I say to them Gentleman, what grounds have you for your fears. Have you ever known Andrew Johnson to use extreme Executive Power. If so was it when you charged him in the Gentry Campain for Governor, when you tried to make him out the worst man in the world because he used the Pardning Power too freely, when you charged him with being the grand Jaiol[3] deliverer, having Pardened more men than all his Predecessors put together.[4] Then he used the Pardning Power too freely now not enough. But since your Proclamation appeared they say you are the man after all, and that they are for you, but you know I dont bet high on your Old Enemies, but I do bet on your Clemmancy. I would like to see you and have a good old fashioned chat with you, but you are of course very busey and I am too poore to waist time. Let me hear from you.[5]

Yours, Gorham

ALS, DLC-JP.
1. Clarksville hotel keeper and clerk.
2. Probably Robert T. (b. c1844), who served in Woodward's Ky. Cav., CSA. 1860

Census, Tenn., Montgomery, N & E of Cumberland River, 108; William P. Titus, ed., *Picturesque Clarksville* (Clarksville, 1887), 51.

3. Possibly a corruption of the combination *gaol* and *jail*.

4. Johnson's generous pardoning policy during his first term as governor was an issue in his reelection campaign in 1855 against Meredith Gentry. *Johnson Papers*, 2: 301, 306n.

5. Gorham was still seeking an appointment in November. Gorham to Johnson, November 18, 1865, Johnson Papers, LC.

From William M. Pollan

June 3, 1865, Memphis, Tenn.; ALS, DLC-JP.

Having previously signed the petitions of John W. Wood, for military governor of Mississippi, and John M. Dickinson, for U.S. marshal, Pollan, a Mississippi Union veteran who knows "all about loyalty" in his home state, now writes to withdraw his name, since both petitioners have "affiliated themselves with rebelious leaders" and their sons, unlike himself and his own son, refused to fight for the Union cause.

To Edwin M. Stanton

Executive Office, Washington, D.C.,
June 3d, 1865.

Hon E. M. Stanton Secretary of War
Dear Sir:

Will you please give Mr Joseph E Brown of Georgia a short interview?[1]

I would suggest that he be permitted to return upon his parole and that free transportation be furnished him.[2]

I discover in conversation that you have succeeded in making a decided impression upon him.

I think that his return home can be turned to good account. He will at once go to work and do all that he can in restoring the State.

I have no doubt that he will act in good faith. He can not under the circumstances act otherwise.

Truly Yours Andrew Johnson

LS, DNA-RG94, Lets. Recd. (Main Ser.), File W-1131-1865, Joseph E. Brown.

1. The recipient of a "parole in the city" from Johnson on May 29, Brown had been permitted to leave his quarters in Carroll Prison during the day and to report to the President from time to time. Brown to Johnson, May 23, 1865, Felix Hargrett Col., Joseph E. Brown Papers, University of Georgia; Parks, *Brown*, 332; Roberts, *Brown and Politics*, 31.

2. On June 3, Stanton granted Brown an interview and issued him a "parole of honor," releasing him from prison. Consequently Brown left Washington with the intention of reaching Georgia eventually. Lets. Recd. (Main Ser.), File W-1131-1865, Joseph E. Brown, RG94, NA; Parks, *Brown*, 332.

I do solemnly swear or affirm, *in presence of Almighty God, that I will henceforth faithfully defend the Constitution of the United States and the union of the States thereunder, and that I will, in like manner,* ABIDE BY AND FAITHFULLY SUPPORT ALL LAWS AND PROCLAMATIONS *which have been made during the late rebellion with reference to the emancipation of slaves.* SO HELP ME GOD.

Par_ _ E Arnold

Sworn to and subscribed before me, at Atlanta Georgia *this* 22_nd_ *day of* July 1865 E Johnson

Capt _ Pro Marshal

AMNESTY

OATH.

An Amnesty Oath
Courtesy National Archives

Executive Mansion,

WASHINGTON, D C.

May 2 9th 1865.

Permission is hereby granted to Joseph E Brown of Ga, who has given his parole of honor to report to the President from time to time or whenever required to pass to and from his quarters in this City without interruption, in reporting as aforesaid, until otherwise ordered.

Andrew Johnson President U. S.

Copy of Joseph E. Brown's City Parole
Courtesy University of Georgia Library

From Henry Watterson[1]

Cincinnati June 3rd 1865

His Excellency The President of the United States.

After sincerely and gratefully acknowledging the kindness with which you have treated father, at a time when he had so much need of your good offices,[2] I want to ask your perusal of the enclosed notice of your proclamation.[3]

It embraces my honest convictions; and, if I am not mistaken I have grouped together some of the facts and principles upon which you built your system of amnesty. Looking to these I can not see how any unprejudiced rebel can complain, and I believe it will strike the common sense of the loyal masses. It is certainly liberal enough to cover all who deserve, or may commend themselves to clemency. In a word—and here you must overlook the appearance of a disposition to play the courtier—it is the act of a Statesman and not of a partisan; and this I conceive to mean, that it is the act of a fair-minded man, who has divested his heart of all violence and passion.

I may be in Washington during the trial of Davis, and when I come about the White House—as I am going to ask your permission to do—I dont want you to suspect that I have any other design upon you, than to show you how sincerely I thank you for the many evidences of friendly regard you have shown to me and mine.

I remain, Mr President
With Great Respect Henry Watterson.

ALS, DLC-JP.
1. Watterson, later editor of the *Louisville Courier Journal*, was at this time editorial manager of the *Cincinnati Evening Times*.
2. The President had just dispatched his old friend and fellow unionist, Harvey Watterson, on an official southern tour to report on conditions in the defeated Confederate states. See *Advice*, 39–60.
3. Watterson probably enclosed his June 3 editorial, entitled "The Guilty and the Innocent." Joseph F. Wall, *Henry Watterson* (New York, 1956), 55.

From Robert Morrow[1]

Headquarters District of East Tennessee,
Knoxville, Tenn., June 4th 1865.

Sir

Since returning to Knoxville, and thinking over your Excellency's kindness to me while in Washington, I am constrained to comply at once with your request to write, and in this letter I desire to convey to your Excellency an expression of my earnest desire to be in a position where I can be of service to you. May I not, without incurring censure for egotism, state what position I feel myself best qualified to fill? From my experience in staff duty both in the field and in bureau, with Major Generals Burnside, Schofield and Stoneman,[2] I feel confident that in a very short time I would be able to give your Excellency entire satisfaction as Private Secretary, Aide-de-Camp, or Assistant Adjutant General, and from the respect that my Father encouraged me to entertain towards yourself, I know your Excellency will find in me a faithful and zealous executor of your wishes and views, in *whatever* position I may be placed.

The death of my Father left upon me the care and support of my Mother and a large family, and this prevents me from continuing my studies and cultivating my mind as I would like, unless I am in a position to do so by study and by association with men of superior intellect and cultivation, and at the same time be earning enough by daily exertion to contribute to the comfort of my Mother's family. I am certain that the positions with your Excellency referred to herein would enable me to accomplish both of these objects far beyond anything that I could wish for, much less obtain elsewhere.

Before your Excellency should determine how you will use me, I would respectfully request your attention to a letter in reference to me which General Stoneman kindly offered to write.[3] Should you determine to take me with you, the order to join you will be, as soon as received, promptly and gladly complied with. I can be spared by General Stoneman from my present duties in about twenty days, probably sooner.[4]

With sincere wishes for your continued health and success, on which depend the life and prosperity of the whole nation, and renewed assurances of my earnest desire to serve you.

I have the honor to be, Very respectfully,
Your obedient servant R. Morrow

His Excellency,
The President of the United States,
Washington, D.C.

ALS, DLC-JP.

1. Morrow (1846–1873), the son of banker Samuel Morrow, had risen from captain to brevet colonel in the volunteer ranks. Laura E. Luttrell, tr., *United States Census 1850 for Knox County, Tennessee* (Knoxville, 1949), 51; 1860 Census, Tenn., Knox, 1st Dist., 96; WPA, "Tennessee, Knox, Tombstone Records: Old Gray Cemetery" (Typescript [Nashville], 1938), 86; Powell, *Army List*, 494.

2. Ambrose E. Burnside, John M. Schofield, and George Stoneman.

3. Stoneman wrote to Johnson on June 8: "I know of no one amongst all my acquaintances who I can more highly recomd. or who I consider more worthy of reward." Stoneman to Johnson, June 8, 1865, Johnson Papers, LC.

4. On June 15 Johnson responded: "When you get ready you will come to Washington and I will try to make some arrangement that will suit you." Although Morrow replied that he could leave on June 22 if the President would send him orders, which Johnson did, Morrow had not yet arrived in Washington by July 8, when a telegram asking his whereabouts was forwarded to Stoneman. Morrow became one of Johnson's

secretaries in mid-July. Johnson to Morrow, June 15, 1865; Reuben D. Mussey to Morrow, June 18, 1865; Mussey to Stoneman, July 8, 1865, Tels. Sent, President, Vol. 2 (1865), RG107, NA; Morrow to Johnson, June 17, 1865, Tels. Recd., President, Vol. 4 (1865–66), RG107, NA.

From A.O.P. Nicholson[1]

Columbia Tenn June 4th 1865

President Johnson
Dear Sir:

I hope you will pardon this intrusion upon your time and attention. I know how greatly you are oppressed with matters of national importance and hence how annoying to you must be the minor individual affairs of those who approach you with their personal concerns. Notwithstanding the painful embarrassment of my situation, I should not add to your annoyance, but for one sentence in your late Proclamation—I refer to the *Proviso*, in which special applications are promised attention. According to my understanding of the 12th excepted class, my case falls within its provisions; tho' some others, who are similarly situated, take a different view of its meaning. You are aware, that I am under indictment for Conspiracy, and that I am under bail to appear and answer the charge, at the Oct. Term of the court. Altho' I am not in *actual custody* yet in legal contemplation I think I am in *legal custody* and therefore embraced in the 12th excepted class. Others insist that the true interpretation of the language confines its meaning to *actual custody*, and therefore that I may lawfully apply for the benefits of the amnesty, and plead it in bar of the indictment. Upon the supposition, that my construction is the true one, I desire to be considered as making a special application for pardon for whatever offence I am charged with, or of which I may be guilty. I am ignorant as to the specific facts, for which I am under indictment, but I assume that facts were sworn to, which rendered my guilt, at least probable, in the estimation of the grand jury. Whatever the facts sworn to were I desire to be allowed to meet and repel by your special pardon. At the suggestion of Mr. Church[2] I enclosed to you[3] a petition addressed to the late President Lincoln, but I am not advised as to whether you ever received my letter. If so I hope you will allow me to refer you to that document as my present application. If it never reached you, and it is necessary for me to send another, I will be obliged if you will let me know. Of course if my construction of the Proclamation is incorrect, I would thank you to let me know that fact, and upon getting that information, I should at once proceed to avail myself of Amnesty.

I repeat that I trouble you with my individual concerns with much reluctance and I throw myself upon your indulgence for thus troubling you. You are aware that my son Alfred has been a prisoner for nearly two years at Johnson's Island. It grieved me not to find in your Proc-lamation some provision which would enable him to obtain his release. He writes to us that he, with other prisoners, had applied for the privi-lege of taking the oath, and being released. May I so far trespass on your kindness as to ask your attention to his case. I submit my own case and that of my son to your clemency and anxiously await the result.[4]

Very Respectfully Your obt sevt.

A. O. P. Nicholson

P.S. Pardon me for adding that I have a half-brother Col. Wm. M. Voorhies,[5] who is a prisoner at Johnson's Island. He has made appli-cation for the privilege of taking the oath. May I ask your kind consid-eration of his application.

Very truly yours A.O.P.N.

ALS, DNA-RG94, Amnesty Papers (M1003, Roll 50), Tenn., A.O.P. Nicholson.

1. Johnson's old friend and former U.S. senator.
2. M. C. C. Church, former Nashville editor.
3. See Letter from A.O.P. Nicholson, March 28, 1865, *Johnson Papers*, 7: 540.
4. The senior Nicholson was pardoned by order of the President on August 28, 1865. Alfred was presumably freed under General Orders No. 109, June 6, 1865, which pro-vided for the release, upon taking an oath of allegiance, of all imprisoned Confederate army personnel with the rank of captain and under. No individual pardon for him has been found. Docket of Pardon Cases, Vol. B, p. 20, RG204, NA; *OR*, Ser. 2, Vol. 8: 641.
5. Voorhies (1815–1896), colonel, 48th Tenn. Inf., CSA, was the son of Nicholson's mother and her second husband, Garrett Voorhies. Although Voorhies wrote on his own behalf to Johnson on June 18, 1865, no pardon date has been found. Jill K. Garrett, ed., *Confederate Soldiers and Patriots of Maury County, Tennessee* (Columbia, Tenn., 1940), 344; Amnesty Papers (M1003, Roll 51), Tenn., William M. Voorhies, RG94, NA.

From Thomas Shackelford

June 4, 1865, Near Demopolis, Ala.; ALS, DLC-JP.

Mississippian, claiming to have been a unionist threatened with arrest, and whose plantation was severely damaged by Confederates, wants appointment as judge, marshal, or circuit court clerk in Mississippi. Reminds Johnson of their train conversation in May 1861, in which Shackelford expressed his "ab-horrence of the heresy of secession" and his belief that Lincoln would not be able to interfere with slavery in the states. Quoting Johnson at length as he remembered it, he notes: "You remarked to me 'We had a decided majori[t]y in both houses of Congress opposed to the supposed policy of the Administra-tion and that if the Southern Members had remained in their Seats, we could have had a frolic through Lincolns administration.'" He cites Johnson as say-ing "that the people would volunteer fast enough—now—(when they knew nothing of war) . . . but when the cold & bloody realities of it, were upon them—they would desert," and "that there was an antagonism between the Slave owner, and the poor . . . that the poor man disliked the negro and his prejudice extended to his master." Remembers Johnson's recounting that when he was governor, "a poor man came hurriedly into your office, one morning and desired you to give him a gun from the State Arsenal," wanting it "to shoot a d——d negro fellow, who had been stealing his turkies. . . . You advised him to go home catch the negro & then he could get pay for his turkies." The man "dissatisfied and breathing vengeance against the negro & his master" was, according to Johnson, an illustration of "this prejudice against the negro & his owner by the poor and illiterate non slave holder." Recalls the threat to Johnson's life in Lynchburg, when the letter writer did not leave his seat, remaining with Johnson until Greeneville and Johnson's departure from the train. [Shackelford did not receive a federal appointment.]

To Edwin M. Stanton

Washington, D.C., June 4th, 1865.

Hon E M Stanton Secretary of War
Sir:

General Ewell[1] cannot be paroled or permitted to take the Oath of Amnesty at present.

At a proper time let him apply for a Pardon and if the facts given in his application are deemed sufficient one will be granted.

As to permitting Mrs General Ewell[2] to pay General Ewell a visit while in prison you will exercise your discretion.

I do not understand Mrs General Ewell as being under arrest now[3] in Saint Louis but permitted to go at large—though not to return to Nashville Tenn.

If they were to go beyond the limits of the United States and there remain it would no doubt be the best disposition we could make of them at this time.[4]

Very Truly Yours Andrew Johnson

LS, DNA-RG107, Lets. Recd., EB12 President 2406 (1865).
   1. Confederate General Richard S. Ewell, imprisoned at Fort Warren.
   2. Johnson's former friend, Lizinka C. Brown, who had married Ewell in 1863.
   3. When she left St. Louis for Nashville in April, Stanton had ordered her arrest and return to St. Louis. See *Johnson Papers*, 7: 601; Basler, *Works of Lincoln*, 8: 372.
   4. The secretary of war had forwarded to the President all of Lizinka's correspondence, including letters of application for parole or amnesty written to Grant and to Montgomery Blair.

From Samuel D. Baldwin

Nashville Tennessee June 5th 1865.

To his excellency Andrew Johnson
President of the United States;
Dear Sir:

It is but just, that you should receive the congratulations of your admirers on your accession to your illustrious position, no matter how much your predecessor be lamented. In common with many of my friends, I believe you were called of God to preserve a democratic government to *mankind*, not only in form but in fact. In you, thank God, the people have a representative, the States a guardian, "the American

empire" a president, the rebels mercy; and (I hope) the despotisms of
Europe the predicted "*Rod of Iron.*" My *faith* in the final unity of our
country never faltered; my *conduct* has been controlled by duty to those
I wished to save, by the final interests of religion rather than those of
civil polity, leaving the management of political matters where it exclusively belongs, with the people, the laity.

The laity and the preachers of our church throughout the south wish,
promptly to avail themselves of your proffered amnesty and under it to
reinstate their church relations and to pass resolutions of fidelity to the
government, as soon as possible. To do this the restoration of their
churches and church property is essential as without these they have
no place of meeting. Can you not order the restoration of all? Certainly
by so doing you risk nothing and may win thousands of friends and do
great good.

Most respectfully Yours S. D. Baldwin.

P.S.   Our trustees called on the new preacher[1] sent by Bishop Simpson[2] to McKendree church, and he said:

1st That your decission did not revoke that of Mr Stanton:

2nd That he would not give up the property without *your* special
order:

3d That he would not give it up even *with it.*[3]

S.D.B.

P.S. Your opinion on the following questions is greatly desired by
many.

1st Are great consolidated national churches desirable in a *free*
government?

2nd Do not great hierarchies tend to great national despotisms as did
the national church of Rome?

3d Is the reunion of the two great methodist hierarchies of America
desirable in view of the religious liberty of our country: as a duality will
they not neutralize any despotic tendancies, either civil or religious,
rather than as a unity?

S.D.B.

ALS, DLC-JP.
1. Allen A. Gee (b. c1828), a prewar pastor at LaPorte, Ind., had been superintendent of northern missionary work at Nashville. 1860 Census, Ind., LaPorte, City of
LaPorte, 46; Ralph E. Morrow, *Northern Methodism and Reconstruction* (East Lansing,
Mich., 1956), 46, 68.
2. Matthew Simpson.
3. See also Telegram to Matthew Simpson, August 10; Letter from Simpson, August
16; Letter from Allen A. Gee, August 23, 1865.

From Thomas Cottman

June 5, 1865, West Point, N.Y.; ALS, DLC-JP.

An associate of J. Madison Wells asserts that, on the basis of his observations in New York and Philadelphia, "All the conservative element of the country will enter actively upon an open support of the Government." Confident that "the good citizens" will "rally to your support as they did to General Jackson," Cottman believes that "prudence & policy require a little delay" before the commencement of public demonstrations in support of the President— although many are "very eager for a public expression of their sympathies or affinities"—and expresses his pleasure that the "small pestiferous element" of Radicals in Louisiana has been rendered powerless by the removal of General Banks.

From Andrew G. Curtin

June 5, 1865, Harrisburg, Pa.; LS, PHarH.

In his concern about the discharge of volunteers, the Pennsylvania governor makes two points: 1) that men were being paid only to the day they arrived at camp for discharge and were not receiving pay if their muster out was not imminent, and 2) that recruits had received only one-third of the $100 bounty at the time of their enlistments and were to receive the remainder at their discharge. Present *modus operandi*, however, to make only partial payment "because the government does not require their services for the full term . . . appears to be a breach of contract." The bounty had been offered by the government "as an inducement to *enlist*, not as additional pay for services rendered."

From Benjamin B. French

June 5, 1865, Washington, D.C.; LS, DNA-RG59, Misc. Lets., 1789–1906 (M179, Roll 225).

Commissioner of public buildings at Washington reports that, in compliance with the civil and diplomatic appropriation act of the previous summer providing for a renovation of "the old Hall of the House of Representatives" into a memorial statuary hall, the "*entire Hall* is completed and stands ready to receive such statuary as the States may send." Suggests that the President "cause a circular to be printed and sent to the Executive of each state," soliciting, in compliance with said act, two statues of deceased citizens "illustrious for their historic renown or from distinguished civic or military services."

From Huntsville, Alabama, Citizens

June 5, [1865], Huntsville, Ala.; Mem, DLC-JP.

"Manufactores, Machanics" and other citizens, twenty-six in all, feeling "the time has come when original union men can without hazard express their undeviating loyalty to the old Flag and their undiminished love of the old Government," send resolutions giving thanks for the restoration of peace, requesting continuation of some military presence subordinate to a provisional governor, promising to aid in the loyal restoration of the state, and expressing sorrow on the death of Lincoln and support for his successor.

From Richard M. Mitchell

June 5, 1865, Chicago, Ill.; ALS, DLC-JP.

Believing that "those who advocate negro suffrage have gone from the extreem of slavery to the extreem of making them our masters," Mitchell, "a Republican ever since the formation of that party at Pittsburgh," suggests that the "question be one of education instead of color. Let those only vote who can read and write. Let the same law that gives the right to vote to the few blacks that can read and write, take away that privilege from the whites who cannot."

Reception of Alabama Delegates [1]

[June 5, 1865][2]

The president's reception of the joint delegations was cordial and hearty. He entered at once upon the subject of the restoration of civil government to the State of Alabama, and presented his views and the future policy to be pursued in relation to States hitherto insurrectionary, in a methodical, and business-like manner, concluding, after a conference of an hour and half, with a suggestion that the members of the delegation should consult together and propose or recommend such persons from among the friends of the National Government in Alabama, any one of whom might be acceptable for the appointment of provisional governor, to guide him in the appointment of such officer.[3]

He desired in the first place to know that the gentlemen of the delegation came as representatives of the people, otherwise they could not be recognized. He was emphatic in the declaration that a delegation from any organization in the State of Alabama, in any way connected with the old order of things, during the period of the rebellion, could not be recognized by the executive, nor any propositions for restoration, from such party or organization be for a moment entertained. He had been called a demagogue, he said, and had come in for no little share of political censure from various political enemies—nevertheless, he was still the true friend of the people, for whose benefit and protection, they themselves had created the government. He came from the people himself and desired nothing which should not conduce to the public welfare. He had found himself suddenly and unexpectedly occupying the highest official position in the gift of the American people. He had but one other ambition, and that was, to go out of his present position, with his whole country once restored and all her people once again prosperous and happy.

The president added that, he cherished the kindest feeling towards the people of the Southern States. He was a Southern man himself, and, he had been a slave owner. Slavery was dead, beyond resurrection. The war had effectually disposed of that institution and the sooner the people of the South should come to the realization of this fact, the more readily and the more harmoniously would they come to accept the new order of things, and assist in the re-establishment of civil government. He differed from those persons who bewailed the condition of the Southern States. He thought the future of the South more brilliant than ever. The dawn of her prosperity had only begun.

The president seemed desirous of impressing upon the minds of the members of the delegation the determination of the government not to entrust the management of its affairs to its enemies. None but men who had proved themselves true and devoted friends to the Union should be appointed to offices of trust and responsibility. With regard to the policy of the administration towards the States hitherto in rebellion against the general government, he would refer them to his North Carolina proclamation, which, he said, to use a homely expression, was a specimen brick of his future policy, the question of suffrage to be left with the people of a State themselves.[4]

Augusta Constitutionalist, July 8, 1865.

1. Alabamians, headed by Joseph C. Bradley and Lewis E. Parsons, presented Johnson with resolutions, adopted at a May 11 meeting in Montgomery, in favor of restoring the state to the Union and of the President's permitting the legislature to call for a constitutional convention. *Savannah Daily Herald*, June 7, 1865; see Petition from Alabama Citizens, May 8, 1865.

2. Although there were at least two Alabama delegations in the capital having interviews with the President during the first two weeks of June, this is probably the report of the meeting mentioned by Parsons and Bradley as being "on Monday last." See Letter from Parsons and Bradley, June 10, 1865.

3. Among those recommended by the delegates for the position of provisional governor were Parsons, William H. Smith, and John J. Seibels. *New York Times*, June 9, 1865; *New Orleans Picayune*, June 13, 14, 1865; Alabama Citizens to Johnson, June 6, 1865, Johnson Papers, LC. See also Letter from Parsons and Bradley, June 10, 1865, and Letter from Seibels, June 30, 1865.

4. Although the President concluded his long, friendly interview by leaving his audience "with the firm conviction that Andrew Johnson was the true friend of the Southern people," in a follow-up meeting on June 8, he indicated he had not reached a decision on the "propositions urged by the delegation." *Augusta Constitutionalist*, July 8, 1865; *New York Times*, June 9, 1865.

From Samuel R. Snyder[1]

Petersburgh Ind June 5th 1865

His Excency Andrew Johnson
President of the United States

Dear Sir I am only a private citizen & have no aspirations to any thing more than an american citizen but have as great an interest in the welfare of our common country as any of you & consequently take the liberty to address you as our honored Chief and while I claim not to know more about how to deal with traitors than your honor yet I will say I differ with you about the treatment of our Indiana traitors for certainly if there is any men in our State who deserve the halter certainly Bowles & Miligan did & as far as my knowledge extends you never done an act in your life that was so much disapproved by loyal men as to commute their punishment to imprisonment for life for who does not know men of wealth can find means to get rid of that kind of punishment pretty soon. It was the principal fault of our late lamented chief that he was too lenient. But from the treatment you have had at the hands of the Rebels & from your declarations since your elevation we had a right to expect a little more nerve about you. Now you know that it is an old adage that small rogues get punished while great rogues go free & while it is not your province to pass sentence on crime it certainly is wrong to step in to save the lives of such monsters in crime as these with many others even in the northern states. My Dear sir is all our expenditure of blood & treasure all the sufferings of our brave boys in the field & hospital (to say nothing of the thousands that have been starved to death in Southern prisons) to go for nothing. Are we to receive back with open arms the murderers of our sons & brothers, and forgive all their crimes & thereby make rebelion honorable? Now while President Lincoln had no warmer friend than your humble servant yet I did believe that in the Providence of God he had filled his mission as we all know that he was too lenient to punish rebels according to their deserts. Now my dear sir when a man has had a fair & impartial trial by his peers & is sentenced to death or banishment or whatever his sentence is I think the most popular course for you and in most cases you would be sustained by the laws of God would be to see to it that the laws are obeyed.

It would certainly be imprudent to pursue a milk and water course with rebels now when the rebelion is crushed. Our peace must be no patch work but you have rightly said on several ocasions that treason must be made odious & now that the arch traitor Jefferson Davis is about to be put on trial if he has a fair trial & is sentenced to death for Heavens sake don't step between him and justice. I agree with you that all the rebels that were ignorant and were misled into the rebelion should be gently dealt with but certainly all well informed and designing rascals should be severely punished and if they are treated otherwise I would not give a fig for our government. We will neither be respected at home or abroad & we will still be nursing a viper that will soon sting us again. President Jackson said the greatest mistake of his life was not having had John C Calhound hung & our experience has abundantly prooved the truth of the assertion & now with all these facts before our eyes and after having reaped the bitter fruits of that mistake let us not be guilty of a like blunder. I have no feelings of revenge towards any one but I do think it would be for the good of our country that all leading well informed rebels should be handled without gloves. I am told that in some neighborhoods in Tennessee where the loyal inhabitants who had to flee their country and are now returning their old rebelious neighbors treat them with utmost contempt which shows that the power to do harm is only wanting & not the will & in my judgment it never will be otherwise so long as we are so tender with traitors and as far as the case of Bowles & Miligan are concerned I need hardly tell you that you have made more enemies than friends in this community.

I am about your own age & altho I have not had the opportunities politicaly that you have had I thought I had a right to shew you mine opinion.

But shall remain as ever
Yours Samuel R Snyder

ALS, DLC-JP.
1. Snyder (b. c1812) was a miller. 1860 Census, Ind., Pike, Petersburgh, 125.

From Alexander N. Wilson [1]

Nashville, Tenn. June 5th 1865.
Andrew Johnson, President of the United States,
My Dear Sir,

On reaching Nashville, I learn that several men from Georgia have passed through on their way to Washington. Hon. Joshua Hill goes as an applicant directly perhaps, for the position of Provisional Gov.; with him, Wm. F. Herring[2] of Atlanta, an ass, a lick-spittle, an infernal secessionist. He never adhered to any thing that required manliness. J. W. Duncan,[3] of Atlanta, who was an old democrat, a good Union man, and has the propensity to find out evry thing and make himself usefull to the persons in authority. R. Peters[4] of Atlanta, originally from Philadelphia, a rich man, who, though, no politician gave freely of his money to fight against Secession, while it did good, but seemingly, went over to the enemy, after Georgia seceded, and blowed for Jeff's crowd; he is a humble penitent, and a worthy & sensible man.

Judge O. A. Lockrane[5] of Macon, Georgia is one who will show for himself, an outspoken Irishman. He filled an important mission as Judge before I left, having decided against Conscription, the impressment of property in any shape and against putting Foreigners into the Confederate service, and in the Spring of 1863, determined to resign his position because he was holding an office within a government, which, he totally abhorred, but was prevailed upon to remain in office by the Union men, to shield them so far as he could.

The day after I left Washington, I met Isaac Scott,[6] of whom I spoke suggesting him as a proper man for Gov. He said the Rebellion had ruined him physically, and he could not entertain the idea of undertaking the labor.

It seems to me, that if the Governors in prescribing, who shall vote for members of state Conventions, require no *other oath* than the one in your general Proclamation, the Rebels will out of sympathy for each other and hatred to Union men, be likely to elect their own men, to all the State offices and "run the machines."

Mr. S. D. Dickson,[7] an old citizen of Savannah, Geo, a very worthy man & a Substintial one, will be likely to write you items from Geo.

I commend to your most favorable consideration Amherst W. Stone,[8] of Georgia, a genuine Union man, who will be an applicant for the office of District Attorney of United States Court for Geo. He is a good Lawyer of fifteen year practice, and will be faithfull to the interests of the Government.

Yours truly Alex. N. Wilson

ALS, DLC-JP.

1. Wilson (c1829–fl1888), a teacher who lived in Atlanta on the eve of the war, was appointed collector of internal revenue at Savannah (1865–73, 1885) and subsequently served in the same city as appraiser and as clerk, U.S. customs (1875–81). 1860 Census, Ga., Fulton, Atlanta, 2nd Ward, 60; *U.S. Off. Reg.* (1865–79); Savannah directories (1873–88).

2. Herring (b. c1834) was a clothier. 1860 Census, Ga., Fulton, Black Hull Dist., 239.

3. John W. Duncan (c1822–1869), an attorney, had been a delegate to several prewar Democratic conventions and served as a Confederate depositary in Atlanta during the war. 1850 Census, Ga., Baldwin, Exclusive of Milledgeville, 227; *Atlanta Constitution*, Jan. 6, 1869; Isaac W. Avery, *The History of the State of Georgia from 1850–1881* (New York, 1881), 33, 109–10, 121. See Letter from Duncan, June 14, 1865.

4. Richard Peters (1810–1889), civil engineer, in 1835 moved to Georgia to work on the Georgia Railroad. While a resident of Atlanta, he suggested the city's name, built the first flour mill in the state, and developed 1,500 acres in Gordon County. Although an opponent of secession, he organized a blockade-running company to aid the Confederacy. William J. Northen, ed., *Men of Mark in Georgia* (7 vols., Atlanta, 1906–12), 3: 495–98.

5. Osborne A. Lochrane (1829–1887) studied law and established a practice in Macon. A Confederate judge during the war, he later became judge of the circuit court and of the state supreme court (1871–72). Ibid., 203–5.

6. Scott (b. c1810) was a Macon merchant and banker. 1850 Census, Ga., Bibb, Macon, 286; *Savannah Herald*, June 15, 1865.

7. Samuel D. Dickson (c1803–fl1871), grocer-merchant, was briefly employed in the Savannah Customs House (1870). There is no record of his writing Johnson. 1860 Census, Ga., Chatham, 3rd Dist., Savannah, 197; Savannah directories (1867–71).

8. Stone (c1824–fl1878), a Vermont-born Atlanta lawyer, while in self-imposed exile in the north, was arrested in New York City in January 1864, "on suspicion of being a rebel emissary" and confined at Fort LaFayette until July, when he was released without trial. After the war he held a number of minor positions in Savannah, and in the mid-1870s was an associate justice of the Colorado supreme court. 1860 Census, Ga., Fulton, Atlanta, 4th Ward, 138; Schofield to Secretary of Treasury, Dec. 21, 1868, Lets. Sent to President, Vol. 8 (M421, Roll 4), RG107, NA; Savannah directories (1866–71); Denver directories (1876–78).

From James B. Bingham

Memphis, Tenn., June 6, 1865.

Dear Governor:

I have only time to congratulate you. Thus far every thing goes right. Your amnesty gives satisfaction to all fair-minded men, and you have struck the true keynote on reconstruction. Your position on the question of negro suffrage is impregnable. It belongs, under the constitution to the States. Wendell Phillips, Greeley & Chase will kick against that in vain. The country will sustain you. I find a great re-action going on in your favor. Fellows who used to curse and damn you begin now to talk sweet about you, and to do you justice. Lincoln never was as popular with Tennesseeans as you are to-day; and I believe what is true of Tennesseeans is equally so of the people of the loyal States. I enclose you a few articles from the *Bulletin* showing how we argue the question down here. I call your attention to the article suggesting Maynard for Catron's place.[1] I really think it would suit Maynard, and believe that he will reflect credit upon you in the position as the appointing power.

Yours, truly, in great haste,

J. B. Bingham

P.S. Please attend to Leoague's application[2] as soon as you have time, and do not entirely forget mine.[3]

Yours JBB

ALS, DLC-JP.

1. Bingham's *Bulletin* of the 6th carried a notice of Catron's death and the editor's recommendation of Horace Maynard for the vacancy.

2. See Letter from Bingham, May 28, 1865.

3. Requesting Johnson's aid in obtaining the West Tennessee marshal's post since September 1864, Bingham, when finally nominated for the post in April 1867, found his appointment rejected by the Senate. Appt. Bk., 4: 227, 228, Ser. 6B, Johnson Papers, LC; *U.S. Off. Reg.* (1865), 117.

From Charles O. Faxon

Clarksville Tenn June 6th 1865

Hon Andrew Johnson Prest U S.

Dr Sir:

You will no doubt be somewhat surprised at the resumption of a correspondence so long since discontinued,[1] but I trust that you will, in consideration of the relations which formerly existed between us, be disposed to read what I write with patience, and that you will permit your judgment to be controlled by that mercy which should always "Season justice."

You are no doubt aware that for the past two years I have been a resident of the revolted States. I have just returned to my family and my home. A brief statement of the causes which drove me for the time to abandon my family and my home will show you that I was moved by circumstances beyond my power to control.

You will remember perhaps how earnestly I struggled to prevent the conflict between and the separation of the sections. How I fought secession in my paper (the Jeffersonian) and out of it, and that I sustained your course in the Senate against Davis Benjamin, Wigfall & Co. until that period when a popular phrensy took possession of the whole people and carried the State out of the Union in a tempest of popular enthusiasm. I was overwhelmed by the fury of the storm and went down before it. I was the Postmaster at Clarksville and was required to turn over my office to the new government and Davis and his advisers would not permit me to retain the office because I had adhered to you and to the cause of the Union until so late a day. I was required to keep the office going for a few days until my successor could be appointed. In a short time my successor was appointed and I vacated the office. But it is a question whether or not my occupancy of the office for the few days I did occupy it under the orders of the Confederate government, though I never held its commission, as for the reason assigned, had any chance of obtaining it, does not place me among the exceptions mentioned in your recent amnesty proclamation.

For fourteen months after the fall of Donelson I remained in the country in the vicinity of Clarksville. I was kept in constant apprehension by the attempts of the goverment agents to arrest me, and in the Spring of 1863, seeing little prospect of being permitted to remain with my family in peace, and having exhausted all of my means I proceeded South to obtain employment in my business (Printing). Soon after my arrival there I obtained employment as foreman of the office of the "Rebel" at Chattanooga and up to the fall of Selma had occupied that position continuously.[2] As I have determined to be candid with you I will state that during that time I wrote much for the paper, and a portion of the time—while at Marietta—had the exclusive editorial control. I was entirely without resources, had a large family of small children depending upon my industry. I had offended the authorities of the U S goverment and was compelled to rely upon my trade and profession for a support. I am still thus dependent, and I desire to be relieved of any liabilities which I may have incurred by my connection with this unfortunate war in order that my energies and talents may have full play. I feel that with my long experience in the editorial profession, and my earnest desire to efface as rapidly as may be all traces of the devastations of the last four years, I can be, if unmolested, a useful member of society. If you can do so consistently with the duties of your exalted station I desire that you will interpose the shield of your clemency between me and the responsibilities I have incurred.

I shall await your response to this communication with anxiety. I am left financially prostrate by the war with a large family upon my hands. I cannot embark in business so long as the avenging Nemesis of the law is dogging my footsteps, threatening to halt me at every turn. At present I have no plans for the future but cannot long remain idle. Trusting that this may command your early attention and elicit a favorable response[3]

I am with high respect
Your obedient servt C. O. Faxon

ALS, DNA-RG94, Amnesty Papers (M1003, Roll 18), Ga., C. O. Faxon.

1. The last correspondence from Faxon found in the Johnson Papers, LC, is dated March 20, 1861.

2. Established in August 1862, the *Chattanooga Rebel* became a very popular southern organ. The office was moved to Marietta, Ga., in August 1863, when Federal forces approached Chattanooga, then to Selma, Ala., by way of Griffin, Ga., as Gen. William T. Sherman moved south. James W. Livingood, "The Chattanooga *Rebel*," ETHS *Pubs.*, 39 (1967): 42–55.

3. Endorsed: "Needs no pardon."

From William Johnson[1]

New York, June 6th 1865

Prest. Johnson

You *pretend* to leave the right of Sufferage to the States. Yet none are so simple as not to see in the North Carolina Proclamation that *you* take it from the States & say who *shall* & who shall *not* vote.[2]

The enormity of your crime is that you put a ballot into the hands of Rebels stained with the blood of *loyal* men, & you deny it to loyal men who have fought for the *right* of *Suferage*.

You *pretend* to be devoted to the fundamental basis of our Government viz "Consent of the governed" yet you (not the State) particularize who shall, & who shall not vote, & deprive 3,500,000 loyal blacks from any voice.

You pretend to *protect* loyal men from Rebels, yet you turn over 3,500,000 loyal people to the *absolute* control of Rebels.

You pretend, & say you will make Treason odious. The way you do it is by giving Rebels votes & denying it to loyal men!

You are commiting the *blackest* crime of the Ages.

Yours in Sorrow William Johnson
35 E 12th St N.Y.

ALS, DLC-JP.

1. Probably the William Johnson listed as a broker in city directories. He was using the stationery of L.G. and J.O. Quigley, brokers at 26 Broad Street. New York City directories (1865–68).

2. Said proclamation specified that only those people who took the oath (as found in Amnesty Proclamation of May 29) and who were qualified voters "as prescribed by the Constitution and laws of the State of North Carolina in force immediately before the 20th day of May, A.D. 1861," could vote. *The Constitutions of the Several States . . . in the Year 1859* (New York, c1879), 263.

From George W. Jones

June 6, 1865, Washington, D.C.; ALS, DNA-RG94, Amnesty Papers (M1003, Roll 49), Tenn., George W. Jones.

Following a personal interview, one of Johnson's oldest friends applies for pardon, being excluded from the May 29 proclamation because of his service in the Confederate Congress. Suggesting that his character and public service before the rebellion "were as well known and understood by you as any other living human being," he refers to his loyalty to the federal government as having been "uniform, consistent, and unwavering." He had labored "diligently and faithfully for its preservation and perpetuation until hostilities *existed*," but "bourn down, along and into the terrible current which was sweeping through the country," following Lincoln's call for troops, "I did not lead, but went with my friends and section," believing that the "more united, harmonious and firm the people of the southern or rebel states, the sooner the conflict would terminate." Refusing to run again for the Congress in 1863, he spent the remainder of the war in Georgia and North Carolina. [Pardoned by order of the President on June 16, 1865.]

From Sterling Y. McMasters

June 6, 1865, St. Paul, Minn.; ALS, DLC-JP.

Former U.S. chaplain, and native of North Carolina, knowing "something of the character of the negro," writes: "We all consent that Slavery must now cease; but you are going to have trouble, with, the Freedmen; and, this, trouble will be increased by the ultra views of ultra men, of both extremes. . . . you have struck a noble keynote; and I think, the heart of the nation will respond in unison with it." McMasters encloses a copy of his sermon "preached on the national Fast day" and asks if he may send "a new book, little known in America;—'Earl Gray's administration in Jamaica &c.,'" in which the author relates his involvement with "the Freedmen of the West Indies." McMasters describes Gray as a "most sanguine abolitionist," whose experiences forced him to "modify ma[n]y of his views, in regard to the capability of the negro of self-government."

From Carl Schurz

Bethlehem Pa. June 6th 1865.

To his Excellency A. Johnson, President of the United States.

Dear Sir,

The passage in your Executive order concerning the Provisional Government of North Carolina, to which I had the honor to call your attention at our last interview, has, as I then anticipated, been generally interpreted as a declaration of policy on your part adverse to the introduction of negro suffrage.[1] So far it is treated with calmness by most of the papers, but it is sure to become a subject of general and fierce discussion—not only among extremists but among men of moderate views—as soon as the old pro-slavery and disloyal element, I mean the oath taking rebels, will have reasserted their influence in the Southern States. This will be the case as soon as, under the present system, any independent political action is allowed in the South, as it is now in Virginia. The question of negro suffrage will then become the burning issue and is likely to have great influence upon the attitude of political parties and upon the relations between Congress and the Executive. It will depend upon events whether any difference of opinion will assume the character of direct opposition to the Administration, and events, if we may judge from present symptoms, bid fair to give sharpness to the controversy.

This would be an unfortunate thing. It is important that your views on this point should not be misunderstood by the country. There will soon be an opportunity for an open declaration. The line of policy you have followed with regard to North Carolina, cannot be applied to her neighbor South Carolina. The reason is simple. The elective franchise and eligibility are limited by the old South Carolina Constitution by a property qualification consisting in the ownership of a certain quantity of land and a certain number of slaves. Suppose then, when the turn of South Carolina comes, you order that, whereas the property qualification prescribed by the old Constitution of South Carolina can no longer remain in force in consequence of the emancipation of the slaves, and there being no other rule in the laws of that State to guide the Executive, the task of restoring the State of S.C. be placed in the hands of her *whole* people, and that at the election of delegates to a convention *all* loyal inhabitants of S.C. without distinction be permitted to vote. The reasons for this course will be clear and acceptable to every fair minded man, and, as the order applies to *South Carolina*, not even the Democrats will find fault with it.

This will be consistent with the theory that secession never carried the State out of the Union, and also with the fundamental principle, that all constitutive action must proceed from the people. In theory as well as fact, this procedure will be far more *democratic* than the policy you have adopted with regard to North Carolina. It may be argued without doing violence to the rules of logic that, although secession never carried any of the States out of the Union, it did break up the existing State Governments and completely suspended the constitutional relations of the seceded States with the Government of the United States. This was a revolutionary proceeding, which placed the Government of the U.S. in a condition, and imposed upon it a task, not foreseen in the Constitution. Nor does the Constitution point out any remedies except those lying within the sphere of the military power. Strictly speaking the appointment of a civil governor for a State by the Executive of the U.S. is an extraconstitutional act; nor has according to the accepted constitutional theory, the President the power to order a Governor of a State to call a convention of the people. You rely upon the implied powers and obey the necessity arising from extraordinary and unforeseen circumstances. Now I ask, is not in this extraconstitutional condition of things the most natural, and also *the most democratic* remedy to be found in a direct appeal to the original source of sovereignty, the whole body of the people of a State? And in what way can that be done more effectually than by calling State conventions to be elected by *all* the inhabitants of the respective States without distinction of rank, property, or color, excluding only those who have disqualified themselves by acts of rebellion?

I think of elaborating these ideas and laying them before the public in a series of letters. By the time Congress meets, the necessity of taking a broad ground will probably have so far disclosed itself, that views like the above will be shared by a large majority of that body, and it would be very desirable to have a cordial understanding and cooperation established between that body and the Executive. When publishing those letters I should like to address them to you, unless it be disagreable to you. It would not commit you in any way, but prepare the public mind for what inevitably must come. Have you any objection to it?[2]

Meanwhile pardon me for saying, that, under existing circumstances, every measure which does not place the business of reconstruction upon the *broadest* ground, will, in my humble opinion, tend to increase the difficulties which necessarily must arise, and hamper your future action.

It seems you have dropped the idea of appointing some one to supervise and aid the political action of our military commanders in the South. I still think it would be an excellent arrangement for keeping the Government well informed of what is going on, for keeping the military commanders well advised of what is expected of them, for facilitating business generally and for preventing a great many mistakes which otherwise are very likely to be made.

I am, dear Sir, very truly and respectfully yours
C. Schurz

ALS, DLC-JP.

1. See Proclamation Establishing Government for North Carolina, May 29, 1865.

2. In response, Johnson invited Schurz to the White House on June 8. There the President proposed that the general make a tour of the South, an offer which, after some hesitation, Schurz accepted. The correspondence of the ensuing tour is found in *Advice*, 61–150.

From George A. Trenholm [1]

Columbia, S.C. June 6, 1865

To his Excellency Andrew Johnson,
President of the United States of America

The petition of George A Trenholm respectfully sheweth that he was a member of the late cabinet of Jefferson Davis, and by reason thereof is excluded from the benefit of the amnesty proclaimed on the twenty ninth day of May 1865. But it is provided by the same proclamation "that special application may be made to the President for pardon by any person belonging to the excepted classes, & that such clemency will be liberally extended as may be consistent with the facts of the case, & the peace & dignity of the United States."

Your petitioner was a member of the cabinet, as aforesaid, about nine months viz from July 1864 to April 1865. Upon the surrender of General Lee he regarded the struggle as ended, and having resigned his place, returned to Abbeville So Ca, & afterwards repaired to Columbia, in the same state. He made no attempt at flight or concealment, being resolved at once to submit to the authority of the United States, and conform to its policy & laws.

Your petitioner is prepared, when permitted, to take the oath prescribed by the amnesty proclamation, with the firm intent to abide by its terms religiously. He was a large owner of slaves, and entered immediately upon the execution of the plans of the Government, causing the members of his family, qualified to act, to enter into contracts with them. Your petitioner is persuaded it is an error to suppose that the change in the status of the negro laborer will be necessarily disastrous to the planting interest, but believes that the cordial and generous support and co-operation of the people in the measures adopted for its accomplishment is essential to ward off the dangers by which it is attended. He has endeavoured to act in this spirit.

Your petitioner has been very little in public life, and on every occasion it has been against his inclinations. His choice has always been in favor of private pursuits, and nearly his whole life has been devoted to commerce. He is profoundly attached to his country and deliberately chose to rely upon the clemency of the President, in preference to taking any chance that might end in expatriation. He conscientiously believes that if this petition is favorably received, and the proffered clemency extended to him, the Country will gain much by the influence of his example amongst his fellow citizens, and his efforts to promote the restoration of order, and to put in motion the slumbering elements of prosperity. Wherefore, your petitioner respectfully prays that he may be admitted to the benefit of the amnesty announced by the proclamation of 29 May 1865. And your petitioner will ever pray &c.[2]

G. A. Trenholm.

ALS, DNA-RG94, Amnesty Papers (M1003, Roll 47), S.C., George A. Trenholm.

1. Trenholm (1807–1876), wealthy Charleston merchant, supported secession, financed a flotilla during the war, and was the Confederacy's last secretary of the treasury. Wakelyn, BDC.

2. Arrested sometime after writing this letter, Trenholm was incarcerated at Fort Pulaski, Georgia, whence on August 10 and September 7 he appealed for release. He was paroled by special order in October 1865 and finally pardoned October 25, 1866. Amnesty Papers (M1003, Roll 47), S.C., George A. Trenholm, RG94, NA; House Ex. Docs., 39 Cong., 2 Sess., No. 31, pp. 4–8 (Ser. 1289); Richardson, Messages, 6: 352.

From Jesse R. Wikle

June 6, 1865, Cartersville, Ga.; ALS, DLC-JP.

A Georgia merchant, former rebel captain, and now acting secretary of a June 6 mass meeting of Cass County citizens, forwards resolves expressing a desire for a convention to elect a governor and reorganize the state, as well as their appreciation for relief and the restoration of order. Resolution 6 warns that blacks, in view of the recent "great Social change," must "remain with their former masters, who in most cases are their best friends" and suggests that the latter "institute as Soon as our destitute condition will allow a system of wages in money or in kind which retain the servants with them and thus avert evils which must otherwise accrue to themselves and families and the Country at large." Asserting that local inhabitants, who "gave an anti-secession majority in the County in 1861," were "dragged" into the war by "a set of political knaves," he concludes: "Our people yield, with scarcely an exception, a ready and cheerful obedience to the authorities of the United States," for they "now feel and see that the Government of the United States is the only power on earth that can give them adequate protection and a guarantee of their freedom and personal rights."

From John E. Wool

June 6, 1865, Troy, N.Y.; LS, DLC-JP.

Having noted that while mourning the loss of President Lincoln, the people "rejoice to find in his place a true patriot" who has "their entire confidence and support," General Wool suggests the enlistment of "a suitable guard and a sufficient number of faithful Aides-de-Camp" to protect the President from "rebel hate." Observes that while army generals are well guarded, "not one of these are half as much exposed to the Assassins dagger as yourself."

From John B. Castleman [1]

Indianapolis Ind. June 7th 1865

To the President of the U.S.
Sir.

In the Summer of the year 1862, being then less than Twenty one years of age and living near Lexington Kentucky, I was induced to engage in the Rebellion, and joined the Rebel Army. I continued in that service, and was arrested in Southern Indiana in the month of September 1864, and have been since that time a prisoner and held under charges for trial.[2] In what I did, I was led to believe, and at the time thought, I was doing my duty. I am now convinced that my action was wrong from the beginning, and that I have committed grievous errors.

For what is past, I can only express my sincere regret, and promise to strive by my future action to atone for it by faithful efforts to discharge my duty as a citizen of the United States.

With this preliminary statement, I desire now to ask that I may be permitted to take the Oath of Allegiance, and be released on such terms as may to you seem best. And if it is not possible or proper in your judgement that this should be done, I ask that I may be allowed to become a voluntary exile to some other country, for life or such shorter time, as may be deemed by you sufficient, Subject to such penalties for returning as may be imposed, and giving my obligation in such form as may be required, to observe strictly the terms of the order and to do no act of hostility in any way to the United States.

I hope it will be found consistent with your views of duty and of the public interests to grant my request.[3]

I am, Very Respectfully
Your Ob't Sv't J. B. Castleman.

ALS, DNA-RG107, Lets. Recd., Gen.-in-Chief, 66 EB13 (M494, Roll 81).

1. Castleman (1841–1918) rose to the rank of major while serving with John H. Morgan's command. After the war he commanded the Louisville Legion, an elite Kentucky militia unit, and was brevetted a brigadier general in the regular army for its service in Puerto Rico during the Spanish-American War. He also served as adjutant general of the state in the 1880s and again in 1900. *Who Was Who in America* (5 vols., Chicago, 1943–73), 1: 203; Perrin et al, *Kentucky*, 8A: 761; *Louisville Courier-Journal*, May 24, 1918.

2. Following Morgan's capture, Castleman made his way to Canada and was assigned by Jacob Thompson in August 1864 to take part in an expedition to free Confederate prisoners held in the Northwest. When the Sons of Liberty failed to deliver their promised support, the attempt collapsed. Subsequently, Castleman joined a small group that unsuccessfully attempted to burn army steamboats docked at St. Louis. He was arrested September 30, 1864, while planning yet another escapade, and held in the military prison at Indianapolis awaiting trial. John B. Castleman, *Active Service* (Louisville, Ky., 1917), 152–59, 172–74; Castleman to Johnson, Oct. 9, 1865, Amnesty Papers (M1003, Roll 25), Ky., John B. Castleman.

3. Johnson endorsed Gen. Alvin P. Hovey's recommendation that Castleman's request be granted, and in late June the prisoner was released into Canada. After more than a year abroad, Castleman's exile was rescinded by the President, but he received no individual pardon. Castleman to Johnson, June 7, 1865 (endorsements of Johnson and Hovey), Commissary General of Prisoners, Lets. Recd., RG249, NA; Castleman, *Active Service*, 188–205 passim.

From Thomas Ewing, Sr.[1]

No 12 N A Street Apl[June][2] 7th/65

To the President
Sir

I think the 10th exception to your proclamation of amnesty too extensive.[3] It will exclude about 50,000 young men in Maryland Kentucky & Missouri who were mere material of war—who never reasoned on the subject of allegience paramount or subordinate but were borne by the tide of fashion in their own confined circles into sympathy & cooperation with the rebellion. They are morally no more culpable than the like class in states which actually seceded & it were better that they—perhaps with a few marked exceptions—should be restored at once & suffered to engage in industrial pursuits, with a feeling of confidence & security.

I am very truly yours T. Ewing

ALS, DLC-JP.

1. Ewing (1789–1871), Ohio lawyer, had been twice elected U.S. senator, and briefly served as secretary of the treasury and of the interior. A conservative on reconstruction, he was nominated secretary of war (1868) by Johnson but was not confirmed by the Senate. *BDAC*.

2. According to a date stamp, this was "Received by the President June 8, 1865"; furthermore, Johnson was not yet President on April 7, and the Amnesty Proclamation, alluded to by Ewing, was not issued until May 29.

3. Special presidential pardon was required of those who left their homes within the jurisdiction of the United States and went into the Confederate states to aid the rebellion.

From James Harlan [1]

Washington D.C. June 7th 1865

To the President:

I feel it to be my duty to inform you that I cannot be responsible for the business of the Indian Bureau in the hands of the present incumbent Wm. P. Dole.[2]

If the President does not deem it best to appoint Hon. Mr. Edmonds[3] Com. *ad interim*, as requested by me on yesterday, I respectfully recommend the appointment, of Dennis N. Cooley.[4]

He is now Tax Commissioner for South Carolina—was Secretary of the Cong. Union Committee during the last Presidential Campaign. He is a man of correct habits, large business experience, unblemished reputation, and superior ability.

I most earnestly request the early attention of the President to this subject.

With the greatest respect, Your ob'd't Ser'vt, Jas. Harlan, Secretary of the Interior

ALS, DLC-JP.

1. Harlan, appointed secretary of the interior by Lincoln on March 9, 1865, had, by agreement with the late President, delayed his assumption of office until May 15.

2. Dole (1811–1889), New England native whose family migrated to Indiana, served as a Whig representative and senator. Relocating in Illinois in early 1850, he was a Lincoln supporter at the 1860 convention and was appointed commissioner in 1861, from which post he resigned in July 1865. Robert M. Kvasnicka and Herman J. Viola, eds., *The Commissioners of Indian Affairs, 1824–1977* (Lincoln, Neb., 1979), 89–96.

3. James M. Edmunds.

4. Cooley became commissioner of Indian affairs in July 1865, serving until the next year. Kvasnicka and Viola, *Commissioners*, 99–105.

From Mississippi and Tennessee Refugees

June 7, 1865, DeSoto, Ill.; LS, DNA-RG60, Appt. Files for Judicial Dists., Tenn., J. M. Jones.

Twenty-two Illinois residents, planning to return home and "feeling keenly the necessity of the laws being enforsed," recommend Lt. J. M. Jones of the 1st Middle Tenn. Inf., formerly a citizen of Corinth, Miss., for an appointment as marshal in north Mississippi or West Tennessee, if available, or "Such other office . . . as the Government may have at its disposal." Although he lost his business and residence, the first when rebels destroyed his printing office because of his Union sentiments, and the second when General Rosecrans was fortifying the town, petitioners suggest Jones's appointment "not So much as a Recompence for loss as for fitness for position," for he "cold have a good effect in Restoring Confidence in the Stability and equity of the administration of law as men of all parties have for him a high personal Regard." [Jones failed to receive a marshal's appointment in either Mississippi or Tennessee.]

From Martha Patterson

Nashville June 7 1865.

Hon Andrew Johnson Prest U.S.

I leave Cincinnati the morning seventeenth (17). Will there be a special car provided to take us from Cincinnati? All well.[1]

Martha Patterson

Tel, DLC-JP.
1. Johnson responded the same day: "The necessary arrangements will be made. I will telegraph you further." Tels. Sent, President, Vol. 2 (1865), RG107, NA.

From James S. Rollins

June 7, 1865, Columbia, Mo.; ALS, DLC-JP.

A Columbia lawyer, having read "intimations" of Secretary of War Stanton's resignation in the newspapers, suggests Frank P. Blair of Missouri—"young, energetic, talented, self-reliant brave, patriotic, and incorruptibly honest"—as his successor. "He is a border state man, a section of the country, which . . . has been greatly overlooked during the rebellion. His appointment . . . would give universal Satisfaction not only to the border states, but to the Union men, of the entire South, as well as to the North."

From Harvey M. Watterson

June 7, 1865, Richmond, Va.; ALS, DLC-JP. See *Advice*, 44–47.

Directed by the President to observe conditions in Virginia and North Carolina, Watterson initially reports that the former Confederate capital "is as quiet as before the Rebellion. You may walk the streets for days, and not witness one act of disorder or violence." Virginians, surprised and pleased with northern leniency, have accepted the results of the war, including emancipation. "The submission is complete and sincere." Moreover, they are "heartily sick of the peculiar institution" and now say "we shall be better off with hired than with slave labor." Although the press assesses the elections as "a 'general sweep' by the disunionists," he assures Johnson that "Every member known to be elected is known as a decided friend to the restored Government." Because Jeff Davis "clung to the Confederate cause long after he knew its fortunes to be desperate," he "has fallen into great disfavor, if not odium." While universally regretting Lincoln's assassination, the Virginians give "unqualified approval" to Johnson's aim to crush the rebellion fully, yet not make the nation into "a great federal consolodation." They also support his North Carolina proclamation and welcome his "purpose to refer the matter of negro suffrage to the loyal voters of the states." In short, "They are looking, with lively interest, to your policy, and the feeling is one decidedly of hope."

From Joseph C. Bradley

June 8, 1865, Washington, D.C.; ALS, DNA-RG94, Amnesty Papers (M1003, Roll 2), Ala., Joseph C. Bradley.

Northern Alabama unionist seeking amnesty asserts that he and a large number of others submitted to secession "*in our action* . . . but not in our feelings & opinions, which we openly and publicly declared"; that he briefly served as a CSA tax collector, having been "persistly importuned by the best union men," but after "appointing sub Collectors and assessors, resigned . . . & refused to accept one Cent of the salary of office"; that he has been in the legislature but voting with conservative unionists; and that he "on all occasions aided with money & advice, the Families of union men who had to flee from Confederate to Federal lines." [Pardoned June 17, 1865.]

From William G. Brownlow
Private

Nashville, June 8th, 1865.

President Johnson:

We shall close out our Session in two days more. We have done some good things, and left others undone, that ought to have been done. We have had a troublesome minority in the House, some of whom have acted worse than Rebels would have done. Among these I name old man Heiskell, Hood, and Steele[1]—the two former, I regard as having acted in violation of the known and expressed wishes of the counties they are pretending to represent—voting, in every instance to save and protect rebels. Until the two last weeks of the Session, I have regarded Cooper[2] as the House of Representatives; and the men I have named, and others, have done work for Cooper, which his good breeding, gentlemanly instincts, and sense of honor, would not allow him to do.

It has been our misfortune in the House, that too many members had rebel kin in trouble; that others wanted to make a record upon which they could get back to the Legislature on, or into Congress. Upon no other principle can I account for the wild votes and speeches of some of them. True, some, through *sheer cowardice* were afraid to vote their sentiments here, and meet rebels on their return home.

The Senate is a noble body, and has done its whole duty. They will be approved by their constituents, whilest those of the House are true and reliable men, but they have been without a leader, whereas, the minority were led by Cooper, a talented, artful man, and so gentlemanly in his bearing, as to win over others.

Inclosed in another envelop I send you the "Dispatch" containing Trigg's long opinion[3] against the law of Congress prescribing an oath for Lawyers practicing in Federal Courts. He declares the law unconstitutional, null and void. Thus any and all rebel Lawyers are admitted to practice before him. Our only hope now is, that you may appoint Maynard in lieu of Catron.[4]

We are all sorry that the noble old Thomas[5] is to leave us. He is vastly popular with loyal men in Tennessee, and is respected by rebels, for his ability, integrity, and manly bearing.

I have the honor to be,
Very truly, &c, W. G. Brownlow

ALS, DLC-JP.

1. Speaker William Heiskell, James R. Hood, and Abner A. Steele, all unionists, had voted against the Radicals' franchise bill. Heiskell (1788–1871), a Maryland native, resided in Virginia, serving in the house of delegates before moving in 1833 to Monroe County, and ultimately in 1865 to Knox County, Tenn., and being twice elected to the legislature, where he presided as speaker (1865–67). Brownlow complained that Heiskell had shifted "clear over on the Copperhead side." *BDTA*, 1: 355–56; White, *Messages of Govs.*, 5: 431–33.

2. Edmund Cooper had presented a more conservative franchise bill and, in a legalistic, but courtly, manner, exerted considerable influence for the minority view. Ibid., 434.

3. Calling it an *ex post facto* law, and doubting for other reasons the constitutionality of the act of January 24, 1865, requiring all lawyers to subscribe to the ironclad oath of July 2, 1862, Judge Connally F. Trigg, in a lengthy decision at the federal court sitting in Nashville during May 1865, ruled against Maynard, and in favor of John Baxter, that the latter could practice in federal court without taking the oath. *Nashville Dispatch*, June 8, 1865.

4. Catron's seat was never filled. Johnson nominated Stanbery, but Congress on July 23, 1866, reduced the court from ten to nine. Charles Fairman, *Reconstruction and Reunion, 1864–88, Part One* (New York, 1971) [Vol. 6 of *History of the Supreme Court of the United States*], 3, 161–62.

5. Thomas, who had won Johnson's respect, did not leave Nashville. Visiting the President in late May, after actively seeking a command "suitable to his rank," he was assured a larger territory, which encompassed an area stretching from the Ohio River to the Gulf of Mexico and including half the states in the rebellion. His headquarters remained in Nashville. Francis M. McKinney, *Education in Violence: The Life of George H. Thomas* (Detroit, 1961), 450–54.

From David Dudley Field

June 8, 1865, New York; LS, DLC-JP.

Renowned lawyer, conservative Republican, and brother of Supreme Court Justice Stephen J. Field, recommends Frank P. Blair, Jr., for secretary of war, if there is to be a change in the cabinet, citing his war record, antislavery record, and "democratic education and principles"; but suggests, more importantly, "his appointment would be very acceptable to that portion of the republican party in this state, on which I think your administration will have principally to rely for support." Apparently in reference to the military trial of the Lincoln conspirators, Field concludes: "This is a matter of great embarrassment to all of us who have been educated to dread encroachments upon the Constitution. We think a military trial is, to say the least, of questionable legality."

From J. George Harris

Key West, Florida June 8, 1865

My Dear Sir—

Honor and gratitude to you for the wisdom, justice, and mercy, displayed in your late Proclamation of Amnesty.

It saves us. It is a perfect safeguard against the preponderance of rebellious influences at the polls.

Loyalty is secured—and at this moment loyalty is "the one thing needful." I have not feared negro suffrage, for the freedmen are loyal. I *have* feared universal amnesty, for there are thousands of unrepenting rebels, who still talk defiantly in our midst.

The Proclamation comes to us like a new revelation. Repentant rebels hail it with joy—but it is like a blister to the skin of those whose loyalty is merely on the lips, for it burns and brings treason from their hearts to the surface. Its wise provisions enable us to reap where we have been diligently and prayerfully sowing for the last four years—and secures us the harvest.

Your North Carolina plan of restoration is admirable. The civil and military authorities are kept in their appropriate spheres—distinct and yet co-ordinate and co-operative under your command. The people will like this feature of it—and if Governor Holden possesses administrative ability I should suppose he would experience little or no difficulty in harmonizing the popular elements.

Pardon the freedom with which I write you.

Ever your friend J. Geo. Harris

Andrew Johnson President of the U States

ALS, DLC-JP.

From John B. Luce

June 8, 1865, Bladensburg, Md.; ALS, DNA-RG94, Amnesty Papers (M1003, Roll 13), Ark., John B. Luce.

A Confederate receiver of sequestered property for the western district of Arkansas until 1863, when Federal forces occupied Fort Smith, applies for amnesty. Attests that his duties were "almost entirely nominal, being confined with but two exceptions"—both relating to the sale of abandoned property—to the registration of property belonging to northern citizens and of statements of indebtedness owed to northern merchants. Although his assessed property had been worth over $20,000, most of it was in slaves, belonged to his mother-in-law or was reassigned to her during the war, and the remainder otherwise disposed of, so that since late 1863, he "has not had, and has not now any taxable property but the watch he wears." Because of bad health, he spent 1864 in Philadelphia with relatives and since January 1865 has been staying with another brother-in-law at Bladensburg. [Pardon granted June 13, 1865.]

From Francis H. Peirpoint[1]

The Commonwealth of Virginia,
Executive Department, Richmond, June 8 1865.
To His Excellency The President of U S.
Washington D C.
Sir.

I am clearly of opinion—that an [inteligent?] commission[er] should be appointed here to take testimony in regard to persons who fall under the exceptions in your Proclamation—And make report to you. This will facilitate and simplify the information.[2]

I am yours &c F. H. Peirpoint

ALS, DLC-JP.

1. This letter was forwarded by Thomas Williams, who wanted to nominate Gen. David H. Williams as the within-mentioned commissioner. Williams to Johnson, June 19, 1865, Johnson Papers, LC.

2. Because provisional governors were authorized to review pardon applications, recommending or withholding approval, perhaps Peirpoint believed such a commissioner could lighten his work, as well as that of the President.

From Alexander H. Stephens

June 8, 1865, Ft. Warren, Mass.; ALS, DLC-JP.

Having learned of Johnson's Amnesty Proclamation of May 29 while reading a newspaper in "close confinement," the Confederate vice president applies for a pardon under the first and twelfth exceptions, adding that he is willing to comply with its provisions and reminding Johnson of his earlier unionism. However, brought up in the states' rights school of politics, which affirmed his duty to secede with his state—for in "no sense was I ever a citizen of the United States except as a citizen of Georgia—One of the 'States united' under the Compact of union of 1787"—he felt it was "right both morally and legally" to go with his native state. To do otherwise would have been to commit an act of treason against the state. His *"misguided patriotism,"* his belief that it was no "sentiment of *disloyalty"* to the Constitution, and his acceptance of a trust in the Confederate government was an "earnest desire to rescue, secure and perpetuate these [constitutional principles] in the convulsions about to ensue." In acquiescing in the inevitable consequences of the war—the defeat of the South and the abolition of slavery—he avers that the war "was inaugurated against my judgment. It was conducted on our side against my judgment. I do not feel myself morally responsible or accountable in any way for any of the great appalling evils attending it." [There is no evidence that Johnson granted Stephens an individual pardon.]

From L. Q. Thompson

June 8, 1865, Mobile, Ala.; ALS, DNA-RG60, Off. of Atty. Gen., Lets. Recd., President.

Draws Johnson's attention to the plight of many widows and orphans, who had inherited property from "honest and hard working men who lived and died in the Union years before the inception of this fratricidal war." Owing to the fortunes of war and the "exorbitant taxes levied on that species of property," they had been forced to sell in exchange for Confederate notes and bonds, and were now reduced to penury. Those who had gained from these distress sales—a "certain class of persons—Speculators—blockade runners, and others who, under various pretexts remained at home to batten on the necessities and sufferings of the people"—are now "enjoying the fine rentals from the estates of their deluded victims." [Johnson referred this letter to Attorney General Speed.]

From Henry P.H. Bromwell

June 9, 1865, Washington, D.C.; ALS, DNA-RG56, Appts., Internal Revenue Service, Assessor, Ill., 7th Dist., George W. Rives.

Illinois congressman, after a conversation with Johnson on June 3, seeks replacement of the incumbent assessor of the 7th district, George W. Rives. Having "been urged continually to procure his removal," and assuring the President that "the interests of the union cause in the District requires his removal," he recommends Col. B. Smith of Champaign County, "a vigilant, *active whole soul* man true to the Country and administration." [Although Johnson nominated William M. Chambers to replace Rives, the Senate failed to confirm the appointment.]

From Delegation Representing the Black People of Kentucky[1]

[Washington, D.C., June 9, 1865][2]

Mr. President   Haveing been delegated by the colored People of Kentuckey to wait upon you and State their greiveances and the terrible uncertainty of their future, we beg to do so in as respectfull and concise a Manner as Posible. First then, we would call your attention to the fact that Kentuckey is the only Spot within all the bounds of

these united States, where the People of colour have No rights *whatever*
Either in Law[3] or in fact—and were the Strong arm of Millitary power
no longer to curb her—her Jails and workhouses would groan with the
Numbers of our people immured within their walls.

Her Stattutes are disgraced by laws in regard to us, too barbarous
Even for a community of Savages to have Perpetrated. Not one of those
laws have Ever yet become obsolete. All have been Executed Promptly
and Rigoursly up to the time the government intervened—and will be
again Executed in the Most remorseless Manner and with four fold the
Venom and Malignanty they were Ever heretofore Enforced—the Very
Moment the government ceases to Shield us with the broad aegis of
her Power.

Not only that—but the brutal instincts of the mob So Long restrained will Set no bounds to its ferocity but like an uncaged wild
beast will rage fiercely among us—Evidence of which is the fact that a
member of the present common council of the city of Louisville[4] [(]who
when formerly Provost Marshall of that city caused his guards to carry
bull whips and upon Meeting colored Men, women or children in the
Public high ways any time after dark to surround them and flay them
alive in the public Streets) is allready a petitioner to *Genl. Palmer*[5] to
remove the Millitary Restrictions that he and others May again renew
the brutaleties that Shocked humanity during that Sad Period. Therefore to Prevent all the horrible Calamities that would befall us and to
shut out all the terrors that So fiercely Menace us in the immediate
future—we Most humbly Petition and Pray you that you will not Remove Marshall Law from the State of Kentuckey Nor her Noble Millitary commander[6] under whose Protection we have allmost learned to
Realise the Blessings of a Home under the Safeguard and sancktion of
law for in him and him alone do we find our Safety. We would Most
Respectfully call your attention to a few of the laws that bear most
cruelly upon Us.

1st we have No Oath
2nd we have no right of domicil
3rd we have no right of locomotion
4th we have No right of Self defence
5th a Stattute law of Kentuckey makes it a penal crime with imprisonment in the Penitentiary for one year for any free Man of colour
under any Sircumstances whatever to pass into a free State Even although but for a Moment. Any free man Not a Native found within her
Borders is Subject to the Same penalty and for the Second offence Shall
be sold a slave for life.

The State of Kentuckey has contributed of her colored Sons over
thirty thousand Soldiers[7] who have illustrated their courage and devotion on Many battle fields and have Poured out their blood lavishly—in
defence of their country and the country's flag and we confidently hope

this Blood will be carried to our credit in any Political Settlement of our Native State. Yet if the government Should give up the State to the control of her civil authorities there is not one of these Soldiers who will not Suffer all the grinding oppression of her Most inhuman laws if not in their own persons yet in the persons of their wives their children And their mothers.

Therefore your Excellency we most Earnestly Petition and pray you that you will give us some security for the future or if that be impracticable at least give us timely warning that we may fly to other States where law and a christian Sentiment will Protect us and our little ones from Violence and wrong.[8]

Chas. A Roxborough—chairman—
R M Johnson Thomas James
Jerry Meninettee Henry H. White
Wm. F. Butler Sec.[9]

ALS (Roxborough), DNA-RG107, Lets. Recd., EB12 President 1957 (1865).

1. Meeting in Louisville in June, a group of blacks and their supporters selected a delegation to present their grievances to the President. Howard, *Black Liberation*, 146.

2. Johnson received the delegates and this address on June 9. *Chicago Tribune*, June 15, 1865.

3. Since Kentucky had remained in the Union, it was not affected by the Emancipation Proclamation. Although the families of black soldiers had been freed in March 1865 by congressional legislation, others remained in bondage. Howard, *Black Liberation*, 79.

4. Not identified.

5. On May 11 John M. Palmer, Kentucky commander, was approached by the Louisville mayor and council with a request for enforcement of the vagrancy law against blacks, who in fleeing the countryside were congregating in large numbers in the city. Howard, *Black Liberation*, 80.

6. Palmer supported the blacks, encouraged their army enlistment, and worked to undermine the institution of slavery as it persisted in Kentucky before the 13th Amendment. Efforts to remove him failed when Johnson sustained him. Ibid., 78–88.

7. At war's end Kentucky's black recruits numbered over 25,000, with enlistments continuing through May at the rate of 70–100 a day. Ibid., 82.

8. In acknowledging their representation, Johnson, according to press report, assured them that "the colored men of Kentucky ... need have no apprehension as to their protection; that martial law would still continue in Kentucky, and that Gen. Palmer with an army would still be maintained there until Kentuckians should learn more truly their position and their duty to the nation. They shall be obliged to treat even their slaves according to humanity." At the same time, he warned them that they "must not expect progress to be too rapid." *Chicago Tribune*, June 15, 1865.

9. Charles A. Roxborough, a steward; Richard M. Johnson, a dry goods merchant; Henry White, a laborer; and William H. Butler, a steward on the steamer *Tarascan*, were all black Louisvillians. Jerry Meninettee and Thomas James are unidentified. Louisville directories (1866–71).

From J. George Harris

Key West, Florida June 9, 1865.

My Dear Sir—

Chief Justice Chase[1] was here—as you know—a few days ago. He assured me and others that there is a perfect understanding between you and himself—that you perfectly understand each other &c.

He was very anxious to see Brig. Gen. Newton[2] who was in command of Key West and Tortugas and who has since been assigned to the entire Florida military district by Gen. Canby.[3]

I could not refrain from the conviction that the Chief Justice was looking forward to the vote of Florida one of these days—yet I would not do him injustice for he manifested sincere friendship for you and spoke of your purposes and policy in handsome terms.

I hope the foundations of new Florida will be firmly laid in the principles of your own sterling record and antecedents—and without even the aid of any partisan jobbers who make private speculations in public affairs.

I really think the Provisional Governor of Florida who will have so much to do with shaping its destiny should be one of your own friends who understands your policy.

Pardon me, again—and believe me,

Very Truly Yr friend J. Geo. Harris

Andrew Johnson President of the U. States

ALS, DLC-JP.

1. Salmon P. Chase, dispatched by the President on a tour of the South, had reported from Key West on May 23. *Advice*, 36–38.

2. John Newton commanded the District of Key West from October 15, 1864, to July 1865. Boatner, *CWD*.

3. Edward R. S. Canby, commander of the Army and Department of the Gulf. Ibid.

From Russell Houston

Washington June 9 1865

Mr President.

I have a message from my wife to you. She asks you to grant a pardon to her brother Lucius E. Polk[1] late of Arkansas. He is a young man—entered the rebel service as a Lieutenant, & was not therefore a leader, & was regularly promoted to the position of Brig. General. He is badly wounded having lost the use of one of his legs, & he will have to use a crutch during his life. He desires a pardon & I will be responsible in every way, for his conduct in the future. Of course, I would be gratified at his release; but the appeal to you is from my wife, & knowing as you do, her steadfast position & its trying peculiarities[2] I do not doubt that you will grant the request. She wishes the pardon enclosed to her, to present to him, that he may see that the Government is not unmindful of the ardent wishes of its faithful citizens. To grant this pardon will be a favor to her never to be forgotten—a pleasure justly due her, when to grant there is no detriment to the Country.[3]

It was my purpose to see you in person about this matter, but you are too busy to see me. I therefore mentioned the subject to the Attorney General. By the way, you are laboring too constantly. Economize your life.

If agreeable, East & I will call tomorrow at 10. A M.

Very Respectfully Russell Houston

ALS, DNA-RG94, Amnesty Papers (M1003, Roll 14), Ark., Lucius E. Polk.

1. Polk (1833–1892), an Arkansas planter and a nephew of Leonidas Polk, was a Confederate brigadier, who settled in Columbia, Tenn., after the war and served in the legislature (1887). Wakelyn, *BDC*; *BDTA*, 2: 731–32.

2. While she and her husband and some of her Polk kinfolk had remained unionist during the war, Grizelda Polk Houston had tried to alleviate the suffering of her Confederate relatives. See Letter from Grizelda Polk, July 15, [1864], *Johnson Papers*, 7: 31–32.

3. Polk was pardoned on June 12, 1865. Pardons and Remissions, Vol. 8 (T967, Roll 3), RG59, NA.

From Backus W. Huntington

June 9, 1865, New York, N.Y.; ALS, DLC-JP.

New York lawyer, a prewar Alabama resident for fourteen years, applies for provisional governorship, citing his service in that state's legislature, as well as in the circuit court of a nonslaveholding district, an area which had paid for its unionism during the war. Its residents "were hunted down with dogs for the rebel army" and "were violently torn from their allegiance and, in effect, rammed like the Sepoys into the cannon of treason and shot like waste powder at the Constitution, the Flag and the Life of their country." He feels these survivors, including widows and orphans, should be allowed to recover damages in the civil courts. Supporting Johnson's restoration plan as reported, he suggests that the President "should be regarded as the master of power . . . and that the administrative agent of your views should be one who can use influence without having been implicated in the late dissensions"; one who could "rally all the true and proper Unionists by the first intention and draw away from the dynastic secessionists such as would like to quit their company forever."

From William H.C. King

June 9, 1865, New York, N.Y.; ALS, DLC-JP.

Editor of the *New Orleans Times*, having had a "recent interview" with Johnson and concluding that the President's views were "greatly in accordance" with his own, reports that he has hired John Savage, of New York, to editorialize "entirely in reference and support of your policy." Suggests that "Information proper and agreeable for you to place within his reach, will further me greatly." In a postscript: "I sent dispatches to N.O. warning them that Mr. Chase was going further than he should, in which he was only tending to embarrass you." [Savage had earlier written on Johnson's life and services (1860, 1864) and was at work on a revised and enlarged edition of *The Life and Public Services of Andrew Johnson* (New York, 1866).]

Order Revoking Cotton Marketing Permits

Executive Mansion,
June 9, 1865.

Whereas, certain special permits, signed by the Secretary of the Treasury and approved by the President, have been heretofore granted to certain persons[1] to enable them to transport to market cotton alleged to have been theretofore purchased by them, but which they were unable to so transport by reason of changes in the military lines and the progress of military operations; and *whereas*, it is believed that sufficient time has elapsed since the issuance of such permits to enable the persons holding them to carry out in good faith the legitimate objects for which they were granted; and *whereas*, it is shown that private interests are prejudiced, and the public good in no way promoted, by the existence thereof, it is therefore ORDERED, that all special permits of the character above cited be vacated, and the same are hereby revoked and annulled, and no transportation will be allowed under them or any of them after Tuesday, the 20th day of June, 1865.

It is also ORDERED, for the same reasons, that after receipt of this order or an official copy thereof all agents and officers of the Treasury Department shall refrain from reviving old permits, as provided by amended Treasury Regulation LV, dated January 4, 1865; and all permits so revived shall be null and void after the 20th inst.

Andrew Johnson

DS, DNA-RG56, Misc. Div., Claims for Cotton and Captured and Abandoned Property.

1. As an example of such a permit, see Order *re* Cotton of William L. Vance, April 24, 1865, *Johnson Papers*, 7: 629. Other examples include orders to James Fish, Jr. & Co. and to W.E.A. Mackintosh & Co., both on May 16, 1865. Misc. Div., Claims for Cotton and Captured and Abandoned Property, RG56, NA.

From William Price[1]

Baltimore June 9th 1865.

His Excellency President Johnson.
Sir.

I have not united in any of the raids, which have been kept up for the last month or two from this city upon your time & patience in reference to appointments.[2] My position in regard to the rebellion from first to last, is known to Mr. Seward, Mr. Montgomery Blair, Mr. Bates[3] late attorney General, & measurably to Mr. Speed. If I have any character for loyalty & fidelity to my country, I prefer to let it speak for itself.

For your information Mr. President, I take the liberty of placing in

your hands, an address of mine[4] to the people of my native state, before
Mr. Lincolns first inauguration. And can only say that the stand I then
took I have maintained steadfastly to the present day.[5]

With great respect Yr friend & svt.

Wm. Price

ALS, DNA-RG60, Appt. Files for Judicial Dists., Md., William Price.

1. Price (c1794–1868), lawyer and legislator, was U.S. district attorney (1863–65).
NUC; Thomas J.C. Williams, *A History of Washington County, Maryland* (2 vols., Baltimore, 1968[1906]), 1: 426.

2. Johnson's office was under siege as the patronage struggle in Maryland intensified
with Radicals under Henry Winter Davis' heirs and Conservative unionists under Montgomery Blair's leadership vying for favor. *Baltimore Sun*, July 26, 27, 1865; Beale,
Welles Diary, 2: 343–44; Charles L. Wagandt, "Redemption or Reaction?—Maryland
in the Post-Civil War Years," Richard O. Curry, ed., *Radicalism, Racism, and Party
Realignment: The Border States During Reconstruction* (Baltimore, 1969), 152–53.

3. Edward Bates.

4. Not found.

5. Despite Price's protestations of loyalty, Johnson replaced him with William J.
Jones in a recess appointment in July, with Senate approval in January 1866. Less than
a year later, Price was again a candidate for district attorney, but his nomination by
Johnson was rejected by the Senate in January 1867. Appt. Bk. 4: 106; 5: n.p., Ser. 6B,
Johnson Papers, LC.

From Miles R. Bohannan[1]

Headquarters Employment Agency

Lynchburg Va. June 10th/65

His Excellency Andrew Johnson
President of U.S.
Sir.

I have the honor of representing to you that I have been a steadfast
supporter of the Union during the wholetime of the late Rebellion, and
from my childhood up. That in September last I sought relief from the
persecutions of the so called confederacy, by going North, where I remained until about 3 weeks since. I have returned home to find all I
possessed, sunk in the dreadful wreck treason has left behind it. With
a family upon my hands I have to commence life de novo. The Government has been ever kind to me. I am now temporarily engaged as Physician to the freedman at these Hdquarters and assistant to Col Richard
F Moson[2] Commanding. I had the honor of knowing our late lamented
President, who kindly told me he would place me in some position in
order to support my family, but before I could make application the
hand of the assassin had stricken him down. I now respectfully ask at
your hands the position of assessor of Internal Revenue for this City or
District.[3]

I have been living here for Ten years and my qualifications are well
known. I was born and reared up in this State.

I am very Respectfully

Your Obt Servant M R Bohannan

ALS, DNA-RG56, Appts., Internal Revenue Service, Assessor, Va., 5th Dist., Miles R. Bohannan.

1. Bohannan (b. *c*1828), Virginia native, was a Lynchburg physician. 1870 Census, Va., Campbell, E. Div., 39.

2. Richard F. Moson (b. *c*1827), lt. col., 21st Pa. Cav., until early July 1865, when he was mustered out, was briefly in charge of the Freedmen's Bureau at Lynchburg. CSR, RG94, NA; *Lynchburg Virginian*, June 2, 1865.

3. He did not get the appointment.

From Committee of Richmond Blacks [1]

[Richmond, Va., June 10, 1865] [2]

Mr. President:

We have been appointed a committee by a public meeting of the colored people of Richmond, Va., to make known to your Excellency, as our best friend, the wrongs, as we conceive them to be, by which we are sorely oppressed.

We represent a population of more than 20,000 colored people, including Richmond and Manchester, who have ever been distinguished for their good behavior as slaves and as freemen, as well as for their high moral and Christian character; more than 6,000 of our people are members in good standing of Christian churches, and nearly our whole population constantly attend divine service. Among us there are at least 2,000 men who are worth from $200 to $500—200 who have property estimated at from $500 to $5,000, and a number who are worth from $5,000 to $20,000. None of our people are in the poor-house, and when we were slaves, the aged and infirm who were turned away from the homes of hard masters, who had been enriched by their toil, our benevolent societies supported while they lived, and buried when they died; and comparatively few of us have found it necessary to ask for government rations, which have been so bountifully bestowed upon the unrepentant rebels of Richmond. The law of slavery severely punished those who taught us to read and write, but notwithstanding this, 3,000 of us can read, and at least 2,000 can read and write, and a large number of us are engaged in useful and profitable employments on our own account.

During the whole of this slaveholder's rebellion we have been true and loyal to the United States Government. Privately and collectively we have sent up our prayers to the throne of Grace for the success of the Union cause. We have given aid and comfort to the soldiers of freedom, (for which several of our people, of both sexes, in Richmond, have been severely punished by stripes and imprisonment). We have been their pilots and their scouts, and have safely conducted them through many perilous adventures, while hard-fought battles and bloody fields have fully established the indomitable bravery, the loyalty, and the heroic patriotism of our race.

We rejoiced with exceeding great joy at the fall of Richmond and the termination of the war, which we supposed broke the last fetter of the American slave. When the triumphant Union army entered the city of Richmond, we alone gave it a cordial welcome, receiving it with hearts bursting with joy and thanksgiving; and when our late beloved and martyred President made his *entree* into our city, we alone hailed his advent with enthusiastic shouts of acclamation, and of all the citizens of Richmond, we alone, with a few solitary exceptions, wear the exterior badges of mourning, as truthful expressions of our grief for his untimely death, and it is therefore with sorrowing hearts that we are compelled thus to acquaint your Excellency with our sad disappointment, for our present condition is, in many respects, worse than when we were slaves, and living under slave law. Under the old system we had the *protection* of our masters, who were financially interested in our physical welfare. That protection is now withdrawn, and our old masters have become our enemies, who seek not only to oppress our people, but thwart the designs of the Federal Government and of Northern benevolent associations in our behalf. We cannot appeal to the laws of Virginia for protection, for the old negro laws still prevail; and, besides, the oath of a colored man against a white man will not be received in our State courts, so that we have nowhere to go for protection and justice but to that power which made us free.

We would call the attention of your Excellency to the condition of our church affairs. By the laws of Virginia, colored churches were compelled to accept of white preachers, who, of course, were uncompromising friends of Southern institutions—and again, our church property, which we have paid for, out of the scanty earnings of years of toil, according to law must be deeded to white trustees. Now, in the reconstruction of our church matters, we wish to employ clergymen of our choice and faith, and to hold our own property. The obnoxious clergy we may gradually get rid of, but how to get possession of our church property, passeth our understanding.

In the city of Richmond, the military and police authorities will not allow us to walk the streets by day or night, in the regular pursuit of our business, or on our way to church without a *pass*; and passes do not in all cases protect us from arrest, abuse, violence and imprisonment, against which, we have thus far had no protection or redress. Men have not only been arrested in the streets, but the police, in conjunction with the provost guard, have entered our dwellings and workshops, and have taken them from the work-bench, and put them in prison, because they had no pass, or because they would not recognize the pass presented as genuine or sufficient.

In numerous instances, our people have been driven from their old homes, or have sought employment elsewhere, where justice to themselves or families demanded that they should make such a change, and many of these people have been rudely arrested—thrust into prison, and hired out by military authority, for the most insignificant sums. A number of men who have been employed upon plantations, have visited Richmond, in search of long lost wives or children, who had been separated by the cruel usages of slavery. Wives, too, are frequently seen in our streets, anxiously inquiring for husbands who had been sold away from them; and many of these people, who ignorantly supposed that the day of passes had passed away with the system which originated them, have been arrested, imprisoned, and hired out without their advice or consent—thus preventing the reunion of long-estranged and affectionate families.

Respectable and educated strangers from distant States, visiting Richmond for pleasure, business, or for benevolent purposes, have, like all the rest of us, been subjected to the insults and oppressions of which we complain. In some of these cases, the parties arrested have exhibited their passports with the broad seal of State stamped upon them, but in every such instance these passports were contemptuously ignored, and the parties holding them subjected to imprisonment.

In addition to the annoyances to which we have been subjected by the pass system, some of our people have been subjected to the most cruel punishments, the like of which was never heard of even in the slave-pens of Southern traders.

For the further practical working of this pass system, we respectfully refer your Excellency to the accompanying documents,[3] being statements made to an authorized committee by respectable colored men, who have been the victims of this system.

A few days ago General Gregg,[4] whose headquarters is at Lynchburg, published an order to the Freedmen, in which he tells them that they "have all the rights at present that free people of color have heretofore had in Virginia, and no more." We were sorry to see this announcement, for we supposed that the recently freedmen were a class of persons unknown to the laws of Virginia, or to any other State, but that they were to be subjected only to special acts of Congressional enactment.

The recent re-establishment of Mayor Mayo[5] and his old police force is deeply regretted by us. During the whole period of the rebellion, Mr. Mayo, as the chief magistrate of the city, and as a private citizen, exerted all his influence to keep alive the spirit of treason and rebellion, and to urge the people to continue the contest. The cruelties perpetrated upon sick and defenceless Union prisoners, in Libby Prison and upon Belle Isle, were openly and shamelessly approved by him. For a long series of years he has been the Mayor of Richmond, and his administration has always been marked by cruelty and injustice to us; and the old rebel police, now again in power, have been our greatest enemies. It was Mayor Mayo who, in former days, ordered us to be scourged for trifling offences against slave laws and usages, and his present police, who are now hunting us through the streets, are the men who relentlessly applied the lash to our quivering flesh, and now they appear to take special pleasure in persecuting and oppressing us.

In justice to Governor Peirpoint, in whom we recognize a true friend, it is proper to say that the reappointment of the rebel authorities in Richmond was not authorized by him, nor are they in power by his advice, consent, or desire.

When we saw the glorious old flag again streaming over the capitol, we thought the power of these wicked men was at an end; and, however sad our hearts may be over the present state of our affairs, we have lost none of our faith and love for the Union, or for yourself as its Chief Magistrate; and, therefore, as oppressed, obedient, and loving children, we ask your protection, and upon the loyalty of our hearts, and the power of our arms, you may ever rely with unbounded confidence. And, in conclusion, let us respectfully remind your Excellency of that sublime motto, once inscribed over the portals of an Egyptian temple, *"Know all ye who exercise power that God hates injustice."* [6]

Fields Cook,
Richard Wells,
Wm. Williamson,
Wm. T. Snead,
T. Morris Chester. [7]

Washington Morning Chronicle, June 17, 1865.

1. Accompanied by "Mr. Van Vleet," president of the Richmond Union League, a black grievance committee organized in Richmond on June 8 and chaired by "Fields Cook (colored)" met with Johnson on June 16. *Washington Morning Chronicle*, June 17, 1865; *New York Herald*, June 17, 1865.

2. The provenance and date were provided in an abridged version of this petition published in the *Cincinnati Gazette* on June 19, 1865.

3. Reprints of these depositions appear with this petition in the *Washington Morning Chronicle*, June 17, 1865.

4. David M. Gregg (1833–1916), West Point graduate, participated in numerous engagements in the eastern theater as colonel of the 8th Pa. Cav. and as brigadier general. Warner, *Blue*.

5. Joseph Mayo (1795–1872), commonwealth attorney of Richmond for thirty years, served in the legislature before his election as mayor (1853–65, 1866–68). He left office after surrendering the city on April 3, 1865, but was reinstated by Peirpoint. *Richmond Dispatch*, Aug. 10, 1872; *New York Herald* June 17, 1865; Michael B. Chesson, *Richmond After the War, 1865–1890* (Richmond, 1981), 91–94.

6. "T. M. Chester (colored)" read this petition, which had been written by Van Vleet. In response, the President pointed out that Mayo had recently been removed from office again. He assured the Richmond blacks that "every proper step will be taken to afford you whatever protection can be given you. But while you are in this transition state there will be a great many things we would all prefer to have different, that must for the present be submitted to as they are, till they can be remedied." He immediately forwarded their petition to Gen. O. O. Howard, Freedmen's Bureau chief, "for his consideration and report as to the action necessary and proper to be had in view of the within statements." Ibid., 92; *Washington Morning Chronicle*, June 17, 1865; *New York Herald*, June 17, 1865.

7. Cook (c1817–fl1877), a property owner and jack-of-all-trades, reportedly a waiter, barber, minister or doctor, manumitted in 1853, was one of the first blacks to serve on a

grand jury before running unsuccessfully as an independent for Congress in 1869; Wells (*fl*1883) was pastor of the Ebenezer Baptist Church; Williamson (*c*1820–*fl*1883) was a barber; Snead (*fl*1877) was a physician; and Chester is not further identified. 1860 Census, Va., Richmond, 2nd Ward, 205; Henrico, E. Div., 185; Richmond directories (1866–83); Alrutheus A. Taylor, *The Negro in the Reconstruction of Virginia* (New York, 1926), 187, 188, 214, 254.

From James Duggan

June 10, 1865, Chicago, Ill.; ALS, DNA-RG153, Court-Martial Records, MM-2185.

Appealing for clemency in the case of Charles Walsh, one of the Chicago conspirators who was sentenced to five years' imprisonment in the Columbus, Ohio, penitentiary, the Bishop of Chicago asserts that "Nearly all of the members of the Military-Commission . . . at the time of their finding and sentence, aske for an immidiate remission of such sentence." [Walsh was released under General Court-Martial Order No. 305 on June 17, 1865.]

From Addison A. Hosmer

June 10, 1865, Washington, D.C.; LBcopy, DNA-RG153, Lets. Sent (Record Books), Vol. 15.

The acting judge advocate general, reporting on the pardon petition of Mrs. Bessie Lee Perine, who was tried and sentenced to three months' incarceration for aiding and abetting a party of rebel cavalry in its attack on a train between Baltimore and Philadelphia, substantiates the charges that she consorted in "animated conversation" with these officers, exhibiting "greatest excitement and delight," and that, after saving her own luggage, she helped identify that belonging to Federal officers for plunder by the raiders. Her petition was accompanied by an affidavit of a witness who stated he was with her throughout the incident, during which time "her deportment" was "dignified and proper, and in all respects befitting an accomplished and cultivated, true, woman," but his testimony was "somewhat inconsistent" with that of Mrs. Perine in her application, wherein she "virtually admits the facts conclusively established against her at her trial, and ascribed them to extreme agitation of mind, and to the fact that she was a widow and orphan, on her way with a sick child to the sea shore, in search of health." The judge advocate general's office "sees no reason for any change of opinion touching the leniency of the sentence" in its recommendation. [On June 18 Stanton, apparently at Johnson's behest, directed that her sentence be "suspended during her good behavior."]

From Isaac Naff[1]
Private

Monroe La June 10th 1865

To his Excellency Andrew Johnson
President U.S of America Washington D.C
Sir.

Under your amnesty proclamation, I am in doubt whether an assessor commissioned by the State Collector of C.S. Tax is included or not.

You say *all* civil officers will be excepted from taking the Amnesty Oath.

Sometime in September last I was Commissioned as District assessor for the District of Morehouse La by R. M. Lusher[2] State Collector of C.S. Tax for the State of Louisiana. I have not the commission with me or I would send it to you.

I have been Parish Recorder of Morehouse nearly eight years, was commissioned when first elected under the U.S. & State constitution & have been acting under the same commission ever since, but was required to take the oath of allegiance to the C.S. about four years ago.

If the election comes off next fall at the time prescribed by the laws in force before the state seceded, I wish to be a candidate for re-election, and should I be among the exceptions in your proclamation, I will thank you for your pardon as soon as convenient—so that I may know what to be at.

I herewith send my exemption from the enrolling officer with its approval. You will see by it that I am a native of your County—but you have no doubt forgotten me, as it is nearly 25 years since we were together.

The last time I saw you was at Aaron Gentry's[3] on Beaver Creek in Knox County. You were then on your way to west Tennessee, to canvass the state at large, on the electoral ticket for Van Buren. You met me on the road and requested me to go with you down to Gentry's and get dinner which I did. The dinner was not very nice or good if you recollect. You were riding a fine young bay gelding which had been raised by my father.[4]

I have tried to profit by the advice you gave me that day. When we parted I never expected to see you again and I remember I was much affected by your Kind and affectionate farewell. I still have the Keep sake you gave me, (a pocket book, we exchanged). You have long since worn the one out I gave you & forgotten it and me too I fear.

You made your first political speech I think on the steps of my father's porch, where John Crawford[5] now lives. It was the year old Fed White was elected to the Legislature, when yourself Tom Bell the singing master—Russell the Lawyer, White the stone cutter, Feasle the farmer,[6] and others were candidates. I think you will now be able to identify me.

I am dear sir your friend & by your
permission will be your *fellow citizen*
Isaac Naff

Please direct your answer to me at Bastrop La Via New Orleans & I will be sure to get it.

I have never been in the army and have done what I have in the civil service because I was nearly compelled to do it.[7]

ALS, DNA-RG94, Amnesty Papers (M1003, Roll 28), La., Isaac Naff.

1. Naff (b. c1822) was a Tennessee-born teacher, who became a Louisiana planter. 1850 Census, La., Morehouse, 3rd and 4th Wards, 813; (1870), 4th Ward, 46.

2. Robert M. Lusher (b. c1818), who served as commissioner of the U.S. Circuit Court before becoming a Confederate tax collector, was appointed state superintendent of education (1865–67) and was elected to that office in the 1870s. 1850 Census, La., New Orleans, 4th Ward, 530; Taylor, *La. Reconstructed*, 73, 142, 236, 465, 483; Amnesty Papers (M1003, Roll 28), La., Robert M. Lusher, RG94, NA.

3. Probably Aaron Gentry (b. c1775), a Knox County farmer. Byron Sistler, tr., *1830 Census East Tennessee* (Evanston, Ill., 1969), 109.

4. Possibly Abraham Naff (1797–1874), who was married in Greene County in 1820. Bennett, *Washington County*, 2: 144; Goldene F. Burgner, comp., *Greene County, Tennessee, Marriages, 1783–1868* (Easley, S.C., 1981), 52.

5. Possibly John H. Crawford (1809–1893), a Greene County farmer. 1860 Census, Tenn., Greene, 15th Dist., 8; Buford Reynolds, comp., *Greene County Cemeteries* (Greeneville, Tenn., 1971), 351.

6. Frederick T. White (1783–1844), Greene County farmer and legislator; Thomas Bell, not otherwise identified; Alfred A. Russell, who, like Johnson, had been alderman and mayor of Greeneville; White, unidentified; and Samuel Feazel (d. 1841), who served in the legislature. Richard H. Doughty, *Greeneville: One Hundred Year Portrait, 1775–1875* (Greeneville, Tenn., 1975), 63; *BDTA*, 1: 244, 776.

7. Naff was pardoned, by Johnson's order, June 29, 1865. *House Ex. Docs.*, 39 Cong., 2 Sess., No. 116, p. 24 (Ser. 1293).

From R. McK. Ormsby

June 10, 1865, Bradford, Vt.; ALS, DLC-JP.

Convinced that the Civil War and emancipation were primarily the result of a British conspiracy to end the southern monopoly of cotton production, a northern lawyer, seeing Johnson "surrounded by the inveterate haters of the South," advises him to ignore the "bigotted feelings" of the Radicals, who do not reflect the current of northern conservatism, and adopt a course of magnanimity. "We must help the South: show her that we regard her as precious to us. Instead of tearing down, we should build up." Although the South erred by seceding, it was not without provocation, for the North, which "passed laws abrogating the Constitutional rights of slaveholders to their property" and "mobbed" southerners legally pursuing fugitive slaves into New England, was not blameless.

From Lewis E. Parsons and Joseph C. Bradley

June 10, 1865, Washington, D.C.; ALS, DLC-JP.

Having met with Johnson "on Monday last" [June 5] as members of a delegation of Alabama unionists, they now recommend for provisional governor of Alabama John J. Seibels of Montgomery, a former Confederate colonel who "opposed secession with all his might & after the ordinance was adopted acquiesced because it was not in his power to resist." [Seibels, who died two months later, did not receive the appointment.]

From Edwin M. Stanton

Washington City June 10th 1865

Mr. President:

I am informed that frequent applications are made to you, by refugees from Rebel States, for transportation back to their homes. This subject properly comes within the jurisdiction of the Bureau for Freedmen and Refugees, of which Major General Howard is Commissioner. He has authority to supply transportation in all proper cases; and I therefore submit that, in order to relieve yourself from any trouble upon the subject, all such applications be referred directly to Major General Howard, Commissioner of the Freedmen's Bureau.

I have the honor to be, Very respectfully,
Your obedient servant, Edwin M. Stanton
Secretary of War.

LS, DNA-RG107, Misc. Lets. and Papers (1804–67).

From Texas Refugees

June 10, 1865, New Orleans, La.; LS, DLC-JP.

Believing that they "speak the sentiments of nine tenth of our truly loyal people," twenty-four Texas refugees assert that slavery is "incompatable with Republican Government" and must be extinguished; only loyal citizens should be placed in charge of state reconstruction, because, should Texas be organized at present under the North Carolina plan, "it would result in surrendering *all* into the hands of the enemies of freedom and of the Government." Preferring loyal military rule to disloyal civil government, the refugees conclude that reconstruction should be "deferred until the truly loyal feel that it can be successfully accomplished."

From the Union League Club of New York City

June 10, 1865, New York, N.Y.; ALS (Otis D. Swan, secretary), DLC-JP.

Officers transmit to the President and cabinet members a resolution, adopted June 8, asking the federal government to establish "a System of Suffrage, in the late rebellious States, which shall be Equal and just to all, without distinction of Color."

From Eber B. Ward[1]

Detroit, Mich. June 10 1865

His Excellency Andrew Johnson
President of the U.S.
Sir

The Lawyal people of the north begin to fear that our government will not be vindicated by the trial by Military tribunals and the conviction and Execution of the Leading Rebels.

An almost unanimous sentiment demands such a course. The unmitigated simplisity of the Greeleys Sumne[r]s[2] and others of sentimental proclivities is not shared by the people. Chandler Wade Howard and Dickinson[3] know how the lawyal masses feel. The Halter for Traiters is the only remedy for our accursed enemies.

Respy E B Ward

ALS, DLC-JP.
1. Ward (1811–1875) lived in Detroit, where he engaged in shipbuilding, invested in railroad ventures, and built rolling mills in Chicago and Milwaukee. *NCAB*, 13: 125.
2. A reference to Horace Greeley and Charles Sumner.
3. Zachariah Chandler, Benjamin Wade, Jacob M. Howard, and Daniel S. Dickinson.

From James C. Wetmore and Robert J. Walker[1]

Executive Department,
State of Ohio, Military Agency.
Washington June 10th 1865

To His Excellency The President:

I have the honor to state that this will be presented by Miss Mary E. Walker, M.D.[2]

Miss W. desires to bring to your Excellency's notice, business which concerns herself.

I take great pleasure in commending her to your favorable consideration.

Though I have not had her personal acquaintance, save in an official way, I can say that I have always heard her spoken of with respect and high commendation. She has been untiring in her efforts for the relief of the sick and wounded soldiers, both in Hospital and Field.

She was for some time attached to the 52d O. Regt. as a Surgeon and while on duty rendered, I have been credibly informed, very efficient service. During the time she was with the 52d Ohio, she was called upon by General Dan: McCook[3] to perform a hazardous enterprise within the enemy's line: the object of her mission was accomplished, though it cost her many months of imprisonment in Libby Prison.

It would afford me much satisfaction to see her services recognized by the Government, so far as it could be done consistent with public interests.[4]

> I am, Mr President With Great Respect
> Your Obedient Servant. James C Wetmore
> O. S. M. Agent.

P.S.   Miss Mary E. Walker M.D, has been well known to me for several years. She desires to be commissioned and assigned to a position in the Refugee and Freedmans bureau as Medical Inspector for a state. I think she is *well qualified* for this position, and her great services to the Union, and her sufferings as a Union Prisoner at Libby entitle her to high consideration. The services of this young Lady are recognized by the Army and the country and her assignment to this position would in my opinion give general satisfaction. Most respy.

> R. J. Walker

President Johnson

LS with ALS, DNA-RG94, Volunteer Services Div., File W-2068-VS-1863, Mary E. Walker.

1. Wetmore (1813–*fl*1881) was an Ohio state military agent and claims attorney. Walker, President Polk's secretary of the treasury, was currently a Washington attorney. *NUC*; Washington, D.C., directories (1863–70); Wetmore to Garfield, April 15, 1881, James A. Garfield Papers, LC.

2. Walker (1832–1919), who graduated from Syracuse Medical College and practiced in Rome, N.Y., sought an appointment as an army surgeon during the war. Her services as an unpaid volunteer, and then as a practitioner without official standing, on northern Virginia battlefields were recognized when in September 1863 Gen. George H. Thomas appointed her an assistant surgeon in Tennessee. Captured by Confederates and imprisoned in Richmond, she was exchanged in 1864. Edward T. James et al., eds., *Notable American Women, 1607–1950: A Biographical Dictionary* (3 vols., Cambridge, 1971), 3: 532–33.

3. Daniel McCook, Jr. (1834–1864), a Kansas lawyer, was colonel of the 52nd Ohio until appointed brigadier at the time of the Atlanta campaign. He was mortally wounded in an assault on Kennesaw Mountain. Warner, *Blue*.

4. Along with numerous other testimonials, Johnson referred this request to the secretary of war with his signed endorsement that "It would seem . . . that she has performed service deserving the recognition of the Government, which I desire to give if there is any way in which or precedent by which this may be done." Despite the adverse reports from the surgeon general that, aside from her payment as a contract surgeon, "there is no manner in which [recognition] could be accomplished consistently with law and regulations," Johnson persisted, first in pursuing "an honorary or complimentary Brevet," and later at Stanton's suggestion conferring upon her in January 1866 the newly-created Medal of Honor, making her the first and only woman recipient of that award. *Above and Beyond: A History of the Medal of Honor from Civil War to Vietnam* (Boston, 1985), 39; endorsements, Volunteer Services Div., W-2068-VS-1863, Mary E. Walker, RG94, NA; R. Morrow to secretary of war, October 27, 1865, Lets. Recd., EB12 President 2495 (1865), RG107, NA.

From Congressional Committee on Indian Affairs [1]

Fort Lyons June 11th 1865

His Excellency A Johnson
President of U.S.

We have received no answer to our telegram from Lawrence Kan.[2] Send this by express. Our messenger waits a reply at Denver.

From all we learn we can probably have peace with the Indians on the New Mexican routes without further hostilities south of the Arkansas if we are authorized to treat with the chiefs. Will you authorize us to do so?[3]

If offensive war is to go on against the Camanches, Kiowahs, Cheyennes and Arrapahoes it will cost probably forty millions and require near 10,000 troops to make it effectual.[4]

J R Doolittle Chairman
L F S Foster[5]
L W Ross[6]

Tel, DNA-RG107, Tels. Recd., President, Vol. 4 (1865–66).

1. In an attempt to stave off a crisis mounting between Indians and settlers, Congress had appointed a joint committee "to inquire into the condition of the Indian tribes and their treatment by the civil and military authorities." Senator James R. Doolittle, chairman of the Senate Committee on Indian Affairs, Senator Lafayette S. Foster, and Congressman Lewis W. Ross were appointed as the committee. Francis Paul Prucha, *The Great Father: The United States Government and the American Indians* (2 vols., Lincoln, Neb., 1984), 1: 485–86; *United States Statutes at Large*, 13: 572–73.

2. The committee had requested authority to "make peace with hostile Indians." Stanton replied on June 15 that at the President's direction, he had wired a response May 29, authorizing them "to make peace, if you can, with hostile Indians—the treaty to be subject to his approval." Doolittle to Johnson, May 27, 1865, Lets. Recd., President, Vol. 4 (1865–66), RG107, NA; Stanton to Committee, May 29, June 15, 1865, Gen. Records, Lets. Recd. (M234, Roll 198), RG75, NA.

3. The President directed Stanton "to make the same answer" as to the original telegram. Stanton's wire assured the committee that the President desired to establish peaceable relations with the various tribes, and that Johnson was empowering them as special commissioners to make such treaties as would suspend hostilities and afford "security to our citizens, settlements, and travellers on the frontier." Ibid.

4. In an interview with Johnson and his cabinet on August 18, 1865, the committee members protested strongly against further attacks on the southwestern tribes. Stanton, in response, reported that General Grant "had already written to restrict operations." Beale, *Welles Diary*, 2: 362.

5. Foster (1806–1880) served in the legislature and as Connecticut senator (1855–67). *BDAC.*

6. Ross (1812–1895), Illinois lawyer, was a state representative and congressman (1863–69). Ibid.

To John W. Garrett[1]

Executive Office, Washington D.C.
June 11th 1865.

J. W. Garrett Esq.
President Baltimore & Ohio R. R. Co
Baltimore.

My family will be in Cincinnati en route for this city on the seventeenth instant.

Can there be arrangements made for them from Cincinnati.[2]

Andrew Johnson
President U.S.

Tel, DNA-RG107, Tels. Sent, President, Vol. 2 (1865).

1. Garrett (1820–1884) became president of the Baltimore and Ohio in 1858, a position he retained throughout the war and into the postwar decades. *DAB*.

2. Garrett responded the next day: "I will take great pleasure in making all requisite arrangements for your family from Cincinnati to Washington." Garrett to Johnson, June 12, 1865, Johnson Papers, LC.

From Winfield Scott Hancock

June 11, 1865, Washington, D.C.; ALS, DNA-RG56, Appts., Customs Service, Surveyor, Philadelphia, Benjamin F. Hancock.

Having received assurances from Lincoln during the previous winter that his father, Benjamin F. Hancock, would be appointed surveyor of the port of Philadelphia, the general now requests that the late president's intentions be fulfilled. Appointment of his father, a War Democrat and "firm supporter of the administration," would be "popular" and "easily established." [Although the petition was endorsed "special attention called to it by Prest. Johnson," Hancock was not appointed.]

From Richard J. Oglesby

June 11, 1865, Springfield, Ill.; ALS, DNA-RG107, Lets. Recd., EB10 President 1789 (1865).

Having learned that Gen. Stephen A. Hurlbut, an Illinoisan "whose reputation so far as any of us know stands without a blemish," has been arrested by federal authorities in New Orleans and charged with cotton speculation, the governor of Illinois requests that Hurlbut receive "a fair Trial by the ordinary military tribunal to clear himself of the charges." [Johnson referred Oglesby's letter to the secretary of war; Hurlbut was allowed to resign, without a trial, and was honorably mustered out June 20, 1865.]

From John M. Palmer[1]

Louisville Ky June 11th 1865

His Excellency Andrew Johnson
Prest U.S.

Dispatch respiting Marshall P. Stewart[2] until the 23rd inst received.[3] The proof before the Military Commission convicts him of deliberately murdering Captain Johnson[4] of the Home Guards, shooting him after he was wounded and helpless. I ask the record may be examined before his sentence is changed. Applications in such cases coming from here are to be regarded with great suspicion.[5]

Jno M Palmer Maj Genl

Tel, DNA-RG107, Tels. Recd., President, Vol. 4 (1865–66).
1. Commanding the Department of Kentucky.
2. Stewart, a home guard member, was charged with being a guerrilla and with murdering three fellow members of the home guard in Grayson County on February 10, 1865. Tried by military court on May 22, he was found guilty and sentenced to be hanged on June 13. Court-Martial Records, MM-2157, RG153, NA.
3. Johnson to Palmer, June 11, 1865, Tels. Sent, President, Vol. 2 (1865), RG107, NA.
4. David Johnson, not otherwise identified, was captain of a home guard company in Grayson County, Ky. Court-Martial Records, MM-2157, RG153, NA.
5. Although he was rescheduled to be hanged on August 5, Stewart's respite was continued. In late July, in "compliance with the recommendation of the Judge Advocate General," Johnson continued the suspension of execution until September 21, when he ordered Stewart released. Johnson to Palmer, July 31, 1865, Tels. Sent, President, Vol. 2 (1865), RG107, NA; Johnson's endorsement to secretary of war, Aug. 14, 1865, Court-Martial Records, MM-2157, RG153, NA; Gen. Court-Martial Order No. 529, Sept. 21, 1865, RG94, NA.

To John M. Palmer

Executive Office, Washington, D.C.
June 11 1865.

To Maj Gen John M. Palmer,
Louisville, Ky.

The application for the Reprieve of T. W. Evans[1] stated that you were absent and would not return before the time fixed for his execution.

The day of execution was therefore postponed.[2]

I hope you will put things through in Kentucky as understood when you were here.

Andrew Johnson
President U.S.

Tel, DNA-RG107, Tels. Sent, President, Vol. 2 (1865).
1. Thomas W. Evans was one of eight men captured near Harrodsburg, Ky., on January 29, 1865, by Kentucky state troops after a brief skirmish. Evans and his companions

insisted they were soldiers from the 4th Mo. Cav., CSA, dispatched on a raid into the area, but after six of them escaped, Evans and the other remaining prisoner were condemned for operating as guerrillas while disguised as Federal soldiers and for murdering Frank Cunningham, a lieutenant in the 13th Ky. Cav., USA. Court-Martial Records, MM-788, RG153, NA.

2. Palmer had protested Johnson's postponement of Evans' execution, which the President wired to Louisville during the general's absence on June 9. Despite Palmer's assertion that Evans was indeed guilty of an "atrocious murder," Johnson on June 23 ordered a second reprieve of fifteen days after receiving a direct appeal from Evans: "I did not kill Cunningham. Allen Palmer of Independence of Missouri is the man. Give me time & I will prove it by twenty (20) witnesses. If I fail then execute me." Johnson to Commanding Officer, June 9, 1865, Dept. of Kentucky, Tels. Sent and Recd., 1865, RG393, NA; Palmer to Johnson, June 11, 1865, Tels. Recd., President, Vol. 4 (1865–66), RG107, NA; Evans to Johnson, June 22, 1865, Johnson Papers, LC; Johnson to E. H. Hobson, June 23, 1865, Tels. Sent, President, Vol. 2 (1865), RG107, NA.

From Henry K. Burgwyn

June 12, 1865, Boston, Mass.; ALS, DNA-RG94, Amnesty Papers (M1003, Roll 37), N.C., H. K. Burgwyn.

Wealthy North Carolina planter, visiting Boston, applies for pardon, citing his subscription to Lincoln's oath of allegiance and pledging "to demean himself during the residue of his life" as a loyal citizen. Having been a unionist before the war, he became convinced that it would be better to exist under two governments—one free, one slave—"allied to each other offensively & defensively against all foreign countries," but had remained firm in the belief that a peaceful separation could occur. His service to the Confederacy was as an agent to appraise the value of agricultural products for governmental purchase. While he was the owner of about 150 slaves before war's end, he doubts that his property, mainly now in real estate, is worth $20,000. [Governor Holden originally recommended suspending action on this petition, which was filed June 20, 1865, but in February 1866 reversed his decision, clearing the way for Burgwyn's pardon on May 26, 1866.]

From James M. Leach

June 12, 1865, Lexington, N.C.; ALS, DNA-RG94, Amnesty Papers (M1003, Roll 40), N.C., J. M. Leach.

Former U.S. congressman, excepted from Johnson's Amnesty Proclamation for having served in the Confederate Congress, cites his record against secession in the 36th Congress, where he "denounced *it*, & *disunion* in a speech" delivered the day after Johnson's "very able speech on the same subject (of the 7th of February)," when he "took the same ground that you did, tho' enforced with vastly less ability." Although Leach went with his state, he "was the first *public man* in the state . . . that took ground boldly on the stump for *peace*" and vowed that he "never supported a measure asked for by Jeff Davis, but was hated by him & his subservient tools." [Pardoned by Johnson on June 19, 1865.]

From James R. Matthews [1]

Cincinnati June 12th 1865

Mr. Andrew Johnson
President of the United States
My Dear Sir—

I was born in Newton County Georgia in the year 1828. Had been for several years and untill the March 8th 1862 with my family,[2] a resident of Atlanta Ga. When traitors and conspirators attemted to consummat the dissolution of the Union by the act of Secession I for one opposed the principle and strove with all my energy to avert if possiable the horrible deed that I well new would flung the country into Civil War. But I was a poor man—my intretes [entreaties] avaled nothing. In the hast and rapid spread of this mania of rebellion I saw the dear old flag go down to the dust by the hands of those whom Slavory had brutalized. From that day forward, the hands of patriots were fettered and their mouths were gagged, but the hearts of some still waxed warm and throbbed with pulsations of loyalty. My love of country made me forget the dangers around me and I wold not abandon my principles for the mere sake of property or the secrurity of my person. I held not my own life dear to me—that I might prove fathfull to the spirit of the constitution and true to the flag of my country. On the 4th of March 1862—Myself and family receved a notice from the Safety committee of Atlanta saying to us—that we Sympathized with the enemies of the Confederate States—and tharefore we would have to leve the Country or be errested and imprisoned. This order to leve was signed by the president of the committee and I new that the non compliance to the order would consign me and family to prison and likly to death. I shuffled the cards to my liking and under grate privations Safely reched the union lines. My wife emediatly took sick from exposue on the way, and has been under the care of physicians the grater potion of our pilgrimage north. I loved my country too well to stand edley by, and see it insulted without linding my ade in its suport. So I sholdred my gun and went foth to meet the cowards who had run me away from my native home be cause of my attachment to the government of my fathers. I was the first and probably the only native Georgian who represented that state in the grate contest for freedom and equal rights. I did not receive a cent of bounty for my servises. I asked for none. It was enough that I should leve a honorable discharge from the Union army, as a rich leggacy to my children—that they might know that I did not disgrace them by committing the attrocious crime for having fought to inslave a human being for life. Now as a union Soldier and a citizen of Georgia, my solicitude is for the wellfare of the poor of my State—

Black and white. I know that you will be over run with applicants for Federal appointments from that State. Some have called on you allready as though they was worthey. I know them. Their hands are red with blood—let them go there way for me. It is indeed refreshing to me to know that you intend to act towards Ga. the same policy as applied to North Carolina. May God in murcy protect you—in all time to come— And make you wise to the performance of the duties that will so much affect the future wellfare and happiness of the people at large.

I am Sir your most obediant and umble Servant
J. R. Matthews

No 647 Sycamore Street

ALS, DLC-JP.
1. Matthews (1828–*fl*1872) was a tinner who moved from Georgia to Cincinnati during the war and continued his trade. Cincinnati directories (1865–73); 1860 Census, Ga., Fulton, Atlanta, 1st Ward, 11.
2. Wife Mary A. (*c*1830–*fl*1881) and at least one child, Benjamin. Ibid.

To Martha Patterson

Executive Office, Washington, D.C.,
June 12th 1865.

To Mrs Martha Patterson,
Nashville, Tenn.

Arrangements have been made to receive you at Cincinnati on the Seventeenth (17th) instant. Let me know when you leave Nashville.[1] I have recieved a long letter from your brother Robert not as pleasing as I would like.[2] He had better come with the family than to go to East Tennessee.

It can be no worse than it has been.[3]

Andrew Johnson

Tel, DNA-RG107, Tels. Sent, President, Vol. 2 (1865).
1. On June 14 both Martha Patterson and Johnson sent telegrams to each other. Mrs. Patterson informed her father that she would leave that evening at 6 o'clock. The President inquired whether she would arrive in Cincinnati in the morning or evening of June 17 and whether she would arrive by mail stage or by boat. Martha Patterson to Johnson, June 14, 1865, Johnson Papers, LC; Johnson to Martha Patterson, June 14, 1865, Tels. Sent, President, Vol. 2 (1865), RG107, NA.
2. Not found.
3. As late as May 31, Robert was planning to go to Washington with the family. Apparently the missing letter indicated a change of plans.

From James B. Steedman

Cincinnati, Ohio June 12, 1865.

My Dear Sir,

This will be handed to you by my friend, Washington McLean[1]— proprietor of the Cincinnati Enquirer, whom I have known and respected for twenty years. He is a true man—worthy of your confidence in all respects. His paper, as you must have observed, is supporting you, and, I doubt not, will continue to support your Administration vigorously. He has opposed the war,[2] in which I think he was wrong; but our difference on the war, has never broken our friendship. We have been life long Democrats together, never differing for twenty years except in the war, and as I know him to be sincere, earnest and honest, I desire he should give you the support of his influential paper. He will either do it cordially, boldly and effectivly, or oppose you fearlessly.[3] I am satisfied all his predilections are in favor of your Administration, and from the prisent indications I have but little doubt about the "Enquirer" being the organ of your Administration in Ohio. McLean has the good sense to know that the party—the masses will have to go over to you—without any assurance from you except that contained in your policy, on the only questions that will divide parties for the next four years.

I think I can see plainly foreshadowed in all directions, disintegration of present organizations and formation of new parties, the one supporting your Administration, the other opposing, and McLean and I agree. He desires to talk with you fully.

I anticipate a more clear developement of the growing opposition to you on the Republican side, by the time he presents this letter than is visible at this time—for I am certain it is coming—and trust this growth may bring him nearer to you than he appears, publicly to be at this time.

All is well among the people. You will be sustained in your policy as enunciated in your North Carolina proclamation, by the masses, overwhelmingly.

With Esteem your friend
James B. Steedman M Gen

Andrew Johnson President U. States.

ALS, DLC-JP.

1. McLean (1816–1890) was the publisher of the *Enquirer*, a prominent Democratic newspaper. Charles T. Greve, *Centennial History of Cincinnati and Representative Citizens* (2 vols., Chicago, 1904), 2: 840.

2. Under the management of McLean's brother, S. B. Wiley McLean, and editor James T. Farran, the *Enquirer* had strongly opposed Lincoln and his administration's war policies, while Washington McLean had been the leader of a peace movement in Ohio during the war. Frank L. Mott, *American Journalism* (New York, 1962), 459n; Bonadio, *North of Reconstruction*, 8.

3. Washington McLean supported Johnson's stand against black suffrage but by the fall of 1865 had repudiated the President's overall Reconstruction program as "unconstitutional." Ibid., 45, 83, 90; *Cincinnati Enquirer*, June 29, 1865.

From Joseph A. Wright

4 Broad St New York June 12th. 1865

His Excellency, Andrew Johnson,
President of U States,
My Dear Friend,

I have just returned from a weeks absence on business in Vermont. You know the ultra character of the politics of Vermont. They have a State Convention the last of this month, and will nominate our old Democratic friend, Paul Dillingham[1] for Governor who was with us in the 28th Congress, and elect him by more then 20,000 majority. *Vermont will endorse* your administration, including your North Carolina proclamation. In my short address at Burlington, I recieved more cheering in the discussion of *your views* of reconstruction, than any other topic. Her people are not in great haste about reconstruction, they are prepared to let time do its work, they say let commerce & trade do *their* work, and we shall more clearly see the proper remedy. It is certainly wisdom, in the great work of reconstruction, to take one step at a time. Vermont is the great sheep state of the Union, and as I am determined not to be a drone in the hive while abroad, I have been making arrangements to exchange the productions of our Country of individuals and State organizations, in Germany, for their superior stock & productions. I will see you in a day or two, trusting by that time the State Department will have heard from Mr Judd.[2] I have nearly completed my arrangements for departure, and can leave in ten days.[3] Please let the appointment to the Post Office in Indianapolis rest till I see you. I am sure I can give you some valuable and reliable information. Mrs. Wright writes in kindest regards with myself, for you and your family. Accept the kindest assurances of your unchanging friend

Joseph A Wright

ALS, DLC-JP.

1. Dillingham (1799–1891) served in the Vermont legislature, in Congress, as lieutenant governor (1862–65), and as governor (1865–66). *BDAC*.

2. Norman B. Judd (1815–1878), a Chicago lawyer who nominated Lincoln for President at the 1860 Republican convention, had been minister to Berlin during the war. He was later congressman and collector at the port of Chicago. Ibid.

3. Wright, minister to Berlin under Buchanan, had strongly hinted that he wanted to return to Berlin as minister. He finally got his wish when Johnson reappointed him. Letter from Wright, Dec. 13, 1864, *Johnson Papers*, 7: 338; Wright to Johnson, Mar. 24, 1865, Johnson Papers, LC.

From M. Elizabeth Young[1]

Nashville June 12" /65[2]

My dear Friend—

I have Just been introduced to General Prince Slam[3] and been to call upon his wife with whom I am very much pleased—indeed delighted. I take the opportunity of writing by them as I know that it will be placed in your hands—unread. I wrote to you under cover to Col Brownig asking him to place it in your hands—unopeed—as I understand that all letters addressed to you are opened and read by your secretaries. Do give orders that all letters marked *private*—will be placed in your hands *unopend*. I should not like letters written [awkwardly?] by me to be read by them. This has [kept?] me from writing as I wished. I was [afraid?] it was inspected. This I know you will get. When shall I see you again—is this [accession?] of Power to separate us entirely? Let me know what I am to expect. I am sad and lonely and miss you more than I can express—and I am made to feel every day by these people that I am *your friend*—and then my Pecuniary condition is very limited. In a month or two I shall have nothing. Aunts[4] health is failing and I need your *aid* and *assistance*. Will you not give it to me. Will change of circumstances change your feeling. Do not let me feel that I have placed my faith in a broken reed. Do not desert us now that you have the power—to place me above—want and above my enemies. Oh you do not know how depressed I am and so fearful of the future. Certainly you will not desert me and leave me to be trodden into the dust. I have placed all faith and confidence in you—do not let me be disappointed. I have always told you that I had complete faith and confidence in you. Do not Oh do not let me be disappointed. It will Kill me—for I have no one to look to but yourself. Write me a few Lines saying [illegible] and I read [illegible] but I am very sad and desponding. You do not know how these people treat me. Remember your promises—and remember above all Aunts long and faithful friendship to you—and aid her now that you have the power. Oh how she misses you and greves over the seperation. She never expects to see you again. She has shed many tears about it. There has bien remarks made about you in this community with regard to Lincons death that you ought never to forgive. They pander to your face and abuse you behind your back. Do not give the Judgeship to Houston.[5] These Polks hate and dispise you. Do not aid anyone—connected with them as he is one [of] them. He is a third rate Lawyer. Give it to some man of character and ability. The persons who take this letter say you have promised to aid her husband. Do it. He seems to be a fine soldier. Who are you going to place over me? So you have rewarded General Miller[6]—for his [illegible] to me. He is no friend of yours. I wish you would bring Granger[7] back again. What is Robert? I am glad Thomas[8] is to remain. He is Just. That is better than any thing else. Do not give yourself into the hands of those ultra Northern Men. Use them but remember that the south is your home. Do you remember saying that you expected to live and die in Nashville? What now are your intentions and what am I to expect? All power is in your hands now.

Aunt says that she feels entirely unpotecte here since you left—and can never ceese to regret your absece—and I—I am afraid to express all I feel. Be assure it is more than I can express or write. Do give me some comfort—and write at least a few lines by this lady. I told her you had promised me a mission to Europe years ago. Will you give it to me—or at least some office under Government that will yield me a support? I am very tired of being in this dirty house surrounded by men. Robert can tell you how disagreeable it is. The men sit in the door smoking in their shirt sleeves [illegible] once respected by [illegible] up its nose at us. I have no visitors now at night and no one to dress for and am very [illegible] and sad.

I am trying to get to the country for a few weeks on account of Aunts health which is very bad. Let Mrs. Slams bring me an appointment to some office. I am in earnest for I cannot st[ar]ve—and have no one to aid me but yourself. Be sure and write what I am to expect.

Yours, etc. L[i]zz[i]e

ALS, DLC-JP.
1. "Lizzie" Young was one of Johnson's fellow boarders at the St. Cloud in Nashville during his governorship in the 1850s.
2. The Library of Congress has misdated this letter as an 1868 document.
3. Prince Salm-Salm (1828–1870), Prussian nobleman who came to America in 1861 and offered his services to the Union army, was colonel, 68th N.Y., when breveted brigadier in Nashville. His wife, Princess Agnes (1842–1881), was an American-born circus rider and actress. For her hospital service in Tennessee, Governor Yates of Illinois rewarded her with a captain's commission and pay privileges. Boatner, *CWD*; *DAB*.
4. Martha Somerville.
5. Russell Houston, Tennessee supreme court judge (Jan.-Aug. 1865). His wife, Grizelda, the daughter of William Polk of North Carolina, was a kinswoman of the former President and of two Confederate generals.
6. John F. Miller.
7. Robert S. Granger.
8. George H. Thomas.

From Henry W. Hilliard[1]

Woodlawn. Near Augusta. Ga.
June 13th 1865.

My dear Sir,

Recalling with sincere pleasure our former relations in the House of Representatives, I write to you without hesitation in regard to some subjects of interest to me, both personal and political. It is true that we sat on different sides of the Hall; but I very well remember that we agreed in opinion as to some important subjects at that time under discussion in Congress: the *Tariff*—and your *Homestead Bill* to which I gave my support. These recollections, and the fact that you occupy at this time a position so exalted and influential as to enable you to control to a great degree the destinies of the country for years to come, induce me to write with frankness confident from my knowledge of your character that the letter will be kindly recieved. I assure you that no one experiences a deeper satisfaction at the restoration of the Union than myself. I have been unswervingly devoted to it from my boyhood. In 1851 I encountered the fiercest opposition from Mr. Yancey[2] and others in Alabama; and succeeded in achieving a complete triumph for the Union cause. In the recent struggle through which we have passed—a struggle without a parallel in history—my attachment to the Union was unconquerable. I canvassed the State of New York in 1860 at the request of the conservative committee who desired to concetrate the friends of the several candidates (Mr. Douglass, Mr. Breckenridge, & Mr. Bell) upon a single ticket: and at the close of the canvass returned to Alabama to oppose the secession movement. I did oppose it vehemently, but was overwhelmed by numbers. I took no part in any of the movements of those who were engaged in orgainzing a new government; but returned to the City of New York where I remained until about the middle of Feb: 1861, in consultation with such gentlemen as Wilson G. Hunt, Judge Roosevelt, and Genl. Scott.[3] Returning by way of Washington, I was acting in concert with those who were endeavoring to save the Union. It was not until hostilities broke out, that I took any part in behalf of the South. Differing from those who thought that force was essential to the restoration of the Union, I felt it to be my duty to resist that mode of settling our troubles. But still I was so earnest in my wish to reestablish the government to which I was ardently attached, that I drew upon me the hostility of those who controlled public affairs at the South. For some two years or more I have been awaiting here the blowing over of the storm; practising law; and cultivating a small place that I own near Augusta. I have never relinquished my residence in Alabama; but thought it best to see where the tempest would leave us, before making any change in my *status*.

I am now disposed to return to public life. I retired from Congress voluntarily, believing that the affairs of the country were at that time settled for many years. But everything now inclines me to an active participation in politics. The field is an inviting one—for those who are really attached to the institutions of the country. I am profoundly so. I do not belong to that class who profess to believe that the country is ruined by recent events. On the contrary, I firmly believe that it will attain a higher prosperity than it ever enjoyed before. The substitution of *compensated* labor, for *slave* labor is acceptable to me. So far from

being disposed to thwart the measures inaugurated for the accomplishment of this great change in our industrial system, I shall give them my
hearty support.

All that the South wants is time to adjust itself to the new system.
Then we may look for the happiest results. It would be very unwise
statesmanship that undertook to incorporate slavery once more into our
social, and industrial system. Independent of every other consideration—
the black race has passed beyond the reach of servitude. The idea of
freedom has entered the brain of the negro: it will never pass out of it.
Henceforth he *is* free! There is of course a large class of our people who
will do all that they feel at liberty to do to restore the old *status* of the
slave. It will be lost labor. They might as well try to turn back the
shadow on the face of the dial: as to reverse the progress of civilization.

I observe with pleasure that you are adopting measures for the restoration of civil government in the several States lately engaged in war
with the United States. I like your plan. The provisional Governor—
the Romans would have called him *Proconsul*—can guide the movement of the returning States. New Legislatures—new political bodies—
new members of Congress: all this will make a loyal State. Henceforth
the Republic will rise to grander destinies. "The Federal Union" will
stand. There will be a nobler spirit in the legislation of Congress than
ever before: larger views of Statesmanship: and a higher consecration
of all that the country possesses to the advancement of its glory and
prosperity.

I need not assure you that whatever I can do either here, or in Alabama, to advance your views, I shall be most happy to do.

With my best wishes for the success of your Administration, and for
your personal welfare,

I am, Very respectfully Very truly Your's
Henry W. Hilliard.

His Excellency, Andrew Johnson—President.

ALS, DLC-JP.
1. Although Hilliard strongly opposed disunion as a Whig Congressman from Alabama, after Fort Sumter he served as Confederate commissioner to Tennessee and briefly
in Bragg's army, before resigning in December 1862. *DAB*.
2. Alabama congressman William L. Yancey was Hilliard's lifelong political opponent
and one of the South's most avid secessionists. During the debates over southern unity
and the compromise of 1850, the two took diametrically opposite positions. Ibid.;
Thelma Jennings, *The Nashville Convention: Southern Movement for Unity, 1848–1851*
(Memphis, 1980), 21–201 passim.
3. Wilson G. Hunt (b. c1805), a New York City merchant; James I. Roosevelt
(1795–1875), New York congressman and ex-officio judge of the state's court of appeals;
and Winfield Scott, general in chief of the U.S. Army at the beginning of the Civil War.
1860 Census, N.Y., New York City, 18th Ward, 160; *BDAC*.

From William W. Holden

Raleigh June 13 1865

His Excellency A Johnson

Col D Heaton[1] treasury agent is about removing a lot of Cotton belonging to this state at Graham Depot N C. This Cotton was not Captured prior to the surrender of Genl Johnston. Genl Schofield favors
its restoration to the state but does not feel empowered so to order.[2] I
earnestly hope that none of the property owned by the state will be
claimed as forfeited to the United States. Enough of Payments can be
collected to pay the Expenses of the provisional Government including
the Convention & first meeting of the General assembly. In view of the
destitute Condition of our people I beg you not to enforce Confiscation
of state property.[3]

Very Respy W W Holden Prov Govr

Tel, DLC-JP2.

1. David Heaton (1823–1870), who moved from Minnesota to North Carolina during the war, where he was appointed special treasury agent and U.S. depositary at New
Bern, later served as a member of the North Carolina constitutional convention (1867)
and as a Republican in Congress (1868–70). *BDAC.*

2. The previous month Schofield told a subordinate, "Army officers cannot settle any
question of confiscation. The desire of the commanding general is that most officers have
as little as possible to do with such matters." However, on May 28 he ordered Heaton to
return to its owner a Wilmington house used as a headquarters. Schofield to I. N. Palmer,
May 16, 1865, and to Heaton, May 28, 1865, Schofield Papers, LC.

3. Following an interview with Jonathan Worth, North Carolina's provisional treasurer, whom Holden had sent to Washington, Johnson issued an order on July 8 for the
state to take over the property not previously seized by the army by that date. Holden
was able to use the income not only to support the provisional government but also to
pay for the constitutional convention in the fall. Harris, *Holden,* 176; Raper, *Holden,* 67.

From Robert E. Lee[1]

Richmond 13 June '65

His Excl. Andrew Johnson
President of the U. States
Sir

Being excluded from the provisions of amnesty & pardon Contained
in the proclamation of the 29th Ulto:[2] I hereby apply for the benefits,
& full restoration of all rights & privileges extended to those included
in its terms.

I graduated at the Mil: Academy at W. Point in June 1829. Resigned
from the U.S. Army April '61. Was a General in the Confederate
Army, & included in the surrender of the Army of N. Va: 9 April '65.[3]

I have the honour to be

Very respt. your obt Servt. R E Lee

Richmond 13 June '65

His Exc.y Andrew Johnson
    President of the U. States

    Sir

            Being excluded from the
provisions of amnesty & pardon contained in
the proclamation of the 29.th ulto: I hereby
apply for the benefits, & full restoration of all
rights & privileges extended to those included
in its terms.
        I graduated at the Mil: Academy
at W. Point in June 1829. Resigned from
the U. S. Army April '61. Was a General in
the Confederate Army, & included in the
surrender of the Army of N. Va: 9 April '65
        I have the honor to be
            very respy. your obt Servt
                R E Lee

Robert E. Lee applies for pardon
Courtesy Illinois State Historical Library

ALS, IHi.

1. While preparing to file an application for pardon, Lee learned of a treason indictment against him. Thereupon, he wrote Grant on June 13 that, though willing to face trial, he believed the Appomattox terms precluded such action and enclosed this letter to Johnson, which Grant forwarded on June 16. Lee to Grant, June 13, 1865, and Grant to Stanton, June 16, 1865, Illinois State Historical Library; Elmer Otis Parker, "Why Was Lee Not Pardoned?" *Prologue*, 2 (1970): 181.

2. Lee fell in the third, fifth, and eighth exceptions of Johnson's May 29 proclamation.

3. Unaware of Attorney General Speed's June 7 circular, requiring that pardon requests be accompanied by a signed amnesty oath, Lee did not forward one until October 2, 1865. As a result, the two documents necessary for a presidential pardon were not filed together, and though Lee never received a personal pardon, he ultimately fell within the provisions of Johnson's amnesty proclamation of Christmas Day, 1868, which restored "all rights, privileges, and immunities under the Constitution." Parker, "Lee Not Pardoned?" 181; Richardson, *Messages*, 6: 341–42, 708.

From Edwin D. Morgan

New York June 13, 1865

Dear President

Presuming that the New York Times of this morning is correct in its statement that "President Johnson has determined to issue a General Proclamation putting an end to the present system of purchasing cotton, and other Southern products by Government Agents," I can Scarcely express to you the pleasure I feel at the announcement, of this decision of the Administration.

I have not the slightest pecuniary interest in any of the productions named. But I have felt, as I expressed when I last had the pleasure of a personal interview with you (being the day that you removed to the Presidential mansion), that it was just & proper that the restriction of 25 per cent should be at once removed and that every body, except those, in some way interested in, or controlled by Treasury Agents, would say it was the proper thing to be done.

Every interest called for it. Every interest will sustain and approve it, except the Treasury agents and their friends.

I have the honor to be with high esteem
Your obt svt E. D. Morgan

ALS, DLC-JP.

From Charles A. Smith

June 13, 1865, Memphis, Tenn.; ALS, DNA-RG48, Patents and Misc. Div., Lets. Recd.

Recommends that Congress order a new census for 1865, so that "the loss of property in the South since 1860 will be a lasting admonition to count[less] generations of the result of rebellion."

From William E. Arnold[1]

Weston W.Va. June 14. 1865

Hon Andrew Johnson
Dr. Sir:

There are at this time two companies of West Virginia Veteran U.S. troops stationed in this town: also two companies at Bulltown Braxton County, and two at Glenville Gilmer County, whose terms of service do not expire till 1867. The keeping of these troops at these places must necessarily cost the Govt. a considerable sum (as provisions have to be hauled from Rail Road, over bad roads from 25 to 50 miles in wagons.) The present quiet and good order of all our citizens (returned rebels and our own discharged soldiers,) together with the civil and efficient administration of public justice, in this part of West Virginia, make it wholly unnecessary, at this time, to keep U.S. Soldiers at these places.

We hold it to be the duty of every man, who has the good of his country at heart, and especially its *financial* condition, to aid the administration, by giving it such information as will enable it, to retrench the expenses of the government as rapidly as the public tranquility will permit. No good loyal man acquainted with the facts (except it be one *in office*, or *enriching* himself) desires U.S. troops stationed here at this time. If their services can not be employed at some other place, where they are needed, they should be discharged without delay, and stop the expenses incident, by their further retention.[2]

I am Your Obt Sert Wm. E Arnold

N.B. I fear subordinate military commanders, are too much inclined to find excuses, for stationing U.S. troops at points, where they are not *now* needed, for the sake of the emoluments of Office, rather than any real good they would at this time render the public.

Of all others, this is *the time*, that a most rigid scrutiny into the military affairs of the country, should be strictly enforced. The blood suckers are going to hold on to the public treasury, with a death grasp.[3]

Wm. E. Arnold

ALS, DNA-RG108, Lets. Recd. *re* Military Discipline.

1. Arnold (1817–1890), a lawyer who served in the Virginia legislature as a Union Democrat, was subsequently a member of the West Virginia legislature (1877). Atkinson and Gibbens, *Prominent Men*, 528; Roy Baird Cook, *Lewis County in the Civil War* (Charleston, W. Va., 1924), 11, 23.

2. The last Federal troops in Weston, part of the 8th Ohio Cavalry, were mustered out on July 30. Ibid., 92.

3. After this letter, Arnold was arrested on unspecified charges and confined by order of Gen. William P. Carlin, but on July 8 was ordered released. E. D. Townsend to William H. Emory, July 8, 1865, Lets. Sent (Main Ser.), Vol. 40 (M565, Roll 27), RG94, NA.

From William G. Brownlow

Nashville, June 14th, 1865.

President Johnson:

As the *brevitting* an officer Maj. General is no additional expense to the Government, if I were you, I would *brevit* Brig. Gen. Donalson,[1] of this city. He desires it, he *merits* it, and he is a warm friend of yours.

Before you grant a pardon to Jesse G. Wallace,[2] you ought to see his *wicked* and *infamous* letters[3] we have found among the papers of Harris,[4] captured at Augusta, with the State archives. Among them are the correspondence with *Lawrence* by *Charlton*, in your name, forging your name and signature.[5]

Let *Clabe Kain* be sent here in the care of the Military.[6]

There are men here, calling themselves *Union men*, who are seeking to overthrow the present State Government, and clamor for another election under the *old State Constitution*, asking that the *amended Constitution* be set aside and the elections with it. They are writing in the "Dispatch," *revolutionary* and *seditious* articles, calling on Rebels to assert their rights at the polls.[7] They ought to be imprisoned.

Yours &c, W. G. Brownlow

ALS, DLC-JP.

1. James L. Donaldson, chief quartermaster of the Department of the Cumberland, was brevetted major general, June 20, 1865. Boatner, *CWD*.

2. A Maryville lawyer, Wallace (c1827–fl1887) had served as Confederate district attorney for East Tennessee (1862–65). 1880 Census, Tenn., Williamson, 236th Enum. Dist., 48; *Athens Post*, Apr. 18, 25, 1862; Goodspeed's *East Tennessee*, 830. For more information on his pardon, see Letter from Wallace, July 6, 1865.

3. Wallace's captured letters (of May 29 and June 7, 1861), supportive of the Confederacy, were published in Brownlow's *Whig and Rebel Ventilator*, July 5, 1865.

4. Isham G. Harris, governor of Tennessee until Federal occupation in early 1862.

5. In May 1861 Knoxville Confederate postmaster Charles W. Charlton, intercepting a letter to Johnson from Boston philanthropist and businessman Amos A. Lawrence, had engaged in a correspondence with the latter by forging Johnson's name. For more on the incident, see *Johnson Papers*, 4: 476–85 passim.

6. Five days later, Johnson's secretary telegraphed Brownlow that William Claiborne Kain had been sent to Nashville "under guard" on June 17. Reuben D. Mussey to Brownlow, June 19, 1865, Tels. Sent, President, Vol. 2 (1865), RG107, NA.

7. Probably a reference to "Senex," whose long letter to the editor, printed three days earlier, had questioned the constitutionality of the April elections for governor and legislators and the exclusion of a portion of the electorate. *Nashville Dispatch*, June 11, 1865.

From Thomas Cottman[1]

Washington June 14th 1865

Mr. President

At the risk of being considered importunate: I take the liberty of suggesting to you the propriety of placing Louisiana & Arkansas on the same footing with North Carolina & Mississippi. In the first place to establish a uniformity among the Rebellious States & in the next to rid us of the embarrassments occasioned by the irregularity of the prior attempts at organizing State Government. The States will start a new with a perfect knowledge of what they have to do and it will afford the entire *Loyal* population comprized within the geographical limits of the State an opportunity to participate in making the organic law for its own government. Speaking for Louisiana alone, the irregularities have been so great, that it would be a task in my humble opinion beyond the power of her citizens to rid her of the mosaic, with which she has been paved;[2]—for what purpose I will not allow myself to say. The ap-point[ment] of J Madison Wells, the acting governor to the position of Provisional Governor, would rid the State of multitudinous embarrass-ments in the State as well as in its connection with the general Govern-ment. It is unnecessary for me to say that my recommendation on this subject will meet the hearty concurrence of the State authorities, the present official incumbents. Upon the receipt of my letters from New Orleans I consulted with Judges Sharkey[3] & Yerger[4] from Mississippi and they cordially agree in the above suggestion & advised that I should submit it before leaving which I had intended to do this evening.

Very Respectfully Your Obt Servt. Thos. Cottman

His Excellency Andrew Johnson
President of the United States

ALS, DLC-JP.

1. A conservative Louisiana unionist.

2. Cottman probably refers to the layers of military and civil authority in Louisiana since its occupation by Federal troops in late April 1862. The overlapping of responsi-bilities between commanding generals and governors, first military and subsequently civil, and between agents of the Treasury Department and of the Freedmen's Bureau, frequently resulted in friction. Dawson, *Army Generals and Reconstruction*, 5–28.

3. William L. Sharkey (1798–1873) practiced law in Vicksburg, served in the leg-islature and as circuit and supreme court judge, and opposed secession as a states' rights Whig. Johnson appointed him provisional governor, June 13, 1865. *DAB*.

4. William Yerger (1816–1872) had practiced law in Jackson and served as supreme court judge. Although an opponent of secession and a unionist, he nevertheless sat in the Confederate legislature. Ibid.

From John W. Duncan

[Washington, D.C., June 14, 1865][1]

To His Excellency Andrew Johnson
President U.S.
Sir

During the interview you did us the honor to hold with the Delega-tion from Georgia on last Friday,[2] I took occasion to present to you the facts connected with my own case, under the Amnesty Proclamation issued May 29th 1865: to-with That after the passage of a Conscription measure by the authorities at Richmond embracing all persons within certain ages as subject to military service in the rebel armies I had no choice as one within the prescribed age, but to enter a service in opposition to my feelings & judgment or accept another position. I therefore as a Banker in charge of a Banking Institution, consented to receive the public deposites & act as Depositary in the City of Atlanta. You were kind enough to express your doubt, as to whether I could be considered one of the excepted classes. But to place the case beyond all question in reference to the above facts, & in reference to some contributions made by me from friendly motives to my neighbors who entered the military service, I respectfully ask that your Excellency will grant full & complete amnesty in the premises with the assurance of my desire to be, in the future—as it was my anxious wish in the past—a loyal citizen of the United States.[3]

Respectfully John W Duncan
Atlanta

ALS, DNA-RG94, Amnesty Papers (M1003, Roll 18), Ga., John W. Duncan.
    1. Duncan's oath which accompanied this application was signed and dated Washington, D.C., June 14, while he was in Washington with the Georgia delegation.
    2. According to the *Washington Morning Chronicle* of June 10, on the preceding day the President had been "waited upon by another delegation from Georgia."
    3. He was pardoned on June 19. *House Ex. Docs.,* 40 Cong., 2 Sess., No. 16, p. 113 (Ser. 1330).

From Ambrose Fowler[1]

New York June 14th 1865

Honored Sir

The New York Herald which until the last year has been ever the most intensely pro slavery paper published in the North had in the month of May on two occasions Editorial articles in favor of including suffrage to the Blacks in the government policy of reconstruction.[2] Soon afterwards it transpired that you Sir were averse to doing so. The Herald then shifted its ground & advocated the submission of the question to the white people recognized as loyal voters in the States being reconstructed.[3] Yesterday however it takes the ground that the government in reconstructing should not withhold the franchise from the following four classes of colored people

    1. All who have borne arms in defence of the Union
    2. All who have property
    3. All who can read & write
    4. All who have been church members for four or five years past.[4]

The New York Observer the organ of that large influential & highly conservative denomination the old School Presbyterians advocates the extension of the suffrage to loyalists without distinction of color. The Papers representing the new School Presbyterians the Independents the Methodists and the Baptists all seem to be in favor of it also.

Very respectfully Your obdt Servt
Ambrose Fowler

ALS, DLC-JP.

1. Not identified.

2. Only one such editorial has been found. On May 3, 1865, the *Herald* suggested granting black suffrage, which would serve the purpose of defusing extremist rhetoric both North and South.

3. Fowler probably refers to the *Herald*'s comments of May 13: "In regard to the question of negro suffrage, we infer that President Johnson will follow up his policy," established as military governor in Tennessee, in providing for the election of a convention to "frame a new State constitution, declaring slavery abolished and interdicted, but will leave the question of negro suffrage at the discretion of the Legislature."

4. While correct in his first three classes, the writer slightly garbles the fourth. As put by the *Herald*, those blacks who were church members four or five years *before the war* should be eligible to vote. *New York Herald*, June 13, 1865.

From James Hickman [1]

Nashville, Tenn. June 14th 1865

To His Excellency Andrew Johnson
Presdt. of U.S.
Dear Sir,

Genl. L. P. Walker has returned home to Huntsville Ala. He is on parole. He has come back in good faith, and is anxious to see the state come back into the Union, and is willing to use all of his influence to bring it back into its original status. I know that Walker has denounced the Richmond government more than two years ago, when he was my counsel, when I was tried for treason for levying war against the so called Confederate government, and said very hard things about Davis' administration, which came very near causing him to be arrested. And for defending me and other union men he was threatened to be taken out and hanged. If it had not been for Walker's influence, and his legal ability, Union men could not have lived in North Alabama. He denounced the Richmond government, as he called it, to me personally, and confidentially, for at that time no one was allowed to speak his sentiments publicly without being in danger of loosing his life. And they would now rather see him hung than any man in the state of Alabama. But I hope he may yet live to do as much good for the Union and the Government as he has ever done against it, and not only pay the debt he owes an offended government, but with interest. He says he is determined, henceforth and forever, to stand by and support the government of the United States at all hazards, and to the last extremity. And if his hands were not tied, he would now be on the stump, preaching to the people to come back to their first allegiance. I have this assurance from himself, and what he promises, you can rely upon. And such a man as Genl. Walker can wield a wonderful influence in the state of Alabama. I have talked to a great many Union men of the northern part of that state, and they are anxious for him to be pardoned and set at liberty, in order that they may have the benefit of his influence in that state, in organizing the state government; all of which I

most respectfully submit to your Excellency, hoping you will duly consider the matter, and act as favorably as the circumstances of the case
will admit.[2] I have the honor to be your

                                        Obedient Servant James Hickman

ALS, NNPM.
    1. Hickman was a Huntsville, Ala., resident who moved in 1864 to Nashville, where
he operated a dry goods store.
    2. See Letter from Daniel B. Turner, June 1, 1865.

From Benjamin H. Hill

June 14, 1865, Fort Lafayette, N.Y.; ALS, DNA-RG94, Amnesty Papers
(M1003, Roll 19), Ga., B. H. Hill.

Former Confederate senator requests a parole to return to Georgia to take the
oath and make a formal application for pardon. Although originally opposed to
secession, he did "act in good faith" in discharging his responsibilities to the
Confederacy, but he had looked for a settlement "procured by peaceful means
not by bloodshed." Wants now to "renew my obligations to the Union . . .
accepting fully the new condition of things according to your programme for
reorganization." [This petition was filed on June 19 with the notation: "Petition very imperfect." Paroled in July 1865, he was ultimately pardoned May
10, 1867.]

From Henry Homer

June 14, 1865, Boston, Mass.; ALS, DNA-RG45, Subj. File N, Subsec. NO,
Courts-Martial, Box 316, Jacob T. Homer.

Assistant superior court clerk seeks pardon for his nephew, Jacob T. Homer,
who, while serving on the *South Carolina*, "was convicted by a court martial
and sentenced to three years solitary imprisonment . . . for saying some words
while on watch in the night against the government," and who has now served
two-thirds of his time. Young Homer was eligible for prize money, and "in
Philadelphia a few days before he was put in irons the Capt of the South Carolina gave him . . . a prize ticket for Fifteen hundred dollars, but he has never
had a chance to get it." [On July 19 the President remitted "the unexecuted
portion of the sentence."]

From Spofford D. Jewett[1]

                                            Middlefield Ct June 14th 1865
Dear Sir—
    Now that the northern Copperheads and the southern secessionists
are defeated in arms—Every effort is being made by them, to reconstruct the old malignant pro slavery democratic party & get the control
of the Ballot Box. *Woe be to us*, poor abolitionists, if they succeed! President Lincoln defeated them in war. May President Johnson be wise to
disappoint their schemes in peace. If the seceded states be permitted to

elect, at will, disloyal members, Congress is theirs & the war has been invain. Be not cheated by sophists & pettifogger as Sherman was.[2]

New England asks of the President a vigorous, "old Hickory" administration. Mr. Stanton enjoys the confidence in his department of all our Loyal men. Dont heed the preaching of foxes.

S. D. Jewett

No relation to "Colorado["].[3]

ALS, DLC-JP.
1. Jewett (c1802–fl1881), a Congregational minister, became postmaster of Middlefield in 1861, a post he held until 1881, with a brief interruption during 1868–69. 1870 Census, Conn., Middlesex, Middlefield, 22; *U.S. Off. Reg.* (1861–81); A. D. Jones, *Gazetteer and Business-Book of Connecticut* (1857–58), 116.
2. A reference to the terms of surrender given by Gen. William T. Sherman to Gen. Joseph E. Johnston on April 18, 1865, which had been repudiated by the President. As endorsed by both officers, this document had guaranteed that the existing governments of the southern states would be recognized upon the administering of a loyalty oath, and that all persons in the South would retain their "political rights and franchise . . . so long as they live in peace and quiet." William J. Ulrich, "The Northern Military Mind in Regard to Reconstruction, 1865–1872: The Attitudes of Ten Leading Union Generals" (Ph.D. dissertation, Ohio State University, 1959), 187–88.
3. William C. Jewett, known as "Colorado" Jewett, had been instrumental in setting up a peace meeting at Niagara Falls, July 20, 1864, between Confederate commissioners and newspaper editor Horace Greeley. *Johnson Papers*, 4: 177n.

From Daniel Mace[1]

La Fayette, 14 June, 1865

Sir

Inclosed find an invitation to be with us on the 4 July.[2] The occasion will be imposing, and largely attended. Should time permit, please give us a letter, to appear in the proceedings of the day. Gov Morton[3] will deliver the Oration.

It gives me pleasure to state that your administration thus far gives our people general satisfaction. Some few ultras, and but few, object to your North Carolina policy as to the rights of Coloured men to vote.

Your Obt Sert Danl. Mace

To the President Washington, D.C.

ALS, DLC-JP.
1. Mace, Indiana delegate to the 1864 National Union Convention, had placed Johnson's name in nomination.
2. Johnson did not attend the celebration at the Tippecanoe Battle Ground.
3. Oliver P. Morton.

From Thornton F. Marshall

June 14, 1865, Augusta, Ky.; ALS, DLC-JP.

Kentucky state senator, regarding Johnson's plan for the reconstruction of North Carolina as "so eminently appropriate, politic, wise & constitutional" that he could not "refrain from contributing my humble, but most hearty endorsement," adds that his constituents "almost universally" have approved his proclamation. Sees as "plain & incontravertible" that "no state has ever been out of the Union" and that the rebellion was "simply opposition to laws & [to] the prosecution of the war to enforce submission & obedience thereto."

From Solomon Parsons [1]

Boston June 14, 1865

His Excellency Mr President

Last Fall as a member of the National Democratic Committee appointed at the National Convention in New York, I wrote to you at Nashville,[2] sending some documents stating why some of us had deemed it necessary to give our whole support to Mr. Lincoln—and I also stated that having done so I labored with my western friends to secure the nomination of yourself as Vice President, (never dreaming that in so short a period of time you would be called to the Presidency)—because I felt as an old democrat that much was due to you as so distinguished a member of our party, and much due to those members of the old Party who could not forget principle and right but were willing to join a Party we had so strongly opposed. By the Providence of God you are now Chief Magistrate of this Country, and you need the support and cooperation of the old Friends who were instrumental in placing you where you now are—and as there are symptoms of some opposition among some of those who have been identified with the Party who elected you, and who appear determined to force you to act in accordance with their views—I with others old friends are as decided under God to stand by you. On the 15th of this month the National Democratic Committee meet in New York, and as a member of that Committee I intend to offer the enclosed resolutions[3] and hope by an unanimous adoption to rally every true friend in the Country to sustain your Administration. I have written to Genl Logan[4] and my old colleagues & friends in Illinois and anticipate their entire concurrence.

I write now that you may feel that you are now as ever before, entitled to our confidence and trust and you may rely on the people to sustain you.

Very Respectfully Your Obt Servant
Solomon Parsons.

ALS, DLC-JP.

1. Parsons (fl1881), former Illinois resident, was currently secretary of the Tremont Temple in Boston. Boston directories (1866–81); Parsons to Lincoln, Oct. 27, 1864, Lincoln Papers, LC.

2. Not found, though he did write to Johnson in July. See Letter from Solomon Parsons, July 25, 1864, *Johnson Papers*, 7: 52.

3. One of these, attached to this letter, affirms support for Johnson as "Chief Magis-

trate on whom the Nation may safely rely for extrication from present perils, and the speedy reorganization of order, industry, and general prosperity."

4. John A. Logan.

From James W. Schaumburg

June 14, 1865, Philadelphia, Pa.; ALS, DNA-RG60, Appt. Files for Judicial Dists., La., James W. Schaumburg.

A refugee since the "cecession ordinance" was adopted, and a former U.S. Army paymaster, seeks to return to Louisiana as marshal for the western district. Believing that as a native he would be "more acceptable" and "could greatly influence the people" in that part of the state "to the entire submission to the changed condition of things," he cites his personal property losses in "negroes horses cattle &c &c" to Confederate sequestration as a result of his brief service as a Union officer. [He was not appointed; the merger of the western and eastern districts left the state with only one set of judicial officers.]

From Edwin M. Stanton

War Department Washington City,
June 14th 1865.

Mr. President:

I have the honor to acknowledge the reference to this Department of two complaints—one in respect to the restrictions upon the sale of spirituous liquors in the City of Richmond;[1] the other in relation to the regulations governing the sale of spirituous liquors in the City of Savannah.[2] These restrictions are undoubtedly in conflict with the general regulations recently established by your authority. All trade regulations are, and always have been understood to be, subject to the military necessity existing in any particular locality; and where they come in conflict with such police regulations as, in the judgment of the Commander of the post, detachment, or army, are required for the safety of his command, the public safety is itself jeoparded. By express authority from this Department, General Halleck was authorized to restrict the traffic in spirituous liquors in the City of Richmond, or even to prohibit it altogether, should such a course be found necessary for the military safety of that place.[3] The same general authority belongs to any military commander, and is the occasion of the restriction upon the liquor trade in the City of Savannah. In my judgment, as the Government holds the commanding officers of those two important places responsible for their security, it would not be wise to control them in the exercise of that discretion which they alone can properly exert. The small gains that would accrue to one or more liquor dealers, on the profits they might realize from this traffic, can be no consideration for a riot, a mob, or a military tumult, endangering arsenals, depots, and millions of public property. I would therefore advise that no action be taken in reference to these complaints, but that the matter be left, where it now is, entirely in the hands of the Military Commanders.

I have the honor to be, Very respectfully,
Your obedient servant, Edwin M. Stanton
Secretary of War.

LS, DNA-RG107, Misc. Lets. and Papers (1804–67).

1. Two Philadelphia liquor importers had complained to Johnson that the wine shipped "to a *loyal* citizen of Richmond" in conformity, they thought, with the terms of the President's "proclamation" of April 29 "removing restrictions on all goods not considered contraband of war," had been prevented from landing by order of General Halleck. Louis Lang and Alfred E. Massman to Johnson, May 29, 1865, Lets. Recd., EB12 President 1768 (1865), RG107, NA. See Executive Order Removing Certain Restrictions on Trade, April 29, 1865, *Johnson Papers*, 7: 669.

2. A New York whiskey exporter, having had thirty barrels denied access to the Savannah market, observed that Johnson's April 29 executive order "is rendered of no effect by military orders, which confine Trade to a few favored individuals." Colin Matheson to Johnson, June 5, 1865, Lets. Recd., EB12 President 1768 (1865), RG107, NA.

3. See Telegram to Henry W. Halleck, May 3, 1865.

From Joseph C. Barnard

June 15, 1865, Philadelphia, Pa.; ALS, DLC-JP.

A Texan, an "old Sailor" and a former blockade runner—a duty he "was oblidged to do, or run the risk of been pressed into Service or quit the country, leaving my Wife and Neice behind"—applies for pardon, having taken the oath before the Havana consul, but "Having some doubt whether I am excluded or accepted by your Proclamation of 29th of last month." Avows his unionism and offers for credit his assistance to the dying Gen. Sam Houston with whom "durring His sickness and up to His Death I had frequaint interviews . . . and know He lived and Died a sound Union Man." [A personal pardon has not been located.]

From Benjamin H. Hill

June 15, 1865, Fort Lafayette, N.Y.; ALS, DLC-JP.

Having read Johnson's proclamations establishing reconstruction in North Carolina and Mississippi, Hill asserts that during the war many southerners feared that the existence of their "States as states" would be ignored by the North, thereby reducing them to territories, a belief which "impelled many to do all in their power to uphold and encourage a struggle commenced in spite of their earnest-oppositions and against their life long convictions." Encouraged that the President's plan has left the right of suffrage in southern hands, making them "the architects of their own future," he avers that this recognition of the "identity of the Separate States" will save southerners from "the keenest of humiliations" and make Johnson "the benefactor of the Southern people in the hour of their direst extremity," entitling him "to the gratitude of those living and of those yet to live."

To John M. Schofield

Executive Mansion June 15, 1865

Major General Schofield
Comdg. Dept. North Carolina
Raleigh N.C.
Dear Sir,

I have just seen your General Order No. 74 C.S.[1]

I thank you for so fully efficiently and promptly recognizing the design and scope of my Proclamation for the re-establishment of Civil Government in North Carolina.

I am with high regards
Very Truly Yours
(Signed) Andrew Johnson

LBcopy, DLC-JP3A.
1. Dated June 5, Schofield's order announced Holden's appointment and directed military authorities to "render all proper and needful aid to all executive officers . . . in the discharge of the duties devolved upon them by law." *OR*, Ser. 1, Vol. 47, Pt. 3: 625.

From Herman Walther[1]

New York June 15. '65

To His Excellency Andrew Johnson
President of the United States.
Sir,

A minister of the gospel, 60 years old, begs to address Your Excellency. Some ten years ago, when a Missionary in the West I had the honor to make Your personal acquaintance. Since then I have watched your life, until it has pleased the Ruler of the Universe, to elevate you to the Presidency. I do not seek any benefit for me from my acquaintance with you, but I beg to give you, in my humble position, a word of advice or rather of warning. A man in so high a station, as yours, has less occasion, than we have, to learn the public opinion. Even such papers, as are the honest exponents of the sentiments of the nation, are often withheld from a President.

The man I warn you against, is not personally known to me, but I judge him from his transactions, which lay before the world. It is "Edwin M. Stanton." I consider him one of the most dangerous fellows living. He will ruin you, if not prevented in time. His infamous acts, his persecutions of innocent persons, his arbitrary arrests, his military trials of civil offences, his treatment of prisoners, especially of Jefferson Davis, who as a political offender was put in irons, all these and more acts of his have brought disgrace and ignominy on our country before the whole world. If not stopped, his acts will fall back upon you and you have to atone for it. And that is just the thing, that he wants. He will ruin you, to save himself. May God enlighten your mind, that you—while it is yet time—get rid of the scoundrel, who is cursed by a whole nation, who was a traitor from beginning and is still a traitor against you and the whole country.

With my earnest prayers to God for Your Excellency and with love and regard I remain

Your most obedient Servant Herman Walther
Methodist Missionary.

ALS, DLC-JP.
1. Not further identified.

From Alfred Austell[1]

St Nicholas Hotel N Y June 16th 1865

His Excellency Andrew Johnson
Prst. of the U States
Dear Sir

I am a citizen of Atlanta Geo; lived there for many years; Borned in Jefferson Co Tenn; Called on you last week[2] in compay with Isaac Scott & others; from Geo; I am desirious of having the appointment of marshal for the state of Geo; for my stattus I will Refer you to Mr J Erskin,[3] Hon. Joshua Hill A N Wilson Isaac Scott and men of that order. I was a large property holder in Geo. made it by my industry & Economy; by this unnatural war I have lost a great deal of it. Trusting that when you make the appointments for Geo you will take my application into consideration.[4]

Yours with high Esteem Alfred Austell
My Political Status a Duglas Democrat.

ALS, DNA-RG60, Appt. Files for Judicial Dists., Ga., Alfred Austell.
1. Austell (1814–1881), a planter and merchant, relocated in 1858 to Atlanta, where he became a successful banker, cotton broker, and railroad developer. Kenneth Coleman and Charles S. Gurr, eds., *Dictionary of Georgia Biography* (2 vols., Athens, 1983).
2. He was apparently with the Georgia delegation which had called on Johnson the previous Friday, June 9. *Washington Morning Chronicle*, June 10, 1865.
3. Following Austell's recommendation, John Erskine (1813–1895), lawyer and unionist, was appointed a district judge by Johnson on July 10, 1865, and served until 1883. Northen, *Men in Ga.*, 3: 169–71, 360; Appt. Bk. 4: 162, Ser. 6B, Johnson Papers, LC.
4. Austell allegedly declined an appointment as provisional governor of Georgia; William G. Dickson was appointed marshal on July 30, 1865. Northen, *Men in Ga.*, 3: 360; Appt. Bk. 4: 162, Ser. 6B, Johnson Papers, LC.

From Montgomery Blair

Washn. June 16. 1865

Dear Sir

I send another letter from Barlow,[1] also a paragraph from the Cincinnati Enquirer written by Geo Pendleton[2] I presume from the endorsement.

I will mention also that Chanler[3] the M.C from the city of N.Y. whom I introduced to you some time ago, & who talked to you about his visit to S.C. On going home he attempted a movement for you with the city Democracy. He told me yesterday that he got on swimmingly with it, but that weed (Thurlow)[4] defeated it finally. It is well known in N.Y that Thurlow & the leaders of the Demoralized *City* Democracy Cooperate. The County Democracy of New York are under the lead of Dean Richmond[5] & it was through him we carried the Constitutional amendment last winter.[6] He was utterly opposed to the Chicago platform which was carried by the other wing of the party headed by Seymour.[7] The result is that the Richmond party are now in the ascendant, & they are the progressive & honest War Democracy by whom the Constitutional Amendment was voted here last winter. I have always stood well with them, & beleive had some influence in persuading them to go the Amendment which they did on exclusively patriotic & party considerations, & yet I know that Mr. Seward made Lincoln beleive that he had carried that Amendment by Corruption. The only man so influenced was Anson Herrick whose vote was paid for by an appt[8] & was not needed for we had a dozen more votes that were not cast for it that would have been cast if they had been needed.[9]

Yrs truly M Blair

The President

P.S. Dont suppose in laying these matters before you that I do so to urge you to act otherwise than your judgt. prompts. You see by what Barlow writes, that I have no apprehensions that either Seward or Stanton or any body else would rule you, & in time I am sure others will see it as I do. These people are indeed obnoxious to me & to every one & it will be a relief to me and will be to the Country when they are dismissed from public employment. But you see the whole ground & I have confidence that you will do what is best, & at the right time.

M. B.

ALS, DLC-JP.

1. Samuel L. M. Barlow (1826–1889), successful New York City lawyer, was an ardent Democrat and McClellan supporter, who had purchased a controlling interest in the *New York World*. His letter to Blair warned that Johnson "day by day, allows himself to be placed in an antagonistic position, not merely to the whole democratic party but to a large portion of radicals." *NCAB*, 3: 259; Barlow to Blair, June 15, 1865, Johnson Papers, LC.

2. McClellan's running mate. This clipping has not been found.

3. John W. Chanler (1826–1877) was a Democratic congressman (1863–69). *BDAC*.

4. Thurlow Weed (1797–1882), a powerful Republican boss, was seeking to influence the President's policies while nullifying the influence of Barlow and other New York Democrats. *DAB*; LaWanda and John H. Cox, *Politics, Principles, and Prejudice, 1865–1866: Dilemma of Reconstruction America* (New York, 1963), 73–75.

5. Richmond (1804–1866) was a commission merchant and railroad promoter, serving as president of the New York Central (1864–66). Leader of the upstate Democracy and a War Democrat who supported McClellan, he was a prominent figure in New York state politics. *DAB*.

6. On January 31 in the close House vote on the Thirteenth Amendment, six New York Democrats of the Richmond stamp allied with ten other Democrats to make possible a two-vote margin of success. Cox, *Politics, Principles, and Prejudice*, 25.

7. Horatio Seymour, ex-governor of New York, became the Democratic standard-bearer in 1868. The Chicago platform, adopted with the McClellan-Pendleton ticket in 1864, contained a controversial peace plank.

8. The appointment, allegedly used as bait for Herrick's vote, was the assessorship of the 9th District of New York for his brother Hugh. Despite appeals to Johnson after Lincoln's death, the incumbent was not removed. Letter from Anson Herrick, [May] 5, 1865; Letter from Guy R. Pelton, Apr. 27, 1865, *Johnson Papers*, 7: 648; Herrick to William Dennison, July 1, 1865, Appts., Internal Revenue Service, Assessor, N.Y., 9th Dist., RG56, NA.

9. "Blair's contention that the Amendment had votes to spare does not square with contemporary accounts." Cox, *Politics, Principles, and Prejudice*, 26.

From James W. Downey

June 16, 1865, Petersburg, Va.; ALS, DNA-RG60, Office of Atty. Gen., Lets. Recd., President.

Conscripted late in the war and serving in the 13th Va. Cav., CSA, before his parole, a wealthy farmer seeks restoration of "Downey Farm" near Hampton, from which the government "dispossed him and made the farm a Got. farm." Subsequently, the property, with his furniture still in the house, was auctioned in March 1865 "for a nominal sum" to the former owner, to whom Downey still owed three payments. Having heard that the government would like to buy the farm, Downey offers to sell it "upon reasonable terms," if it is restored to him. [Presumably, his property was restored when he was pardoned September 26, 1865.]

From Alexander N. Wilson

Chattanooga Tenn, June 16th 1865.

Andrew Johnson, Pres. United States.

My Dear Sir,

I have been in Georgia one week, as far down as Macon, & I have been pleasingly surprised at the spirit manifested by the people. They are as tame as sick kittens. The cry is, "What shall we do to be Saved." They manfully acknowledge they are whipt, and have a wholesome fear of that Government, which they have been fighting.

I see no disposition to be turbulent, on the part of any. The original Ranters are most humble. If the directing power be placed in the hands of judicious men, order can soon be brought out of present confusion. Through Middle Geo. there is & has been a strong disposition to give expression to their wishes in [Primary?] meetings, but have been discouraged by the military through a misapprehension on the part of Gen. Wilson,[1] as I think, in his instructions to prevent political meetings; otherwise the military power could not have been directed more judiciously.

The impression is general that Hon. Joshua Hill will be made Provisional Gov. from the fact, as is said, that you had requested his presence in Washington. The people have confidence in his ability, also in his fidelity to the Government and interest in them. I am not personally acquanted with Mr. Hill, and consequently have but one fear in regard to him, and that is, he may play Brownlow.[2]

A great many of old party affinitives in opposition [to] the Democracy, seem to think that democrats will be kept on the back shelves by Hill, because the Democracy destroyed the count[r]y.

Among the rank & file in Georgia, there are as many good Union men democrats as among the opposition.

I shall be in Washington soon.[3]

Yours most truly Alexr. N. Wilson

ALS, DLC-JP.

1. James H. Wilson.

2. Wilson probably refers to Governor Brownlow's public stand in favor of vengeance, rather than conciliation in regard to Confederates, a course not endorsed by other unionists. E. Merton Coulter, *William G. Brownlow: Fighting Parson of the Southern Highlands* (Chapel Hill, 1937), 270–73.

3. A week later Johnson recommended Wilson to the secretary of the treasury for "as good a position under your control as there may be for him in the State of Georgia"; though he was on duty as collector of internal revenue by September, his appointment was not confirmed until May 1866. Johnson to McCulloch, June 23, 1865, Appts., Internal Revenue Service, Collector, Ga., 1st Dist., Alexander N. Wilson, RG56, NA; *U.S. Off. Reg.* (1865), 62; Appt. Bk. 4: 162, Ser. 6B, Johnson Papers, LC.

From Thomas E. Burriss

[ca. June 17, 1865], Philadelphia, Pa.; LS(X), DNA-RG94, Amnesty Papers (M1003, Roll 37), N.C., Thomas E. Burriss.

Captured aboard a British steamer, the *Deer*, which was returning from Cuba, a Wilmington, N.C., steamer pilot, now a prisoner aboard the "Receiving Ship Princeton," seeks pardon for blockade running. Forcibly pressed into Confederate service "against his will and consent" in 1862, he claims that he "never willingly bore Arms, or done any act or thing against the lawful Authority of the Government of the United States." [Although his name appears on a list of pardon cases in the Office of the Pardon Attorney, his pardon date is missing.]

From H. Talbot Cox[1]

Lynchburg Va June 17th 1865

Sir

I learn much to my astonishment and regret that quite a reign of Terror still exists in East Tenn.—that persecutions in allmost every conceivable manner are prosecuted against men of property and those who heretofore—had some position in Society—regardless as a general thing of their acts during the war—provided they were in any way identified with the southern party—and that none who are absent from Home are to be allowed to return to their families—regardless of the cause of their absence, &c. My Union friends in East Tenn. whom I am grattifyed to know I have many advise me not to come Home now—that by a certain class I and my property are being persecuted with shameful procedures, &c—and tis possible that you have been misinformed as to my true position during the war. Hence I am induced to trespass on your time simply to set myself right and to open the way to fully Vindicate my position and true sentiments and acts—during the deplorable war we have passed through.

No one Sir deplored the war more than myself and no one strived harder in an humble way to avert it than myself. I was opposed to secession and so expressed myself and at the beginning of our troubles whilst in Georgia—opposed secession even at my perril. At the first Election in Tennessee I voted for Seperation conscientiously believing that if Tenn then took a stand with the South as Virginia had then but recently done—that it would surely result in compromize and an amicable settlement in this however I was mistaken. Soon after I seen that the war would continue—and still maintaining my oposition to Secession—I did not believe that coercion was the most practicable mode of settling the difficulty—and came to the determination to remain as near passive and neutral as it was possible for a man to do in East Tenn. The vote for seperation identifyed me to some extent with the southern cause, and I suffered it to be so from the fact it placed me in a position the better to protect and defend Union men and their families—from the many acts of wrong that were done them, and the time spent and labor performed by me in endeavoring to protect Union men their property &c is well known in East Tenn as well in other parts of East Tenn as in my own immediate section—before whom and by whom I can fully vindicate myself and fully establish what I here assert. No man can in truth say they ever heard me utter a word of persecution towards a single individual in East Ten or elsewhere but on the other hand often at my perril, and especially since I left my Home Have remonstrated at abusive language uttered against my old finds [friends] of the Union party in East Ten—and in a prudent way vindicate their course—which facts I can well establish here where I have lived for near 12-mos, as well as at other places—and when I first came to this place—I found the public mind very much abused as to your private and public character, and on all occasions I endeavored to disabuse the public mind as to your political course and I feel warrented in saying that I have been the means of producing a great change in public sentiment here both before as well as since the War ended—and as an evidence of that fact the Virginian a leading public Journal of this City notices the facts in a leading Editorial which I here enclose for your perusal.[2]

You may ask why I left my Home in Tennessee. It was to look after my interest of business in the south—and to live quiet and place myself in a position where I could not even be suspicioned for taking any part in or in any way encouraging the unfortunate sectional and neighborhood strifes existing then. I became horror struck and disgusted at the many acts of violence and crime, committed in detail by both parties and disapproved by the more peaceful and humane of both parties. I fear judging from a late proclamation issued by the Govr of Tennessee[3] that peace quiet and prosperity Cannot soon be restored in East Tenn— unless other influences are brought into requisition.

I well know that the party there who unjustly seek my property destruction if not life are the same who persecuted you with so much vindictiveness years past—and my only crime is that I aided in an humble way in causing their shafts of calumny to fall harmless at your feet that and the crime of success to a limited extent in my business vocation of life. If such are crimes then I am guilty.

I desire to return to my Home and family in East Ten at the earliest convience—and have the protection that peaceable Law abiding citizens have a right to expect from their Govnment and to this end as well as the general good of our beloved country East Tenn. I expect to be in Washington in [a] few days to ask the favor and honor of an interview with you as an old frind unabated with me—as also to appeal to you for such relief as in your judgment under the circumstances you may deem proper and I may merit. I also desire to detail in short other facts than expressed in this that would two much lengthen this communication to refer to.[4]

I have the honor to be Verry truly your frind
& obt Servt H. T. Cox

To His Excellency Prest. A. Johnson
Washington City D.C.

ALS, DLC-JP.
1. Cox (1814–1894), a merchant postmaster at Louisville, Tenn. (c1839–65), had conducted business with the Confederate government in grain, meat, and poultry. Edith B. Little, comp., *Blount County, Tennessee Cemetery Records* (Evansville, Ind., 1980),

109; Confederate Papers *re* Citizens or Business Firms (M346, Roll 202), H. T. Cox File, RG109, NA; Burns, *Blount County*, 267; *U.S. Off. Reg.* (1851–65).

2. Not found.

3. Brownlow's proclamation of May 30, while taking cognizance of the difficulties exacerbating postwar relations between unionists and southern sympathizers in East Tennessee and recommending the use of the courts to mediate, excoriated the latter element for heinous crimes against unionists, and as men who "had forfeited all rights to citizenship, and to life itself"; he all but decreed their banishment from the state. *Knoxville Whig and Rebel Ventilator*, June 7, 1865.

4. There is no evidence that Johnson either saw Cox personally or responded in writing to this letter.

From J. Rhodes Mayo[1]

Brooklyn N.Y. June 17th '65

Hon. A. Johnson
Your Excellency

Ever since the Announcement by the Press, of the appointment of Mr Holden, as Provisional Gov. of N. Carolina, I Said "The President has taken a step at once cruel and unjust towards 4,000,000 of loyal American Citizens, inasmuch as he has practically thrown the helpless Negro under the iron-heel of his oppressor—his late Master—with no redress for himself at the ballot box.["] You Sir, know as well as I do, (We are both Southeren men,) the former Status of the Negro, and the intense hatred, or at least prejudice, of the Whites towards him. What rights, then are to be expected from such men towards the black man, in the re-organization of Governments in the late rebellious States? Sir, who are the men, you are permitting to re-construct the new Government? I answer, to all intents and purposes, they are as much "States rights-men" and rebels to day, as they were prior to the overthrow of the Jeff Davis dynasty, their oaths of allegiance to the contrary notwithstanding.

Sir, it is not for me an humble individual, to dictate to the Chief Magistrate of my beloved Country what should, or should not be his State policy. Yet, I may humbly suggest what duty would point out to me, as State Policy, were I the Nation's Executive, To wit. No conquered state should be permitted to have a voice in Congress, until an article in each returning State's Constitution, should make all men free and equal at the ballot box—the political franchise to the loyal black man, as well as to the semi disloyal white man. Failing in such an article, let such a state be under the rule of a Military Governor until Congress in its wisdom, should dispose of the matter. Sir, that power is invested in you. But sir, persist in your present policy, and next Dec. every Southern State will ride into full power again on the backs of their blatant, disloyal Senators & Representatives to Congress. And after that gang of *traitors* and "nest of unclean birds," are once more in power,—then Sir, farewell to the loyal Negro's rights at the South.

Should such prove the case, and it must, from the very Nature of things, if you continue to pursue your present unwise policy towards those states.

Then Sir, the last four years of anarchy, war, and suffering, will be re-inaugerated, after a few years respite. For the Negro will have his political rights, in spite of unfriendly Presidents, disloyalists political hacks, and ex parte Constitutions. Sir, I voted for you, as the candidate for the Vice Presidency, But your unwise policy in the matter of Negro sufferage and sending questionable *Unionists* back into power at the south, where they were known as notorious Secessionists—Holden for instance, makes me more than ever regret the death of the black man's friend and honest protector—Abraham Lincoln.

Pardon me sir, for my extended remarks, I really had no intention to do otherwise than to call attention to the inclosed letter,[2] I cut from the N.Y. Herald of this date.

Dr Bingham's[3] views I fully endorse.

I am Sir, Your humble and Obt Servant,

J. Rhodes Mayo

The "Percy Walker"[4] refered to by Dr Bingham, you dubtless know all by anticedents while he was in Congress.

While residing in Mobile Ala, from 1854 to '57, I was one of his Constituents; and my knowledge of the man, rather surprised me, to see his endorsement of that "address."[5]

"He intimated he was not in favor of Negro Sufferage at present."

Ah, if not at present, What Power will the President have over the matter after the states are reorganized, and back in the Union? J.R.M.[6]

ALS, DLC-JP.

1. Mayo was a Brooklyn book dealer. Brooklyn directories (1866–71).

2. In his letter dated June 15 and directed to the *Herald*'s editor, Daniel H. Bingham deplored any return of governing power into the hands of those responsible for the war and its continuation. Insisting that Lewis Parsons, rumored to be Johnson's choice for provisional governor, was not a strong Union man, the writer, himself an applicant for the governorship, claimed that most of the delegation which recently called upon the President were not "inactive agents" in fomenting rebellion. *New York Herald*, June 17, 1865.

3. Bingham (b. c1802), a New York native and editor who lived 32 years in Alabama, was a strong unionist, driven out by the war. Upon his return he became a member of the Union League, of the State Republican executive committee, and of the 1867 state constitutional convention. 1860 Census, Ala., Limestone, Div. No. 1, Athens, 81; *New York Herald*, June 17, 1865; Sarah W. Wiggins, *The Scalawag in Alabama Politics, 1865–1881* (University, Ala., 1977), 9, 26, 143, 151.

4. Walker (1812–1880), physician-lawyer and brother of Leroy P., began medical practice in Mobile but switched to law, serving in the state legislature, in Congress, and as adjutant general for the state during the war. *BDAC*.

5. The "Address," mentioned in Bingham's letter as endorsed by Walker as well as by a Confederate congressman, "both new converts to loyalty," was directed to the President from Mobile.

6. Mayo also attached a newspaper clipping containing two brief reports headed: "The Quakers and Negro Suffrage," which described the June 12 meeting of New York Quakers, who urged the President to lend his influence for the adoption of black suffrage, and "The President Not in Favor of Negro Suffrage." According to the latter, Johnson

responded that "he was fully acquainted with the negro race . . . and that the question was one surrounded with very grave difficulties. He intimated clearly that he was not in favor of negro suffrage, for the present at least."

From Ambrose E. Burnside

Fifth Avenue Hotel New York—
June 18" 1865.

His Excellency—Andrew Johnson President
My dear Sir

In conversation the other day you were kind enough to give me permission to forward an application of the rebel Genl Henry Heth[1] for pardon, and restoration to his civil rights, which I have the honor now to enclose.

I am satisfied, from correspondence with the applicant, that he will well and truly observe the obligation taken, and will prove himself worthy of any clemency you may see fit to show him.

We at the same time spoke of the promotion of Genl John G. Parke[2] to the position of Brig Genl in the "Regular Army." The Genl is now in command of the 9th Corps near Washington, is Maj Genl of Volunteers, and Major, or Lieut Col in the Engineer Corps. He is one of the most valuable officers in the service, and in my opinion is second to none in his deserts for promotion. I speak from personal knowledge, as he has served with me constantly since I went to North Carolina. This application would not be made did I not know that his retiring disposition would prevent him from making any effort, in any quarter in his own behalf.

In the hope that the interests of the public service, may permit you to grant these requests, and with my best wishes for your health, happiness and success I remain

Sincerely your friend A. E. Burnside

ALS, DNA-RG94, Amnesty Papers (M1003, Roll 62), Va., Henry Heth.
1. Heth (1825–1899), a former classmate of Burnside's at West Point, served during the war in Tennessee and Virginia and was major general when paroled at Appomattox. In January 1863 he issued orders that led to the massacre of thirteen alleged unionists at Shelton Laurel, N.C. Johnson pardoned Heth on June 18, 1867. Warner, *Gray*; Phillip S. Paludan, *Victims: A True Story of the Civil War* (Knoxville, 1981), 34, 36, 85–88, 104–5; Amnesty Papers (M1003, Roll 62), Henry Heth, RG94, NA; Amnesty Record, Vol. 3, Ser. 8C, Johnson Papers, LC.
2. Parke (1827–1900) served after 1861 on Burnside's staff, rising to major general of volunteers and chief of staff. In 1866 he returned to the regular service but was not promoted to brigadier. Warner, *Blue*; Powell, *Army List*, 518.

From Mary R. Hunter

June 18, 1865, Baltimore, Md.; ALS, DNA-RG107, Lets. Recd., EB12
President 1845 (1865).

Wife of a Baltimore coachmaker, struck by "the condition of a number of Rebel
Soldiers who are now in our City without Friends or means," seeks help for
them. Observing that most were recently conscripts paroled from East Tennessee, Kentucky, and Louisiana in need of transportation to their homes, she asks
permission for the "Ladies" of Baltimore to supply them with "such Food and
Clothing as their necessities call for" now that peace has come, for "we should
not look upon these Men as Enemies, but try by kindness to soften the bitterness which still to a certain degree, must exist." [Johnson referred the letter to
Stanton.]

From Gazaway B. Lamar, Sr.[1]

Old Capitol Prison
June 18 1865

To His Excellency Andrew Johnson
President of the U States,
Sir,

I was arrested at my residence in Savannah on 28 April, & brought
here & have been confined ever since.

I had been very unwell for 8 weeks before my arrest & am still liable
to attacks from chronic disease.

I crave to be allowed an interview with your Excellency, being confident, I could satisfy you that there has been no cause for my arrest &
imprisonment.

I took the oath[2] & resided for three months unmolested in my
house—where I can be found—if not in search of restoration of my
health.

But I can be much more explicit, if allowed to see your Excellency.[3]

I am Very Respy
Yr Obt Servt
G. B. Lamar

ALS, DLC-JP.
    1. Lamar (1798–1874), Georgia commission merchant, blockade runner and Confederate financier, was suspected by Stanton to have been an accomplice in Lincoln's
assassination. Thomas R. Hay, "Gazaway Bugg Lamar, Confederate Banker and Business Man," *GHQ*, 37 (1953): 89–128.
    2. He did so on January 6, 1865. See Lamar to Johnson, June 26, 1865, Johnson
Papers, LC.
    3. Upon receipt of this, on June 18, Johnson referred it to Stanton, who returned the
letter to the President with the recommendation that Lamar not be granted an interview
until certain incriminating evidence had been forwarded. Stanton to Johnson, June 18,
1865, Johnson Papers, LC. See Letter from Lamar, July 17, 1865.

From John F. Poppenheim

June 18, 1865, Charleston, S.C.; ALS, DLC-JP.

South Carolina physician-planter, a "consistent National Democrat" who had
seen "the best part of the hard earnings of a life of industry . . . swept away,"
warns Johnson about a state delegation en route to Washington to present a
petition soliciting the appointment of a civil governor. Although the petition
itself is valid, he explains that the committee is "a self appointed one" whose
members "involved the country in its present distress, by their former political
opinions, and actions," held "high political and military rank in the Rebellion,
[and] now attempt to represent loyal sentiment of people of South Carolina."
Listing the delegates, he identifies Col. William Whaley, Fred. Richards, Col.
Joseph Yates, and Judge Frost (the latter, however, a "gentleman of high character") as "violent" or "rank" secessionists; George W. Williams, J. I. Mc-
Carter, Rev. Joseph Seabrook, William H. Gilliland, and Isaac E. Holmes as
unionists, but "unexceptionable"; and the rest "not only Secessionists," but
many of them "actively engaged in Blockade running, and in gambling and
defrauding the goverment in this disreputable business." Andrew G. Magrath
is "the bogus Governor," while the real power lies with his advisor, James B.
Campbell, a member of the legislature, and in Col. John Phillips, who passes
as a Union man, but who attended the secession convention, albeit after the
ordinance was passed.

From George A. Goodman[1]

U.S. Military Prison
Fort Delaware [Delaware] June 19th 1865

To His Excellency Andrew Johnson. Presdt. U.S.A.

Understanding that no application would be considered, unless made
directly to yourself, I therefore earnestly hope that you will consider
favorably the following petition. I reside in Louisa County, State of
Virginia, was captured near Winchester State of Va, on the 19th Sept
1864 and have been a prisoner of war ever since.

I was not educated at a military or Naval School of the U. States,
have never held Military or Naval office thereunder. Never held Civil
office under the Confederate Government, and am not possessed of
property to the Value of twenty thousand dollars. No charges are pending or have been preferred against me, neither have I at any time mal-
treated prisoners of war, white or Colored, nor am I exempt in any
manner, from the benefits of your late proclamation except being a prisoner of war. I have taken the oath of Allegiance to the United States,
and respectfully solicit permission to take the oath of Amnesty, and be
allowed to return home—where it shall ever be my earnest endeavor,
to obey & support the laws of the U. States.

Very Respectfully Your Obt Servt G. A Goodman
Lt. Col. 13th Va. Infty

ALS, NcD-Andrew Johnson Papers.
    1. Goodman (b. *c*1830), a farmer-teacher who rose from lieutenant to lieutenant col-
onel before his capture, obtained his release from prison on July 15, 1865. No record of
an individual presidential pardon has been found for him. 1870 Census, Va., Louisa, No.
Dist., 199; CSR, RG109, NA.

From Ulysses S. Grant

Washington, June 19th 1865.

His Excellency A. Johnson
President of the United States
    The great interest which I feel in securing an honorable and perma-
nent peace whilst we still have in service a force sufficient to insure it,
and the danger and disgrace which in my judgment, threaten us unless
positive and early measures are taken to avert it, induces me to lay my
views before you in an official form.
    In the first place, I regard the act of attempting to establish a monar-
chical government on this continent in Mexico, by foreign bayonets as
an act of hostility against the Government of the United States.[1] If allowed to go on until such a government is established, I see nothing
before us but a long, expensive and bloody war, one in which the enemies of this country will be joined by tens of thousands of disciplined
soldiers, embittered against their Government by the experience of the
last four years.
    As a justification for open resistance to the establishment of *Maxi-
millian's* Government in Mexico, I would give the following reasons:
    1st. The act of attempting to establish a monarchy on this continent
was an act of known hostility to the Government of the United States,
was protested against at the time and would not have been undertaken
but for the great war which was raging, and which it was supposed by
all the great powers of Europe, except possibly Russia, would result in
the dismemberment of the country and the overthrow of Republican
institutions.
    2d. Every act of the Empire of *Maximillian* has been hostile to the
Government of the United States. Matamoras and the whole Rio
Grande, under his control, has been an open port to those in rebellion
against this Government. It is notorious that every article held by the
Rebels for export was permitted to cross the Rio Grande and from there
go unmolested to all parts of the world,[2] and they in return to receive
in pay all articles, arms, munitions of war, &c. they desired. Rebels in
arms have been allowed to take refuge on Mexican soil, protected by
French bayonets. French soldiers have fired on our men from the south
side of the river, in aid of the rebellion. Officers acting under the authority of the would-be Empire have received arms, munitions and
other public property from the Rebels, after the same has become the

property of the United States. It is now reported, and I think there is no doubt of the truth of the report, that large organized and armed bodies of rebels have gone to Mexico to join the Imperialists.[3] It is further reported, and too late we will find the report confirmed, that a contract or agreement has been entered into with Dr. *Gwinn*,[4] a traitor to his country, to invite into Mexico armed immigrants for the purpose of wrenching from the rightful government of that country, States never controlled by the Imperialists.[5] It will not do to remain quiet and theorize that by showing a strict neutrality, all foreign forces will be compelled to leave Mexican soil. Rebel immigrants to Mexico will go with arms in their hands. They will not be a burden upon the States, but on the contrary, will become producers, always ready, when emergency arises to take up their arms in defense of the cause they espouse. That their leaders will espouse the cause of the Empire, purely out of hostility to this Government, I feel there is no doubt. There is a hope that the rank and file may take the opposite side, if any influence is allowed to work upon their reason. But if a neutrality is to be observed which allows armed Rebels to go to Mexico, and which keeps out all other immigrants, and which also denies to the Liberals of Mexico belligerent rights, the right to buy arms and munitions in foreign markets and to transport them through friendly territory to their homes, I see no chance for such influence to be brought to bear.

What I would propose would be a solemn protest against the establishment of a monarchical government in Mexico by the aid of foreign bayonets. If the French have a just claim against Mexico, I would regard them as having triumphed and would guarantee them suitable award for their grievances. Mexico would no doubt admit their claim if it did not affect their territory or rights as a free people. The United States could take such pledges as would secure her against loss. How all this could be done without bringing on an armed conflict, others who have studied such matters could tell better than I.[6] If this course cannot be agreed upon then I would recognize equal belligerent rights to both parties. I would interpose no obstacle to the passage into Mexico of emigrants to that country. I would allow either party to buy arms or any thing we have to sell and interpose no obstacle to their transit.

These views have been hastily drawn up and contain but little of what might be said on the subject treated of. If however they serve to bring the matter under discussion they will have accomplished all that is desired.

Sgd U S Grant,
Lieut. General.

LBcopy, DNA-RG108, Lets. Sent, Let. Bk. B, No. 22 (1865).

1. British, Spanish, and French troops had jointly occupied Veracruz in 1861. The following year, after the first two withdrew, the French overthrew the Mexican government and set up a government under Austrian Archduke Ferdinand Maximilian.

James M. McPherson, *Ordeal by Fire: The Civil War and Reconstruction* (New York, 1982), 344.

2. Matamoros became a major outlet for Confederate trade, circumventing the Union naval blockade. Robert W. Delaney, "Matamoros, Port for Texas During the Civil War," *SWHQ*, 58 (1955): 473–87; Alfred J. and Kathryn A. Hanna, *Napoleon III and Mexico: American Triumph over Monarchy* (Chapel Hill, 1971), 159.

3. As early as 1862, Confederates had sought refuge south of the Rio Grande. After Appomattox, Marshal Bazaine, commanding the French forces, quietly enlisted volunteers from those Confederates who fled to Mexico. Ibid., 223–26.

4. Former U.S. Senator William M. Gwin, whose southern sympathies landed him in prison for two weeks in 1861, after his release went to Paris, where he interested Napoleon III in a mining settlement venture in Mexico. His plan aborted after Appomattox, he was arrested in New Orleans. Lately Thomas, *Between Two Empires: The Life Story of California's First Senator, William McKendree Gwin* (Boston, 1969), 298–305, 351–52, 354.

5. The goal of Gwin's Mexican project was the subject of widespread speculation, usually suggesting that the doctor plotted to detach various Mexican states along the Rio Grande to form a new country. Ibid., 303.

6. In 1861 U.S. Minister to Mexico Thomas Corwin had proposed that the U.S. guarantee Mexico's payment of interest on debts owed France, England, and Spain to prevent European military intervention under the London Convention. Hanna, *Napoleon III*, 54–56.

From John Hogan

June 19, 1865, St. Louis, Mo.; ALS, DLC-JP.

St. Louis merchant, Democratic congressman, and "an old personal friend of President Lincoln," assures Johnson that "the Democratic masses will come out and triumphantly sustain you, as their own President, in the restoration of the right." Although apprehensive about the pitfalls of the Tennessean's position, he observes that "happily you have had the discretion So far to Stear clear of the chief difficulties." Not only does the "old Democracy of this region . . . fully endorse—your course," but the conservative Republicans feel Johnson will "carry out the plans and policy of their late chief . . . in restoring harmony, with Freedom, in all the States late in Rebellion." At the same time "the majority of the Radical party are preparing themselves for opposition to the Reconstruction policy which you are endeavouring to inaugerate."

Lincoln had proposed that Hogan retain his "political affiliations, so as if possible to bring the Democratic members [of Congress] into such union with his Conservative friends, as might insure an ample majority of the House to carry out his consiliatory purposes." Hogan comments: "if Such cooperation could have been brought about with or under the lead of Mr. Lincoln who had never been a Democrat, it will be much easier to accomplish under your lead— always a Democrat." Advises that southerners be "allowed quetly yet securely to restore by industry the damage done themselves and country by their own mad acts against a paternal Government," without the fear that "their destiny will . . . be placed in the hands of strangers." The goal: "tranquilizing the country and bringing all together again in a 'Union of hearts & hands.'"

From North Carolina Friends Yearly Meeting[1]

[June 19, 1865]

Petition

To Andrew Johnson, President of the United States
From the Meeting for Sufferings of North Carolina yearly Meeting of Friends, held 19th of 6 mo 1865.

We respectfully petition that members of the religious society of Friends be excused from taking the oath or affirmation prescribed for all citizens of those states which have been in rebellion against the United States government.

Our reasons are, first, that we believe said obligation, as to us, to be unnecessary, from the fact that our religion prevents us from ever placing ourselves in rebellion against the government under which we live, or from ever offering violent opposition to the execution of its laws. And, accordingly, we do not know a single instance among the members of our Society, of any who were in favor of a rupture of the U.S. Government, or who were in favor of the war which was waged against it. On the contrary, we were much opposed thereto, and many of us suffered both in property and person rather than give any aid therein. Some were imprisoned for months, some were whipped on the bare back, suspended for hours by the thumbs and suffered other personal indignities and abuse; Some were kept for days (in two instances for five days and nights) without a particle of food or a drop of water—for refusing to take up Arms. Their firmness and constancy, in this respect, were and are heartily approved by the whole body of the Society. Hence, for us, we believe said obligation to be unnecessary.

Secondly, we have felt a scrupulous tenderness as to taking affirmations "to defend" any government lest it may be construed that we could bear arms in its behalf—a practice in direct violation of one of our primary principles, and a principle which has characterized our Society from its very origin, now more than 200 years ago.

If it should not meet the approbation of the President to release us entirely from said affirmation we ask that it may be so modified as not to violate our conscientious scruples.[2]

Signed by direction and on behalf of the meeting aforesaid.

Nereus Mendenhall, Clk.[3]

Pet, DLC-JP.

1. This petition was forwarded through Governor Holden, whose covering letter in support of the Friends' request assured the President that "This Religious Sect in North Carolina, have been true and faithful union men during the rebellion." Holden to Johnson, June 27, 1865, Johnson Papers, LC.

2. In his forwarding letter Holden spelled out the acceptable oath prescribed by North Carolina statutes, which assures loyalty in a variety of circumstances without reference to defensive activities. The governor's support was not effective; Johnson did not

exclude Quakers, and others of similar religious scruples, from taking the oath. Dorris, *Pardon and Amnesty*, 193.

3. Mendenhall (b. *c*1820), a Guilford County physician, was principal of the New Garden Boarding School (subsequently Guilford College), which he managed to keep open during the war, and after the war was appointed superintendent of schools for blacks in North Carolina. 1850 Census, N.C., Guilford, No. Div., 836; Rufus M. Jones, *The Later Periods of Quakerism* (2 vols., London, 1921), 2: 603, 694.

From Hendrick B. Wright[1]

Wilkes-Barre Pa. June 19/65

My dear Sir:

I have been confined to my room with severe indisposition for the last three months, but am now quite recovered. Since your inauguration as President, I have carefully looked into, and examined all your Executive acts; and you cannot conceive, the pleasure it affords me, to say, that I see no one of them to censure. The good men of the land, irrespective of party, must and will sustain you, in the course you have so clearly and so happly foreshadowed. The radicals of both partis may condemn: but their censure is better than their approbation. I deeply regret that I am not in congress to do you yeomans sevice.

An indiscriminate negro Suffrage would destroy, at least, four of the Southern States. Your policy of permitting the loyal men of the Seceding States to manage this question is entitled to all praise. The old parties are things of the past. It is in your power, under your views of reconstruction, to make a grand, conservative national party that shall rule every thing, *and Save every thing*.

My dear Sir, you are right and my only hope and prayer is, that the mind which can conceive such a course may have the bravery and fortitude to maintain it.

I foresee the influences that will be brought to bear upon you to change your views: but I have an abiding confidence in your judgement which makes me feel Easy.

Before the meeting of congress, the work can all be done. It is easy now to Settle the whole question. Congress, you are aware, is a restive body, and will have more whims & caprices than you can possibly gratify.

I look on from a distance; asking no favors for myself or friends. I can therefore well afford to speak as I think. What I have said, are the views of the best men, with whom I meet. May God preserve you, is the prayer of

My dear Sir Yr V. Obt Hendrick B. Wright

His Excellency Andrew Johnson
Prest of the U.S. Washington

LS, DLC-JP.

1. Wright (1808–1881) was a Pennsylvania lawyer and former Democratic congressman (1853–55, 1861–63). *BDAC*.

From Simon Cameron

Harrisburg, June 20, 1865.

To the President:

Sir

I have pleasure in recommending the re-appointment of Mr. Mill-ward,[1] the present U.S. Marshal for this District. He is a most efficient officer and a true man in all respects. No one can be selected who will give more satisfaction in the discharge of the duties,—& I sincerely hope for the sake of the party that he will be retained.[2]

Very respectfully Simon Cameron

ALS, DNA-RG60, Appt. Files for Judicial Districts, Pa., William Millward.

1. William Millward (1822–1871), a former congressman (1855–57, 1859–61) who was appointed as U.S. marshal by Lincoln in 1861, failed to win Johnson's endorsement. The President did nominate him in September 1866 to be director of the Philadelphia mint, but his appointment was not confirmed, and Millward stepped down after serving only six months. *House Ex. Docs.*, 39 Cong., 2 Sess., No. 67, p. 10 (Ser. 1292); *BDAC*.

2. Sacrificed in the feud between Congressman "Pig-Iron" Kelley and Cameron, Millward was replaced by Peter C. Ellmaker, whose July recess appointment the Senate confirmed in January 1866. Erwin S. Bradley, *Simon Cameron: Lincoln's Secretary of War* (Philadelphia, 1966), 256–57; Appt. Bk. 5: n.p., Ser. 6B, Johnson Papers, LC.

From William G. Crenshaw[1]

Liverpool June 20. 1865

To his Excellency Andrew Johnson
President of the United States
Sir.

Your petitioner respectfully represents that he is a citizen of Richmond, Virginia, 41 years of age, and doing business as a merchant.

In the fall of the year 1861, I accepted a commission as Captain of Artillery in the army of the so called Confederate States, and acted in that capacity until December 1862, when I embarked for England, where I have since resided.

Since my departure from America I have held no commission, appointment or other official connection with the government of the so called Confederate States, but have been the owner of an interest in a line of vessels which have been engaged in blockade running. The estimated value of my property is more than twenty thousand dollars, but I am not excluded from the benefits of the amnesty proclamation of May 29th upon any ground other than is herein set forth.

I respectfully ask permission to take the oaths prescribed in the proclamation of President Lincoln of December 8, 1863, and in that of your Excellency dated May 29th 1865, and I pledge myself to faithfully observe and abide by the same in all respects as a loyal citizen of the United States.

I hereby renounce and disclaim any title or interest which I may have heretofore held in slave property and petition your Excellency to grant me an amnesty or pardon, according to the terms of your proclamation of May 29th.[2]

Respectfully submitted Wm G Crenshaw

ALS, DNA-RG94, Amnesty Papers (M1003, Roll 59), Va., William G. Crenshaw.

1. Crenshaw (1824–1897), a Richmond importer-exporter who had equipped a Confederate artillery battery, remained in England until 1868. William W. Scott, *A History of Orange County, Virginia* (Richmond, 1907), 184–85.

2. Falling under exceptions 11 and 13, he was pardoned July 13, 1865. *House Ex. Docs.*, 40 Cong., 2 Sess., No. 16, p. 50 (Ser. 1330).

From J. G. Dodge[1]

Office Superintendent of Freedmen
Port Royal S.C. June 20th 1865

To His Excellency Andrew Johnson
President of the U.S.
Dr Sir

Having been instructed to forward you the following *Preamble* & *Resolution*, passed at a regular business meeting of the "Council of Administration" of the Town of Mitchelville,[2] a community of some sixteen or eighteen hundred *Freedmen* gathered from various localities since *emancipation* was proclaimed who have been authorized by the Military commandant to organize a government amongst themselves which after some months trial has been found to work well, producing an orderly, thriving, condition of things, from which older towns of educated whites might draw profitable lessons. I take pleasure in complying therewith & would improve the opportunity, by commending to your especial care & *protection* that portion of our citizens of which these people are the representatives.

When we remember the spirit of the people who have heretofore controuled these southern communities, & the disposition they have to trample upon the *rights* of the Negro, the propriety and necessity of the request of the resolution must be quite apparent, & it need not surprise us that at this most critical hour in the life of our country they are filled with fear & anxiety lest the government permits them to pass again into the hands of their enemies.

I pray you Sir to give the *Loyal* inhabitants of this State the protection of the *ballot*, as their only security against those whose hands are still red with the life blood of the Nation, in their attempts to destroy it, & who have no heart yet, notwithstanding the terrible scourging

they have received, to do *justly* by those whom they have so long outraged & oppressed.

With due consideration for the perplexities by which you are surrounded & hopeing for the exercise of that wisdom which shall secure
justice to all I remain My dear Sir

Most Truly Your Obt Sert J. G. Dodge

Supt of Freedmen

Copy, DLC-JP.

1. Dodge, hired in March 1865 by the quartermaster department to serve as general
superintendent of freedmen at Hilton Head, is not otherwise identified. Chief Disbursing
Officer, Monthly Report of Persons and Articles Hired, S.C., May 1865, RG105, NA.

2. A settlement named for Gen. Ormsby M. Mitchell, located some ten miles south
of Port Royal. The residents, meeting on June 9, adopted the following preamble and
resolution: "Whareas we believe all efforts for the reorganization of the States recently in
rebellion on any other basis than that which secures the *elective Franchise* to all loyal
citizens to be unwise & unjust therefore be it

Resolved That we respectfully request His Excellency President Johnson to so organize the State of *S. Carolina* as that all persons, be they black or white who have been
true & loyal to our country during the dark hours of the rebellion may be authorized
to vote."

From William Gregg, Jr.

June 20, 1865, New York, N.Y.; ALS, DNA-RG94, Amnesty Papers (M1003,
Roll 45), S.C., Wm. Gregg, Jr.

Owner, along with father William, Sr., and brother James J., of the Van-
cluse and the Graniteville cotton mills in the Edgefield District of S.C.,
near Augusta, Ga., solicits pardons under the 13th exception for himself, his
father—who had been a member of the secession convention, but had never
"meddled with politics before," and who had been a "strong Union man up to
time of the last troubles"—and his brother. Pleading that "our machinery is
nearly worn out and we desire & will refit our mills . . . giving employment to
about one thousand poor people," Gregg cites the need for full pardons in order
to raise the necessary capital. [With the endorsements of Senators William
Sprague of Rhode Island and Henry Wilson of Massachusetts, the Greggs were
pardoned on June 28, 1865.]

From William W. Jones

June 20, 1865, White Hall, Ky.; ALS, DLC-JP.

A Madison County doctor, having read newspaper notices "of a proposed
change of Cabinet—Secretary of War," recommends the appointment of Cas-
sius M. Clay, "promised the place [by Lincoln] unsolicited during his first
race," but not appointed "for the dissatisfaction it would have produced at that
time—in the border states." Clay, he suggests, "has labored lake yourself for
the freeing the white man from the slave power." Claiming to have seen "letters
of Mr Lincoln to Mr Clay upon the subject," Jones adds a postscript: "Mr
Private secretary please do not tumble this into a basket of waste paper . . . and
I will use my influence to have your appointed Assistant sec of War—as I was
introduced by Mr Johnson to Mr Lincoln" and had visited the former in Wash-

ington, where "I saw him in tears myself—over his Tennessee—in his room at the hotel."

To James W. Scully

Executive Office, Washington, D.C.,
June 20 1865.

To Colonel J. W. Scully
Greenville Tenn.

Will you be kind enough to try and bring Robert with you to Washington?[1]

Please answer.

Sincerely Andrew Johnson

Tel, DNA-RG107, Tels. Sent, President, Vol. 2 (1865).
1. Robert did not finally arrive in Washington until early August, despite Johnson's repeated urgings that he get there sooner.

From Harvey M. Watterson

June 20, 1865, New Bern, N.C.; ALS, DLC-JP. See *Advice*, 48–54.

"No people were ever more thoroughly conquered and subdued," observes Watterson, than those in this section of North Carolina. Yet the presence of thousands of blacks and black troops, the behavior of treasury agents, and the confiscation of abandoned property present obstacles to reconciliation. He urges that Gen. Innis N. Palmer (removed by Gen. Charles J. Payne earlier) be placed in command of the Department of North Carolina, for not only is there "no officer who would be more acceptable to her citizens," but "Like yourself, too, he is for a white man's government, and in favor of free white citizens controlling this country." Transmits, with approval, General Palmer's letter describing his efforts to restore abandoned property to those "who had taken no active part in the rebellion, but who had been dragged from this place at the time of its capture."

From William Windom[1]

Warwick Masstts. June 20 '65

Andrew Johnson President U S.
Sir:

Having been informed that an effort will be made to remove one of the Land officers, at Winnebago City, in my District, I have to request, that I may be heard before any change is made. Two Land officers in my District, have already been removed,[2] since the 4th of March, last, at the instance of Senatr Norton,[3] for no other reason than, that they were *my friends*. Of course I make no complaints against the Administration on this account, but believing that, having been four times elected to represent that Dist. gives me a right to be consulted concerning its patronage. I desire to say that Senator Norton does not speak for me in any of these matters, and I earnestly desire to be heard before any more removals are made. The two removals, above referred to, were made by President Lincoln, dubtless under a misapprehension of the facts.

> I have the honor to be Very Respectfully
> Yr obt Servant Wm. Windom
> M. C. 1st Dist Minnesota

ALS, DNA-RG48, Lands and Railroads Div., Misc. Lets. Recd. (1840–80).

1. Windom (1827–1891) served as Republican congressman (1859–69), senator (1870–81, 1881–83), and secretary of the treasury (1881, 1889–91). *BDAC*.

2. Presumably the "removed" persons were lesser officers, since the *Official Register* for 1865 lists the same register and receiver at Winnebago City as two years previously.

3. Daniel S. Norton (1829–1870) served in the state legislature of Minnesota before becoming U.S. senator (1865–70). *BDAC*.

From Truman Woodruff[1]

Saint Louis—Mo. June 20, 1865

President Johnson
Dear Sir—

I came up from Memphis the other day—and I must confess I was never so struck with the damneble diception of human beings than I was with some of those damm trators—who now pretend to be good union men. I overheard them say when they were talking about you— "we must keep in with that damm scoundrel *Andie*—and let him make appointments of our own men; let us get the upperhand of him—then we will give him particular hell["]—says they Judge Sharkey[2] is one of our men etc. They said many other things. I cut this slip out of a paper they had when this conversation took place.[3] You may rest assured that, you will be much more safe in being determnd with those, who are now pretend to be your best frends. They are your worse enemies. Look to this before it is to late.

> From Yours & Truman Woodruff

ALS, DLC-JP.

1. Woodruff (b. *c*1810) was a commission merchant and active Republican, currently serving as city auditor in St. Louis. 1860 Census, Mo., St. Louis, St. Louis, 5th Ward, 98; Woodruff to Lincoln, Apr. 9, 1863, with clipping, Lincoln Papers, LC; St. Louis directories (1860–66).

2. William L. Sharkey.

3. The enclosed clipping quoted the *Cincinnati Times*' account of a prewar case in which Judge Sharkey had decided in favor of the collateral heirs of a planter against the widow, a former slave freed by her husband, and her mulatto children, by decreeing that the marriage "was a fraud upon the law of slavery." As a result, the legal heirs sold the widow and her children as slaves. Undated clipping, Johnson Papers, LC.

From Eli M. Bruce

June 21, 1865, New York, N.Y.; ALS, DLC-JP.

Former Kentucky Confederate congressman, having received his pardon, writes "with the feelings of deepest gratitude . . . to tell you how much I thank you, and how much I appreciate your magnanimity toward me, and to assure you with what *fidelity* I will adhere to you, and *your cause* in all future time." Admitting that he had been "a very bad rebel," he indicates he is "now *cured*" and is one of the President's "most loyal subjects, only desiring the way, to be indicated, in which I can serve you." Since seeing Johnson and visiting Richmond, he reports that the President is "winning golden opinions of all—all concur in, and heartily cooperate with you in your plan of reconstruction—the only dangerous question being now the 'Negro suffrage.'" He adds that he desires to talk with the President again to "make some suggestions as to the future which I am *very sure* will be valuable to you, and your party." [Bruce was pardoned June 12, 1865.]

From Daniel T. Chandler

June 21, 1865, Baltimore, Md.; ALS, DNA-RG94, Amnesty Papers (M1003, Roll 30), Md., Daniel T. Chandler.

Former political prisoner applying for pardon states his case. After resigning his U.S. commission in 1862, he was arrested and confined in Old Capitol Prison on "no specific charges," until exchanged in 1863 for Johnson's nephew, Andrew Johnson, Jr., then a prisoner in Richmond, Va. Serving as a colonel in the Confederate adjutant general's office assigned to the charge of a "Sanitary camp" and subsequently to "General Inspection duty," he refused promotion and tried to obtain a passport north when he learned of Lincoln's amnesty offer. [There is no evidence he received a special presidential pardon.]

From Citizens of Abbeville District, South Carolina

June 21, 1865, Abbeville Court House, S.C.; Mem, DLC-JP.

Pledging "in good faith, ready and unreserved submission and obedience to all lawful authority," the memorialists present a catalog of conditions which include either too much or too little military control, leading to "Crime, outrage and wrong" to innocent citizens; a demoralization of labor efficiency; the "devastation of whole districts . . . by armies or raiding parties"; the disruption of postal and rail facilities; and the "total absence of any circulating medium," even to pay taxes, which results in forced property sales. They further warn of the great potential for a clash between the white and black races with "its horrors" in consequence of "the superior numerical strength of the blacks over the whites." While weapons are denied the latter, "many of the former are in the possession of fire-arms." Hoping for mitigating measures, they ask that "our Legislature may be allowed to hold its usual sessions"; that a convention be permitted to assemble; that Congress "may exhibit the magnanimity and statesmanship which the difficult posture of affairs requires"; that the President "may so exercise the high powers entrusted to him," which will subsequently give him renown; that the courts "may again exercise their beneficent powers," so that "crimes be restrained—contracts inforced"; that postal facilities and public offices may be reopened; and "private avocations safely and profitably re-sumed," so that the Union can be speedily reestablished.

From East Tennessee Citizens

June 21, 1865, Knoxville, Tenn.; Pet, DNA-RG60, Appt. Files for Judicial Dists., Va. (West), Edward C. Trigg.

Twenty-eight petitioners, including T.A.R. Nelson, O. P. Temple, Blackston McDannel, L. C. Houk, and John Baxter, recommend Col. Edward C. Trigg, deputy marshal of East Tennessee, for U.S. marshal of southwest Virginia. They remind Johnson that "he is well known to your Excellency; being the same person who, in the Summer of 1861, conveyed your Excellency in a buggy from Knoxville to Greenville and from Greeneville to Barboursville Kentucky" on Johnson's escape north in the early days of the war. [Trigg did not receive the marshal's appointment in Virginia.]

From Robert W. Latham

June 21, 1865, Richmond, Va.; LS, DLC-JP.

New York financier recommends Robert J. Walker of Mississippi for the Su-preme Court vacancy and warns Johnson about Chief Justice Salmon P. Chase: "From this man you have more to fear than from any other man in this nation. He is a restless perturbed spirit, whose vaulting ambition knows no bounds"; to become President he would use all the influence his position on the court would give him, acting "upon the principle that corruption *wins more* than honesty." Knowing Chase well, the writer continues that he "is an unmitigated coward . . . as insensible to every generous impulse, as a Porcupine or Rhinoc-eros," and his sole object in life "is to gratify his selfish ambition for place, power, and plunder."

From Stephen R. Mallory

June 21, 1865, Fort Lafayette, N.Y.; ALS, DNA-RG153, Lets. Recd. (1854–94), File 1891.

Ex-senator from Florida, petitioning for pardon, claims never to have been a disunionist, but, when his state seceded, he "withdrew from the Senate . . . and retired to private life." While still in Washington, he had successfully inter-vened by telegraph to forestall the attack upon Fort Pickens by "armed bands of Alabamians and Floridians . . . assembled at Pensacola"; for this act he "en-dured the bitter hostility of leading men in my own state." Accepting the office of secretary of the navy under the provisional Confederate government, he at-tempted to resign when the permanent government was inaugurated in Feb-ruary 1862, only to have President Davis refuse his resignation. Defends his position: "Though opposed to Secession, I nevertheless regarded the com-mands of my state as decisive of my path of duty; and I followed where she led." Acknowledging that the Confederacy "contained the fruitful elements of its own destruction; and . . . recognizing its death as the will of Almighty God, I regard and accept His dispensation as decisive of the questions of slavery and Secession." Commends the President for his "large views and patriotic labours" for restoration and offers "to aid, so far as a private citizen, by precept and example might, in conforming my state to her new status under the policy which you have adopted." [Paroled in March 1866, Mallory was finally pardoned by Johnson, July 5, 1867.]

From James Ready

June 21, 1865, New Orleans, La.; ALS, DLC-JP.

Tennessee-born physician, resident of New Orleans for 25 years, expresses concern about government in the city and state. There are enough loyal citizens to fill the vacancies in public offices, but their "power has gradually been userped by Copperheads and Traitors . . . and the old aristocratic influence." Among the latter he includes Governor Wells, a "cotton speculating refugee who came into the lines about Two years ago pretending to be a very radical Union man" when he was elected lieutenant governor, but who "turned a complete sommerset and allied himself with a notorious Copperhead, wire-pulling pro-slavery party" when he became governor. His appointments are from "the scum of the Copperhead party down to the meanest rebels in the State." As proof of Wells's malfeasance, Ready denounces—among others—District Court Judge Edmund Abell, an "avowed Rebel sympathizer"; Sheriff Charles Bienvenu, a "notorious Rebel and one of the signers of the Ordinance of Secession"; and New Orleans Mayor Hugh Kennedy, "who never was loyal" and "turned every loyal man out of office that he could remove, and appointed Traitors in their place." Other disloyal or incompetent officials include Collector of Customs William P. Kellogg and Naval Officer Thomas M. Wells, the "rattle brained horse racing . . . son of Governor Wells." Too, the quartermaster's department was full of "rebel Clerks," while "nearly all" of the contractors as well as any official appointed by Judge Edward H. Durell were "rebels and Copperheads." As evidence of his own loyalty, Ready recalls that he raised a black home guard which was mustered out after 60 days without receiving "anything for their services, except the cloths they wore while in service."

From William B. Compton[1]

Staunton, Augusta Co. Virginia
June 22d 1865.

Mr. President,

I desire to make special application for your Amnesty & pardon—if I am not already entitled to the benefit of your proclamation. The circumstances of my case are briefly these: I was convicted & sentenced to be hung in May 1863, having been captured within the U.S. lines bearing a commission to recruit a company for the Confederate Army. I was reprieved by the President but retained in close confinement until May 1864, at which time I made my escape from Fort McHenry, and since then have been serving as a private in the 20th Va. Cavly. I am now on parole—and herewith enclose the amnesty oath which I have taken in accordance with instructions from the Atto. Genl.[2]

I have the honor to be
Vey Resptly W. B. Compton

His Excellency Andw. Johnson President U.S.[3]

ALS, DNA-RG94, Amnesty Papers (M1003, Roll 58), Va., W. B. Compton.

1. As an escaped prisoner, William Boyd Compton, of Fairmont, W.Va., a cousin of Belle Boyd but otherwise unidentified, applies for pardon, probably under the 12th exception of Johnson's May 29 proclamation. Captured and exchanged in 1861, he was retaken as a spy in 1863 while recruiting a company of irregulars for Confederate service. John Bakeless, *Spies of the Confederacy* (Philadelphia, 1970), 143, 174, 178–80.

2. He obtained his pardon, July 13, 1865. *House Ex. Docs.*, 40 Cong., 2 Sess., No. 16, p. 49 (Ser. 1330).

3. Compton listed as references, Governor Peirpoint, Judge Edward Pitts of Accomac County, Va., and Maryland Senator Reverdy Johnson.

From Michael Cunningham

June 22, 1865, New Orleans, La.; ALS, DLC-JP.

Despite his arrest by rebel authorities in 1861 as a consequence of his refusal "to obey military orders in this city," Cunningham, an adopted New Orleans citizen, recommends a lenient policy of reconstruction. Recalling the loyalty of southerners during the Mexican War, he advises: "In order that our land and laws and Constitution—and *Powerful* government may be Loved—*not* feared, Restore the old order of things as far as possible. Let no confiscation, or gallows or guns—be the means of making loyal men out of the blood and seed of the late rebels."

From Andrew G. Curtin

June 22, 1865, Harrisburg, Pa.; ALS, DLC-JP.

Pennsylvania governor, expressing his "earnest desire" to support Johnson's administration and wanting "to produce harmony in the Union party" in Philadelphia, requests a change in postmaster for that city. Although remaining neutral regarding the candidates applying for the post, Curtin complains that the present incumbent, Cornelius A. Walborn, has consistently opposed him; and, while not asking control of his state's patronage per se, he does ask that "men bitter in their hostility to me shall not fill places of important trusts in the State." [Walborn, reappointed February 1866, was replaced the following September.]

To James Harlan

Executive Mansion, Washington, June 22d 1865

It having been deemed expedient to send the Hon: William P. Dole, Commissioner of Indian Affairs, to visit and treat with the Indian tribes in the territories of Dakota, Idaho, Montana and Colorado, with a view, if possible, to terminate hostilities, and to secure a more cordial and lasting peace with them, the Secretary of the Interior is hereby directed to furnish to the Secretary of War a copy of the instructions he has this day given to Mr. Dole,[1] and the Secretary of War will, immediately, communicate them to the Commanders of the proper Military Departments, and require them to cooperate and assist the Commissioner in the discharge of the duties, which have been devolved upon him.[2]

Andrew Johnson

LS, DNA-RG108, Lets. Recd. *re* Military Discipline.

1. The letter, which Interior Secretary Harlan did forward to Stanton the next day, directed Dole to make treaties to settle the Indians "upon suitable reservations," impressing upon them "the alternative of permanent peace or annihilating war." Harlan to Dole, June 22, 1865, Harlan to Stanton, June 23, 1865, Lets. Recd. *re* Military Discipline, RG108, NA.

2. In an endorsement of June 26, 1865, Stanton referred the matter to General Grant "with instructions to issue orders to Military Commanders in conformity with the Presidents directions." Harlan to Dole, June 22, 1865, ibid.

From Robert M.T. Hunter

June 22, 1865, Fort Pulaski, Ga.; ALS, DNA-RG94, Amnesty Papers (M1003, Roll 63), Va., R.M.T. Hunter.

Assuring Johnson that if pardoned "my object will be to devote myself to the pursuits of private life, and to the labor of supporting my family and restoring to some extent my fortune which has been so much wasted and shattered by the war," the former Confederate senator and secretary of state, in his third application, asks: "What possible harm could arise from allowing me to return to my family? . . . Could an example of liberality in my case have other than a good effect in Virginia?" He acted from "a sense of right and a conviction of duty," having been "reared in the Virginia states rights school of politics . . . taught to believe that the allegiance of the citizen was first due to his state and that the state had a right to secede whenever in her opinion her duty to her citizens required it." Moreover, he was simply loyal to the "de facto" government in the portion of his state in which he lived. Even "in states where there were two legally established governments and a conflict of authority between them," surely "a citizen ought not to be held answerable with his life and fortune for making a mistake as to the government to which he might render his obedience," especially now when there is "no necessity to do so in order to maintain the Union and secure the authority of the General Government." He had advocated that cotton states hold a convention to ask for such guarantees as they "thought would have saved the Union & their rights together." "Failing in this," they would "have gone out in a body . . . making the separation peaceable if possible." He had envisioned "two Confederacies to be united in such Constitutional bonds as would secure an alliance offensive & defensive and perfect freedom of trade and intercourse between the two." If Johnson does not concur in his petition for amnesty, he asks "for permission to go abroad not to return to the Country without the leave of the Government." [Hunter was pardoned October 1, 1867.]

From James A. Seddon

June 22, 1865, Fort Pulaski, Ga.; ALS, DNA-RG94, Amnesty Papers (M1003, Roll 68), Va., James A. Seddon.

Applying for pardon, the former Confederate secretary of war, currently under arrest, points out that, prior to the "late convulsions," he held no office and that, during the 1861 Peace Conference, he urged a settlement to avert "a fearful war with all its train of horrors." However, he had been in the Provisional Congress and had accepted a cabinet position "Under the conviction of duty," discharging his office "with as much of Liberality and humanity, as the unhappy nature of the struggle, the straitened resources and stern necessities of the Confederacy allowed." He feels that he served only under an "established *'De facto'* Government of admitted authority" and that "public and international Law would Justly preclude the application of the doctrines of Treason to the action of a citizen aiding the *'De Facto'* Government."

A Christian concern for the fate of the blacks, whom he sees as free laborers constituting "a permanent colored Peasantry," prompts him to warn that "there may be serious danger in the future of hostility and perhaps conflict of races." He also believes that the "late owners . . . [who] have the strongest motives" are the blacks' "truest friends and counsellors" and will provide the "best means of allaying animosities and preventing conflicts."

Recognizing the overthrow of the Southern Confederacy, the emancipation of slaves, the complete submission of his state, and the "triumph of the Federal arms," he has taken the oath. In promising loyalty, he concludes that—"Almost ruined by the disasters of War, of infirm health, and with a large family of young children"—he wants only "to spend the residue of Life in private industry." If further punishment is deemed necessary, however, he prefers "exile (temporary I trust)." [Paroled in November 1865, Seddon did not receive his pardon until three years later.]

From Thaddeus Stevens

St. Lawrence Hotel, Chestnut St. above Tenth.
Philadelphia, June 22, 1865

His Excellency Andrew Johnson
Sir

E. R. Myer Esr[1] is surveyor of the port of Phila. I do not suppose any person will be proposed to supersede him. But I wish to say that if such application should be made I think it would be unwise to grant it, as I do not believe a single objection can be fairly made to his reappointment. He is intelligent honest and industrious. He was selected from the country as the choice of the most loyal portion of the people. Such preference continues. I think his removal would be very unpleasant to our friends especially in the rural districts.

I trust you will not be called upon to decide between him and an other; or if you should be that you will feel it your duty to continue Mr. Myers.[2]

With great respect your obt svt
Thaddeus Stevens

ALS, DNA-RG56, Appts., Customs Service, Surveyor, Philadelphia, E. Reed Myer.

1. E. Reed Myer (1818–*fl*1874), former state legislator and surveyor from 1861 until his resignation in 1866, was the almost unanimous choice of the state's congressional delegation. *The Biographical Encyclopaedia of Pennsylvania of the Nineteenth-Century* (Philadelphia, 1874), 489; *U.S. Off. Reg.* (1861), 62; E. Reed Myer to Hugh McCulloch, Sept. 21, 1866, Appts., Customs Service, Surveyor, Philadelphia, E. Reed Myer, RG56, NA.

2. Reappointed by Johnson in August 1865, Myer promised his "Earnest and Stead-

fast Support." Thirteen months later he resigned because the secretary of the treasury had directed him to fill the deputy surveyor's position with a person named by the President. Myer approved of "the Policy of Congress," he explained, but not "that of the Administration." Ibid.; Myer to Johnson, Aug. 16, 1865, Johnson Papers, LC.

From Ausburn Birdsall[1]

Binghamton N.Y. June 23d 1865.

Dear Mr President

I would not willingly lay one straw in the way of pardon to any really repentant rebel, but I hope Mr. President, that you may deem it proper to let South Carolinians *wait a little*.

After the death of Mr. Petigrew[2] I do not believe there was left in the whole state of South Carolina, except in Mr Petigrew's family, one man or woman, whose heart remained true to the Union.

I am personally acquainted with Edward Frost,[3] who heads the delegation from that State, which recently called upon your Excellency and also with Geo. A Trenholm late rebel Secretary of the Treasury, and from my own knowledge of their characters before the rebellion I venture the assertion, that there is not on the face of the earth a set of men, more Jesuitical, faithless and unscrupulous than they and their associates in South Carolina,—and as South Carolina, and South Carolinians & these men among the foremost with treason long rankling in their hearts, inaugerated the rebellion, should they not remain a good long while under stern military rule, before being restored to rights which they so wickedly threw away—thereby involving the Country in civil war, with all its inconceivable horrors?

I hope Mr President, that you will not regard these suggestions as officious. I could not resist their expression.

I am glad to see by the papers that Executive clemency has been extended to Geo. W. Jones[4] of your state, whose friendship, as well as your own, I greatly prized, when Andrew Johnson and Geo. W. Jones represented the real democracy of Tenn. in the House of Representatives.

Sincerely & Truly Yours Ausburn Birdsall

His Excy Andrew Johnson

ALS, DLC-JP.

1. Birdsall (c1814–1903), a New York lawyer, had been a Democratic congressman and U.S. naval storekeeper at New York City. *BDAC*; *New York Tribune*, July 11, 1903.
2. James L. Petigru (1789–1863), Charleston lawyer, had been a state legislator and a U.S. district attorney. As leader of the local Union party, he strongly opposed both nullification in 1832 and secession in 1860. *DAB*.
3. Frost (1801–1868), a lawyer, served in the legislature, as superior court judge, and subsequently as a delegate to the 1865 South Carolina Constitutional Convention. *Cyclopedia of Eminent and Representative Men of the Carolinas of the Nineteenth Century* (2 vols., Madison, Wis., 1892), 1: 143–44.
4. Jones, who visited Johnson on June 8, was pardoned June 16. *House Ex. Docs.*, 39 Cong., 2 Sess., No. 116, p. 43 (Ser. 1293).

From George D. Blakey

June 23, 1865, Bowling Green, Ky.; ALS, DNA-RG56, Appts., Internal
Revenue Service, Collector, Ky., 1st Dist., Nimrod B. Allen.

Bowling Green physician, currently Internal Revenue collector for the 2nd district, protests the appointment of Robert M. Hathaway, a non-administration
man, as 1st district collector, and recommends the selection of Nimrod B. Allen
of Owensboro in his place. If true Union men "are passed by and Copperheads
appointed to office the practical effect will be to add to the social odium which
already in too many places attaches to their position." He argues for a change
in policy—"We are struggling against the old Fossilized Politicians of the State
for a new and higher order of things." Although "used to persecution from
Rebels—we hope for nothing from Quassi-Union men but pray do not 'wound
us in the house of our friends.'" [Hathaway retained his appointment.]

From Arthur I. Boreman

June 23, 1865, Wheeling, W. Va.; LS, DNA-RG153, Court-Martial Records,
MM-1652.

West Virginia governor seeks pardon for Private Anderson Walker, Co. C, 7th
W. Va. Cav., who, as a lad of about seventeen with two years of faithful service,
"while extremely fatigued [and] required to stand guard . . . fell asleep," was
court-martialed and sentenced to one year in prison. [On July 27 the President
remitted the "unexecuted portion of the sentence."]

From William W. Boyce[1]
In Confidence

Winnsboro So Ca June 23d 1865

His Excellency The President
My Dear Sir

On arriving at home I found the people as well disposed as could
possibly be expected. In my part of the State they were waiting my
return in order to know what to do. I immediately took such steps as
were best calculated to encourage public meetings. A meeting has been
held since my return in Fairfield County, where I live, in which resolutions were unanimously adopted, making for the establisment of the
State Government. A meeting of the same character has been held at
Columbia. Proceedings are being taken in Chester and York Counties,
for the purpose of applying for a State Government.[2] The rail roads
being generally broken up and no mail communications existing it is
difficult to get into operation a combined system of public demonstrations. I am perfectly satisfied from what I see & know of the public
sentiment, and I have taken every opportunity of ascertaining it that
the public are prepared by an overwhelming majority to act the part of

peaceful and loyal citizens. There are a few dissentients, but they are powerless. Public sentiment is now ripe for the establishment of a State Government.

I tell the people that Slavery is gone, and try to reconcile them to that idea. The majority acquiesce in this idea readily, a few still cling to the idea that slavery in some mysterious way may still be continued. I tell the people that slavery being gone the result of a political and military necessity, you wish to be kind to them. I try to strengthen your administration with the people, and I predict to them that they will be your supporters, and that before the end of your administration some of the members of the cabinet will be from the Southern States.

I have talked to some about the changes which should be made in our State Constitution. I find a pretty strong sentiment in the up country for getting rid of the oligarchical provisions in the constitution. These are two great changes which should be made

1st To get rid of the Parish representation.[3]

2nd To give the election of Governor to the people.

Other changes may be desirable, but these should certainly be made. Our old and aristocratic families are pretty well ruined.

My general idea of the policy to be pursued here is

1st To harmonize the State thoroughly with the General Government

2nd To lop off all the aristocratic features of the State Government, and make it a people's State.

3d To build up a party favourable to your administration, and then controul the State Government for the best purposes.

In mentioning these points I have said nothing about slavery, for that is being gotten rid off as fast as possible, under the Federal authority. On that point I would say let the slaves go free, but do this with as much gentleness to the whites as possible. I inculcate this idea as to the duty of the planters, that they should recognize emancipation with all its logical consequences and act towards the negroes with liberality & kindness. One very important matter I think is for judicious men to be put at the head of the emancipation movement. Men who understand the negro character & who while they feel for the negro are not hostile to the late masters.

Mr Orr[4] is making speeches in his part of the State to reconcile the people to the existing order of things. Mr Orr is one of the few men who have been in public life in the State of late, who has much common sense. He comprehends the condition of things and is disposed to take a wise course for the country. His ideas I am confident will agree with ours. He is not fanatical about slavery, was always at heart for the Union, desires the State Constitution modified as we do, is from the Up Country, & like myself does not belong to the old families. With his aid we can mould the State institutions like wax. I respectfully submit that you should pardon him & use him. He and I acting together could answer for this State, and be of more service to you than any number of other people could be.

I could say much more but as I know what an immense amount of business you have to go through with, I will conclude

With highest regard, Yours Sincerely
William W. Boyce

ALS, DLC-JP.

1. The Confederate congressman appears to have been detained in Washington, along with other political prisoners after the fall of Richmond, for on June 8 Johnson issued him a parole to return home and "cultivate and diffuse a loyal sentiment among the people of his State." Six days earlier Boyce had discussed and presented to Johnson his petition for pardon, which the President finally ordered granted on September 7, several months later than the South Carolinian had expected. Johnson to Boyce, June 8, 1865; Boyce to Johnson, July 12, 1865, Johnson Papers, LC; Boyce to Johnson, June 2, 1865, Amnesty Papers (M1003, Roll 44), S.C., William W. Boyce, RG94, NA; *New York World*, June 3, 1865; *Winnsboro News*, June 27, 29, 1865; Bell, "Presidential Reconstruction in South Carolina," 355–56.

2. The Fairfield (Winnsboro) meeting, which Boyce described briefly in an attached note, sent its resolutions to Johnson, as did the Chester and York meetings. See petitions from Citizens of Fairfield District, June 22; York District, June 22, Johnson Papers, LC; and Memorial from Chester District Citizens, July 12, 1865.

3. For over twenty years upcountry conservatives like Boyce had favored abolishing the old parish system which fixed the number of representatives in accordance to the number of church parishes within an electoral district. Since the lowcountry districts contained several parishes apiece, that region wielded greater political power. At the constitutional convention held in Columbia in September 1865, Boyce would join the majority of his fellow delegates in voting to base the number of legislators in both houses on population and taxation, thereby providing more equal representation. *Senate Ex. Docs.*, 39 Cong., 1 Sess., No. 26, pp. 124, 158, 174 (Ser. 1237); David D. Wallace, *South Carolina: A Short History* (Columbia, 1961), 341–42, 563–64; Bell, "Presidential Reconstruction in South Carolina," 355–56; Francis B. Simkins and Robert H. Woody, *South Carolina During Reconstruction* (Gloucester, Mass., 1966[1932]), 40–41.

4. Like Boyce, James L. Orr (1822–1873), U.S. congressman and Confederate senator, had been a leader of the peace movement, was appointed by Johnson as a special commissioner to establish a state provisional government, and would serve as a delegate to the state constitutional convention in September 1865. Shortly afterwards he joined the Republican party, serving as governor (1865–66), 8th circuit judge (1868–70), and minister to Russia (1872–73). *BDAC*; Warner and Yearns, *BRCC*; *Senate Ex. Docs.*, 39 Cong., 1 Sess., No. 26, p. 174 (Ser. 1237); Robert K. Krick, *Lee's Colonels: A Biographical Register of the Field Officers of the Army of Northern Virginia* (Dayton, Ohio, 1979).

From Joseph W. McClurg

June 23, 1865, Linn Creek, Mo.; ALS, DLC-JP.

Believing that Johnson's "sympathies are with the *radicals* of Missouri," Congressman McClurg seeks the removal of Postmaster Allen P. Richardson of Jefferson City, who was "appointed under the *Blair influence*, and . . . retained by *that influence*." Continues: "*That influence* has been long on the wane. . . . We once looked upon the Blairs as free-soilers. Now we regard them as corrupt demagogues." Having heard that Johnson "would be governed by the wish of the Member of Congress" in such appointments, the writer asks "whether or no" this is correct. [Richardson retained his office.]

From Levy J. Moses

June 23, 1865, New York, N.Y.; ALS, DLC-JP.

Charleston, S.C., bookkeeper, merchant, and unionist, unable to travel to Washington owing to a "slight indisposition," warns that a Charleston delegation now at the capital, "praying for the appointment of A Provisional Governor," is composed largely of "the most embittered secessionists in the State." Concerned that the "avowed enemies of our Glorious Republic" might become "the recipients of Government favor," the writer urges that loyal men, even "from other States," receive government appointments, rather than those "tainted in the least with disloyalty."

From Sarah C. Polk

Polk Place Nashville.
June 23, 1865.

His Excellency, Honl. A. Johnson,
President of the U.S.
Dear Sir,

Will you allow me most respectfully to ask your consideration in behalf of my Brother, Mr. John W. Childress, who visits you to solicit consideration relative to his Home & property, a subject on which I confered with you so often in his absence, and you so kindly rendered me aid & advice.

My brother now desires to get possession & the rents for his place, which has been entirely devastated by the War, having nothing left but the Land. The rents would in some degree renumerate him for his losses, & furnish means to support his large family.

I have previously stated to you the circumstances which induced him to leave his home. The locality was such he was compelled to remove his family out of the *way of the armies*, and he left when the Confederates were occupying that region, some months before the battle at Murfreesboro'.

Through your kindness & agency I was enabled to save from destruction some of his Furniture. I now Mr. President, ask your consideration to his application.

My brother has had nothing to do with the late war in any manner & has always been your personal & political friend, and will be ever grateful for a decision in this matter, in conformity to his wishes. The favor will renew my obligations to you for much kindness.[1]

I return my acknowledgments for the dispatch relative to cotton restrictions which I received.

With much consideration & respect
I am verry respectfully
Mrs. James K. Polk

ALS, DNA-RG94, Amnesty Papers (M1003, Roll 48), Tenn., John W. Childress.

1. Childress did in fact go to Washington, where he took the oath of allegiance on July 3 and then was granted a pardon by Johnson on July 11, 1865. See Amnesty Papers (M1003, Roll 48), Tenn., John W. Childress, RG94, NA; and *House Ex. Docs.*, 39 Cong., 2 Sess., No. 116, p. 36 (Ser. 1293).

From John A. Andrew

June 24, 1865, Boston, Mass.; ALS, DLC-JP.

Assuring the President of "a sincere welcome," the governor of Massachusetts, as ex officio president of the Board of Overseers of Harvard College, extends an invitation to attend commencement exercises on July 19 and ceremonies in honor of the soldiers of Harvard on July 21. Such a visit could serve "a thousand advantages of a public nature . . . the character and magnitude of which will most readily occur to yourself. I am sure that at no moment in the history of the Union has any concurrence of circumstances yet happened where more good could be done by any such means." [On July 18 Johnson, apologizing for the lateness of his response, wired that "it is impossible for me to leave here."]

From Christopher C. Andrews

Hd. Qrs. 2d Div. 13th A.C.
Mobile, Ala. June 24, 1865.

To Andrew Johnson President U. States Washington:

Will be glad if you have time to look at the enclosed address.[1]

Every thing is quiet around here. In the country however we occasionally hear of acts of lawlessness, among citizens.

The weather is very warm. The most of my command is *waiting* as it has been for two weeks, for transportation to Galveston.[2]

There are 500 colored children attending school here.

A great many people cherish the hope of reestablishing slavery.

With great regard. C. C. Andrews.

ALS, DLC-JP.

1. Although the enclosure has not been found, Johnson's secretary's endorsement indicates it was a copy of Andrews' General Orders No. 25, "To Officers and Soldiers of the Second Division," issued June 20 to quell unrest among the troops, disappointed at their retention in service. *OR*, Ser. 1, Vol. 49, Pt. 2: 1019–20.

2. The majority of Andrews' division began moving from Mobile to Galveston by ship between June 25 and 28. Ibid., 1034; Dyer, *Compendium*, 1057–58, 1062, 1078–79, 1088, 1128–29, 1334.

From Jonathan Cory, Jr.[1]

Beaufort S C June 24th 1865[2]

Pres. A. Johnson,
Sir

Your proclamation making James Johnson[3] Gov. of Ga. has fallen like a flash of lightening from clear sky upon us. The most intelligent

colored preacher, in speaking of it began to talk of war against the U.S.
The plan of educating the colored men in South Carolina before the
4th day of Dec. next is ruined If congress receives the States with the
negroes disfranchised. The Republican party will be disfranchised.

We were expecting to get the within printed and circulated. The Ga.
proclamation[4] renders such an undertaking useless.

J.C.

To His Excellency, Andrew Johnson, President of the United States of
America

We the undersigned, True and Loyal Citizens of the United States
and residents of   in said State of South Carolina, do humbly pray,
that you would order the said State of South Carolina to be divided into
50 Constitutional Districts for the purpose of electing, on the 4th of
December 1865 50 Delegates (one from each District,) whose duty it
shall be to meet, on the 8th of January, 1866, at the Capitol of South
Carolina, and form a Constitution for said State of South Carolina; and
that you will make all necessary regulations, to secure the free votes of
all the Loyal Citizens of the United States, whether white or black, for
said Constitutional Delegates; provided said Loyal Citizens of the
United States, are at the time of said Election, residents of the Districts
of said South Carolina in which they offer their votes and also provided,
they can read and write.

And thus will we ever pray

"The measure ye mete shall be measured to you again."[5]

J. Cory Jr Box 38.

ALS, DLC-JP.

1. Cory, commissioned by the Presbyterian Church to work with freedmen, later
moved to Jacksonville to continue his work. Cory to O. O. Howard, Oct. 20, 1866,
Records of the Commr., Lets. Recd. (M752, Roll 37), RG105, NA.

2. Received by the President on July 1, the letter was written on stationery of the
"United-States Sanitary Commission, N.E. Women's Auxiliary Association, No. 18,
West Street, Boston."

3. Johnson (1811–1891), Columbus lawyer and congressman who was currently
serving as Georgia's provisional governor (June 17-Dec. 19, 1865), was subsequently
collector of customs at Savannah (1866–69) and judge of the state superior court
(1869–75). *BDAC*.

4. The Georgia proclamation establishing a provisional government was issued on
June 17.

5. Matt. 7:2.

From Henry A. Farnsworth

[June 24, 1865, Greeneville, Tenn.]; LS, DNA-RG94, Amnesty Papers
(M1003, Roll 49), Tenn., Henry A. Farnsworth.

Indicted for treason in the federal court at Knoxville and currently free on bond,
petitioner claims that "said prosecution was instituted . . . for the purpose of
harassing him, and through personal malice, and not for the public good." A
unionist at the time of Tennessee's secession, and so continuing to the present,

he "has never voluntarily, aided, abetted or assisted" the Confederacy in any way. Having "complied with all the Laws of Congress," he "voluntarily went forward and took the Oath of Amnesty" and now seeks presidential pardon. [Johnson, without recommendation of the governor, pardoned Farnsworth, October 12, 1865.]

From Harvey H. Helper[1]

Washington, D.C. June 24th, 1865

To the President

The Secty. of the Treasury has to day, signified a willingness to appoint me Assessor of Revenues in my own district—the 3rd—in N.C. but desires, out of deference to Gov. Holden as the Chief Agt. of the Government for that State, that my application should be endorsed by him.

In consideration of my suffering and services, military and civil, during the late rebellion, I think this desire of the Secretary might justly be waived and the appointment made. May I ask your favorable endorsement of my wishes, thereby avoiding further delay.[2]

Very Truly, Yours, H. H. Helper

ALS, DNA-RG56, Appts., Internal Revenue Service, Assessor, N.C., 6th Dist., Hardin H. Helper.

1. Helper (c1821–fl1872), native North Carolinian, abolitionist, and older brother of Hinton R., returned home from his northern exile to become assessor (1865–71) at Salisbury. 1870 Census, N.C., Rowan, Salisbury, So. Ward, 4; U.S. Off. Reg. (1865–73); James A. Padgett, ed., "Reconstruction Letters from North Carolina: Part X, Letters of James Abram Garfield," NCHR, 21 (1944): 140n.

2. A distrust of Holden's unionism was probably the reason Helper wished to circumvent the governor's office and to appeal directly to the President. Respecting this request, Johnson endorsed Helper's letter: "I hope the Secretary of the Treasy will have it [in] his power to do something for Mr Helper," which was followed by McCulloch's initialed note: "Let Mr Helper be Commissioned." Appts., Internal Revenue Service, Assessor, N.C., 6th Dist., Hardin H. Helper, RG56, NA.

Interview with South Carolina Delegation[1]

June 24, 1865

The introduction over, the President requested the gentlemen of the delegation to resume their seats, and smilingly remarked, as he sat down among them himself, that in the days of old there used to be a class of men called Augurs, who never met each other without smiling in each other's faces; but that now the rebellion is over, and they would better look each other right in the face and speak clearly as to the future.

This Government, if it be preserved at all, must be preserved on the principle of equality, and if we have States therein, they must be States occupying and preserving certain clear relations to the Government of the United States. Hence, continued the President, I proceed upon the idea that a State cannot go out of the Union; and now that the rebellion is over and has been put down, the Southern States must come back with a proper understanding of these relations, and upon proper principles. Do you know that I believe I am a better State rights man than some of you are? <A general though subdued laughter greeted the remark.> I used always to believe that slavery could not be maintained outside of the Constitution of the United States, and did we not find when the experiment was made that slavery was lost? I was always for the Union, always; and I saw that when slavery attempted to control the Government, slavery must go down. The institution of slavery made the issue; it set up to control the Government and it fell. All institutions must be subordinate to the Government or it cannot stand. The great object now is to restore and preserve the Government that we all once loved and respected.

The present relation of slavery is changed, and if so disposed we could not remand it back; and so we must dispose of it as prudent, discreet, and wise men should. You have heard me spoken about as a great people's man, a rabid man, and all that sort of thing. I will not disguise from you that there are certain things to which I have always been opposed. I have always been opposed to monopolies, entails, &c; and for this I used to be denounced as a demagogue; but going back to that Magna Charta, from which, after all, we get all our liberties— liberty of speech, liberty of the press, protection from unreasonable search, &c., I believe in its doctrines, and am not going to deceive you now, gentlemen; when I tell you that, as far as in me lies, I intend to exert the power and influence of this Government to develop, and when developed, to place in power the great heart of the nation—the people— that *is* the heart of the nation. I look upon this nation as one sent upon a great mission, not a thing springing like an ephemeral mushroom, and I believe we will fall short of our duty unless we carry that mission out.

The Constitution of the United States says that persons shall be chosen for Congress by persons qualified in the several States, Congress acting for the whole. Now in some of the States a portion of the people have rebelled, and to some extent suspended, and even paralyzed the operations of the State governments; but there is a constitutional obligation on the Government to suppress rebellions, repel invasions, and to secure to every State a republican form of government. The Government may seem (and I will not undertake to enumerate the reasons) to have been tardy to protect the Union men in the South, but they are protected now, and having reached that protection they should come forward and stand upon all equality with the other loyal men everywhere in the country.

When the South went into this rebellion, the slaves went in as slaves, they came out as freemen of color. The rebellion has rubbed out the nature and character of the institution, and the loyal men of the South are compelled, therefore, to bow and submit to this result, and stand simply as equals to the other loyal men of the country everywhere. There can be nothing wrong in that.

Now, in the work of reconstruction, we have tried to begin at that point. You understand it—understand it perfectly; but understand also that I am not here to subserve any particular clique. I am here simply to serve the country and no particular interests; to use the power entrusted to me to bring the country back to the peace and harmony it owned before the rebellion commenced.

I will again say to you that slavery is gone. Its status is changed. There is no hope you can entertain of being admitted to representation either in the Senate or House of Representatives till you give evidence that you, too, have accepted and recognized that that institution is gone. That done, the policy adopted is not to restore the supremacy of the Government at the point of the bayonet, but by the action of the people. While this rebellion has emancipated a great many negroes, it has emancipated still more white men. The negro in South Carolina that belonged to a man that owned from one to five hundred slaves, thought himself better than the white man who owned none. He felt the white man's superior. I know the position of the poor white man in the South, compelled to till the barren, sandy, and—poor soil for a subsistence. You cannot deny how he was, in your eyes, of less value than the negro. Some here in the North think they can control and exercise a greater influence over the negro than you can, though his future must materially depend on you. Let us speak plainly on this subject. I, too am a Southern man, have owned slaves, bought slaves, but never sold one. You and I understand this better; we know our friends are mistaken, <here the President rose up and continued emphatically,> and I tell you that I don't want you to have the control of these negro votes against the vote of this poor white man. I repeat our friends here are mistaken, as you and I know as to where the control of negro vote would fall. When they come to talk about the elective franchise, I say let each State judge for itself. I am for free government; for emancipation; and am for emancipating the white man as well as the black man.

A Delegate.—I see you are for maintaining the Government and the Constitution.

The President.—Yes, sir; intact.

Delegate—We are at the present moment without law. You have the power.

President—Don't let us proceed upon the idea of power, but upon that of right. My opinion is that, for the present you must have an agent of the Government—a military or civil Governor, call it what you will; then have a convention, amend your Constitution, abolishing slavery, adopting the amendment to the Constitution of the United States.

After that, as far as white and black man are concerned, they come into market as laborers, subject to the same general law of supply and demand.

Delegate.—But is it necessary to have a convention pass upon the question.

President.—Certainly; and then it remains with the Government to receive them, or "leave them out in the cold," to use a common expression.

Delegate.—Then our admission or rejection would depend upon our adopting or not adopting what you think right?

President.—No; I only advise; I would have you understand me more correctly. In the first instance we proceed upon this idea, that the Constitution guarantees to every State a republican form of government. Now there comes a rebellion which has suspended the functions of the State Government; in order to restore to the State its republican form of government which it has lost, it is necessary to take some initiative step. A civil or military governor is appointed the agent of the Government; through him the Government may say convene yourselves, send your delegates, but we expect you to amend your Constitution and abolish slavery. You may refuse, but then Congress can say we have the right to judge of the eligibility of our own members, and if you don't submit it you must remain under military rule. You may send your two Senators, but it is for that body to admit or reject them, not for me; but here, as Executive of the nation, I can only take the initiative to enable you to do these things.

Delegate.—But there is the fact that slavery is not mentioned at all in the Constitution of the State.

President (smiling).—But there is the fact that it has existed in the State, and you can amend the Constitution so that it will say it does not exist there.

Delegate.—Then this is a *sine qua non* to precede our being restored.

President.—You must see that the friction of the rebellion has rubbed slavery out, and I assume it would be better for the people through that convention, to make it legally and constitutionally dead. The people, in coming forward, would better recognize that fact.[2]

. . . .

The President.—I will just say that you may name whom you would prefer.

Delegate.—It may be that those in whom we might have confidence might be objectionable; but there is Mr. Aiken.[3]

Other Delegate.—Or Mr. McKinley.[4]

Another.—Mr. Boyce, or Colonel Manning, or Mr. Perry.[5]

President.—B. F. Perry.

Delegate—Yes, sir.

President.—What part has he taken in the rebellion?

Delegate.—He was for awhile judge in one of the Confederate courts.

Benjamin F. Perry
Courtesy University of South Carolina Library

William W. Holden
*Courtesy North Carolina Division
of Archives and History*

J. Madison Wells
Courtesy Louisiana State Library

William L. Sharkey
Courtesy National Archives

Four of Johnson's Southern Governors

President.—Perry used to be rather too much of a people's man for you South Carolinians over there. Well, is he an acceptable man? I will not disguise anything from you. I am going right to the people as far as I can. I have a strong prejudice that way, you know. Ere you go let me assure you that there is no feeling of vindictiveness or revenge on the part of the Government, and I want you to feel that it is so. On Tuesday I will submit the substance of this interview to the Cabinet, and will see you again if you remain so long.[6]

Washington Evening Star, June 26, 1865.
1. At three o'clock on Saturday afternoon, Johnson met with this delegation of Charlestonians, headed by Judge Edward Frost. They had evidently presented their petition asking for the reestablishment of civil government to the President on Wednesday the 21st, and now returned for a more lengthy interview. *Washington Evening Star*, June 26, 1865; *New York Herald*, June 23, 1865; Bell, "Presidential Reconstruction in South Carolina," 358–59; Kibler, *Perry*, 377–78. For an unfavorable description of the petitioners, see Letter from John F. Poppenheim, June 18, 1865.
2. At this point Judge Frost spoke, telling the President that the "people of the South had come out of the struggle wiser than they went into it" and would make the best of the circumstances, though there was concern that the freedmen, "inflamed by their newly-conquered liberty," were "too apt to confound it with licentiousness; and to adopt the idea that freedom means exemption from labor." He concluded by requesting the appointment of a provisional governor at the "earliest convenience."
3. Emma Holmes, a niece of Judge Frost, recalled that William Aiken seemed "quite in favor with the ex-*tailor* & renegade, Andy Johnson, who has worked in this state & made clothes for Mr. Hamilton Boykin." John F. Marszalek, ed., *The Diary of Miss Emma Holmes* (Baton Rouge, 1979), 456.
4. A reporter's error, it actually is a reference to Samuel McAliley, Chester, S.C., lawyer, whom the Democrats subsequently nominated for Congress in 1868. Ann P. Collins and Louise G. Knox, eds., *Heritage History of Chester County, South Carolina* (Chester, S.C., 1982), 323; Bell, "Presidential Reconstruction in South Carolina," 359.
5. William W. Boyce, John L. Manning, and Benjamin F. Perry (1805–1886), a Democratic editor and unionist who resisted secession but stood with the state after its withdrawal from the Union. Appointed provisional governor on June 30, Perry would bitterly oppose congressional reconstruction. *DAB*; Kibler, *Perry*, 378. For other nominations see: B. B. French to Johnson, June 17, 1865; Adam T. Cavis to Johnson, June 21, 1865; South Carolina Districts to Johnson, June 29, 1865, Johnson Papers, LC; and Augustin L. Taveau et al. to Johnson, June 17, 1865, Augustin Taveau Papers, Duke University Library.
6. Diarist Emma Holmes reported: "Andy Johnson, whom Uncle knew in Congress, behaved much better than reported. He treated them courteously & spoke plainly." Johnson, who was ill—"feeling the effects of intense application to his duties, and over-pressure from the crowd"—cancelled his next cabinet meeting. There is no report of a discussion of South Carolina before his proclamation of June 30 appointing Perry and specifying the conditions for restoration of the state based on the North Carolina model. Marszalek, *Holmes Diary*, 461; Beale, *Welles Diary*, 2: 324.

From George Leslie[1]

Chicago, June 24th 1865

President Johnson
Respected Sir

In my capacity of a citizen, allow me to say that your position on the Reconstruction of the Revolted States, is not approved, but condemned by 9/10th of the best friends of the Administration in this Section of the Country.

You have had a grand opportunity to settle the Negro question now and forever and we fear that you have missed it.

It will not satisfy us to say that you did not have the power to do so, for your right over this matter is just as legal, as any of the steps you have taken, in setting up a Provisional Goverments. The people do not care so much about the mere fact of the Negro voting (although only right) as they do about a settlement of the question on a just, fair, and progressive basis; and thus removing the cause of future agitation.

But Dear Sir it is perhaps not yet too late at least, for a satisfactory compromise.

Why not apply the principle to the two States not yet provided for[2]—that all citizens have equal rights before the law, making your tests as high as you please only do away with all invidious distinctions, and thus cary out the principles of a *true Democracy*.

Save us we pray you as a nation, from the shame of denying the rights of suffrage to those who *fought* and *bled*, that the nation might *live*, and of giving it to those who fought, that it might *be destroyed*. Justice, Honor, Right, here indicate the true policy.

I am Your obt Servt Geo Leslie

ALS, DLC-JP.
    1. Leslie (*fl*1881), a salesman for John H. Dunham's Commission Sugar House, later worked as a "merchandise broker." Chicago directories (1863–81).
    2. The remaining southern states to be reorganized under presidential proclamation were South Carolina (June 30) and Florida (July 13).

To Sam Milligan

Executive Office, Washington, D.C.,
June 24 1865.

To Hon Sam. Milligan
Judge Supreme Court Tennessee
Knoxville Tenn
(If not there forward to Greenville Ten[)]

Your letter has been received and read.[1] I thank you for it. I trust in God you can do something with R——[2] for I have almost despaired. If any one can exert any influence with him you can. Give my sincere regards to Mrs Milligan.[3]

Andrew Johnson

Tel, DNA-RG107, Tels. Sent, President, Vol. 2 (1865).
    1. Not found.
    2. Johnson, obviously concerned over son Robert's failure to arrive in Washington with the rest of the family, turned to his old friend Milligan, who had been especially close to this second son.
    3. Tennessee-born Elizabeth R. (1826–1909), daughter of Jacob and Sarah R. How-

ard, married Sam Milligan, February 22, 1849. Memoir of Samuel Milligan (microfilm), TSLA; Reynolds, *Greene County Cemeteries*, 270.

From Albert Pike

June 24, 1865, Memphis, Tenn.; ALS, DNA-RG94, Amnesty Papers (M1003, Roll 14), Ark., Albert Pike.

Confederate brigadier, commissioner to the Indians, and judge of the Arkansas supreme court, applies for pardon, having accepted "that construction of the Constitution against which I contended." In addition to his Confederate services, he falls under the $20,000 exception of the May 29 proclamation, as well as having confiscatory proceedings already instituted against his property. Claiming he "yielded reluctantly to an inexorable necessity"—that is, secession, which he did not regard as treason, "but as the exercise of a lawful right"—he wishes now only "to pursue the arts of peace, to practice my profession, to live among my books, and to labour to benefit my fellows and my race by other than political courses." Reminding Johnson of the historical uses of amnesty and of the legacy of dead heroes, such as Jefferson and Madison, in fostering the war just fought—"'civil commotions have long roots in the Past'"—he suggests that southerners will not feel the guilt of treason because "Neither defeat nor condemnation changes convictions." [Pike's letter was forwarded to Johnson by B. B. French, July 1, 1865. On August 30 Johnson gave Pike permission to return home, provided that he take the oath and consent to the parole conditions. The Arkansan was pardoned April 23, 1866.]

From David L. Yulee

June 24, 1865, Fort Pulaski, Ga.; ALS, DNA-RG153, Lets. Recd. (1854–94), File 1891.

Former U.S. senator from Florida, now a prisoner at Fort Pulaski, seeks amnesty under the provisions of Johnson's May 29 proclamation, noting that he had no official connection with the Confederate government, nor any responsibility in its formation. He had considered passage of Florida's secession ordinance as a "mandate," however, and retired from his seat in the Senate on March 4, 1861, because "I could not honorably have done otherwise." Having staunchly defended the doctrine of state sovereignty before the war—"the political school to which I had always from youth adhered"—he acknowledges the abolition of slavery and the supremacy of the national government. [The date of a special pardon for Yulee has not been found.]

From William G. Brownlow

Knoxville, June 25th, 1865.

President Johnson:

James W. Sheffy,[1] of Marion, Va. has forwarded to you for pardon, a petition. He has never been in arms, but was a member of the convention that voted out. When my family and Maynards were sent out,[2] he denounced the act, and tendered to them, at Wytheville, all the money he had in his pockets. I would like to see him pardoned.

W. C. Kain was ordered here, to meet an indictment against him in Hall's circuit court,[3] for the murder of Haun and the Harmons.[4] Trigg[5] has determined to take him in hand, and to turn him out on bail. We cant do anything here, while Trigg's court is in the way, and on the side of the Rebellion, as it is.

Respectfully &c, W. G. Brownlow

ALS, DNA-RG94, Amnesty Papers (M1003, Roll 68), Va., James W. Sheffy.

1. Sheffy (1813–1876), Virginia lawyer and opponent of secession, served one term in the house of delegates (1875–76). Falling under the 13th exception, he was pardoned initially on Brownlow's recommendation on July 5 but reappears as pardoned with Governor Peirpoint's recommendation on August 7, 1865. William H. Gaines, Jr., *Biographical Register of Members Virginia State Convention of 1861: First Session* (Richmond, 1969), 69; *House Ex. Docs.*, 40 Cong., 2 Sess., No. 16, pp. 89, 91 (Ser. 1330).

2. The Brownlow and Horace Maynard families in April 1862 were given thirty-six hours "to pass beyond the Confederate States lines" and traveled north under escort. Oliver P. Temple, *East Tennessee and the Civil War* (Cincinnati, 1899), 318.

3. Elijah T. Hall, judge of the 3rd judicial circuit.

4. Unionists Jacob Harmon, his son Thomas, and A. C. Hawn, "bridge-burners" of the November 8, 1861, episode, were captured and hanged by the Confederates for the destruction of the bridge over Lick Creek in Greene County. Ibid., 384; *Johnson Papers*, 5: 42n.

5. Connally F. Trigg, U.S. District Court judge.

From Simon Cameron

Harrisburg June 25 1865

His Excellency, Andw Johnson,
Prest. of the U.S.
Dear Sir.

I know this repentant man.[1] His family are natives of, and reside in this state. My beleif is that what treason he did commit was of an involuntary character, and in a measure forced upon him by a pressure which it would have been impossible for a Northern man to withstand at the time of his fall from grace.

I respectfully enclose this request of his for pardon, without comment on its merits, to you who have shown so much mercy since your elevation to the Presidency, and will rest satisfied with such action as you may take in the matter.[2] His family here are thorough going unionists in Pennsylvania.

Yours Truly & Sincerely Simon Cameron.

LS, DNA-RG94, Amnesty Papers (M1003, Roll 13), Ark., John J. Clendenin.

1. John J. Clendenin (1813–1876) of Arkansas was a longtime state circuit court judge who retained his office after secession. Unsuccessful in his attempts to take Lincoln's amnesty oath, he applied to Johnson under the 13th exception after his land was seized by federal authorities; Cameron enclosed his petition in this letter. John Hallum, *Biographical and Pictorial History of Arkansas* (Albany, 1887), 274–75; Clendenin to Johnson, June 12, 1865, Amnesty Papers (M1003, Roll 13), Ark., John J. Clendenin, RG94, NA.

2. Cameron's recommendation undoubtedly helped; Johnson pardoned Clendenin on July 7. *House Ex. Docs.*, 39 Cong., 2 Sess., No. 116, p. 81 (Ser. 1293).

To Thomas C. Fletcher

June 25 1865

Hon Thomas C. Fletcher
Governor of Missouri
Governor.

I respectfully transmit through you to the officer in charge of the Missouri State Penitentiary an this order for the immediate enlargement of William P. Rogers,[1] late 7th Minnesota Volunteers now and for some time past, confined in said penitentiary, whose sentence is hereby remitted and all disabilities attaching to him therefor removed.

May I trouble you to forward this at once?[2]

I am Governor with high regards
Very Resp'y Yours Prest U.S.

LBcopy, DLC-JP3A.
1. Rogers (b. *c*1837) was a carpenter when he enlisted in 1862 in the 7th Minn. Vols. Discharged in February 1864, he was arrested for larceny in April, when another soldier, allegedly intoxicated, accused Rogers of robbing him. CSR, RG94, NA.
2. On July 8 Rogers was released by order of the President with his ten-year sentence remitted and "his enlargement ordered." Gen. Court-Martial Order No. 356, RG94, NA.

From Duff Green

Washington City 25th. June 1865

Confidential
To His Ex Andrew Johnson
President U States

Judge Bailey,[1] had been, for many years, my personal and political friend. You were Comparatively a Stranger. When he prompted by corcoran[2] made in Congress a false and malicious charge against me and my son you defended us, proving the falsity of his charge.[3] For that Vindication we have been ever grateful and ever ready to serve you.

You are now in a Situation Calling for the Sympathy and Support of your friends, for no one in your position, with a proper regard for his reputation, can be indifferent to the opinion of his Country men and that opinion will be indicated by the Election in 1868.

That extraordinary efforts will be made to organise an unscrupulous opposition to your administration and to your Election in 1868 you cannot doubt. That Chase or Sherman[4] or both will be opposing Candidates is clearly indicated, and that the vote of the South will control the Election in your favor, if you act wisely is to me now manifest.

The democracy of the north look to the South to reinstate them in power. If you identify yourself with the ultra abolitionists, in thier warfare on the South, then the democracy will rally on Sherman, and, aided as he will be by his brother's influence in Ohio, he will carry the conservative Whigs and organise the North West & the South against New England. If you so act, towards the South, as to command thier Confidence and Support you will carry the democratic party and unite the North West & the South in your support and Secure an overwhelming majority.

Do you ask what the South want? They desire to be reinstated as loyal, patriotic members of the Union. They want your proclamation restoring the people of the South to thier rights as loyal citizens and to thier rights of property.

Let the fourth day of July be a day of Jubilee. Throw wide open the prison doors. Send home the Captives to thier anxious friends at the public expense. Recal the Exiles and rest assured that there will be one unanimous loyal grateful response throughout the South and that no one can compete with you for thier confidence or Support. I would make no exceptions among those who are guilty of political offences only. No not one. But if exceptions are made they should be few. I would be glad to see and converse with you but will not obtrude.

Your Sincere freind Duff Green

ALS, DLC-JP.

1. Thomas H. Bayly, former Virginia congressman.

2. William W. Corcoran (1798–1888), successful Washington, D.C., banker, retired in 1854 to devote himself to managing his investments and pursuing philanthropic projects. During the war, though a southern sympathizer, he spent most of his time abroad. *DAB*.

3. On January 21, 1852, during House debates on the annual payments to Mexico for the Mexican Cession, Thomas Bayly singled out Duff Green and his son Benjamin, who had sought to get the contract to handle the transfer of payments, by implying that Green's wealth had enabled him to bring unusual pressure in governmental circles. Johnson defended the Greens' actions. See Speech on Indemnity Payment to Mexico, January 21, 1852, *Johnson Papers*, 2: 4–16.

4. Salmon P. Chase and William T. Sherman.

From Anthony M. Keiley [1]

Petersburg Va. Sat. June 25th 1865.

To His Excellency Andrew Johnson
President of the United States

About one P.M. yesterday, Capt. Brown A.D.C. to Major Gen. Hartsuff,[2] commanding in this city, handed me a dispatch received by Gen. H. from the Adjutant of Maj. Gen A. H. Terry,[3] Commanding the Department of Virginia, ordering the "immediate suppression" of the Petersburg *News* of which I am the editor. No cause was assigned for this act, and I therefore proceeded at once to Richmond and waited on Gen. Terry to ascertain the reason of this interference with a recognized, licensed pursuit in which the publishers had embarked much of their means, and in the prosecution of which they are protected in the country by the most solemn sanctions of law. I went prepared, as I am now prepared, to engage to forego all unfriendly criticism upon public acts while the state is without civil government, as is substantially the case at this time, rather than provoke conflict with the military authorities who govern Virginia, or if required to withdraw my pen entirely from the editorial columns of the paper, during the same interval, rather than entail upon the publishers the heavy loss which the destruction of their business, as of any business in this impoverished land must occasion. Gen. Terry would listen to no explanation or proposition but said with the greatest violence of language that he would neither suspend rescind or modify the order: assigning as a reason for issuing it "that the course of the paper in calling Clement Clay a chivalrous gentleman and designating the Military Commission now in session a Star Chamber was cause enough for the suspension of 40 journals"—that he would not suffer such things to be said much less published, and that a paper that would circulate such treason ought not to be suffered to exist a day.

In such an exigency, I feel there is no recourse but to your Excellency. As the military as well as civil superior of Gen. Terry, I know you have the power and as the sworn custodian of the people's rights, as the Executive Officer of that Constitution which secures to the American citizen free speech and a free press, as the arm of that Law which guarantees rights of property by sanctions as solemn as those which secure rights of person, I assume that you have the disposition to defend even the humblest of your fellow-citizens.

I invoke your powerful aid to vindicate those rights, that constitution and that law, against the unwarrantable infringement of all by this officer, with the same confidence that I would call upon you, if a foreign power the greatest as well as the least should dare invade my privileges as an American citizen. I invoke it in the name of the duty of Protection which by virtue of your Proclamation I have a right to claim as correlative to the duty of Allegiance which I frankly tendered and propose to yield hereafter. I invoke it in the interests of that Peace Order and Freedom which you have avowed to the world to be the ends you seek to attain in your official conduct. I invoke it in behalf of the South, your native section and your constant home whose ghastly wounds it is your happy province to bind up, but which, acts of such tyranny as this so necessarily irritate and inflame that it is difficult to acquit their authors of this as their deliberate design.

Let not, I conjure you, the insignificance of the individual excuse you from interference. For justice in rights so fundamental, no claim is unimportant, no claimant insignificant.

In conclusion it is proper to say that I have preferred at once to lay the matter before Your Excellency because I had rather appeal first to the Chief Magistrate of this most powerful nation who holds his seat by virtue of the Constitution whose protection I ask and the law to whose judgment I submit the question of my rights, than to appear to seek the vulgar honor of notoriety based on political martyrdom.[4]

I have the honor to be
Your fellow citizen A M Keiley

ALS, DNA-RG107, Lets. Recd., EB12 President 1925 (1865).

1. Keiley (1835–1905), editor of the *News* and founder of its successor, the *Index*, and of the *Norfolk Virginian*, served in the Confederate army and was briefly a prisoner of war. In 1870 he moved to Richmond, where he opened a law practice and served as mayor (1871–76). James H. Bailey, "Anthony M. Keiley and 'The Keiley Incident,'" *VMHB*, 67 (1959): 65–81; Tyler, *Va. Biography*, 3: 255.

2. Edward O. Brown (*c*1834–1899) was born in New York but resided in the midwest before the war. Mustered out in September 1865, he subsequently relocated to Toledo, Ohio, where he worked as an insurance agent. George L. Hartsuff (1830–1874), chief of staff for General Rosecrans in West Virginia (1861–62), commanded the XXIII Corps and headed the District of Nottoway, headquartered in Petersburg. Pension Records, Weltha A. Brown, RG15, NA; Heitman, *Register*, 1: 250; Warner, *Blue*.

3. Alfred H. Terry (1827–1890) of Connecticut commanded the X Corps under Butler and Schofield in eastern Virginia and North Carolina. After the war he held departmental commands in the Indian territory. His adjutant was Maj. Charles H. Graves (1839–1928), Massachusetts native, who settled after the war in Duluth, Minn., where he was a businessman and politician. Warner, *Blue*; *NCAB*, 22: 228.

4. Johnson's action, beyond referring the matter to the secretary of war, is not known. Federals suspended the paper on June 23, arrested Keiley in Petersburg on July 1, and confined him in Castle Thunder at Richmond until his release on parole July 3. *Washington Evening Star*, July 5, 1865; Bailey, "Anthony M. Keiley," 69.

From Walter Lenox

June 25, 1865, Fort McHenry, Md.; ALS, DNA-RG107, Lets. Recd., EB12 President 1899 (1865).

Former mayor of Washington, D.C., arrested as an "agent of the Confederate goverment" and imprisoned at Fort McHenry for eighteen months without trial, asserts that the charges against him are "without the *Shadow of a foundation*," his crime being that he crossed federal lines without permission, in order to return to Maryland to take care of business affairs and the estate of a deceased sister. Seeking release, he asks: "Is not the punishment I have undergone not only adequate to cover the offense, but is it not far beyond it?" Noting that "the entire residue of Southern Citizens lately in opposition to the U S (with few exceptions) are at large without parole," Lenox contends that the "accident of my being in custody should not be made the occasion of imposing upon me the oath of allegiance." Accepting the South's defeat as an "established fact" and the abolition of slavery as "an inexorable, unalterable necessity of the War," he concludes that he only wants "*the speedy restoration of the Union*" and "peace and happiness" for the South. [Johnson took no action other than forwarding Lenox's letter to the War Department, where it was filed.]

From William W. Holden

Raleigh, N.C. June 26, 1865.

Hon. Andrew Johnson:

My dear Sir:

I should have written to you before, but I have been so pressed with business that I have found it impossible to do so at any length. And I do not intend now to inflict a very long letter upon you, for I know that your engagements are greatly more pressing than mine.

I began at once the work of reorganization as soon as I had freely and fully consulted our leading friends. My proclamation seems to receive general approval, and the best disposition exists among the people. Of course there are exceptions, but they are not numerous or formidable. The truth is, the hearts of our people were never in the rebellion, and as soon as the pressure of military power was removed the old spirit of Unionism manifested itself every where.[1] The true friends of the Union are elated and hopeful, while the rebellious are subdued and ready to submit to lawful authority.

I have already appointed Justices of the Peace in some forty Counties out of the eighty-five. These Justices are to organize the County Courts, and from them I am selecting Enrolling Boards[2] for each County to administer the amnesty oath to the people. These Boards will sit until every one shall have had an opportunity to be heard. It is impossible to say now when the Convention can be called. The great West is comparatively untouched. The people of that region are for the most part devotedly attached to the government, and it is important that they should have a fair hearing. In the absence of mail facilities the work must proceed slowly in the Western Counties.

Our people have but little money. In the greater portion of the State they have none. I fear the tax now being collected will distress many of them.[3] Could it not be suspended for a time?

Much complaint exists in the Eastern part of the State in relation to colored troops. The people of Wilmington appear to fear a collision. Several outrages have been committed, and many loyal and peaceable citizens have been molested and insulted by colored soldiers. I would suggest that the white and colored troops be intermixed in the same localities, or rather that a body of white troops be stationed at points where there are large numbers of colored troops. Indeed, I do not perceive that we need any considerable number of troops in this State. Certainly we shall not, after the Local Police shall have been fully organized and armed. I have no complaint to make of Gen. Schofield or Cox[4] in this respect, but the sooner the Local Police is organized and armed the sooner the great bulk of the regular troops can be withdrawn.

Jonathan Worth,[5] Esq. the State Treasurer, who will hand you this, is an able financier and every way reliable. He visits Washington to have a thorough understanding as to what property the State is entitled to. I leave the whole matter in your hands without argument, as I am satisfied you will do right.

I have been operating for nearly a month without one cent of money. I trust you will place some funds in the hands of Mr Worth, the Treasurer. I shall be obliged, with your consent, to devote a small portion of these funds to the support of the Deaf and Dumb and Blind and Insane Asylums. These charities must be sustained, and the State has no money, and no means of raising any. I will send soon an official estimate of the probable expenditures of the Provisional Government from 1st June to 1st Sept. 1865.[6]

In the matter of pardon I am exercising care and caution. The worst cases have not yet gone forward. I may be in error as to some, but I will endeavor in each case to inform you as to the peculiar character of the applicant.[7]

Some of our people are complaining that although they are restored by the proclamation to their rights of property, they are kept out of possession by Treasury Agents. Some action by which loyal persons could be restored to possession of their property in such cases, would be gratefully received.

I have had several interesting conversations with Mr Watterson.[8] He will no doubt post you fully in relation to affairs in the State.

I am glad to say that your administration is constantly gaining on the confidence and affection of our people. They look to you as a *friend*, and they feel they will not be disappointed.

I cannot ask you to write me, for I know you are incessantly and most laboriously engaged but if you see that I am making mistakes or taking the wrong path, admonish me.

Very Truly Your friend, W. W. Holden.

ALS, DNA-RG59, Misc. Lets., 1789–1906 (M179, Roll 225).

1. During the war, many North Carolinians were critical of the Confederacy. A strong peace movement, headed by Holden, made an impressive showing at the polls in the 1864 gubernatorial election. Raper, *Holden*, 45–59.

2. Holden attached a printed form, which he sent to prominent unionists, requesting that they suggest the truly loyal from their county's magistrates and "designate six . . . to act as a Board or Boards for administering the amnesty oath."

3. Holden sought remission of the two and one-half cents a pound on cotton and postponement of other taxes, such as the direct tax on land. Suspension of the first enabled farmers and planters to receive considerable savings on cotton sales; the second gave needed relief from default. Raper, *Holden*, 67; Harris, *Holden*, 177.

4. John M. Schofield and Jacob D. Cox.

5. Worth (1802–1869), lawyer and state senator, strongly opposed secession but nevertheless served as a state representative under the Confederate regime. Briefly state treasurer in 1865, he was subsequently elected governor (1865–68). Worth delivered this letter to the President and argued against seizures of state property. *DAB*; Richard L. Zuber, *Jonathan Worth: A Biography of a Southern Unionist* (Chapel Hill, 1965), 194.

6. With Johnson's July 8 order allowing North Carolina officials to resume possession

of the state's property, the governor saved some $300,000 in "cotton and naval stores" for the state treasury, thereby enabling him to fund the provisional government. Harris, *Holden*, 176–77. (Raper, *Holden*, 67, says that the amount was only $150,000. In any event, both authors agree that Holden had more than enough money to cover the government's expenses.)

7. On June 23 the President, through the attorney general, had warned Holden, as he was warning other governors, to be especially careful in administering the amnesty proclamation, particularly to those excepted classes who would be making direct appeals to him. The governor was to screen all such petitions, indicating his recommendations for deferral or release, before forwarding them to Washington. Dorris, *Pardon and Amnesty*, 190–92, 194; James Speed to James Johnson and Other Governors, June 23, 28, July 11, 1865, Office of Atty. Gen., Lets. Sent, Vol. D (M699, Roll 10), RG60, NA.

8. Harvey Watterson, touring the South for the President, had been in North Carolina since June 20. *Advice*, 42.

From William Lawrence

June 26, 1865, Washington, D.C.; ALS, DNA-RG56, Appts., Internal Revenue Service, Assessor, Ohio, 4th Dist., James Walker.

Ohio congressman requests the removal of James Walker, the 4th district assessor so "that the National officers might be better distributed over the Dist—the Assessor and Member of Congress—both being in the same county." He agrees to Walker's resignation the next year (June 1866) if "this arrangement can be carried out in good faith; *but if an effort* be made by those not satisfied with it, I hope *to be notified before any change is made*" in order to recommend a successor. [David M. Fleming replaced Walker in June 1866.]

From Levin R. Marshall[1]

Pelham, Westchester Co., N. York
26 June '65,

My Dear Sir,

When I had the pleasure of calling upon you in Washington I mentioned to you that I held some Bonds of the U. States Govt. due last Decb'r, upon which the interest coupons were paid, but the Bonds refused; and you were kind enough to give me a Line to Mr. Sec: McCulloch, who said that, if the question was presented to him as an original one, He would decide upon their payt. at once. But as Mr. Chase, his predecessor, had taken a different view, He would prefer to reflect further and requested me to make a written application to him which I have complied with by the present mail.

These Bonds are part of a series issued by the Govt. of the U. States to the State of Texas, distinguished as Indemnity Bonds, bearing 5 pr. ct. interest and made payable to *bearer*—the interest coupons payable semi-annually.

The ground taken by Mr. Chase, for refusal of payt., I understand to be the want of endorsement by a Loyal Governor; altho' the interest coupons attached to the Bonds are acknowledged and paid. I purchased these Bonds—Forty two in number of $1,000. each and in preference to sterling Bills which I could have purchased at less premium. I preferd. the security of my own Govt., and never doubted for a moment the faithful payment of them when due. They state upon their face "Transferable on delivery" and payable to "*Bearer*" which, of course disarmed me of any suspicion of the necessity of any endorsement—none being needed by the face of the instrument—besides, I purchased them of a highly respectable party and had no knowledge of any inaccuracy on the part of the agents of the Texan Govt, if any existed. I have owned them about 4 years and worn them in the lining of my vest to conceal the knowledge from the Rebels. As you are aware, all my Property has been destroyed by the Rebels in consequence of my Union sentiments—and these Bonds I secured and looked to as a suppot for my Family in my now reduced circumstances and advanced age. Even if it is admitted that these Bonds were paid out by the Rebel Governor of Texas—still he was the embodiment of the State of Texas being elected by the People of Texas, and altho' the state was disloyal to the Govt, still it was the state of Texas and his act could bind the state for property belonging to the state altho' he could not take it out of the Union—and I think you will agree with me that no act of a disloyal Governor, could affect the obligation of the General Government. It would place the General Govt. in a false position before the world to repudiate its solemn obligations because of the wrongful act of the state authorities. May I ask your kind consideration of this claim, and confer with Mr. McCulloch, to whom I write by this mail. This fund is of the utmost importance to me, having lost all except my Land, and no means to cultivate that unless I can collect these Bonds. I am aware that your time is very much taxed and I feel great reluctance in trespassing upon your important duties; but, I am encouraged to hope for a favorable consideration of my peculiar case so similar to your own trials of the last four years.

I hope Judge Sharkey, will soon have the wheels in motion in Mississippi. The appointment of the Judge, I am glad to say, gives great satisfaction in New York as well as at home; and I may add, as I do with great pleasure, that your measures for bringing the southern states back to their allegiance is approved by all except the ultras who desire to elevate the negro into a sphere for which he is wholly unfit. These People will clamor, but in vain. As a Party, it will sink into insignificance before your present term expires, and with the southern states which you will assuredly get entire and the Democratic vote of the North & West superadded to the conservative Republicans your reelection is assured beyond doubt by a large majority.

Persevere in the course you have marked out and the Country will sustain you and *Thank* you.

I am, My Dr' Sir Yr's Very Truly, L R Marshall
of Natchez, Missi—

Hon: Andrew Johnson,

P.S. I enclose an article cut from the New York Evening Post which covers much of the ground in my case.[2] Please allow me to call your attention to it. I scarcely think, however, that you will need much argument to decide my case. It seems to me too plain a business matter to doubt.[3]

ALS, DNA-RG60, Office of Atty. Gen., Lets. Recd., President.

1. Marshall (1800–1870), wealthy native Mississippi planter and banker, had for years maintained a residence in New York, where he also had investments. Goodspeed's *Biographical and Historical Memoirs of Mississippi* (2 vols., Spartanburg, S.C., 1978 [1891]), 2: 397; L. R. Marshall to Johnson, Feb. 26, 1866, Johnson Papers, LC.

2. Not found.

3. Johnson referred this matter to Attorney General Speed, who issued an opinion asserting that Chase's requirement of an endorsement "was an impairment of the contract" with the bondholders and "was, therefore, of no effect in law." McCulloch redeemed many unendorsed Texas indemnity bonds before the Supreme Court in 1869, under Chief Justice Chase, forbade further redemption of those that had been sold by the Confederate government of Texas and ordered restitution of the securities or the proceeds therefrom to Texas. William W. Pierson, Jr., "Texas *Versus* White," *SWHQ*, 18 (1914–15): 345, 353–360; 19 (1915–16): 1, 142–44, 147–48.

From Sidney C. Posey[1]

Florence Alabama June 26th 1865

His Exl Presd Johnson
Dr Sir

Perhaps it would be agreeable to you to hear what we a portion of the people have to say and to think of the measures adopted by the President for our benefit.

Several of our citizens have just returned, who were admitted to an interview with you,[2] and every man of them well pleased, and give us confident assurances that you are doing & will continue to do, all that the President of the U States, can or should do for the people of these unfortunate States.

Permit me to assure you there is no want of confidence in nine tenths of the people in your administration. No reasonable man can expect any thing more than the course you have marked out indicates.

The people of Alabama are heartily sick and tired of secession, Southern Independence, & the whole concern. To get back again into the good old Govermt. they are willing to give up the negro, to be placed once more under a Government, the best in the world, in exchange for the very worst Govmt. in the world.

I know of only one man of influence[3] who has been contriving to get back negroes & all, by holding that the State has never been out of the Union, & that the election of members to Congress, will take the State back *ipso facto*. He, I presume after seeing his Bro. at Washington recently (R Houston Esqr[4] who knows better) will give up that delusion.

I assure you, Mr President, from all I can hear from every part of the State, when the time comes a convention will be called to amend the Constitution in conformity with the well known policy of the Govermt.

As you have labored & suffered much to uphold the Union, & may have more toil & persecution ahead, before yr great work is finished, I hope it will help you somewhat, to whisper into your ear, that the people of the South, (if they ever did) do not now consider it "a *calamity*" to them that the administration of the Fed Govt. is in yr hands.

Very Respectfully Yr Obt Svt. S. C. Posey

ALS, DLC-JP.
1. Posey (1805–1868), lawyer and prewar legislator, though a member of the 1861 secession convention, had opposed the movement and refused to sign the ordinance. Henry S. Marks, comp., *Who Was Who in Alabama* (Huntsville, 1972), 144.
2. See Reception of Alabama Delegates, June 5, 1865.
3. Former U.S. Congressman George S. Houston.
4. Russell Houston.

From St. Louis Citizens

Saint Louis June 26th 1865

Mr President
Dear Sir

The undersigned respectfully recommend the appointment of their distinguished fellow Citizen Maj Genl. Blair[1] to the position of Secretary of War.

We think it is manifest that the nation is directly to be involved in a struggle scarcely less portentous than that of the War which has closed. A powerful political organization has already risen up to demand a mighty change in the form of the Goverment. The fundamental idea of this new Party is to make the lately emancipated slaves the governing class in the South. They propose to take away suffrage from the Conquered white and bestow it on the ignorant inexperienced black.

As a means to the end they expect to overthrow the state goverments resting their powers mainly if not wholly in a great central consolidated power realizing what some of the party have been bold to proclaim "The new Nation."

In our Opinion this party is already formidable and by means of appliances continually at work particularly in the border states is growing. Most certainly it is uncommonly active and determined.

To defeat the aim of this party is to save the Country.

At the same time we are free to declare we believe nothing will defeat them but wise counsels & prompt and decisive action. The administration should lose no time in marshalling its freinds on the great issues. Whatever of moral or intellectual power it can apply should be combined and brought to bear and judicious and prudent steps should be taken without delay in directing the popular mind. We have assumed

that a reorganization of the Cabinet is unavoidable, and it is this beleif
we have ventured to name an incumbent for the War Office.

Genl Blair is a person of great sagacity prudence and resolution. He
was the first soldier who inlisted in the National army west of the Mississippi and having once "put his hand to the plow" never looked back.
He has never failed to adhere to the right regardless of the smiles or
frowns of the giddy multitude. Only such men in times like these are
valuable to their Country.

We have the honor to be sir
Your Freinds & Fellow Citizens

Saml T. Glover	Jas. O. Broadhead
J M How	Barton Able

Danl. M. Grissom, Editor, St. Louis Dispatch.[2]

Hon Andrew Johnson Washington DC

LS, DLC-JP.
  1. Francis (Frank) P. Blair, Jr.
  2. Glover (1813–1884) was an attorney whose law partner and fellow state legislator
Broadhead (1819–1898), district attorney for eastern Missouri, served in Congress
(1883–85); John M. How (1813–1885), an owner of a profitable leather business, had
twice been mayor of St. Louis; Able (1823–1877), a former steamboat pilot, commission
merchant, legislator, and now city gauger, became customs collector (1866). Grissom
(1829–1930) later edited the *Missouri Republican*. All had served on Congressman
Frank Blair's Committee of Safety early in the war. William Hyde and Howard L. Con-
rad, eds., *Encyclopedia of the History of St. Louis* (4 vols., St. Louis, 1899), 2: 905–6;
St. Louis directories (1863–66, 1870, 1881); *BDAC*; *House Ex. Docs.*, 39 Cong., 2
Sess., No. 67, p. 7 (Ser. 1292); Robert J. Rombauer, *The Union Cause in St. Louis in
1861* (St. Louis, 1909), 148, 190, 191; Howard K. Beale, ed., *The Diary of Edward
Bates, 1859–1866*, in *Annual Report of the American Historical Association*, 1930, Vol.
4 (Washington, D.C., 1933): 58, 82n, 124; *NUC*; J. Thomas Scharf, *History of Saint
Louis City and County* (2 vols., Philadelphia, 1883), 1: 604; Holli and Jones, *American
Mayors*, 171.

From Lewis Texada

[ca. June 26, 1865], New Orleans, La.; ALS, DNA-RG94, Amnesty Papers
(M1003, Roll 29), La., Lewis Texada.

Although he took Lincoln's amnesty oath of December 1863 during the Federal occupation of his parish (Rapides), Texada served in the Confederate reserve corps under special orders from the Conscript Bureau after Federal forces
evacuated. He does not feel that this non-voluntary service should put him
within the exceptions of the May 29 proclamation, for he was never "commissioned or sworn in, nor has the company ever been armed or ordered to the
field." If he falls within the 14th exception, he hopes his documented testimony
of his protests to Confederate military duty will sufficiently support his petition.
[With Governor Wells's strong endorsement of the petitioner's "truthfulness
and integrity of character," Texada received his pardon on July 11, 1865.]

From Robert W. Johnson [1]

Galveston Texas June 27th 1865

To His Excelcy. Andrew Johnson
Mr. President

I will make no attempt to embellish my case, or multiply words.

This War is over; and enclosed I hand you a duplicate of my letter of surrender to Gen Granger,[2] together with the Oath which is required.

I am now ruined & stripped of all means of support. My wife & young daughter are with me.[3] I can not well leave them to go into exile; and it has appeared to me to be in the true line of my duty to my people & country, to surrender myself into your power.

It is proper that I should now present respectfully, as I do, my petition for the benefits of your Amnesty Proclamation of June 3rd 1865. No one could well know me, personally & politically, through the last twenty years, better than yourself, & to that knowledge I appeal. My actions have been open & conscientious, the results of the avowed principles of a life-time. I submit myself to your judgement, as cheerfully as may be, under all the surrounding circumstances.

What I have done & now do, is in good faith. I give in my adhesion to the Government of the United States—accept it with its powers as it now construes them—and abandon all claim to the right of Secession, until & unless the Government shall itself declare differently, & thus change my obligations.

The Slave holding institutions of the South are destroyed, & all the consequences however distressing & incalculable are incurred. Our States & *great* Statesmen, our *great* Offices & *great* Armies, and our people have submitted. I, Sir, submit in good faith & without reserve, & it is but feeble expression to say I lament & deplore this War.

It is idle to say more, and I think of nothing, not already familiar to yourself to add, in justification or extenuation; but leave all to your political knowledge & your personal knowledge of myself, & to your best judgement.

My address is at Marlin—Falls Co—Texas & I ask respectfully an answer, with permission to visit Washington City next fall, if my bad health & small means will allow me.[4]

I am Sir very respectfully

Your Obt. Svt. R W. Johnson

P.S. Gen Granger holds me under parole.

ALS, DNA-RG94, Amnesty Papers (M1003, Roll 13), Ark., R. W. Johnson.

1. Arkansas Confederate senator, whose terms in the U.S. House and Senate overlapped President Johnson's.

2. R. W. Johnson to Gordon Granger, June 19, 1865, Amnesty Papers (M1003, Roll 13), Ark., R. W. Johnson, RG94, NA.

3. Johnson had recently married Laura Smith of Louisville, Ky., the sister of his first wife, who had died during the war. *DAB*.

4. Enlisting the help of the President's friend Preston King in August, and finally obtaining Arkansas governor Isaac Murphy's endorsement in October, Johnson received a presidential parole on November 8, and a full pardon on April 23, 1866. George H. Thompson, *Arkansas and Reconstruction* (Port Washington, N.Y., 1976), 46–47; *House Ex. Docs.*, 39 Cong., 2 Sess., No. 31, p. 23 (Ser. 1289).

From James B. Lambert[1]

Doylestown, Bucks Co., Pa., June 27, 1865

His Excellency Andrew Johnson,
President of the United States,
Dear Sir,

Before this reaches you you, will probably have been apprized of a movement in favor of the appointment of Mr. A. S. Cadwallader[2] as Collector of Internal Revenue for the Fifth District of Penna.,—of which this county forms a part,—in place of Mr. Cowell[3] the present incumbent. So long as those who are and have been the earnest adherents of the administration were alone consulted we felt that there could be little doubt in regard to the result. But an organization has been effected, composed largely of persons who have been the most unwavering and violent opponents of the present and past National Administrations asking for the retention of Mr. Cowell.[4] So true is this that his retention can hardly fail to be construed as a triumph of our most inveterate political opponents. Lest this *appearance* of *strength* thus presented should be mistaken for an indication of the will of the friends of the government in this district, I feel constrained to call your attention to the fact above stated, and to remind you further, that much of the opposition to Mr. Cadwallader's appointment comes from persons who do not reside in this District and whom we feel should permit us to determine questions like this for ourselves.

I have been at some pains and have had considerable means of ascertaining the wishes of our citizens, and believe I speak advisedly when I say that a large majority of those who have labored and voted to sustain the government during the late rebellion are desirous of seeing the proposed change effected, and that their interests will be most decidedly promoted by its being made.

Mr. Cadwallader's qualifications will be questioned by no one at all acquainted with him. A man of strict integrity, active and thorough business habits, and earnestly devoted to the interests of his country, I consider him especially fitted for and deserving of the position to which he aspires.

Believing that his appointment will give very general satisfaction and materially advance the interests of your supporters in this locality; I sincerely hope you may find it consistent with your convictions of duty to make the proposed change.

I remain, very truly,

Your obt. Servant, James B. Lambert,—
Member of Union State Central Committee for Bucks Co.

ALS, DNA-RG56, Appts., Internal Revenue Service, Collector, Pa., 5th Dist., Algernon S. Cadwallader.

   1. Not further identified.
   2. Algernon S. Cadwallader (1828–*fl*1905), a merchant and local Whig-Republican politico who attended the Republican national conventions of 1864 and 1868, was appointed collector, September 12, 1865. Warren S. Ely and John W. Jordan, eds., *History of Bucks County* (3 vols., Baltimore, 1975[1905]), 3: 604; Appt. Bk. 1: 50, Ser. 6B, Johnson Papers, LC.
   3. John W. Cowell was collector (*c*1863–65). *U.S. Off. Reg.* (1863–65).
   4. A veritable avalanche of signatures appended to many copies of a petition in support of Cowell's retention descended upon Johnson during July. These petitions not only lauded Cowell's performance in office but also declared him to be "an efficient and zealous advocate of the principles of the Administration, and a loyal and Union loving citizen," whose removal "would be prejudicial to the interests of the Government, impolitic and injurious to the future success of the party in the District." In August Johnson was assured that Cowell was "far more popular in the Union Republican Party, than is his opponent Mr. Cadwallader." Appts., Internal Revenue Service, Collector, Pa., 5th Dist., John W. Cowell, RG56, NA.

From Hugh L. McClung

June 27, 1865, Saltville, Va.; ALS, DNA-RG94, Amnesty Papers (M1003, Roll 65), Va., Hugh L. McClung.

Unable to avail himself of the amnesty oath before a writ was served on him for having "given aid and comfort to the enemy," McClung, a longtime Knoxville resident, attests that his wartime activity was solely related to the production of salt, most of which benefited the Union families of Tennessee, saving them over $2,000,000. "This salt, too, was distributed per capita by agents appointed by the several county Courts, at least four fifths of whom were union men," and, he reasons, because "three fourths of the people of East Tenn. are union citizens of course three fourths of the salt made was consumed by union citizens." [Indicted for treason and worth over $20,000, McClung was pardoned November 30, 1865, with Governor Brownlow's recommendation.]

From Hugh McCulloch

June 27, 1865, Washington, D.C.; Copy, DNA-RG56, Lets. Sent *re* Customs Service Employees (QC Ser.), Vol. 2.

Treasury secretary sends commission for John S. Loomis as Richmond, Va., collector, advising that he be appointed in place of Joseph Humphreys, previously recommended, inasmuch as the former seems the more popular choice and meets Governor Peirpoint's approval. Though not long a Virginia resident, Loomis, as acting collector, is well acquainted with the property "abandoned by and captured from the rebel government," which will be turned over for customs collection the first of July. [Humphreys was ultimately appointed the next year (June 1866), while Loomis remained in Richmond as an assistant special agent in the Treasury Department.]

From J.G.M. Ramsey[1]
(Copy)[2]

Charlotte N.C. June 27, 1865.

To His Excellency Andrew Johnson
President U.S.A.
Sir

You will perceive from the date of this letter that I am no longer at my old home at Mecklenburg T. At the time of the invasion of East Tennessee in August 1863 I thought it necessary in fidelity to my public duties to come away. My residence was soon after reduced to ashes & the ladies of my family a few months later followed me. We are here in Mecklenburg county but desire to return to our native state where a widowed daughter, several grandchildren & other relatives still reside.

I have seen your proclamation & observe from its tenor that persons belonging to certain specified classes therein enumerated are excepted from the amnesty & pardon extended to those who have participated in the late rebellion & that in such cases "special application" may be made to the President for Executive clemency.

I have no wish to attempt to conceal from you all the facts in my own case. When Tennessee declared in 1861 for seperation I went with her & became an earnest & faithful confederate. Nay more when Mr. Memminger[3] without solicitation on my part asked me to serve as Depositary at Knoxville I accepted that position & executed its duties to the best of my abilities & with the utmost good faith. When Genl. Lee surrendered I handed over my office & its assets to [Major] Nutt[4] the agent of the Treasury then in Georgia & became again a private citizen engaged in the practice of physic for the maintainance of a helpless family houseless & in exile.

I have always as you perhaps know desired to be useful to my age & to my country—have been especially proud of Tennessee—her patriots—her heroes—her statesmen & her excellent people & have borne some humble part in her improvement educational material & moral & now when nearly three score & ten desire to return to the place of my nativity a law abiding man & a good citizen & have taken the prescribed oath of allegiance. In all I have done since 1861 I know I was honest & believed I was patriotic. Such is my consciousness. If I have erred, the error was honest—it was the error of the head—not of the heart I am sure.

My case is before you—briefly but truthfully stated & I submit it to you.

Wishing you very sincerely a successful & prosperous administration that will reflect honor to the Union lustre to Tennessee & credit to your self.

I am Very Respectfully
Your Obt. Sert J. G. M. Ramsey

Post Scriptum July 12, 1865

I shall not be able for a year or more to return to Tennessee having engaged in company with my kinsman Doctor J. M Knitt Henderson[5] in the practice of medicine in this county.

In conformity with what I understand to be the rule in similar cases this application is forwarded to you through Hon. W. W. Holden Provisional Governor of North Carolina.[6]

Very Respectfully J. G. M. Ramsey

ALS, DNA-RG94, Amnesty Papers (M1003, Roll 42), N.C., J.G.M. Ramsey.
    1. Knoxville physician and Confederate Depositary for East Tennessee.
    2. Although Ramsey clearly marked this letter as "Copy," nevertheless this is the letter that eventually was forwarded to Washington and placed in the Amnesty Papers of North Carolina.
    3. Christopher G. Memminger, Confederate secretary of the treasury.
    4. Not identified. This person is referred to as "Major Butt" in the account of this incident found in William B. Hesseltine, ed., *Dr. J.G.M. Ramsey: Autobiography and Letters* (Nashville, 1954), 226–27.
    5. Joseph M. Henderson (1828–1877) was the son of Ramsey's cousin. Ibid., 3–4; Worth S. Ray, *The Mecklenburg Signers and Their Neighbors* (Austin, 1946), 395.
    6. On July 20, 1865, Governor Holden endorsed the Ramsey letter and referred it to Johnson, "who is much better acquainted with Dr. Ramsey than I am." A copy of Ramsey's amnesty oath, dated June 12, 1865, also accompanied Ramsey's letter and Holden's endorsement. It should be noted that on June 27, 1865, Ramsey also wrote a letter to Johnson which was apparently sent to Tennessee, for eventually it became a part of the Amnesty Papers of that state. This so-called Tennessee letter differs stylistically from the North Carolina one at various places. Johnson pardoned Ramsey on November 13, 1865. Amnesty Papers (M1003, Roll 50), Tenn., J.G.M. Ramsey, RG94, NA; Amnesty Record, Vol. 2, Ser. 8C, Johnson Papers, LC.

From Harvey M. Watterson

June 27, 1865, Raleigh, N.C.; ALS, DLC-JP. See *Advice*, 54.

Submits a brief message reiterating his support of Johnson's positions—"that the Southern states are in the Union, and have never been out . . . that the suffrage question belongs to the States alone"—and assures him that "All is politically right in North Carolina."

From Enoch W.S. Greene[1]

Washington June 28/65

His Excellency, Andrew Johnson
President of the United States
Dear Sir,

That I did Judge Kelley[2] no injustice, in stating to you last Thursday that he had no heart in the present policy of the administration but would array himself against it—*no matter what you might do at his desire*, his speech enclosed will show.[3] It was delivered that very night at Concert Hall, Philadelphia. He is against you, depend upon it; & time will show that such patronage as may be entrusted to his friends & fellows will, in due season, be directed to the overthrow of your policy with the people. Whatever may be your determination respecting me— I do not want you to be deceived by enemies in disguise "who crook the pregnant hinges of the Knee that thrift may follow fawning."[4]

With my best wishes, I am, as always,
Your Friend E. W. S. Greene
Sunday Transcript Philadelphia

ALS, DLC-JP.
1. Greene (c1828–1877), publisher of the *Philadelphia Sunday Transcript*, became the local pension agent under Johnson (1865). *New York Times*, Dec. 28, 1877; *Bangor Whig and Courier*, Oct. 23, 1865.
2. William D. Kelley, Pennsylvania congressman.
3. Although not found in the Johnson Papers, the speech delivered June 22, as it appeared in the *Philadelphia Press* the following day, was an attack upon racial prejudices and the exclusion of blacks from the political process. Kelley maintained that the President should demand equal rights before restoring state governments in the South.
4. *Hamlet*, Act 3, sc. 2, line 65.

From James S. McClelland

June 28, 1865, Crawfordsville, Ind.; ALS, DLC-JP.

An Indianian, who as a delegate to his party's state convention in 1864 reported the Lincoln-Johnson ticket for the nominating committee, reminds Johnson of this service. A War Democrat impressed with Johnson's views, "especialy in relation to the emancipation of the white men of the South, the dignity of labour and the final results of the great contest," he had insisted that loyal Democrats, having supported the Lincoln administration, were "entitled to the second place on the ticket. . . . 'We had a man for the place who had been tried as by fire, whose head, and heart were right, one that every loyal man should delight to honor,'" and he then placed "*Andrew Johnston* of Tenn, as our candidate for Vice president." This action, though evoking "strong, almost bitter opposition," caused McClelland to announce that, if Johnson's nomination failed in the majority report to the convention, "if I could not get your name before it in any other maner I would make a *minority report*." This announcement carried the day, the committee reporting the ticket as "Lincolin and Johnston." He closes with the prediction that Johnson will win the nomination in 1868.

From Sam Milligan

Greeneville Ten. June 28. 1865

To/His Excellency Andrew Johnson,
President of the United States:
Dear Sir:

Through the solicitation of my friends, I have to trouble you more than is agreeable; and the only apology I can offer is that if I did not trouble you some body else would. Your life, I know is nothing but trouble, and if I overburden it, you must just thow my letters aside.

The accompanying letter is from the Rev. John W Elliott.[1] He desires to be reinstated as Chaplain in the United State's Army, and if practicable, stationed in Lincoln Hospitle at Washington, or as Chaplain to the Hospitles at Knoxville. But if not convenient at one or the other of these points, anywhere else he can be useful.

I confess freely, I would be very glad you could provide for him. He needs the office, and will work in it. His wife is dead—and he has three children to support; and I am sure you never had a more devoted friend, or a greater admirer. As proof of this I will trouble you with an extract of a speech he delivered in Pennsylvania on the 1st of Feb. 1864.

After describing your great efforts to save E. Ten., from rebellion, and the scene at Rogersville, when you were about to be mobbed, he says:

Andrew Johnson arose. I was filled with admiration at the cunning hand, with which he began to play upon the Harp of a thousand strings—the adroitness with which he set to work to calm dow[n] the excited multitude. His tones were as soft as the tones of a girl. And his words were as sweet as the words of Plato, upon whose lips the Bees of Hemettus delighted to linger. It was like the Siren coming forth from her Ocean cave to charm the winds and the waves to sleep.

In this way he continued until he saw he had tamed the fierce Democracy—until he felt he had thrown the spell of his genius over the excited audience. Then he began to thunder! And his thunder peals shook the house. His speech was like an unchained Tornado. It prostrated every thing before it. And like some mighty Storm Spirit, he rode upon the whirlwind and directed the Storm, which he had conjured up. Such a piece of soul stirring Eloquence I never listened to. Evey element of the man's fearful and wonderful nature was aroused. And his arguments went like chained lightning through the ranks of the enemy. And his firy bursts of passion fell like Greek-fire upon the rottenness of the Southern Confederacy. No wonder Jefferson Davis and his compeers feared Andrew Johnson more than they feared an army with Banners.

You will excuse this extract as it is given both to show the man, and his strong attachments.

I believe he is a worthy man, and if you can aid him, you certainly will assist a worthy man, who will be true to the country, and greatful to you. I do not know that there are any vacancies, but when the President indicates his wish, vacancies readily appear.[2]

Your obt Sevt. Sam Milligan

ALS, DNA-RG94, ACP Branch, File E-395-CB-1865, John W. Elliott.
1. Elliott also wrote from Greeneville, chronicling his difficulties as a result of his exile in 1862 from his duties as pastor of the Greeneville Presbyterian Church. While serving as an army chaplain at Hilton Head, S.C., he became ill, was discharged, and was unsuccessful in his efforts for reinstatement. Elliott to Johnson, June 23, 1865, ACP Branch, File E-395-CB-1865, John W. Elliott, RG94, NA.
2. Readmitted to the service in June 1867, Elliott was appointed a hospital chaplain. *Official Army Register* (1867), 21.

From Richard J. Oglesby

State of Illinois Executive Department.
Springfield June 28th 1865

The President of the United States
Dear Sir

I desire to write you a letter in refference to State matters which specially affects us here. D L Phillips our present Marshal for the Southern District of Illinois who has held the office for four years has received six thousand dollars a year and besides this large salary is independent I may say rich.[1] It is true he is a good enough union man but he has been a citizen all through the war. I think in all fairness he aught to be willing without hesitation to yield to the wishes of all of those who feel a deep responsibility for the success of our cause In this State hereafter, and consent to the appointment of a new and worthy man. I did favor the appointment of Thomas Quick[2] who has given the Life of his son to our cause but when I Learned that Mr Lincoln prefered to appoint Colonel John Logan,[3] as good a man as we have in the State, who has been a faithful soldier through the war and a brave and gallant one I at once yielded my preference for Mr Quick and now wish to be understood as favoring and urgeing the appointment of Col Logan for Marshal of the southern District of Illinois and candidly state to you that such is my personal wish and will regard it as a private and public favor if you will appoint him at the expiration of the term of Mr Phillips in July. It will be difficult to get along in this state if we continue to elect or appoint all civilians and so few soldiers to responsible offices.[4]

Very respectfully Your obt servant
R J Oglesby Govenor

ALS, DNA-RG60, Appt. Files for Judicial Dists., Ill., John Logan.
1. Marshal Phillips, according to John Logan's supporters, had become rich from fees collected. Basler, *Works of Lincoln*, 3: 521n; Appt. Files for Judicial Dists., Ill., John Logan, RG60, NA.
2. Quick (b. c1824) was a farmer who became president of the board of trustees for Illinois Agricultural College at its founding in 1861. 1860 Census, Ill., Washington,

T1SR1W, Centralia P.O., 81; George W. Smith, "The Old Illinois Agricultural College," *Journal of the Illinois State Historical Society*, 5 (1913): 476, 478.

3. Logan (1809–*fl*1879), a physician who commanded the 32nd Ill. Inf., replaced Phillips in 1866 and served until 1870. *History of Macoupin County, Illinois* (Philadelphia, 1879), 95; Appt. Bk. 2: 180, Ser. 6B, Johnson Papers, LC.

4. Over the governor's objections, Phillips was reappointed July 12, 1865. Speed to Seward, July 12, 1865, Office of Atty. Gen., Lets. Sent, Vol. D (M699, Roll 10), RG60, NA; see also Letter from Richard Yates, May 20, 1865.

From Robert Purdy

June 28, 1865, Cumberland, Md.; ALS, DNA-RG153, Lets. Recd. by Col. H. L. Burnett (Apr.-Aug. 1865).

Former scout warns Johnson that two "desperadoes from the South west," Jim Blevans and Jake Sparrow, are reportedly in Washington, armed with "those heavy globe sighted whitworth rifles," with plans to assassinate the President and secretaries Stanton and Seward, "by shooting at long range." Once imprisoned as the result of "some indiscretions incident to my business," and still a fugitive, the writer asserts that his scouting and detective experiences have given him "first rate chances to get information."

From Milton L. Rice [1]

Lancaster Ky June 28 1865.

His Excellency Andrew Johnson.

Sir

Geo. A. Bowyer[2] of Lexington Ky has been a union man of the right stripe from the Commencement. He was in good circumstances when the war broke out. Was engaged in the Merchant Tailoring business—when Camp Dick Robinson[3] was established. The soldiers & officers were generally destitute of cloathing & had not the means of supplying themselves. Mr Bowyer furnished them upon credit. All the recommendation that he asked was that they were in the federal service. Every dollar he was worth was thus credited out, and while many paid him, perhaps all that Could, yet from death & other Causes large numbers were unable to pay & Bowyer lost heavily in the transaction. Besides Bowyer was at Cumberland Gap when Kirby Smiths forces were in Lexington and the rebels on account of Bowyers active loyalty took & destroyed almost every thing he had, in Consequence of all of which Bowyer has been greatly reduced in circumstances & has been nearly broken up. You will yourself probably remember the assistance Bowyer rendered as he furnished a large number of Tennesseeans in whose welfare you were taking a deep interest. Mr Bowyer is a Competent thorough business man, reliable & qualified and any position which you could confer upon him that would help him in his present time of need would be gratefully received by him & his friends generally and especially by the hundred whom he has assisted when they were in necessity. I hope you will find it Consistant with your duty to do a good part by him in this way of some appointment. I ask nothing for myself & shall ask for no friend unless he is worthy.[4]

Yours Truly M. L. Rice

ALS, DNA-RG56, Appts., Internal Revenue Service, Collector, Ky., 7th Dist., George A. Bowyer.

1. Rice (b. c1825) was a lawyer. 1860 Census, Ky., Garrard, Lancaster, 6.

2. Bowyer (b. c1815) made a formal application in August for the position of collector for the 7th District in Kentucky. Ibid., Fayette, Lexington, 4th Ward, 76; Bowyer to Johnson, Aug. 10, 1865, Appts., Internal Revenue Service, Collector, Ky., 7th Dist., George A. Bowyer, RG56, NA.

3. Located near Danville, Ky., Camp Dick Robinson was established in 1861 for recruiting unionists, including Tennessee refugees, to serve in military units.

4. He did not receive the appointment. The next year he reapplied, asserting that the incumbent, William Davis, was opposed to Johnson's policy, as were "almost all the Federal office holders in this State." Bowyer to Johnson, July 25, 1866, Appts., Internal Revenue Service, Collector, Ky., 7th Dist., George A. Bowyer, RG56, NA.

From Thomas A. Scott

June 28, 1865, Philadelphia, Pa.; LS, DLC-JP.

The vice president of the Pennsylvania Railroad Company, noting that Johnson "will likely be present at Gettysburg on the coming 4th. of July," suggests "that you take Philadelphia in your route" and offers "to provide special accommodations for yourself and party from Philada. to Gettysburg, and thence to Washington." If the suggestion is adopted, he wants "a quiet intimation to that effect" with "probable time & number of party leaving Philada." so that he can make the arrangements. [Secretary R. D. Mussey responded on the 30th that the President would have to take the shortest route, bypassing Philadelphia, if he went to the Gettysburg celebration. Ultimately, because of illness, Johnson was unable to attend.]

From C. L. Brown [1]

New York June 29th 1865

President A. Johnson
Dear Sir

There are a great many Southern men at present in this city and I have made it my business to learn from them their ideas about the state of affairs with them. They all seem perfectly submissive and say that even those who were most ultra during the war are so, also, but they complain of the treatment of Mr Davis their late president. This seems to be the great barrier to a complete restoration of good feeling. Some of them are also uneasy about confiscation not knowing what to expect in this respect and fearing the worst. I have deemed it my duty to call your attention to these facts believing that it is your desire to establish good feeling and permanent peace, as soon as possible.

With great respect Your obt. servant C. L. Brown

ALS, DLC-JP.
    1. Possibly Charles L. Brown, jeweler, who lived at 117 W. 16th St. *Trow's New York City Directory* (1865), 115.

From Robert P. Dick[1]

Raleigh N C June 29th 1865

His Excellency, Andrew Johnson.
President of the United States.
Sir.

Gov Holden has just informed me that the difficulty in relation to my qualifying as Judge of the U.S. District Court,[2]—has not, and in the opinion of the Cabinet, cannot be removed. I greatly desired the position, as it would be an endorsement by you of my fidelity to the Government of the United States. If the appointment in any way embarrasses you in the discharge of your official duties, let it be withdrawn as I am willing to make any sacrifice for the public good.

I deeply regret the difficulty as my removal from office will seriously injure me in public opinion, as it will be regarded as a disapproval of my past political career by your administration. My appointment is generally known through out the state and universally approved of by loyal men. I have been opposed to secession all my life. I took an active and prominent position against the rebellion. I have never for a moment either expected or desired the success of the Confederate Government. I held office under the state government, not for the purpose of aiding the rebellion, but to try and assist in extricating my state from the impending ruin of treason. I have always loved the Union, and ever desired to see it restored, and I have constantly labored (indirectly) to that end. I could not throw myself in *direct* opposition to the overwhelming torrent of rebellion without loosing my life. For four years I have endured proscription and persecution, in church, society, and status, and I have ever fought as good a fight against treason as it was possible for any one to do *and live*. If I cannot hold office in North Carolina no one else can, who remained at home in the midst of the storm. Those who left may have shown *loyalty*, but they exhibited little true courage. If I cannot hold office, then every federal appointment must be made from the Northern States. Nine tenths of our people are earnestly desirous of returning to the Union with their whole soul,— but foreign tax gatherers and northern judicial officers will necessarily greatly try their patience and retard the restoration of genuine fraternal feeling.

There is no northern man—who has not entered the army—who has endured more for the Union than I have—or who has *loved* it with a deeper and fonder affection.

My *loyal people* know this and they were rejoiced when they heard that I had received the endorsement and approval of the President of the United States.

There are many difficulties yet ahead. I have given up a hundred slaves—*my whole estate*—cheerfully and cordially because the peace and quietude of the country demanded it. I have entered the field for immediate and complete emancipation. I shall sustain with my whole strength your policy for I am satisfied that it is the wisest and best course that can be adopted. I want to elevate the negro as rapidly as possible by education and christian influences, and I want to see him kindly and generously treated. I fully approve of your position on the question of negro suffrage.

As Judge of this District I would exert a wholesome influence upon our people, which cannot be done by a foreigner.

I do sincerely trust that some way can be devised by which guenuine North Carolina men can hold the federal offices in this state. Secession and rebellion have destroyed nearly all of the property of a people who, at heart, have ever been loyal to the union of their fathers,—and I do hope that a great and magnanimous government will not *long make* them feel the humiliation of subjugation in seeing foreign *tax gatherers* "sitting at the receipt of customs"—and strange judges administering *law* and *equity*.

But let this matter end as it may,[3] be assured that I am the firm and steadfast friend of your administration, as I honestly believe that you will do all you can for our *loved* and common country.

Your kindness to me while in Washington will ever be remembered as one of the most pleasant recollections of my life. With the best wishes for you and yours—I am with high regard your true friend & servant.

Robt. P. Dick

ALS, DLC-JP.

1. Dick (1823–1898), native North Carolina lawyer, had been a member of the secession convention and a peace candidate state senator (1864–65). A member of the state convention of 1865–66, he later aligned himself with the Radicals and aided the organization of the local Republican party. *DAB*.

2. On Governor Holden's advice Dick was appointed federal district judge by Johnson but had to resign because he felt unable to take the test oath, a requirement for the judgeship. Ibid.; *Cyclopedia of the Carolinas*, 2: 635.

3. George S. Brooks was appointed judge on August 21. Appt. Bk. 1: 20, Ser. 6B, Johnson Papers, LC.

From Thomas Ewing, Sr.

Washington No 12 N A St
June 29/65

To the President
Sir

I suggested in a letter[1] to you some time ago the free pardon of A H Stevens & Judge Campbell. The merits of Stevens are quite as well

known to you as to myself—his demerits better—of him I have nothing
more to say.

As to Judge Campbell the country owes him much, though perhaps
he may have more than cancelled the debt. I had frequent conferences
with him in the winter of 60/61 and he gave me much information of
the points of danger in the then unguarded condition of the City. He
expressed a strong belief that the public offices were about to be captured by a combined movement of the Clerks within and the Knights
of the Golden circle,[2] who held chapter on 4 1/2 Street, without. I
called & communicated the information to Genl. Scott[3] who told me
had no military force with which to defend the City but its own militia
& thirty five Marines—that he had applied to Floyd[4] Secy of War for
authority to order a sufficient force to the City but he denied him. On
consultation he determined to call personally on the President & demand the means of defence or a discharge from his duty—this he did
promptly and a thousand men were brought in the next day from Ft
Washington. That the City was not captured at that time I think we
owe to Campbell as fully & absolutely as we owe to Stanton that it was
not surrendered to the rebels by the President & cabinet a few weeks
later.

I am very truly Yours T. Ewing

ALS, DNA-RG94, Amnesty Papers (M1003, Roll 23), Ga., Alexander Stephens.
    1. Ewing to Johnson, May 29, 1865, Johnson Papers, LC. In addition to suggesting
pardons for Alexander H. Stephens and John A. Campbell, Ewing had urged "an additional guard over Davis & take off his manacles."
    2. A secret organization, originating in the South and spreading north and midwest
during the war as a pro-southern, anti-war movement, eventually identified with the
Copperhead movement and the Peace Democrats. *Johnson Papers*, 5: 10n.
    3. Winfield Scott.
    4. John B. Floyd.

From John W. Ford[1]

Jacksonville Al June 29, 1865

His Excellency Andrew Johnson:
Hon Sir:

Having filled one sheet[2] with matters purely personal to myself I hear
that it would not be uninteresting to you to learn something in reference to the present status of things in this state.

Since the surrender of the Rebel Armies East of the Mississippi,
things have been greatly settling down. There has not been a single
outbreak so far as I have heard. The Negro question was a subject of
considerable discussion for a few weeks; Slave holders seemed to be at
considerable loss to know what would be the final issue of that question. In the meantime, their Negroes were constantly runing away, and
going to the Military posts at Taladega, Montgomery and Selma, and

those that remained at home became so perfectly worthless, that their former masters chased them off their plantations, and they were compelled to go to the Military posts to get something to eat. In other cases, the Negroes were hired by their former Masters, the Negroes agreeing to take a certain portion of the Crops. Slave owners are finally coming to the Conclusion that the abolition of Slavery is a fixed fact, and they seem disposed to submit to that Conclusion, with the best grace they can. After you were first installed into office, there was a great disposition manifested to abuse you, but I told those with whom I was in the habit of conversing, that they had better wait until your Administration policy developed itself—that I was convinced from personal knowledge of you that you would be as lenient to the South, in all things, as you could possibly be, consistent with your duties to the whole Country. That you found a certain set of things existing when you came into power, and that you would be compelled to deal with them, for the present, as you found them. I have told them that no man or set of men could control you—that you would emphatically be *the* President— that you had as much of the nerve of Andrew Jackson in your Composition, as any man I ever knew, and your course, as far as it has unfolded itself is making you scores of friends.

The appointment of Parsons[3] as "Provisional Governor," if it has not been made, would give great satisfaction to all parties. I write what I know. There is no other man that would prove as acceptable. I have felt it to be my duty to say this much to you.

I am most Respectfully John W. Ford

ALS, DLC-JP.
    1. Ford was a former McMinnville and Chattanooga newspaper editor. *Chattanooga Times*, Nov. 19, 1882.
    2. Not found.
    3. Lewis E. Parsons (1818–1895), a New York-born lawyer, an Alabamian since 1841, and a unionist who had considerable political experience—including service in the legislature—when Johnson appointed him on June 21. Supporting presidential reconstruction, he was elected to the Senate in 1865, but was denied a seat. *DAB*; Sarah Van V. Woolfolk, "Five Men Called Scalawags," *AR*, 17 (1964): 47.

From Edward W. Gantt[1]

Little Rock Ark June 29th 65

His Excy A. Johnson
Dr. Sir.

I have been here for some days & have carefully noted public sentiment. The work of organization progresses well. In ninety days, the most radical will not have the nerve to say that *Arkansas is not a state*. I shall quietly but energetically endeavor to see that we get good sound men for congress—those who will strengthen the hands of the administration in the great work before it.

No office holder, and determined never to be, I can only hope to get all the strength you can give me as a private citizen, and promise you that much or little it shall be used for the welfare of the Country.

I beg leave to say here as I said in another letter,[2] that I think Mr Garland[3] ought to be pardoned at the earliest possible moment, & hope you may find it consistent so to do. At the same time that I recommend this, I am inclined to think that as a general rule, there should be but as few pardons as possible before the character of each has been sifted. Many bad men might thus be thrown upon us & control the elections in the fall.

I think also that no *general officer* from the state should be pardoned *for the present*.

I shall start on a trip through the Southern portion of the state in a few days & will write you definitely about the situation of affairs.[4]

Very respectfully Your obt St E. W. Gantt

ALS, DLC-JP.
    1. Gantt (d. 1874) was a Little Rock attorney. *Athens Post* (Tenn.), June 19, 1874.
    2. Probably Gantt's letter to William H. Seward, June 29, 1865, in which he urged Garland's pardon "at once," noting his Union stance at the secession convention, his defense of Lincoln's first message as a "Constitutional document," and his conservative sentiment, even as a Confederate officeholder, which held "an ultimate return to the Union" as a possibility. Amnesty Papers (M1003, Roll 13), Ark., A. H. Garland, RG94, NA.
    3. Augustus H. Garland (1832–1899), lawyer, Confederate representative, and senator, who at the close of the war returned to Arkansas and attempted to negotiate easy peace terms with Federal authorities. *DAB.*
    4. See Letter from Gantt, July 4, 1865. Garland was pardoned July 15, 1865. *House Ex. Docs.*, 39 Cong., 2 Sess., No. 31, p. 23 (Ser. 1289).

From William W. Holden

State of North Carolina, Executive Department,
Raleigh, N.C., June 29th, 1865.

To His Excellency The President.
Sir:

You will find herewith a letter from Judge Dick in relation to the oath he is required to take to qualify him for his office. Allow me to invite your careful attention to his letter. Mr. Mason,[1] the District Attorney, is in a similar situation. If it be at all possible I would be greatly gratified to see it so arranged that these gentlemen could fill these places. The oath required is, it is true, the law of the land, but it seems to have been framed for a state of war, and not of peace. This State is now at *peace* with the federal Union and with all the world. If such men are to be deprived of the right to hold office, it will be difficult to fill the federal offices in this State with any but strangers.

I need not add more. Judge Dick and Mr Mason are warmly attached to the administration and to you personally, and they are anxious to occupy positions in which they can most effectually serve the administration and the country.[2]

Very Respectfully, W. W. Holden.

ALS, DLC-JP.
1. William S. Mason (c1829–fl1880), a Raleigh attorney, had been a unionist, holding only a minor commissioner's office during the war, and in May 1865 was among those who accompanied Holden to Washington to advise with the President. A few weeks later Holden suggested Mason for the North Carolina district attorney position. Amnesty Papers (M1003, Roll 41), N.C., William S. Mason, RG94, NA; Elizabeth McPherson, "Letters from North Carolina to Andrew Johnson," *NCHR*, 27 (1950): 343, 344; John W. Moore, *History of North Carolina* (2 vols., Raleigh, 1880), 2: 318.
2. Darius H. Starbuck was appointed district attorney on August 21, 1865. Appt. Bk. 1: 300, Ser. 6B, Johnson Papers, LC.

From Joseph Holt

June 29, 1865, Washington, D.C.; *OR*, Ser. 2, Vol. 8: 684–89.

Judge advocate general offers opinion upon the proceedings of the military trial of the Chicago conspirators, reviews the testimony, and recommends carrying out the sentences of Charles Walsh (5 years), Buckner S. Morris and Vincent Marmaduke (acquittal), and Richard T. Semmes (3 years). For the two defendants convicted and condemned to death (Charles T. Daniel and G. St. Leger Grenfell), Holt, in upholding the tribunal, avers, "there can be no doubt that [Daniel] was one of a large number of rebel fugitives sent from Canada to aid in the hideous projects of the conspirators" and that Grenfell was correctly convicted on charges of conspiracy "after a most patient and doubtless absolutely impartial investigation." Concludes that if in the "altered position of public affairs . . . the President will feel justified in sparing even so unworthy and dishonored a life" as that of Grenfell and commutes his sentence, "it is believed that the punishment substituted should be severe and infamous." [On July 22 the President commuted the sentence for Grenfell to life in prison at hard labor and he was sent to Dry Tortugas.]

From Charles D. McLean[1]

Memphis, Tennessee, June 29th 1865

To Hon Andrew Johnson,
President of the United States
Dear Sir,

I met many of your old personal and political friends within a few days—Wm C. Dunlap, Phillip B. Glenn, W. T. Avery, Judge King, Pitser Miller, Fraser Titus[2] and many others.

One object we had in view was to select candidates for Congress, the Legislature, &c and on next Monday we hope to meet at our county Court House, in Raleigh, and arrange the right sort of men.

You, no doubt, recollect, that it was at Raleigh that you were nominated for President, by our County Convention in 1860, which course was *unanimously*, adopted at Nashville, afterwards.

Many of those who composed those Conventions have passed from the stage of action, but those of us who are left, so far as I know, or believe, are your personal and political friends, and will give your administration our cordial support.

In regard to the "negro sufferage" question, as defined by you, we are all well satisfied.

My own family negroes were worth $100,000 in 1860, which has been a heavy loss to a man of my age, (70 years); but as the thing has been done, I submit. I would have much preferred "*gradual emancipation*," as I have about 15 children on my farm, under ten years, and some very aged, which classes, must suffer under the present system, as the men who are able to work are demoralized, and will not take care of their aged fellow servants, nor have they thrift enough to support and raise their young children; and so far as Tennessee is concerned, the regulations of the "Freedman's Bureau" are a perfect failure.[3] The Northern People do not understand managing "Sambo."

I feel deep solicitude for my former slaves; 50 of whom are yet with me, but at my time of life, I feel at a loss to do them justice, for they have but little self reliance and no management, unless directed by some person of experience, and having a correct knowledge of their *character*.

Pardon my intrusion on your time, and believe me, as ever,

Your friend Charles D. McLean

ALS, DLC-JP.

1. McLean (1795–1881) had been a newspaper publisher in Clarksville, Nashville, and Jackson, Tenn., before moving to a plantation near Memphis. *BDTA*, 2: 1043–44.

2. Dunlap (1798–1872), a lawyer, had served as Democratic congressman, circuit court judge, and state legislator; Glenn (b. c1813) had been a state representative; William T. Avery was a Shelby County lawyer; E.W.M. King was a Memphis judge; Miller was a Bolivar, Tenn., merchant; and Frazer Titus (1800–1870) was a wealthy Memphis cotton factor and merchant. Ibid., 1: 219, 289; Amnesty Papers (M1003, Roll 51), Tenn., Frazer Titus, RG94, NA; 1870 Census, Tenn., Shelby, Memphis, 1st Ward, 118; Memphis directories (1866–70); *Memphis Appeal*, July 1, 1870; *Elmwood . . . History of the Cemetery* (Memphis, 1874), 159.

3. Because the Bureau office was not officially set up in Tennessee until July, McLean might refer here to the regulations and operations of the Freedmen's Department of the Army of the Cumberland, which had been involved in overseeing mandatory contract labor arrangements for blacks, if they were not working independently. *House Ex. Docs.*, 39 Cong., 1 Sess., No. 70, p. 48 (Ser. 1256); Cimprich, *Slavery's End*, 66–70, 120, 125, 143–46.

From Gideon J. Pillow

June 29, 1865, Nashville, Tenn.; LS, DNA-RG94, Amnesty Papers (M1003, Roll 50), Tenn., Gideon J. Pillow.

In a follow-up to his original pardon application, sent before the attorney general's requirements were issued, former Confederate general forwards his oath and explains his intention "to be understood, as accepting the *whole duty* of a loyal citizen," pledging "to perform those duties, *in honor* and *good faith*" and to use his influence "in favor of the restoration of the authority of the Government." [Falling under the 3rd and 13th exceptions of the May 29 Amnesty Proclamation, Pillow was pardoned August 28, 1865.]

From Taliaferro P. Shaffner

June 29, 1865, Washington, D.C.; ALS, DLC-JP.

Learning from Dr. Albert G. Mackey, recently appointed collector of Charleston, that a "self styled, and self appointed" delegation of "anti-Union and pro-slavery" South Carolinians is now in Washington to recommend the appointment of a provisional governor, Shaffner, an inventor and author, urges the President to withhold the appointment until "the Union men of South Carolina" can "be heard from upon the subject." Adds: "I am of opinion that the time has not arrived when a Provisional Governor can with propriety be given that state."

From South Carolina Black Citizens [1]

[June 29, 1865] [2]

To his Excellency Andrew Johnson
President of the United States of America

The petition of the subscribers being colourd Citizens of the State of South Carolina, most respectfully asketh of you—that in the organization of a State Goverment for South Carolina that they be granted the Inestimable and protective rights of the Elective franchise; which privalage we regard as the only means by which our class of the population of the State, will have the power of protecting ourselves and our interest, against oppression and unjust legislation.

Your humble petitioners would here promise Sir, that no Statesman knows better than you do, that the power to tax, and legislate generally by one class only of a commonwealth, distroys the safeguard of the disenfranchised, and undermines the piller of Civil liberty upon which rests their prosperity happiness and improvement, and impairs the quietude and Strength of the Goverment. Born and Raised in this country, we claim it as our native land, and regard the United States Goverment, as our common parent, intitled to our fealty love and affection, and we glory in the name of American Citizens. Our Loyalty and warm affection for the Goverment, needs no special proof at our hands, for it has been tested before the Eyes of the World on many a hard fought battle field for the Restoration of the Union, and integrity of the Goverment.

Your humble petitioners further makes the Solicitation for the grant of the Elective franchise to them, upon the ground of the important fact of their very large numerical Majority in the State. Without pretending to precission, but based upon the Estimated population of the United

States, according to the Eigth Census, the approximate population of the State of South Carolina in 1860 Stood thus[3]

Free population	308,186
Deduct for the estimate number of Free Colored	10,456
Leaves the number of White population	297,730
Bondmen	407,185
add Free Colored	10,456
Total Colored population	417,641
Deduct white population	297,730
Leaves a Majority, Colored	119,911

Exclusive of the increase since 1860.

And your humble petitioners would most Respectfully aver, that with so large a Majority in their favor, to be deprived of the Elective franchise and political Right given exclusively to the Minority, would place them in a anomelous position as citizens, and all together at the mercy of that class of the commonwealth; and a Goverment thus formed your humble petitioners are of the opinion would not be the true Representative and organ of the whole people.

For the foregoing and other cogent reasons, your humble petitioners anxiously desire to be put, by your excellency politically, in a position that would inable them to protect their Rights and interest against the probable Encroachments of a power that would have no nutralizing influences should they (Your humble petitioners[)] be denied the right of suffrage.

And your humble petitioners do further pray that in the appointment of a provisional Governer for this State. You will be pleased to make the selection from the following very competent Gentlemen

> Gen John C. Freemont of South Carolina
> Wm. H. Brisbane[4] of South Carolina
> Brevt Major Gen Saxon[5]
> Gen B F. Buttler of Massachusetts

And your petitioners as in duty bound will ever pay &c

Pet, DLC-JP.

1. This petition had 1,456 names. In a covering letter dated June 29, Ednah D. Cheney, secretary of the executive committee of the New England Freedmen's Aid Society at Boston, wrote that the superintendent of schools, James Redpath, brought the petition, which "is Entirely the work of the colored people themselves and we respectfully ask your Earnest attention."

2. Cheney's date was used, although the petition was obviously prepared earlier.

3. South Carolina did have a black majority, but, according to the 1860 Census, these figures are slightly inaccurate. Joseph C. G. Kennedy, comp., *Population of the United States in 1860 . . . the Eighth Census* (Washington, D.C., 1864), 452.

4. Brisbane (c1803–1878), native South Carolina Baptist minister and planter who became an abolitionist in the 1830s and freed his slaves, settled in Cincinnati and published a number of antislavery pamphlets. Moving to Wisconsin, where he was chief clerk

of the state senate and pastor of a Madison church, he returned briefly to South Carolina in 1862 as a direct tax commissioner. *Appleton's Cyclopaedia.*

5. Rufus Saxton, assistant commissioner for the Freedmen's Bureau in South Carolina and Georgia.

From Alexander H. Stephens

June 29, 1865, Fort Warren, Mass.; ALS, DLC-JP.

After seven weeks in custody, having doubts about the reception of his June 8 application for pardon, but not wishing to be "obtrusive or forward," Stephens writes to withdraw his application, feeling Johnson's long silence reflects on the inappropriateness of his case under the proclamation. Not wishing to appear as a "supplicant for mercy" and having no sense of being a criminal nor of guilt for the "most lamentable war between the States," he comes "not as a suitor for a probable voluntarily tendered favor but as a claimant for my clear legal rights." Citing Johnson's use of the Magna Carta "as the source from which you imbibed some of your political principles," he asserts that his imprisonment is a denial of the rights so embraced and wants the government to bring what charges it has against him or allow him parole until such charges can be readied; the "appearance and answer of the accused will be punctual—*Deo volenta.*"

From Harvey M. Watterson

June 29, 1865, Raleigh, N.C.; ALS, DLC-JP. See *Advice*, 54–56.

Pleased to discover "the extent to which the Southern people were subjugated," Watterson declares that "None can be found so insane as to think of further resistance to the authority of the United States." He feels "a lively sympathy" for North Carolinians who, like Tennesseans, were "literally dragged into the Rebellion." Praising the performance of provisional governor Holden, "a calm, clear-headed, systematic, laborious gentleman," he advises the reestablishment of mail facilities, the restoration of property, and the suspension of the collection of the federal direct tax as measures conducive to the success of Johnson's policy. "You can scarcely have an idea of the present poverty of these people."

From LeRoy M. Wiley

[ca. June 29, 1865, New York, N.Y.]; LS, DNA-RG94, Amnesty Papers (M1003, Roll 24), Ga., L. M. Wiley.

Longtime New York City merchant and owner of cotton plantations in Alabama and Georgia, who in 1861 "proceeded South for the purpose of protecting and preserving both his own property and that which he held as assignee" for several northern firms with overextended credit in the South, applies for amnesty, pleading his age and losses in slaves and other property, worth over $450,000, including "forced contributions" to the Confederacy. [With the recommendation of New York Senator E. D. Morgan and a number of prominent New York merchants, he was pardoned under the 13th exception on July 20, when the President directed the attorney general to issue a pardon "immediately."]

From Lizinka C. Ewell

Baltimore 30th June 1865

His Excellency—the President
Sir—

In obedience to the commands of your Excellency I beg leave to submit the following statement. On the 24th March the following Telegram was received by Genl. Dodge[1] at his Hdqts in St. Louis.

Washington 23rd March 1865
Genl. Dodge—Allow Mrs. Ewell the benefit of my amnesty proclamation on her taking the oath. (Signed) A Lincoln—

In accordance with this special amnesty on or about the 20th April the U.S. District Court for the state of Tennessee decreed to me possession of all my property in that state—but on the 22nd of the same month I was arrested by order of the Secy. of War & sent under military surveillance to St. Louis & kept there under arrest until the 22nd of June & the District Court of St. Louis has thus far failed to render a decree in accordance with the expressed wishes of the late lamented President & the authorities in Tennessee to give me possession of my property there. Now as your Excellency has distinctly assured me[2] that there is no charge whatever of disloyalty against me since the date of Mr. Lincoln's amnesty I hereby appeal to your Excellency to give me such further pardon & protection as may be necessary to render valid & carry into execution the amnesty of the late lamented President Lincoln— intended by him to give me possession of my property & to protect me as every other loyal citizen is protected from military arrest.[3]

Very Respectfully L. C. Ewell

ALS, DNA-RG94, Amnesty Papers (M1003, Roll 30), Md., Mrs. L. C. Ewell.
   1. Grenville M. Dodge.
   2. Although no documentation has been found, Mrs. Ewell apparently had not only direct access to the President but also the active intercession of the Blairs. It is possible that assurances came through them. To an unknown correspondent on May 10, Montgomery Blair wrote: "Now I think Andrew Johnson really likes Mrs. Ewell but he resents the want of national feeling he thinks he finds in her letters." George Washington Campbell Papers, LC.
   3. On July 17 Johnson directed that, having met the provision of the Amnesty Proclamation, Mrs. Ewell be allowed to return to Nashville, "free from arrest or other detention," and take possession of her property. Office of Atty. Gen., Lets. Recd., President, RG60, NA.

From Joseph S. Fowler and Others [1]

State of Tennessee, Comptroller's Office,
Nashville, Tenn., June 30th 1865.

Andrew Johnson President United States
Respected Sir,

Gen. Fisk,[2] who has charge of the freedmen and refugees of Tennessee, needs the services of a man competent for the services. Few men have the qualifications needed. Mr. Farwell[3] we think has them.

We have known him for about two years and know that he is admirably calculated for the duties. He has rendered us most valuable assistance in the case of refugees and is intimately acquainted with their wants and habits and devotes himself most kindly and in the spirit of true Christian Charity to the work. As Gen. Fisk can use only military men we would request of your Excellency to commission Mr. R. E. Farwell as a Major in some of the colored regiments and have him detailed for the service.[4]

Very respectfully Jos. S. Fowler

ALS, DNA-RG107, Lets. Recd., EB12 President 1963 (1865).

1. Other signers were: James Cameron; E. Root, agent, U.S. Sanitary Commission; R. H. Allen, pastor Second Presbyterian Church of Nashville; E. S. [Mrs. James] Cameron and Mrs. M. E. Allen, president and secretary, Nashville Ladies Union Aid Association; T. M. Goodfellow, late hospital chaplain; and T. R. Devine and Mrs. E. P. Smith, agents U.S.C.C., Department of the Cumberland.

2. Clinton B. Fisk (1828–1890), a former St. Louis businessman, held the post of assistant commissioner of the Freedmen's Bureau in Tennessee and Kentucky. In that capacity, he sponsored the establishment of the "Fisk Free Colored School," now Fisk University. Joe M. Richardson, *A History of Fisk University, 1865–1946* (University, Ala., 1980), 3–4; Warner, *Blue.*

3. R. E. Farwell, an agent of the American Union Commission, had been involved with transporting southern white refugees to the North. *Louisville Journal*, Dec. 9, 1864; *Knoxville Whig and Rebel Ventilator*, Apr. 5, 1865.

4. This letter was referred "by order of the President" to the War Department on July 10. Two weeks later, on the 26th, the adjutant general's office refused the request, noting that "all vacancies in the colored troops above the grade of 2d Lieutenant [are to] be filled by promotion in the respective regiments. . . . It would be a manifest injustice to appoint a person, not in service, to a field position in an old organization over the heads of the officers already in such organization." C. W. Foster endorsement of July 26 on William A. Browning to Adjutant General, July 26, 1865, Lets. Recd., EB12 President 1963 (1865), RG107, NA.

From Francis H. Peirpoint

The Commonwealth of Virginia,
Executive Department,
Richmond, 30th June 1865.

To His Excellency Andrew Johnson
President of the U.S.
Sir:

The twenty-thousand dollar clause in your Proclamation of the 29th May 1865, has had the most paralizzing effect, upon business and trade of every character, throughout the state of Virginia, as I have learned from gentlemen from every section.[1] No person seems to be willing to invest or give credit upon real estate, whatever may have been the sentiments of the party owning it during the rebellion; nor does it effect only the state of those worth twenty thousand dollars. Strangers cannot investigate the taxable wealth of a party even if they had opportunity to do so.

I have considered much upon this subject, and am satisfied that all the ends of justice and sound policy, will be conserved by modifying that clause of your late Proclamation, and extending general amnesty to all persons in Virginia who have not held office under the Confederate government. The officers of that government all came under the exceptions in your Proclamation, and their cases can remain for future consideration.

I am yours &c F. H. Peirpoint

LS, DNA-RG94, Amnesty Papers (M1003, Roll 71), Va., Misc.
   1. The governor's request was principally spurred by a June 28 memorial to the President from Richmond businessmen owning land in the the "burnt district." Stating that their titles were now "insecure" under the attorney general's opinion nullifying all previous oaths of allegiance and by Johnson's proclamation containing the exception of general amnesty to those worth over $20,000, they discovered that "credit founded on the title necessarily went down." Without credit to rebuild, business would stagnate. Amnesty Papers (M1003, Roll 71), Va., Misc., RG94, NA.

From John J. Seibels [1]
Private

Montgomery June 31[30], 1865

My Dear Sir

Believing that you would like to be kept informed as to the sentiments of the people of Alabama, as well as other Southern States, regarding the course & policy of your administration, as developed by your acts so far, I venture to write you this letter.

I must say to you frankly, that our people were at first greatly apprehensive that a severe, retaliatory & proscriptive, if not a revengeful and vindictive policy might characterise the acts of your administration; but with equal frankness I say to you that, those apprehensions are rapidly giving way to a most hopeful and cheerful confidence that justice, sound sense, and a wise statesmanship will be characteristic of all you do.

Your reception & treatment of the informal delegation recently sent to you from this State,[2] was at once so kind, cordial, and frank that they were all made your friends, & have done and are still doing much to bring our people to the same mind.

Your *amnesty proclamation* of the 29th May ult., & your proclamation reorganising North Carolina (which I presume is a specimen of your policy regarding the other Southern States) are all that could be desired. Generosity, magnanimity & wisdom are their distinguishing characteristics, and in carrying out their policy, I feel perfectly safe in assuring you of the most cordial & zealous support on the part of the people of this State; and the indications are very decided that a similar feeling and determination exists throughout the South generally.

We are anxiously awaiting your action to allow us to begin in earnest the work of restoration in Ala. But little interest is felt among *Loyal men* regarding the *person* whom you may select to be the provisional governor, and any one of those prominently mentioned thro' the papers— Parsons, Humphreys or Smith[3]—all good & true men—would be entirely satisfactory to the loyal people of the State. (Geo. S. Houston, Pryor, or Wm. O. Winston[4] all reliable Union men, would also be satisfactory).

Upon this point allow me to add my *entreaties* that you give *my name* no further consideration in that connection.[5] This appointment, under all the circumstances, might give the enemies of your administration an opportunity—& at least a plausible excuse for assailing *you*; and *I*, nor any other man must not be allowed to stand in the way, or to impair or weaken the wise & generous policy which I feel sure will govern you in a restoration not of the Union politically, only, but morally & socially.

In conclusion allow me to say, that I sympathise deeply in your success, in connection with your anticedents. I myself was once a poor, a very poor boy, and for *many years* in my early youth *followed the plough*; and the good fortune that has blessed me since, has not deprived me of a pleasure & pride in recurring to those days of manual labor, which assisted fond & doting parents to give me that education which has been the chief means of giving me what little prominence I have among my fellow men; and the success of one simelarly situated always imparts to me unwonted satisfaction.

I pray that Heaven may smile upon and bless your efforts to heal the wounds; & restore the prosperity & happiness of your country, so wantonly and unnecessarily interrupted by Southern demagogues, malcontents, and traitors in their late attempt at Secession.

I am with the most perfect respect your friend, & very obedient servt.

John J. Seibels

To/ His Excellency Andrew Johnson
Washington D.C.

ALS, DLC-JP.
1. Alabama prewar cooperationist.
2. See Reception of Alabama Delegation, June 5, 1865.
3. Lewis E. Parsons, David C. Humphreys, and William H. Smith. The latter (1826–1899), a Randolph County lawyer and farmer, who had opposed secession and two years later escaped through Union lines, served briefly upon his return as a circuit court judge, was an organizer of the Republican party in the state, and was elected governor on that ticket (1868–70). Wiggins, *Scalawag in Ala.*, 38; Marks, *Alabama*, 166.
4. Athens lawyer Houston; his partner, Luke Pryor (1820–1900), state legislator, later U.S. senator (1880), and congressman (1883–85); and Winston (1807–1871), also a lawyer, legislator, and state senator (1865). Ibid., 195; *BDAC*.
5. See Letter from Lewis E. Parsons and Joseph C. Bradley, June 10, 1865.

From Charles Sumner

Boston 30th June '65

My dear Sir,

I have received the enclosed petition[1] from three hundred colored citizens of Georgia with the request that I would present it to you.

The petitioners humbly ask that they may be allowed to exercise the right of suffrage. Profoundly convinced, as I am, that they have a right to the suffrage—that the peace & tranquility of the country require that *they should not be shut out from it*, I present their petition & most sincerely unite in its prayer.

Faithfully Yours, Charles Sumner

ALS, DLC-JP.
1. The printed petition read: "We, the undersigned, COLORED CITIZENS OF THE STATE OF GEORGIA, respectfully represent, that we are Loyal, always have been Loyal, and always will remain Loyal; and, in order to make our loyalty most effective in the service of the Government, we humbly petition to be allowed to EXERCISE THE RIGHT OF SUFFRAGE." Johnson Papers, LC.

From Washington C. Whitthorne[1]
Private

Columbia Tennessee. June 30th 1865.

To/ Honl. Andrew Johnson,
Prest U.S. Washington City D.C
Dr Sir:

A delay of Messenger's prevented me from receiving earlier the evidences of your kindness to Mrs. Whitthorne and myself.[2] I have just returned and the kind greetings of friends and the welcome home, (the sense of which deeply impresses me with feelings of gratitude to your-self) give me a new interest in life. I avail myself of the first opportunity and this means of returning thanks to you, which I will take pleasure in tendering to you personally as soon as I can raise means to visit the capitol. I know that you appreciate what I feel and what I would say. Allow me to say that if I can in a private and unofficial way, aid, in the work, in which, your head and heart is engaged—the restoration of peace and harmony to the Union—I am ready to obey your command & wishes. I feel that I owe you much, and every impulse of my heart is to meet that obligation.

Our mutual friend Dunnington,[3] is in Alabama, and has been so se-riously sick, that he could not travel. He is expected, as soon as Rail roads are opened.

Your policy as far as indicated meets with the approval of the masses of the people—though I have only been in the State of Mississippi where the appointment of Judge Sharkey is universally popular. If, in all other appointments your administration is as fortunate as in this, you will be assured of success.

Allow me so far to trespass on your time, as to ask what further or other step is necessary upon my part to secure pardon. Of course, I am ready to comply with the terms laid down by yourself in your procla-mation of the 29th ult.

Assuring you of my wishes to do all that I can in restoring peace harmony and prosperity to the people of Tennessee,—of my willing-ness to do whatever I can to convince you of my grateful feelings to yourself,[4]

I am respectfully Yr obt Servt.
W. C. Whitthorne.

ALS, DLC-JP.

1. Columbia lawyer, who had been Tennessee's Confederate adjutant general.

2. Whitthorne's amnesty application indicates that "by the kindness of the Executive, under Executive order No. 14, he was allowed to return to his home." Other "evidences" of Johnson's concern, either for Whitthorne or his wife, Jane, have not been found. Whit-thorne to Johnson, undated, Amnesty Papers (M1003, Roll 51), Tenn., W. C. Whit-thorne, RG94, NA.

3. Frank C. Dunnington, another Columbia lawyer.

4. Having taken the oath in early July and having received the support of A. M. Hughes, Whitthorne presumably went to Washington to present his application to the President. Johnson endorsed and signed Whitthorne's undated amnesty application letter on July 22 and referred it to the attorney general's office. There a secretary noted on the file that Whitthorne was "Personally known to the Prest." Whitthorne received his pardon on July 25, 1865. Whitthorne to Johnson, undated, and A. M. Hughes to John-son, July 13, 1865, Amnesty Papers (M1003, Roll 51), Tenn., W. C. Whitthorne, RG94, NA.

From Edward Winslow[1]

Boston June 30/65

Sir

It is with great regret that we have heard of your illness[2] & while wishing your speedy recovery we beseech you to be most careful of your health & a life so valuable to our country. The progress of reconstruction will not perhaps be retarded seriously, if less labor is applied to it & more care is given to health—indeed the delay may be better, as was the custom with our late beloved President to wait the unfolding of events & the leadings of Providence—one of these leadings seems to be the great increase of immigration & of a class superior to any former years. This country seems provided by Providence for the surplus population of Europe, & it would seem to be a good, if not the best element for reconstruction, but time is required for its introduction into the Southern States & it must have *full protection* there, as must also the loyal population. The poor whites, & ignorant portion is disloyal, but not so malignant & bitter as that of the Southern aristocracy, but sufficiently so to make a residence at the South very uncomfortable if not imposible & this can be done in various ways without direct and positive infringement of law. Already Loyal persons who have returned to their possessions have been obliged to leave them & resort to the cities. The poor whites are cruel to the negro & easily excited against the emigrant who has no prejudice against him & will cheerfully labor together, but the prosperity arising from this cooperation will only excite the envy & hatred of *all* the whites who have rebelled. If the latter got the controul of the States, or local power the emigrant & loyal white will avoid the country. I would suggest therefore a plan of confiscation & settlement of Emigrants & northern whites by means of societies and organizations similar to that of the Emigrant Aid Society[3]—that saved Kanzas to Freedom. This Society exists now & if it had the means wd undertake the plan, but if the disloyal element gains the ascendancy in any place it will then be too late & the poor whites will certainly favor the disloyal & educated classes against the free negro & against the emigrant from any quarter who favor him.

with great respect Your Obt St E Winslow

To His Excy A Johnson Presdt. U S—

ALS, DLC-JP.

1. Winslow (*fl*1881), an importer, was at this time agent of the American Emigration Company and subsequently of the Industrial Aid Society, Charity Bureau. Boston directories (1864–81).

2. Johnson had been ill and indisposed since June 27. Randall, *Browning Diary*, 34–35; *New York World*, June 28–30, 1865.

3. The New England Emigrant Aid Company, organized in Boston in 1854 for the purpose of settling Kansas with free-staters, was actively pursuing a plan to set up colo-

nies in Florida. Samuel A. Johnson, *The Battle Cry of Freedom* (Lawrence, 1954), passim.

From Francis H. Peirpoint

[ca. July 1865]; *New York Herald*, July 9, 1865.

Virginia's governor, in an extended public letter, argues in favor of Johnson's "early . . . recognition of the validity and efficacy" of the pardons and amnesty granted under Lincoln's several proclamations. Points out that during the war, as part of the effort to suppress the rebellion "by any and all means—by the overthrow of its armies, by encouraging desertions from rebel armies, by converting or neutralizing all in hostile attitude to the Union," Lincoln had pledged "the faith and honor of the Union to all persons who accept and respect the terms tendered." Lincoln considered his offer of "pardon to the rebels was continuous . . . that at any time . . . any offender might effectually embrace the tender." Believing that over 10,000 Virginians, as well as citizens of other states, have subscribed to such pardons, he contends not only that the "national faith" has been pledged to such parties, but that there would be much "vexation, expense and labor involved in the repudiation of these, and the procurement of other pardons." Many of these "valuable citizens . . . are still subject to all the pains and penalties of treason, because they fall within one or more of the exceptions" of Johnson's May 29 Amnesty Proclamation; yet they had returned to loyalty before war's end, while R. E. Lee and "multitudes of inferior offenders," who were continuously guilty, once pardoned, are not "liable to a hundred prosecutions."

From Cora A. Slocomb and Daughters

[New Orleans, ca. July, 1865][1]

To his Excellency Andrew Johnson
President of the United States
Sir.

The petition of Cora A Slocumb and of her daughters Ida A. Slocumb and Caroline Augusta Slocumb wife of David Urquhart, all residents of the city of New Orleans,[2] Respectfully shows

That for many years they have resided in the City of New Orleans and were residing in that city on the 23d of June 1862 at which time they were in the peacable and undisturbed possession of their property. That being desirous of going to their usual summer residence in the mountains of North Carolina, they applied for and obtained permission of Major General Butler, then commanding the Department of the Gulf so to do, which permission was accompanied with an assurance that their common residence the property of Mrs Slocumb, one of your petitioners should not be disturbed during their absence, and that they might leave the city without fear that their property should be interfered with by any exercise of military right and would be safe under the laws of the United States, and your petitioners aver that but for this assurance they would not have left the City of New Orleans.

Your petitioners represent that as long as Genl Butler remained in command of the Department of the Gulf, their property remained undisturbed,[3] but that shortly after he was relieved of his command, not only was their residence taken into possession by the military authorities by whom it has been ever since and is now occupied, but all of their property of whatever description was seized by the agents of the Government, either military or civil and all the rents and revenues arising therefrom were collected and have been retained by them up to the present time.

That a portion of the property belonging to one of your petitioners, to wit, Ida A Slocumb, having been destroyed, the Insurance money upon the same to the amount of $14,330 was collected by Capt John McClure[4] of the Quarter Masters Department under a military order to the Insurance Company to pay it over.

Petitioners aver that all the rents and revenues of their property from the date of their seizure, more than two years ago, have been received by B. F. Flanders[5] Supervising Agent of the Treasury Department in the city of New Orleans, and are now held by him, and that in the meantime the taxes due to the city of New Orleans, the State of Louisiana, and the U.S. Government have been permitted to accumulate and remain unpaid until they now amount in the aggregate to $35,000, or thereabouts, your petitioners being deprived of the means of paying them.

Petitioners aver that when they departed from the city of New Orleans, they left their property under the control and management of their duly authorized agent and that their property was in no sense abandoned by them, that they are not amenable for any violation of the laws of the United States, nor have any judicial proceedings been instituted against them or their property on the part of the Government.

Petitioners represent that they are without adequate redress in these matters under the law, wherefore they respectfully ask that the accompanying certificates and vouchers in support of the statements[6] herein contained being considered, that they may be restored to the possession of their property, and your Excellency will order the same to be delivered to them and that the Special Agent of the Treasury Department and the officers of the Quarter Masters Department may be ordered to pay over to your petitioners such moneys, rents and revenues as they may have received as above stated, all—which is respectfully submitted.

> Cora A. Slocumb[*sic*]
> Ida A. Slocumb.[*sic*]
> Augusta Urquhart.

Pet, DNA-RG56, Misc. Div., Claims for Cotton and Captured and Abandoned Property.
1. On July 19, 1865, this letter was received in the President's office and forwarded

to the Secretary of the Treasury. Index to Lets. Recd., Ser. 4A, Johnson Papers, LC.

2. Slocomb (b. c1811), the widow of a wealthy iron merchant, had aided the rebellion by equipping the Washington Artillery Battery, in which her son and son-in-law served, and by subscribing $3,000 to the defense of New Orleans, for which she was fined $750 by Federal authorities after they captured the city. Ida A. (b. c1830) later married Confederate surgeon T. G. Richardson. David Urquhart (b. c1828), the husband of Caroline Augusta (b. c1834), was a prewar commission agent who became a Confederate lieutenant colonel, an aide to the governor of Louisiana, and an assistant adjutant and inspector general. Robert Tallent, *The Romantic New Orleans* (New York, 1950), 94–95, 109, 261; Benjamin F. Butler, *Butler's Book: Autobiography and Personal Reminiscences* (Boston, 1852), 423; *OR*, Ser. 1, Vol. 6: 625; Vol. 10, Pt. 1: 469; Vol. 15: 540; Ser. 2, Vol. 7: 39, 1046.

3. General Benjamin Butler was impressed with Slocomb, in part because, though a supporter of the Confederacy, she refused to repudiate the debts her husband's company owed to northern creditors, insisting that she would redeem them when she could. Butler, *Butler's Book*, 423–25.

4. John W. McClure, captain and assistant quartermaster, was mustered out in June 1865. Heitman, *Register*, 1: 658.

5. Benjamin F. Flanders.

6. Slocomb had apparently hired William M. Evarts of New York and enlisted help from General Butler. Accompanying this claim and copies of the amnesty oaths of each lady was a statement from General Butler. On August 5 Johnson endorsed this claim: "In this case I have to direct that the real estate mentioned be restored to the parties as recommended by Major General Butler." They were pardoned, also on Butler's recommendation, on August 3, 1865. Misc. Div., Claims for Cotton and Captured and Abandoned Property, RG56, NA; Amnesty Papers (M1003, Roll 29), La., Cora A. Slocomb et al., RG94, NA; *New Orleans True Delta*, Sept. 17, 1865.

White House Grocery Account for June 1865

[July 1865]

Presidents House

1865   To A. S. Chamberlin & Co[1] Dr

June	8	To	35 lb cut loaf sugar @25¢	8.75
	"		50 lb B Coffee @20¢	10.
	"		1 Sack Flour 1.75 1 sack salt .20	
			1/4 Gro Matches .75	2.70
	"		1 lb White Pepper .80 1 Bot mustard .85	
			10 lb Pow Sugar 2.20	3.85
	"		10 lb Pro Coffee 5.00 24 lb Ham @25¢ 6.00	
			6 Bots yeast Pow 1.80	12.80
	"		1 Bot Oil .75 1 Bot Chow Chow 1.00	
			1/4 nutmegs .56	2.31
	"		1/2 lb Allspice .50 6 Bars Soap 1.20	
			1 nest spice Boxes 1.75	3.45
	"		1 lb Oolong Tea 1.75 1 lb Imp Tea 2.50	
			1/2 Doz mackerel .60	4.85
	"		2 Sugar Buckets @1.50	3.00
	9 "		10 1/2 Cheese @.30 3.15 10 lb Crackers 2.00	
			3 [Mats?] 3.00	8.15

	"	2 Galls Whiskey 10.00 1 Gall Sherry 4.50	14.50
10	"	1 meal Bucket 1.00 10 lb meal .50	
		1 Bot Worcestershire 1.00	2.50
	"	1/4 lb Pepper .40 1/2 lb Soda .15	
		7 lb Starch @.16 1.12 5 Sal soda .50	2.17
	"	2 oz Washing Blue	1.20
13	"	1 Buckets .75 11 lb Rice 1.98	
		1 Box Raisins 6.50	
		1 lb cream Tarter 1.00	10.23
14	"	1 Kit Mackerel 3.50 62 lb Soap 12.40	
		1/2 Cinnamon .60	16.50
"	"	1/2 ginger .60 1 Bot Ext Vanilla .40	
		1 Bot ex Lemon .40	1.40
15	"	1/2 Gall Mollasses .75 1/2 Bbl Flour 3.25	
		1 Jug .40	4.40
17	"	2 Cans Peaches .80 1 do Tomato .40	1.20
19	"	4 Lemons .40 1 Bot Wine 1.50 1/4 mace .70	
		1/4 Cloves .20	2.85
20	"	1 Bot Pickels 1.25 2 Bots chow chow 2.00	
		5 lb Cheese 1.50	4.75
"	"	5 lb Crackers 1.00 3 lb do .60	
		1/2 Gal Syrup .75	2.35
"	"	1 Demijohn 1.00 1[?] Tea 2.75 1 lb Tea 1.75	5.50
"	"	10 oz Sal Soda 1.00 1 Box .30	
		2 Clothes Lines .80	2.10
22	"	2 Gal Vinegar 1.20 1 Bucket .75	
		10 lb Pulv Sugar 2.30	4.25
	"	5 lb Coffee 2.65 10 lb Lard 2.50	
		1/2 lb Cloves .63	5.78
24	"	7 1/4 lb Starch 1.16 1 Box Salt .25	
		17 lb Meal .85	2 26
26	"	1 Kit mackerel 3.50 1 lb Butter .40	
		2 lb mackerel .25	4 15
"	"	4 Boxes Blacking .50 2 Brushes 1.20	1.70
27	"	1 Bbl Flour 12.00	12.
28	"	37 cut Loaf Sugar 9.25 1 qt Whiskey 1.25	10.50
29	"	5 lb Coffee 2.65 1 Box Cooking Salt .48	
		1/2 B Coars do .80	3 93
30	"	1/2 Gall Syrup .75 1 Stone jar 1.00	
		3 1/2 Castile Soap .63	2 38
	"	1 pape Brick Dust .20	
		55 Cut Loaf Sugar 13.75	13 95

" 11 lb Pulvd do 2.31 1 lb Oolong Tea 1.75
    1 lb Imp Tea 2.75   6 81
" 1 Pepper .75 1 Can Peaches .45   1.20
                                                 $200.42

                Recd Payment
                A S Chamberlin & Co

D, DLC-JP10.
    1. Arthur S. Chamberlin, a grocer on Pennsylvania Avenue. Washington, D.C., directories (1862–68).

From Charles Beasely

July 1, 1865, Lancaster, N.Y.; ALS, DLC-JP.

Expecting that Johnson would "relentlessly punish the wretches of every degree who brought such sorrow, ruin, and mourning on our fair land" through this "scandalous, wicked, and wholly inexcusable rebellion," Beasely expresses disappointment at the President's choices of governors in Alabama and Mississippi and at his not having by now hanged numbers of rebels. Republicans "*saved this nation*, and their views ought to be adopted. We elected you. We thought you reliable. We hope you will prove so, although you have made a bad start." Argues that those who aided or did not actively oppose the rebellion were responsible for the death of every man who defended the nation and thus deserve "extermination."

From Nathan Bedford Forrest

[ca. July 1, 1865, Miss.]; LS, DNA-RG94, Amnesty Papers (M1003, Roll 49), Tenn., N. B. Forrest.

Former Tennessean and Confederate lieutenant general, since February 1861 a citizen of Mississippi, applies for special pardon. A states' rights advocate who supported Breckinridge, and who in June 1861 believed he "owed his first allegiance to his state," he entered the army as a private. As long as that army remained in the field, he "fought the ones who were opposed to it—in arms—when ever and whereever I could find them," but upon the surrender he "acquiesced in the fate of war . . . and withdrew to my plantation," counseling "all soldiers under my command to pursue the same course—to lay aside all ideas of '*guerrilla*' warfare—and to return at once to the peaceful avocations of citizens." As a believer in the Monroe Doctrine, he is determined "in the event of a foreign war . . . to draw my sword in behalf of my country." In the struggle just over he was not a political leader but fought "for his faith" to the best of his ability. Having been "fairly whipped," he now asks that "amnesty may be granted me." [Although Forrest's oath and this petition were forwarded by Mississippi governor Sharkey, the general did not receive his presidential pardon until July 17, 1868.]

From Benjamin B. French

Office of the Commissioner of Public Buildings,
Capitol of the United States,
Washington City, July 1, 1865

His Excellency Andrew Johnson
President of the U.S.
Sir,

I recd. by the mail of this day the enclosed application of my old and dear friend Albert Pike for a pardon.[1] I have read his application. It is an eloquent & manly paper, and I do not doubt that should the Executive clemency be extended to my Masonic Brother he will be one of the best of citizens of the U.S.

It happened, curiously enough, that Capt. G. A. Schwarzman,[2] whom you have pardoned, came into my office to get his pardon to day, and was sitting at my side speaking of Pike, with whom he went to Arkansas at the beginning of the war, and telling me how Pike had been belied, when the letter containing his application was handed me. Capt. Schwarzman told me that he was present when an Indian was brought in who had killed and scalped a union soldier in cold blood. That Pike ordered the execution of the Indian, & he himself saw the Indian shot in a few hours after he had murdered & scalped the soldier.

I know, of my own knowledge, that Albert Pike was, prior to the rebellion, the very soul of Truth, Honor and Mercy.

I leave his case in your hands sincerely hoping that a man capable as Pike is, of great & good things may be saved to the literature of his country if nothing else.

With very high regard your obt. Servt.
B. B. French

ALS, DNA-RG94, Amnesty Papers (M1003, Roll 14), Ark., Albert Pike.
    1. See Letter from Albert Pike, June 24, 1865.
    2. Gustavus A. Schwarzman (1812–*fl*1882), a Washington, D.C., postal clerk before the war, was on Pike's staff in 1862 and apparently left the army for Confederate civilian employment. Johnson requested his pardon on June 10. Relocating in Baltimore after the war, Schwarzman became an insurance agent. 1860 Census, D.C., Washington, 4th Ward, 257; Washington, D.C., directories (1855–60); Baltimore directories (1870–82); *List of Staff Officers of the Confederate States Army 1861–1865* (Washington, D.C., 1891), 146; Amnesty Papers (M1003, Roll 68), Va., G. A. Schwarzman, RG94, NA.

From William Gray[1]

Boston July 1, 1865.

Dear Sir.

I have had the pleasure of joining with some gentlemen, in inviting you to visit Boston this summer.[2] We trust that you will accept the invitation.

In the course of Commencement week, on the 21st of July, there is to be a Commemoration at Cambridge, in honor of the students of Harvard University who have served in the army and navy in the war. I am Chairman of the Committee of the Alumni Chapter with the arrangements. After several discussions it has been decided to extend no formal invitations to official persons excepting Governor Andrew, who is the presiding officer of the Board of Overseers. This decision was made from an apprehension that a different course might change the character of the occasion, intended to be of a private and personal description, in commemoration of our fellow graduates and students. I cannot therefore address you on the part of the Committee, but I am at liberty to say that it will give me great gratification if you will pass Commencement week at my residence in Brookline, and accompany me to the Commemoration at Cambridge. If two or three friends, of your own selection, will accompany you as my guests it will increase my pleasure. I am quite sure that you will be gladly welcomed in Massachusetts, which, in addition to other reasons, will cordially receive the representative of East Tennessee, already known to our people by her peculiar sorrows.[3] In the retirement of the Country you will secure some rest which you must greatly need. My residence is within five miles of Boston and Cambridge.

Will you be kind enough, at your convenience, to inform me whether I may expect you.

I am Very respectfuly Yours
Wm. Gray

To the President of the United States

ALS, DLC-JP.

1. Treasurer of the Atlantic Cotton Mills, Boston, Gray graduated in 1829 from Harvard and served on the first Board of Overseers (1866–72). Boston directories (1864–70); Harvard University, *Historical Register* (Cambridge, 1937), 37, 232.

2. See Letter from John A. Andrew, June 24, 1865.

3. In 1864 Edward Everett, former president of Harvard, had chaired a committee which raised over $100,000 in relief funds for "the loyal and suffering East Tennesseeans." *Johnson Papers*, 5: 479n.

From Gustavus A. Henry [1]
(Private)

[Charlotte, N.C.] [2] July 1st 1865

His Excellency Andrew Johnson
President of the United States
Sir

I have the honor to inform you I have forwarded to you, through my son, my application for amnesty accompanied with my oath to defend the constitution of the United States as prescribed in your proclamation of the 29th may 1865. The war being now at an end and the union being virtually restored I am very anxious to return to Tennessee that I may support my family by the practice of my profession, who are sadly in need of any assistance I may be able to render them.

The respectful manner in which we conducted our political conflicts in Tennessee and the friendly feelings that have prevailed since that time, so far as I am aware, between us, justify me now to make this private appeal to you.

I will not sacrifise my own self respect, and incur your disgust, as I am sure I would do, by saying I was forced into the course I have lately pursued by the public opinion of my State against my judgement & that I did not go willingly, into the measures that led to the temporary seperation of the Southern, from the northern States, as I am told a great many are now doing, who were the most ardent advocates of it, in the beginning, & for years before, while I was earnestly advocating the Union.

On the contrary, truth compels me to say, what I did, I did voluntaraly and from a conscientious conviction, that the time had come, when the tranquility of the whole country, north and south, would be promoted by that Seperation, most especially if it could have been effected peaceably which I hoped for, to the last moment before, the bloody arbitrament of battle was resorted to. With me it was a desire to promote no partial evil, but universal good.

Recent results have however overthrown my theory, and I submit like a man to my inevitable destiny, and have taken in good faith all the steps that are prescribed for readmission into the old union, have sworn to support the constitution of the United States and ask the privilege to enjoy the protection it confers on every citizen.

I had, as I think you know, at the beginning of the war, a very handsome estate. It is now nearly all gone from me and my heirs forever, and the best I can hope for in the future is, to place my family above the contingencies of want by close and vigilant application to my private business. The opportunity to do this will however be denied me unless you grant me the amnesty I here solicit at your hands.

I have in good faith taken the oath prescribed, and I believe you will do me the justice to think, I will not be likely to violate it, such at least is my fixed determination. I have now done all I can do and leave the result to your magnanimity & to your sense of justice, and feel confident you will do what you believe will be consistent with the peace and dignity of the United States.

If you approve of this application, I will be obliged to you if you will at once grant my amnesty and have it placed into the hands of my son that I may return to my family in Tennessee.[3] I have the honour to be respectfully your friend & obedient servant

G A Henry

ALS, DNA-RG94, Amnesty Papers (M1003, Roll 49), Tenn., G. A. Henry.

1. Tennessee Confederate senator and Johnson's opponent for governor in 1853.

2. Henry took the oath two days earlier in Charlotte. Amnesty Papers (M1003, Roll 49), Tenn., G. A. Henry, RG94, NA.

3. Although he suggests that either Gus Henry, Jr., or Thomas F., both Confederate officers, might be the bearer, Henry himself went to Washington and visited Johnson about the middle of the month, but Johnson did not issue his pardon until November 27, 1866. Wakelyn, *BDC*; *Nashville Union*, July 14, 1865; *Richmond Enquirer*, Jan. 31, 1865; *House Ex. Docs.*, 39 Cong., 2 Sess., No. 31, p. 11 (Ser. 1289).

From Joseph E. Johnston

Buffalo Springs, Mecklenburg County,
July 1st 1865

His Excellency the president
Sir,

The terms of the amnesty proclamation encourage me to apply for the removal, in my case, of the exception from its benefits.

When Virginia seceded like many others I believed the division of the country permanent, &, preferring to live in the section which contained all my kindred & friends, I joined it. The war has decided the questions at issue—I hope & believe, permanently. I accept the decision—& have urged all those over whom I could exert influence, to do likewise.

I regret to be unable to advance any special claim to indulgence. Perhaps, however, your excellency may think it worth consideration, that while an officer of the United States army I served faithfully for many years—& gave my blood & offered my life in that service, many times.[1]

Most respectfully Your obt. sert.
J. E. Johnston

ALS, DNA-RG94, Amnesty Papers (M1003, Roll 63), Va., J. E. Johnston.

1. President Johnson did not grant the general's pardon until June 25, 1868.

From Amos A. Lawrence[1]

(near) Boston. July 1st. 1865.

Dear Sir

As it is possible that the fear of heat & of crowds may deter you from coming to Boston, I will venture to offer you & your family an asylum from both in my house at Nahant. This is a rocky promontory near the Town, running out four miles into the sea: occupied by about fifty families. I shall esteem it a great privelege to recieve you there, & to do what we can for yr comfort during yr stay here, or any portion of it.

Some of the N York newspapers have asserted that the recent meetings at Faneuil Hall & elsewhere[2] are called by men of extreme views, to create an opposition to yrself & yr Administration. I will take this opportunity to assure you from my own personal knowledge, that the reverse of this is the case. The discussion was started, & has been carried on with great propriety, by some of the best legal minds here. And the opinion is becoming fixed, that under a republican Govt. there should never be any disfranchisement owing to race. Many think that the higher the standard of qualifications required of the electors, the better it will be for all.

All understand what yr position is, & some of its difficulties, & are desirous to support you in carrying out a doctrine which lays at the foundation of our Govt. The fact that the negro vote of the Southn. States would be cast in sympathy with the old aristocracy does not alter this principle: & it may perhaps induce the latter to adopt it at a future time.

Respectfully & truly Yr Obt Sert
Amos A Lawrence

His Excelly. Andrew Johnson.

ALS, DLC-JP.
  1. Boston merchant, Cotton Whig, and philanthropist.
  2. On June 21 Bostonians convened at Faneuil Hall and passed resolutions endorsing black suffrage; members of the New York Union League also announced their support of the measure. Benedict, *Compromise of Principle*, 110–11; *Boston Advertiser*, June 22, 1865; *New York Herald*, June 27, 1865.

From Richard J. Oglesby

July 1, 1865, Springfield, Ill.; ALS, DNA-RG60, Appt. Files for Judicial Dists., Ill., Lawrence Weldon.

The Illinois governor, writing on behalf of Lawrence Weldon, attorney of the southern district of the state, "very much" desires the President to reappoint him "for the next term of four years." He lauds Weldon as "an efficent and strictly honest public officer" who has the "full confidence of the whole District both as Lawyer and citizen." [The Senate confirmed Weldon's reappointment on January 18, 1866.]

From Robert M. Patton

[ca. July 1, 1865, Lauderdale County, Ala.]; ALS, DNA-RG94, Amnesty Papers (M1003, Roll 8), Ala., Robert M. Patton.

Former Alabama legislator, who "comes within the first and thirteenth exceptions" of the amnesty proclamation, declares that before the war he "was always an ardent and faithful supporter of the Union"; in 1860, as a delegate to the Charleston Democratic Convention, he supported Douglas. As president of the state senate at the time of secession, "he exercised all his influence to prevent that fatal step." However, "in common with nearly all the union men in Alabama," he "fell into the current, and sided with the Rebellion," holding for a short period "an agency for the sale of Confederate Bonds." In late 1862 he resigned his position in the senate and returned home to North Alabama, "where he has ever since quietly remained." He acquiesces "in good faith in the change in the institutions of the South effected by the war" and gives "his cordial support" to Johnson's policy "so far as it has been developed in reference to the restoration of the insurrectionary states to there former place in the union." [Patton was pardoned August 8, 1865.]

From Henry M. Rector

July 1, 1865, Little Rock, Ark.; ALS, DNA-RG94, Amnesty Papers (M1003, Roll 14), Ark., Henry M. Rector.

The first Confederate governor of Arkansas, applying for special pardon, presents a lengthy statement in his own defense. Believing in states' rights, he "supposed the right of Seperation existed as a legel proposition" and approved the legislature's call for a convention. He claims he was never a "Secessionist *Per Se*," did not believe separation "would enhance the happiness or prosperity of the South," and did not think Lincoln's election was just cause for disrupting the government, but accepted secession as an "unfortunate necessity" for Arkansas, since many other states had already withdrawn from the Union. While governor he "neither imprisoned nor persecuted men for opinions sake." Although he negotiated the surrender of the Federal arsenal at Little Rock, he did so only to "prevent bloodshed [and] destruction to the city and the people." Conceding that the right of secession is an "exploded Theory," he hopes that the demise of slavery, which he accepts "cheerfully, nay with pleasure," will prove to be a "blessing to both races and gratifying to the civilized world." [Rector's pardon was issued October 27, 1865.]

White House Butcher's Account for June 9–17, 1865

Washington July 1/65

Thomas Stackpole for Presidents House

To James Hazel[1] Dr

June	9	Qr of Lamb	$ 2 75
"	"	10 lbs Beef	2 50
"	"	12 " Loin of Beef	3 60
"	"	12 " Lard	3 00

"	"	9 1/2	"	Beef Steak	2 85
"	"	11	"	"	3 30
"	"	12 1/2	"	Salt Beef	2 60
"	"	10	"	Bacon	2 50
"	"	9	"	Pork	2 25
"	12	5	"	Veal	1 50
"	"	4	"	Cheese	1 20
"	"	14	"	Beef	4 20
"	13	12	"	" Steak	3 60
"	"	11	"	Loin Beef	3 30
"	"	7	"	Beef	1 75
"	"	Qr		Lamb	2 50
"	14	12	lbs	Beef	3 60
"	15	10	"	Salt Beef	2 50
"	"	Qr	of	Lamb	2 50
"	"	6	lbs	Steak	1 80
"	"	12	"	Beef	3 60
"	"	12	"	Lard	3 00
"	"	6	"	Pork	1 50
"	16	6	"	Beef	1 80
"	"	3	"	Chops	90
"	17	16	"	Beef	4 80
"	"	Qr	of	Lamb	2 50
"	"	5	lbs	Cutlet	2 00
"	"	Cash			5 00
"	"	10	lbs	Salt Beef	2 50
"	"	8	"	Beef	2 00
"	"	4	"	Steak	1 20
"	"	10	"	Veal	3 00
		Amt Carried fow'd			$ 87 60 [2]

ADS, DLC-JP10.

1. James H. Hazel, whose butcher shop was located at "52 1/2 Centre Mkt." Washington, D.C., directories (1858–73).

2. The actual butcher's account continues on from this point to include the remainder of the month of June. The total amount owed and paid was $187.97.

From Peter F. Young

July 1, 1865, [Cleveland, Ohio]; ALS, DNA-RG56, Appts., Customs Service, Assessor, Fla., 1st Dist., C. L. Robinson.

The former provost marshal for the District of Florida discusses two of the candidates for that state's provisional governor: Calvin L. Robinson, "a prominent business man," and Judge S. L. Burritt, both of Jacksonville. Young favors Robinson, "a self sacrificing, energetic Union man, in every sense meritorious," who at the beginning of the war "was obliged to flee the country on account of his bold denunciation of secession" and later "was the most prominent in introducing secret Loyal Leagues in the State." Burritt's loyalty, on the other hand, was "questionable"; he did not take the oath of allegiance until the summer of 1864. [Johnson selected neither man for the post of provisional governor.]

From James L. Dunning

Atlanta Geo July 2nd 1865

Mr President:

Since I saw you in company with others on the 19th of May Last[1] I Returned to my Home at this Place, and have Tried to study the Public sentiment of the Peopple of this State.

So far as the masses are concerned they have Enough of War and its consequences and Realy Desire to conform to the new order of things in Good Faith.

There is However Among us the *Old* Leaders a Large Portion of which are Among your Excepted Classes Named In Your Proclamations. It is this Class who Clamor on the Streets About their *Disabilities* under which they Labor and who Talk constantly About the Oath of Allegiance, Amnesty, and *Special Pardons* which they Desire to obtain *at once* In order that they may vote at our coming Elections. Their Zeal about this is wonderful and before long a Shower of Petitions will Rain on your Head at Washington.

The Truth is these men are no Better *now* then Before Although their *Present Status* Prevents them from Interfering as they would were they *Forgiven.*[2]

Respfly Jas L. Dunning
Atlanta Geo

ALS, DLC-JP.

1. See Comments on the Restoration of Georgia, May 19, 1865.

2. Until pardoned, their property was liable to confiscation, their political franchise denied, and treason indictments were pending. Six weeks later Dunning wrote again that nothing had changed in community attitudes and that "Early Pardons Will Prove Injurious enabling as it Will most of our former leaders to Again controll our coming Election to our state convention." Dunning to Johnson, Aug. 19, 1865, Office of Atty. Gen., Lets. Recd., President, RG60, NA.

From Jeremiah S. Black

July 3, 1865, Washington, D.C.; ALS, DLC-E. M. Stanton Papers.

Hired by Mrs. Clement C. Clay, Jr. to defend her husband, now confined at Fortress Monroe and charged with "the crime of murder," Black, a prominent

Democratic legal authority and former attorney general, seeks an order allowing him to meet with Clay, his client, so "that I may know what his case is, what evidence exists against him or for him, and to what extent I can serve him without thwarting the administration of public justice." [Johnson denied Black's request.]

From Charles H. Lewis [1]

The Commonwealth of Virginia,
Executive Department,
Richmond, July 3d 1865.

His Excellency And: Johnson President, U.S.

Dr Sir

My friend, Hon J T Harris [2] is about to visit Washington, & has called on me for such information in regard to the status & prospects of our State Government as will enable him to give you a fair idea of our progress in the work before us: My official position has brought me in contact with men of intelligence & character from every part of the State, & I can assure you that the very strong manifestations of earnest determination to support the Federal & State Governments, from every quarter, furnish abundant & cheering evidences that Virginia will be, henceforth, one of the most loyal States in the Union. The people, with a *few* mischievous exceptions, cheerfully acquiesce in the Constitutional provision abolishing slavery, & many of the slaveholders declare that they would vote for it if the question were now to be submitted to them. We have some mischievous Secessionists amongst us, who, abstaining from open demonstrations of disloyalty, confine their efforts to desseminating disloyal articles from London & New York papers, & growling at every measure of the Federal or State authorities. But I am convinced that these people have little influence with the masses of the people. Our only trouble is with those ill advised people who are endeavoring to excite dissatisfaction amongst the freedmen, & to persuade them to agitate for the right to vote, when the great question with many of them, as well as the white people, is how are they to get bread? I apprehend no difficulty in regard to enactments by the next Legislature, which will afford to the free colored people every protection, that will be needed, to their rights as to person & property, & thus I think, if the extreme radicals will but let us alone, or we shall be successful in preventing them from producing riots & turbulent demonstrations among the colored people, until the assembling of the Legislature, we shall be able to dispose of this vexed question to the satisfaction of loyal & well disposed men of all parts of the Country.

Very Respectfully Ch. H Lewis
Sec'y Com'w'th Va:

ALS, DLC-JP.
    1. Lewis (b. 1816), Staunton, Va. lawyer, was appointed by Peirpoint in 1864, serv-
ing until congressional reconstruction commenced. *NCAB*, 12: 121.
    2. John T. Harris (1823–1899), Democratic congressman (1859–61, 1871–81),
served in the Virginia House of Delegates (1863–65) and as judge of the 12th circuit
(1866–69). *BDAC*.

From Wall Street Baptist Church Deacons

July 3, 1865, Natchez, Miss.; Pet, DNA-RG105, Records of the Commr.,
Lets. Recd. (M752, Roll 13).

Four black deacons of a congregation originally "composed of white & Colored
members" report that when the rebellion began, the meeting house was closed
for two years, and "we had to do the best we could in getting a p[l]ace to
worship God in." The Union forces opened the church, partly to preach to the
soldiers, and partly to gather a white audience. They soon discovered, however,
"that our citezens was such strong Rebals that they would rather hear the Devil
then a yankee." "When all efforts too gether white audience failed," E. G.
Trask, agent of the Baptist Home Mission Society, allowed the deacons and
other black members to return, but "we know not how long it will be so." If
"preferance" is to "be given to Unionest above Rebals, we the colored members . . . are entitled to it." Therefore, they petition the President to turn over
the "Meeting house & ground [to] only loyal members." Signed by Edward
Claton, Tony Jones, Daniel Holley, and Henry Johnson, who represent "between 80 & 90 Members." [On July 15, 1865, Col. Samuel Thomas, assistant
commissioner, Freedmen's Bureau, state of Mississippi, ordered the meeting
house turned over to the petitioners.]

From J. Madison Wells

New Orleans July 3d 1865

Sir

On my return from Washington on the 6th day of June I immediately
again resumed my Gubernatorial duties bearing in mind steadily
then and since your views and injunctions as to the proper mode of
proceeding.

Dr Kennedy returned on the evening of the 26th June and on the
1st inst resumed his office of Mayor.

The visit of Judge Chase the machination of Gn Banks and the en-
difatigable endeavors of the plunderers who adhere to the cause of the
latter in expectation of a new saturnalia of plunder were he to obtain
power again in Louisiana have produced some uneasiness among the
timid and inexperienced in politics who fears that a noisy and venal
faction backed by the two gentlemen named and their party in the Eastern States would organize here an opposition of some strength to your
administration—than such an opposition nothing is more groundless.
The federal offices here with four exceptions these are the Recv. of
Customs Naval Marshal and Post Master[1]—are it is true in the hands

of persons devoted to what is called the Chase interest, and negro suffrage—but their power is not formidable and the general sentiment is so unequivocally in favor of an earnest support of your Government that I have not a doubt of their utter discomfiture when a trial of strength at our first general Election takes place.

I am most happy in being able to assure you that the returned soldiers as well as the Civilians who have come into our lines in this state manifest the greatest readiness to comply with the requirements of your amnesty proclamation and to submit themselves to the laws and I do not know nor have I heard of in any quarter any threat or even empty bravado signifying *vindictive* or *resentful* feelings.

In consequence of this, in reorganizing parochial machinery for administrative and Judicial purposes I have been less exacting in regard to the antecedents of some candidates and in remote sections where trouble was feared from disbanded soldiers run away negroes and other outlaws who might seek to disturb society—I appointed some few men of resolution and intelligence—who had seen military service in the rebel ranks.

I will however guarantee their fidelity to the nation and to you its Executive and I have not the slightest doubt that they will give a good account of themselves.

I regret it is still deemed necessary to give the power of interfearence in civil matters to the General Commandg here.[2] It has led to no unpleasant conflict of authority and I am determined it shall not. Yet it is to be deprecated as it weakens my power and produces a belief in the public mind which disturbs artfully exerts that the commanding General can in certain circumstances set aside whatever I may order to be done. As this is contrary to what I understood when in Washington to be your intention or desire I mention it in the hope that you may order its correction.

A Mr. Cavode[3] of Pennsylvania and other missionaries of his school are coming and going hence. I am assured they are much discouraged and carry off with them the conviction that this state is now inseparably attached to those principles of government of which through life you have been a champion. In my opinion alike result will be experienced in all the Southern States. Your frank determined and generous declarations are received in their true spirit and will be sustained to your entire satisfaction.

The Chase people are now endeavouring to overthrow the State government from the creation of which after the Banks plan they derived so much plunder. Hahn late Governor Shaw sheriff—and Fish[4] late Clerk of the 2nd district Court all of whom were partners in & exclusive owners of the True Delta news paper and encumbents of office its great power and pecuniary profit, are, now, the leaders of the agitation.

These men contrived to secure from the convention printing alone over two hundred thousand dollars and from profits every way, enhanced possibly as much more, from their other places secured to them under the Banks rule. The special Commission of Gen Smith and Mr James T. Brady[5] I think can throw some light upon their operations. They propose through petitions they have hawking about for signatures to obtain the appointment of a Provisional or Military Governor. Enclosed you will find the printed heading of one of their documents.[6]

In answer to the charges the radicals make against my appointment are untrue and that Hahn was himself a state officer under Confederate authority. Shaw & Fish his associates were notorious as sympathizers the latter being in addition chief detective at the time to Mazureau[7] sheriff, who was sent to fort Lafayette—and is still a prisoner at large at the north and was also the secret clerk of a vigilance committee. Such are the men who charge me with making appointments of disloyal persons.

> I have the honor President to be
> your most obt servt J Madison Wells
> Gov La

To His Excellency Andrew Johnson
President United States Washington D C.

ALS, DLC-JP.
    1. William P. Kellogg, collector of customs (not receiver); Thomas M. Wells, J. Madison's son, acting naval officer; Cuthbert Bullitt, marshal; Robert W. Taliaferro, postmaster. *U.S. Off. Reg.* (1865), 120, 122, 295, *127; Tunnell, *Crucible of Reconstruction*, 239; McCrary, *Lincoln and Reconstruction*, 60.
    2. Gen. Edward R. S. Canby, who assumed command on June 3, 1865. Max L. Heyman, Jr., *Prudent Soldier: A Biography of Major General E.R.S. Canby, 1817–1873* (Glendale, Calif., 1959), 280.
    3. John Covode (1808–1871), former Pennsylvania congressman and Radical Republican, who was sent by Stanton to investigate conditions in Louisiana, would write Benjamin F. Wade that Wells had abandoned the unionist element. *BDAC*; Covode to Wade, July 11, 1865, Wade Papers, LC. See also Letter from Loyal Citizens of Louisiana, July 10, 1865, and Letter from Cottman, July 20, 1865.
    4. Michael Hahn, Alfred Shaw, and William R. Fish.
    5. See Letter from Wells and Others, May 26, 1865.
    6. Not found.
    7. Adolph Mazureau (c1806–fl1874), New Orleans lawyer who was sheriff before Federal occupation, had been arrested in May 1862 and sent to Fort Warren, Mass., for being "president and leading man of a secret society known as the Southern Independence Association." He was paroled to Boston six months later. 1870 Census, La., Orleans, New Orleans, 6th Ward, 152; New Orleans directories (1849–74); *OR*, Ser. 2, Vol. 3: 616; Vol. 4: 760.

To David Wills [1]

Executive Mansion, July 3, 1865.

Mr. David Wills, Chairman, &c. &c, Gettysburg, Pa.:

Dear Sir:

I had promised myself the pleasure of participating in person in the proceedings at Gettysburg tomorrow. That pleasure, owing to my indisposition, I am reluctantly compelled to forego.[2]

I should have been pleased, standing on that twice consecrated spot, to share with you your joy at the return of peace, to greet with you the surviving heroes of the war who come back with light hearts and heavy laden with honors, and with you to drop grateful tears to the memory of those that will never return.

Unable to do so in person, I can only send you my greetings and assure you of my full sympathy with the purpose and spirit of your exercises to-morrow.

Of all the anniversaries of the Declaration of Independence, none has been more important and significant than that upon which you assemble.

Four years of struggle for our nation's life have been crowned with success: armed treason is swept from the land; *our ports are reopened*; our relations with other nations are of the most satisfactory character; our internal commerce is free; our soldiers and sailors resume the peaceful pursuits of civil life; our flag floats in every breeze, and the only barrier to our national progress—human slavery—is forever at an end.

Let us trust that each recurring Fourth of July shall find our nation stronger in numbers, stronger in wealth, stronger in the harmony of its citizens, stronger in its devotion to nationality and freedom!

As I have often said, I believe that God sent this people on a mission among the nations of the earth, and that when He founded our nation, He founded it in perpetuity. That faith sustains me now that new duties are devolved upon me, and new dangers threaten us. I feel that whatever the means He uses, the Almighty is determined to preserve us as a people. And since I have seen the love our fellow-citizens bear their country, and the sacrifices they have made for it, my abiding faith has become stronger than ever that a "government of the people" is the strongest as well as the best of governments.

In your joy to-morrow I trust you will not forget the thousands of whites, as well as blacks, whom the war has emancipated, who will hail this Fourth of July with a delight which no previous anniversary of the Declaration of Independence ever gave them. Controlled so long by ambitious, selfish leaders, who used them for their own unworthy ends, they are now free to serve and cherish the Government against whose life they in their blindness struck. I am greatly mistaken if, in the States lately in rebellion, we do not henceforward have an exhibition of such loyalty and patriotism as was never seen nor felt there before.

Where you have consecrated a National Cemetery you are to lay the corner-stone of a National Monument, which in all human probability will rise to the full height and proportion you design. Noble as this monument of stone may be, it will be but a faint symbol of the grand monument which, if we do our duty, we shall raise among the nations of the earth upon the foundation laid nine and eighty years ago in Philadelphia. Time shall wear away and crumble this monument; but that, based as it is upon the consent, virtue, patriotism, and intelligence of the people, each year shall make firmer and more imposing.

Your friend and fellow-citizen,
Andrew Johnson.

PL, DLC-JP20. Clipping in unidentified scrapbook.

1. Wills (b. *c*1831), a Gettysburg attorney, was the founder-president of the Soldiers' National Cemetery. Having conceived the idea of the memorial park and been placed in charge of the reburials, he had been Lincoln's host when the President dedicated the cemetery in November 1863. 1860 Census, Pa., Adams, Gettysburg, 50; Frank L. Klement, "'These Honored Dead': David Wills and the Soldiers' Cemetery at Gettysburg," *Lin Her*, 74 (1972): 123–33.

2. Invited to attend the July 4 dedication of a monument to the Gettysburg dead, Johnson presumably had intended to go to the ceremonies, but his lingering illness precluded his attendance. Although reported better on June 30, he did not entertain visitors or hold a cabinet meeting until July 7. Gettysburg National Cemetery Board (Wills) to Johnson, June 2, 1865, Johnson Papers, LC; *New York World*, June 29–July 7, 1865; Randall, *Browning Diary*, 34, 35, 36.

From Richard P.L. Baber[1]

Cincinnati Ohio July 4, 1865.

His Excellency Andrew Johnson,
President of the United States:

A day or so before our Union State Convention in Ohio, on June 21st, I had a long interview with the Honorable Joseph S. Fowler, one of the Senators from Tennessee, an old friend who was with me, at the Burnet House in your room, when you were on your way to the inauguration at Washington. I told him, that whilst the mass of the people sustained your proclamations, declaring that the regulation of the elective franchise rightfully belonged to the legal loyal voters in each State, that many of the leading policians could not be *trusted*. Under the Lead of Chase and Sumner, they were actually organizing a party in Congress, to *reject* all the Senators and Representatives elected from the South, until negro suffrage was *forced* on their acceptance. From my knowledge of the Army, having served in every Department from the Potomac to the Rio Grande, and the feeling in the West, I knew our people would repudiate such a *test*, that would exclude Ohio and other States from Congress, whose Constitutions confined suffrage to white men. I submitted to Senator Fowler the enclosed article, published in the Ohio State Journal, the morning of the Convention, as a correct interpretation of your policy;[2] and also a communication in the Commercial, containing President Lincoln's Columbus speech,[3] (of which I speak from personal knowledge) on the negro suffrage question, which should be published everywhere, as sustaining your action. I know that in the Chicago Convention in 1860, both Seward and Chase were beaten, because of their record on this question, for I am thoroughly posted in the whole *secret* history of Lincoln's nomination, which I detailed to you at Washington in the winter of '62. I attended the Ohio State Convention as an army delegate, and found their delegation (143) from every army in our service, and all sections of our State, a *unit* for your policy, and determined to use up the *home* politicians who are carping at your proclamations. The resolution I offered the Army caucus, demanding an *unequivocal* endorsement of your policy, passed with a shout, and the Chase men who were figuring for a GENERAL resolution, *omitting* a commitment of the Union party of Ohio to the support of your *policy*, could raise but five or six votes out of the committee of twenty-four on Resolutions. Your friends refused to yield an *inch*, and also determined amongst themselves to submit, through our legislature, the negro suffrage issue to popular vote, by proposing an *amendment* to our own Constitution, refusing, at the same time, to make it a *party* question. This will get rid of trouble in the future, as the amendment will be *voted down* by two hundred thousand majority.[4] I understand this state tolerably well, having served on the State Central Committee for years, and during the late Convention, I inquired particularly from delegates on this subject, and am satisfied that *outside* of the Western Reserve (twelve counties) not a half a dozen counties out of the 88, would give a majority for negro suffrage. In the Columbus District, where I reside, and which gave Lincoln and yourself 4,000 majority—not 2,000 votes, out of 24,000, could be polled for negro suffrage, and the party is thankful for your saving them such a *suicidial* issue. No Senator can be elected in Ohio, until the people know how the aspirants vote next winter on the measures of your policy—old party hacks will not be permitted longer to lead—reliable men from the *returned* army will be chiefly nominated and elected to the Legislature. The Chase-Ashley party[5] have already made propositions to unite with the Copperhead Opposition—a happy riddance for they *opposed* you at the Baltimore Convention that would be more than compensated by accessions from the rank and file of the War Democracy. The negro faction will adopt a system of *bullying* in Congress, but if, Jackson-like, you appeal to the people, the honest masses will sustain you, and your friends will triumph in the revolution of politics which always occurs after a war. But it is important that the Treasury appointments be forthwith *overhauled* as Secretary Chase has stocked every place with his partizans, who are bitterly working *against you*. In the Columbus District, A. P. Stone,[6] who is now under charges for taking stock in a company, trading in "Contraband" at Matamoras, under a pass from Jeff. Davis, is shown by the *suppressed* testimony, just found by Alex. Reed,[7] your Revenue Agent at Toledo, appointed to investigate the matter, to have been *shielded* by the late Secretary of the Treasury from exposure. If you will have this testimony, now in the hands of Mr. Reed, published, it will bring to light such a case of *corruption*, that the admirers of the Chief Justice, will have enough to do to *defend* him, instead of attacking you. I write at the suggestion of Senator Fowler, as an original friend of President Lincoln and yourself, to assure you that Ohio will *stand* by you, no matter what certain *weak kneed* politicians at Washington may say or do. I am a member of the Union State Central Committee, appointed by the late State Convention, and in conjunction with Congressman Eggleston,[8] of Cincinnati, and others, am busy *organizing* the friends of your policy. The Commercial, a paper of the largest circulation in the State, has been *secured*; and being on duty at Camp Dennison, near here, I have abundant opportunity of learning the sentiments of the returned troops, and working in the cause. Hoping for the speedy restoration of your health, and that you will stand by your friends in the Union Party, and *expose* fully the corruptions of the Treasury Chase-faction, by investigating thoroughly their cotton contraband speculations,

I am, Very Respectfully,
Yours, R. P. L. Baber

LS, DLC-JP.

1. Columbus, Ohio, attorney.
2. Meeting in Columbus on June 21, Ohio Republicans selected a ticket for state offices headed by Gen. Jacob D. Cox for governor. The group issued a statement in praise and support of Johnson, and adopted a Conservative platform advocating peace and prosperity for the South, as well as for the North, and the abolition of slavery without an endorsement of black suffrage. *Ohio State Journal* (Columbus), June 21, 1865; Eugene H. Roseboom, *The Civil War Era, 1850–1873* (Columbus, 1944), 449–50.
3. On September 16, 1859, Lincoln addressed a gathering at Columbus, denying that he had spoken in favor of black suffrage in his debates with Stephen A. Douglas the previous year, and quoted extracts from the debates in support of his contention. Basler, *Works of Lincoln*, 3: 400–425.
4. No such amendment was voted on until 1867, when it was defeated by some 38,000 votes. Benedict, *Compromise of Principle*, 273.
5. A faction of Ohio Republicans represented by Chief Justice Salmon P. Chase and Congressman James M. Ashley, who had been unsuccessfully challenged by Independents (ex-Whig Republicans) and Democrats in 1864. Bonadio, *North of Reconstruction*, 1–8.
6. Alfred P. Stone (1813–1865), Columbus merchant, former Democratic congressman, and sometime proprietor of the *Ohio State Journal*, was appointed collector of internal revenue in 1864. Accused of gambling away over $90,000 of government funds, he committed suicide August 2. *BDAC*; *New York Times*, Aug. 13, 1865; *New Orleans Picayune*, Aug. 16, 1865.

7. Reed (fl1878), a Toledo clerk and auditor, was appointed a revenue agent (1865–67) and postmaster (1868–70). Toledo directories (1858–78); *Ohio State Journal* (Columbus), May 12, 1865.

8. Benjamin Eggleston (1816–1888), Ohio entrepreneur and Cincinnati merchant, was in the wartime state senate when elected to Congress (1865–69). *BDAC*.

From Albert G. Brown

July 4, 1865, Terry, Miss.; ALS, DNA-RG94, Amnesty Papers (M1003, Roll 31), Miss., A.G. Brown.

Former U.S. senator asks for special pardon after a long explanation of his beliefs and actions. Although reluctant to see the southern states secede, once it was done "he ardently desired their success." He quit the Senate and returned to his plantation, expressing the opinion that a "long bloody and disolative war" was imminent, and preparations should be made "to take up arms." He commanded a company of volunteers for six months, then after resigning learned that the legislature had elected him to the Confederate senate. All of his "political actions" stemmed from being an "earnest believer" in state sovereignty and the right of secession if a state "failed to get her constitutional rights in the Union." He maintains that "systematic attacks on the South & its institutions" by the North, the latter's refusal to give up fugitive slaves, and the "election of a President by a strictly sectional vote" justified the "organization of a seperate Nationality." He nevertheless "continually predicted the most fearful consequences from the constant agitation of dangerous sectional issues" and was "most anxious to adjust all such issues on broad & solid principles." The contest so long waged in Congress has been settled by the sword, and he is prepared to abide by the result in "good faith." He admits that when his state seceded he lost all rights under the Constitution but, asserting that it is the conqueror's right to impose terms, he "finds no impediment in the way of his taking the oath prescribed in Your Excellencys' Amnesty Proclamation." [Attorney General Henry Stanbery recommended amnesty for Brown on October 1, 1866, and his pardon became effective on that date.]

From James D.B. DeBow

July 4, 1865, Winnsboro, S.C.; ALS, DNA-RG94, Amnesty Papers (M1003, Roll 44), S.C., J.D.B. DeBow.

Southern economic journalist and superintendent of the 1850 U.S. census has taken the amnesty oath and is anxious to "devote himself henceforward to the pursuit of letters and to the elevation in every way of the great interests of the United States." His past positions were the result of states' rights doctrines "as expounded by Calhoun, Randolph, Crawford, Macon McDuffie & others"; he "never did *per se* desire the dissolution of the Union." He advocated secession "as a remedy for evils" but did not regard it as "*permanent*," believing "it would lead to a new understanding & new compact in which the rights of all the States would be protected." He had not thought war was possible or desirable, yet after it began he "regarded it to be the duty of every citizen to stand by his government." During the Hampton Roads Conference, he advocated acceptance of reconstruction and, upon Richmond's fall, he was "for immediate submission." DeBow "now regards secession as a remedy [never] again to be countenanced" and encloses endorsements from William W. Boyce and William Aiken. [DeBow, included in the thirteenth exception to Johnson's proclamation, was pardoned on August 29, 1865.]

ANDREW JOHNSON,

PRESIDENT OF THE UNITED STATES OF AMERICA,

TO ALL TO WHOM THESE PRESENTS SHALL COME, GREETING:

Whereas, *George M. Murrell,* of *Lynchburg, Virginia*, by taking part in the late rebellion against the Government of the United States, has made himself liable to heavy pains and penalties:—.—

And whereas, the circumstances of his case render him a proper object of Executive clemency:———,———

Now, therefore, be it known, that I, ANDREW JOHNSON, President of the United States of America, in consideration of the premises, divers other good and sufficient reasons me thereunto moving, do hereby grant to the said *George M. Murrell,*

Done at the city of Washington, this *Third* day of *July,*—A. D. *1865,* and of the Independence of the United States the *Eighty ninth.*

By the President:

Andrew Johnson

Will H. Seward
Secretary of State.

A Virginian pardoned by the President
Courtesy James F. Ruddy, Rancho Mirage, California

From Thomas Ewing, Sr.

Washington July 4/65

To the President

The suspension of the writ of Habeas Corpus & the Judgment of
military commissions in the case of persons not "in the land or naval
service of the U S" is now as I suggested it would soon be, in our late
brief conversation a matter of contest between the Judicial tribunals &
the secy of war.[1] I regret that he attempts to sustain the Military. There
is no possible foundation for it, & so it must end. It will be a subject of
serious investigation, not only before our courts but in Congress—
parties will form & divide on the question. The constitution & law &
enlightened public opinion are all on one side, and those who have no
fixed opinions on the subject will concur in this—that the rights of the
citizen are better protected by our constitutional tribunals than by military commissions. You I think have never sanctioned, by your signature
the finding and sentence of one of these commissions, against any one
not a spy—not taken in arms—not in the land or naval service of the
U S. *Your* administration has not upon it the *"damned spot."*[2] The appointment of the commissions as we all well know, though in your
name, is but an act of the Department. It is now in your power to set
this matter right at once, by desolving all military commissions appointed for the trial of citizens, *"not &c."* Set aside all their unexecuted
sentences & transfer the causes to the regular judicial tribunals, and by
a general order direct all military officers having citizens in custody to
obey the writ of *Habeas Corpus.*[3]

I am very truly yours
T. Ewing

ALS, DLC-JP.
    1. When courts were reestablished under Johnson's provisional governors, judicial
authorities expected to resume their normal functions. However, as the South remained
under martial law, wartime suspension of the writ of habeas corpus still applied, and U.S.
military commanders frequently circumvented the civil courts in cases relating to the
maintenance of law and order, thereby leading to questions of jurisdiction. Michael Perman, *Reunion Without Compromise: The South and Reconstruction, 1865–1868* (Cambridge, 1973), 132–34.
    2. Shakespeare's *Macbeth*, Act 5, sc. 1.
    3. Johnson failed to issue an order reinstating the habeas corpus privilege until Sep-
tember, after endorsing Governor Sharkey's request that his judicial appointees have
such authority. Beale, *Welles Diary*, 2: 366–67; Richardson, *Messages*, 6: 333.

From Edward W. Gantt

Little Rock Arks July 4th 1865

His Excy——A Johnson
President &c:
Dear Sir:

Since my letter of June 29th I have carefully watched the course of leading rebels here, many of whom have returned since the date of that letter. I have also read the opinion of Atty Genl Speed in reference to pardons[1] & had several interviews with Genl Reynolds and Gov. Murphy.[2] Without abating in the least the sentiments contained in that letter, I desire to say that if it can be done, a pardon, *except as to franchise*, would be safer in all cases that may come up from this State among prominent men from the Army or in civil life.

Gov. Murphy has but little political experience & is not a strong, though a most excellent man, & I fear they may induce him to recommend too many persons for pardon. The fewer the better with us, just now. In this connection, I beg leave to say with all deference to Gov Murphy that Genl Reynolds seems to apprehend much more clearly the proper course to be pursued in reference to pardons & treatment of rebels & therefore I think his recommendations ought to receive much consideration. While I say this, it may be as well to say that I have defended & sustained Gov Murphy in every thing connected with our free State movement. But Genl Reynolds seems to be a forcible, quiet, clear headed man, who has accomplished much and said little, & whose administrative ability surpasses that of any of the General officers under my observation.

Our state Government is as thoroughly acquiesced in and as generally sustained as that of any in the United States. We will present to the country such a united, harmonious & complete state government that I cant see how any can assail it.

With the kindest wishes for your health &c I am

Your obt St—
E. W. Gantt

ALS, DLC-JP.
1. See Letter from James Speed, May 1, 1865.
2. Joseph J. Reynolds and Isaac Murphy.

From Peter W. Gray

July 4, 1865, Houston, Tex.; ALS, DNA-RG94, Amnesty Papers (M1003, Roll 53), Tex., Peter W. Gray.

Virginia-born lawyer and Confederate congressman, a Texas resident since 1838, petitions for amnesty. A Democrat of the "conservative States Rights school," he "sincerely believed in the right of Secession . . . as a last resort." He also believed that if any state or states seceded, "the reconstruction of the Government on a more permanent basis of fraternal Union and interest" was not only possible "but could and should be effected by peaceable means." After John Brown's raid and the "triumph of a sectional party," he "honestly and earnestly" supported secession, hoping that "peaceable reconstruction" would occur. Consequently, he was a member of his state's secession convention and, after a peaceable settlement failed and the war began, "there seemed to me no other course than to contend to the best of our ability; and to abide the decision of arms." He served as congressman from February 1862 to February 1864 and afterwards was treasury agent west of the Mississippi. Recognizing that the appeal to arms "has been decided against us," he accepts the decision "as legitimate and final" and "heartily" desires to help restore the country and sustain the constitution of the United States. He has returned to his home, given his parole, taken the amnesty oath, and "as far as practicable resumed my vocations." However, since the lack of civil rights "must greatly embarrass one's efforts and impair his usefulness," Gray desires a restoration of his "status as a loyal citizen." [Gray was pardoned November 1, 1865, thanks to the personal and direct intervention of Johnson on that date.]

From H. B. Sherman

July 4, 1865, Titusville, Pa.; ALS, DLC-JP.

An advocate "since 1833 in behalf of the slave and his rights" begs the President to read an enclosed article by a black man, T. A. White of Brockport, Pa., on suffrage and "the true policy of our Government." Sherman and "thousands" with whom he has been acting are "exceedingly pained" by what they see in the papers regarding the black in the chief executive's reconstruction plan. They are "mortified" to hear that the "very men" they had been urging the black man to fight "have all the rights of American Citizens, while he who *saved* his Country is deprived of them—and left at the mercy of these traitors." Friends of the black man will "fight on until this relic of barbarism is completely eradicated," and Johnson is beseeched "to see that justice is done to this poor degraded Class."

From William W. Boyce

Winnsboro So: Ca July 5th 1865

His Excellency Andrew Johnson
My Dear Sir

Since I wrote you[1] public meetings have been held in Abbeville and Newberry Districts, and in Pickens District and at two places in the low country[2] expressing the desire of the people for the establishment of civil government. The fact of the rail roads and mail communications being broken up render it very difficult to communicate with distant parts of the State, and get up concerted action. I am more and more confirmed in the opinion that the great majority of the people desire the establishment of civil government and are prepared in good faith to cooperate in restoring the State to its rightful relations to the Federal Government.

Any thing like an outbreak or a renewal of the war is considered nothing less than madness. There is a great scarcity of money, and a very large number of persons who were well off before the war are very poor now.

I had a long interview with Ex Speaker James L. Orr. He talks like Governor Brown of Georgia, did in Washington.[3] He acquiesces completely in the emancipation policy, and is willing to carry it out to logical consequences. He is fully alive to the importance of amending the State constitution so as to abolish the Parish system of representation, and to get rid entirely of all the aristocratic elements of our State Government. I consider him capable of being used by you to carry out your ideas of policy to more advantage than any other man in the State. I am certain his intentions are all that you would desire. In accomplishing the changes desired in the State Government, it is important to use men from the up-country. Charleston is low country. I inclose you an abstract of a speech I made in a public meeting.[4] You will see from it I hope that I am moving in the right direction.

With sentiments of the greatest kindness [and] regard I remain

Sincerely Yours William W. Boyce

ALS, DLC-JP.
    1. See Letter from Boyce, June 23, 1865.
    2. For results of these meetings, see petitions from citizens in the Abbeville (June 21), Newberry and Pickens (July 3), and Edgefield (July 4) districts, Johnson Papers, LC.
    3. See Letter from Brown, May 20, 1865.
    4. Although the abstract has not been found, Johnson's clerk indicated on the cover sheet of Boyce's letter that the speech was the one given at Winnsboro. According to the local newspaper account, Boyce in his June 21 speech urged public support of the President's "conservative" reconstruction policies. *Winnsboro News*, July 4, 1865.

From William J. Demorest

July 5, 1865, New York, N.Y.; ALS, DLC-JP.

An abolitionist inquires whether, after a war to secure a republican form of government, the people were willing that the President "practically ignore the only just object of the war, and put us back where we were four years ago." Would it not be seen that Johnson "is surrendering to the rebels," who by "strategy" are doing what could not be accomplished by arms? Demorest accuses the Chief Executive of denying representation to "nearly half of our native-born and indisputably loyal citizens." By winning the war the opportunity to remedy this was secured, but the government "from choice, not necessity, pleads the wicked prejudices of the former rebels" and adheres to Judge Taney's philosophy: "Black men have no rights that white men are bound to respect." The New Yorker warns that if this policy is continued, "it will prove that we as a nation are capable of a blind and wicked reversion of our fundamental laws." Noting that the attorney general had recently "decided that all native-born persons are citizens," he observes that the government does not act "in accordance with this decision." Demorest insists that the national policy must be to give "absolute justice to all" and queries, "Cannot the President be made to see this?"

From John W. Forney

Philadelphia July 5, 1865.

My dear Sir—

I write you to Say as your devoted friend, having no personal object to Serve, that the disregard of the United voice of the Union members of Congress from this city,[1] in the matter of the Post office would be most unfortunate for the interests of the common cause. My own wishes on this subject are before you.[2] I have now been at home for several days, and Speak with a full knowledge of public opinion. Nothing but a desire to protect you from the influence of wrong counsels and to save you from the complaints of good men has induced this letter.

Yours Truly J. W. Forney

To the President

ALS, DLC-JP.

1. Philadelphia's three Republican congressmen—Charles O'Neill, Leonard Myers, and William D. Kelley—and the lone Democrat who had supported the war and served in the Union army—Samuel J. Randall. *BDAC*.

2. Presumably Forney, while in Washington, had verbally conveyed his advocacy of a "Mr. Brown," a Union Democrat, for postmaster. See Forney to Johnson, July 1, 17, 29, 1865, Johnson Papers, LC.

From Charles F.M. Garnett[1]

Richmond July 5th 1865

His Excellency Andrew Johnson
President &c

As my near relation Mr R. M. T. Hunter[2] is under arrest and is therefore unable to take any active steps to secure a release, I have ventured to bring his case to your notice. He is too well known to need any argument in his favor. I hope his uniform moderation, his long & arduous services, & ardent zeal for the good of the whole Union, while a member of the United States Congress, and his general character as an honorable gentleman will be remembered in his favor.

I am authorised to say that he is ready & desirous to use all the influence he possesses in favor of order & submission to the Laws & the Constitution of the United States.

His family are sadly in need of his presence at home & his wife particularly has suffered greatly in health from anxiety. I will mention that there are on his farm ninety people of color who were formerly his servants. Only 25 of these are capable of performing any labor at all—so that there are 65 absolute Paupers. Mr Hunter has been making every effort to take care of these helpless people & will do so as long as he is able. But his captivity must greatly impair his ability to carry out his intentions in this matter.

I would respectfully ask that, if he cannot be fully released, he shall be parolled to report from time to time, at the nearest Military Post.

Very respectfully Your ob. Servt

Chas. F. M. Garnett

ALS, DNA-RG94, Amnesty Papers (M1003, Roll 63), Va., R.M.T. Hunter.

1. Garnett (1810–1886), Hunter's cousin, had been chief engineer of the East Tennessee and Virginia line and, more recently, Confederate commissioner, with the rank of colonel, for collecting railroad iron. William G. Chisolm, "The Garnetts of Essex County and Their Homes," *VMHB*, 42 (1934): 175; 1850 Census, Va., Campbell, Lynchburg, 240; *OR*, Ser. 1, Vol. 30, Pt. 4: 496.

2. See Letter from Robert M.T. Hunter, June 22, 1865.

From John T. Harris

Washington July 5' 1865.

His Exy. Andrew Johnson Prest. U.S.

Dear Sir:

I have heard a report that an effort is being made to supercede Gov. Pierpoint of Va. by the appt. of a Military Govr. If such is the case, I beg to assure you that the course of Gov. Pierpoint, gives great satisfaction to *almost evry loyal* man in the state, to say nothing of others. He is progressing admirably with the inauguration of civil law & we most earnestly hope that we may not again be thrown into chaos by his removal. His course meets the hearty approval of the friends of the Administration and in a few weeks, we shall have the old State righted again and evry thing moving on in unison and harmony with the Federal Govt.

With the best wishes for your speedy recovery

I am Truly Yours

John T. Harris.

ALS, DLC-JP.

From Joseph Holt

July 5, 1865, Washington, D.C.; ALS, DNA-RG153, Court-Martial Records, MM-2251.

The judge advocate general officially reports the conclusions of the military commission which, between May 9 and June 29, tried the Lincoln conspirators. Those found guilty of the main charge—conspiring to kill the President, vice president, secretary of state, and lieutenant general of the army—were sentenced as follows: David E. Herold, George A. Atzerodt, Lewis Payne [Powell], and Mary E. Surratt, death; and Michael O'Laughlin, Samuel Arnold, and Samuel A. Mudd, life imprisonment. Edward Spangler, found not guilty of the main charge, but guilty of aiding the escape of J. Wilkes Booth after the murder of Lincoln, received six years' imprisonment. Holt deems it "unnecessary" to discuss the "immense mass of evidence" from a trial where hundreds of witnesses were examined and the rights of the accused were guarded by "able counsel." He does not review the record because assistant judge advocate Henry H. Bingham's examination of the questions of law in the case was "part of the record." The "proceedings were regular," the findings "fully justified by the evidence," and the sentences should be executed.

From Hugh Kennedy

July 5, 1865, New Orleans, La.; ALS, DLC-JP.

Recently resuming his position as New Orleans mayor following receipt of Johnson's pardon, Kennedy reports that during his absence his economic plans had been frustrated, contracts annulled, and city expenditures increased by $200,000 a year. The treasury is "absolutely bankrupt," and outlays to keep the "municipal machinery" afloat are supplied by "issuing shin plasters, based upon the faith of the City," of which $2,700,000 are extant. Complicating this, the plates from which the first $1,200,000 were made are lost. The amnesty oath was monopolized by the clerk of the federal district court and U.S. commissioners, who respectively charged $2.10 and $3.00 to each person, which in effect excluded the poor. Consequently, Kennedy as mayor performs the duty free of charge, and now about two hundred people a day "avail themselves." Each day he talks with "every description of men" and the sentiment is a "sincere regret for the past" and an "earnest desire to make amends." Many are now registering to vote who have been politically inactive "for eight or ten years past." Explanations of the President's "kind feelings" for the state and promises of aid reassure the people. Fears, expressed while he was in Washington, about opposition to state authority being fostered "under federal auspices" are now confirmed, with "the Customhouse taking the lead." Louisiana will support the administration as much as Tennessee, and will "exercise an immense influence over public opinion throughout the entire South & upper Mississippi Valley." Governor Wells is rapidly proceeding in "parochial and district organization." A "great outcry" will be made about his appointments, but "disinterested persons" observe that "in the main" the appointments are satisfactory. Both governor and mayor support the President and request directions for their "official guidance."

From Isaac Murphy

Executive office Little Rock Ark
July 5th 1865

Andrew Johnson pres. U.S

I most respectfully ask your Excellency, that all the recommendations given by me for the pardon of Traitors since the date of your Amnesty proclamation be considered as entirely withdrawen as events have occurred here in connection with the celebration of the 4th,[1] that have fully proved, that I have acted prematurely and done wrong, in recommending those men as proper subjects for the exercise of the pardoning power. I further ask, that for the present, no pardon be issued to any one in the excepted classes, belonging to this State. Give them time to show that they are disposed to be loyal hereafter.

with high respect, your Excellencys obt ser &c
Isaac Murphy
Gov Ark

Please cause the receipt of this to be acknowledged.

ALS, DNA-RG94, Amnesty Papers (M1003, Roll 14), Ark., Misc.

1. It is unclear which "events" had upset Murphy. The local paper described the Fourth of July celebration—where citizens, Union and ex-Confederate soldiers, the Hook and Ladder Company, and Masons participated—as one with "an enthusiastic and becoming character," which "passed off as quietly as heart could wish," without "the least disturbance." *Arkansas State Gazette* (Little Rock), July 8, 1865.

Order re *Lincoln Assassins*

Executive Mansion
July 5th 1865.

The foregoing sentences in the cases of David E. Herold, G. A. Atzerodt, Lewis Payne, Michael O'Laughlin, Edward Spangler, Samuel Arnold, Mary E. Surratt, and Samuel A Mudd are hereby approved,[1] and it is ordered that the sentences in the cases of David E. Herold, G. A. Atzerodt, Lewis Payne, and Mary E. Surratt be carried into execution by the proper military authority under the direction of the Secretary of war, on the seventh day of July 1865, between the hours of ten o clock A.M & two oclock P.M of that day. It is further ordered that the prisoners Samuel Arnold, Samuel A. Mudd, Edward Spangler and Michael O'Laughlin, be confined at hard labor in the Penitentiary at Albany, New York, during the period designated in their respective sentences.[2]

Andrew Johnson
Prest.

DS, DNA-RG153, Court-Martial Records, MM-2251.

1. Herold (c1842–1865), a Washington, D.C., druggist clerk; George A. Atzerodt (c1832–1865), a Port Tobacco, Md., carriage maker; Lewis T. Powell, alias Payne or Paine (1845–1865), a Florida resident and former Confederate soldier, who attempted to assassinate Secretary of State Seward; O'Laughlin (d. 1867), a former Confederate soldier from Baltimore and Washington, D.C., feed salesman; Spangler, originally from Baltimore, was a stage hand at Ford's Theater in Washington, D.C.; Samuel B. Arnold (c1834–1906), another Baltimore County, Md., resident and former Confederate soldier, was recently a clerk in a sutler's store near Fortress Monroe; Surratt (1823–1865), widowed in 1862, moved to Washington, D.C., where she operated a boarding house; Mudd (1833–1883) was the Maryland doctor who set John Wilkes Booth's leg. Benn Pitman, comp., *The Assassination of President Lincoln and the Trial of the Conspirators* (New York, 1865), 96, 102–4, 222, 231–32, 236, 240; Jerry H. Maxwell, "The Bizarre Case of Lewis Paine," *Lin Her*, 81 (1979): 224–27; *Montgomery Advertiser*, Nov. 22, 1865; *DAB*; *New York Times*, Sept. 22, 1906; Joseph George, Jr., "A True Child of Sorrow: Two Letters of Mary E. Surratt," *MdHM*, 80 (1986): 402–5; Leech, *Reveille in Washington*, 362–63, 407, 450.

2. On July 15, 1865, Johnson changed their place of confinement to the military prison at Dry Tortugas, Fla. Richardson, *Messages*, 6: 348.

From Campbell Wallace[1]

Athens Ga July 5th 1865.

Dear Sir

I have prepared my petition for pardon. The Officer in command at this Post[2] says he is not authorsed at present to administer the requsite oath in such cases, but will be in a few days as he has written for instructions. When that is done I will send forward my papers to the Honl. Secy. state for your consideration.[3] This application I would present in person but I have not the funds to pay expenses and must therefore beg you to allow me, in this way, to tresspass on your allready overtasked time.

I have been a zealous rebel during the war from an honest conviction that it was my duty, but I have never indulged in personalities or a persecuting spirit. Time and experience has sattisfied me the doctrine of "the right of a state to secede from the Union" is not only a fallacy but an unmittigated evil and moreover I firmly beleive *that even if the South had succeeded in the conflict, the confederated states would not have held together ninety days.* Under these convictions I sought the earliest opportunity to take the oath of amnesty and the day an office was opened here I availed myself and subscibed to that of the 8th Dec 1863, yours of the 29th may not having then been promulgated. Since the tender of your amnesty many are of the opinion that it is requsite to subscibe to that also in order to a full pardon and a restoration to citizenship. There is one clause only in that of the 29th May that causes any hesitation on my part. I do not know whether I have taxable property to the amount of Twenty Thousand dollars or not. I have not land worth that much. I have or had, when I left Tennessee some Two Hundred shares Rail Road stock, (exempt by charter from Taxation). If this stock and land are both taxable I would be excluded by the 13th clause as they are worth more money. Under these circumstances I submit my case to your clemency, promising to make as good a citizen in the future as I hope you held me to be before the war.

In justice to myself I must say that the charges I hear have been made against me from time to time, in a certain paper in Tennessee, are without the shadow of foundation.[4] I have had nothing to do with either the arrest, imprisonment or hanging of men and have all the time to the extent of my ability discountenaned and discouraged guerrillas and their raids in East Ten, contending that no greater curse could be inflicted on the people of that section of both parties and I can give you multitudes of instances in which I exerted my influence for the release of union men.

On the subject of arrests allow me to mention one case, as that will shew the principle on which I acted all the time. In May 1862 The Provost Marshall at Knoville[5] enclosed to me and requested my opinion on an anonymous letter he had recd. giving information about an attack to be made on Rail Road Bridges and charging Judge Patterson[6] with being the instigator and advising and requesting his arrest &c. I reinclosed the anonymous letter with the following ansser.

Knoville May 5 1862

Dear Col

If the men now guarding our bridges are watchfull they are all sufficient to protect us against incendiaries or any neighborhood clubs, but of course not enough to resist an organised enemy. In case of the approach of regular troops he would allways have notice in time to reinforce, if he had the men to reinforce with.

The "*anonymous*" is evidently from Greenville and should have attention so far as to increased vigilence at the bridges. No doubt one part of the plan of attack on E. Ten will be to cut off re-inforcements by burning bridges. *As to arrests being made on such letters. It ought not to be done. A man who is not willing to face charges he makes against his fellow man, ought not to have the power of depriving his fellow of his liberty.*

It would be well for you to have the "Register" state by *authority* that the Prvost Marshall gives no heed to anonymous letters or verbal charges against disloyal parties. It would stop many petty anoyances and moreover give confidence in your determination to do right.

Truly yours Campbell Wallace

Col Wm. M. Churchwell
Pro. M. Knoville.
P.S. The letter is written either by an Editor or some one in the habit of writing for the press.

C. W

You will bear with me while I allude to one other matter. I do not mention these things supposing they will have any bearing on the case, but I am anxious not only to have the opportunity of doing right as a good citizen but of meriting the confidence of old friends and renewing old friendships. The sins for which I am now to atone were committed *before* the war and no one understands this, in my case, better than yourself. But to the other matter mentioned—I have been charged with trying to instigate a mob against you at Lynchburg in the Spring of 1861. The facts are that Sam Tate[7] and myself returning from the North were by accident detained 12 hours at Lynchburg. There was an excitement there about some dispatch you had sent to Tennessee.[8] At my instance Tate went with me to see some of the staid men of the city and remonstrate against such an outrage and proceeding as we understood was threatened if you passed that way home. We did remonstrate and found the good citizens as much opposed to such a procedure as we were. This being the fact you will readily immagine how much surprised and mortified I was when told that you gave full credit to the charge. I presume however now that you possibly may never have heard of it as I have found within the last 30 days many things *untrue* that I have not doubted for the last 3 or 4 years.

I have now been living in this state for two years and expect to make it my home. (Alltho I would rather live in East Tennessee than any place in this world.) I have made many acquaintans and know a good deal of public sentiment and I am sure there will be no difficulty in reorganising a state Goverment with such a constitution as you have indicated. The large mass of the citizens have given up slavery as dead and are quietly and in good faith adapting themselvs to the new condition of things. The great desire now is to be saved from Negro Suffrage and you would be amused to hear the multitude of questions asked me (being a Tennessean) with regard to yourself. I tell them that when the policy of the Goverment on slavry is once cheerfully acquiesd in all our troubles will be at an end and that the South will be perfectly sattisfied with your administration and that the Radicals Can never move you from your position on the question of Suffrage.

Truly & Respectfully Yours
Campbell Wallace

To His Excellency Andrew Johnson
President United States of America

ALS, DNA-RG94, Amnesty Papers (M1003, Roll 24), Ga., Campbell Wallace.
    1. President of the East Tennessee and Georgia Railroad.
    2. Either Captain Alfred B. Cree, 22nd Iowa Inf., appointed provost marshal and commandant of Athens May 29, 1865, or James Mack (1842–1892), a native New York City stonecutter and 1st lieutenant, 156th N.Y. Inf., who held the same job by mid-July. *Athens Southern Watchman*, June 14, 1865; Amnesty Papers (M1003, Rolls 23, 24), Ga., Samuel P. Thurmond and Campbell Wallace, RG94, NA; CSR, RG94, NA; Pension File, Jane C. Mack, RG15, NA.
    3. Wallace prepared his formal petition, to accompany his oath, on July 10. His pardon was issued on October 2, 1865, but he did not receive it. He therefore applied again under the 13th exception and was pardoned a second time May 12, 1866. Amnesty Papers (M1003, Roll 24), Ga., Campbell Wallace, RG94, NA.
    4. Wallace had written to Brownlow on May 10, 1865, proposing that he turn over to the governor, as the "proper representative of the State of Tennessee," all the property of the East Tennessee and Georgia Railroad at Knoxville or at Social Circle, Ga., where it was located. Brownlow's response, published along with Wallace's query in the *Knoxville Whig and Rebel Ventilator* on May 31, 1865, agreed to the transfer, but added that Wallace's "high crimes" could not be expiated by the "return of a few old passenger cars and trucks, and a few new ones thrown in." He furthermore warned Wallace not to return to Knoxville, because those persons who had been imprisoned and the sons of men who had been executed in response to his directives were waiting for him there; "and they will make your home anything but a 'social circle' for you." In his *Sketches of the Rise, Progress, and Decline of Secession* (Philadelphia, 1862), 256–58, Brownlow had also implicated Wallace in the lynching of unionists.
    5. William M. Churchwell.
    6. David T. Patterson.
    7. Prewar president of the Memphis and Charleston Railroad.
    8. Johnson's "infamous and traitorous telegraph" to a person or party in Tennessee had been stopped on or about April 19, 1861. *Nashville Patriot*, Apr. 20, 1861.

From J. Madison Wells

State of Louisiana, Executive Department,
New Orleans, July 5th 1865.

To Andrew Johnson
President of the United States.

    You are I doubt not Mr President fully aware of the terrible losses of property and the wide spread destitution and wretchedness caused in Louisiana by the breaks in the Levees and the consequent inundation of an immense Extent of the most productive and Valuable lands in the State.[1] The loss of every vestige of crops and the destruction of cattle leaves a large and industrious population wholly dependent on precarious relief for existence; while pestilence on the other hand on the subsidence of the waters menaces such as may be compelled to encounter the Malaria emenating from the decayed matter left by the flood. Local efforts will even in our present exhausted State, it is to be hoped relieve, if not fully, measurably so, the deficiency of food; but the pecuniary means indispensable to put the Levees in proper repair are utterly beyond the State government to procure and furnish. Many of the breaches too were produced by the military in pursuance of orders for defensive or aggressive purposes; therefore I am Sure Mr President there is nothing unreasonable in my making an appeal to the government to aid us in the reparation to such an extent as justice and the great exigencies and the urgency of the case require.

At a later period, I intend to place this matter more fully before the Government, for to my mind nothing is more dearly established than the necessity for the national government's taking this whole matter of Levees and the Levee System under its supervision and Control exclusively.[2] If left to the States individually as heretofore there will be neither security or promptitude and experience has demonstrated how ineffectual the safeguards proved when local bodies were charged with this great riparian duty.

The immediate urgency of repairing the Levees is the fact that unless done before winter, no crops Can be made next year more than this and then a very great outlay of money will be required by the Cultivators of the Soil to fit the land for tillage, to say nothing of the fences and buildings.

Submitting this matter for the kind consideration of government.[3]

I have the honor to subscribe Mr President

Your obt Servant, J Madison Wells

Governor of Louisiana

LS, DLC-JP.

1. Previous to the war, flooding had been controlled by levees kept in repair by abutting owners. During the conflict, however, many plantations were abandoned and levee repair virtually stopped. Although severe spring floods in 1862 and 1865 created the most damage, levees were also destroyed in military operations, most notably when General Grant's forces cut the levee at Lake Providence in 1863. At war's end it was estimated that repairs in the Mississippi Delta alone would cost over half a million dollars. Robert W. Harrison, *Alluvial Empire* (Little Rock, Ark., 1961), 96–97; Taylor, *La. Reconstructed*, 319; *Senate Ex. Docs.*, 40 Cong., 1 Sess., No. 8, p. 12 (Ser. 1308); *Senate Reports*, 40 Cong., 1 Sess., No. 2, p. 3 (Ser. 1309).

2. In 1866 the state took over the burden, when repeated requests for federal aid were denied. Sixteen years later the latter government finally became involved in flood control assistance. Walter Pritchard, "The Effects of the Civil War on the Louisiana Sugar Industry," *JSH*, 5 (1939): 329–30; Harrison, *Alluvial Empire*, 87, 96.

3. The record fails to reveal any Johnson response.

From James A. McDougall[1]

[Washington, D.C., July 6, 1865][2]

Mr. Pres:

You do not design to permit Mrs. Surratt to die by the cord.

I think & trust not. I do not know any of her kin or friends. With me what I say I think is for the common good of all and will be in all respects consistent with opinions conclusions & judgments—common (I think) to yourself & myself.

Extend to her *your grace*. I presume you have done it. If you have not, then do it. It will be a noble christian act—whatever the sin.[3]

Yours now in kindness
J. A. McDougall

ALS, DLC-JP.

1. California senator.

2. The date "July 6 or 7?" was added later, possibly by someone on the Library of Congress staff. The letter could have been written anytime between June 30, the day the trial of the conspirators ended, and July 7, the date of execution. The letter must have been written in Washington, perhaps even at the White House, as a number of people, McDougall among them, sought to intercede for Mrs. Surratt on the last two days of her life. It would not have been unusual for McDougall to have remained in Washington; some congressmen and senators probably anticipated an extra session. Turner, *Beware the People*, 172; Letter from Thaddeus Stevens, May 16, 1865.

3. Johnson received other appeals on behalf of the conspirators, including one from Congressman Charles Mason, enclosing an affidavit of John P. Brophy repudiating much of the testimony of one witness. Mason to Johnson, July 7, 1865, Johnson Papers, LC.

From Humphrey Marshall

July 6, 1865, Waxahatchie, Tex.; ALS, NHi-Andrew Johnson Papers.

Confederate brigadier general and congressman inquires whether it is safe for him to return to his family, or to bring them to Texas and live under Federal jurisdiction. Not wishing to leave the country, he would do so rather "than yield a great principle." Never a secessionist, he "remained quietly" at his son's farm in Kentucky, until Gen. Robert Anderson suppressed a newspaper and arrested former governor Charles Morehead. This he "So opposed" that he "was willing to offer armed resistance," but always "inside" the state and Federal governments. Even though he had not aided the Confederate government and "neither in sentiment nor act" desired separation, he left Kentucky in September 1861 to "avoid an undeserved arrest." He took service with the Confederacy "as a means . . . of *reaching Kentucky*" and as a way through which he hoped the people would resist the U.S. invasion of "the slaveholding States and . . . the principle of *coercion*." Resigning in May 1863, he practiced law in Richmond and nearly a year later was elected to Congress by Kentuckians who, under "Confederate regulations and laws, had the right to vote." Wishing "to be answered Explicitly and at once," Marshall is "perfectly willing" to take the oath and be a peaceful citizen if he can remain in the U.S. "by doing so free from arrest." If so, he will probably live in Texas. If not, he wants a "pass port and Safeguard" for himself and family "to seek an assylum in some foreign land." [Marshall was not pardoned until October 1, 1866.]

From Thomas A.R. Nelson

Knoxville Tenn. 6 July 1865.

His Excellency Andrew Johnson
President of the United States
Sir.

I herewith enclose the Petition of A. G. Mason[1] of Jonesboro for Pardon, which I, as his counsel, advised him to present, in view of the fact that there are more than a thousand presentments in the Federal Court here for treason, and rendering aid and comfort, and that it is not probable his case will be tried in five years.

Mr. Mason is personally known to you as a respectable and industrious mechanic and you personally know his *endorsers* to be men of good character.[2]

Very respectfully, Thos. A. R. Nelson

ALS, DNA-RG94, Amnesty Papers (M1003, Roll 50), Tenn., A. G. Mason.

1. Archibald G. Mason (1813–1895) of Jonesboro, a blacksmith and constable, served briefly as Confederate assessor and in a home guard company. Penning his application on June 28, he was pardoned on September 22, 1865. Bennett and Rae, *Washington County*, 2: 4; 1860 Census, Tenn., Washington, Jonesboro Dist., 148; Amnesty Papers (M1003, Roll 50), Tenn., A. G. Mason, RG94, NA; CSR, RG109, NA.

2. Among the 13 signatories who endorsed Mason's pardon application were Seth J.W. Lucky and Samuel B. Cunningham. See Mason to Johnson, June 28, 1865, Amnesty Papers (M1003, Roll 50), Tenn., A. G. Mason, RG94, NA.

From B. R. Peart[1]

Clarksville Tennessee July 6th 1865

Andrew Johnson President of U.S
Dear Sir

Accept my Harty Greeting, then purmit me to call your attention to the fact that many of the Rebels have Returned home, who were residents in this County, Some of whom have (as I am informed) made application to you for a Special-Pardon. My purpose in addressing this note to you is to call your attention to the fact that the Political Status of this portion of Tennessee is not yet well or purmanently Established. Hence the great necessity of Caution in granting Pardons to any of the Leaders in this Portion of the State. I would direct your mind Particularly to the following cases in this County viz D. N. Kenedy,[2] one who assisted in the getting up of the first Secession meeting that ever was held in this County. He was Elected a member of the Rebel Legislature in August 1861. Traveled about with I G Harris & Co. until since the Surrender of Lee. Another Was John F House[3] who was a member of the Provissional Congress at Richmond in 1861. He allso has been South too until after Lee's surrender. House was in the Rebel Army with Gen. Hood and fought at or near Franklin Ten. James E Bailey is another who went quite early in to the Rebellion Was one of the State Military Board, in 1861. In November of the Same year he Raised a Co. then with others formed a Regt. & Was made its Col. He has verry lately came here to his Home. Yet another is Gen Wm. A Quarles. He was early in this Rebellion was Colonel of the 42d Reb Regt. He is now on parole. In my judgment the interest of the Union Cause would be better secured by letting Such Men Remain for the present as they now stand. It Seemes to me that to pardon such as they, at this time would be throwing another stumbling Block in the Road of Loyal Union men which would be hard to remove or overcome.[4]

I hope you will pardon me for the liberty thus taken.

My only apology is that I do it for my Countrys Good.

I Remain Truly your Friend B R Peart

ALS, DLC-JP.

1. A Montgomery County unionist and state senator (1865–66).

2. In 1843 David N. Kennedy (1820–1904) moved to Clarksville, where he was a businessman. During the Civil War he served in the Confederate Treasury Department. *BDTA*, 2: 490–92.

3. House (1827–1904), a Montgomery County lawyer, had served in the legislature as a Whig and had supported John Bell in the 1860 election. After the Civil War he served in Congress (1875–83). Ibid, 1: 379; *BDAC*.

4. There is no direct evidence of Johnson's response to this letter. Kennedy was already pardoned (June 29), but House and Quarles were not pardoned until December 27, 1866. Bailey's pardon has not been found. *House Ex. Docs.*, 39 Cong., 2 Sess., No. 116, pp. 42, 43 (Ser. 1293); Amnesty Papers (M1003, Roll 50), Tenn., William A. Quarles, RG94, NA.

From James M. Rutland

July 6, 1865, Longtown, S.C.; ALS, DLC-JP.

Native South Carolina lawyer and unionist who escaped hanging by three mobs reports various personal and state problems. Understanding that the President intends to appoint a provisional governor, withdraw the army, and reestablish civil law, Rutland thinks a majority of South Carolinians "are not ripe for such a measure." He has observed that "there is a strong under current of feeling" against the United States; though people "are taking the oath of allegiance freely," they "look upon it as a sort of necessity, and do not love the Union any the more." Recent public meetings proclaiming allegiance to the United States are "illusory" because the people see that as a way "to get rid of what they call a military despotism." Without military courts, "many criminals will go unwhipt of justice" because "*secession*" juries "convict with reluctance" those who murdered Union prisoners and stole U.S. property acquired by the surrender of Confederate armies. Many freedmen, "intoxicated by the idea of freedom," caring little "for their former owners or the white race," and "disposed to . . . become insolent and disorderly," require the presence of troops "at least until after the first of January next." "The mortification of defeat" and "immense loss of property" have left South Carolinians prone to "excessive legislation," and thus not "capable of judiciously governing ourselves." "A little delay" in appointing a provisional governor "will be of service to South Carolina."

From Thaddeus Stevens

St. Lawrence Hotel, Chestnut St. above Tenth,
Philadelphia, July 6, 1865

His Excellency Andrew Johnson
Sir

I am sure you will pardon me for speaking to you with a candor to which men in high places are seldom accustomed. Among all the leading Union men of the North with whom I have had intercourse I do not find one who approves of your policy. They believe that "restoration" as announced by you will destroy our party (which is of but little consequence) and will greatly injure the country. Can you not hold your hand and wait the action of Congress and in the mean time govern them by military rulers?[1] Profuse pardoning also will greatly embarrass Congress if they should wish to make the enemy pay the expenses of the war or a part of it.

With great respect yr obt svt
Thaddeus Stevens

The Prest.

ALS, DLC-JP.

1. By June 30 Johnson had appointed provisional governors and set the guidelines for restoration in six Confederate states not partially reestablished with wartime Union governments. In mid-July he made similar arrangements for Florida.

From Ten New York City Marine Insurance Companies

July 6, 1865, New York, N.Y.; LS, DLC-JP.

They concur in the request of Florida citizens that District Judge William Marvin be named provisional governor, averring that: "his personal influence and efforts were of great value in retaining Key West in the possession of the United States Government at the breaking out of the rebellion; and that his long residence in the South, his high character, his cautious and prudent temperament, united with his great legal learning and acquirements, together with his popular and pleasing manners, render him eminently suitable and worthy of the appointment."

From Jesse G. Wallace

Knoxville, Tenne. July 6 1865

His Excellency Andrew Johnson,
President U.S.

The undersigned in the year 1863, in part at the solicitation of Union men of E Tenne. accepted the appointment of District attorney for said

District under the late rebel government. My predecessor, J. C. Ramsey[1] had given universal dessatisfaction by his course towards the Union men of the country, and they & moderate minded southern men were anxious that he should be displaced & succeeded by some one who would not persecute or mistreat them. It was under these circumstances I agreed to accept of the position. And the ferst act I did after being inducted into office was to dismiss every indictment on the docket against Union men. I never during the whole of my official career brought the ferst single indictment against a Union man for any political offence and I never had any thing to do with the execution of the Confederate Confiscation Law or received a cent in way of fees or commissions from that fund. I appeared in only two indictments against Union men, one in case of R. R. Butler,[2] which I dismissed & the other in case of Judge Lucky[3] which I attempted to dismiss but was not permitted by the court, whereupon I retired from the case & refused any further to prosecute it.

I do not dispute the fact that I was an open & avowed rebel, but I never did any thing towards persecuting, annoying or mistreating Union men. On the contrary my course was mild & conciliatory—Insomuch that I became unpopular & lost influence with the rebel authorities. I have hailed with gratifycation the termination of our political troubles, and am anxious to do all I can as a loyal citizen of the U.S. to promote the integrity & common interest of the country. I am within the excepted classes, and make this application to be permitted to avail myself of the benefit of your Excellency's amnesty proclamation, if your Excellency considers me entitled to it. If your Excellency will be pleased to grant the special pardon herein prayed,[4] will you please direct it to this place care of F. S. Hieskell.[5]

Very Respectfully Yr Obt Servant,
Jesse G. Wallace

ALS, DNA-RG94, Amnesty Papers (M1003, Roll 51), Tenn., Jesse G. Wallace.
    1. John Crozier Ramsey.
    2. Roderick R. Butler.
    3. Seth J. W. Lucky, chancellor of the eastern judicial circuit.
    4. Although included in the President's list of pardons sent to Congress on November 13, 1865, Wallace received word that his original application had been lost. Reapplying through the governor's office on November 17, 1865, he was still without pardon in hand two years later, when he wrote Johnson that his first application had been lost and that he had heard nothing from the second. Wallace to A. J. Fletcher, Nov. 17, 1865; Wallace to Johnson, undated and Sept. 12, 1867, Amnesty Papers (M1003, Roll 51), Tenn., Jesse G. Wallace, RG94, NA.
    5. Frederick S. Heiskell (1786–1882), founder of the *Knoxville Register*, was an antebellum state senator. *BDTA*, 1: 353–54.

To Winfield Scott Hancock

Executive Office, July 7, 1865.—
10 o'clock AM.

To Major Genl W. S. Hancock,
Commanding, &c.

I, Andrew Johnson, President of the United States, do hereby declare that the writ of Habeas Corpus has been heretofore suspended in such cases as this, and I do hereby especially suspend this writ, and direct that you proceed to execute the order heretofore given upon the judgment of the Military Commission, and you will give this order in return to this writ.[1]

Andrew Johnson
Prest

DS, CSmH-Misc. 1986.

1. Seven hours earlier, on the petition of the defense counsel, Supreme Court Justice Andrew Wylie had ordered Mrs. Surratt to appear before the Criminal Court of the District of Columbia at 10:00 that morning. The writ, delivered at 8:30 to General Hancock, who had charge of the prisoners, was forwarded through the secretary of war and the attorney general to the President. Joseph Holt Papers, LC; *Cincinnati Gazette*, July 8, 1865; Turner, *Beware the People*, 172.

From Mrs. J. Richards Nicklin

July 7, 1865, Richmond, Va.; ALS, DNA-RG56, Appts., Customs Service, Sub-Officer, J. R. Nicklin.

The wife of an unemployed and impoverished Virginian who had allegedly saved Johnson's life as he passed through Lynchburg in 1861, by placing himself between the vice president and his assailants and by throwing "aside the weapon, that was aimed for your destruction," seeks a government post for her husband. [Marked "*for special consideration*," the request was forwarded by Johnson's office to the secretary of the treasury. Nicklin, however, received no appointment.]

From James L. Scudder

July 7, 1865, Shelbyville, Tenn.; ALS, DLC-JP.

Reports on conditions in Tennessee, assuring the President that the "disposition of the people to acquiesce in the state of things and return to their allegience and restore the Government . . . is manifest every where." He, an old Democrat, approves Johnson's policy "as developed by your North Carolina proclamation." Believes the great masses in Tennessee "will before long, most heartily give you and your administration their support," as "all say, that if they had taken your advice, enunciated in your speech in the Senate . . . *denouncing rebellion* and *disunion*, they would not have been in their present situation."

From Charles Albright

July 8, 1865, Tamauga, Pa.; ALS, DNA-RG56, Appts., Customs Service, Naval Officer, Philadelphia, Charles Albright.

A brigadier, lawyer, and former bank president seeks position as naval officer or surveyor of the Port of Philadelphia, citing as credentials that he was "one of the pioneers to Kansas" in the 1850s, a delegate to the Republican convention in 1860, and has served in the army since 1861. Complains of the lack of federal patronage in his district (11th Pa.) "the most disloyal . . . in the entire North," where it is "up hill work to be a Union man." [Albright did not receive an appointment.]

From Kedar Bryan

July 8, 1865, Duplin Co., N.C.; ALS, DNA-RG94, Amnesty Papers (M1003, Roll 37), N.C., Kedar Bryan.

Believing, like most citizens of his section, that the Constitution sanctioned states' rights doctrines, Bryan accepted secession and "felt bound" by the ordinance passed by the state convention of May 20, 1861. As a former Confederate county tax assessor, he is "satisfied" of the failure of secession "practically," and desires to "yield obedience" to United States authority, praying that a "full pardon" will be granted for his offence. [Bryan was issued a pardon on August 21, 1865.]

From Lydia Dickinson

July 8, 1865, New York, N.Y.; ALS, DLC-JP.

Writing on behalf of her husband, the wife of former U.S. Democratic senator Daniel S. Dickinson, "who has been severely ill with fever," she expresses his "high gratification and satisfaction . . . with regard to the conspiracy trials, and the final termination and executions." Thanking the President and the administration for the "course you have pursued," which "crushed, forever, treason at home and silenced despotic sympathy from abroad," she adds: "any yielding to sickly sentimentality, in such a crisis, would have occasioned irreparable injury, and degraded us before our own people and the nations of the earth."

From Enoch W. Eastman[1]

Eldora Hardin Co. Iowa July 8, 1865

Hon. And. Johnson Washington D.C.

Dear Sir.

We have this evening recd. the glad tidings that you have refused to commute the sentence or pardon the murderers of Mr. Lincoln & that they have been *hanged*.

I write to say that the great mass of the people in this part of Iowa has manifested a strong desire that you should do as you have & they will most heartily approve your acts in this case.

Allow me to further say that while the people of Iowa do not thirst for blood, they *do* hope that Jeff. Davis & every other member of congress who left his seat in congress to engage in the rebellion & accepted office in it and every officer in the Army & Navy of the U.S. who was educated at West Point & resigned his commission & took a commission in the rebel Army or navy; may each *& every one be hanged* and that you will permit every sentence which may be pronounced in either of their cases, to be executed as pronounced.

Feeling a deep anxiety for your personal health & prosperity and that your Administration may be as popular as that of your predecessor,

I am Very Respectfully Your Friend
E. W. Eastman
Leut. Gov. Iowa

This is written not for a reply but to *stay up your hands* in a holy cause.

ALS, DLC-JP.

1. Eastman (1810–1885), lawyer and Iowa resident since 1844, was a prominent Democrat who became a Republican over the slavery issue. Many years after the war he was a state legislator. L. F. Andrews, "Life Story of Governor Enoch Eastman," *Des Moines Register and Leader*, Apr. 17, 1910; Morton M. Rosenberg, *Iowa on the Eve of the Civil War* (Norman, Okla., 1972), 182.

From Charles C. Fulton [1]

Office of the American and Commercial Advertisers,
No. 128 Baltimore Street.
Baltimore, July 8, 1865

His Excellency Andrew Johnson
President of the U.S.
Sir.—

Mr. J. A. Cowarden,[2] late proprietor of the Richmond Despatch being an applicant for Executive Clemency, I take pleasure in testifying to the fact that during the year 1863, I appealed to Mr. Cowardin on the score of humanity and old personal friendship to aid me in having promptly delivered to our prisoners in Libby and on Belle Isle large quantities of provisions and money. He promptly responded to my appeal, and in all cases personally delivered my remittances, and forwarded me receipts from the parties to whom they were sent. Many of these prisoners afterwards spoke to me of the many acts of kindness extended to them by Mr. Cowardin.

The Dispatch, although it became, after the rebellion was inaugurated and enthusiastic upholder of the Richmond Government had previously been strictly a newspaper, the most prosperous in the State, having taken no part in "*firing the Southern heart.*"

I am satisfied that no man in Richmond done more for our prisoners than Mr. Cowardin.

Very respectfully, yours,
Charles C. Fulton

ALS, DNA-RG94, Amnesty Papers (M1003, Roll 58), Va., J. A. Cowardin
  1. Fulton (1816–1883), associated for three decades with the *Baltimore American*, was its sole proprietor from 1862 until his death. During the war he twice accompanied the Army of the Potomac, as well as the naval expedition against Charleston. *Men of Maryland and District of Columbia*, 23–24; Dawn F. Thomas, *The Green Spring Valley: Its History and Heritage* (2 vols., Baltimore, 1978), 1: 344.
  2. James A. Cowardin (1811–1882) worked in various capacities on several newspapers, most notably as partial owner of the "independent in politics" *Richmond Dispatch*, which at mid century he helped found. He was pardoned July 13, 1865. *NCAB*; Amnesty Papers (M1003, Roll 58), Va., J. A. Cowardin, RG94, NA.

From Quincy A. Gillmore[1]

Hilton Head S.C. 3 P.M. July 8, 1865.

His Excellency The President, U.S.

Mr Perry was regarded as an union man up to the secession of the State; was a member of the Legislature which called the Convention which passed the secession ordinance, but rather quietly opposed calling that Convention.

He took no active part for or against the United States during the first year of the war but accepted the position of Judge of the Confederate District Court vacated by McGrath[2] when the latter became Governor. I judge Mr Perry to be as good an union man as any citizen of South Carolina of equal ability and power, but his course during the war would not [stand] before a rigid test of loyalty. Rumors of his appointment as Provisional Governor have reached Charleston and give evident satisfaction to the more moderate of the former secessionists.

This information is furnished me by Genl _____[3] whom I sent to Charleston to obtain it.

Q. A. Gillmore Maj. Gen. Cmdg.

Tel (in cipher), DLC-JP.
  1. Gillmore (1825–1888), a West Point graduate who had won renown for his successful reductions of the harbor defenses at Savannah and Charleston, had been reinstated as commander of the Department of the South and breveted a major general near the end of the war. This wire is in response to Johnson's "confidential" inquiry "whether the course of Benjamin F. Perry . . . has been consistently for the Union as is represented to him." Warner, *Blue*; R. D. Mussey to Gillmore, July 2, 1865, Tels. Sent, President, Vol. 2 (1865), RG107, NA.
  2. Andrew G. Magrath (1813–1893), Charleston attorney, Federal and Confederate district court judge (1856–60, 1861–64), and governor (1864–65), had been impris-

oned in Fort Pulaski on May 28, where he remained until November 23, 1865. *DAB*.
   3. The original telegram omitted this general's name.

Interview with Richmond Merchants [1]

[July 8, 1865] [2]

The President reminded them that the amnesty proclamation did not cause this distrust; [3] it was the commission of treason and the violation of law that did it. The amnesty proclamation left these men just where they were before; it did not add any disability to them. If they had committed treason they were amenable to the confiscation law, which Congress had passed and which he, as President could not alter nor amend. In the amnesty proclamation he had offered pardon to some persons, but that did not injure any other persons. Would they like to have the amnesty proclamation removed altogether? Would they feel easier in that case?

One of the deputation—No; but it would assist us very much if you would extend the benefits of the proclamation to persons worth over twenty thousand dollars.

The President replied that in making that exception, he had acted on the natural supposition that men had aided the rebellion according to the extent of their pecuniary means. Did they not know this?

One of the deputation—No; I did not know it.

The President—Why, yes you do—you know perfectly well it was the wealthy men of the South who dragooned the people into secession. I lived in the South, and I know how the thing was done. Your State was overwhelmingly opposed to secession, but your rich men used the press and bullies, and your little army, to force the State into secession. Take the $20,000 clause: Suppose a man is worth more than that now the war is over, and the chances are ten to one that he made it out of the rebellion by contracts, &c. We might as well talk plainly about this matter. I don't think you are so anxious about relieving the poor. You want this clause removed so as to enable you to make money don't you? If you are very eager to help the poor why don't you take the surplus over the $20,000 you own and give it to them? In that way you will help them and bring yourselves within the benefits of the proclamation. I am free to say to you that I think some of you ought to be taxed on all over $20,000 to help the poor. When I was Military Governor of Tennessee I assessed such taxes on those who had been wealthy leaders of the rebellion and it had a good effect.

One of the deputation—It so happens that none of us were leaders. We staid out as long as we could, and were the last to go in.

The President—Frequently those who went in last were among the worst after they got in. But be that as it may, understand me gentlemen, I do not say this personally; I am just speaking of the general working of the matter. I know there has been an effort among some to persuade the people that the amnesty proclamation was injuring them by shutting up capital and keeping work from the poor. It does no such thing. If that is done at all, it is done in consequence of the violation of law and the commission of treason. The President concluded by saying that he would look at the papers they presented, but, so far, had seen no reason for removing the 13th exception.

New York Times, July 10, 1865.
1. James A. Jones, Robert A. Lancaster, William H. Hazall, and James L. Apperson, wishing to have the Amnesty Proclamation amended by striking the 13th exception, the twenty thousand dollars clause, called upon the President.
2. This date is based upon that supplied in the *New York Times*, July 10, 1865.
3. The "distrust" had been exhibited by northern investors, who refused to lend money to those falling under the 13th exception.

From Bradley T. Johnson

July 8, 1865, Raleigh, N.C.; ALS, DNA-RG94, Amnesty Papers (M1003, Roll 30), Md., Bradley T. Johnson.

Former Confederate officer who in 1861 "abandoned his residence in Maryland," then served "continuously" in the military until his May 1, 1865, parole under General Johnston's surrender terms, now resides in and wishes to become a citizen of North Carolina. He has taken the amnesty oath and "respectfully submits" that he does not come under the tenth and third exceptions of the recent amnesty proclamation. When he left home, there were no military lines established "beyond which he could pass" and his only "real rank" had been colonel; for his June 1864 appointment as brigadier general had been temporary. However, should his "conclusions not be agreed to," he asks the Chief Executive "for such relief as his case may require & the Presidential prerogative afford," pledging "to keep & maintain true allegiance to the United States." [There are, inexplicably, two pardon dates for Johnson: November 1, 1865, and January 13, 1866.]

To Robert Johnson

Washington July 8 1865 [1]

To Col Robt Johnson
Your letter just received.[2] I was glad to find you in such good Spirits. Anything I can do I will. All I desire of you is to let me know what you want done and when. Let me hear from you.[3]

Andrew Johnson Prest

Tel, DLC-JP.
1. The copy of this wire in Tels. Sent, President, Vol. 2 (1865), RG107, NA, dated July 9, is addressed to Greeneville.
2. Not found.
3. Robert on the 14th responded: "Your dispatch of 8th received—will answer in full

by letter. I now have possession of the entire office, and will have the Library arranged in a short time, after which, if advisable will go to Washington." Johnson Papers, LC.

From Isaac Murphy and Others

Little Rock Ark July 8 1865

To His Excellency Andrew Johnson President

Sir

There is no longer any insurrection against the U S within the limits of this state. Not only has the open war heretofore waged against the Government ceased but it is believed there is not today a single guerilla company or rebel organization of any kind in the state.

What is now wanted for the peace & best interests of the state is a speedy & successful reestablishment of civil authority. The organization of the several counties in the state is about completed by the appointment or election of loyal officers and Judges have been appointed or elected for the several circuits.

But the fact that the state stands proclaimed in insurrection against the Government and the rejection of our congressional delegation for that, among other reasons, has the effect to beget distrust and want of confidence in the authority and stability of all the civil departments of the state.

This want of confidence is particularly felt with reference to the state Courts where confidence is most needed. Rogues hope and honest men fear the present civil government of the state will fail and that all judgments, sentences and prosecutions will fail with it. It is desirable that something should be done to inspire confidence in the strength and authority of the civil government of the state.

This distrust and want of confidence would be removed by a proclamation from your Excellency declaring this state no longer in insurrection and counselling obedience to constitutions laws and civil authorities of this state. Believing that such a proclamation from your Excellency, would lessen the labor and remove the chief difficulty in the way of restoring civil law & order throughout the state in all its pristine force and vigor, we respectfully ask that such proclamation may be issued. We beg your Excellency not to construe this petition into a request for the removal from the state of the U.S. forces now here; they are needed to suppress sporadic cases of violence and to aid the state & U S Civil authorities in the reestablishment of civil law. Much of the success that has attended the efforts in that direction is due to the efficient administration and admirable action of Maj Genl Reynolds[1] commanding this Department and whom we pray your Excellency not to remove from among us so long as we need the aid of the U S military forces. Your Excellency will accept our thanks and the thanks of the people of the state for the removal of trade restrictions and the suspension of the sale of lands for direct taxes.[2]

We are with great respect Your Obt Servts
Isaac Murphy Gov Ark
Henry C Caldwell District Judge U S
Orville Jennings[3]
U.S. Dist Aty Eastern Dist. Ark

In addition to what is said in my communication herewith inclosed I take great pleasure in indorsing all that is here said of Genl Reynolds and the hapy manner in which he has managed the affairs of this Dept.
E. Baxter.[4]

LS, DLC-JP.
1. Joseph J. Reynolds.
2. On June 24, 1865, Johnson had lifted restrictions on trade west of the Mississippi. In June 1862 Congress had authorized the collection of a war tax in the insurrectionary states. Land owners were to pay a levy based on the 1861 assessed value of their property, plus a penalty of fifty percent. If they defaulted, their land was to be confiscated. Attorney General Speed in May 1865 suspended confiscation proceedings, but within a few months they began anew and continued until June 1866. James G. Randall, *Constitutional Problems Under Lincoln* (rev. ed., Urbana, Ill., 1951), 320–23, 328–32.
3. Caldwell (1832–*fl*1887), a lawyer and state legislator who had been colonel, 3rd Iowa Cav., USA, and Jennings (b. *c*1826), a Maine native. *U.S. Off. Reg.* (1865–77); Hallum, *Arkansas*, 481–82; 1860 Census, Ark., Hemphill, Washington, 4.
4. Elisha Baxter (1827–1899) was an Arkansas attorney who served in the legislature but fled the state during the war to avoid Confederate conscription. He raised and commanded a Union regiment until appointed by Governor Murphy to the state supreme court. In his enclosure, senator-elect Baxter sought an executive proclamation "declaring the State of Arkansas no longer in a State of inserection or rebellion." *DAB*; Baxter to Johnson, July 7, 1865, Johnson Papers, LC.

From William W. Peebles[1]

Jackson, N.C., July 8th, 1865.

His Excellency Andrew Johnson, President of the United States of America;

I would respectfully ask your Excellency whether or not the *tax in kind* officers and agents of the pretended Confederate government are exempted from the benefits of the amnesty proclamation of your Excellency, dated the 29th day of May 1865?

Some lawyers of the south give it as their opinion that said officers and agents are *military* officers and agents under the rank of General, and not "pretended civil or diplomatic officers and agents." Hence, the question raised.

The tax in kind was raised exclusively for the support of the army, was authorized by an act separate and distinct from the general tax bill; and was assessed, collected, and distributed by a separate and distinct class of officers and agents. The head of the department in each State received the rank and pay of Major, and in each congressional district the rank and pay of Captain. All of said officers and agents were responsible to the Quartermaster General, and were subject to the army rules and regulations prescribed for the Quartermaster's Department of the pretended Confederate government.

Should said opinion be correct, and if the government would so declare, it would save many petitioners the cost and trouble of petitioning for special pardon and amnesty and your Excellency much trouble in the examination and consideration of their petitions.

May I respectfully ask your Excellency to cause a letter in answer to said question to be directed unto me at Raleigh, N.C., care of Mrs H. W. Miller?[2]

I have the honor to remain your Excellency's loyal fellow-citizen and humble and obedient servant,

W. W. Peebles.

ALS, DNA-RG60, Office of Atty. Gen., Lets. Recd., President.
1. Peebles (b. c1833), lawyer and Confederate receiver, who was not pardoned until November 15, 1865, was nine years later a Republican state senator. 1860 Census, N.C., Northampton, 5th Dist., 45; Amnesty Papers (M1003, Roll 41), N.C., W. W. Peebles, RG94, NA; Samuel A. Ashe, *History of North Carolina* (2 vols., Raleigh, 1925), 2: 1185.
2. Frances J. (b. c1819) was the widow of Henry W. Miller, a lawyer and "ardent Union leader in Wake County." 1860 Census, N.C., Wake, Raleigh, 49; Johnston, *Vance Papers*, 148.

From K.W.R.[1]

Cincinnati July 8th 1865

Mr. Johnson Washington, D.C.

You have approved the sentence of Payne, Mrs. Surratt, Harrold, and Atzeroth and where hung July 7th and are now dead. Mr Johnson I now wish to say to you that this will cost your life, and perhaps your wifes to.

I am the man that will kill you. You must be murdered. Do you believe that you will die a natural death? No, no, never. If I cannot do it in months time let it be then years. It will cost your life only. There are also several others there in Washington that will be served the same way as you will be done. And should I be caught while in the act of murdering you I am willing to die, but will have Plenty of friend behind me that will serve others as I will have served you. Our society is Strong yet north and South. Oh the Sorrows that you have done. But you must suffer suffer for all of that. You ought to thanked god a thousand times so that Black harted sonofabitch Lincoln Was killed. He ought to have been killed 3 years ago. Would of been much better for the people in general. You have shown yourself now that you are not worth a god dam more then old Lincoln Was. We thought you was a different man but now we see. Your Penalty is death, and not by a natural death but a cold Blooded murder. It will be accomplished as soon as possible. A member of the secret society

yours K.W.R.

ALS, DNA-RG94, Baker-Turner Papers.

1. One of several anonymous letters Johnson received and forwarded to the War Department during the aftermath of the conspiracy trials and executions. Some were brief: "Murder is on Thy Head," signed "Mrs Surratt's Ghost"; others, such as this one, contained personal threats by the writers to act as Johnson's executioner. Baker-Turner Papers, RG94, NA.

From Kenneth Rayner

July 8, 1865, Raleigh, N.C.; ALS, DLC-JP.

Former North Carolina congressional colleague of Johnson, prompted by Harvey M. Watterson, assures the President that he has been such "an active, vigilant, and devoted advocate of the Union" that he has been "denounced . . . by fire-eating secessionists *as an Abolitionist*." Reports that the "most perfect quiet, order and calmness prevail" in the Tar Heel State, but the people suffer from "utter and absolute poverty," and he calls on Johnson to delay collecting taxes assessed on property, to forestall a complete collapse. Southerners look toward the new chief executive with "confidence and hope." He predicts that "honest and patriotic men," who "will defy all the carpings of the factions, and all the intrigues of envious political aspirants," will rally around Johnson. Rayner hopes "that time and reflection may soften and allay the acerbity of Northern feeling" and suggests that were northerners able to see the South, they would agree with the Union general that "'The South had been punished enough.'"

From Joseph J. Reynolds

Hd Quarters Department of Arkansas
Little Rock Ark July 8th 1865

Respectfully forwarded and earnestly recommended that the Proclamation be issued as Requested.[1] The State of Arkansas contains fifty six (56) Counties. Civil Government is in full operation in all except Eighteen (18) and these will probably be reorganized before this paper can reach the President, delay being caused only by the difficulty of Communicating with some of the Counties. The State of Arkansas is, in *fact*, no more in insurrection today than is the State of Indiana. The present State Government is recognized and respected throughout the State. The Military forces usurps none of the functions of the Civil Officers of the State. The issuing of a Proclamation by the President in accordance with the request of Senator Baxter would remove the last ground for Cavil with a few malcontents and would prove of incalculable benefit in the encouragement which it would afford to continuous efforts on the part of a loyal people who have proved faithful to their government amid persecution and discouragements that can hardly be appreciated by those who have not witnessed them.

J. J. Reynolds Maj Genl Comdg.

ES, DLC-JP.

1. Reynolds' endorsement appears on Elisha Baxter's petition, which in turn was enclosed in the Letter from Isaac Murphy and Others, July 8, 1865. See also Baxter to Johnson, July 7, 1865, Johnson Papers, LC.

From Harvey M. Watterson

July 8, 1865, Wilmington, N.C.; ALS, DLC-JP. See *Advice*, 57–60.

Echoing his previous reports of southern submission, Watterson concludes that North Carolina's "future loyalty is as certain as that of any State in the Union," although not all men can take the oath required for holding office, since "nearly everybody in North Carolina, from 17 to 55 years of age . . . may have, in some form or other, been mixed up with the Rebellion." He has taken pains to credit Johnson with having abolished the enormous tax on cotton, as well as other benefits for the southern people, so that they are beginning "to realize the pleasing fact that they have a friend instead of an enemy in the Presidential Chair." He has reminded others that the President cannot do more "Because it would array against him an overwhelming majority in both branches of Congress, and thus render him utterly powerless to help the South." Warns of Chase's presidential ambitions based on his advocacy of black enfranchisement.

From William W. Boyce

July 9, 1865, Winnsboro, S.C.; ALS, DLC-JP.

Reports that affairs in South Carolina are doing "as well as could be expected." People have a "great horror" of black troops; better use can be made of white troops under "discreet commanders." The inauguration of civil government has caused "great gratification," and Perry's appointment [as governor] "is extremely acceptable to the people." The state should be rebuilt "on the right basis." A convention organized "on the basis of population" will abolish slavery. Then, repeating his earlier recommendations, certain changes should be made in the state constitution: do away with parish representation; popularly elect the governor; give the governor power to veto and, with senate approval, power to appoint state officers; and have presidential electors chosen by the people. Noting that in this state "the secession idea" is dead, the writer wishes "to pluck up by the roots" all "institutions adverse to the most harmonious working" of state-federal relations. Boyce hopes the President can extend kindness to the "great mass" of people in order to become "the object of public attachment within southern states." Closes with a plea for Johnson to take care of his health, observing that the President was "working entirely too hard when I saw you in Washington."

From James A. Stewart[1]

Louisville Ky July 9th 1865

His Excellency: Andrew Johnson:
President United States:
Dear Sir:

A recent and rather protracted visit to middle Georgia has satisfied me that the release of Hon. A. H. Stephens and his early return to his native State,[2] would be attended with good results. It would accord with the earnest desire of all with whom I conversed; whilst on the contrary, if Hon Howel Cobb were held in custody, or punished to the full extent of the law for his political offenses we would scarcely hear a murmer of disapprobation.

The appointment of James Johnson as provisional Governor has given general satisfaction; and a large majority of the people are perfectly willing to acquiesce in any reasonable measures for the restoration of civil athority under the Constitution. They look upon slavery as existing heretofore, as at an end, and will not hesitate to cooperate with the Federal Government in all measures essential to the proper regulation of free labor.

The extreme abolition program in reference to Negro equality (political and social)—negro suffrage &c, meets with no favor; and if attempted to be imposed by the national authority, would result in no good. I see no way to establish a permanent peace except by a scrupulous observance of the reserved rights of the States under the Constitution. The United States Government, is now recognised as a government in fact for National purposes, and to that extent, as the supreme law of the land; and hence we need have no fears of any renewed advocacy of the unconstutional and extreme states rights doctrine of Secession and nullification. The higher law faction of the South has effectually played out.

POST OFFICE IN ATLANTA

I learn that Thos. Sims[3] of Atlanta is a petitioner for the position of P.M. of Atlanta. I hope he may be favored with the appointment. He has been an uncompromising Union man, and is in every respect qualified for the office.

Yours most respectfully—J. A. Stewart
Rome Georgia
Formerly of Tennessee

ALS, DNA-RG94, Amnesty Papers (M1003, Roll 23), Ga., Alexander H. Stephens.

1. A former slaveholder who opposed secession, he offered his Atlanta mills and residence for sale in early 1864, in order to open new mills in Louisville. He returned to Georgia after the war. *Memphis Appeal*, Jan. 23, Feb. 24, 1864; *Louisville Journal*, Feb. 27, 1865; Atlanta directories (1867–79).

2. See Letter from Stephens, August 16, 1865.

3. Thomas G. Simms (*c*1829–*fl*1876), a merchant, was appointed in July 1866 and served until May 1869. 1860 Census, Ga., Fulton, Atlanta, 4th Ward, 126; Atlanta directories (1867–76); Appt. Bk. 4: 162, Ser. 6B, Johnson Papers, LC; *U.S. Off. Reg.* (1865–69).

From William M. Daily

July 10, 1865, St. Louis, Mo.; ALS, DLC-JP.

Former congressional chaplain, perennial office seeker, and an "ardent friend, and admirer," concerned about Johnson's "protracted *indisposition*," warns: "do not *overwork* yourself. Remember your life is precious—and belongs to this great nation which needs your guiding and governing hand." Endorses Johnson's handling of the "question of '*Negro Suffrage*,'" noting that "you occupy the only *true, tenable* and *Constitutional ground*—It is a question that must be settled by *the states*, severally, for themselves." Closes with a request for "*some position*," when mustered out of the army, "where I can serve my *country*, serve *you*, and secure a good support for my young *family*." [By September 1865 Daily was appointed a special agent in the Post Office Department for Louisiana and Texas.]

From Margaret Donelson [1]

Near Nashville July 10th 1865

To his Excellency Andrew Johnson, President of the U.S.

Dear Sir,

You will recognise in the signature the name of the wife of an old acquaintance & friend. My husband, Maj Genl. Daniel S. Donelson,[2] was for many years a warm personal & political friend of yours, as you know. My husband died at Montvale Springs near Knoxville Tenn. on the 17th day of April 1863. You will pardon me for saying he was a man of education, honest in all his words & actions, beloved by all who knew him. He lived the life of an upright man. He died the death of a Christian. In making his will he gave to me the farm in Sumner Co Tenn, on which he was born & lived for many years & after my death to be divided between our children. You know the place. I left my home to be with my husband then in bad health. I was with him when he died & afterwards went to Florida to live near my brother, sister & daughter, carrying nothing but my wearing apparel. The farm was left in charge of a relative living near & the overseer living on the place. Soon after I left, the Commander of the post at Gallatin[3] took possession of the farm removing the forage, farming implements, furniture, bedding &c., & held the farm, until the close of the year 64. Application was, made for permission to return to Davidson Co. to live with my daughter, which was refused by the Military authorities at Nashville. On my return from Florida, eight days, since with the hope of getting possession of my farm, to make it a home for life I find it in possession of Genl. Fisk. I have made application to him in person & in writing asking possession of my farm. In answer, He says, he has no power to grant my request, & has sent my petition to Genl. Howard at Washington. I am informed by many persons that the dwelling, barn &c, are greatly damaged, Most of the fences are burned, every tree of any size has been sawed into lumber. This farm is the only home I can have for myself & children. Living on it we could all go to work, enclose some ground, sow some wheat this Fall & endeavor to make an honest living. My old neighbors, say they will help me. Now in conclusion. I the widow of your old friend make an appeal to you praying you to issue an order giving me & my orphan children possession of our once happy home. You have the power to grant this request & I believe it would be an act of justice for you to exercise it & a just & merciful God will bless & reward you.[4]

Yours most respectfully
Margaret Donelson.

ALS, DNA-RG105, Records of the Commr., Lets. Recd. from Executive Mansion.

1. Daughter of North Carolina Governor John Branch, Margaret (1804–1871) married Daniel S. Donelson in June 1825. Goodspeed's *Sumner*, 872; *BDTA*, 1: 206.

2. Donelson (1801–1863), a West Point graduate, farmer, and minor Democratic politico, served in the legislature and in the Tennessee militia and Confederate armies until his death. Ibid.

3. Probably Benjamin S. Nicklin.

4. According to Jackson B. White, attorney for Mrs. Donelson, Johnson ordered Fisk to release the property, but the latter, thinking it a "bogus" dispatch, ignored the order. "Confiscating Private Property," *Con Vet*, 1 (1893): 43. See Telegram to Andrew J. Martin, August 29, 1865.

From Thomas Ewing, Jr.

July 10, 1865, Washington, D.C.; LS, DNA-RG204, Pardon Case File B-596, Samuel A. Mudd.

Counsel for Samuel A. Mudd at the recent conspiracy trial encloses the affidavit of the doctor's wife, Sarah F., and three corroborating depositions. Ewing laboriously outlines Mrs. Mudd's statement: 1) The testimony of two witnesses that Dr. Mudd asked for Booth in Washington, D.C., March 3, 1865, was false. 2) Dr. Mudd had not been in Washington, D.C., between December 23 and March 23; therefore the testimony that he talked to Booth there in mid-January was false. 3) On Tuesday after Lincoln was killed, Dr. Mudd "could not have denied" to two detectives that "two strangers had been at his house, as they swear he did." 4) A week after the assassination Dr. Mudd "*voluntarily*" spoke of the finding of Booth's boot, and not after a threat to search his house, as previously claimed. 5) The boot was discovered only on Thursday. 6) Neither Mrs. nor Dr. Mudd recognized Booth on April 15, because of his haggard appearance and disguise. 7) Herold could not have gone with Dr. Mudd to Bryantown, eight miles away, since Herold "was gone not one half an hour." 8) Dr. Mudd "pointed out the short route through the swamp (to Parson Wilmers) to Herold *before* going to Bryantown & *before he learned of the assassination*"; and when he returned, Booth and Herold were gone. 9) Dr. Mudd's suspicions were first aroused an hour after they had gone, when his wife told him "the whiskers of the crippled man were false"; but he was prevented from reporting the information to the authorities "by her fears and entreaties."

Therefore, he delayed until the next day and sent the information through a relative. 10) Dr. Mudd did not hide Booth and Herold "in the woods Saturday night." 11) John H. Surratt had never been at the Mudd house. Of the preceding, number 8 was the "only act" by Mudd "which could have implicated him had he from the first known the crime & the criminal." Ewing suggests that if the President would "cause the record to be carefully & impartially examined by any one who has not a preconceived opinion," it would "show no tenable ground for conviction." Furthermore, since Dr. Mudd had the "disadvantages of a military trial," with many false witnesses, it was but "just that you hear & weigh the sworn statements of his wife . . . whose testimony, if it could have been heard, would have *triumphantly acquitted* the accused." [Johnson, through secretary Mussey, responded that the "petition for the remission of the sentence passed upon Dr. Samuel Mudd has been received and read and . . . can not be granted." Just before leaving office, however, Johnson ordered Mudd's release, which took place March 8, 1869.]

From Thomas C. Fletcher

Jefferson City, Mo. July 10th 1865

To the President:

The party which gave to the union candidates nominated at Baltimore for President and Vice President, a majority of forty one thousand votes in Missouri, and which has given Freedom to Missouri, is unanimous in the wish that the usual fruits of victory may not be withheld from it.

Representing the wishes of the Union party of the State, I take the liberty of asking that the Federal offices within this State be filled with men who have co-operated with the Union party.

The Surveyor of the Port at St. Louis, R. J. Howard,[1] appointed in 1861, has not, since 1863, acted with the Union and Freedom party of the State, but with the conservatives, "Copperheads," and rebels. I beg that he may be removed and that his place be filled by the appointment of John McNeil[2] of St. Louis.

John McNeil, has done glorious service in the army; rose to be Brig Genrl of Volunteers; is an old citizen of St. Louis, and eminently qualified for the position. Has earned it by service in the cause of the Country, and the loyal men of the State will rejoice at his appointment.[3]

I am very Respectfully Your obt Servt.

Tho' C Fletcher Gov' Mo'

ALS, DNA-RG56, Appts., Customs Service, Surveyor, St. Louis, Richard J. Howard.

1. Politically allied with the Blairs, Richard J. Howard (c1815–fl1881) was collector, as well as owner of a firebrick company. 1850 Census, Mo., St. Louis, 3rd Ward, 625; St. Louis directories (1850–81).

2. McNeil (1813–1891) served in the antebellum Missouri legislature. Warner, *Blue.*

3. Howard continued in office. The administration's policy, as explained by McCulloch's assistant secretary, was to reappoint "existing incumbents . . . where it did not seem to be perfectly clear, that a change should be made"; or if one were, "there did not seem to be entire unanimity . . . the President of course intending in all such cases, if satisfied before the meeting of Congress that new appointments should be made, to pro-

ceed with the same notwithstanding the continuance in office of the existing incumbents."
William E. Chandler to Henry T. Blow, Aug. 3, 1865, Appts., Customs Service, Collector, St. Louis, Richard J. Howard, RG56, NA.

From Speed S. Fry

Stanford Ky. July 10 1865

To His Excellency the President of the United States,
or Hon E. M. Stanton Sec. of War.
Washington City D.C.
Sirs

I take pleasure in recommending to your favorable Consideration Mr Saml T. Hays[1] a citizen of Fayette County Ky.

Mr Hayes is one of the most unflinching loyal men in the Blue Grass region of Ky. having stood by the govt. in the midst of all its troubles during the great rebellion which we trust has been forever crushed.

He visits Washington City for the purpose of procuring a situation as Commissioner to assess the value of slaves of loyal men in this state who have gone into the army.[2] Mr Hays has been a large slave owner himself and is in my judgment one of the best men for the position that could be selected.

I request that in the selection of Commissioners his claims may be considered, or if the commissioners have already been selected I ask for him some other position which you may have to confer.[3]

He will ask for nothing which is beyond his capacity.

I am very Resflly Your obt Servt
Speed S. Fry Brig. Genl.

ALS, DNA-RG94, U.S.C.T. Div., Lets. Recd., File P-365-1865.
1. Hayes (b. c1816) was a prosperous farmer. 1860 Census, Ky., Fayette, 1st Dist., 21.
2. By a congressional act of February 24, 1864, loyal owners of slaves who enlisted in the Union army received for each inductee a $100 bounty and a certificate redeemable after the war. Commissioners in each slave state were appointed by the secretary of war to determine the awards. General Orders No. 34, issued on April 18, 1864, and approved by the War Department, specifically authorized the compensation plan for Kentucky. *U.S. Statutes*, 13: 11; *OR*, Ser. 3, Vol. 4: 233–34.
3. No record of an appointment for Hayes has been found.

From Charles E. Haas[1]

[Lexington, Va., July 10, 1865][2]

To His Excellency Andrew Johnson
President of the United States

Your petitioner Charles E Haas of Rockbridge County Virginia aged Thirty five years and by profession an attorney at law, respectfully represents that in July 1863 he was a citizen of Illinois, that about that time his wifes father (John Hamilton[3] of Rockbridge County Virginia) sent word to her to return home and take charge of her mother who had been stricken down with paralysis (her mother being without white help). Thereupon your petitioners wife returned to Virginia and in october following your petitioner as a natural consequence followed her to Virginia where he has since remained. During the fall of 1864 your petitioner served as a clerk in the Quarter Masters department. He is included in the 10th exception to your Excellency's proclamation and to no other—and no proceedings have been instituted to libel or confiscate my property. Your petitioner has taken the amnesty oath prescribed in said proclamation, the original of which is herewith filed & which he intends to observe in good faith. He asks for Executive clemency & makes this special application for amnesty & restoration to his original rights of citizenship.

Cha E Haas

ALS, DNA-RG94, Amnesty Papers (M1003, Roll 62), Va., Charles E. Haas.

1. Haas, a Chicago attorney, was a quartermaster agent procuring horses for the Confederate army. He was pardoned one week later, on July 17, 1865. Chicago directories (1859–63); Confederate Papers *re* Citizens or Business Firms (M346, Roll 389), RG109, NA.

2. At the end of the letter there is a notation that on July 10, 1865, it was "Sworn to & subscribed before" J. Wilson Hess, captain and provost marshal. Hess was then stationed in Lexington.

3. Hamilton (b. *c*1789) was a farmer who furnished teams and wagons for hauling grain for the Confederate army. 1860 Census, Va., Rockbridge, 2nd Dist., 173; Confederate Papers *re* Citizens or Business Firms (M346, Roll 397), RG109, NA.

From William K. Hall

Columbus Ky July 10 1865.

Andrew Johnson, Prest of the U S.
Dear Sir.

Lt Col. P P Dobosey[1] Com'd'g Post Columbus Ky has arrested and brought to Columbus Emerson Etheridge[2] of Weakley County Tenn for making incendiary & treasonable speeches in Tennessee against the Govt's of the U S & the State of Tennessee & the authorities thereof.

He is doing great harm to reorganization of civil law in Tennessee. I have telegraphed the fact to Governor Brownlow and General Thomas for their action. Yours most Respectfully

By order Lt Col P P Dobosey.
W K Hall
Senator 23'd Dist Tenn

Tel, DLC-JP.

1. Hungarian-born Peter P. Dobozy (*c*1833–1919), who had served under Kossuth and Garibaldi, came to the U.S., and after serving as lieutenant colonel of the 4th U.S. Cld. Heavy Arty., settled on a farm near West Plains, Mo. Pension Records, Peter P. Dobozy, RG15, NA.

2. Former Tennessee congressman and a conservative unionist.

From Loyal Citizens of Louisiana

July 10, 1865, [New Orleans, La.]; Mem, DLC-JP.

One hundred eighty-nine citizens, mostly from Rapides Parish, who endorse the President's Amnesty Proclamation and reconstruction views, represent "that various schemes and combinations exist" in Louisiana by "evil disposed persons, disappointed office-seekers and political adventurers" to destroy the government's confidence in Governor J. Madison Wells, who "hazarded everything for the cause of the Union" and "willingly gave up one hundred and fifty slaves." Five-sixths of "all classes of loyal citizens," plus those who have taken in good faith the amnesty oath, favor and "warmly support Governor Wells in his measures to restore Civil Government," which "have been fully approved by the highest military authority in this Department." They, therefore, "protest that any report to the contrary emanating from any agent [John Covode] sent here recently to ascertain the condition of the affairs of this State, which may seek to impair" Governor Wells's authority or lower the chief executive's confidence in his loyalty "is untrue, unjust and without any foundation in fact," and it is hoped the "aid and confidence of the Administration will not be withdrawn from him in this noble work so near accomplished." [A second memorial, dated July 19, signed by 113, is also in the Johnson Papers, LC.]

From Hugh McCulloch

Treasury Department. July 10th 1865.

My dear Sir,

I have been for some weeks corresponding with some of my New England friends for the purpose of preventing them from taking an antagonistic position to your policy for re-establishing federal authority in the South, and bringing back the recently insurrectionary States into harmonious action with the General Government.

I am this morning in receipt of a letter from our mutual friend, J. M. Forbes,[1] which I shall be glad to have you read and return.[2]

Mr. Forbes is very anxious that you should visit New England. In my last letter I stated to him that I was apprehensive that the state of your health would prevent it.[3] I have now to say that in my opinion a trip to New England would not only be of great benefit to you physically, but might have a beneficial influence in a political point of view.

I am, Very truly, Your friend,
H. McCulloch

The President.

LS, DLC-JP.
1. John M. Forbes (1813–1898), Boston businessman and railroad promoter, helped raise black regiments during the war, served as a consultant to both state and federal administrators, and organized the Loyal Publication Society, a propaganda agency. On June 27 McCulloch had urged Forbes to "use your influence to prevent our radical friends in the North from taking such ground, in regard to the policy of the administration, as will inevitably bring about a breach in the party." DAB; McCulloch Papers, LC; Benedict, Compromise of Principle, 110–11.

2. On this same day McCulloch notified Forbes that his letter had been forwarded to Johnson "to post him in regard to the opinions of his true friends." The following day Mussey returned Forbes's letter to McCulloch. McCulloch Papers, LC.

3. On July 3 McCulloch had informed Forbes that Johnson had been so ill over the last week that the President was "unable to attend to business." Ibid.

From Hugh McCulloch

Treasury Department. July 10, 1865.

Sir:

I have the honor to enclose herewith a memorial signed by certain citizens of Tullahoma, Tenn.,[1] and approved by Maj Gen Milroy,[2] asking for permission to transport thither ammunition, etc.

As the shipment into Tennessee of articles of that class is prohibited by Executive Order, I have no power to act in the premises, and accordingly refer the case to you for such action as you may think proper.[3]

With great respect, H McCulloch
Secretary of the Treasury.

The President.

LS, DNA-RG393, Dept. of Tenn., Lets. Recd. (1865).

1. Ten citizens requested that a supply of ammunition be shipped for sale to the "loyal citizen . . . for his protection against Horse thieves and maurarders—and the great increase of wild game that are damaging the crops." R. D. Rathbone et al., to McCulloch, June 17, 1865, Dept. of Tennessee, Lets. Recd., RG393, NA.

2. Following a disastrous defeat, Robert H. Milroy (1816–1890) had been remanded to administrative assignments in Tennessee. He reported, in his endorsement on the enclosed memorial, that he had given "small amounts of ammunition to known loyal men for self defence," and assured McCulloch that munitions could be sold "on guarded military permits with much benefit." Warner, *Blue*.

3. Johnson's secretary, William A. Browning, had wired the commander at Nashville on June 16, 1865, that, because an executive proclamation on June 13 had declared Tennessee no longer in insurrection, a "special permit" was not required in order to ship ammunition into that state. Through secretary Reuben D. Mussey, the President replied to McCulloch on July 11 that he was "not aware that any order forbade the shipment thither of such ammunition and in such amounts as the Commander of the Department of Tennessee may authorize." McCulloch subsequently issued a circular allowing articles previously proscribed as contraband to be shipped to Tennessee only, with the prior approval of the commanding general. Browning to James A. Boyd, June 16, 1865, Tels. Sent, President, Vol. 2 (1865), RG107, NA; Mussey to McCulloch, July 11, 1865, Dept. of Tennessee, Lets. Recd., RG393, NA; Circular to Officers of Customs, July 11, 1865, Lets. Sent *re* Restricted Commercial Intercourse (BE Ser.), Vol. 10, RG56, NA; Richardson, *Messages*, 317–18.

From Sam Milligan

Greeneville Ten July 10 1865

To His Excellency Andrew Johnson
President of the U.S.
Dear Sir:

You will scarsely excuse me for the number of letters I have forwarded and written to you.[1] I have refused I may say hundreds, but these I was compelled to write. You can of course do as you think best about each case, and I am sure I will be content with your decision.

On the opposite page of this letter you will find a letter in behalf of Judge Robert L Caruthers.[2] That too, is to be treated as your sound judgement may dictate. Nothing, in my opinion, but a sense of duty to the public, will justify the pardoning of such men as he is; but the quiet of the Country is above almost evry other consideration, and if it is promoted thereby it would be wise to do so.

Robert is with us, and doing some better than a week ago. Poor fellow I do from my heart pity him. I hope he will be soon straight again.[3] I will cheerfully do all I can for him.

I hope your health is good—and that God will spare you to wind up this war—and stanch the bleeding wounds of the Nation. I am anxious to see you, and it is possible I will be in Washington before long. I have no "axe to grind," but I want to get the hang of a few things. Excuse trouble

Your *friend* Sam Milligan

P.S. Gov W B Campbell is making speeches in Middle Tenn if reported correctly that ought to arrest him.[4]

S. M.

ALS, DLC-JP.

1. During the first three months of Johnson's presidency, Milligan had written several letters of recommendation.

2. Caruthers, former state supreme court judge, had served the Confederacy as a member of the Provisional Congress and as a brigadier in the state militia. He was pardoned August 20, 1866. Amnesty Papers (M1003, Roll 48), Tenn., Robert L. Caruthers, RG94, NA.

3. Remaining in Nashville and Greeneville to arrange his father's books and papers, Robert had apparently been further delayed by his perennial drinking problem. See Telegrams to Robert Johnson, May 6, July 8, 31, 1865; see also *Johnson Papers*, 7: 560, 601.

4. In his speeches for Congress as a conservative unionist candidate, former governor William B. Campbell denounced emancipation without just compensation, denied the legitimacy of the Brownlow government, and attacked the legislature and its franchise law in what one report termed an indication of advocating a "revolutionary policy in state affairs." *Washington Morning Chronicle*, July 21, 1865; *Nashville Press and Times*, July 13, 1865.

From Michael O'Sullivan

July 10, 1865, Rochester, Wis.; ALS, DNA-RG59, Lets. of Appl. and Recomm., 1861–69 (M650, Roll 36), Michael O'Sullivan.

A "stanch supporter" and tailor relates an 1843 or 1844 visit to New York City by "Andrew Johnson of Tenn" to obtain "the Report of Fashions & hire a hand to work." At the time a "Foreman Cutter at Van Dozen," O'Sullivan had met the visiting Johnson "at the Porter house at Dye St." When an English tailor "commenced to abuse the South," Johnson countered "by drawing a pistol." O'Sullivan claims that his "quick interference saved the mans life"—for which Johnson later, when his temper had calmed, pledged "eternal friendship." The writer desires an appointment as consul to Dublin, Ireland, "if your Excellency is that same A Johnson." [O'Sullivan did not replace William B. West as the Dublin consul.]

From John C. Underwood

U.S. District Court, Alexandria, Va.,
July 10 1865

Mr. President

Ten thousand thanks for your plain talk with the rich rebels of Richmond.[1] It will give joy to the hearts of all true men of this State who since the cruel desertion of Pierpoint[2] began to fear that they were abandoned by all the powers of Earth. I went up on Friday to see you & ask you to do precisely what you have done in this case. Not being able to see you I called on the Atty Genl.[3] & found to my sorrow that he was against the 13th exception & like Pierpoint in favor of universal amnesty & of turning the worst rebels loose to devour & prey upon us. Therefore I say again thanks for the hope you have given us. Let me however state one apprehension & my reason for it. I learn that the Atty Genl. in case of special applications for pardon has asked the aid of our District Atty Mr. Chandler.[4] Mr. Chandler is a very clever gentleman & my friend, but being remarkably social in his disposition & long an aspirant for a seat in Congress, the rich rebels have urged him to come out for Congress & have induced him to do so in opposition to a candidate nominated by a convention of union men[5] promising him their hearty support which of course is equivalent to his election. Hence my apprehension that his gratitude will lead him to join Pierpoint & the Atty Genl. in recommending every bodys pardon.

I feel that a sincere regard for truth & justice & our old acquaintance & companionship in exile for our loyalty to the union demand this explanation & that it will be received in the spirit in which it is made by Your Excellency's

Very Obt Servant John C. Underwood

ALS, DLC-JP.

1. See Interview with Richmond Merchants, July 8, 1865.

2. Upon Governor Peirpoint's recommendation, the state legislature in June 1865 restored the franchise and officeholding privileges to Virginians who would take the President's amnesty oath, angering many unionists. Charles H. Ambler, *Francis H. Pierpont* (Chapel Hill, 1937), 272–74, 278.

3. James Speed.

4. Lucius H. Chandler (c1812–1876), Norfolk lawyer and U.S. district attorney, was elected with the aid of both Democrats and Republicans to Congress in October 1865 but not seated. In 1868 he joined the Radicals. 1860 Census, Va., Norfolk, Norfolk, 69; *U.S. Off. Reg.* (1863), 267; Thomas J. Wertenbaker, *Norfolk: Historic Southern Port* (Durham, N.C., 1931), 263, 270.

5. A notice for this convention has not been found. However, Chandler's first opponent for Congress was a "Mr. Buttz," and his final opponent was John S. Millson, a former congressman who had taken no part in the war. It was reported in September

1865 that a convention at Isle of Wight Court House had nominated John R. Kilby for Congress. *Richmond Whig*, May 30, 1865; *National Intelligencer*, Oct. 13, 1865; *BDAC*; Benjamin Perley Poore, comp., *The Political Register and Congressional Directory . . . of the United States, 1776–1878* (Boston, 1878), 535; *Charlottesville Tri-Weekly Chronicle*, Sept. 14, 1865.

From Montgomery Moses

July 11, 1865, Sumter, S.C.; ALS, DNA-RG60, Appt. Files for Judicial Dists., S.C., Franklin J. Moses.

A lawyer and former Confederate tax collector recommends his brother, Franklin J. Moses, for the U.S. judgeship of South Carolina. The latter, "the architect of his own fortune & fame," was "Admitted to the Bar from the office of the late distinguished James L. Petigru." Opposed to nullification in 1832 and secession in 1851, he had long been a state senator. Although Moses "went with the State" in 1860, he "has now taken the oath of allegiance" and "is doing what he can to instruct the people" in their "new obligations." [George S. Bryan, who endorsed Moses' petition, received the appointment.]

From Lucius B. Northrop [1]

Castle Thunder
Rhd Va July 11th [1]865

Sir

I have to ask your personal consideration to my application because delay will work very great if not fatal injury to my family which requires my immediate attention.

I premise my application by urging on your consideration the fact that the question of divided and ultimate sovereignty had agitated this country from its origin that the opposing opinions had been maintained by such an array of talent & influence and so numerously as to have become sectional and men grew up in their respective creeds and few could if they would, study the controversy of a half century—nor were they obliged to.

I even believed that the state was sovereign and that in the last extremity a man must sustain her.

Then without any aspirations or political antecedents—with the certainty of ruin if the south failed, and inevitable loss if successful, I answered to the call made on me for service and continued—till thrown off—to render service without fear or favour—irrespective of persons or authorities.

Last February I was by a legislative ruse & concurrence of the Executive & cabinet, manipulated out of service.

My family was large including a delicate wife and four daughters, among six children, every one of which, needs my care or supervision and depend on me. I rented some land to work on shares, till more permanent arrangements could be made. The War has impoverished me.

Repeated fevers and a severe attack of opthalmia were the results of my efforts at field work.

The proclamation of May the 29th was read to me while my eyes were closed and incapable of use in a darkened room.

This was the first indication I recieved of the course to be pursued.

As soon as my eyes permitted I arranged to take action under that proclamation—because I could conscientiously take the oath: Having repeatedly declared before, that state rights and slavery—the two points involved had been finally settled by a resort to arms.

Two days after I was arrested brought here and cast into prison.

If I was in the service of the C States then I had a right to take the parole, if not then to take action under the proclamation of May 29th as a civilian.

I am 54 years old on the 8th of Sept. Am crippled and an invalid which can be verified by the Medical Dept here, and unfit for the life of a Jail.

My large family is one to which some consideration of its previous life, and associations is vital. My imprisonment estop all my efforts in thier behalf and if continued will ruin them.

No charges have been presented to me, none disreputable can be specified.

I ask to complete that which I begun. I ask to be released, so that I may take the oath, and seek the provisions under the amnesty proclamation.

If released I will pledge my honor—and if desired—give here any amount of security to be forthcoming whenever charges are ready. Investigation can only be beneficial to me.

I have several times come in contact with the federal authorities. All the facts of my movements since last February, show that I had no idea of avoiding notice, which is known to the officers at Raleigh and Fayetteville.

The bearer of this letter is fully able to meet any points which brevity required not to be fully set forth.[2]

> I have the honor to be Very respectfully
> Your Obt Sert L B Northrop

His Excellency Andrew Johnson
President of the United States

ALS, DNA-RG107, Lets. Recd., EB12 President 2469 (1865).

1. Northrop (1811–1894) was Confederate commissary general but resigned in early 1865 amid controversy. Arrested by federal authorities on charges of deliberately starving prisoners of war, he was released on parole November 2, 1865. Warner, *Gray*; Thomas R. Hay, "Lucius B. Northrop: Commissary General of the Confederacy," *CWH*, 9 (1963): 22.

2. On September 26, 1865, acting secretary of war Thomas T. Eckert endorsed this petition: "Release not expedient at the present." Lets. Recd., EB12 President 2469 (1865), RG107, NA.

From E. H. Stainback

July 11, 1865, Petersburg, Va.; ALS, DNA-RG60, Office of Atty. Gen., Lets. Recd., President.

A Jacksonian Democrat and unionist who held a minor post under the Confederacy is concerned that the oath requirement "will be sure to act as a *deadlock* to secessionists . . . those *blood hounded hot spurs* in the South, who would have *licked* and *sucked out* the *very life blood* of this people to carry out their designs," and who now have the audacity "to seek office at the hands of the very government they have tried to break up." Expressing confidence that Johnson will not enforce the oath so rigidly on loyal southerners who opposed the war but aided it only from necessity, he now applies for office as inspector of customs and wants to take the traditional oath; for "if this test oath is to be administered and the same enforced to the letter . . . it will be a most difficult matter to find persons in the South . . . to fill these offices." On the other hand, to appoint northerners is to court disaster; for "strong parties and associations will commence to be organized, a bad state of feeling will almost be sure to be engendered and . . . cause a bad state of things to exist, which may terminate in something that nobody dreams of at present." [Available evidence indicates that Stainback did not receive an appointment.]

From Chester District Citizens [1]

[July 12, 1865] [2]

To His Excellency Andrew Johnston, President of the United States

The Undersigned residents of Chester District S.C. and Citizens of the U.S most respectfully memorialize your Excellency to obtain the restoration of Civil government in this State.

The great Civil War which has swept away one half of our young Men, desolated our homes, bankrupted our people, reduced to abject poverty & want, the many thousands of Widows and Orphans, and left us in utter political & social confusion is at an end.

Our State, contrary to the earnest remonstrances of many of us, appealed to the God of battles, to shield us from an anticipated danger. It has been decided against us by the Divine Will. We therefore humbly submit. In good faith we affirm our fidelity to the Constitution of the U.S. and earnestly desire to return peaceably to a position in the Union in which, we may enjoy the privileges of our Sister States.

We are satisfied that the determination is almost universal to be truly loyal and to do every thing in our power to promote the welfare of our Common Country.

Your Memorialists therefore pray that a Provisional Government be appointed for the state of South Carolina.

And your petitioners will ever pray &c. &c.

Mem, DLC-JP.

1. There are 622 memorialists.

2. The Library of Congress assigned this date to the memorial because it was accessioned in the President's office on July 12. But on July 6, when two of the memorial-

ists—A. P. Wylie and James Hemphill—were in Washington, they wrote to Johnson
that they desired to present the Chester District petition to him. Therefore, the actual
date of the memorial should be sometime in late June or early July. Chester District
Citizens to Johnson, July 6, 1865, Johnson Papers, LC.

From Thomas Cottman

July 12, 1865, Washington, D.C.; ALS, RG60, Appt. Files for Judicial Dists.,
La., Edward Ames.

After "most serious consideration and due reflection," Cottman concludes that
the best nominees for Louisiana marshal and New Orleans postmaster are Edward Ames and Robert J. Ker. The former is "not erudite or versed in abstruse
science" but is honest and a "thorough business man." The latter, whom
Cottman has known since 1830 as a printer, notary's clerk, and notary,
would "make a most competent & efficient officer." [Neither man obtained an
appointment.]

From Frederick County, Virginia, Citizens

July 12, 1865, Washington, D.C.; ALS, DLC-JP.

Transmitting resolutions condemning Governor Peirpoint's proposal to grant
ex-Confederates the right to vote and hold office as "mistaken leniency or political intriguery," and claiming that in every county there are "at least enough
of *competent* loyal men to fill the offices," 103 southern loyalists praise unionist
John Minor Botts as the "soundest and most practical statesman of Virginia"
and call for a convention of northern Virginians to select a "suitable" congressional candidate and "to secure harmony and unanimity" among unionists.

From Edwin A. Keeble

July 12, 1865, Murfreesboro, Tenn.; ALS, RG94, Amnesty Papers (M1003,
Roll 50), Tenn., Edwin A. Keeble.

Ex-Confederate congressman invokes Johnson's attention to his amnesty application, trusting that "you have known me favorably enough to believe that I
would not countenance or promote a further factious opposition to the Government." Explaining that his family requires his "prompt and undivided attention
and labor," Keeble asks that his petition be given "an early attention." He adds
that Edward H. East had advised that it was "unnecessary" for his papers "to
pass under the supervision of the Governor of Tennessee" and that Keeble
"should always appeal directly to you who knows me the best." [Keeble was
pardoned September 18, 1865.]

From Alexander Rives [1]

Charlottesville—12 July 1865

His Excellency, Prest. Johnson,
Dear Sir,

I have read with satisfaction your reply to the delegation from Richmond.[2] It will not do for wealthy men in private life, who by their

station in society have aided in coercing or suppressing the will of the people, and have stifled their true voice by threats of violence, to escape without some mark of the Govt's displeasure.

Allow me to suggest, whether confiscation—a tedious and expensive process—might not be substituted by *fines*, proportioned to the offender's estate & guilt, as the *condition* of pardon. I see, some have been pardoned from this State, who little deserved it, such as Harvie, Edmunds, Crenshaw &c.[3] but of course, I should wish to see you lean to mercy.

I have ventured to write Govr. Pierpoint's secretary of State[4] on the danger of too great facility of passing applications through his hands, and to suggest the propriety of conferring with tried Union men in the various counties.

Fearing to obtrude on your time, I am, truly, Yr. Obt. Sert.

Alexr: Rives

ALS, DLC-JP.

1. Rives (1806–1885), a state legislator "bitterly opposed to secession," became judge of the Virginia Supreme Court of Appeals (elected 1866) and a Grant appointee to the U.S. District Court. J. Rives Childs, *Reliques of the Rives* (Lynchburg, Va., 1929), 599–600.

2. See Interview with Richmond Merchants, July 8, 1865.

3. Lewis E. Harvie (1809–1887), who served in the House of Delegates and as a member of the Secession Convention, was pardoned June 29, 1865. John R. Edmunds (b. *c1812*), of Halifax County, a wealthy planter who constructed a vital link of railway for the Confederacy, was pardoned June 16, 1865. William G. Crenshaw (1824–1897), senior member of a Richmond import-export firm, who supported secession and the Confederacy and went as a special procurement agent to England, was pardoned July 13, 1865. Gaines, *Biographical Register*, 43; Wakelyn, *BDC*; Tyler, *Va. Biography*, 3: 369–70; 1860 Census, Va., Halifax, Southern Dist., 121; (1870), Bunch Creek Twp., 92; Wirt J. Carrington, *A History of Halifax County* (Baltimore, 1969 [1924]), 171; Amnesty Papers (M1003, Rolls 59, 60, 62), Va., William G. Crenshaw, John R. Edmunds, Lewis E. Harvie, RG94, NA.

4. Charles H. Lewis.

From William D. Snow

July 12, 1865, Washington, D.C.; ALS, DLC-JP.

Reporting on the rapid reorganization of county and state government in Arkansas, Snow notes that the archives, as much of the state's money "as remained unexpended by the late rebel legislature," and the records of the supreme court and auditor's office "have been surrendered to the legitimate government." Because the "late occupants of the pretended civil offices . . . have abandoned all pretentions to the exercise of their respective official functions," the senator-elect requests Johnson to consider the "propriety of issuing . . . a proclamation similar to that issued in the case of Tennessee, declaring the insurrection in that state suppressed & withdrawing its loyal citizens from the disabilities arising therefrom." [Snow's request was not granted. Johnson did not declare insurrection in Arkansas at an end until his general proclamation for the entire South, April 2, 1866.]

From Baltimore Unionists

July 13, 1865, Baltimore; LS (James Young, president), DNA-RG56, Lets. Recd. from Executive Officers (AB Ser.), President.

A convention representing the "unconditional union Party" of Baltimore expresses, in the form of resolutions, its approval of "the course pursued by Andrew Johnson . . . and that we do especially and emphatically applaud, as wise, just and patriotic, his views and conduct in relation to the restoration of the late rebellious States to their proper position in the National Government."

From Thomas J. Durant and Henry C. Warmoth[1]

New Orleans. 13. July, 1865.

To His Excellency Andrew Johnson
President of the United States Washington City
Respected Sir,

The apparent state Government in Louisiana exists solely by the sufferance of the military authority of the United States.

Its Senators and Representatives obtained no admission to the Halls of Congress.

Its Governor appeals to the President of the United States, as the fountain of his power.

Shortly after the return of his Excellency Governor Wells from his recent visit to Washington, the Picayune Newspaper of this city, esteemed his official organ, in an article of the 14th June said

Doubts have been expressed in high quarters, in the Congress of the United States and elsewhere as to the constitutionality and regularity of the existing state Government. The President has guarded against all such doubts by reorganizing and designating Govr. Wells as Military Governor.

The powers of Gov. Wells no longer rest upon his election by the small number of legal votes cast for the Government, which Senators Sumner and Wade declared in Congress to be a bogus Concern, but upon the appointment of the President. His authority is as lawful, valid and unquestionable as that of Genl. Banks and Genl. Shepley or as that of Gov. Holden of North Carolina.[2]

The truth of these emphatic declarations have never been denied in any quarter. They are Conclusive as to the power of Governor Wells to comply with the prayer of the memorial lately presented to him[3] by those who now have the Honor to address you.

We ask in the most respectfull manner your attention to the memorial of this Committee to Governor Wells and his reply,[4] Copies of which are herewith enclosed, and which were published by the governor without the formality of Conveying to us a written reply.

We now appeal from the Presidents officer to the President himself, most respectfully pray that if you should determine to exert any interference in Louisiana affairs, in advance of the action of Congress, that you will make it in the path indicated by this memorial.

We have the Honor to be
With great respect Your most obdt Servents.
Thomas J. Durant President
H. C. Warmoth Corresponding Secretary

ALS (Durant), DLC-JP.

1. Warmoth (1842–1931), Illinois-born Union soldier, began practicing law in New Orleans in 1865 and served as Republican governor (1868–72). *DAB*.

2. Banks, former commander of the Department of the Gulf; George F. Shepley (1819–1878), post commander (1862–64) at New Orleans who became military governor of Louisiana in June 1862; and Holden, provisional governor since May 29. Warner, *Blue*.

3. Signed by Durant, Warmoth, and twenty other members of the "Central Executive Committee of the Friends of Universal Suffrage," the letter, probably written about July 1, requested that "a complete registration . . . be made, in every parish of the state, of all loyal citizens, without distinction of race or origin, who have resided twelve months in Louisiana." A copy in Durant's hand was enclosed.

4. On July 10 Governor Wells in a lengthy reply refused to comply with the committee's request, deeming it neither "wise or expedient" to grant the emancipated slave the right of suffrage. His response, together with the committee's original petition, appeared in the *New Orleans Picayune*, July 12, 1865.

From Emerson Etheridge

COLUMBUS, Ky., July 13, 1865.

To His Excellency, ANDREW JOHNSON,
President of the United States:

The Hon. Horace Greeley—the wisest and among the best of your present friends—once addressed your distinguished predecessor through the columns of his newspaper. He wrote in behalf of the "colored race;" I am emboldened by his example to invoke your attention to the condition of the unfortunate whites. Besides, I know how you are surrounded by political and religious patriots who daily approach the throne of Executive grace to assure you of their love of country and detestation of place; and to offer up their fervent prayers for the restoration of your health, and the prolongation of your invaluable life. Perhaps some one of these may see this communication and present it to the attention of your Excellency. In this press upon precious time, I make no estimate of the intervals you so cheerfully devote to the crowds of contrabands who constitute so much of the *elite* of the Capitol.

I know the magnanimous nature of your Excellency, and I fear the sad announcement I have to make will prove injurious, if not fatal, to the delicate sensibilities of your noble and generous heart. I was arrested at my home in Dresden, Tennessee, on Friday last[1] (hangman's day) by a detachment of armed soldiers whose deportment and appearance would do honor to any service. They are known in the Army Regulations as "colored troops," but, to their shame be it spoken, your old friends still persist in calling them "niggers." They were commanded and directed by four or five white men, who arrested me as Mr. AD-DER-RIG, from which, I infer, they claim a lager beer nationality.[2] I deem it my duty to report that your old friends of the sesesh persuasion still persist in the treasonable practice of calling the *personnel* of such expeditions "d——d Dutch and niggers." You will doubtless be relieved to hear that the expedition was a success. Though I had timely warning of the approaching raid, I preferred surrender to hopeless resistance, and the command reached this city without material loss, treating me, since my arrest, with courtesy and kindness, for which I am grateful.

I have been here five days, and though I have not yet been able to obtain the names of my accusers, or a copy of the charges, if any, upon which I was arrested, I have obtained from other sources information upon which I rely, of the causes and motives of my arrest. I am charged with using *treasonable language* against the Government of the United States, and the Government of Tennessee, and with speaking disrespectfully of your Excellency, and of the Right Reverend William G. Brownlow, who, unmindful that the Constitution of Tennessee excludes all ministers from civil office, is now claiming to have successfully secured the office of Governor of said State. Further and truly that I have given a professional opinion declaring that the slaves in Tennessee have not been made free by law. As I will, no doubt, be held a prisoner *until after the pending election farce in Tennessee is over*, I propose to indulge a portion of my leisure, in giving you a concise statement of some things I *did* say and the circumstances under which I have provoked the military displeasure of that Grand Army, of which you are the Commander-in-Chief.

A public meeting of all the citizens of Weakley county, Tennessee, was called at Dresden on Saturday, the 1st day of July last to consider the best course to be adopted for the interests of all. That meeting was very large, and was addressed by William P. Caldwell[3] and myself. The object of the meeting, the character of Mr. Caldwell's speech, and much of my own, may be easily inferred from the resolutions,[4] which were unanimously adopted at the close of the meeting—all but the last having been reported from the Committee on Resolutions.

On the following Monday, July 3d, a very large meeting was held at Trenton, Gibson county, which I addressed for three hours. Isaac Sampson, one of Brownlow's newly appointed Circuit Judges, having as he said, full civil and criminal jurisdiction to arrest and try all offenders, was present. He had one of Brownlow's Sheriffs and several of the Justices of the Peace present, and in their presence he addressed the multitude from the same stand I had occupied; yet he did not as much as hint at my arrest; he only threatened the people *with an invasion of Federal troops* (meaning negroes,) to deter them from voting for me. At the close of the meeting, resolutions precisely similar to those passed at Dresden were unanimously adopted. I was unanimously nominated for Congress, and the pretended Senator and Representative[5] from that county were unanimously requested to resign.

I was to have addressed a similar meeting at Paris, Henry county, on Saturday last, and would have done so, had I not been arrested. As the offensive words are alleged to have been spoken in my Dresden speech (they were substantially repeated at Trenton,) I will give you accurately and concisely as I can, what I said of you at Dresden. Indeed, I will give you the precise words of my exordium in which *you* were first personally alluded to. Addressing myself to the audience, I said:

You have witnessed the rise, culmination and overthrow of a rebellion, in all respects the most astonishing in the world's history; astonishing because of the numbers engaged, the resources it so suddenly improvised, and the duration and intensity of the conflict. It was only less astonishing than the numbers and resources it encountered. It has ended as all rebellions must end when opposed by greatly superior resources and numbers. The rebellion is over. Its leaders are captives, exiles, or supplicants for pardon; its armed adherents have saluted their flag for the last time, and its friends throughout the South have yielded the contest. Their submission has been graceful, unanimous, and in all apparent good faith. Not an armed Confederate is to be found within the limits of the State. The Federal Government professed to draw the sword only for the sole purpose of enforcing its Constitutional authority wherever it was opposed; it is this day supreme within the entire limits of the United States. No opposition is anywhere attempted; nor indeed, can any be organized. Why, then, I ask, are we threatened with a despotism as inexcusable as rebellion? Why are free elections denied to the Union men and qualified voters of the State? Why have non-residents and loungers around Federal camps, without your knowledge or consent, and in defiance of your protests and appeals, been permitted to usurp the high and responsible places of power, and to declare themselves your oppressors and masters—and this, too, in contempt of that Declaration of Rights, whose sacred principles are inviolable, and, by your Constitution, *"excepted out of the general powers of Government?"* Why are offensive rulers being set over the loyal people of the State by those who are jointly responsible for the war? Why are bands of armed negroes permitted to roam over the country, plundering and insulting the timid and defenceless? And more than these, why are you and I, whose souls are unstained by treason, compelled to drain this cup of shame at the hands of those who were *the original instigators of the rebellion?*

I beg leave to assure your Excellency that, in using the words "ORIGINAL AGITATORS OF THE REBELLION," I alluded to *you*; further, that I spoke in no Pickwickian sense.[6] And now that I may invoke your clemency, not for myself, but for those who listened to my remarks, I frankly confess that I submitted certain proofs of the truth of my charges. I told the people that the first time I ever saw you, you were harranguing the multitude to prove me an Abolitionist; that it was a somewhat "raw and gusty day," and that your vehemence in the open air caused you to contract a throat desease, from which, unfortunately for the country, you profess not to have recovered. I alluded to your early speeches in Congress in which you resorted to the bitterest personal abuse of John Quincy Adams because of his religious, anti-slavery opinions; to your reverential confession that God had killed off Gen. Harrison because he was an Abolitionist. I also told the people that you had, in 1856, in the State of Tennessee, proposed that every Southern man should "join in the fraternal hug"—and plunge into rebellion, if Fremont and Dayton were elected. In addition to this, I informed the audience that I heard you, in the Senate, in December, 1859, denounce Mr. Seward and the Republican party, as wholly responsible for the murderous raid of "this old man Brown," whom you then stigmatized as "nothing more than a murderer, a robber, a thief and a traitor."[7] I said, also, that you not only supported Breckinridge, the candidate of the avowed disunionists, but that after the election of Lincoln, *after* the meeting of Congress in December, 1860, and only *one* day before the assembling of the Convention which declared South Carolina *out of the Union*, you had, in the Senate of the United States, made a labored speech, embracing a part of two days, in which you positively pledged yourself, in a contingency which has long since happened, to join these same rebels, "*to perish in the last breech*," to "*burn every blade of grass*," and to make your grave in "*the last intrenchments*" of rebel freedom.[8] I told the people that I heard this speech, (during the delivery of which Jefferson Davis offered you a most unprovoked insult, the effect of which I will not now attempt to state,) and that every word of it was designed to convince the people of Tennessee that they were an oppressed people and you their champion; that their constitutional rights were in imminent danger and that they ought "to demand additional securities;" that you then and there submitted the following "basis," upon which you declared an unalterable purpose "*to fight the great battle for our rights:*"

Resolved, That we deeply sympathize with *our sister Southern States*, and freely admit that there is good cause for dissatisfaction and complaint *on their part*, on account of the recent election of sectional candidates to the Presidency and Vice-Presidency of the United States; yet we, as a portion of a people of a slave-holding community, are not for *seceding* or *breaking up the Union* of these States until every fair and honorable means has been exhausted in trying to obtain *on the part of the non-slaveholding States*, a compliance with the *spirit* and *letter* of the Constitution and *all* its guarantees; and when this shall have been done, and the States *now* IN OPEN REBELLION against the laws of the United States, *in refusing to execute the Fugitive Slave Law*, shall persist in their present unconstitutional course, and the Federal Government shall fail to execute the law in good faith, it (the Government) will not have accomplished the great design of its creation, and will, therefore, in fact, be a practical dissolution, and *all* the States, *as parties*, be *released* from the *compact* which formed the Union.[9]

In commenting on the foregoing "*basis*" I said it proved that you did then "*deeply sympathize* with our sister Southern States;" that you particularly alluded to South Carolina, whose treasonable representatives were then assembled, and who, one day after, inaugurated the rebellion, that you did then and there "freely admit * * good cause for dissatisfaction and complaint," because of the election of your illustrious predecessor and the Hon. Hannibal Hamlin, who the Rev. Mr. Brownlow represented as a free negro. I said, also, that you were then only a *conditional* Unionist; that you declared yourself, "not for seceding or breaking up the Union of these States UNTIL every fair and honorable means had been exhausted in trying to obtain on the part of the non-slaveholding States a compliance with the spirit and letter of the Constitution and all its guarantees." And I further stated that you, at the same time, had assured your rebel friends, with whom you did so "deeply sympathize" that "when this shall have been done and the States now IN OPEN REBELLION" (meaning Vermont and Massachusetts) "against the laws of the United States * * * shall persist in their present unconstitutional course, it * * * (the Government) will not have accomplished the great design of its creation, and will therefore, in fact, be a practical dissolution of the Union." I repeat, I told the people that this speech, so made as aforesaid by you (assisted by Senator Latham who was kind enough to read for you,)[10] was *designed* by you to foment rebellion among your constituents. I selected certain passages from that speech to prove the above general statement. I referred to that part in which you said "there is no power conferred upon the Congress of the United States, by the Constitution, to coerce a State." I pointed to your "*demand*" for "*additional securities*" for slavery; to your statement that Vermont was, at that time, guilty of "nullification," of "resistance to the laws of the United States," which you pronounced "OPEN REBELLION." I commented upon your statement that the conduct of Vermont had been such that "the Government was at an end." Nor did I omit to tell the people that you then and there (18th and 19th of December, 1860) had submitted an opinion in regard to your general "complaint." I did not, like Beecher, pronounce you *drunk*, nor did I, like Wilkes, say you had been *poisoned*,[11] I permitted you to speak for yourself by reading the following from your speech:

We have *complained* that their intention is to hem slavery in, so that, like the scorpion when surrounded by fire, if it did not die from the intense heat of the scorching flames, it would perish from its own poisonous sting.[12]

You further promised your rebel friends what Tennessee should do, if new guarantees for slavery were refused. You said, "Tennessee will be found standing as firm and unyielding in her DEMANDS for those guarantees * * * as any other State in the CONFEDERACY." I asserted, also, that you had declared the election of Lincoln and Hamlin "sectional," that you avowed your purpose to PUT DOWN Mr. Lincoln and DRIVE BACK his advances upon SOUTHERN INSTITUTIONS; that you promised not to abandon your "Northern Democratic friends and leave all to Lincoln's *cohorts*;" that you solemnly pledged yourself not to "permit Mr. Lincoln to come with his *cohorts*, as we consider them, *from the North*, to *carry off everything*." All the foregoing, and much more, I charged upon you and proved by your speech of 18th and 19th of December, 1860.

Continuing my address, I said that if you were a credible witness—I beg you to believe I so regard you—I could prove that every political supporter and admirer of your Excellency, and every follower of the saintly Brownlow then and there present, was a *disunionist*. In doing this, I read from a speech made by you at Columbia, Tennessee, on the 2d of June, 1862. It was revised by yourself, and published in your own organ, the Nashville *Union* of June 9, 1862, then edited by your friend Mercer,[13] who is best known as "quinine Mercer," because of his sympathy with the rebel sick, to whom, it is alleged, he kindly smuggled that invaluable medicine while he sojourned within the Federal lines.

I read the following:

Now I will prove very briefly that a secessionist is as great an Abolitionist as Sumner. Both the secessionist and disunionist are for breaking up this Union. I will state the argument in a *syllogism* thus: AN ABOLITIONIST IS A DISUNIONIST. A disunionist is a secessionist. A secessionist is a disunionist. A disunionist is an Abolitionist. Therefore, a secessionist is an Abolitionist. There is not a particle of difference between them.[14]

I repeat, I read the foregoing, after which I was so irreverent as to say, in regard to your syllogism, that I could find the *silly* but not the *gism*; but you were distinct and positive in the allegation that "*an Abolitionist is a disunionist.*" All this and much more did I say, may it please your Excellency, for the many pious purposes herein after enumerated; chiefly however, with the design of quieting the hearts and consciences of a few of your old rebel friends, office holders and Trade Agents, who desire to join you in your late but earnest championship of the rights of the colored race. They have some pride of consistency; having always been rebels, at heart, they dislike suddenly to become Abolitionists, fearing they may be required, in following your illustrious example, to deal harshly with those who, from a false sense of shame, are still unwilling, by turning Abolitionists, to incur the rebel reproach of apostacy. They urge that they dislike to be called Judases; and yet they "wish to be with *you*, and at rest." Hence the struggle between their old party and rebel pride, and their *love for you*; their dire necessities and *love of cash*. With all such I adopted this mode of reasoning: That the popular judgment is often wrong, and traditionary or hereditary prejudices rarely right. For example, I would take two celebrated cases, those of Pilate and Judas, that the Christian world affected, nay, felt great horror of their name and characters, that they were associated with the murder of our Saviour, and therefore, no one supposed it possible to find any thing in their natures to extenuate the severe judgment of mankind; whereas, in fact, Pilate was bitterly opposed to our Saviour's persecutions and ignominious death, and protested he "found no fault in him," while the mob (may Heaven protect your Excellency from all mobs) hurried him away to execution, without even the dignity of a military arrest! That Judas, from all we had been able to ascertain in regard to *his* character, was a very unobtrusive reticent man, better fitted by nature for a trade agent or contractor than a Disciple, that, though he "turned his back upon his friends," nay, *betrayed* them, he was neither the first nor the last who had yielded to temptation; that *his* reward was *hard money*—thirty huge pieces—and long before Chase had inflated the currency, or California had augmented the coin; that he was a man of sensibility, that he repented, and so suffered from remorse that he burst his bowels. I assured the secessionists and office-seekers, however, that they need not wait for quarantine before joining the army of Sumner and John Brown; that you had done so, turned your back upon them—betrayed them, and that, although the official health-bulletin represented you in a precarious condition, I had yet seen no mention of any morbid distension of your bowels. Nor did I fail to remind the audience of the radical change in your opinions of John Brown and Mr. Seward, since you denounced the one as "a murderer, a robber, a thief and a traitor," and the other as his political tutor. I pointed to the remarkable ease and elegance with which you fraternize with the original Browns; how you now piously regarded his gallows as only less sacred than the Cross of Christ; how benignantly you smiled at his apotheosis, and how divinely you could sing,

"John Brown's body lies mouldering in the dust."

In the foregoing, I can give you only a brief outline of that portion of my speech which was devoted especially to yourself. I rose doubtless "to the full height of the great argument," and many of your old sesesh friends pronounced my speech truly eloquent and convincing. Several are known to have declared positively, for you and Brownlow, while among the office seekers, trade agents, and those who have "lost fortunes by the war," there seemed to be a general inclination to join the grand army of universal freedom so bravely led by yourself. I found none reluctant to do so except a few original Union men who still declare themselves ardent supporters of "THE Union of the Constitution." Ordinary compassion requires me to say, in their behalf, that they read but few newspapers, and do not know that old fogy parchment is wholly "played out."

Now for this eulogium upon your life, character and public services—and because the Union men of that portion of the State in which I live have nominated me for Congress—I am held, like Napoleon, a prisoner of State. Napoleon at Helena!! Ad-der-rig at Columbus!! How history will repeat itself! For the benefit of subsequent travellers who may visit this classic city in search of relics, I will here state that I am at the Columbus Hotel, room No. 1, directly opposite a butcher's establishment, where thirteen chained dogs, hundreds of unchained contrabands and millions of musquitoes nightly mingle their music to lull me to repose.

A few words more and I will suspend all further recital of those afflictions which I am sure will greatly affect your Excellency's compassionate heart. I am very unhappy here. "The noblest river in the world" lies just before me; its waves dance merrily and unrestrained. Unbleached ladies and gentlemen crowd the streets, moving with graceful and elastic tread, while arrayed in robes of loveliest blue. The air is fragrant with the sweet odor which they only can exhale, and all around is gayety, happiness and FREEDOM. I alone, of all the denizens of this great emporium, pine in captivity. Do not forget, I pray you, that our foreign relations are in a most critical condition. A blunder may not only prove fatal to your Administration, but it may light a torch to set the world on fire. Though I am personally friendly to Mr. Maximillian and his schemes, still I am fully advised of the embarrassments he has caused to yourself and Cabinet. Remember it is the last hair that breaks the camel's back. Will not my arrest cause a sensation at St. James, St. Cloud and St. Petersburg—indeed, throughout all Europe? Will not the Sublime Porte[15] be aroused? And will not those great powers, who so anxiously await a pretext to interfere in behalf of Maximillian, be urged to extreme measures, when informed that his chief American ally is under arrest? I will no further enlarge upon the danger; a wise statesmanship alone can save your Administration, and, what is of the first importance to every office-holder, secure your re-election. I suggest this expedient as the best; Brownlow has any number of Courts in Tennessee. His Judges (although our Constitution requires that they be elected by the people) have been appointed by himself. They are as true as steel to you and your glorious Administration. Their jurisdiction is coextensive with their own wishes and Brownlow's necessities. They are all sworn to execute his pious will. Besides, you have Federal Courts in full operation all over Tennessee. Courts are regularly held at Memphis, Nashville and Knoxville for the Judicial Districts which embrace the State, in each of which District Attorneys, who are good Abolitionists, reside. The Judge, Hon. C. F. Trigg, is *your* friend, and was appointed upon your and Brownlow's urgent recommendation. He voted for you. I never belonged to "the land or naval service," and I suggest, with great diffidence, it is true, that, by transferring me to some one of these many tribunals for a "speedy trial," the sensibilities of the legal profession will not be shocked beyond recovery. Failing in this, am I asking too much when I avow myself willing to swallow a dose of that universal panacea for all doubtful cases, the Military Commission at Washington? Doubtless it has jurisdiction of my case, as I am accused of conspiracy. I know it is competent to inflict that punishment which many of your old rebel friends say I deserve—hanging—as it has recently hung a woman.[16] Don't fail to write soon. Direct your *private* letters to Paducah, Kentucky.

May our Heavenly Father speedily restore your Excellency's health, enlarge your already powerful judgment and understanding, save you from being again *poisoned*, as on the 4th of March last, and finally crown you in Heaven with "the old man Brown" and all the mighty hosts who await you there.

Your Excellency will again accept renewed assurances of the high consideration in which you are ever held by

Your very humble servant, sincere admirer and affectionate friend.[17]

EMERSON ETHERIDGE

The Missouri Republican (St. Louis), July 19, 1865.

1. While campaigning for Congress as a Conservative, Etheridge was arrested on unspecified charges and taken to Columbus, Ky. Alexander, *Reconstruction*, 87–88.

2. By referring to a distinctly German method of brewing introduced into the U.S. shortly before the Civil War, Etheridge identifies the arresting officers as Germans. William L. Downard, *Dictionary of the History of the American Brewing and Distilling Industries* (Westport, Conn., 1980), 106.

3. Caldwell (1832–1903), Dresden lawyer, served in the antebellum legislature, in Congress in the 1870s, and later in the state senate. *BDAC*.

4. The resolutions stated the circumstances of the reestablishment of civil government in Tennessee and concluded by lambasting the "self-constituted convention and legislature," including Governor Brownlow, for acts "scarcely less treasonable, revolutionary, and lawless" than those of the "original authors and instigators of the rebellion." If the federal government, by use of troops, backed these "usurpers," it too was guilty of "usurpation." *House Misc. Docs.*, 39 Cong., 2 Sess., No. 72, p. 38 (Ser. 1302).

5. W. K. Hall, state senator for Gibson, Carroll, and Dyer counties, and James E. McNair (b. *c*1835), a North Carolina-born farmer who served as a lieutenant in the 6th Tenn. Cav., USA. *BDTA*, 2: 584–85; *Knoxville Whig and Rebel Ventilator*, Apr. 26, 1865; *Report of the Adjutant General of the State of Tennessee on the Military Forces of the State from 1861 to 1866* (Nashville, 1866), 469.

6. With this reference to Charles Dickens' *Pickwick Papers*, Etheridge makes it clear to Johnson that he meant exactly what he said and was not making such an inflammatory statement in an off-hand or flippant fashion. Charles Dickens, *The Pickwick Papers*, ed. James Kinsley (Oxford, 1986), 7.

7. Speech on Harper's Ferry Incident, December 12, 1859, *Johnson Papers*, 3: 318–50.

8. Speech on Secession, December 18–19, 1860, ibid., 4: 3–46. Quoted passages from the Irish patriot Robert Emmet are found on pages 45–46. Davis' "unprovoked insult" probably came during the exchange on pages 39–40. Etheridge was then a member of the House.

9. Johnson quoted this resolution—promulgated at a Greeneville "State Rights" meeting in November 1860—during his Speech on Secession, December 18–19, 1860, ibid., 4: 6, 46n. For the full text, see U.S. Congress, *The Congressional Globe* (23 Congress to 42 Congress, Washington, D.C., 1834–73), 36 Cong., 2 Sess., 117–18.

10. Milton S. Latham, senator from California (1860–63), read several passages for Johnson, who explained that he could not "see by this light." *Johnson Papers*, 4: 18, 31, 37.

11. Although Henry Ward Beecher's comments have not been found, George Wilkes, in his *Spirit of the Times* on April 29, 1865, had opined that Johnson had been under the influence of a "deadly poison" on inauguration day, administered by the same group of assassins who later killed Lincoln.

12. Speech on Secession, December 18–19, 1860, *Johnson Papers*, 4: 32.

13. Samuel C. Mercer. The June 9, 1862, *Union*, in which Johnson's speech appeared, is no longer extant.

14. Johnson offered a similar syllogism in his Speech at Columbus, Ohio, October 4, 1861. *Johnson Papers*, 5: 18.

15. The court of the ruler of the Ottoman Empire. Burton Stevenson, ed., *The Home Book of Quotations* (New York, 1967), 2061.

16. Mary E. Surratt.

17. Not until September 26 did Etheridge have his day in court before a military tribunal. Charged with "Encouraging resistance to the enforcement of the laws" and with "Inciting sedition and insurrection," he was found not guilty on both counts. *House Misc. Docs.*, 39 Cong., 2 Sess., No. 72, pp. 38–40 (Ser. 1302).

From Lizinka C. Ewell

Wakefield Rhode Island
13th July 1865

Andrew Johnson—President of the U. States

You told me to address you not with the formality due to your high office but with the freedom of a friend. I do so with fear & trembling.[1] You have treated me so harshly & cruelly that I scarcely dare approach you with any petition but I am very miserable. I have seen my husband & son haggard from their months confinement in Stone-celler & the former debilitated & almost helpless from injury to his leg & the effects of poor diet & imprisonment. Without them life is barren of interest to me. When my little girl[2] can get along without me—I would rather die than live—if indeed I am to be separated from Richard & Campbell[3]—my husband & my child. A single line from you can give them back to liberty & me to happiness. Will you write it? Or are your professions of kind feeling towards me merely air—intended to deceive one too miserable & insignificant to be worthy of such artifice from such a man. I am afraid to write to you—afraid of rendering their confinement harder—by making some mistake as in my note to Mrs Johnson[4]—but I am too miserable & restless to be quiet & I appeal to you—as a weak woman to a strong man—& entreat you by all that makes life dear to you—to give me back my husband & my child. I am afraid to write more—I could not write less—but if Richard dies in Ft. Warren—how I will hate you—wicked as it is to hate any one.[5]

Your miserable friend Lizinka C. Ewell

ALS, DLC-JP.

1. Because she had moved from Baltimore to Wakefield, Mrs. Ewell did not know that a week earlier Johnson, in response to her appeal, had wired, "If you will visit Washington on tomorrow or Monday, I will see if some arrangement cannot be made in reference to the release of General Ewell and your son." Discovering that she did not receive the wire, the President, the day previous to this letter, had his military secretary write a letter to Rhode Island repeating the earlier invitation. Johnson to Ewell, July 7, 1865, and Reuben D. Mussey to Ewell, July 12, 1865, Polk, Brown, and Ewell Family Papers, Southern Historical Collection, University of North Carolina.

2. Harriot Brown.

3. Confederate Gen. Richard S. Ewell and Capt. Campbell Brown, both imprisoned at Fort Warren.

4. In the hope of reoccupying some portion of her home in Nashville, then occupied by Johnson's family, Mrs. Ewell had delivered a note to Mrs. Johnson, requesting "the use of one or two rooms in my own house." She received no reply and, according to her daughter's later account, concluded "from subsequent events . . . that Mrs. Johnson showed it to her husband, who took offence at the request or the manner of making it." See Letter from Martha J. Patterson, April 15, 1865, *Johnson Papers*, 7: 560, 561n; Harriot S. Turner, "Recollections of Andrew Johnson," *Harper's*, 120 (1909–10): 174.

5. An exchange of wires brought Mrs. Ewell an interview with Johnson on the 17th followed by a presidential parole to the general and his stepson, conditioned upon their taking the oath of allegiance and giving bond. L. Ewell to Johnson, July 15, Tels. Recd., President, Vol. 4 (1865–66), and Johnson to L. Ewell, July 16, 1865, Tels. Sent, President, Vol. 2 (1865), RG107, NA; Johnson to Commanding Officer, Fort Warren, July 17, 1865, Johnson Papers, LC.

From Amos Kendall[1]

Washington July 13th 1865

President Andrew Johnson
Sir,

Twice I have called to see you, the first time to thank you for rejecting the present offered by your New York friends,[2] thus aiming a blow at one of the most prolific causes of corruption which beset this government. On that occasion you were not in. On the second occasion, I had the same object in view with the addition that I desired to thank you in the strongest terms for the sound principles enunciated by you in relation to the States whose people have recently been in rebellion, and especially for your determination to regard that legitimate State Right which underlies all our institutions, the regulation of the right of suffrage.[3] Having on that occasion waited over two hours, I left intending to call again. Seeing that since your recovery from your late indisposition, you are again overwhelmed by visitors, I take this method to express my hearty thanks for the efforts you are making to purify our government and save its fundamental principles from being swallowed up in the waves of a fanatical revolution.

Your task, though a difficult, is still a most important and honorable one; of its faithful performance the most exalted may well be proud; and as feeble and powerless as my voice is, I cannot be content without raising it to cheer you on in your glorious work. I am sure God and the people will sustain you.

With the highest respect Amos Kendall

Present

ALS, DLC-JP.
1. Fourth auditor of the treasury and postmaster general under Presidents Jackson and Van Buren.
2. See New York Citizens to Johnson, May 17, 1865, *Washington Morning Chronicle*, May 26, 1865; Letter to New York City Merchants, May 22, 1865.
3. See Interview with South Carolina Delegation, June 24, 1865.

From Rolfe S. Saunders
Private

Nashville, July 13, 1865

My Dear Sir:

I have just completed a canvass of Fayette, Tipton, Haywood, McNairy, Shelby & part of Hardeman, and it gives me pleasure to assure you that never before did you have so many & such ardent friends in those Counties. With scare an exception they are all for you. Your course meets their most hearty approval.

I have no fears but I will get a large maj over any of my opponents for Congress; and I think I will beat *all* of them.[1] I am now on my way to see Col. Hurst's Regt.[2] at Pulaski with letters from him urging them to give me their entire vote. You may count at least on *one* steadfast friend if I am elected—a friend anyhow.

Urge up on your P.M. Genl.[3] to reestablish the Post routes in W. Tenn. [as] soon as possible. They are greatly needed. The best of feeling pervades all classes except a few secesh, who wanted the war & never took any hand in it. Some of them yet grumble; but they are few & insignificant. The returned soldiers all speak well of you; & only regret they have not the same priviledges you grant in Miss. & other Southern States.[4] They hope patiently & confidently that they will be placed on the same footing. It would produce a most excellent effect.

Pardon this, & believe me as ever, Yrs. truly
Rolfe S. Saunders.

To His Excellency, Andrew Johnson

ALS, DLC-JP.
1. Saunders' optimism was unjustified, for he came in third in the election returns. Alexander, *Reconstruction*, 90, 261n.
2. Fielding Hurst, of the 6th Tenn. Cav., USA.
3. William Dennison.
4. Under Johnson's proclamations establishing provisional government in these states, returned soldiers who did not fall within the several exceptions of the Amnesty Proclamation could vote after subscribing to the amnesty oath of that proclamation, whereas Tennessee's Confederate non-com soldiers had been disfranchised for five years and officers for fifteen years by the Brownlow government. Alexander, *Reconstruction*, 74–75.

From Eliakim P. Walton[1]

Montpelier, Vt., July 13, 1865.

To the President of the United States:
Sir:

Perhaps you will recollect that, immediately after the first inauguration of President Lincoln, a large party of *very* "black Republicans" invaded your room one day, and through myself as their representative in Congress and spokesman, expressed their admiration of the patriotic and fearless stand you had taken and ably maintained in the Senate. Most of these same Green Mountain Boys have recently been in council, in State Convention, and have attested anew their confidence and friendship for you, as you will observe by the resolutions I enclose.[2] The people of a State which, from its first constitution, in 1777, abolished all political distinctions founded in color or race, have of course very decided opinions as to the true policy of the Southern States; and in expressing them they have a real regard for the future peace and prosperity of those states, and the perpetuity of the Union: but at the same time they understand perfectly well that it is for the people of those states to form their own Constitutions, subject only to the supervision of Congress under its power to admit Senators and Representatives, and its obligation to secure Republican government to the people of each state. While they are doubtless many who believe that the freedmen constitute a part of the people and are now entitled, theoretically at least, to a voice in reorganizing the states under amended constitutions, they do not quarrel with you for committing the work in the first instance to the white citizens. It is best that those who, for generations, have denied the colored man his natural rights, should now repair the wrong by their own act. If they do not, the opinion of Vermont is that Congress should bar its doors against them until they do. Our people do not, I think, anticipate a satisfactory solution of the question at any early date. The ruling whites of most of the Southern states probably need quite as much time to unlearn their radically wrong political notions, as the poor whites and blacks do to fit themselves for intelligent citizenship. Time is their teacher.

Respectfuly, Your ob't sv't. E. P. Walton.

ALS, DLC-JP.
1. Walton (1812–1890), journalist and editor, served in Congress as a Republican (1857–63) and later in the Vermont state senate. *BDAC*.
2. Not found.

From William J. Bloomer[1]

State of Ill. Cass Co.
Ashland Ill July the 14th 65/

Mr Andrew Johnson President of these U.S.
Verry Dear old Friend

I take the pleasure to address you a few lines.

I am sorry to hear that you have bin in such bad health for some time past. I rejoice to notice that your health is improving. I do pray to Almity God that you may live to see our onct happy Government in a Better condition than what it has bin for the last four years. It is my un shaken opinion Judging from the Start you have made as our chief magistrate that you are the verry man to bring a bout A restoration of peace and hapeniss & prosperity in our Distracted nation. It is likely I had better Tell you who I am and how I come in the State of *Ills*. I am your old friend William J Bloomer of Hawkins County. Settlement of old Christian Pearson[2] on Clinch. The last time I saw you we met to geather in the City of Washington. I was un well. You and I Traveled to geather to Bluntsville *Tennesse*. Thare we parted. I shall never forget the kind attention you paid me while Traveling to geather. You went off at Bluntsville & Baught me some medicin so I got home all right. You had one of your front Teeth Taken out at withville (Va) on our way. That same yeare you become A candidate for govner. I rode severl weaks thro my county to aid you in your Election. I made it Tell (Too).[3] I have the pleasure to say that I have voted for you for all the offices you Ever run for before the People from State senate to (Vice President). A fee years before the Rebelion I mooved to Missouri while you was I believe Serving Your last Term as govner. I lived in Mo. until this Rebelion come up & I Taken sid with the (Union) and Constitution. Gerrillers come in my Town & Broke me all most up. I was Merchandiseing. I left Warsaw Mo. in the fall of 63/ me and famly and mooved to Ashland Ill. I am old & crippled with Rheumatism, But I have Plenty friends & acquaintance. I live in a Democrat county and that suits me verry well.

I often Told the whigs in Tennesse when you was canvassing that I should live to see you President of these (U S). It was a centiment from my hart. I all ways craved to see you president But the assinnation of Mr Lincoln was a Horable Bad act. President I well know you have a big job, before you. More to do A greater Responsibilly than any President before you. But I am fully persuaded and I Tell Every person so that I Talk with that your administration will be one of the most Lasting administrations held in Rememberance by the people of this government. We see that you let fanatics know that you are President of these (U S). Mr Johnson I have Two much respect for you to preach politics to your (Honor) But I feel like Talking as I did in my native state Tenn. I will say one thing to you & the Verry moment you come out a gainst Negro Suffrage you immortalized your self in this nation & all the nations of the Earth. Thare is a party a raid a gainst you in Politics But that Party will soon play out. I believe you will be the peoples choise for our next president from all that I can learn. I hope you will be a ble to organise all the seceded States in time for them to send thare Representatives to our next Congress. I hope you will write to me on the Reception these awkerd lins. I am verry Desirous to know how your health is. Also your famly. Please do not forget me. I know you have a press of Busyness on hand. If you fail to write the Post master in my Town will Laugh at me for writing to you.[4]

Your True friend W. J. Bloomer

ALS, DLC-JP.
    1. Bloomer (b. c1815) owned a grocery in Missouri. 1860 Census, Mo., Benton,
Warsaw, 144.
    2. Probably Christian Pearson (b. c1787), a Hawkins County farmer who resided in
an area north of Rogersville. 1850 Census, Tenn., Hawkins, 2nd. Dist., 624.
    3. Johnson carried Hawkins County in both the 1853 and 1855 gubernatorial elec-
tions by approximately 300 votes. White, *Messages of Govs.*, 4: 521, 628.
    4. Bloomer's letter of April 17, 1866, indicates that Johnson sent a reply on July 22,
1865, but the latter document is not extant. Appts., Internal Revenue Service, Collector,
Ill., 10th Dist., William J. Bloomer.

From Elbert H. English

ca. July 14, 1865, Little Rock, Ark.; ALS, DNA-RG94, Amnesty Papers
(M1003, Roll 13), Ark., E. H. English.

Chief justice of Arkansas, in a lengthy pardon application, states that he opposed secession "both on principle and expediency" but acquiesced in Confederate rule and continued to serve as judge. "I frankly confess to you, Sir,
however, that after Arkansas had seceded, and the deplorable Civil War had
commenced, my feelings and sympathies became enlisted on the side of the
southern people—though I took no part in the war, and deeply regretted its
existence." Seeks return of his house, which had been libelled, along with some
furniture. Although he deeded the family residence to his wife prior to the
Confiscation Act, the judge ruled that the proof of the delivery of the deed prior
to the Act was "deficient"; this decision is now under appeal in the U.S. District Court. English further states that he has been informed that some 250
persons, including state officers, have been indicted, and that he is probably
among them; having neither seen the indictment nor been arrested, he hopes
for a special pardon to "be so framed as to relieve me from prosecution in
such indictment if any has in fact been found." [He was pardoned November
13, 1865.]

From Joseph E. Brown
(Copy)

                                                    Milledgeville July 15th 1865
His Excellency Andrew Johnson President &c &c
Dear Sir
    On my return home I came across the country from Savannah to
Macon in a buggy with a view to see and converse with as many as
possible of the people of the section of the country between. The exposure to the sun and rain brought upon me an attack of billious fever
which has confined me to my bed most of the time since I got home. I
am now convalescent and hope in a few days to be able to travel.
    I write you a short letter (feeble as I am) to say that I conversed with
many persons on the way and many friends have called to see me since
I got home from different parts of the state, and I am satisfied your
policy will be carried out in the state. The Convention[1] will abolish
slavery in my opinion though there will be in it an element of opposition. It is hard for our slaveholders to realize the facts as they exist, and

to accept them. I send you a copy of my address to the people of Georgia[2] which so far as I am able to judge has had a good effect. The people were in much confusion and no leading man had indicated to them any course. They have read my address with interest and have I believe generally acquiesced in its suggestions. I shall do all in my power to have the Convention incorporate into the state constitution a clause forever prohibiting slavery and to pass a resolution concurring in the proposed amendment of the constitution on that subject. I am satisfied under all the circumstances by which we are surrounded that this is best for our people and will promote the future prosperity of the state. If I could be a member of the Convention I believe I could be of service but this can not be on account of the disabilities under which I labor. I will do all I can to get the right sort of men elected where I have influence and hope and believe all will work right.

Gov Johnson has arrived here and has called on me. He will board with me. We shall act harmoniously and I shall do all I can to sustain him in carrying out your policy.[3] He puts a very limited construction upon his powers—thinks about all he has to do is to call a convention and to take care of the public property till it meets. Comparatively few of our people have yet had an opportunity to take the oath. The Governor holds that only the military officers have power to administer it and that he can appoint no one to do it. There are 132 counties in the state, many of them remote from a R R or military post. If officers are not sent to these counties to administer the oath few will take it. I respectfully suggest that this subject is worthy of immediate attention and action. In all these backwoods counties the people are well disposed towards the Government, and should have an opportunity to take the oath, and vote. They will from all these counties send delegates for immediate abolition. I will write you more fully when I have more strength and see more of our people. As we have no mails I send this by Express.[4] I should be very happy to have any suggestions you may think proper to make. I wish to see or communicate with Senator Patterson.[5] Please telegraph me when this reaches you where he is. I feel under great obligations for your kindness and courtesy and shall always be most happy to serve you.

I am very truly your friend Joseph E. Brown

ALS copy, GU-Felix Hargrett Col., Joseph E. Brown Papers.

1. The state constitutional convention that would meet three months later.

2. This was his farewell address of June 29, 1865 (twelve days after James Johnson's appointment as provisional governor) in which Brown had urged support for the President's reconstruction policies. Allen D. Candler, ed., *The Confederate Records of the State of Georgia* (6 vols., Atlanta, 1909), 2: 884–92.

3. See Letter from James Johnson, August 14, 1865.

4. He also sent a dispatch reiterating the urgency of appointing oath administrators. See Telegram from Brown, July 21, 1865.

5. Senator-elect David T. Patterson, the President's son-in-law, who would offer to use his influence to obtain a pardon for Brown. Parks, *Brown*, 340.

From Ulysses S. Grant

Head Quarters Armies of the United States,
Washington D.C. July 15th 1865

His Excellency, A. Johnson,
President of the United States,
Sir:

Looking upon the French occupation of Mexico as part and parcel of the late rebellion in the United States, and a necessary part of it to suppress before entire peace can be assured, I would respectfully recommend that a leave of absence be given to one of our General officers for the purpose of going to Mexico to give direction to such emigration as may go to that country.

I would not advise that emigration be invited or that such officer should go under special instructions. He would probably take service under the Liberal Government of Mexico and by giving head and shape to the foreign and native element already there would insure the restoration of the Liberal or Republican Government.

Mexico has men enough if she had Arms to defend herself. With the large surplus on hand I do not see why we should not sell her them. I presume there would be no objection raised to sell the English or French Government Arms. I do not see therefore why we should not be allowed to sell them to the only Government we recognize on Mexican soil.

I write this for instructions because I will not do or authorize anything not receiving the proper sanction. Of the sale of arms I have nothing to do. I speak therefore in reference to giving leaves of absence for the purpose stated.

I send this direct the Sec. of War being absent from his office to-day.[1]

Very respectfully Your obt. svt.

U. S. Grant Lt. Gen

ALS, NHi-Andrew Johnson Papers.

1. Grant had already approached Gen. John M. Schofield with his idea, and Johnson apparently approved it. However, Seward, who opposed the use of military force as a first resort, convinced Schofield to journey instead to Paris and inform the government of Napoleon III that a continued French presence in Mexico would not be tolerated by the United States. Glyndon G. Van Deusen, *William Henry Seward* (New York, 1967), 491–92; James L. McDonough, *Schofield: Union General in the Civil War and Reconstruction* (Tallahassee, Fla., 1972), 162–66.

From Samuel Hartz[1]

Office of the Commissary General of Prisoners,
Washington, D.C., July 15th, 1865.

To his Excellency, Andrew Johnson
President of the United States.

Having presented a petition from my son late Captain Edward L. Hartz,[2] U.S.A. I am requested by him to say, that if he can not be restored to his former position in the regular army, he is willing to join Genl. Hancocks Corps.[3] if he can be permitted to do so.

He is Government property, having been Educated at the Expens of the Goverment, and to serve the Government, I believe it is required by the army regulations, that a Board of Survey should be held on all property before being condemned, as useless, and Court Martials on officers for Violation of any of the Articles of War, and think it a hard case that he should be dropped on Expart Evidence—without an oppertunity of defence, and placed in a possition that he can not again Enter the Service of the Governmnt.

The Constitution guarrantees to Every man a fair trial, which has not been allowed him. Even a Government Horse is honored with a Board of Survey before being condemned. There being no charges against him to my knowledge of infidelity, malfesence, or being a defaulter, having disbursed several millions of Dollars, while in the service, and not owing the Government one cent, that I am aware of. I hope that his case may meet your full and favorable consideration, and submit this in connection with his petition now pending before you, and ask nothing but a fair hearing, and that Justice may be done him.[4]

I am with great respect Your Excellencies
Obedient Servant Saml. Hartz

ALS, DNA-RG94, ACP Branch, File Q-62-CB-1868, E. L. Hartz.

1. Samuel Hartz (b. *c*1808), former Pottsville, Pa., justice of the peace, was a War Department clerk. 1850 Census, Pa., Schuylkill, Pottsville, N.W. Ward, 613; Washington, D.C., directories (1863–65).

2. Edward L. Hartz (*c*1831–1868), a West Point graduate, was a chief assistant quartermaster at Chattanooga. According to his father's petition of June 23, 1865, young Hartz, upon the recommendation of the quartermaster general, had been dismissed from service for drunkenness in July 1864, "without a hearing, or assigned cause." The West Point Alumni Foundation, Inc., *Register of Graduates and Former Cadets of the United States Military Academy: Cullum Memorial Edition* (West Point, 1970), 249; Edwin M. Stanton to Johnson, July 1, 1865, Lets. Sent, Mil. Bks., Exec., 56-C, RG107, NA; Samuel Hartz to Johnson, June 23, 1865, ACP Branch, File Q-62-CB-1868, E. L. Hartz, RG94, NA.

3. Gen. Winfield S. Hancock's Veteran Reserve Corps.

4. Writing on his own behalf, young Hartz reported that, after becoming ill in June 1864 and requesting a "respite from duty," he learned that he had been discharged from the army. He reiterated that the charge "was not the result of regular official investigation but of casual report." Explaining the nature of his illness, he sought restoration or, failing

that, an honorable discharge. He was reinstated in 1866. Edward L. Hartz to Johnson, June 18, 1865, ACP Branch, File Q-62-CB-1868, E. L. Hartz, RG94, NA; *West Point Register* (1970), 249.

To Hugh McCulloch

Executive Office, Washington, D.C.
July 15th 1865

To the Hon Secretary of the Treasury
Sir

Any arrangements that you may make with Genl. Geo P Estis[1] in reference to securing and promoting the interest of the goverment in regard to cotton captured or surrendered to the United States will meet with my approbation.

Most Respectfully Andrew Johnson

LS, DNA-RG56, Misc. Div., Claims for Cotton and Captured and Abandoned Property.
    1. Estey (Este) (1829–1881), commander of the 2nd Bde., 3rd Div., Army of the Tennessee, was stationed at Louisville, Ky. Resigning in December 1865, he practiced law in Washington, D.C. Warner, *Blue*; *OR*, Ser. 1, Vol. 49, Pt. 2: 1065.

From William G. Wyly[1]

Washington City D C
July 15th 1865

President Johnson
Dear Sir:

Permit me to apply for the office of Judge of the U.S. District Court for the Western District of Louisiana.

I have been practising law in that District for the last ten years & graduated in the law School of New Orleans under Judge Roselius.[2]

I enclose herewith a letter from Judge Roselius in relation thereto.

I have stood fast to the old flag & the government of our ancestors, amidst the widespread treasonable infection of the south.

I have lost every thing by this horrible Rebellion, but my patriotism & my profound reverence for the constitution & laws of my country.

The letters of Gov Wells & other distinguished Louisianians which I handed you yesterday bear evidence of my uniform loyalty & patriotism.[3]

I have the honor to be very Respectfully Yrs
W G Wyly

ALS, DNA-RG60, Appt. Files for Judicial Dists., La., W. G. Wyly.
    1. Wyly (b. c1832) was an East Tennessee-born lawyer, practicing in Floyd, La. 1860 Census, La., Carroll, 4th Ward, 19. See Letter from Wyly, August 10, 1865.
    2. Christian Roselius (1803–1873) was one of the state's leading lawyers, as well as a professor at the University of Louisiana, later Tulane. *DAB*; Tregle, "Thomas Durant and Reconstruction," 496–97.
    3. Wyly's application, forwarded to Attorney General Speed on July 21, 1865, was endorsed by Johnson: "This young man has been known to me from his infancy and I

respectfully commend him to the favorable attention of the Attorney General." The two
judicial districts of Louisiana, however, were combined in 1867, with Judge Edward H.
Durell, rather than Wyly, receiving the appointment. Wyly to Speed, July 21, 1865,
Appt. Files for Judicial Dists., La., W. G. Wyly, RG60, NA; *U.S. Off. Reg.* (1867), 318.

From William G. Brownlow

Knoxville, July 16, 1865

President Johnson:

I have several letters from Gov. Foote and Ben. Hill[1] asking my
friendly interference in obtaining for them pardon. You are in possession of more facts in regard to their cases than I am, and I cannot feel
at liberty to urge upon you any particular action.

I respectfully suggest, that you let both of them return home on *parole*, trusting to their good behaviour, and having them to understand,
that a future pardon is suspended upon the condition of their good
conduct. This is but a *suggestion*, and is made on the supposition that
there are no *serious and specific* charges against them.

I am, Very truly, &c,
W. G. Brownlow
Gov. of Tenn.

ALS, DNA-RG94, Amnesty Papers (M1003), Roll 51), Tenn., Misc.
   1. Henry S. Foote, Tennessee Confederate senator, and McMinnville resident Benjamin J. Hill (1825–1880), a merchant and lawyer, who had been a southern brigadier.
The letters to Brownlow and pardon dates have not been found. *BDTA*, 1: 365–66.

To William G. Brownlow

Executive Office,
Washington, D.C., July 16th, 1865.[1]

To Gov W. G. Brownlow,
Nashville, Tenn.

I hope, as I have no doubt, you will, see that the laws passed by the
last Legislature are faithfully executed and that all illegal voters in the
approaching election be kept from the Polls and that the Election of
members of Congress be conducted fairly. Whenever it becomes necessary for the execution of the law and the protection of the ballot box
you will call upon General Thomas for sufficient military force to sustain the civil authority of the state. I have just read your address which
I most heartily endorse.[2]

Andrew Johnson President U.S.

Tel, DNA-RG107, Tels. Sent, President, Vol. 2 (1865).
   1. The recipient's copy of this telegram is dated July 10, 1865, but subsequent
correspondence indicates that July 16 is the correct date. Johnson to Brownlow,
July 10, 1865, A. Johnson Corres., TSLA. See Telegram from George H. Thomas, July
20, 1865.

2. On the 20th Johnson dispatched a second, slightly modified copy of this wire, with the following addendum: "I have recd your recent address to the people of the State, and think it well timed and hope it will do much good in reconciling the opposition to the ammendment of the constitution and the laws passed by the last Legislature. The law must be executed and the civil authority sustained. In your efforts to do this if necessary, Genl. Thomas will afford sufficient military force. You are at liberty to make what use you think proper of this dispatch. Please furnish Genl. Thomas with a copy." Tels. Sent, President, Vol. 2 (1865), RG107, NA.

From John S. Carlile

July 16, 1865, "Waverly Near Fredk Md."; ALS, DLC-JP.

Former Virginia congressman offers written advice in lieu of a personal interview, which he had sought on several occasions. "Solicitious" for Johnson's re-election, he believes "nothing can defeat you unless the patronage of your administration should be wielded against you," for the "Treasury War Attorney General's and Post office Departments" with all their agents and appointees "can elect anybody." Carlile warns that "already the Chief Justice is in the field on the stump!!!" He has "always supposed" that Secretary Stanton "had a supreme admiration for Edwin M Stanton and his aspirations," adding, "whether he could cordially sustain the hand that retains him in position and place I know not."

To Edward H. East

Executive Office, Washington, D.C.
July 16th 1865.

To Hon. Edward H East
Nashville Tenn

I dislike to be importunate & over urgent. You know that I desire you to be with me, and beleive in the end your interest would be promoted as well as mine. I still desire you to come if you can reconcile it to your feelings and interest to do so.[1] Your friend

Andrew Johnson.

Tel, DNA-RG107, Tels. Sent, President, Vol. 2 (1865).
1. East replied: "Sickness of my Mother and helplessness of family . . . prevents a definite answer at present." Although East made a visit to Washington in June, he never became part of Johnson's White House staff. East to Johnson, July 16, 1865, Johnson Papers, LC.; see also Letter from Horace Maynard, May 2, 1865; Johnson to East, July 9, Tels. Sent, President, Vol. 2, RG107, NA.

To Alvin Hawkins[1]

Executive Office. Washington, D.C.
July 16 1865

Hon Alvin Hawkins
Memphis Tenn

I have been advised that 1600 Bales of Cotton claimed by Parkman Brooks & Co[2] was seized by the Treasury agent and after investigation by the Treasury Department it was determined that the transaction was fair and that the Agent deliver the Cotton back to the claimants, and that it was then seized by the District Attorney and is still held by his instruction.[3] I desire to know upon what proof the Cotton was seized and is still held and what is the state of the proceedings up to this time.[4]

Andrew Johnson. President U.S.

Tel, DNA-RG107, Tels. Sent, President, Vol. 2 (1865).
1. U.S. district attorney for West Tennessee, appointed in 1864, reappointed the next year, and subsequently elected governor of Tennessee.
2. Edward Parkman and Franklin W. Brooks (c1838–fl1872), a Memphis attorney who became a claims agent in Washington, D.C. 1860 Census, Tenn., Shelby, Memphis, 5th Ward, 77; Memphis directories (1860–69); Washington, D.C., directories (1867–72); see also Letter from James B. Bingham, May 28, 1865.
3. The claimants had originally contracted to purchase 15,000 bales from the Confederates. Parkman himself in September 1864 went with a vessel to buy the cotton at Shreveport. He was captured on his return by Federal troops and sent to Memphis. Although he had obtained a permit from Treasury Secretary William P. Fessenden to bring 15,000 bales out of the South, Federal military authorities believed he had "fraudulently" purchased the cotton and was guilty of "complicity" with Confederate officials. According to the latter's records, Parkman had indeed offered to buy the cotton for about 30¢ a pound from the Confederates and had delivered $16,000 in supplies to them. OR, Ser. 1, Vol. 41, Pt. 4: 629–30; Johnson, "Northern Profits," 103–5.
4. In reply to Johnson's query, Hawkins wired that the claimant's cotton had been seized "upon proof that it has been purchased and transported in violation of law and has been acquired by the late rebel government for the purpose of aiding the rebellion." Hawkins to Johnson, July 18, 1865, Tels. Recd., President, Vol. 4 (1865–66), RG107, NA.

From Benjamin H. Brewster

July 17, 1865, Philadelphia, Pa.; ALS, DNA-RG56, Appts., Customs Service, Collector, Philadelphia, Thomas Webster.

A prominent lawyer writes in behalf of his friend Thomas Webster, a merchant and shipping agent, who desires "to be Collector of this Port." He is "the person most fit," and his services during the war "were of more value to the Government than those of any other man" in Pennsylvania. Black enlistments were inaugurated by his efforts and "made a practical success." He started, presided over, and "was" the Philadelphia Supervisory Committee for Recruiting Colored Regiments. "The draft was a practical failure," and without "those negro regiments the war would still be raging." Webster and the writer are former Democrats who, with other sometime Democrats, rescued the "falling fortunes" of the Republicans during the war. Thus, because of "his former political position," Webster can not "command a cordial help from those who now help others from a sense of partizan duty." [Webster failed to obtain the appointment.]

From Martha Deery Churchwell [1]

Winchester Tenn.
July 17th 1865.

To His Excellency Andrew Johnson,
President of the United States.
Sir.

May I entreat of you to read this communication yourself. Strangers cannot understand it. Do I ask too much? Read and judge for yourself.

I come to you as an old acquaintance of my Father & Brother's,[2] they who have so often rallied under the Democratic Banner for you as their choice, and so successfully too, as your own memory and history will prove. I repeat I come to you as to a friend, who will not turn a deaf ear to my short statement of facts, which will in some degree put you in possession of my *situation*.

I have just returned from Knoxville. I went over with Gov. Brownlow by invitation, and from whom I received every attention & politeness that a lady can so much *feel and appreciate*.

The object of my visit, was to gather something from the wreck of *my own property, on which to live*.

My Husband[3] having died insolvent, the personalty was all I could derive benefit from, and this being *small*, the greater *the necessity* for me having my portion of it.

A Law & Miscellaneous Library have been destroyed by the Federals, valued at more than five thousand dollars by one or two Genls. of the Federal Army. The Sword & Gun was taken from his Father's where I had left them, not having a home to place them in.

My Husband, was made Trustee of my Estate, and the only portion of it ever in my hands, was at his urgent request invested in a family of Negroes in September 1862 the year of his death. Mr. Cs. brotherinlaw Mr Jos. Mabry,[4] immediately attached those Negroes, & brought suit against myself & the Bank. President Lincoln abolished Slavery, the War ended, and I have lost both money and Negroes. I will remark that Mr Mabry *was and is now*, a man of wealth & large resources. He has taken from me the Widows mite, while I am I fear reduced to beggary.

The feelings of my own heart have prompted me without consulting any one, to write and ask you if your large heart & magnanimity will not cause to be restored to me what the war has taken from me; I refer to books &c.

I could write pages that would *enlist your sympathies*, but I feel that you know who I am and that nothing but pressing necessity would compell me to make this communication.

While I sincerely deplore the death of President Lincoln, Allow me

to congratulate you that an East Tennesseean, & that one yourself, occupies the proud position.

With much Respect,
Mrs W. M. Churchwell.

ALS, DLC-JP.
1. Churchwell (1830–1897) later resided in Bristol, Tenn. Herschel Gower and
Jack Allen, eds., *Pen and Sword: The Life and Journals of Randal W. McGavock* (Nashville, 1959), 91, 350n.
2. William Deery (c1765 or 1770–1843 or 1845), a wealthy Blountville merchant
and large landowner, had three sons: James A. (c1820–1857), William Bruce (c1822
or 1828–1892 or 1898), and Robert E. (c1829–1892), the first two of whom moved at
mid-century to Williamson County and established a textile mill. Ibid., 62, 663, 664;
WPA, *Sullivan County Tennessee Tombstone Records* (1936), 12; Worth S. Ray, *Tennessee Cousins* (Baltimore, 1966[1950]), 172. There are discrepancies in the last two
sources regarding the Deerys' dates.
3. William M. Churchwell.
4. Joseph A. Mabry, a Knoxville businessman, had married Churchwell's sister,
Laura. Lucille Deaderick, ed., *Heart of the Valley: A History of Knoxville, Tennessee*
(Knoxville, 1976), 564.

From Sherrard Clemens

Shreveport La July 17th 1865
His Excellency Andrew Johnson Pres. U.S.
Sir

In virtue of the written authority extended by you to me I am here:[1]
and I am compelled to say, that the state of things resulting from the
acts of various local agents, has taken me utterly by surprise: and is I
am bold to say, rapidly bringing the government itself into disrepute.
The circumstances as near as I can gather them up to the present moment, are as follows.

The agents at Memphis Little Rock, Vicksburg and Natchez, have
delegated authority before and since the 15th day of June last to collect
confederate cotton, to sub agents, on various terms, of one half, one
third and one fourth of the proceeds.[2] The local agent divides these
proceeds with the sub agents, or fails to make any return to the Treasury Department at all, putting in many instances the Cotton in the
hands of factors who share the unlawful plunder.

The regular outlet for this country, and Arkansas is New Orleans,
but as the case is now presented, there is conflicting jurisdiction by sub
agents, from Little Rock, Memphis, Vicksburg, Natchez and New Orleans. The consequence is they go to remote points, call upon some
post Commander for an escort of Cavalry, and seize all Cotton at accessible points, under the pretext of securing Cotton and thus defraud
honest Citizens. The whole Country is therefore in a state of alarm,
resulting in a feeling fatal to the organization of any civil policy at all.

Many of these sub agents I know to be disgraced or dismissed officers of the army, in consequence of peculations and frauds, during the war, in this nefarious business. They and the local agents I believe have presumed upon the fact that their designs can be consumated before justice can reach them.

I cannot in this hurried communication go into particulars, but my standing with you will I know, be a sufficient guarantee of my declarations. I will send you hereafter a full and extended communication upon the subject, but in the meantime, prompt and decisive measures are indispensable.

I recommend therefore that the agencies at Memphis, Vicksburg, Natchez and Little Rock be immediately abolished: that they be instructed to report the names of each sub agent appointed by them, to collect Cotton, the amount collected, where and by whom and the terms on which the said Cotton was received where deposited, to whom consigned &c.[3]

The Office at New Orleans under Mr Flanders[4] ought possibly to be retained as well as the sub agency here.

Knowing your detestation of all malversation in Office, I have as succinctly as possible given you my honest advice. If it is not acted upon at once, it will be far better to abolish the whole system, and leave to individual Capital, Enterprise and Energy, the whole question, abandoning all hope of securing a tithe of the vast amount of Cotton which belongs to the government. If it is to be lost at all it better be in the hands of Capitalists who will pay for it, than to be stolen by sworn officers of the Government, who in their cupidity disgrace their profession and show they are capable of the basest turpitude.[5]

In confirmation, of what I say, I Enclose papers, marked respectively from No 1. to No 9.[6] Mr. Little,[7] the Agent at Vicksburg professes to be the brother in law, of the Secretary of the Treasury. If he is, I am humiliated by the fact, as his deputies here, are of the most mercenary description, among whom is Gen Hovey[8] of Illinois, whose history in cotton, is now part of the public records, & who retired from the army in disgrace. My Experience of Two years in the South has given me great advantages. Under the present state of things, I say in pain, that the Federal government, is in utter disrepute. Under all the circumstances, perhaps the most prompt measure, will be for Major Gen Canby,[9] whom I know to be an honest gentlemen, to assume military control & drive out all Treasury Agents, in Louisiana and Arkansas, Except Mr. Jewell,[10] who is here & compel him to report to Mr. Flanders in New Orleans. Both of these gentlemen I believe to be beyond a bribe.

To give more force to this statement I make it under oath.[11]

Your Friend. Sherrard Clemens

L and ALS, DLC-JP.

1. A month earlier Johnson had authorized Clemens to purchase cotton. William A. Browning to H. A. Risley, June 7, 1865, Seventh Special Agency, Lets. Recd., RG366, NA. See also Letter from Clemens, May 20, 1865.

2. Clemens enclosed a permit from a "Local transporting agent" at Shreveport to A. J. Dabbs, authorizing him to "collect and transport (to this point) any and all Confederate cotton" he found in Lamar and Red River counties, Texas. He would receive one-half of the proceeds at the time of the sale. J. M. Berry to A. J. Dabbs, June 24, 1865, Johnson Papers, LC.

3. None of these agencies was closed. Although Secretary McCulloch on June 27 had issued a directive to recall all agents engaged in receiving and disposing of captured cotton, turning such collection over to the military, arguments against such closing prevailed. Actual sales of Confederate cotton captured after June 1865 reached nearly $5,000,000. *House Ex. Docs.*, 39 Cong., 2 Sess., No. 97, p. 27 (Ser. 1293); James G. Randall, "Captured and Abandoned Property During the Civil War," *AHR*, 19 (1913): 77–78.

4. Benjamin F. Flanders. This letter was forwarded by Flanders to Johnson. See Letter from Flanders, July 27, 1865.

5. The remainder of the letter and the witnessing statement are in Clemens' hand.

6. Aside from the permit to Dabbs mentioned above, the only other enclosure found is a printed copy of a July 5 order issued by an Arkansas post commander limiting cotton seizures in that state to the duly authorized treasury agent and prohibiting out-of-state agents and subagents from removing any cotton. Enclosure with Letter from Benjamin F. Flanders, July 27, 1865.

7. George L. Little (*c*1820–*fl*1875), a Fort Wayne, Ind., merchant, was before the war a next-door neighbor and partner of Hugh McCulloch. 1860 Census, Ind., Allen, Wayne Twp., 330; Fort Wayne directories (1858–75).

8. Alvin P. Hovey.

9. Edward R. S. Canby.

10. Probably Edwin L. Jewell (1836–1887), an accountant, subsequently editor of Governor Wells's organ, the *Daily Southern Star*, a state senator, and author of a history of New Orleans. Lowrey, "Wells," 1041; Richard H. Wiggins, "The Louisiana Press and the Lottery," *LHQ*, 31 (1948): 723, 727.

11. Gen. James C. Veatch, commanding at Shreveport, witnessed Clemens' oath.

From John W. Forney

Phila July 17 1865.

His Ex Andrew Johnson

The fact that the Phila Congressional delegation has not named a single war Democrat for federal offices here creates great and Just indignation.[1]

J. W. Forney

Tel, DLC-JP.

1. The next day Forney recommended Thomas Webster for collector at Philadelphia. Forney to Johnson, July 18, 1865, Appts., Customs Service, Collector, Philadelphia, Thomas Webster, RG56, NA.

From William W. Holden

Raleigh July 17 1865.

Prest of the US
Sir

I have appointed about three thousand magistrate & Mayors & Commissioners for all the towns. County courts have been organized & I am now prepared to issue a proclamation for a convention. I will write you at length by a special messenger in the course of a few days. I desire your approval of a plan for administering the amnesty oath to the people of the state[1] & also your approval of my proclamation before it is issued. I will send them with my letter.[2] I think a convention could be assembled on the tenth day of October.[3] It could be called sooner but in so important a matter I think I ought to proceed deliberately & carefully. Please ans so that I may know this has been received.

W W Holden

Tel, DLC-JP.
1. Because of illness Holden did not forward his plan until July 26. Raper, *Holden*, 73.
2. See Letter from Holden, July 26, 1865.
3. The convention first met on October 2.

From Russell Houston

Louisville July 17, 1865

To The President U.S.
My Dear Friend—

I enclose you an application which I hope will not add too much to your present labors.[1] It will not be necessary to send your decision to me, whether favorable or unfavorable, as I will probably be in Washington between the first & fifth of August. I presume, however, that if the application be granted the order to dismiss the proceedings will be sent to Mr. Harrison[2] who is not now in Nashville; & if any order is to be made upon the Military, I suppose it will be forwarded, after ascertaining from Genl. Thomas whether or not the property is needed longer for military purposes. The marshal seized the property before it was taken by Genl. Donaldson[3] & all the personal property had been replevied upon the bond of Mr. Abbey[4] & others & was in the custody of Abbey subject to the order, of the Court; & if the application receive a favorable response & an order is to be made upon the military, I would like for it to be done at an early day in order that Mr Abbey may rent the property as he needs all available means to pay the debts of the Concern, which amounts to a large sum. I know myself of judgments to the amount of about $20,000.

There is no news of interest in this State. I think the result of the approaching election will be adverse to the Constitutional Amendment,[5] but still there is a growing feeling among intelligent & leading men in favor of the prominent measures of your Administration & decidedly in favor of yourself individually & as President of the nation. The Amendment does not seem to be connected with the Administration in the minds of the people & none of its unpopularity attaches to the Executive.

I regret to see so much said & written about the present rebellious disposition of the people of the South inasmuch as I do not believe that it is true. I have seen & conversed with many returned rebel soldiers & have not found a rebellious one among them & I have the same report from others from different parts of the South. They all say the war is over—that they have been fairly whipped—that secession & revolution are a failure, & slavery abolished by the war & that they have come back to be quiet, good & faithful citizens of the United States. I do not expect or wish them to say that they love their government, as their truth might then well be doubted. But they say just enough to show that they are sincere & to create the most cheering hopes for the future. If I thought the charges true, I should not so write, & would be for settling the matter now & so as not to be disturbed hereafter. But as I discredit them, I feel assured that they will be used to the injury of the Country. I have no doubt that these letters, proclamations & addresses will be collected & filed away to be forthcoming in December, in order to defeat, the applications of the Southern States, to be represented in the Congress of the United States on the ground that they are yet thoroughly disloyal as proved by Southern testimony. Many of the authors of these unfortunate documents do not intend any such use of them or such results to follow them, as I suppose; & it is not my purpose to question their honest purposes—but I do very much question their wisdom in the premises.

I learn from East that his mother is quite sick. I believe he had almost made up his mind to go to your relief from what he wrote me & others have told me. He wrote that he had received a telegram from you[6] but that he had not then answered it. I hope he will be able & willing to give you a favorable answer.

With highest regards Russell Houston

ALS, DLC-JP.

1. Houston, attorney for the Methodist Publishing House in Nashville, which had been confiscated in the early part of 1862 and used by the army for printing purposes, sought restoration of the property to the church owners. Houston to Johnson, July 17, 1865, Johnson Papers, LC.

2. Horace H. Harrison, U.S. district attorney.

3. James L. Donaldson.

4. Richard Abbey (1805–1891), Mississippi minister, who in 1858 became the financial secretary of the Methodist Publishing House and remained during the war to

serve as custodian of the property. He was the author of numerous religious works. Horace M. DuBose, *A History of Methodism* (Nashville, 1916), 97, 152; *NUC*.

5. Republicans had unsuccessfully pushed for Kentucky's ratification of the 13th Amendment in the winter and spring of 1865; the "Amendment" was the chief issue of the August election and failed to pass. Coulter, *Civil War Kentucky*, 260–61.

6. Although Johnson had wired East on July 16, the reference here must be to Johnson's earlier request: "When may I expect you? Answer." Johnson to East, July 9, 1865, Ser. 3A, Johnson Papers, LC.

From Gazaway B. Lamar, Sr.

Old Capitol Prison
July 17 1865

To His Excellency Andrew Johnson
President of the United States
Sir,

The order in regard to me, granted by your Excellency, was left on Saturday, in the absence of the Secy of War, with his Assistant Maj. Eckart[1]—who assured me he would deliver it as soon as the Secretary returned. Since then, I have heard of no action in regard to it—& I am still in prison.

May I claim of your Excellency the especial favor of an effectual interposition for my release & the restoration of my Books & papers[2] & also for transportation to Savannah without delay—or—that your Excellency will afford me the honor of another interview, which will enable me to explain every point of my life to your satisfaction—at which Mr Stanton may be also present—that he may also be put right in regard to my conduct.

I feel confident that your Excellency cannot deny my petition, founded on the right of every citizen to be heard, before he is condemned or punished.[3]

Very Respectfully
Yr Obt Servt
G. B. Lamar

ALS, DNA-RG153, Court-Martial Records, MM-3469.

1. Gen. Thomas T. Eckert (1825–1910) headed the Military Telegraph Dept. and served as Stanton's ad interim assistant. In 1867 he resigned from government service and became an administrator for Western Union. *DAB*.

2. Some six months earlier Lamar's business ledgers and correspondence had been confiscated by a U.S. treasury agent in Savannah. Lamar to Lincoln, Jan. 27, 1865, Lincoln Papers, LC.

3. The charges implicating him in Lincoln's death obviously dropped, Lamar finally secured his release from confinement by presidential order on July 28, 1865. The bitter and often heated controversy that ensued over the rights to his confiscated property, however, would consume the rest of Lamar's days. Lamar to Johnson, Sept. 27, 1865, Johnson Papers, LC; Robert Neil Mathis, "The Ordeal of Confiscation: The Post-Civil War Trials of Gazaway Bugg Lamar," *GHQ*, 63 (1979): 339–52.

From Edward G. Phelps [1]

New York. July 17th 1865

To his Excellency Andrew Johnson
President of the United States

The petition of the undersigned Edward G. Phelps formerly of New Orleans in the State of Louisiana humbly sheweth That he is now 25 years of age, that he has been formerly engaged in the Military service of the rebellion, and that he has resided in a foreign country engaged in entirprises inimical to the interests of the United States, that he has resided in Havana in the Island of Cuba since the month of January 1865. From that time he has not been engaged in any thing injurious to the United States. He farther shews that he is desirous of returning to his former home in New Orleans but cannot do so with safety unless under a special pardon from the Government.

He therefore asks of your Excellency that a pardon may be granted to him and that he may be allowed to take the Oath of allegience he promising hereafter to be a good and loyal citizen faithfully observing all the laws of the General Government and as in duty bound he will ever pray.

Your Obt. Svt.
Edwd G. Phelps

ALS, DNA-RG94, Amnesty Papers (M1003, Roll 29), La., Edward G. Phelps.

1. Phelps (b. c1832), a wartime blockade-runner, may have been the "steamboatman" who resided at 327 First Street, New Orleans, in 1868. He was pardoned on October 30, 1865, presumably under Exception No. 7, those who left the United States for purposes of aiding the rebellion. 1870 Census, La., Orleans, New Orleans, 3rd Ward, 196; *Gardner's New Orleans Directory* (1868), 348; *House Ex. Docs.*, 39 Cong., 2 Sess., No. 31, p. 13 (Ser. 1289).

From Francis P. Blair, Sr.

Wash. 18 July. 65.

My Dear Mr. President

I recd. this morning the within note from Mrs. Davis.[1] I trouble you with it, because you ought to know the condition of the unhappy, innocent ones who are at your mercy. A few days ago I had from her a letter of 16 pages giving an account of her flight & capture, full of complaints of harsh treatment mixed with bitter & unfounded suspicions. She is phrenzied to the "worst pitch of all, that wears a reasoning show." I will not trouble with it—nor Mr. Seward with her letter of protest against the publication of her private letters to her husband.[2]

In her letter to me, she entreated that her husband may have a fair trial before a Jury. In the note I send, she asks the privilege of leaving

Savannah evidently to come near her husband as all her letters show. I advised her to go abroad, as he seems to have advised through his private Secretary in a note to me, I gave. Justice to which law entitles him (& lenity, at least, to the innocent) is what both may confidently ask from a man of your character & position.

Yo. mo. af. fd. F. Blair

ALS, DLC-JP.
1. On July 10 Varina Davis wrote Blair from Savannah, enclosing a letter meant for Seward. She asked Blair to secure her release from confinement to Savannah, fearing that her already ill baby might succumb to yellow fever and wondering how to support herself after she depleted her meager financial resources. Johnson Papers, LC.
2. Mrs. Davis was referring to a dispatch in a Boston paper headlined "Glimpses into Jeff Davis's Desk. Interesting Correspondence," reprinting the Confederate President's personal correspondence. Hudson Strode, *Jefferson Davis* (3 vols., New York, 1955–64), 3: 251.

From Joseph E. Brown

(Private)   Copy
                                               Milledgeville July 18th 1865
His Excellency Andrew Johnson President &c. &c.
Dear Sir

Since I wrote you a few days since I have seen the Editors of three of the most influential Journals in the state. The Federal Union at Milledgeville, The Telegraph, Macon, and the Intelligencer, Atlanta. They all promise to support your policy. I hope to see others soon as my health is still improving, and think most of our news papers will be put right. You may rest assured I shall spare no pains to succeed. If I were relieved of my disability[1] by the generous tender to which you made allusion in our conversation which you did not then think policy, I am quite sure I could now turn it to good account for the cause. I shall however await your own time without complaint believing you are my friend and knowing you will do what you think best.

I referred in a private note with my other letter to the case of Col Kenan[2] of this place late Congressman and tool of Mr. Davis. I am told his application for immediate pardon will be strongly pressed, that he may get into the Convention.[3] I am sure it is not best for the success of your policy that he be a member of the Convention. I know the influences that sustain him and will in no case deceive you. I suppose you wish to know such points.

I am very truly your friend.
Joseph E Brown

ALS copy, GU-Felix Hargrett Col., Joseph E. Brown Papers.
1. A reference to Brown's desire to be granted a pardon. Parks, *Brown*, 337.
2. Augustus H. Kenan (1805–1870), Milledgeville attorney and Whig legislator, opposed secession, but served in the Confederate Congress. Wakelyn, *BDC*; James C.

Bonner, ed., *The Journal of a Milledgeville Girl 1861–1867* (Athens, Ga., 1964), 8n. Several works erroneously claim that Kenan died on June 16, 1865. See, for example, Wakelyn, *BDC*, and Warner and Yearns, *BRCC*.

3. On August 18, 1865, Kenan himself wrote the President asking for a pardon. The following day Governor Johnson endorsed his request, assuring the President that Kenan would, "if pardoned, prove a loyal and useful citizen." Although Kenan was not pardoned until October 24, 1865, he did attend the state constitutional convention that month. Amnesty Papers (M1003, Roll 20), Ga., A. H. Kenan, RG94, NA; Avery, *Georgia*, 347; Amnesty Record, Vol. 1, Ser. 8C, Johnson Papers, LC.

From Milton Brown

July 18, 1865; ALS, DNA-RG94, Amnesty Papers (M1003, Roll 2), Ala., Milton Brown.

The president of the Mobile and Ohio Railroad reports that recent orders by Generals Canby and Thomas delivered "into the possession and control" of the company "the entire road and all the rolling stock & other property belonging to the company." On May 17 Brown and most of his directors took the U.S. oath of allegiance, and after the May 29 Amnesty Proclamation, he also took the oath required by it. He calls attention to an important clause in Canby's order, which specifically did not bar "*any questions of private interest*" in the property or "*any legal proceedings that may hereafter be instituted*" against the company, the disposition of which is vested in the President. A large force is working on the railroad and Brown hopes that "the entire line . . . will be in running order in five or six weeks, possibly sooner." Since three-fourths of the rolling stock was "destroyed or rendered unfit for use," he has been making large purchases "*on time*." The clause referred to, "while it can be of no practical benefit to the Government . . . *is a cloud hanging over our credit*," but once removed, Brown has "great confidence" that the friends of the road in New York and London will "put this great enterprise once more in healthy operation." Therefore, he "humbly" requests a full pardon for the railroad and himself, declaring, "If we have sinned we will sin no more." [Brown was pardoned three days later, and the railroad was returned to the company August 25, 1865.]

From Joseph R. Flanigen

July 18, 1865, Philadelphia, Pa.; ALS, DNA-RG56, Appts., Customs Service, Collector, Philadelphia, William B. Thomas.

The editor and proprietor of the *Philadelphia Daily News*, who had met Johnson in the city "some two years since," discusses proposed government appointments. Although he has "not favoured the reappointment of Mr. [Cornelius A.] Walborn as Post Master," he has written that Walborn "is infinitely more capable" than William Kern, who is supported by the congressmen "of our several districts." These representatives "desire not only the removal of Walborn but of Mr. [William B.] Thomas the Collector & others." Yet "they *do not represent the sentiments or wishes of our people*." The Union party of the city needs "repose, rather than a disturbance," and the interests of the party and government "will be best promoted by the reappointment of *all those now holding office here* under the administration." Mr. Thomas' retention "is especially desirable." Over three-fourths of the city's party members oppose the current course by the representatives from the four local Union districts. If "removals *are* to be made," an opportunity should be given the people "to indicate their preference," since neither person urged by our congressmen is "calculated to give satisfaction." [Walborn was not replaced until September 1866, and Thomas not until the following year.]

To Joseph S. Fowler

Executive Office, Washington, D.C.,
July 18 1865

To Hon Joseph S. Fowler,
Nashville, Tenn.

Did you attend to my affairs in Cincinnati. Please send by Express the packages in the safe belonging to me.[1]

Andrew Johnson President U.S.

Tel, DNA-RG107, Tels. Sent, President, Vol. 2 (1865).
1. The next day Fowler wired that he had not been to Cincinnati, but "Intend to go with Mr. East who will take the papers with him to Washington," or, "I will send them by express if you prefer." Fowler to Johnson, July 19, 1865, Tels. Recd., President, Vol. 4 (1865–66), RG107, NA.

From John W. Headley[1]

Nebo Hopkins County Kentucky [ca. July 18, 1865][2]

To his excellency the President of the United States

I have the honor to make application, in accordance with the provision of the Amnesty Proclamation issued under date of May 29th 1865, for special Pardon since in an humble way I have rendered some service which has been designated among the exceptions of said Proclamation, under the head of "Raiders from Canada.["]

I entered the Confederate Army in October 1861 at the age of twenty years and served in the army of Tennessee until the expiration of my first term of service (twelve months). A few months afterwards I volunteered in the command of Brig Genl. John. H. Morgan and was made a Lieutenant in the 10th Regiment of Kentucky Cavalry then in Camp at Catoosa Springs Georgia. I moved with the command to the Department of Western Virginia and was on duty during Genl. Morgans raid through central Kentucky in June of last year (1864). While the command occupied the towns of Mt. Sterling and Lexington a few of Genl. Morgans Staff Officers and their accomplices took large sums of money from the banks in those places, without authority and appropriated it to their own private uses, and through the negligence or indisposition of Genl. Morgan these officers and men were not punished or exposed so as to relieve the rest of the command from the burthen of their disgraceful conduct.[3] With this disreputable affair imputed alike to all I determined that, if I could honorably do so, I would terminate my connection with the command.

Having heard that a few young officers of our army were operating in the northern States in connection with a secret military organization [4] and having a fondness for adventure and a partiality for secret service I felt that this duty would afford me the opportunity to pursue the career suited to my inclination.

Accordingly after procuring the endorsement of influential friends I made application to the Hon James A Seddon Secretary of War for assignment to this duty on the grounds that the company to which I belonged was in prison and I had no command. After being informed by Mr Seddon that if detected within the limits of the United States in the garb of a citizen, I could not be protected by my government I consented to the peril and was allowed to pass through the lines of the army September 25th 1864.

Upon my arrival in the North I found that the secret organization which I had come to encourage had been betrayed and exposed, the leaders imprisoned and the people intimidated and feeling that any efforts on my part in this connection would accomplish no good result I decided to abandon this part of my duty. I also had instructions to encourage and take part in any expeditions intended to release Confederate officers or soldiers from prison and hearing that a party of Confederates who made an unsuccessful expedition against Johnsons Island Prison Ohio had fled to Canada [5] and knowing that a number of confederate agents were in that country I set out immediately to connect myself with them for any similar expedition that might be attempted in the future. I was not connected with nor had I any knowledge of the raid of Lieutenant Bennett. H. Young upon the banks at Saint Albans Vermont [6] but I was associated with persons called raiders and accompanied them in various adventures and secret expeditions into the United States, none of which ever proved successful [7] and after these ineffectual efforts to, injure the government of the United States and harrass the people mostly upon the northern border I became convinced that this service was of no benefit to the cause of the South and soon after set out by Rail Road through Ohio and on horseback through Kentucky, to rejoin my old command which had been reorganized under the auspices of Brig Genl. B W Duke successor of Genl. Morgan. I found it encamped near Abingdon Virginia at which place I arrived March 12th 1865. I was then on duty at Lynchburg Virginia until the surrender of Genl. R. E. Lee. From there I marched with the retreating column southward. At Charlotte North Carolina our brigade became a part of President Davis' escort, and accompanied him through South Carolina and as far as the town of Washington in Georgia. I was surrendered and paroled at this place with the brigade according to the terms of Maj Genl. W. T. Sherman. On reaching Nashville Tennessee I appeared before the proper authorities and accepted the prescribed

Oath of allegiance to the government of the United States, and returned to my fathers home near Nebo Hopkins County Kentucky.

The foregoing is a brief and true statement of the character of the offense which excludes me from the clemency of the executive as granted in the said Amnesty Proclamation of May 29th 1865, and though I have not attempted to conceal the ardor with which I supported the unfortunate cause of the southern people, I hope I may not be deemed less earnest or honest in making this application for special pardon on account of that candid acknowledgement, for with the same true sense of honor that inspired me with patriotic faith and fortitude during the war, do I now accept the result achieved by the arms of the government of the United States and in good faith pledge myself to abide by the constitution and laws in like manner with every citizen of the country.[8]

John W. Headley

ALS, DNA-RG94, Amnesty Papers, (M1003, Roll 25), Ky., John W. Headley.

1. Headley (1841–1930) served as secretary of state for Kentucky (1891–96). *NUC*; John W. Headley, *Confederate Operations in Canada and New York* (New York, 1906), 461; "Capt. John W. Headley," *Con Vet*, 39 (1931): 26.

2. This letter was accompanied by a recommendation from George D. Prentiss, which bears this date. Headley, *Confederate Operations*, 441.

3. On June 8, 1864, Morgan's troops plundered the town of Mt. Sterling, Ky., after capturing it from a small Federal garrison. An officer and two enlisted men took $59,057.33 in private funds from the Farmer's Bank of Kentucky. Although this was clearly a violation of international law and Morgan's own orders, he failed to take action against the thieves. James A. Ramage, *Rebel Raider: The Life of General John Hunt Morgan* (Lexington, Ky., 1986), 217–18.

4. Headley and others worked closely with the "Sons of Liberty," a Democratic organization in the northwestern states that opposed Lincoln's policies. Headley, *Confederate Operations*, 217–96 passim; Klement, *Dark Lanterns*, 91–231 passim.

5. John Y. Beall commanded a group that seized two Great Lakes steamers on September 19, 1864, but failed to capture the U.S.S. *Michigan* or release the thousands of Confederates held on Johnson's Island. Beall was later captured while participating with Headley and others in an attempt to free seven Confederate generals who were reportedly traveling through New York. Beall was hanged on February 24, 1865, for his exploits. Headley, *Confederate Operations*, 231–53, 301–06, 340–69; Brandt, *Burn New York*, 60–61, 145–46, 192.

6. Young (1843–1919), who had served with Morgan's command until his capture in 1863, after the war amassed a fortune in railroads and became a prolific author. With the sanction of Clement C. Clay, he led a raid by Confederates across the Canadian border on October 19, 1864, robbing three banks of more than $200,000 and killing at least one civilian. Ibid., 68; Headley, *Confederate Operations*, 256–63; Klement, *Dark Lanterns*, 190; *NUC*; *NCAB*, 11: 571.

7. Headley also took part in the attempt to burn New York in November 1864, setting fire to three hotels, a lumberyard, and some docks along the Hudson River. He later claimed, too, that he had only narrowly failed to kidnap Johnson on his way to Washington in February 1865. Brandt, *Burn New York*, 101, 107, 113, 115–17; Headley, *Confederate Operations*, 264–83, 402–10.

8. Johnson pardoned Headley on September 2, 1865. *House Ex. Docs.*, 39 Cong., 2 Sess., No. 116, p. 11 (Ser. 1293).

From Thomas M. Jacks [1]

Helena July 18th 1865

A. Johnson President
Honored Sir—

The importance of the issue involved is my only apology for adressing you this letter.

We have in Arkansas a class of men *professing* loyalty whose past history proves the contrary. Their actions now afford no proof of the sincerity of their present professions. They are finding fault with all that union men did while, *they* were openly or secretly working for the success of the Southern Confederacy. They wish to repudiate the present state organization. The true source I believe of their objections is their secret hatred to loyal men, and to all, that is truly loyal to the united states government.

They make a lever in their war upon the state government of section 6th (of the election law of the state a copy of) which I send you herewith inclosed.[2]

Their argument is that the whole organization is a nullity because Congress has not recognized it; and that the present President yourself has not formally signified his intention to recognize it.

Would you be so kind as to furnish me in answer to this, in a few words your opinions of, and your intentions towards the existing state government in Arkansas. A direct word from you will be more telling than an elaborate circuitous argument made by me.

Hoping you will be able to devote a few minutes of your time to the consideration of, and in answer to this inquiry, most important to loyal Arkansians[3] I subscribe myself

Most respectfully yours T. M. Jacks

P.S. It is perhaps proper that I should say to you that I was a member elect to the thirty eighth Congress from the first district of Arkansas.

I believe the present organization, admitting its faults, to be better than any thing that could be gotten up in the state under the present excitement. It is loyal. It is the work of loyal men. I may have too much feeling in the matter. I am not willing to be dictated to—to be ruled by those who strove to rule me as with a rod of iron under Confederate Authority. I know them *too well.*

ALS, DLC-JP.

1. Helena physician and druggist, Jacks (c1821–1883), elected to Congress as a unionist in 1864, failed to take his seat. Goodspeed's *Biographical and Historical Memoirs of Eastern Arkansas* (Chicago, 1890), 777; Poore, *Political Register*, 465.
2. Not found.
3. There is no indication that the President responded.

From Charles Marshall

July 18, 1865, Baltimore, Md.; ALS, DNA-RG94, Amnesty Papers (M1003, Roll 30), Md., Charles Marshall.

Former Confederate staff officer, who falls within the tenth exception, applies for amnesty. Born and educated in Virginia, he practiced law in Baltimore until he returned to his father's residence at the beginning of the war. Feeble health prevented military service until March 1862, when he was appointed aide-de-camp to Gen. Robert E. Lee, with whom he was associated until the surrender at Appomattox, where he was paroled as a lieutenant colonel. His opinions were those of the majority of Virginians, "opposed to a rupture of the Union, but no less opposed to coercion as a means of preventing it." He considers all questions between the sections "definitely settled by the late war, and will abide the result in good faith." [Marshall obtained his pardon three days later.]

From Horace Maynard

Burnet House, Cincinnati, July 18, 1865.

Dr. Sir,

I left town Saturday night & arrived here last night. Our friend Miller[1] has diverted his leisure to me, & I take a spare moment to pen these notes.

The "Amendment" party in Ky. will be sadly defeated. They will elect to Congress Randall, probably G. Clay Smith & possibly Rousseau—not likely any others.[2]

Gen. Sherman will not allow himself to be used by the Copperheads, who, he says, are his enemies. I think he will settle down pretty nearly right.

A great struggle for the senate is going on quietly between John Sherman & Gen. Schenck.[3]

Mr. Blair's late speech at Hagerstown has been published here, & is thought by some to be a reflex of your views on the Mexican Question.[4] By-the-bye, I believe I did not mention to you that Mr. Seward offered me the Mexican Mission last Friday, saying I would have to go to Chihuahua to find the Government.[5] That appointment by you, with the relations understood to exist between us, would be taken, in this country & abroad, as pretty significant of your intended policy.

The news from Tennessee is not as good as I would like. Campbell[6] will be elected in the Nashville District. That element is moving strongly for the control of affairs there.

I go on to-day & when I reach there will communicate touching the matters of our late conference.[7]

I am very Respectfully Your Obt. Svt.

Horace Maynard

His Excy. Andrew Johnson President.

ALS, DLC-JP.

1. Former steamboat captain Silas F. Miller (c1821–fl1901) owned the Galt House in Louisville (c1860–64) and the Burnet House in Cincinnati (1865–67), before becoming part owner of a Louisville woolen mill. Louisville directories (1858–64, 1875–1901); Cincinnati directories (1865–68).

2. Of the nine congressmen elected in the August elections, William H. Randall, Green Clay Smith, Gen. Lovell H. Rousseau, and Samuel McKee were Republicans. *American Annual Cyclopaedia* (1865), 465; *BDAC*.

3. Congressman Robert Schenck had begun a campaign for John Sherman's Senate seat. Bonadio, *North of Reconstruction*, 50.

4. Montgomery Blair on July 12 had attacked "American spinelessness" in its reaction to the threat of the French in Mexico. Elbert B. Smith, *Francis Preston Blair* (New York, 1980), 392.

5. By the time a minister could reach the Mexican Republican government, which had occupied the capital of the state of Chihuahua since October 1864, Juarez had been driven northward again, as he evacuated Chihuahua in early August. Charles A. Smart, *Viva Juarez* (Philadelphia, 1963), 326, 339.

6. William B. Campbell.

7. Having lost the senatorship to Patterson, Maynard apparently agreed to accept a Washington or foreign service post. He shortly changed his mind, however, and ran for a Congressional seat instead. Alexander, *Reconstruction*, 76, 82.

From John H. Reagan[1]

In Prison, Fort Warren,
Boston Harbor, July 18th 1865.

His Excellency Andrew Johnson,
President of the United States;

With great respect I beg to make an addition to my former application to your Excellency for pardon and amnesty.[2] I do so under the hope and belief that your policy will be in favour of clemency where the facts show that this can be rightly and safely extended. And as the opinions and feelings of applicants, when known and relied on by your Excellency, may influence your action, I desire to add to what I have heretofore said, after much and prayerful reflection:

That I recognize and believe the fact that if the cause of the south had met the approval of the Almighty its people would have succeeded in the establishment of their independance. Under this conviction, though I was a sincere and earnest supporter of that cause, and believed it was just and righteous, I accept the result of the war as the will of God. And I now acquiesce in the abolition of slavery, and in the principle that the federal government has the right to preserve itself against disintegration, by the secession or separation of the states from it.

If, therefore, your Excellency will accept a sincere and cheerful acquiescence in these results, and a faithful willingness to assist the government, both by example and influence, in sustaining them, and in the restoration of order, and prosperity, and the authority of the government, and fraternal good will between the people of the different parts of the country, as an attonement for the errors of the past, and as indicating a proper disposition for the future, I give these assurances on my part; and pray that you will extend to me a full pardon, or such clemency as will enable me to prove my fidelity to these views, as, in your discretion, you may think best. But I will add that the influence of my example and advise, if that be desirable, would be much greater probably if I had a full pardon.

If your Excellency is not sufficiently advised of my integrity and uprightness of character to know how far to rely on my declarations, and would afford me the opportunity, I could furnish the most satisfactory testimony on this subject. And I make this declaration and request with the stronger hope of securing the favour of your Excellency because I think my past life will ensure confidence in what I say, and because of my consciousness of having done nothing during the contest violative of the laws of war.

I would also say that my property has never been valued at as much as twenty thousand dollars, and is now, as I am informed, from losses and deterioration, worth much less than when the war began. And what property I have consists, for the most part, of wild uncultivated Texas lands. I will also add that I never bought, or sold, or owned a slave in my life, in my own right. A slave woman and some three or four children were given to my wife[3] by her father, which by the laws of the state remained her property. And five or six years ago he gave her and my children eight or ten others, which, owing to my being much from home, were never taken from his place, or in any way under my controll. In mentioning the value of my property, the agregate, to which I refer as being less than twenty thousand dollars, was made up in part of the value of the four or five slaves which belonged to my wife and children, and is, to the extent of their value, less than the amount on which I paid taxes. Of these facts, if it be deemed necessary, proof can be taken, by my own affidavit, or from such other sources as may be deemed advisable.

I beg also to say to your Excellency, if you find reason to act favourably on my petition, as an additional inducement, that I believe the confidence a very large number of the people of Texas have in me will render my example and advise valuable in the restoration of order, and the prompt acquiescence of the people in the new order of things.

I also pray your Excellency's attention to the fact that I have four small motherless children, as mentioned in my former petition, for whose fate I feel the most intense solicitude, if I should not be allowed to return to them. And that my presence, advise, and assistance, is of much importance to other relatives, on account of recent bereavements, and their helpless condition, and on account of the great changes in the fortunes of some of them by the results of the war.[4]

With greatest respect
Your Excellency's obedient servant
John H. Reagan

JULY 1865   433

ALS, DNA-RG94, Amnesty Papers (M1003, Roll 54), Tex., John H. Reagan.
1. Reagan (1818–1905), a former member of Congress from Texas, had served as
the Confederacy's only postmaster general. *BDAC*.
2. See Reagan to Johnson, May 28, 1865. See also Reagan to Johnson, June 2, 1865,
Amnesty Papers (M1003, Roll 54), Tex., John H. Reagan.
3. Virginia-born Edwina M. (1832–1863), daughter of Edwin Nelms, was the second of Reagan's three wives. Ben H. Procter, *Not Without Honor: The Life of John H.
Reagan* (Austin, 1962), 47, 89, 153n.
4. In spite of subsequent letters by influential Texans on behalf of Reagan, he failed
to receive a presidential pardon until April 29, 1867. Amnesty Papers (M1003, Roll
54), Tex., John H. Reagan.

From Amasa Walker [1]

North Brookfield July 18th 1865—

President Johnson
Dear Sir

"Treason is a crime that must be punished. The people must be made
to understand that treason is a crime to be punished." These were noble
utterances worthy of the president of the United States, and the people
every where said "Amen," for they felt that the welfare of the nation
depended upon the maintenance of that declaration and they hoped and
expected that you would make it good. They knew it was in your
power to do so, and had no doubt, could have no doubt that Jefferson
Davis would be tried for *treason*, and if convicted, punished.

The newspapers are however telling us every day that the arch Traitor is only to be tried for *conspiracy* to assassinate President Lincoln,
which if proved, would only convict him of one of his lightest crimes.

I hope there is no truth in all this, for I feel that you owe it to yourself
and your country to bring Jefferson Davis to trial for *Treason*, so that
"the people may understand" that the government recognizes such a
crime; and if convicted, as he cannot fail to be, that he will be punished,
so that the people "may understand" that such is the fate of Traitors. I
do not say what the punishment should be, but whatever it is, let it be
executed promptly and fully.

You may rely upon it the people will be greatly mortified and disappointed if the great chief of the rebellion is never arraigned for his
crimes against the nations life.

Allow me to say on another point, that I hope you will be in no haste
to get the seceded states back into the Union. The great question is,
not *how soon they shall be brought in*, but *how long they can be kept out*.
To admit their delegations into Congress, is to renew a conflict more
irrepressible and dangerous than any we have ever yet experienced.
You can take care of them while under your authority, but allow them
to be your masters, as they will be when restored to power, and neither
your situation nor that of the nation will be a very eligible one.

Excuse the liberty I take, in thus addressing you. I rejoice that you are President of the United States, and hope you will be successful in restoring order and harmony throughout the country.

> I have the honor to be Your Ob St.
> Amasa Walker
> of the Massachusetts Delegation in 37th Congress

ALS, DLC-JP.
   1. Walker (1799–1875), who served in the prewar Massachusetts house and senate, was also in Congress (1862–63). *BDAC*.

From Eleazer Waterman

July 18, 1865, Georgetown, S.C.; ALS, DNA-RG48, Patents and Misc. Div., Lets. Recd.

A Connecticut-born southern resident in his 73rd year, who "for *fifty* years voted the Union ticket," explains that, as deputy U.S. marshal, he was a census taker in 1860. He received half his pay the same year, but over three hundred dollars are still due. His claim "is regularly authenticated," but a congressional act of August 6, 1861, directed the secretary of the interior "to suspend all further payments to all persons under certain restrictions." During the war he continued as deputy "for some two years, and then *resigned it*," recommending as his successor "*a man who was liable to conscription*," which he submits "was not aiding or abeting the Rebellion!!" He has taken the oath and now returns it "with a hope that you will grant the Amnesty and direct the Secretary of the Interior to remit me the balance due, with interest." [There is no record of a pardon for Waterman.]

From East Florida Union Men

July 19, 1865, New York; ALS (C. L. Robinson), DLC-JP.

Aware that "intimations have been made by certain prints that some dissatisfaction exists" regarding Johnson's choice for provisional governor of Florida, three loyal East Floridians—Calvin L. Robinson, Lemuel Wilson, and Samuel T. Ray—sent by local citizens to lobby for a strong union candidate, assure the President "of our entire satisfaction with the appointment of Judge Marvin to that position."

Endorsement re Ford's Theatre[1]

> Executive Office July 19, 1865.

The within mentioned property, Ford's Theatre, was seized and is held by my orders, given to the Secretary of War, who is directed to retain possession thereof, for the use of the Government of the United States, until further order.

> Andrew Johnson

ES, DLC-E. M. Stanton Papers (Wm. Schley and H. Winter Davis to Stanton, July 18, 1865).
   1. Attorneys for the owner of Ford's Theatre sought, through Secretary Stanton, the

return of Ford's property or, failing that, "advice as to the proper remedy to be pursued." It is to their letter that the endorsement is made. Schley and Davis to Stanton, July 18, 1865.

From Fletcher S. Stockdale

ca.July 19, 1865; ALS, DNA-RG94, Amnesty Papers (M1003, Roll 55), Tex., Fletcher S. Stockdale.

A "faithful, earnest, conservative supporter of the cause of Secession," who was a state senator, member of the secession convention, and Texas lieutenant governor (1863–65), applies for pardon. His property on March 2, 1861, exceeded twenty thousand dollars, which places him also "within class 13 of exceptions." During the war he gave "such counsel and votes, at all times," which he "thought would benefit" the South. However, he never "counselled or voted for any violation of the laws of war or humanity" or aided "in any persecution of his fellow citizens for opinions sake," believing those actions "could only injure the cause." He was "an honest believer in the right of a State to Secede" and that it was the "only remedy" to save slavery. The "result of the terrible war" has "definitively" settled these questions, and "if he had foreseen the consequences" of secession, "his action, in the beginning, would have been the reverse of what it was." Questioning what an honorable man's duty ought to be, "in his present situation," he has determined that he should remain in the country of his birth, and that "it is right, honorable, and his duty, to recognize and renew his allegiance to the United States." [Johnson pardoned Stockdale on December 7, 1866.]

To George F. Comfort[1]

Executive Office, Washington, D.C.,
July 20, 1865.

Mr. G. F. Comfort, No. 2 Franzosische strasse, Berlin, Prussia:
My Dear Sir,—

I thank you for your letter of the 30th of June.[2] I shall use my best endeavor to make my administration national, and not partisan. Perverting power or influence to partisan ends is only less criminal than attempting the nation's life.

Our nation has come out of its four years' struggle for existence strengthened and purified, and with a capacity for a growth in the future unparalleled in history. I am pleased to hear from so intelligent an observer as yourself that the fact that our government is a government of the people, deriving all its power from the people, existing only for the people, is being appreciated in Europe. I trust our national success will prove the success of popular principles throughout the world. I am, sir, very truly yours,[3]

Andrew Johnson,
President of the United States.

Springfield Republican (Mass.), September 20, 1865.
 1. Comfort (1833–1910), New York native and art critic, taught modern languages

at Allegheny College in Pennsylvania (1865–68) and later at Syracuse University. *NCAB*, 3: 162; *New York Times*, May 6, 1910.

2. Writing from Berlin, Comfort reported that while there in April, Fernando Wood had asserted that Democrats were "getting hold of Johnson's administration" and would soon control it. Comfort to Johnson, June 30, 1865, Johnson Papers, LC.

3. Submitting this letter to the European press without Johnson's permission, Comfort later attempted to explain his reasons. European editors found good copy in Johnson's letter. Comfort to Johnson, Oct. 17, 1865, ibid.

From Thomas Cottman

Washington July 20th 1865

His Excellency Andrew Johnson
President of the United States
Sir

I exceedingly regret the necessity of annoying you; but Governor Wells requested me to come on here that you might personally ascertain the status of his state government if desirable. There are so many conflicting elements & such a diversity of opinions that he deemed it adviseable to consult you & for that purpose I presented myself here on monday & wait your pleasure to see me. A gentleman called John Covode came to New Orleans representing himself as a Government Agent specially deputed to look after State Administration, in conjunction with one B R Plumley[1] a Voudou Chief & N P Banks a Politician, collogued[2] to intimidate our state authorities. They put forth authoratively the announcement that Wells had been superceded by Banks & Covode wrote Kennedy an insolent letter concerning negro prisoners in the city prison to which a characteristic & proper reply was given.

I still think that the appointment of Wells as Provisional Governor, with similar instructions to those given the Provisional Governors of the other late Insurrectionary States, would be exceedingly adviseable. Besides the uniformity of action therein constituted an infinity of evils would be avoided for the future. Wells admits the vote by which he was elected to have been a fraud & he turned out the Register for perpetrating it. Banks confesses it in his Fourth of July Oration—representing the Banks Hahn party.[3] Durant & his set petition for a Provisional appointment. Wells & all of his friends desire it: no faction, sect or party object to it. Of course each has his preference, but the selection is with your Excellency. As there are several vacancies to be filled in the State & I think recommendations were sent by me & delivered on tuesday[4] I will take the liberty of calling your attention to them. The Western District in Louisiana has lately come under the authority of the United States & of course all the offices are vacant—John E King of S' Landry[5]—has all the time been Loyal, is a Lawyer of high standing & is recommended for U.S. District Judge for Western District. Judge

Martel[6] also of S' Landry for U.S Marshal Edwin Jewell for District attorney. Dr. James L McCormick[7] for Surgeon to the United States Marine Hospital. He was a distinguished graduate of the University of Maryland pursued his studies in Paris & London & for the last three years has been the consulting Physician of the Federal army Surgeons at his Post. The above are all old residents of the State & recommended to fill vacancies. Fergus Penniston,[8] a most worthy citizen & Creole of the State is recommended for Ass Treasurer of U S at N. Orleans the place now held by Thos. May.[9] You have very ardent friends & supporters in Louisiana: but I apprehend very few of them hold Federal appointments. In the Custom House I know two: Cuth-Bullitt the Marshal & young Wells[10] the Naval officer. It may be right & proper to send citizens from other States to hold the Federal offices in our State:[11]—but I really do not think it pleases our citizens & if they were consulted; it would be otherwise. It would give me great pleasure to *shake your hand* before I leave this place which my private matters will require of me in a few days.

I do not know that you will have the time to read it but I enclose the correspondence between Durant & Wells.[12]

With the highest consideration & esteem I have the honor to subscribe myself

Your Obt. Sevt. Thos Cottman

ALS, DLC-JP.

1. Benjamin Rush Plumly.

2. Basically meaning "conferred," the dialectic "intrigued, conjured" is the use here.

3. Ex-governor Hahn and General Banks, leaders of the more moderate Republicans, and their organization, the National Union Republican Club, hosted a 4th of July celebration at the customs house, with Banks as the principal speaker. McCrary, *Lincoln and Reconstruction*, 320.

4. The recommendations on an appended sheet carried a note: "The above are new appointments—nobody turned out—" which is followed by Johnson's pencilled: "Left by Cottman on the 25th dy of July 1865."

5. King, a unionist, raised a battalion for Confederate service, but retired when the city was surrendered. Amnesty Papers (M1003, Roll 28), La., John E. King, RG94, NA.

6. B. A. Martel (b. *c*1819) had been a judge and editor. 1870 Census, La., St. Landry, Opelousas, 1st Ward, 19; Hugh Kennedy to Johnson, July 5, 1865, Johnson Papers, LC.

7. McCormick (*c*1831–*fl*1870) was an Ascension Parish resident. 1870 Census, La., Ascension, 2nd Subdiv., 2nd Ward, 28.

8. Fergis Penniston (b. *c*1827), prosperous native Louisiana planter. 1860 Census, La., East Baton Rouge, 165.

9. Thomas P. May (*c*1842–*fl*1883), wealthy sugar planter and unionist who briefly served in the Confederate army, was part owner and coeditor of the *New Orleans Times*, and a novelist. New Orleans directories (1861–83); Tunnell, *Crucible of Reconstruction*, 221; McCrary, *Lincoln and Reconstruction*, 166, 285; *NUC*; Tregle, "Thomas Durant and Reconstruction," 490. See also Letter from King, July 22, 1865.

10. Cuthbert Bullitt, U.S. marshal for the Eastern District, and Thomas M. Wells, acting naval officer.

11. King, Martel, and Jewell did not receive judicial appointments. Instead, the two districts of Louisiana were combined into one and Edward H. Durrell of New Hampshire, Samuel H. Torry of New York, and Francis J. Herron of Pennsylvania were appointed to the positions of judge, attorney, and marshal, respectively. May was reap-

pointed as assistant treasurer, but by 1867 had been replaced by John S. Walton of New Jersey. *U.S. Off. Reg.* (1865–67).

12. Not found.

From Andrew J. Fletcher[1]

State of Tennessee, Executive Department,
Nashville, July 20th 1865.

Hon Andrew Johnson President U.S.

Honored Sir.

The Governor has been absent and ill for six weeks and most of the Executive duties have fallen upon my office. A sense of the propriety of communicating with you is my apology for this letter.

A crisis is upon this state Government. It was with the utmost difficulty that any Disfranchisement could be had from the Legislature. That which did pass is so indefinite and so easily evaded by disloyal clerks & Judges of election that it will not protect us, and will prove a failure. *Under that law Frank Cheatham[2] could be elected to Congress from this District.*

If your opinions had been known as they now are a better law could have been passed; but such men as Hood and Cooper & D. B. Thomas[3] referred to the Amnesty Proclamation and insisted that that document indicated the extent to which the President desired disfranchisement. Absurd as the point was it so embarrassed the friends of the measure that they had to yield many of the best features of their Bill. Disloyal Clerks register indiscriminately all who apply. Disloyal Judges of election will receive all ballots. All the County and District special elections result in favor of rebels. It is no uncommon thing for a returned rebel soldier with the lice still on him to defeat a Union citizen or soldier for a county or District office by large majorities.

Gov Campbell[4] will be elected from this District to Congress by rebel votes & will represent rebel sentiment in Congress if permitted to take his seat.

Gen. Thomas contemplated his arrest but he came in and took the oath to *support and defend* the Goverment & Laws he had violently denounced as unconstitutional and void.

Gen Thomas is of opinion that it will be impossible for soldiers to keep off illegal votes as they cannot discriminate, but he stands ready to carry out any request from the Governor or from you. At present we dispair of carrying the polls and rely upon measures to be taken after the election is over.[5]

Any suggestions from you Mr. President will be most thankfully received.

Most respectfully A. J. Fletcher
Sec. of State

ALS, DLC-JP.

1. Tennessee secretary of state.

2. Gen. Benjamin F. Cheatham.

3. James R. Hood, Edmund Cooper, and Dorsey B. Thomas. The latter (1823–1897), a lawyer and tanner, served several terms in the house and senate. *BDTA*, 1: 715–16.

4. William B. Campbell was elected, but not seated.

5. Fletcher also wired Johnson on the 20th: "Disloyal clerks, sheriffs and judges of Election will enable the rebels to make the Election in Middle and West Tenn. . . . It is feared that the best that can be done is to treat the election as void in many counties leaving the Contest to Congress." He further speculated that a better law could be passed at the next session. Johnson Papers, LC.

From Thaddeus Stevens

Bedford Springs July 20, 1865

His Excellency A Johnson

I have just heard that the members of congress from the city of Phila. claim the exclusive right to recommend the Collector of the Port. I beg leave most decidedly to protest against that claim. I admit that the Post Master is a local appointment and ought to be at their disposal. But the Marshals and Collector and the other appointments in the Custom House are as much due to the country as to the city—such has always been the understanding, the Collector being frequently taken from the rural Dist. I do not write as the partisan of any man as I was not aware that there was any objection to Mr. Thomas.[1]

Thaddeus Stevens

ALS, DNA-RG56, Appts., Customs Service, Collector, Philadelphia, William B. Thomas.

1. Former Republican congressman John Covode had also telegraphed Johnson on July 19 to protest anticipated changes in customs house appointments. Simon Cameron telegraphed Johnson on July 21 that the central committee of the Democratic party in Pennsylvania had resolved to leave the Philadelphia appointments "untouched" until after the October elections. Cameron was apparently successful in maintaining the status quo in most cases; not until 1866 did Johnson begin to wield the patronage club in Pennsylvania. Covode to Johnson, July 19, 1865, Ser. 2, Johnson Papers, LC; Cameron to Johnson, July 21, 1865, Tels. Recd., President, Vol. 4 (1865–66), RG107, NA; Erwin S. Bradley, *The Triumph of Militant Republicanism: A Study of Pennsylvania and Presidential Politics, 1860–1872* (Philadelphia, 1964), 209, 231–32.

From George H. Thomas

Nashville July 20 1865.

His Excy Prest Johnson

Will you authorize the publication of your telegram of the sixteenth inst[1] to Governor Brownlow advising him to adopt strenuous measures to have the laws passed by the last legislature [en]forced? Its publication will do much good in satisfying many obtuse minds in this state

[that] Gov Brownlow is approved by you. The Rebel element in some portions of this state is very restive under the present state of affairs.

Geo H Thomas Maj Genl

Tel, DLC-JP.

1. The telegram of the 16th, repeated in expanded form on the 20th, was published in the *Nashville Press*, July 22, 1865.

To George H. Thomas

Executive Office, Washington, D.C.,
July. 20th 1865.

To Maj. Genl. Geo. H. Thomas.
Nashville Tenn.

Gov. Brownlow has been authorized to publish my dispatch as requested by you. I hope that you will have it understood that whatever amount of military force is necessary to sustain the Civil authority and enforce the law, will be furnished. This being made known to the public will exert a powerful influence throughout the State and will perhaps prevent the necessity of any Military interference. I am hard pressed here. Every moment of my time is occupied. Accept assurances of my esteem.

Andrew Johnson

Tel, DNA-RG107, Tels. Sent, President, Vol. 2 (1865).

From Thomas H. Watts

July 20, 1865, Montgomery, Ala.; ALS, DNA-RG94, Amnesty Papers (M1003, Roll 12), Ala., Thomas H. Watts.

An erstwhile member of Jeff Davis' cabinet and last Confederate governor of Alabama, applying "for pardon and release from forfeitures," gives a summary of his "past conduct" and "present position." As an old-line Whig, "reared in the school of States Rights," he believed in secession, and as early as 1856 his party in Alabama had declared "that the election of a Black Republican" as President justified withdrawal from the Union. In fact, the state legislature in the winter of 1859–60 provided for a convention "in the event of such election." Afterwards Watts, as a member of such a convention, voted for secession. During the war, as colonel of a regiment, Confederate attorney general (Mar. 1862–Oct. 1863), and governor (Dec. 1863–65), he endeavored with all his powers to achieve the independence of the South. Since independence "has proven a failure," he regards "the South as a conquered people" and slavery as destroyed. Punished for his conduct "by the loss of friends & relatives," the loss of his slaves, and the destruction by Federal forces of over fifty thousand dollars of his property, he is now "sincerely desirous of forgetting the past" and wishes "in good faith to renew my allegiance." [Watts was pardoned October 18, 1865.]

From Yale College Festival Committee

Yale College N Haven Connt.
July 20 1865

Mr President!

I am instructed by the Com[mitte]e in charge, most respectfully and earnestly to request the honor of Your Excellency's presence here on the 26th inst upon occasion of the Festival proposed to be given in honor of the Patriotism of those who have represented this University in the Service of our Country in the late memorable Struggle for National Existence. This Legion of Honor, numbers about Six Hundred of our Alumni in all Departments, and among these are numerous examples of persons whose lives have been and are to be devoted to the Country in Civil Service as well as in Military. Should the Public Service permit, the Committee belive that your Excellency would enjoy the Festival, Academic and National which your presence will so much honor.[1]

I remain with great respect Your Excellency's Obt Svt
B. Silliman[2] Chn.

To His Excellency President Johnson
Washington D.C.

ALS, DLC-JP.

1. Sending his regrets on the 24th, Johnson did not attend, because of "the pressure of public duties." On the same day he also declined Gov. William A. Buckingham's invitation of the 21st for the same occasion. Johnson to "Chairman Festival Committee," July 24, 1865, Indiana Historical Society, Mitten Col.; Buckingham to Johnson, July 21, 1865, Johnson Papers, LC; Johnson to Buckingham, July 24, 1865, Johns Hopkins University Library.

2. Benjamin Silliman (1816–1885), professor of chemistry at Yale Medical College and associate editor of the *American Journal of Science. DAB.*

From Joseph E. Brown

Atlanta Ga July 21" 1865

His Excellency Andrew Johnson
President U S

No opportunity is offered the people of many of the counties of the State to take the Amnesty oath. The back woods counties whose people are most loyal and would send delegates on your line of policy, are neglected.

Please order a person with competent authority into each county in the State to administer it. If this is done soon there will be no difficulty in the convention.

Hope you have received my letters by Express.[1] No mail to Milledgeville. Answer to Atlanta. On my way to Cherokee for a few days. Where is Senator Patterson?[2]

Joseph E Brown

Tel, DLC-JP.
1. Presumably the Letters from Brown, July 15 and 18, 1865.
2. For Johnson's response, see Letter to Brown, July 24, 1865.

From Lizinka C. Ewell

Wakefield [Rhode Island] 21st July 1865

His Excellency The President—

I write you a few lines today to thank you again for the liberation of Genl. Ewell & Campbell & to remind you that in remaining & keeping them a few days at Wakefield I am only availing myself of the verbal permission of your Excellency while slightly infringing the letter of the parole.[1]

On the cars from Baltimore was a gentleman from Brooklyn who spoke regretfully of the State of the President's health & said he had had a long interview with him a fortnight since. I asked what he thought of him & was struck with his reply "Oh—he is a charming man to me—has more executive power than any man in the U.S. & does more work." I suggested that the work might be done by the Cabinet & you only sign the papers. He replied that Cabinets were not now what they had been—your Cabinet was not a unit—consequently every-thing had to be decided by the President & without precedents. I asked what he thought of Staunton. "He did not know him at all" & he became silent & would give no more political opinions.

As Genl. Ewell, Campbell & I left Fort Warren a man came up & told me he was delighted at his release & so were a great many of us. Another thrust a couple of Segars in his hand with some kind wish & at the Tremont the chambermaid told me every one in the house was glad of Genl. Ewell's release—at least every one of the help & there was something very pleasant in the prompt attention & cordial kind[ness] of the waiters. I mention all this as an indication that a large party in Boston & doubtless the rest of the North—are kind to Southern prisoners & desirous to see them all released. I do not even yet realize the horrors of imprisonment in an underground cell & its effect on mind & body—but I see & know enough to beg you earnestly to hasten as much as possible the release of the remainder of our friends— particularly that of Genl. Cabell[2] of Arkansas—who is a poor man— without political friends—with a wife & two young children from whom he has not heard for three months & who are dependent on him not merely for the luxuries but for the necessaries of life. Is it not cruel to keep him in prison one day longer than the safety of your Government demands & you know the release of the whole batch would not cause it one moment's peril. If you were in earnest about the purchase of my house you must write me your views on the subject directing to the care of Wm. Reynolds 131-W. Fayette St Baltimore.[3]

Once more thanking you for the release of my husband & son & desiring my kindest regards to Mrs. Patterson

I remain Very Sincerely
L. C. Ewell

ALS, DLC-JP.

1. Johnson's letter of July 17 to H. A. Allen, commander at Fort Warren, specified that Ewell was "permitted to return to his home in Virginia upon parole to report once a week by letter to the Secretary of War . . . until further orders." Johnson Papers, LC.

2. Confederate Brigadier William L. Cabell (1827–1911), captured in Missouri in 1864, would be released from Fort Warren in August 1865. Warner, *Gray*.

3. Either William Reynolds, Sr. (d. 1873) or Jr. (1842–*fl*1897), both lawyers residing at the same address. The elder Reynolds had married a cousin of General Ewell. *Genealogy and Biography of Leading Families of the City of Baltimore and Baltimore County, Maryland* (New York, 1897), 848–49.

From Andrew J. Fletcher

Nashville July 21st 1865.

Hon Andrew Johnson

Your despatchs of the 16th and 20th[1] thankfully rec'd. The Govr is absent but has instructed me [to] act. The proclamation, & address, arrest of Etheridge, & above all the publication of your dispatch of the Sixteenth, (16) are having salutary effects.

Gen Thomas will send troops to many portions of the state. Still the rebels will elect Campbell and Dunlap[2] & others. The enforcement of the law even by the aid of Military is almost impracticable, but an earnest effort will be made.

A. J. Fletcher Secy State

Tel, DLC-JP.

1. These two dispatches contained essentially the same message. See Telegram to Brownlow, July 16, 1865.

2. William B. Campbell and former congressman William C. Dunlap.

From Hugh Kennedy

Mayoralty of New Orleans
City Hall, July 21st 1865

President,

Since my last letter, sent through Dr. Cottman, State Agent, reporting condition of affairs in this City, nothing has occurred to disturb the public tranquillity or to cause any solicitude for the future.

The political agitation which followed the reappearance of Maj. Gen. Banks in the Dept. of the Gulf as commander, which at one time threatened serious annoyance, has almost entirely disappeared; and the

journals then sustained by largesses from the public purse, which ministered to the purposes of the authors of the commotion, have without
pressure or seduction from authority, been forced to change their
courses.

The public printing for the City I contracted for with the lowest
bidder; and the Governor agreed in opinion with me, that it would be
advisable to allow State & local administration for some little time
longer, at least, to depend upon undirected independent public opinion
alone for support. In this way the people and the national government
will be better able to judge of the merits and demerits of those who
have been entrusted with the management of public concerns, for there
will be no misrepresentations or deceptive coloring given to any thing.

The Rail Roads

Agreeably to your order, verbally communicated to me when in
Washington, I had notices of elections, as follows, published: [1]

NOTICE.

The President of the United States having required, as a step precedent
to the delivery of the New Orleans and Jackson Railroad to its Stockholders by
the military authority, that an election for loyal Directors be held, it is hereby
ordered that an election be held on TUESDAY, the 25th inst., for that
purpose.

                                        HU: KENNEDY, Mayor.
H. BONNABEL,[2] Secretary.

The President of the United States having required as a step precedent to
the delivery of the New Orleans, Opelousas and Great Western Railroad to its
Stockholders by the military authority, that an election for loyal Directors be
held, it is hereby ordered that an election be held on TUESDAY, the 25th
inst., for that purpose.

                                        HU: KENNEDY, Mayor.
H. BONNABEL, Secretary.

The publication of the notice for the New Orleans & Jackson road
elicited, I understand, some feeling in Mississippi, the more, I presume,
because a citizen of that State, Mr Shackelford,[3] had succeeded in getting himself elected to the Presidency by the votes of directors elected
before the rebellion.

Judge Sharkey, the Provisional Governor of Mississippi, doubtless
upon the representations of citizens of his State, telegraphed me in regard to the matter. His telegram and my reply, by same channel,
thereto, marked telegrams 1 & 2, I respectfully enclose.[4]

I have neither feeling or wish in relation to these railroads other than
it is my duty as Mayor of New Orleans, which is a stockholder to the
extent of several millions, to entertain. I represented that interest, as
you will recollect, simply, and you were pleased to direct, and I think
with great propriety and justice, that as an indispensable preliminary
to the surrender by the military of these roads to their stockholders,

new directions, composed of "loyal & reliable men" should be chosen. Beyond compliance with your wishes in this respect, I have distinctly and unequivocally declined to take one step; or in any manner to manifest my personal preference or partiality for any individual or individuals to be connected in the future with these great enterprizes.

A new Agitation

There would seem to be, judging from reports which reach me from various points, remote from each other, in the interior of the State, as well as from indications around me, an organized plan upon the part of a restless faction, which affects to draw its inspiration from the Chief Justice of the United States, to keep up a vexatious & perillous agitation. They hope by exasperating the white & colored population belonging to the country to maintain a constant disquietude, so that the national government will be embarrassed in the earnest & just efforts to restore peace, happiness and unity again, and the hands of its opponents in the free states strengthened.

Thomas W. Conway,[5] Asst. Com. of Bureau Refugees, Freedmen & abandoned lands, and also custodian of all property held for confiscation in place of B. F. Flanders removed, is one of the most active city agitators, and his recent attempts to provoke me into controversy upon the most ridiculous pretences, exhibit the animus of the individual.

I enclose herewith copies of three letters he addressed me,[6] with one from an ally of his, named Fisk,[7] written by the latter to Conway; also copy of the only direct communication he ever had from me.[8] Simultaneously with these experiments of Conway, to create a diversion in the City until their plans in the country are fully ripe, intelligence reaches me that the garrison (colored) of Port Hudson commit, unpunished, every outrage on the residents of the adjacent neighbourhood, for miles. The command of the place is in the hands of Col. Hamlin,[9] a son of the Ex-vice-President, who is charged with connivance at the excesses of his men, and with allowing a sanctuary at the Fort for all run-a-ways from contract labor, and protection to them in disposing of the cattle & other moveable property they carry off from their employers. This Col. Hamlin is said to be a reserve candidate, in the Banks interest, for the State legislature.

It is quite possible there may be errors & exaggerations in these statements; but that there is good foundation for them I myself do not doubt, altho' I am very far from deeming them of the importance many cool-headed persons believe them to be.

Returned Confederates

The young men returning from the confederate armies and military prisons demean themselves most satisfactorily. They are sober, orderly, obedient to the laws & respectful to authority, and in administering the amnesty oath to hundreds of them, not a syllable indicative of resentful or bitter feeling towards the government has ever been heard by me;

but on the contrary, a spirit of thank'fulness & resignation seems to pervade all. It is also due to their officers to state that they on their part are equally contented with the magnanimity of the government. Genls: Beauregard, Hays[10] and others have in person or through friends assured me of their pleasure at seeing me in the Mayoralty, and their determination to do all in their power to strengthen authority in maintaining, against all transgressors, the supremacy of the laws.

The exceptions in this case are to be found among a large class of fellows who have trafficked in the confederacy during the war; have never seen a shot fired in anger or in honorable warfare; who always make themselves conspicuous for ultra-Southern opinions, and proscriptive disposition, and who are now rich. It is needless to add, that they are almost invariably Eastern or Northern men. They assume an insolent swagger, and affect to consider themselves very ill treated & aggrieved because they do not receive large rents and exemption from taxes on property they abandoned for more profitable occupation than watching it. These persons even presume to present their names for offices of trust and responsibility.

Renewal of trade

The removal of almost all the restrictions hiterto imposed on interior trade begins to tell favorably on industry.

I am taking advantage of it to push forward some important public works, so as to give immediate occupation to unemployed labor, until the demands of the Fall & Winter become equal to the supply or greatly exceed it, as I confidently expect.

It was unfortunate for N. Orleans that Genl. Banks should on removing me from office, have overthrown the system of municipal retrenchment I had so successfully inaugurated; and in other ways even more exceptional, sanctioned a great waste of public money. I still am sanguine, however, of being able to restore order out of chaos in our City affairs, and to lay the foundation, deep & indestructible, of a better system than has hitherto existed. For the present I continue to work with the old material of office I found there, unfitted and useless though much of it is, rather [than] to give cause for clamor before the urgency for change cannot be evaded.

I had hoped that the exigencies of government would not still require the interference of the military in affairs purely civil, in the State. The exercise of this power by Genl. Canby is not more assuring than it was when done by his predecessor; and the very fact that he can do it renders the task of civil government difficult, and its administrators are obnoxious to constant disrespect. If a permanent change in this respect were practicable, it would be gladly welcomed here.

Secret Political Associations

These dangerous organisations continue to gain in numbers and efficiency. Their ramification is being pushed, and many dangerous and bad men, the profligate offshoots of both armies, are being initiated. As Genl. Canby has not considered them of sufficient importance to be taken in hand, it is possible he may have better information of their force physically, their aims and their *modus operandi* than I possess; I cannot, nevertheless, reconcile indifference to this matter with my official duty. I hope my apprehensions are groundless.

Govr. Wells is laboring earnestly in the work of getting parochial organization complete, and is, as a great pre-requisite to legislation and thorough re-establishment of State government, putting the judiciary Every where in motion. Of course, complaints are made about appointments, and disappointed suppliants for place and their friends have many harsh things to say of the successful. As, however, every thing is merely provisional, the Gov'r. is less scrutinizing than he otherwise would be, believing that when order reigns again, which he anticipates will soon be the case, the objectionable can be pruned off.

With best wishes for your complete & permanent restoration to health,

> I have the honor to subscribe myself, President,
> Your obdt. servt. Hu. Kennedy
> Mayor

Andrew Johnson Pres. United States

ALS, DLC-JP.

1. The following notices are newspaper clippings attached to the letter.

2. Henry Bonnabel (d. *c*1894) for many years owned a New Orleans chemical works which manufactured bisulphite of lime. New Orleans directories (1866–95).

3. Charles C. Shackleford (*c*1815–*fl*1875), a wealthy Canton, Miss., lawyer-planter and antebellum state legislator, became in 1867 a circuit judge. 1860 Census, Miss., Madison, Canton, 19; Carol L. Mead, *The Land Between Two Rivers: Madison County, Mississippi* (Canton, Miss., 1987), 395; Dunbar Rowland, *Courts, Judges, and Lawyers of Mississippi, 1798–1935* (Jackson, Miss., 1935), 259, 260.

4. On July 19 Sharkey had telegraphed that if the proposed election for directors of the New Orleans and Jackson Railroad was "not in accordance with the charter," he would "take immediate steps to have it declared forfeited." Kennedy replied the same day that the election was ordered by the President, and what Sharkey did in regard to the charter would not affect him. Johnson Papers, LC.

5. Conway (1840–1887), Baptist minister and chaplain of the 9th N.Y. Inf. and 79th U.S.C.T., became Louisiana's superintendent of education after a stormy career with the Freedmen's Bureau. John Howard Brown, ed., *Cyclopaedia of American Biographies* (7 vols., Boston, 1897–1903), 2: 159; *New York Tribune*, April 8, 1887; *American Annual Cyclopaedia* (1887), 578.

6. On July 7 and 13 Conway wrote the mayor regarding a black man named John Martin, who had been arrested for vagrancy. Upon testimony of friends, Martin's sentence had been dropped, but the workhouse keeper would not release him without the signature of the mayor. Conway protested that a "poor white man is deemed industrious till proved a vagrant; a poor black man is deemed a vagrant till proved industrious." On a separate matter, Conway's letter of July 17 reported that city police were breaking up black religious meetings, and he asked Kennedy whether the police had "any instructions from you concerning such meetings." All three July documents referred to here are found in Johnson Papers, LC. See also Letter from Hugh Kennedy, July 29, 1865.

7. Possibly James Fisk (1834–1872), the infamous Boston and New York speculator, who had traded in cotton from the occupied South during the war. *DAB*; J. Fisk to Conway, July 3, 1865, Johnson Papers, LC.

8. On July 8 Kennedy had written Conway: "Neither the style of your letter nor the offensive enclosure of Fisk are warranted by the facts." He had not signed Martin's release form, because it was not correctly filled out. "When the Recorder sends me a release endorsed by him in a proper manner, that is, Martin is entitled to his liberty, I shall sign it"; but until then, he would not violate his duty, even if Conway went to the military to secure Martin's freedom. Johnson Papers, LC.

9. Cyrus Hamlin (1839–1867), colonel, 80th U.S.C.T., and brigadier general of volunteers, remained in New Orleans as a lawyer. Warner, *Blue*.

10. Pierre G.T. Beauregard and Harry T. Hays (1820–1876), Mexican War veteran, attorney, and Confederate brigadier, who became sheriff of Orleans Parish in 1866. Warner, *Gray*.

From Mrs. M. S. Kimbrough

July 21, 1865, Americus, Ga.; ALS, DNA-RG94, Amnesty Papers, Jefferson Davis, Pets. to A. Johnson.

In beseeching Johnson's clemency for Jefferson Davis, Kimbrough reminds the President of their meeting in Nashville in 1857 while he was governor. She and her party had been "very gallantly escorted" through the capital, with the governor's "pointing out its beauties, and various apartments." Kimbrough insists that Davis should not be punished while a "black hearted traitor to his State" such as Joseph E. Brown was pardoned. Should Davis "be the sacrifice, his blood will be to every Southron woman's heart, what the blood of Lamb was to the women of the cross." Asks Johnson to be merciful toward Davis and to thwart the "violent men" who "seek after his soul."

From William J. Murtagh [1]

Office of the National Republican,
Washington, D.C., July 21, 1865

To His Excellency: Andrew Johnson:
Sir:

I respectfully ask the appointment, as Justice of the Peace for the County of Washington of Mr Charles Wilson [2] a citizen of the District. The ward in which I reside, one of the largest, perhaps the largest, has but one resident Justice in it, and the business of the ward would readily occupy the labor of two men. Mr Wilson is a man of integrity and talent, has been a member of the city councils for many years and has all the qualification necessary. I am prompted to ask his appointment at no solicitation on his part, but because I believe the interests of the city will be faithfully attended to. [3]

very truly your obt svt
Wm. J. Murtagh

ALS, DNA-RG60, Appt. Files for Judicial Dists., D.C., William J. Murtagh.

1. Murtagh (*c*1836–*fl*1901), former city councilman (1862–63) and publisher of the *National Republican*, appeared in postwar city directories as journalist, clerk, editor, and lawyer. 1860 Census, D.C., Washington, 7th Ward, 228; Washington, D.C., directories (1858–1901).

2. Wilson (b. *c*1822), a native Pennsylvanian and secretary of an insurance company, had been on the council with Murtagh. Ibid. (1858–67); 1860 Census, D.C., Washington, 7th Ward, 35.

3. Although Johnson's handwritten endorsements appear on a later letter—"Let the appointment be made," and "If an other Justice of the peace is needed let this man be appointed,"—Wilson apparently did not get the position. Murtagh to Johnson, Sept. 4, 1865, Appt. Files for Judicial Dists., D.C., William J. Murtagh, RG60, NA.

From William Winter Payne

July 21, 1865, Washington, D.C.; ALS, DNA-RG94, Amnesty Papers (M1003, Roll 66), Va., William H. Payne.

Former Alabama congressman, now a Virginia resident, laments that, in their "short interval of conversation" the day before, there "was not sufficient time" for him to understand fully *"what the South should do"* to meet the President's reconstruction views. For that object he asks "to be informed, confidentially, or otherwise." Having been pardoned ten days earlier, he thanks Johnson and announces his intentions once again "to enter the [political] arena" in order to aid in "reconstructing the Union." "Indefatigable labor" will be required of the President and all his "sincere friends" who had differed on the slavery question, friends now reunited by the result of the war. Payne wants the President's *"confidence"* and "moral assistance" to "control the citizen every whear within my reach." He observes that the late Confederate soldier, "having been exposed to the hardships and hazards of the war," feels he has a right to lead rather than be led by the citizen. "To this end" the Virginian recommends for pardon his son-in-law, Brig. Gen. William H. Payne. [General Payne was pardoned October 28, 1865.]

From Julio H. Rae[1]

Mineral Springs
Syracuse July 21, 65

His Excelleny Andrew Johnson

By the advice of Hon T. T. Davis M C from our District,[2] I have assumed the liberty to forward you by Express one case of the Excelsior Mineral Water from the recently discovered Mineral Springs of Syracuse. The Water is a tonic laxitive operating directly upon the Liver: also upon the Stomach. If you will use the Water, with the consent & advice of your Physician I truly believe it will be of the greatest benefit to you. In sending you the water my only object is to improve your health.

Respectfuly J H Rae M D.
Syracuse

ALS, DLC-JP.

1. Rae (*c*1822–*fl*1880), an advocate of the "Electropathic Cure," resided variously in New York City, Syracuse, and Philadelphia. 1870 Census, New York, Onondaga, Syracuse, 3rd Ward, 5; New York City directories (1860, 1880); Syracuse directories (1862–73); Philadelphia directories (1878–79).

2. Thomas T. Davis (1810–1872), a Syracuse attorney and unionist member of the U.S. House of Representatives (1863–67). *BDAC*.

From William Smith Reese[1]

Washington July 21, 1865.

To His Excellency the President,

Assured from my interview yesterday with yourself and the Secretary of the Treasury, that your desire in making the appointments for Baltimore is to promote the interests of the union cause, and gratify the wishes of those you recognize as the representatives of the party as far as possible, I sought an interview with both our United States Senators[2] from which I am prepared to say, that meeting my proposition in the same spirit as made they will accept as a compromise the following list giving to each of them one appt and the remaining seven to Gov Swan[3] and his friends.

For	Collector	**D**	Wm. S. Reese Balto.	recommended by Mr
"	Naval officer	**W**	Thos. King Carroll E. Shore	Johnson & Mr Creswell
"	Surveyor	**W**	Mr Fulton	
"	Appraiser at large	**A**	Mr Meredith	Understood to be
"	" local	**A**	Mr Nichols	recommended by Gov.
"	" "	**A**	Mr. Waggoner	Swann Mayor Chapman[5]
"	Postmaster	**A**	Mr Purnel	and friends—
"	U.S. District Attorney	**A**	Mr. Price	
"	" Marshal	**A**	Mr. Bonifant[4]	

This arrangement, will give Mr. Johnson one appointment an union Democrat, Mr. Creswell one a whig, and Gov. Swan and friends seven, one whig and six americans.

This proposition is submitted to your excellency in the belief that it will remove the difficulties heretofore surrounding these appts. be acceptable to the mass of the party throug out the state, and bring to the support of you administration and policy every element of the loyal people of the State. To disregard the wishes of the two senators or of Gov Swan and his friends altogether would be manifestly impolitic while recognizing both will bring to your support the united influence of all.[6]

This arrangement will also secure to the Eight counties of the Eastern Shore one of the principle appts—an important consideration as we must rely to a great extent upon those counties to make up our Union Majority in the next Legislature of Maryland. It will also retain the valuable services in Congress of Mr. Webster[7] whose vote and influence will be required—and we cannot even take the possibility of an opposition member being elected from his district, which is by no means improbable.[8]

Very respt Your obt servt
Wm. Smith Reese

ALS, DNA-RG56, Lets. Recd. from Executive Officers (AB Ser.), President.

1. Reese (*fl*1891), Maryland native and physician, was naval officer (1865–68) and deputy collector (1873–76) at Baltimore. Baltimore directories (1867–91); *U.S. Off. Reg.* (1865–75).

2. Reverdy Johnson and John A. J. Creswell. The latter (1828–1891) was a Republican congressman (1863–65) and senator (1865–67), before serving as Grant's postmaster general (1869–74). *BDAC*.

3. Thomas Swann.

4. Carroll (1821–1900), a doctor and state legislator, was the son of a former Maryland governor; Edington Fulton (*c*1818–1878), a Pennsylvanian, became surveyor (1865–71) and clerk and storekeeper (1877); John F. Meredith was general appraiser (1861–81); William I. Nicholls (*c*1824–*fl*1886), a Baltimore druggist, was assistant appraiser (1861–65) and inspector (1873–78); James F. Wagner (*c*1820–*fl*1901), appraiser under Lincoln, was later a local post office agent; William H. Purnell (*c*1826–*fl*1870), an attorney, became Baltimore postmaster (1865–66); William Price (*c*1794–1868) was a lawyer, legislator, and U.S. attorney (1863–65); Washington Bonifant was marshal (1861–67). 1850 Census, Md., Baltimore, Baltimore, 4th Ward, 149, 153; 2nd Dist., 332; Worcester, Snow Hill, 597; Elias Jones, *New Revised History of Dorchester County, Maryland* (Cambridge, 1966), 299–301; Williams, *Washington County, Md.*, 1:426; *Men of Maryland and District of Columbia*, 24; Baltimore directories (1861–1901); *U.S. Off. Reg.* (1861–81).

5. John Lee Chapman (1812–1880), native Marylander who became Baltimore mayor in 1862, was subsequently appointed naval officer (1867–*c*71). Holli and Jones, *American Mayors*, 64; *U.S. Off. Reg.* (1867–71).

6. See Letters from William I. Nicholls, July 29, 1865, and Reverdy Johnson, July 31, 1865.

7. Edwin H. Webster (1829–1893) served in Congress (1859–65), from which he resigned to become customs collector (1865–69, 1882–86). *BDAC*.

8. After Congressman Webster resigned, John L. Thomas, Jr., a Republican was elected to fill the vacancy. Ibid.

From Edward H. Durell

July 22, 1865, New Orleans, La.; ALS, DNA-RG60, Appt. Files for Judicial Dists., La., N. P. Banks.

Judge of the Eastern District of Louisiana recommends Gen. Nathaniel P. Banks for the "office of U.S. Dist. Atty. in place of Judge [Charles A.] Peabody resigned." Banks, who has become a member of the New Orleans bar, would be "most acceptable" to the "loyal people" of the state.

From William W. Holden

State of North-Carolina, Executive Department.
Raleigh, N.C., 22nd July, 1865.

To His Excellency
The President of the United States

I learn that a Mr. Heddrick,[1] one of the Clerks in the Patent Office at Washington City, is making himself very officious in the matter of appointments to office for the State of North Carolina & I feel it a duty incumbent upon me as the Chief Executive Officer of the State to put you upon your guard against this man & to inform you with regard to his political status. He is an abolitionist of the Sumner type and on that account is very distasteful to the loyal & conservative people of our State and should his views meet with any favour from your Excellency I much fear that a strong prejudice will be aroused against both our National & State Administration. The great body of our people appear to be moving on harmoniously together, with the purpose to yield a generous & hearty support to your Excellency in your efforts to reconstruct a loyal Government in North Carolina and I most sincerely hope that nothing may occur to mar this harmony or chill the loyalty of our people. Of this I have no fears where your Excellency is advised of the political status of those who seek to exert an influence with officials who control the appointments to office. My object now is to secure the appointment of Collector in the 3rd Collection District of North Carolina for Mr. James W. Dick[2] of Guilford County, who is one of our most loyal and reliable citizens & one every way qualified to discharge the duties of that office. Mr. Heddrick I am informed is using his influence against Mr. Dick for no other reason than because he, D, is not fanatical enough in his views to please Mr. H.[3]

I have the honor to be
Yr. Excellency's most Obt. Servt.
W. W. Holden.

LS, DNA-RG56, Appts., Internal Revenue Service, Collector, N.C., 5th Dist., James W. Dick.

1. Benjamin S. Hedrick (1827–1886), North Carolina editor, had taught at the state university. Forced by Holden to resign his professorship, Hedrick joined the Patent Office in 1861 and became a prominent unionist in Washington. Hedrick later assisted Jonathan Worth's successful effort to wrest the governorship away from Holden in the fall election. Raper, *Holden*, 25–26, 93, 260n, 283n; *U.S. Off. Reg.* (1861–65).

2. A bank teller before the war, Dick (b. *c*1823), brother of Holden's close associate, Robert P. Dick, had been conscripted into the 40th N.C. Inf., and detailed as Confederate tax collector. Amnesty Papers (M1003, Roll 38), N.C., James W. Dick, RG94, NA; Raper, *Holden*, 55, 60; Manarin, *N.C. Troops*, 1: 399.

3. Dick was unsuccessful. Samuel H. Wiley was appointed to the collector's position in September 1865 and continued to hold it throughout most of Johnson's presidency. *U.S. Off. Reg.* (1865–67); Appt. Bk. 1: 356, Ser. 6B, Johnson Papers, LC.

From William H.C. King[1]
Private

Office of "The New Orleans Times,"
No. 70 Camp Street.
New Orleans, July 22 1865.

To His Excellency, Andrew Johnson,
President U.S.
Dear Sir

In the interview you were pleased last month to grant me, mention was made of important men and matters in Louisiana. You said: "I should like that you leave with me the names of such of your loyal citizens as you can endorse," etc.

I was then, as I respectfully stated, unprepared to particularize, having sought you entirely in a spirit of personal and political friendship—political only, so far as my humble efforts could possibly conduce in support of your Administration.

I am now, through the generous confidence you manifested in me, induced to address you in regard to the vacancy created in the U.S. Supreme Bench, by the death of Judge Catron.

The opportunity is thus afforded for placing in that Court a jurist versed in the *civil* law, which has now no representative there.[2] The practice and laws of Arkansas and Texas largely partake of a civil law character. In Louisiana the civil code is the law of the State. The importance of the Southwest, as a part of the Union, its resources and interests, entitle it to this recognition of its legal system.

Judge J. S. Whitaker[3] has had judical experience in this State and acquitted himself with great ability in that position. He has *always* been loyal. He acted with the Democratic party before the war, and is an able and earnest supporter of your Administration. No man is more respected here for legal acquirement, soundness of judgment, and personal and political integrity. His appointment to succeed Judge Catron would be highly satisfactory to Louisiana, and, in my judgment, would reflect great credit upon your Administration.

Regarding Gov. Wells, my views, as expressed to you, have undergone quite a change. I do not agree with his friends in the correctness of many of his recent acts, particularly regarding some of his appointments. Recently he has appointed Ex-Lieut. Governor H. W. Hyams as a Director of the Citizens Bank. You must be familiar with his history.[4]

In this connection I will reiterate my last words to your Excellency, made in the presence of Secretary McCulloch. I think the people would be better satisfied with a Provisional Governor until such time as matters could assume a more settled shape. There are two parties here, violently arrayed against each other, and in my opinion neither should be in power. The Provisional Governor should be a man above every personal and party consideration, in no way connected with either of the opposing factions. I am much afraid that matters, as they are now progressing, will assume a serious shape unless checked by your speedy interposition.

My views are thus submitted, candidly, and with due respect to your judgment, and I sincerely trust, in a shape unobjectionable.

With sincere respect for yourself personally, and with renewed pledges that the TIMES which is owned as I informed you, by Messrs. Thos. P. May, C. A. Weed[5] and myself, will support you with all the sincerity your noble policy inspires, and the ability we can command,

I remain, Truly yours,

Wm. H. C. King

ALS, DLC-JP.

1. King (1824–1868), Pittsburgh, Pa., native and former actor, had been associated with various New Orleans newspapers since the 1840s. Fayette Copeland, "The New Orleans Press and the Reconstruction," *LHQ*, 30 (1947): 281–82, 285.

2. The "opportunity" did not last long, for in 1866 Congress reduced the number of justices from ten to nine. Fairman, *Reconstruction and Reunion*, 161–62.

3. John S. Whitaker (1817–1895), New Orleans lawyer, served as judge of the city's second district court. *NUC*; New Orleans directories (1861–96).

4. Henry M. Hyams (c1806–fl1875), a Louisiana lawyer, had been cashier of the Donaldsonville branch of the Canal Bank, state senator, and lieutenant governor (1859–61). In the 1830s he had been a leader at an anti-abolitionist meeting and a member of a vigilante committee to combat antislavery propaganda. Ibid. (1872–75); Bertram W. Korn, *The Early Jews of New Orleans* (Waltham, Mass., 1969), 141, 188–89.

5. Charles A. Weed (c1831–fl1873), a Stamford, Conn., farmer, came to New Orleans during General Butler's regime, managed abandoned plantations, speculated in cotton, and operated a grocery business. By 1869 he was sole proprietor of the *Times*. 1860 Census, Conn., Fairfield, Stamford, 179; *Richmond Enquirer*, Mar. 15, 1864; Copeland, "The New Orleans Press and the Reconstruction," 286; New Orleans directories (1866–73).

Memorial re *Pennsylvania Draft Resisters*

ca. July 22, 1865; Mem, DNA-RG60, Office of Atty. Gen., Lets. Recd., President.

Robert L. Johnston and state senator William A. Wallace list thirty-six names of Cambria and Clearfield County citizens who have been charged with resisting the September 20, 1864, draft. Arrested by the military on December 10, 1864, and confined "at Fort Mifflin and elsewhere . . . one to four months," the accused are now indicted and held by the U.S. Court for the Western District of the state. Since "no overt act . . . was perpetrated" and the men "have borne good characters," it is believed they have already "been sufficiently punished," especially in view of the fact "that the war has ended," and the "necessity . . . of the draft has ceased." Further "punishment of these men can effect no public good," and their pardon is, therefore, recommended. [Senators Edgar Cowan and C. R. Buckalew endorsed the memorial. Johnson's secretary, Reuben D. Mussey, on July 22, 1865, referred the document to the attorney general "for his opinion as to the propriety of entering a nolles in the prosecution against them."]

From John P. Usher

Washington D C July 23rd 1865

To the President;

I trust I may be permitted to express my regret that Mr. Dole should have found himself constrained to retire from the office of Commissioner of Indian Affairs. My regret is occasioned partly out of regard for him, and partly because you have parted with a true, and useful friend, who would have effectually exercised the power in his hands, for your support on the approaching conflict which the old Malcontents of the Government are endeavoring to force upon the already too distracted country. I feel that you will need men who will stand by you and keep the sound and true Union men together.

If Mr. Dole was appointed to the Office of Register of Deeds, in this City, he would be in a position to be useful to you, though not to so great an extent as before, yet it would be gratifying to himself and his friends, and allay the regret felt by them because of the recent events which led to his resignation of Office.[1] I may add that, it would be very gratifying to myself.

I am also very sorry that matters should have taken such a course as to induce Halloway to resign.[2] He is a Representative man of Indiana of those who may be relied upon to sustain you. Men, who, have large and wholesome views of all public m...tters and never fanatical. The latter are faithless and bent upon mischief. They demand Suffrages for the Negroes and will make all possible disturbance to effect their object, but the people will never agree to it, and the Masses of all parties hope you will never yield to their demands. The people would be glad to see you well rid of all these Malcontents.

I have been much over the Country and am glad to know that the masses are for you and earnestly pray that no harm may befal you, and that, you will remain firm in your course.[3]

I need not assure you that you have my earnest support and that I am

Sincerely & faithfully your friend

J. P. Usher

P S. I forgot to thank you for the appointment, of my good friend Gov. Wright.[4]

LS, DLC-JP.

1. William P. Dole remained in Washington as a claims attorney and agent. See Letter from James Harlan, June 7, 1865.

2. David P. Holloway, commissioner of patents since 1861, stayed in Washington as a patent attorney.

3. Johnson endorsed this letter "I[n] reference to the removal of Holloway & Dole."
4. See Letter from Joseph A. Wright, June 12, 1865.

From Mary A. White

Edgefield July 23rd, 65

Hon Andrew Johnson
President of the United States,
My Dear Friend.

I feel a very strong desire this evening to talk to you, and being deprived of that privillage I choose this medium of expressing my wishes to you. I might say much of my gratitude to you for your very great kindness to me in the past, of your patience & forbearance at all times, but I am afraid you would think it, the *cold compliment of ceremony*. I trust you will believe me when I say I have *never* been wanting in a proper appreciation.

Gen Clements and Ben[1] are at present living with John.[2] Ben is in a very feeble, low state of health, it is feared will never recover. I am exceedingly anxious that both of them should receive pardon from your hands.[3] We are all living together as one family. You know the relationship and kindly feeling existing between us. I do hope in your goodness of heart you may see fit to grant this favor. I will receive it as a personal act of kindness from you.

Papa[4] desires the same very much and expressed a wish that I should say as much to you. His health is giving way very rapidly I fear. I shall not write at length for fear of wearying you. Present my kind regards to your family. Papa sends many good wishes. Accept for yourself the assurance of my continued friendship & highest regards.

As Ever Your friend
Mary A White

ALS, DNA-RG94, Amnesty Papers (M1003, Roll 48), Tenn., Jesse B. Clements.

1. Former Confederate marshal of Tennessee, Jesse B. Clements and his son Benjamin N. (c1824–1865), a Confederate postal official who suffered from consumption. Amnesty Papers (M1003, Roll 48), Tenn., Jesse B. and Benjamin N. Clements, RG94, NA; *Index to Interments in the Nashville City Cemetery, 1846–1962* (Nashville, 1964), 16.

2. Mary's brother, John P. White.

3. Both father and son were pardoned August 8, 1865, the latter dying less than a month later. *House Ex. Docs.*, 39 Cong., 2 Sess., No. 115, pp. 35, 36 (Ser. 1293); *Nashville Union*, Sept. 5, 1865.

4. Richard White.

From "Mr. Brown"

New York July 24 /65

Mr Johnson
Dear. Sir

You fucked up Son of a Bitch! If you dont let Jeff go i will Be at your house in less than 24 Ours and Dan me if you dont fet [let] hin of i will Blow you dan Brains out You Son of a Bitch.[1]

Yours Truly Mr Brown

ALS, DNA-RG94, Baker-Turner Papers.
1. A sample of the kind of threat received in Washington and referred to Major Levi C. Turner, associate judge advocate general for the army.

To Joseph E. Brown

Executive Office, Washington, D.C.
July 24 1865

Joseph E. Brown
Atlanta, Georgia

The Governor of the State ought to proceed at once to appoint persons to administer the Amnesty oath. The oath can be administered by any military or civil officer who is loyal to the Government of the United States. I am gratified to know that the people of Georgia are acting so promptly in restoring civil authority, and hope it will be a complete success.[1] The letters referred to by you sent by Express have not been received. Judge Patterson is somewhere in Tennessee. Will be here soon.

Andrew Johnson
President U.S.

Tel, DNA-RG107, Tels. Sent, President, Vol. 2 (1865).
1. Sometime later, Brown, enroute to Augusta, gave James Johnson copies of this dispatch and his July 21 telegram to the President, reminding the governor that the "military are doing very little to have the oath administered." See endorsement of Brown to James Johnson, n.d., on transcriptions of Brown to Johnson, July 21, 1865, and Johnson to Brown, July 24, 1865, Felix Hargrett Col., Joseph E. Brown Papers, University of Georgia.

From Alexander B. Clitherall

[ca. July 24, 1865], Montgomery, Ala.; ALS, DNA-RG94, Amnesty Papers (M1003, Roll 2), Ala., A. B. Clitherall.

A forty-five year old lawyer, who favored "the establishment of a southern Confederacy" and believed that "separation would be peaceable," asks for a pardon for having served as register of the rebel treasury until July 1861, and sequestration judge for the middle division of Alabama in 1863. The latter was a nominal office, and he "did nothing," the only benefit being exemption from the army. He now regards the secession question and "all its issues as forever settled" and "accepts the situation," wishing "in good faith" to be a "loyal, law abiding citizen of the United States." [Johnson issued Clitherall's pardon October 14, 1865.]

From Mrs. H. J. Cowden

[ca. July 24, 1865], Westfield, N.Y.; ALS, DNA-RG60, Office of Atty. Gen., Lets. Recd., President.

Widow of a Union captain seeks help in regaining Texas property confiscated by Confederates. She claims that her husband went to Limestone, Tex., "with a view of makeing that his residence; taking with him a fine flock of thourough bred fine wool sheep; and had carried on the business of raising" such stock, when in May 1861, he had to flee, "leaving his entire property, having onley a very small sum ($120) left." [Johnson sent his "sympathy" through the attorney general's office, whose agent assured the widow that, "as soon as courts are in operation," she could reclaim the land. Furthermore, if a suit against the parties stealing the stock was unsuccessful, she could apply to Congress for indemnity.]

From Christopher C. Graham

July 24, 1865, Crab Orchard, Ky.; ALS, DNA-RG105, Records of the Commr., Lets. Recd. from Executive Mansion.

An aged physician informs Johnson of "what is now going on in Kentucky," pleading against the breakup of slavery there. If we live under a written Constitution "which protects life liberty and property," he argues, then it cannot be "by your approbation that the best of its citizens are, by arbitrary arrests and consequent death . . . deprived" of the same. Johnson has "fought too hard against rebellion" to place himself now "in rebellion against the government," but "there is a party, at Washington, who would be willing to see the Administration take from the states who created it, all their inherent and reserved rights." The Kentucky Constitution "forbids free blacks remaining in the state," but passes issued by Federal authorities encourage them to stay. State laws allow "no public conveyance" to take a slave away without the master's consent, "yet these papers order all conveyances to take them off." This "high-handed and sudden breaking up of all our domestic relations" leaves "our crops to perish for want of help," and "we are forced to suffer." Kentuckians feel that they own "slave property as any other, and any power which may rench it from us without consent or compensation is unjust." Claiming to be an emancipationist who has written upon the subject, Graham asserts that the "turning loose" of four million slaves "is not a remedy, but a grievous evil to both black and white." Those who are "being seduced from their happy homes by the pledge of free papers, at Camp Nelson, assemble in such numbers as to render their condition uncomfortable and unhealthy." Yet the "worst feature about this Camp Nelson business" is that the blacks think their free papers entitle them "to live the remainder of their lives without work, and that the Government will support them, at the expense and labor of the white man." Graham therefore urges Johnson to "proclaim to the blacks and to your Agents, that they must go to work and support themselves, and all will soon go like clock work, for the blacks will then want a home and the whites want their services." Those blacks who do return home seem to want to taunt their previous master "with their free papers and threaten him with military power." He concludes by asking the President to "heed not" the "Moloch howl" of the Radicals, but to "gain the hearts of the people, discharge your armies, tell the idle negroes they must support themselves, pay our myriad-debt, redeem the currency and sustain the credit and the honor of the nation."

From Andrew J. Hamilton [1]

Galveston Texas 24th July 1865

Mr President

After leaving Washington I was twelve or fourteen days reaching New Orleans, where I was detained for two weeks before I could procure transportation for my family and Texas Refugee friends, numbering between forty and fifty persons.

I reached this place three days past and have been compelled to wait for transportation from this point to the city of Austin, the Capitol of the State, for which place I will leave day after to morrow. The time spent here is not lost however. This is the principal Sea Port and commercial city of the State, and I find here, besides the resident population many gentlemen from various portions of the interior from whom I have sought all the information in their power to give; and from their uniform and concurrent statements I think I know pretty accurately the present temper and frame of mind of the different classes of men in the State. The Union men are of course happy and satisfied. They do not use the hackneyed phrase "I accept the situation" but they say the situation is the right one—the one we desired—Civil liberty is secure and the cause which threatened it, is forever crushed. The poor men of the Country who have been the sufferers by the War, whether originally in favor of disunion or Union are now fast friends of the Govt. and will give me a hearty and unswerving support—all of them, who have homes and families, and who have any interest in Government and society. And among these not the least ardent are those who have gone through the war and felt in all its weight and bitterness the yoke of Rebel rule. These men can be trusted, and all being within your general Amnesty are availing themselves of it as fast as possible.

As to those who are not embraced in the general Amnesty I wish to say a few words which I hope Your Excellency will duly consider. I have had many applications for my recommendation for special pardon— so far I have recommended some five or six, all of them men that I know well and upon whom I can rely implicitly—who never deceive and who understand thoroughly the issues that have been settled by the war and will manfully sustain the result. The great mass of the applicants I have refused because they are of a class who yield to what they cannot help, but retain all the bitterness of heart which induced them in the outset to raise their hands against their Government, intensified by the dethronement of their God the institution of Slavery. I of course allude to those embraced in the 13th exception to your Amnesty—those worth more than twenty thousand dollars, most of whom are Planters and Slave Owners, and if we include Merchants and Commercial men embracing nearly all covered by the 13th exception.

These men, especially the planters with few exceptions, come forward in the most confident manner, with a manner and bearing rather patronizing than penitent, and graciously say that they do not intend to fight the Government any more—that they will submit to what they cannot help but they deeply deprecate the want of Statesmanship in the effort of the Government to abolish slavery, and very many of them plainly indicate in conversation their belief in the necessity and propriety of providing in the reorganization of the State Government by Constitutional provision for a Coercive system of labour for the Negro: that slavery in some form will continue to exist under some new name.

None of these seem to think it necessary to make the slightest apology for the past, but rather seem to think they place the Government under great obligation when they say with a lofty sadness "I submit." It is most apparent that this class of men are not at this time in a frame of mind to bring any support to the organization of Loyal Government upon the basis of the extinction of slavery. To prove how far they have respect for the negro as a freeman combinations are forming in the different neighbourhoods and Counties, embracing the large planter, in the form of resolutions by public meetings, pledging themselves to each other not to hire or countenance any negro who shall have left his late Master or to countenance any white man who will hire one who has so left, and the same spirit was manifested a few days ago in a public meeting in the City of Houston, in which was passed resolutions recommending a combination to employ white mechanics to the exclusion of black ones &c. We have here also most painful accounts of the shooting and hanging of negroes by the half dozen at a time, for the crime of leaving their former Masters. These accounts may be exaggerated as such things generally are, but there is too much evidence that such things have occurred. The Military Authorities, before my arrival, had very properly by general orders, notified the whites that the negroes were free, but at the same time recommended to the freedmen the propriety of remaining with their former masters for the time being, if treated with humanity and reasonably compensated for their labour. I intend to recommend to them the same course, but at the same time assure them of their freedom and the ability and intention of the Government to protect them in their rights as freeman.

I have met a number of planters here who say they acquiesce in the results of the war and wish henceforth to be good citizens of the U.S. and who are wanting my endorsement of their petition for special pardon, and who have just taken the Amnesty oath solemnly swearing to support the Proclamation of emancipation, and at the same time talk of the *gradual emancipation* of the slaves as the proper policy for Texas. This will serve to show how far they are to be trusted, with their present feelings in the work of reorganizing Government. And this brings me to the subject which I particularly desire to call your attention to: and it is this—the wisdom of the 13th exception to your general Amnesty and the importance and necessity of adhering to it. The Unionists of Texas could better afford to have every other exception stricken out than that one. It embraces the class of men from whom we are to meet the most determined and powerful opposition to the re-organization of such State Govt as will be acceptable to the people and Govt of the U.S. unless they are kept under bonds for their good behaviour until such time at least as they shall be powerless for harm.

Therefore I do most sincerely hope that you will adhere to the exception, and also to the rule requiring from all applicants for special pardon under each of the exceptions, the recommendation of the Provisional Governor. It is not because I want power for the love of its exercise, but because it is a powerful lever in my hand to repress evil.

There will be many cases which I shall recommend—a few I have already endorsed, because I know the men and they will act with me and not against me: but from all I can see now the majority who are applying would use their restored rights and increased influence directly against the policy of the Govt whose mercy they had prayed for and received—especially is this true of the large slave owners as a class who constitute the largest portion of those who are worth more than twenty thousand dollars.

It is needless to say that any man embraced in any of the exceptions, who has been heretofore respectable can get recommendations for pardon. They have their old friends and correspondents in the commercial cities North and through them can obtain the offices of some respectable politician to urge their claims. Let them wait for a time—it will not hurt them. Let them "bring forth fruit meet for repentance"[2] and ask to be forgiven. They can trust the Govt better than the Govt can trust them.

I am happy to say the Union men of the State are a unit, and they will have the hearty co-operation of most of the poor men who were deluded into rebellion.

I receive the most flattering report from these classes from every part of the State of their unswerving support in the difficult task before me. I shall need their support Mr President, as I shall yours, and as I intend to deserve both I feel assured that neither will fail me. I shall be beset by the enemies of the Govt and possibly by some who claim to be its friends from motives of personal ambition—but the loyal Union Sentiment of the Country is with me and will remain so.

I am preparing a Proclamation which will be issued in a few days a copy of which I will forward you when ready.[3]

I leave here day after to-morrow for the Capitol where I will enter upon the work which you have confided to my hands, with all the ability and energy I possess, with a full knowledge of how much depends for Texas, and for myself, upon my humble exertions.

I will not fail to keep you regularly advised of the true condition of things and the prospects ahead.

I find the people greatly embarrassed because no official announcement of the opening of this Port (Galveston) has yet reached here and no appointment so far as we have heard of a Collector of Customs.

Before I left Washington I recommended for that Office Dr R. R. Peebles[4] one of the oldest and most respectable citizens of Texas— every way qualified and who had suffered long and cruel imprisonment at the hands of the Rebels for his Unionism. But I have heard nothing from it since I left. This is our principal Seaport.

The people are suffering much for many articles of prime necessity which cannot be admitted, and are anxious to send out Cotton, Wool, Hides &c! I hope this may be speedily remedied; and have forwarded by the same mail which bears this, a communication to the Hon. Sec'y of the Treasury upon the subject.

Wishing you health adequate to the demands of your Office

I have the honor to be
Your Excellency's Obt Servt
A. J. Hamilton
Provl Govr of Texas.

T[o] His Excellency Andrew Johnson
President U.S. Washington City D.C.

LS, DLC-JP.
1. In June Hamilton had visited Johnson, who appointed him provisional governor. Carl H. Moneyhon, *Republicanism in Reconstruction Texas* (Austin, 1980), 22–23.
2. Matt. 3:8.
3. Hamilton's "Proclamation to the People of Texas," July 25, 1865, outlined the measures to be adopted for the reestablishment of civil government in the state. Executive Record Book, No. 281, pp. 191–94, Texas States Library, Archives Div. See Letter from Hamilton, August 30, 1865.
4. Arrested by Confederate authorities for his unionist sympathies and deported from the state, Richard R. Peebles (1810–1893) returned in August 1865, to become nominal collector of the Port of Galveston, but ill health prevented him from assuming active duties. Webb and Carroll, *Handbook of Texas*, 2: 356.

From William W. Holden

State of North-Carolina Executive Department.
Raleigh, N.C., July 24, 1865.

To the President.

Sir:

I send herewith a proof-sheet of the Proclamation[1] I propose to issue for a Convention. I could have prepared it ten days ago, but for indisposition, which continues, and which has somewhat unavoidably retarded public business. Please examine the proof-sheet, make such correction as you may deem necessary, and hand or send to Mr. Mason or Dr. Powell[2] to be returned to me. I had thought of several plans for administering the amnesty oath to the people, and the plan adopted in the Proclamation seems to be the best. It would not be safe to confide this power to all the Justices, though I believe they are all loyal, yet there are weak men among them, and persons would be qualified to vote who ought not to be.

If the Convention should assemble on the 2d of October the Constitution could be altered and submitted to the people by the 20th November; and then, in anticipation of the ratification of the Constitution by the people, the Convention could provide for the election of Governor and members on the 15th or 20th December, so that the new or regular government could be inaugurated on the 1st January, 1866.[3]

I have thought it best to begin at the foundation and build upwards. We now have 3,500 Magistrates, Mayors and Commissioners in all the towns, with police, with Sheriffs and Constables in all the Counties. The civil power is now felt in every neighborhood in the State; and the result is, as a general rule, that the people are submissive and quiet, and looking anxiously to the time when the State will be restored to her relations with the government. In addition to this heavy labor, (for the antecedents and present disposition of every man appointed had to be ascertained,) I have had to see to the reorganization of the Banks and the Railroads. This latter work is well nigh accomplished, and these corporations will pass from the hands of traitors into the hands of loyal men.

Many of the oligarchs are still unsubdued. I think it a good plan to hold their pardon in suspense, and, whether their estates are to be confiscated or not, they ought not to be allowed to vote for twelve months to come. But I find, what is a little singular, that the ultra original secessionists who profess to have repented, appear to be really more penitent than the ultra partizans of Vance[4] who were once Union men. By the way, it would not be good policy to extend a pardon to Vance for sometime to come. Your administration is very popular in North-

Carolina, but there are indications on the part of some of the oligarchs and the old Whig leaders to concoct opposition. A firm, discreet use of the pardoning power and the patronage of the government will contribute greatly to keep them down, and thus preserve tranquility and order in the State.

The amount, $7,000, brought by Mr. Treasurer Worth, will probably be enough to defray the expenses of my office until the regular government is established. We shall be able, I think, to realize several hundred thousand dollars from the cotton and rosin you were kind enough to allow us.[5]

My health is very feeble, and I have written this while suffering pain.

I am rejoiced to learn that your health has been restored. May your valuable life long be spared to your friends and your country.

With high respect, W. W. Holden

ALS, DLC-JP.

1. Holden enclosed a draft of the proclamation that he would issue on August 9, 1865, ordering an election for delegates to a state convention. See Telegram to Holden, August 7, 1865.

2. William S. Mason and Robert J. Powell.

3. The election of a governor and legislators was held on November 9, the same day that the convention's recommendations were ratified. Unfortunately for Holden, he was defeated by provisional treasurer Jonathan Worth. Zuber, *Worth*, 206–7.

4. Confederate Governor Zebulon Vance.

5. See Letter from Holden, June 26, 1865.

From John Letcher

Lexington Virginia, July 24th 1865:

Dear Sir:

On my way home through the Valley of Virginia, and since my arrival, I have met with quite a large number of our citizens of all classes, and have conversed freely with them on the condition of the country, and the best and speediest means of securing relief, from existing and future evils. I have availed my self of the opportunities thus presented, to impress upon them the necessity of a prompt and cheerful response to your call for re-organization, and have advised them that your views as expressed in our conversation, were liberal and conciliatory towards the Southern people: that it was both our policy and duty, to meet you in the same generous spirit—effect the re-organization as speedily as practicable—and be prepared to cast their influence in the scale, in your behalf, in the contest, which must occur, at no distant day, between your administration, and the radical element of the North, on the suffrage question. The advice has been uniformly well received, and the people are acting promptly and cheerfully, in taking the preliminary steps, to effect re-organization.

The election here takes place, Thursday next. In the main, we will secure very fair officers. Every thing is proceeding in a quiet and orderly manner, without the slightest exhibition of excitement or ill-temper. Indeed I have never seen our people animated by a better, or more patriotic spirit. After so long and destructive a war, the universal desire of all classes, is for quiet and order—a speedy return to business relations, and a restoration of prosperity to the whole country.

Throughout the valley, the institution of Slavery is regarded as dead, and no man that I know of, seeks to revive it. The result is accepted and acquiesced in without a murmur, and the people are making their arrangements for the future, as if it had never had an existence in our midst. Most of our farmers, are willing to employ as many of their late slaves as they need, but as a general rule, the slaves seem disposed to change their locations and seek new homes, while a very general disposition exists with a large number to crowd into the towns and villages, where it is impossible for them to secure permanent employment. Many have left their former homes, and are now congregated in the lower end of the valley, and owing to the failure of the wheat crop, and the limited corn crop, they will experience great difficulty in passing safely through the coming winter. Numbers of women and children run the hazard of starvation, as employment in that locality, cannot be had, for a vast majority of them.

And now in conclusion permit me to call your attention, to one matter that promises "a harvest of woe," to this country, at no very distant day. I allude to the National Banking system, now spreading itself so rapidly over the land North and South. This bubble is distined to burst, and involve millions in financial ruin, and in this general ruin the government is to suffer with the people. A *specie basis* is indispensable, to a safe system of Banking.[1] Bank credit, cannot rest securely upon any other species of credit and the most uncertain of all credits, upon which to rest it, is that of government credit. Legislation is generally uncertain, and at a time like this more uncertain than at any other time. Unless prudential action is speedily taken, this bubble will burst during your administration, and if it does, the future of the Democratic party, is hopeless.

With the best wishes for the success of your administration, and for your individual happiness and prosperity[2]

I am truly Your obdt: servt:
John Letcher

His Excellency, Andrew Johnson
Pesdt. U.S.A.

ALS, DLC-JP.
1. Congress passed the National Banking Act of 1863 in order to provide a large market for government bonds. The more than 1,600 private banks established under its provisions served as depositories for federal funds and were authorized to issue notes to be used as circulating medium. One of McCulloch's first acts as secretary of the treasury

was to consider a plan redeeming greenbacks and pushing toward the resumption of specie payment. Irwin Unger, *The Greenback Era* (Princeton, 1964), 14–19, 41.

2. An endorsement, possibly by one of Johnson's secretaries, scribbled across the last page of the letter, reads: "John Letcher/Sensible Letter."

From Peter E. Love[1]

Thomasville Ga. July 24th 1865.

To his Excellency Andrew Johnson,
President Of the United States of America.
Sir,

The Fourth exception in your Amnesty Proclamation is as follows: "All who left their seats in the Congress of the United States to aid in the rebellion." I was a representative from the first District of Georgia in the Congress of the United States when the convention passed the ordinance of secession & ordered me & the rest of the delegation home. My status while in Congress was that of a conservative or Union man & on that account I was appointed by the Speaker on the Committee of Thirty three, on which committee I labored faithfully day & night untill I vacated my seat.[2] I was opposed to secession. I believed that it would bring unspeakable calamities upon both North & south & would result just as it has, in the subjugation of the seceding states. I was however educated in the States Rights school of politics & as a mere question of political right I believed that the state could withdraw from the Union. Consequently when a convention embodying as I thought the sovereignty of the state passed the secession ordinance & ordered me home, I thought it was my duty to obey, & did so. During the war I was a quiet & orderly citizen. I did not take up arms against the Government of the United States altho I have reason to believe that I could have done so with a commission in my pocket. During the war I was a member of the Georgia Legislature, Mayor of the Town of Thomasville where I reside, & was at the surrender one of the Judges of the county Court. These positions were all sought for & obtained however, exclusively for the purpose of avoiding conscription.

These are the facts of my case and I earnestly desire to be pardoned for any political offence which they involve.

All of which is respectfully submitted[3]

P E Love

ALS, DNA-RG94, Amnesty Papers (M1003, Roll 21), Ga., P. E. Love.

1. Love (1818–1866), a physician-lawyer, served in the state legislature, as circuit judge and in Congress (1859–61). *BDAC*.

2. Composed of representatives from each state in the Union, this congressional committee in December 1860 produced a resolution for sectional compromise that was later adopted by a two-thirds vote in both chambers. James G. Randall and David Donald, *The Civil War and Reconstruction* (Lexington, Mass., 1969), 148–49.

3. Over a year later, still unpardoned after applying diligently and knowing "no reason why I should be excluded from Executive clemency," Love appealed again; for if "the

radicals should get full possession of the government, which is to be feared I know not what they may do with me." Love to Johnson, Oct. 22, 1866, Amnesty Papers (M1003, Roll 21), Ga., P. E. Love, RG94, NA.

From Joseph E. Brown
(Private)

Canton Ga July 25th 1865

His Excellency Andrew Johnson President &c. &c.

Dear Sir

You were kind enough before I left Washington to invite me to write you in reference to the state of things in Ga. I fear I may weary you by trespassing too frequently on your valuable time. I must ask your indulgence however a little further.

Since I wrote you the other day from Atlanta I have passed through the Country to this place and have Conversed freely with the people and advised them to take the oath and abide by it in good faith, to vote for good men to the Convention who will abolish slavery and give us a good Constitution, and place the state back in the Union as a loyal state. I have also assured them that you are their friend, that it is not your purpose to crush them, but your wish to build them up. They are well disposed and are generally ready in good faith to take the oath and to become loyal good citizens. But they have no opportunity to do so. From Marietta to the North Carolina line over 100 miles I do not hear of any one authorized to administer the oath. In my opinion this large section of Country is now entirely loyal, and will send delegates if the people generally vote ready to abolish slavery and carry out your line of policy. Let me again beg you if not already done, to order one person to each County in the state immediately with power to administer the oath, and with plenty of printed blanks that it may be done at once. If this course is pursued and I am left at liberty to mingle freely with our people and adopt such line of argument with each as I am satisfied will be most likely to influence him in favor of the line of policy you wish carried out, I feel that I can vouch for the result you wish attained. I have used freely and with excellent effect the argument that we should adopt the policy which you lay down, because you are our friend in leaving the question of negroe suffrage &c with the states. I believe your line the true one under the circumstances. Hence I can freely adopt it.

That I may be successful it is essential that I shall not be disturbed by military Commanders in the state. I neither interfere with their business nor prerogatives. I am satisfied that some of my enemies have labored hard to prejudice the minds of the Generals against me, and may to some extent have succeeded.

Since I reached this County an officer followed me with an order from Maj Genl Wilson that I send him a Copy of my parole given [by] the Secretary of War,[1] with any other papers I have from the War Department, and if I did not have them with me that the officer carry me back. He found me in bed too feeble from the fatigue of the trip up to travel and went back without arresting me, on my assurance that I would return to Milledgeville by Macon as soon as I feel able to bear the fatigue, and furnish the papers. My heath is still feeble and I hoped by a short sojourn in this healthy section to restore it, as well as to put all right with the people. This order of Genl. Wilson will compel me to return before I have accomplished either object as fully as I had hoped to do.

You have had experience enough in managing political affairs to know that such order is not only annoying, but tends to lessen my influence with the people. When it is said the General is sending orders after me &c. I do not know what use is to be made of the Copy parole. I have not spoken of it in the state, but have only alluded to my military parole.[2] I think the reasons for this Course will at once strike you as Good. If it is published to the people that I am discharged and sent home under promise or pledge to use my influence to induce them to return to their loyalty, and adopt certain measures, part of my influence is at once distroyed, as they would reply to my arguments by saying these may or may not be your honest Convictions, as you are under pledge to the Government to Come, among us, and do all you can to induce us to take the Course you indicate. Under these Circumstances I beg you to order Genl Wilson to make no public use of the Copy parole. You are so familiar with these matters that I know you will see at once the effect of the publication. As I am laboring to strengthen the government with the people I hope the Government will not weaken me with them, and thereby destroy the influence I am bringing to bear in its favor. I will be greatly obliged if you will telegraph Genl Wilson immediately on the subject.[3] My military parole was returned to me by the Secretary of War and I have spoken of your Just decision in discharging me from arrest upon it.

I know I am not mistaken when I assure you that the people of this state are now well disposed, and that with prudent management there will be no trouble in Ga. It is equally true that military Commanders from other states are not the best Judges of the line of argument or the Course of policy that will influence the people of this state to adopt any particular line of action. I should be glad to have a letter from you.

I am Very truly
Your friend & obdt Servt
Joseph E. Brown

I must beg the President to read this letter long as it is.

ALS, DLC-JP.
1. As a condition of his parole, Brown had pledged on June 3 to "restore the authority

of the Federal Government" by "induc[ing] the inhabitants" of Georgia "to return to their allegiance and fidelity." Lets Recd. (Main Ser.), File W-1131-1865, Joseph E. Brown, RG94, NA. See also Letter to Stanton, June 3, 1865

2. The one granted to Brown by General Wilson on May 5. See Letter from Brown, May 7, 1865.

3. Brown repeated his request on July 29, and on the 31st Johnson wired Wilson: "For the present withhold publication of Joseph E. Brown's parole and telegraph your reasons for desiring to publish it." Tels. Recd., President, Vol. 4 (1865–66), RG107, NA; Tels. Sent, President, Vol. 2 (1865), RG107, NA; Parks, *Brown*, 338–39.

From Joseph S. Fowler

State of Tennessee, Comptroller's Office,
Nashville, July 25th, 1865.

Andrew Johnson Pres. United States:
Dr. Sir,

I have sent all the Papers by Judge Milligan. I wrote to Carson[1] requesting him to pay your interest and send it by him to Washington. I also directed him to pay the interest on the $40,000 and give a new certificate.[2]

I received a letter from the Banks urging the payment of the notes.[3] The letter was pretty sharp. I have not answered. You will do me the pleasure of indicating what course I must take. I think the notes could be bought now as favorably as they can at any time. They must be carefully purchased of course.

I would have settled all my matters up had not my health forbidden my laboring. I will in a few days make my report in full in reference to my United States funds.

Gen Milligan will give you a full account of all that we are doing & will represent my views. I am satisfied that all our old Conservatives are now making an effort to go off into a direct opposition. They have failed to seduce the state officers & now turn against it. I am sorry organization was neglected in my absence. But we will do the best we can.

I cannot now promise much from Middle Tennessee. It is the same old fight continued. The same parties are at work and the same ideas are in issue. I hope you are in good health. My regards to your family.

Yours truly Jos. S. Fowler

ALS, DLC-JP.

1. Enoch T. Carson.

2. For some time Johnson had on deposit in Cincinnati, $40,000 as a "Temporary Loan to the U.S.," an amount he increased by $3,900 in July 1864. See Carson to Johnson, June 9, July 8, 1864, *Johnson Papers*, 6: 718; 7: 24.

3. Not found.

From Annie E. Hutchcroft[1]

Paris Bourbon Co. Ky—, July 25th 1865.

His Excellency Andrew Johnson,
President of the United States.

My dear Sir,

During your stay in Ky—, as a "Refugee" I met you lastly at "Camp Nelson," then Camp Dick Robinson. Perhaps you will remember me, when I remind you, of a pair of Gloves, so kindly given, as a memento, now lying on my "Cabinet." Feel assured, you have not forgotten my dear Father,[2] who was afflicted, with Cancer, and applied to you, for information as to Br. January's[3] whereabouts. You kindly wrote to him, which will ever remain, fresh upon memories Tablet. I beg your attention, for a few minutes. Believeing you are unaware, of the condition of affairs in Ky, I feel as one of the sufferers, that you will give me, a hearing.

To put down the Rebellion, we gave up willingly, all of our able bodied men, excepting one. Now those that were left, are leaveing us, to go to the Millitary Post. There from the Commanders they receive "Free Papers,"[4] then allowed to go, and do as they please. Men come back, and tell us, they are our equals, free as white men.

The women & children, even little Orphans, who have no relations, in the Army, apply and are freed. This morning our only negro, man was missing. When called for, one of the women, said that "he had gone to Paris to get his Free papers—, that there was a man stationed there, for that purpose." Mr. Johnson if this is to be, a Law, from a higher power, then we must submit. Do you sanction this? Are we to be thus robbed, and then insulted by our negros, who our Parents have raised?

Now My Mother[5] is a Widow, with eight children, but one mail member, in the family, my little brother, fourteen years of age—, who is delicate. What is left for us to do? No one left to cultivate our Crop?

Permit me to state, an unfortunate case in our family. My Uncle John,[6] nine years past, became involved in debt, by his only son. At the time, he owned 800 acres, of the best land in Bourbon County, well-stocked. It was a Model Farm. He owned forty negro:s who he had raised, every one of them, kept them all, togather. And when it became necessary—, for a Sale of Land or negro.s, The Land was sold, rather than to have his servant, scattered. Up to two years past, he was able to rent a Farm, which paid family expenses. A call was then made, for aid, to crush the Rebellion. It was given. Since then by degrees his negros, have been taken, till now, none are left, to support my poor old Uncle, 74 years of age. He is extremely delicate, and now he and his single daughter, are homeless, nothing left for them. All has been taken without compensation. Tis hard—hard, to see an old Kentucky Gentleman, thus crushed. Cant something be done? But ah, there are many such, left without, a support whereas if their laborers had been allowed to do their mission, they would be handsomely cared for. Are we Mr. Johnson to stand, all this without a murmur? No—No. I feel something *will* be done, and that speedily. Still worst of all, our negro.s are freed, and allowed to remain, in our State. We cannot, stand that. I appeal to you Mr. President, to aid us, and that quickly. If they are to be freed, Oh! take them beyond our borders. Leave them not in our midst. You were once a Southern Slaveowner—and must know how we feel. Believeing you will rescue, us—I close, hopeing you will do me the honor of giveing advice at your earliest conveniance.

Very respectfully, Miss Annie E. Hutchcroft.

ALS, DLC-JP.
1. Hutchcroft (b. c1837) was a Kentucky native. 1860 Census, Ky., Bourbon, E. Div., 80.
2. Kentucky farmer James Hutchcroft (1800–1863) had amassed a small fortune in the stock breeding business. Ibid.; William H. Perrin, *History of Bourbon, Scott, Harrison, and Nicholas Counties* (Easley, S.C., 1979 [1882]), 70, 472.
3. Probably Robert W. January (1798–1866), a Kentucky-born Baptist minister, farmer, "successful cancer doctor," and longtime resident of Murfreesboro, Tenn., who just before the war moved to Trenton, Tenn. John H. Grime, *History of Middle Tennessee Baptists* (Nashville, 1902), 229–30; *Knoxville Whig*, June 6, 1866; 1850 Census, Tenn., Rutherford, Murfreesboro, 709; (1860), Gibson, 7th Dist., 128.
4. The so-called "Freedom Papers" were really passes issued by Federal officers to blacks who had not been covered by the Emancipation Proclamation, in order to allow them more freedom of movement in seeking employment. Howard, *Black Liberation*, 75, 82–84.
5. Eliza Ann Hutchcroft (b. c1812). 1860 Census, Ky., Bourbon, E. Div., 80.
6. John Hutchcroft (1791–1868), farmer and horse breeder. Perrin, *History of Bourbon*, 483.

From Horace Maynard
Unofficial,

Knoxville, July 25, 1865.

Dr. Sir.

I reached home yesterday & found this state of things. Five candidates are on the ticet for Congress in this District, Cols. Houk, & Byrd, Gen. Cooper, Messrs. F. S. Heiskell & Wells.[1] I was instantly & all day visited upon by persons from differing parts of the district urging me to become a candidate. This did not meet my views. Finally a convention of men from various counties met here to-day & nominated me. I have accepted the nomination, & written a brief circular, of which I will send you a copy.[2] There is now time for little more than to announce my name through the District. The result I think very doubtful. But it will have at least the effect to secure a much better vote at the poll, a point of some importance, just at this time.

This of course will put it out of my power, at present, either to go to Washington, or to go abroad. And quite likely will result as it has resulted to me heretofore, that when the angel troubles the waters, another steps in ahead of me & enjoys the healing benefit.[3]

Saturday at Nashville, the candidates spoke in the court-house. Campbell[4] made a thinly disguised copperhead speech which was applauded a good deal by that style of listeners. "Abolitionists," "Black Republicans," "Negro Equality" & things of that sort abounded in it. He & his class are doing what they did during your administration in the state, seeking to find an issue between the Federal & state policy. In the March Election of last year, you remember, they tried to array Mr. Lincoln policy against yours.[5] Now they are attempting to play off yours, against that of the state. They profess to be great "Johnson" men now just as they were "Lincoln" men then & for the same purposes. John Hugh Smith[6] replied vigorously with some effect, saying in substance that he was a supporter of the Federal Government & the present administration, & appealing to know whether such an one, or one like Campbell could best serve their interests. Campbell will, I think be elected.

I spoke at night to a good crowd in the Market House.[7]

Stokes & Nat Taylor[8] seem likely to be elected in the 1st & 3d districts.

I am very Respectfully Your Obt. Servt.

Horace Maynard

His Excy. The President.

ALS, DLC-JP.

1. Leonidas C. Houk, Robert K. Byrd, Joseph A. Cooper, Frederick S. Heiskell, and Benjamin Wells (b. c1808), a McMinn County farmer. 1860 Census, Tenn., McMinn, 7th Dist., 100; *Knoxville Whig and Rebel Ventilator*, July 5, 1865.

2. Not found.

3. Maynard alludes to the New Testament account, found in John 5: 2–9, of the pool at Bethesda, where, it was believed, an angel stirred the waters at certain times, and whoever first stepped into the pool would be healed of his or her infirmity. Perhaps his recent defeat for the Senate prompted Maynard's complaint, but he did win a congressional seat in August. Alexander, *Reconstruction*, 260n.

4. William B. Campbell.

5. Johnson's imposition of a strict loyalty oath for the March 5, 1864, elections had prompted more conservative unionists unsuccessfully to call for the use of Lincoln's less stringent pledges. *Johnson Papers*, 6: 601, 612, 626, 629.

6. Nashville mayor and congressional candidate from 5th district.

7. Maynard spoke in Nashville on Saturday, July 22. *Nashville Press and Times*, July 22, 30, 1865.

8. William B. Stokes and Nathaniel G. Taylor were both elected.

From Thomas F. Meagher [1]

St Paul July 25, 1865

His Excellency The President

An expedition which I accompany leaves this place for Montana first of August to aid in developing the Territory and making it a state. To insure the Safety and Success of expedition a mounted military escort of not less than One hundred men and section mountain howitzer battery is absolutely necessary. Genl Sibley [2] commanding District of Minn at His Hd Qrs authorizes me to say he will most cheerfully provide the men required should they be replaced immediately from some other command as he has hardly enough at present to hold the frontier. Gov Miller [3] also heartily unites in this request—a reply to which by telegram at the earliest moment is respectfully entreated. [4]

Thomas Francis Meagher

Tel, DNA-RG107, Tels. Recd., President, Vol. 4 (1865–66).
1. Brigadier under Sherman, until he resigned in May 1865.
2. Henry H. Sibley.
3. Stephen Miller (1816–1881), a former newspaper editor who had risen to the rank of brigadier general in the Union army, had been elected governor (1864–66) of Minnesota as a Republican. Warner, *Blue.*
4. Despite subsequent appeals for troops from Meagher, Johnson took no further action after forwarding the July 25 letter to Stanton for "consideration." The brigadier had earlier requested an appointment as governor of Idaho. The President, through his private secretary, offered Meagher the office of secretary for the Montana Territory, which he accepted. Meagher to Johnson, June 20, Aug. 2, 1865, and Meagher to Browning, Aug. 4, 1865, Tels. Recd., President, Vol. 4 (1865–66), RG107, NA; Browning to Meagher, Aug. 2, 1865, Tels. Sent, President, Vol. 2 (1865), RG107, NA; Index to Lets. Recd., Ser. 4A, Johnson Papers, LC; *U.S. Off. Reg.* (1865), 15.

From William R. Patterson

July 25, 1865, Baltimore, Md.; ALS, DNA-RG56, Appts., Customs Service, Appraiser, Baltimore, William R. Patterson.

The recording clerk of the superior court in Baltimore applies for the position of appraiser in the local custom house. A Democrat and "active union man," he sustained the party until 1860 and 1864, when he voted for Bell and Lincoln, respectively. During the first half of the war he was a captain in Purnell's Legion and a quartermaster in Tennessee and Mississippi, before his health became "completely shattered." In his county very few prominent Union politicians or leading men "were original democrats," but the majority of the rank and file soldiers in the Union army were. Feeling that there is "no longer a necessity for a district organization of the union party," Patterson promises, upon its dissolution, to return to his "old faith." [Patterson did not get the appointment.]

Indian Peace Medal
From J. F. Loubat, The Medallic History of the United States of America,
1776–1876 *(New York, 1878), Vol. 2: Plate 75*

From William Thorpe[1]

St. Louis, July 25, 1865

His Excellency Andrew Johnson,
President of the United States, Washington:
Sir—

I take the liberty of addressing you in reference to your friend and mine, Col. J. Warren Bell,[2] formerly of the 13th Ill. Cavalry, but now of this city. Col. Bell, though almost a stranger here, has already, by his unusual abilities, his gentlemanly conduct and manners, and his liberal education, made a wide reputation and gained a large circle of friends who are interested in his welfare. Many of us know of his intimate relations with, and devotion to, you during the past 20 or 30 years, in all the positions of public life which you have filled; and have looked, since your accession to the Presidency, for his appointment to some place where his talents could be of service to his country, to yourself and to your administration.

There are, sir, many here who earnestly sympathize with, and work constantly to sustain, you in your great work, and not a few of our best men feel grateful that Providence, at this particular time, placed you where you now are.

But I respectfully suggest whether your friends will not feel more encouragement and greater confidence upon seeing in office such men as Warren Bell, Horace Maynard, Caleb Lyon,[3] etc., than at seeing Messrs. Seward Chase, Sumner and others giving their friends places where they can be serviceable to their own interests in the next Presidential campaign, while your truest supporters have been left out. I am well assured that this thing is going on. A day or two since a gentleman remarked to me (and I am willing to furnish his name) that "I am going down to see my old friend Chase next month and I think I will take a small appointment abroad. He can walk right up and get it for me. . . . There is no man on this earth that I would rather see in the Presidential chair than he." Now, will this class of men obtain positions, and those whom I have named be left out in the cold? I sincerely hope and believe not.

In a conversation with Col. Bell since his return from Washington I learn that he desires a foreign mission and that he prefers the one to Japan.[4] In that place I know he could make his influence felt for the United States, and at the end of three or four years there he will have gained an influence at home that will be of great service to you, and I am satisfied, from what I know of his devotion to you, that whatever he has is always at your command.

I am, sir, Very Truly Yours,
William Thorpe.

ALS, DNA-RG59, Lets. of Appl. and Recomm., 1861–69 (M650, Roll 4), J. Warren Bell.

1. Thorpe (*fl*1871), a St. Louis reporter, Democrat, and wartime stenographer to the provost marshal of Missouri, soon relocated in Washington, D.C., where he served as secretary of the National Executive Committee. *Edwards' Annual Director . . . St. Louis* (1865); *OR*, Ser. 2, Vol. 7: 321–25, 741; Washington, D.C., directories (1867–71); Thorpe to Johnson, Nov. 20, 1867, Johnson Papers, LC.

2. One of Johnson's fellow Greeneville mechanics.

3. Lyon (1822–1875), former New York congressman and governor of the Idaho Territory (1864–66). *BDAC*.

4. Not receiving a foreign post, Bell became special agent (1867) of the treasury at Brownsville, Tex., and collector of customs at Corpus Christi. *U.S. Off. Reg.* (1867), 137; *Richmond Whig and Public Advertiser*, Oct. 8, 1867.

From William W. Allen

July 26, 1865, Montgomery, Ala.; ALS, DNA-RG94, Amnesty Papers (M1003, Roll 1), Ala., W. W. Allen.

A Confederate brigadier general, whose property "may possibly be estimated at over twenty thousand dollars," applies for pardon. He enlisted in the southern army "from a conviction that her cause was just" and, while in the field, "endeavored conscientiously" to discharge what he conceived to be his duty. Since the issue has been decided against the South, he has taken the oath of allegiance "with the purpose of observing it in good faith." Before the war he "was a planter by occupation and had never been in public life." [Allen received his pardon September 12, 1865.]

To William M. Evarts [1]

Washington D C July 26th 1865.

To Hon W. M. Evarts

Chairman &c "Yale"—

I thank you and through you the graduates of Yale for their kind greeting.[2] In the difficult and delicate duties before me I rely upon the support of the same intelligent patriotism which during the War has given so many noble lives and deeds to our Country. American Scholarship has gained undying honor by its contributions to the literature and the achievements in our recent struggle for National Existence and in the Victories of peace which I trust are now to come. American Scholarship will sustain the reputation it has won.

Very truly your friend   Andrew Johnson

Tel, MdBJ-Daniel Coit Gilman Papers.

1. Evarts (1818–1901), a Yale graduate, later served as principal defense attorney for Johnson's impeachment trial and as attorney general in his cabinet (July 1868-Mar. 1869). Appointed secretary of state by Hayes (1877–1881), he subsequently served in the Senate. *BDAC*; *DAB*.

2. Signing himself as "chairman," Evarts had wired that the graduates of Yale "assembled in commemoration of their associates who have served in the war," sent their "respectful greetings" to the President and their encouragement for a successful restoration of "peace & order for which so many of our brethren have perilled & offered up their lives." Evarts to Johnson, July 26, 1865, Johnson Papers, LC.

From John W. Forney

July 26, 1865, New York, N.Y.; LS, DNA-RG56, Appts., Internal Revenue Service, Assessor, Pa., 1st Dist., Washington Keith.

Forney intimates that "your leading friends" in Pennsylvania's first congressional district, which has "no Union representative in Congress," will "ask you to direct that they should be chiefly consulted in the distribution of the patronage properly belonging to the District, including their full share of the appointments in the Navy Yard." He opposes the removal of Internal Revenue assessor Washington Keith "on the ground or charge that he is not a resident of the District," since Keith "has voted in the District since 1863, and is now an actual resident of it." Forney requests Johnson's "interposition." [Keith remained in office.]

From James R. Hood

Chattanooga July 26 1865.

Andrew Johnson Prest.

Gov. Brownlow and his friends are circulating a telegram of your approving his address and claiming in it you unqualifiedly endorse the act to limit the elective franchise.[1] I simply understood you to be determined as are all loyal men that the act shall be enforced until repealed or declared unconstitutional. The truth is that many of the opponents of this law have been grossly misrepresented by association to the effect that state we desired to overthrow the Gov't. Do I not correctly understand you to mean only that the law must be enforced while it is law without expressing an opinion as to its wisdom of whether it should be modified or repealed? I have been all over the district & the people are all well disposed amply Justifying that remarkable paragraph in your Gettysburg letter.[2] Please answer immediately.

J. R. Hood

Tel, DLC-JP.
1. See Telegram to William G. Brownlow, July 16, 1865.
2. See Letter to David Wills, July 3, 1865. The paragraph to which Hood refers concludes: "I am greatly mistaken if, in the states lately in rebellion, we do not henceforward have an exhibition of such loyalty and patriotism as was never seen nor felt there before."

From George W. Jones[1]

Fayetteville Tennessee July 26. 1865.

Andrew Johnson
President of the United States
My Dear Sir:

I reached home on last friday night, the 21st instant. Our once beautifull village I found with all the evidences of the evils, of that terrible scourge of nations, present on all sides and on all hands—Ruin and devastation all around. The people here are not altogether as bouyant and hopefull of the future as I had hoped to have found them. They are isolated, Cut off almost from the world. No mails yet, and they know but little of what is going on. The people here were your friends in former days, zealous and ardent. Forget their errors and be to them a friend now that you have it in your power to be their friend and can afford to be lenient and magnanimous. Those here and in the State who participated in the late rebellion were for the most part your friends and supporters. Bring them back to the fold by the clemency of the government. Extend the Amnesty by reducing the excepted classes. I assure you it is the better, the true policy. All those whom you intend to pardon ultimately, it will be much better to pardon early and promptly, but I did not disign to trouble you with that subject, and hope you will pardon me for what I have said.

I stopped in Nashville several days on my way home to enquire after my bonds which were in the Bank of Tenn but, of which, I learned nothing, because the gentlemen who had charge of the returned Banks and effects were absent from the City. And also to make some enquiry concerning my books. You told me that Robert had written you that my books were in the Capitol. So I went there, and the Governor being absent I enquired of Mr Fletcher the Secretary of State. He informed me that hearing that such books were down at an Auction House, the Governor ordered them up to the Capitol under the impression they had been taken from the State Library. That they were thrown in a pile in the passage of the Capitol where they remained about twenty four hours, and were then sent back to the U.S. Treasury Agent. John P. White[2] then went with me to enquire of the Treasury Agent, but, ascertained that Mr Davis and Mr Dillon[3] the agent, were both absent from the City, So I could learn nothing definite about them. On my way home in the neighborhood of Lynchburg I was told that some of the books were sold and others given away on the road between this and Tullahoma. Here I learned that the books were through [thrown] into uncovered wagons on a damp rainy day and left for Tullahoma in that condition. The creeks were up it is said and some of [the] books got wet in crossing, altogether I think it probable they are pretty well used up. They did not only take all my books, our book case and a chair, but they also took all my private papers, from the Secretary and table drawers in the room I occupied. Papers and other articles which could be of no use to any other person but to me, and among other papers they took off an acknowledgement signed by James G. Finnie[4] of Memphis that in October 1860 he owed John C. Rives[5] over thirteen thousand dollars, money collected as a lawyer. I was despoiled of books, papers and other things by order of Genl. Milroy[6] then commanding here with Head Qrs at Tullahoma. The order was executed by A. W.

Billings[7] Major 42. Mo. Inft Vol. & Pro. Mar & Sub. Dir. Mid. T. assisted by C. R. Haverly[8] Capt. and Pro. Mar. Fayetteville Tennessee. Major Billings I have been told took the papers from the Secretary and table drawers, tied them up in a handkerchief and carried them away. What he did with them of course I do not know. I should be very glad to have them back. The Library was the most perfect and in better condition than any one of the kind within my knowledge. I had a full set of the American Almanack, the most of Niles Register, The American Encyclopedia, The Democratic Review, Iconographic Encyclopedia, Gales & Seatons Register of Debates, and the Congressional Globe complete, U. States Statutes at Large, American State papers American Archieves, Bancrofts history, McCauley's history, History of Charles fifth, Shakespeare, Cobbetts works, Byrons, Moores, and various other works, all of which were taken and I fear much injured if not destroyed. Now what I desire you to do, is to have an order issued to the Agents of the Treasury at Nashville to return all the *books, papers boxes and other things taken from me and in their possession, to me at this place*.[9] I hope your health is fully restored and reestablished and that you will be able to endure the arduous labors now upon you.

As formerly Your *friend* G. W. Jones

(Genl. Milroy—Major Billings & Capt Haverly were all present when I was despoiled.)

ALS, DNA-RG366, First Special Agency, Lets. Recd.

1. Former U.S. and Confederate congressman, who had been one of Johnson's earliest political friends, had written in May from Charlotte, N.C., seeking and obtaining a June 8 interview with Johnson. Jones to Johnson, May 16, 1865, Tels. Recd., President, Vol. 4 (1865–66), RG107, NA; Johnson to Jones, May 16, 1865, Tels. Sent, President, Vol. 2 (1865), RG107, NA; Jones to Unknown, June 10, 1865, Johnson Papers, LC.

2. Nashville merchant.

3. Charles Davis, commissioner of abandoned property, and Joseph R. Dillin.

4. Attorney John G. Finnie (c1825–fl872). 1870 Census, Tenn., Shelby, Memphis, 8th Ward, 40; Memphis directories (1855–72).

5. Washington editor and founder of the *Congressional Globe*.

6. Robert H. Milroy.

7. Andrew W. Billings (c1838–1898) served as private and lieutenant, 53rd and 42nd Mo. Enrolled Militia regiments before holding his present rank. Pension Records, Sarah E. Billings, RG15, NA.

8. Curtis R. Haverly (c1830–1905), a blacksmith residing in Macon, Mo., was a private in the 10th Mo. Inf. before his promotion and transfer to the 42nd Inf. Pension Records, Curtis R. Haverly, RG15, NA; CSR, RG94, NA.

9. Johnson forwarded Jones's letter to Gen. George H. Thomas, commander of the Military Division of Tennessee, "who will take measures to have the property restored to Mr. Jones whether it be held by Military Officers or Officers of the Treasury." Johnson to Thomas, Sept. 6, 1865, First Special Agency, Lets. Recd.,RG366, NA.

From Jean Alexander Francois LeMat

July 26, 1865, Paris, France; ALS, DNA-RG60, Office of Atty. Gen., Lets. Recd., President.

A resident of Paris for two years seeks pardon from Johnson, claiming that he had "never borne arms in the late insurrection against the United States Government." Yet he had served as a Confederate purchasing agent and had accompanied Mason and Slidell, hand carrying their dispatches after their capture. [The New Orleans physician, famous for the invention and manufacture of the revolver which bore his name, failed to receive a pardon.]

From Bartholomew F. Moore

July 26, 1865, [Raleigh, N.C.]; ALS, DNA-RG94, Amnesty Papers (M1003, Roll 41), N.C., B. F. Moore.

A Raleigh, N.C., unionist petitions for amnesty under the twenty thousand dollar clause of Johnson's May 29 proclamation. After his state seceded he submitted to its laws and those of the Confederate States, but at "*all* times . . . ardently prayed for a reunion of the severed states." His "sentiments were openly spoken" during the war, causing newspapers to advise his arrest and denounce him as a traitor. Moore believes he was saved from prison because of the kindness of his wife and daughters "to the destitute & wounded within their reach, federal as well as confederate." In 1860 he supported Bell and addressed "meetings both by letter and speech in advocacy of the Union." Although he "never for a moment desired a separation of the states," he is advised that he "may by *act*, if not by *intent*, have participated in the rebellion," because he "voted in the elections"; was in 1861 and 1862 auditor of claims against his home state; contributed items to make his son, a Confederate private, more comfortable; and "voluntarily fed and administered to the wants" of hungry or sick Confederate soldiers. [Johnson pardoned Moore August 12, 1865.]

To John M. Palmer

Executive Office, Washington, D.C.,
July 26 1865.

To Major General Palmer
Louisville, Ky.

I have received the following telegram dated Lexington, Kentucky this day. To President Johnson. Our citizens desire to know if it is by your sanction that Provost Marshals are issuing free papers to all negroes who apply. Signed D. L. Price.[1]

Andrew Johnson
President U.S.

Tel, DNA-RG107, Tels. Sent, President, Vol. 2 (1865).

1. Douglas L. Price (b. c1814) was a Lexington physician, unionist, and sometime legislator. 1850 Census, Ky., Fayette, 1st Dist., 338; Lewis Collins, *History of Kentucky* (Louisville, 1877), 171.

From South Carolina Lawyers

[ca. July 26, 1865, Charleston, S.C.]; Mem, DNA-RG60, Appt. Files for Judicial Dists., S.C., George S. Bryon.

Twenty-eight members of the South Carolina bar, who have all taken the oath of allegiance, pray that in the reorganization of the Federal court in their state, appointments of judge, attorney, and marshal be made from local citizens. Their request "is made not only in behalf of the Citizens at large, but . . . on behalf of a numerous & learned profession among whom may be found many loyal Citizens." Noting that in the recent appointment of the provisional governor the President "has made a declaration in favor of this line of policy," they "indulge the hope that the same course" will now be pursued. If their request meets with favor, they "will be prepared to submit . . . a list of names from which fitting and acceptable appointments may be made."

From John L. Blevins

Adams Express Company,
Columbus Miss July 27th 1865

Mr. President

The cotton agent of this Department has Received Seventy thr[ee] Bales of cotton of mine that I Sold to an agent of the So called Confederate States. I Sold It to them the time of Grierson's rade down by Okolona and West Point. The Confederate Soldiers were ordered to Burn the cotton and through the choice of taking a receipt upon the Goverment for my cotton or their money I went into the Sale, and received the money and never did use It atall owing to being wounded in a few months afterwards. [It] therefore died upon my hands. I hoping as by no act of my own this rebelion was brot about that you will have my cotton confiscated. I will Send you a Statement countersigned by Mr. Harrison Johnson[1] agent, and that you th[r]ough your proper Departments have my cotton given over to me or the proceeds. Pleas give me an answer as Soon as convenient at this place. I am here at my place trying to fix up my fragments and the weather very warm and If It is right for me to have my cotton It will help me out of many difficulties and I dont want to leave until I hear from you.

your Friend truly
John Blevins

P S. Enclosed you will find a Statement from Mr. Harrison Johnson Agt. Cant you Telegram me to this place?[2]

J. B.

ALS, DNA-RG56, Misc. Div., Claims for Cotton and Captured and Abandoned Property.

1. The affidavit of Johnston (1815–fl1906), assistant special treasury agent, was attached, as was also a copy of Blevins' signed statement to "take due care of said cotton whilst on his plantation and to deliver the same at his own expense at River Ldg . . . to

JULY 1865

the order of Sec of the Treas or his agents." Browning to McCulloch, Sept. 11, 1865, Misc. Div., Claims for Cotton and Captured and Abandoned Property, RG56, NA; Dunbar Rowland, *Mississippi* (4 vols., Atlanta, 1907), 3: 407.

2. Johnson reviewed Blevins' file in September 1865 and on the 12th, "satisfied the facts are as stated," ordered the secretary of the treasury to release the cotton. By then, however, only 22 bales remained in the agent's hands. Some had been burned with the arsenal at Columbus, Miss., and 32 bales had already been shipped to New York. On November 9, 1866, the proceeds from the latter, $4,800, were also released to Blevins. Misc. . Div., Claims for Cotton and Captured and Abandoned Property, RG56, NA.

From Solomon E. Cohen

July 27, 1865, Philadelphia, Pa.; ALS, DNA-RG56, Appts., Customs Service, Collector, Philadelphia, William B. Thomas.

Editor and publisher of *The Dial*, "who has made heavy personal sacrifices in aid of the administration," protests the removal of Thomas as customs collector. For four years he "has filled his appointment . . . to the complete satisfaction of this whole community" and "more than 19/20ths. of the entire population will hail with delight his re-appointment." Recent opposition to the collector "by a small minority of selfish politicians," including congressmen, does "not reflect the sentiments of their constituents." Cohen hopes the President will not permit the city's Union party "to be disturbed & distracted" and that Thomas, who privately equipped and led a regiment during the war, will be retained in office.

From Benjamin F. Flanders

[New Orleans, La.] July 27th, [186]5

Sir:

I have the honor to transmit the inclosed letter, with accompanying papers addressed to Your Excellency by Hon. S. Clements.[1]

This letter was sent to me, in company with a note requesting me to forward it to you, and likewise containing the following language:

"As it must be some weeks before the President can act officially on this subject, I submit to you, whether it may not be well to telegraph the President, stating the substance of my letter to him, for his prompt action."

Accordingly I have this day telegraphed to you the substance of the inclosed letter.[2]

The statements of Mr. Clemens concerning fraudulent transactions in cotton are too true, and are worthy of serious consideration.

The suggestions of Mr. Clemens, looking to the removal of the evils complained of, had been partially met by certain arrangements entered into between Genl. Canby and myself before the letter of Mr. Clemens reached here.

Mr. Jewell alluded to in the letter is my agent at Shreveport, charged with the duty of collecting Confederate cotton in that District.

I have written fully to the Hon. Secretary of the Treasury on this subject, in reports of the 3rd. and 25th. Inst.

I am, Sir, with great respect
Your obed. servt. Benj. F. Flanders.
Sup. Spl. Agt. 3rd Agency T.D.

To His Excellency Andrew Johnson
President, U. States.

ALS, DLC-JP.
1. See Letter from Sherrard Clemens, July 17, 1865.
2. Although Clemens' letter is dated July 17, Flanders' wire bears the date of its transmittal ten days later. Clemens to Johnson, July 27, 1865, Tels. Recd., President, Vol. 4 (1865–66), RG107, NA.

From Nathan Gammon
PRIVATE

Knoxville, Tenn. July 27. 1865

To His Excellency Andrew Johnson
President of the United States Washington City, D.C.
Dear Sir:

It may perhaps appear strange to you that *one* personally known to you for many years as a steadfast and unflinching friend and supporter of the Government of the United States,—and known by you as a political friend throughout a long and successful career,—and known to have ever supported the Democratic cause and you as its standard bearer through many a bitter contest (in times when friends were needed)—and because of his conscientious belief that the success of that party was necessary to uphold, maintain and preserve the Government and its constitution in *their purity*, should, after so many years of devotion to its interests, be *now* indicted *for treason*![1] And only because he felt that he was only exercising his high constitutional privilege in thinking for himself—and exercising his own judgment as to what was the true interests of the Government & the rights of its people; Yet it is nevertheless true! I have been indicted by presentment of the Grand-jury for treason against a Government which *you know* we as democrats ever desired to uphold and preserve in its purity & to whose constitution—unmutilated—no people ever were more devotedly attached.

Having been deprived of the means, by the results of war, which afforded a comfortable subsistence for my family previous to the advent of the Federal army here, and deprived also, by the trade regulations existing in this State, of the privilege of engaging in any business whatever for a support *here*, and so bound I cannot seek business *elsewhere*, I have been reduced to straightened circumstances, and these considerations, together with my desire to stand again upon the record of my country as a good and loyal citizen to that Government of the United States, (where, allow me to say, I think I have in justice ever *stood*,) urge me to petition your Excellency—at once—for a special pardon, and therefore enclose herewith my petition—which I confidently trust will receive your just consideration.

Very Respectfully Your Obdt. Svt
Nathan Gammon

P.S The war—which has severed, politically, many friends of almost lifelong standing—now being over, & peace restored again to the country—may we not hope for a reunion of friendships as well as States—and the affections of the people won back to their Government? Will you allow me to suggest that it may not be improbable—you, in the course of events, *could* stand foremost in the South on the list of Presidential aspirants.

I shall be pleased to be advised of your Excellency's action in the matter of my petition in any way that may be deemed proper.

Very Respectfully N. Gammon

Augt 3. 1865

N.B. I had intended to get a few names to my petition—recommending your favorable consideration, but being advised it was not necessary—send it with the single indorsement of Col. Wm. Heiskell U.S. Court comr. which he kindly proposed.[2]

Respectfully Your Obt. Svt. N. Gammon

ALS, DNA-RG94, Amnesty Papers (M1003, Roll 49), Tenn., N. Gammon.

1. Gammon, former Jonesboro merchant and clerk of the U.S. circuit court at Knoxville until the fall of 1861, subsequently served as receiver's clerk and court commissioner under the Confederate regime. Indicted for treason in May 1864, he had since been under bond to appear at court. Gammon to Johnson, July 27, 1865 (2nd letter), Amnesty Papers (M1003, Roll 49), Tenn., N. Gammon, RG94, NA.

2. Gammon's pardon was issued September 5, 1865.

To James R. Hood

Executive Office, Washington D.C.
July 27 1865

James R. Hood,
Chattanooga, Tenn.

In reference to the amendment to the Constitution and the laws passed in pursuance thereof my last telegram to Governor Brownlow, which was intended to be published as sent to him, was emphatic and explicit and will speak for itself.[1]

Andrew Johnson.

Tel, DNA-RG107, Tels. Sent, President, Vol. 2 (1865).

1. See Johnson to Brownlow, July 20, 1865, Tels. Sent, President, Vol. 2 (1865), RG107, NA. This July 20 telegram is cited and quoted in the explanatory footnotes which accompany Telegram to Brownlow, July 16, 1865, published above.

From Robert H. McEwen [1]

Nashville July 27th 1865

To His Excellency Andrew Johnson President U. States
Washington City
My dear Sir

I take great pleasure in commending to your favourable consideration & Clemency Dr. Paul F. Eve [2] who before the breaking out of the rebellion resided in our City many years, was Professor of Surgery in our Medical College, of high repute in his profession, in Social life a Gentleman and Christian. In church matters, for many years, we were intimately associated.

Doctor Eve was favorable to the rebellion. In Feb 1862, he left for the South. Seeing the imprudence of his course, some weeks since, he returned to Nashville & is now here with his family, determined to live & die under the Stars & Stripes. Since his return, in public & in private circles the Doctor has in strong terms advocated the cause of the United States, says it is the most powerful Goverment in the world. He advises all returned soldiers & others to submit to the laws of the United States & become good citizens—that for himself he cares not what they call him, a submissionist or abolitionist he is determined to prove by his course that he is a faithful citizen of these United States. In short Dr. Eve is doing much good in the cause of the Union, is a man of great influence. I therefore pray your Excellency, if consistent with your duties of office, that you grant unto Dr. Eve a full pardon for the past, and if he does not live up to the obligations required of him, I give you my head for the block. [3]

May God bless & speed you in your arduous duties is the prayer of

Your friend truly R. H. McEwen
Spruce St

P S. Dr. Eve returns to his Professorship as surgeon in the medical College of this City, as heretofore.

ALS, DNA-RG94, Amnesty Papers (M1003, Roll 49), Tenn., Paul F. Eve.

1. Collection agent and attorney.
2. Former president of the American Medical Association, who had turned down an appointment as surgeon general of Tennessee, Eve later served as a surgeon for the Confederate army. Amnesty Papers (M1003, Roll 49), Tenn., Paul F. Eve, RG94, NA; see Letter from Ogilvie Byron Young, November 21, 1864, *Johnson Papers*, 7: 311–12.
3. In 1858, a year after Johnson suffered a broken arm in a train wreck, Eve recommended that it be rebroken and reset. His subsequent poor management of the procedure left the President with a permanently impaired arm. Despite his alleged antipathy toward Eve, whose petition was endorsed by Governor Brownlow and eighteen New York members of the American Medical Association, Johnson pardoned him on August 28, 1865. Amnesty Papers (M1003, Roll 49), Tenn., Paul F. Eve, RG94, NA; Turner, "Recollections of Andrew Johnson," 171.

From the New Bern Committee on Correspondence

Mayor's Office, New Bern, N.C.,
July 27th, 1865.

His Excellency Pres'd't Johnson
Washington D.C.
Sir

We the "Committee on correspence" appointed by the Board of Commissioners for the Town of New Bern would respectfully direct His Excellencys Attention to the enclosed correspondence between the Provost Marshall Comdg the Post and his Honor the Mayor of the Town.[1]

Under existing circumstances daily conflicts between the civil and military authorities are unavoidable, especially so since the Colored Troops are sustained in their acts of violence and Breaches of the Peace, frequently, by subordinate officers. Among others can be enumerated, the following acts of lawlessness committed by them, and other practices indulged in, in utter disregard of all order discipline, and Soldiers conduct.

To wit, citizens have been shot down in cold blood, by the guard, and officers ordered the arrest of those who condemned the act or sympathized with the victim.

Ladies have been violently elbowed and shoved off the sidewalk, by the guard while officers looked on with approving smiles commending the gallant act. The soldiers armed with Bowie knives and revolvers thereby intimidating the defenceless citizens have committed robberies in open daylight and fired on the Police in the proper discharge of their sworn duties. They have incited Negro civilians to rebellion against the Civil authority, and endeavored to release by violence and force of arms Criminals in charge of Police, stating their determination to "stand by" all colored people. The houses of loyal citizens have been made the Quarters for the soldiers Subordinate Officers in some instances, each, ocupying a whole house, and during the time the town was Policed by the Provost Guard, burglaries and highway robberies were of nightly occurrence in many instances perpetrated by the Negro soldiery. Systematic violation of the sanitary regulations of the Municipal Authorities by all grades of officers and soldiers, and an obvious intention on the part of the subordinate officers to bring about a collision between the civil and military authority by tacit encouragement to the Negro soldiery to commit the acts of violence referred to and many others of an equally grave and aggravated character. In view of all these *facts* and the serious and fearful results calculated to flow from the evil of this state of affairs, can there not be some Clemency exercised by His Excellency and we be relieved of the Presence of this element of discord among us.[2]

Verry Respectfully Your Obdt Servts
James Osgood ⎤
Jno. M. Davies ⎬ Com.[3]
T. B. James ⎦

ALS (Osgood), DNA-RG107, Lets. Recd., EB12 President 2986 (1865).

1. Austrian-born Augustus S. Boernstein (c1831–1900), lt. col., 4th U.S.C.T., and James T. Hough (fl1881), a merchant who had moved from New Jersey. Pursuant to a circular from his superiors, Boernstein on July 25 directed Hough to inform the city commissioners and the chief of police that "immediate steps will be taken at these Head Qrs. to suppress a certain traffic of liquor going on in this city." Boernstein also complained of the "extremely filthy condition of some of the streets." As acting mayor, John M. Davies responded for Hough, reminding Boernstein of the municipal ordinances forbidding "the sale of liquor to soldiers, sailors, or those recently discharged." Davies further claimed that the town's sanitary conditions had improved. CSR, RG94, NA; Pension Records, Jennie E. Boernstein, RG15, NA ; 1870 Census, D.C., Washington, 4th Ward, 221; Jersey City directories (1860–81); *New Berne Times* (N.C.), June 26, 27, July 13, Aug. 3, 1865; Circular, Dept. of N.C., July 11, 1865, Boernstein to Hough, July 25, 1865, and Davies to Boernstein, July 26, 1865, Lets. Recd., EB12 President 2986 (1865), RG107, NA.

2. Governor Holden, in forwarding this letter to Johnson, observed that it "has been understood that when Civil government was established," the military authority would "only be exercised to aid and assist the Civil Officers." As to the enforcement of the military regulations "for the suppression of Gambling Houses, and Liquor Saloons," he saw "nothing to Complain of" except for the "violent language used on both sides." Johnson referred the matter to the secretary of war. Holden to Johnson, July 28, 1865, EB12 President 2986 (1865), RG107, NA.

3. James Osgood, John M. Davies, and Thomas B. James were all newly appointed city commissioners. Osgood (b. c1840) and James (b. c1826), longtime residents of Craven County, N.C., were before the war a law student and an Episcopal minister, respectively. The latter briefly served as a sergeant in the 40th N.C. Inf., CSA. Davies, a former assistant surgeon with the 9th N.J. Inf., chaired the local board of health. 1860 Census, N.C., Craven, 5th and 1st Wards, Newbern, 73, 118; Manarin, *N.C. Troops*, 1: 472; *New Berne Times* (N.C.), June 26, 27, 1865; Dyer, *Compendium*, 1360–61; John M. Davies et al., to Johnson, Oct. 28, 1865, Appts., Customs Service, Collector, N.C., 1st Dist., James T. Hough, RG56, NA.

From John M. Palmer

Head Quarters Dept of Kentucky,
Louisville, Kentucky. July 29[27].[1] 1865.
To His Excellency Andrew Johnson
President of the [U.S.],
Sir:

I have already by telegram,[2] acknowledged your despatch of yesterday containing copy of despatch of Mr *Price* which states that Provost Marshals issue "Free Papers" to negroes indiscriminately. I refer you to my despatch in which I say no "free papers" are issued by any officer in this Department, which, though literally true, does not quite meet the facts as they are.

I forward you my General Orders Nos 32 and 49.[3] Under these orders many passes have been issued by Provost Marshals &c to negroes who hold them; and, I am told in many cases they regard and act upon them as "free papers."

The reasons for issuing Order No. 32. will be found on the face of the order, but the reasons which influenced the Mayor and his friends to apply to me do not.[4] Large numbers of negroes were then in Louisville from the surrounding country, who had escaped, from, or repudiated the authority of their masters.

The Mayor and others desired my approval of a plan they had arranged for the general enforcement of the laws against vagrancy, and the law which forbids slaves to go at large and hire themselves out as free persons. To have enforced these laws would have produced great misery and alarm amongst the blacks. To leave the negroes in the city would have alarmed the fears of the citizens who were before hand taught to think their presence would cause a pestilence. They sought to make me responsible for either consequence.

To avoid both, I issued order No. 32. Under it over five thousand negroes have crossed the Ohio river at this place alone.

Before the 4th of July, an impression got abroad amongst the negroes throughout the state, that on that day they were all to be made free.[5] Inflamed by this belief, thousands of them left their masters houses and came into our posts at different points in the state. Every nook and hiding place at such places as Camp Nelson, Lexington, Frankfort, Bowling Green, Munfordville &c, was filled with them. They were without work or means; and the greater the number, and the more destitute they were, the more the people resisted employing them. I was compelled, from these causes, to issue General Orders No. 49 and the "free papers" referred to in the telegram of Mr Price, are merely passes issued under that order.

I have been greatly embarassed in respect to the colored people by the acts and declarations of politicians and presses in the Anti Administration interest. They have given the negroes extravagant ideas of the purposes of the government by announcing in their speeches and columns that it was the intention of the government to free them all, furnish them with food and clothing, and put them upon an equality with whites. Invariably, a conservative gathering in a neighborhood is followed by a stampede of negroes.

I think and respectfully submit that it is impossible, under the existing state of facts here, to recognize the laws of the state in reference to slaves and slavery.

At the beginning of the war, Kentucky had about two hundred and thirty thousand slaves.

say 230,000
Our reports show number of negro enlistments .... 28,818.
Estimated number of women and children freed by resolution of Congress of March 3, 1865,⁶ 2 1/2 for each man .. 72,045—100,863.
Ballance   129,137.
One half of this residue are presumed to have belonged to rebels, and are, therefore, free,   64,569
                                                        64,568.

From this small number ought still to be taken a percentage for the thousands, who have escaped from the state.

For the sake of keeping the small number in subjection to masters, the whole race in the state are most cruelly oppressed and outraged under color of laws which renders freedom to a negro in Kentucky impossible.

I have felt it my duty to give protection to this large free population as far as possible, but in doing so I have been, on occasions, compelled to do acts which, in effect greatly impair the tenure of the small number of persons who are still technically masters of slaves. Indeed it must be admitted that many slaves have left the state under Orders No. 32 and 49, which are enclosed, and every decision I make in favor of a negro, seems to start a host of individual cases which come within the same principle.

In short, slavery has no actual existence in Kentucky, and if the Constitutional Amendment is defeated at the election, the whole active colored population will fly unless I employ the troops to prevent it, and you have not, and will not be likely to order that to be done.

To illustrate the effect of any fair rule upon the status of slavery in Kentucky I will advert to the effect of one rule which I am compelled to recognize and observe.

By the laws of Kentucky—laws once when all were slaves, just enough in their application, all negroes were presumed to be slaves. Now a large majority are certainly free. To presume slavery from color alone is contrary to justice; to presume freedom without regard to color and give protection accordingly is to end slavery.

I am often called upon to afford protection where there is no proof at hand, and am compelled to presume one way or the other.

I submit these difficulties to meet some of the complaints which will probably reach you from the *loyal people* of Kentucky.⁷

I have the honor to be
Very Respectfully John M Palmer
Major General Comdg.

LS, DNA-RG393, Dept. of Kentucky, Lets. Recd.

1. From the text it appears that this letter was written the day after the President's telegram of July 26.

2. Palmer telegraphed on July 27: "No free papers are issued to any negroes within my Department by any officer by my authority or within my knowledge." This response

was forwarded to Douglas L. Price the following day. Palmer to Johnson, July 27, 1865, Tels. Recd., President, Vol. 4 (1865–66), RG107, NA; Mussey to Price, July 28, 1865, Tels. Sent, President, Vol. 2 (1865), RG107, NA.

3. The first, in May 1865, ordered passes for blacks wishing to leave Louisville for work elsewhere, and the second, on July 20, extended the pass policy to those seeking employment. Howard, *Black Liberation*, 80, 83.

4. Both Philip Tomppert (1808–1873), the German-born mayor of Louisville, and a city council committee, on May 11 had requested Palmer to enforce the vagrancy laws against large numbers of blacks in the city. *Louisville Courier-Journal*, Oct. 30, 31, 1873; Howard, *Black Liberation*, 80.

5. Since it was widely circulated that Palmer on July 4 was going to declare Kentucky blacks free, large numbers crowded into Louisville on that day. The general addressed a large group, assuring them at first that they were "substantially" free and then categorically announced: "My countrymen you are free." Ibid., 83.

6. In a joint resolution on that day, Congress, in order to encourage enlistments and to promote military efficiency, decreed that the wife and children of any person who has been or may be mustered into U.S. service shall "be forever free," regardless of any law or custom to the contrary. *U.S. Statutes*, 13: 571.

7. See, for example, Letters from Christopher C. Graham, July 24, and Annie E. Hutchcroft, July 25, 1865.

From H. B. Allis

July 28, 1865, Bloomington, Ill.; ALS, DNA-RG94, Amnesty Papers (M1003, Roll 13), Ark., H. B. Allis.

Former speaker of the Arkansas House of Representatives, who during the "Entire 'rebellion'" was a "Union man," states that, because of his sentiments, he was confined in the guardhouse at Pine Bluff, while rebels took his animal stock and burned "his *house*, furniture, and provisions." He has no recourse for compensation, "save by petition to Congress" and the President. His neighbor, former U.S. and Confederate senator Robert W. Johnson, who owns "a large am't of lands adjoining his place" in Jefferson County, which was "saved from destruction" by both armies, is now an applicant for pardon. Allis prays that Johnson's "pardon may depend upon his compensating *one* of his neighbors" for "losses caused by the rebellion," which "no man in Arks., did more to produce, and continue" than the said Johnson. The ex-speaker points out that unless the wealthy who aided the rebellion "are compelled to pay for property destroyed by the rebel army around their own property the entire advantage, is with the rebel and against the 'Union man.'" Admitting that Johnson "lost largely by the freeing [of] his negroes"—Allis says he lost "*seven, all he had*"—the senator did aid "in the destruction of cotton, and other property of 'Union men.'" [Allis was pardoned October 24, 1865, and Johnson April 23, 1856.]

From Christopher C. Andrews

Head Quarters 2d Division 13th Army Corps,
and District of Houston.
Houston, Texas, July 28 1865.

To Andrew Johnson President U. States
Dear Sir:

I leave here today in company with Gov. Hamilton and family for Austin, the Capital of the State; and shall return in a few days. I may possibly however go on to San Antonio if I can do any good to the cause.

Gov. Hamilton's proclamation was published yesterday. I think it is very excellent. I never saw him till day before yesterday but think him a man of superior ability. He has been treated with much attention and respect while here by the people of Houston. A handsome dinner was given him yesterday; and last night he made a powerful and grand speech to a large crowd.[1]

Your friend & ob't serv't C. C. Andrews.
Bvt. Maj. Genl.

ALS, DLC-JP.
1. The response to Hamilton's speech was mixed. Many had hoped that he would urge gradual emancipation; instead he declared that slavery was dead. Waller, *Hamilton of Texas*, 62.

From Thomas Cottman

Washington July 28th 1865

Mr President

I am instructed by Govr. J M Wells of Louisiana to represent to your Excellency the propriety of appointing a Provisional Governor for the State; in conformity to the established rule for the other States. It will certainly simplify the proceedings to be hereafter had in the State. The Senate & the House of Representatives at the last session of Congress refused to recognize the existence of State Government in Louisiana[1] and most persons think they acted properly in consequence of the irregularities attending its pretended formation. At any rate Governor Wells is willing to abide their decision and is desirous of freeing you from any embarrassment in the matter; by the request that Louisiana be placed in the same category with the other Southern States regardless of the anomalous proceedings which have been undertaken in the State. I am further instructed to say that Governor Wells does not regard the feigned election under the order of General Banks[2] any impediment to your appointment of any other person to the office of Provisional Governor but that we the people look upon the bonafide votes cast for him as a recommendation for his appointment by your Excellency. The Register of voters appointed under General Banks was turned out of office by Governor Wells for knowingly recording fraudulent voters & the Governor feels that holding office under an election when more than half of the votes were spurious, would imply his sanction of the fraud. Hence he desires a remedy applied, which will place Louisiana on the same footing with Alabama & Mississippi. Speedy action is necessary to enable Louisiana to march pari passu[3] with them in reestablishing relations with the Federal Government. I am directed to await your action on the subject.

Very Respectfully your obt sert
Thos. Cottman

His Excellency Andrew Johnson President

ALS, DLC-JP.
    1. See Letter from Durant, May 1, 1865.
    2. On January 11, 1865, Banks had issued a proclamation ordering the election of a governor and other high Louisiana officials. McCrary, *Lincoln and Reconstruction*, 207.
    3. "In step."

From George K. Fox, Jr.

July 28, 1865, Richmond, Va.; LS, DNA-RG94, Amnesty Papers (M1003, Roll 61), Va., George K. Fox, Jr.

A thirty-two-year-old Loudoun County, Va., court clerk, whose property "has been proceeded against under the confiscation laws," seeks a presidential pardon under the May 29 Amnesty Proclamation. Since his court position during the war exempted him from the army, he had managed to keep "in a place of safety, the papers & records of his court" for the "*Entire War*." His long absence, while hiding the court records, is the only reason for proceedings against him. He has taken both Lincoln's and Johnson's amnesty oaths "in good faith," and "prays that he may have such pardon & amnesty as may relieve him & his property from all pains & penalties & forfeitures heretofore incurred by him." [Fox was pardoned September 9, 1865.]

From Hugh Kennedy

New Orleans City Hall
28th day of July 1865

Andrew Johnson
President of the United States & & &
Sir,

    Permit me to lay before you copy of correspondence herewith which has passed between Maj. Genl. Canby, Comdg. Dept. of La. and Texas and myself,[1] as President of the Bank of New Orleans, and to ask for my views, if they appear to your better knowledge worthy, your sanction, and such action in behalf of the Bank as may seem to you reasonable & just.

In Jany. 1864, I was called to the direction & presidency of the Bank by my fellow stockholders, when its affairs were deemed to be in inextircable disorder. Its liabilities at that time amounted to fifteen hundred thousand dollars.

In twelve months from my accession, this debt was reduced one half; and had I been allowed to proceed with the liquidation, without military interference, I would have paid off every dollar during the current year.

Taking advantage of my visit to you President, in May last, Genl. Banks coerced one of our District Judges, under threat of removal, into the appointment of liquidators for the Bank. One of these liquidators had been his own clerk; the second was a person of no responsibility, and neither of them had any interest in the institution, or had the confidence of either its stockholders or creditors, or in fact any other pretension to the position than might be supposed to attach to his connection with the Genl. Comdg.

It is only necessary to add further, that the property, the management of which was thus illegally & shamefully placed in their hands, would amount to seven or eight millions of dollars. The whole proceeding in the Court was contrary to law & subversive of right, and had no more warrant than the subsequent proceedings of the military authorities.

With these explanations I submit this whole matter, President, for your consideration and decision, confident that you will have such instructions given to Major Genl. Canby as you may deem consistent with the right & justice involved in the case.[2]

> I have the honor to be, President,
> with very sincere respect, Your obdt. servt.
> Hu. Kennedy

ALS, DLC-JP.

1. Not found, but Governor Wells on July 22 forwarded copies of correspondence between himself, Canby, and Kennedy on this topic to Johnson. Canby had ordered Kennedy, as president of the Bank of New Orleans, to become a "liquidator" under military authority. When Kennedy refused to do so, "all the available assets" of the bank—14,000 bales of cotton and bonds worth over $500,000—were seized, and Canby refused to let the stockholders administer the institution's "fragmentary remains." Wells agreed with Kennedy that "there is no longer any necessity for the military interference complained of." Kennedy to Canby, July 20, Kennedy to Wells, July 21, Wells to Johnson, July 22, 1865, Johnson Papers, LC.

2. Five days later Kennedy protested Canby's appointment of three liquidators, not one of whom was a shareholder, calling it an "unwarrantable exercise of military power." Despite Kennedy's repeated protests, Johnson apparently declined to intervene. See Kennedy to Johnson, Aug. 2, Sept. 6, 10, 1865, Johnson Papers, LC.

From Josiah R. Parrott

July 28, 1865, Washington, D.C.; ALS, DNA-RG60, Appt. Files for Judicial
Dists., Ga., J. R. Parrott.

Upon arriving in Washington, Parrott has learned that no U.S. district attorney
has been appointed for Georgia, and he therefore asks for the position. Since
1850 he has been "an unchanging union man" and recognized "as one of the
few true representatives" of "genuine union sentiment in that State." For fourteen years he has practiced law and has been twice appointed solicitor general
for his judicial circuit. A resident of Cass County in central north Georgia,
where "a larger majority of the people have been loyal," his appointment would
"encourage the belief that union men in whom they have confidence will have
control of affairs." Loyal lawyers "are scarce in Georgia," and justice demands
their appointment in order to "form a nucleus around which the union elements
can confidently gather." Claiming that if he held the position it would "give
general satisfaction" and "meet the approval of every sound man in the state"
who was not supporting "some favorite" for appointment, Parrott expresses a
desire for a personal interview upon this and other important Georgia matters.
[Although he eventually gained an audience with the President, Parrott's request was not granted. Three years later, however, he became judge of north
Georgia's Cherokee circuit.]

From Sarah C. Polk

Polk place Nashville Tenn.
July 28. 1865.

To His Excellency, the President of the U.S.
Dear Sir,

I sincerely hope that you will pardon me for intruding on your time,
which I know to be so much occupied.

Some weeks since I addressed you a letter, which I sent by Judge
Walker,[1] in behalf of my friend & relative Genl. Jno. C. Brown[2] of
Giles Co. Tenn. who has made application to you for a pardon.

I am induced to believe that in the great press of business this letter
was not presented to you, but laid aside among the numerous applications for pardon. I therefore Mr. President, most respectfully call your
attention to my letter & to this petition for pardon. I am encouraged to
hope when I see so many from our state receiving your Executive
kindness.

My special interest in Genl. Brown arises from the fact, he is married
to my neice, (Miss Bettie Childress)[3] who you knew, and who now
unites with me in asking a pardon for her Husband.

I stated to you in a former letter that Genl. Brown was a Union man
& cast his influence against secession until after the Proclamation of
Mr. Lincoln calling on Tennessee for troops. He was a District Elector
in 1860 & earnestly advocated the preservation of the Union. The last
Union speech made in his Congressional District before the War was

made by him. He is a worthy man & I am assured will make a good & loyal citizen.

May I indulge the hope on a early decision & a favorable one with a pardon which will be gratefully acknowledged by Genl. Brown Mrs. Brown & myself.[4]

Trusting that your health may be restored and the country long have your services; I am with most consideration & respect,

Mrs. Polk.

ALS, DNA-RG94, Amnesty Papers (M1003, Roll 48), Tenn., John C. Brown.

1. Mrs. Polk's June 30, 1865, missive on behalf of Brown is in his amnesty file but does not indicate to which Judge Walker she refers.

2. Brown (1827–1889), a native Tennessee lawyer, rose from private to major general in the Confederate army and became the state's first postbellum Democratic governor. Warner, *Gray*.

3. Elizabeth was a daughter of John W. Childress, Mrs. Polk's brother.

4. General Brown was not pardoned until January 15, 1867. Amnesty Papers (M1003, Roll 48), Tenn., John C. Brown, RG94, NA.

From John Rice[1]

129. South 7th Street
Philada. July 28th 1865

His Excellency Andrew Johnson
Prest. of the U.S.
Sir—

Upon the receipt of Your telegraph,[2] I called on the Carriage builder,[3] who informs me that He has commenced a new carriage for You, which will be finished in about 10 or 12 weeks. I think without doubt this carriage will suit You better than any you can buy in this City, or New York. He says that the party to whom the carriage he sent you was sold, will hire it untill the new one is finished, or I can hire one here, and send it down immediately.[4]

If You approve, I will go to New York, and if one can be found that will suit, will buy it, and countermand the order, for the one now building.

Telegraph, your decision,[5] and dont hesitate to command the services of,

Your Obedient Servant, John Rice

LS, DLC-JP.

1. Rice (*c*1813–*fl*1880) was a prosperous master carpenter. 1860 Census, Pa., Philadelphia, 10th Ward, 109; Philadelphia directories (1861–80).

2. Johnson had wired: "You know what sort of carriage I want. May I so far trouble you as [to] ask you to get me what in your judgement will suit me—and send it to me with the Bill. I need one daily." Johnson to Rice, July 28, 1865, Tels. Sent, President, Vol. 2 (1865), RG107, NA.

3. Presumably Joseph Beckhaus and John Allgaier, owners of a carriage factory in Philadelphia, about whom Rice wrote again in August. See Letter from John Rice, August 10, 1865.

4. When, on June 29, the President had peremptorily wired, "Please hurry up the coach and harness," the carriage maker had evidently sent a conveyance that did not satisfy Johnson. It is this vehicle to which Rice refers. Reuben D. Mussey to Rice, June 29, 1865, Ser. 3A, Johnson Papers, LC.

5. Johnson replied through Mussey: "Please exercise your discretion as to whether you will get a new carriage from New York or have the work proceed. The article is much needed." Mussey to Rice, July 29, 1865, Ser. 3A, Johnson Papers, LC.

From Carl Schurz

July 28, 1865, Hilton Head, S.C.; ALS, DLC-JP. See *Advice*, 78–89.

In this, the first report on his trip undertaken "In obedience to your request" to South Carolina, Schurz cites his sources: personal observations and conversations with U.S. military and civil officers and with "a considerable number of prominent and intelligent individuals . . . whose views and opinions undoubtedly represent those of large numbers of their fellow citizens." Further, he has asked several military and civil officers—"men who have excellent opportunities for observation"—to give their views in writing, which he appends to this communication. Dismissing the number of the consistent Union white men as being "so insignificant as to make their influence hardly felt," he divides the South Carolina people into two classes: those who during the war came "into direct contact with our forces," and those who did not. The intelligent among the former "acknowledge and submit to the results of the war"; whereas the latter "adhere not only to their former opinions, but to a certain extent also to their former practices." Schurz notes a reluctance to free slaves, with a resort to "contracts" as a device to keep them on the plantation until a restoration of civil government will permit reimposition of "their former condition." He observes a willingness to "return to their allegiance," i.e., take the oath, as a ruse to get "their internal affairs again under their immediate control." He is hopeful that efforts to restore slavery will soon die out, but South Carolinians "are as little as ever inclined to put in the place of slavery a bona fide system of free labor," believing as they do *"that the negro will not work without compulsion."* He makes a case for not permitting the South Carolinians at this time to call a convention to revise the state constitution: "They have no clear conception yet of the true nature of their situation and of the problem they have to solve." Even if civil government were to be reestablished, troops would still have to remain in the state. Schurz explains why "Our military power is looked upon by both whites and blacks as their protector" and further advises Johnson "not to build any hopes upon the restriction of suffrage to those who have given no other evidence of their loyalty than by the taking of the oath of allegiance." He reiterates "the safety of the people demands a continuation of the military rule until the dominant class has in good faith accommodated itself to the results of the war." Schurz concludes by offering suggestions concerning the need to clarify the status of property with respect to confiscation and sale by tax commissioners, to extend the activities of the Freedmen's Bureau and of teachers among the blacks, to pardon Theodore D. Wagner, "a large business operator," and to be vigilant "that the federal offices should be filled with *real* union men," even if they must come from outside the state. He encloses five letters describing conditions in South Carolina.

From William E. Smith

July 28, 1865, Dougherty Co., Ga.; LS, DNA-RG94, Amnesty Papers
(M1003, Roll 23), Ga., W. E. Smith.

Thirty-five-year-old lawyer and longtime resident of Dougherty County, Ga.,
applies for pardon. A member of the Union party in 1850 and 1860, and an
opponent of secession in 1861, he nevertheless "saw no safety" after Fort Sumter "for Southern rights and institutions except in the establishment of seperate
independence." While serving in the Confederate army, he lost his right leg
and was forced to resign. As a member of the Confederate Congress, in cooperation with "others who sought a solution of our troubles by an appeal to
reason and humanity," he made efforts to settle the "existing difficulties" between the North and South. Since the "re establishment of National Authority"
he has abandoned slavery and has "publicly and privately councelled his
friends" to take the amnesty oath and return to peaceful pursuits. [Smith was
pardoned November 8, 1866.]

From Edward G. Webb

July 28, 1865, Philadelphia, Pa.; ALS, DNA-RG56, Appts., Customs Service, Collector, Philadelphia, William B. Thomas.

Understanding that an effort is in progress to remove Thomas as U.S. collector,
Webb, editor of the *Philadelphia Pennsylvanian*, who left the Democratic party
at the start of the war, adds his "voice against so impolitic and unwise a movement." It is important to retain "that portion of the Union party which came
from the Democratic ranks," and in Philadelphia, where "it numbers many
thousands," its aid is essential to prevent "both the City and State" from passing
under the "control of the old Democratic organization." The collector is the
only prominent Philadelphia officeholder "who had a Democratic training" and
also headed a regiment in defense of the country. If the only former Democrat
who holds office in Philadelphia is struck down, it "will have a very bad effect,
as there is strong ground of complaint at the exclusive manner in which the
present City administration disposes of its patronage." The loss of Philadelphia
would mean the state legislature would pass "into the hands of the Democrats,
and an opposition United States Senator will be the consequence."

From York, Pennsylvania, Union Committee

July 28, 1865, York, Pa.; ALS (G. A. Maish), DNA-RG56, Appts., Internal
Revenue Service, Assessor, Pa., 15th Dist., Stephen L. Barnett.

"Feeling assured, by the late change in Postmasters in this place, that the Government is determined to look after those of its citizens who have suffered the
loss of limbs" during the war, the Committee recommends Stephen L. Barnett,
who "in his line of duty as a soldier . . . lost his left Arm" at Antietam and who
is "a fit and proper person" for Internal Revenue assessor for their district.
[Barnett did not get the appointment.]

From David F. Caldwell

July 29, 1865, Greensboro, N.C.; ALS, DNA-RG56, Appts., Internal Revenue Service, Assessor, N.C., 5th Dist., Nathan B. Hill.

Desiring "to see your administration increase in usefulness and popularity" and believing that the application for tax collector of Dr. Nathan B. Hill, formerly of North Carolina but currently a resident of Minnesota, "has given great offense to some very prominent men," Caldwell wants his name and that of his brother William withdrawn from Hill's petition "and transfered to that of James W Dick." [Neither Hill nor Dick secured the appointment, which went to Samuel H. Wiley.]

From James W. Harold[1]

Greeneville Tenn July 29th 1865

His Excellency A. Johnson,
President *United States*
Dear Sir

I take the liberty of addressing you a few lines at the earnest request of Mrs. Reynolds[2] who is a neice of my wifes[3] as you are aware as she is contemplating a trip to Washington on an Errand of mercy and to beg at your hands Clemency for her husband John T. Reynolds[4] who is now in prison and has been for some 14 months.

The object she stated in wanting me to write to you was simply to state who she was & also to state what I knew of John T. Reynolds. I can do that in a verry few words, fully, frankly, & Truly.

I became acquainted with J. T. Reynolds a short time before the commencement of the war. He seemed to be a clever man and profesed at the start a decided Union Man but went into Rebelion & was Verry ultra ever after. His conduct towards union people throughout the country I know but little about to *my* certain knoledge although I have heard much alleged against. Whether true or not is more than I can tell, doubtless some true & some false which is generally the case. I can only speak certainly as to what I know certainly myself. In the dark days of the Rebellion he always treated me kindly and courtiously & I have heard some other ultra Radical union men speak of him as having treated them in the same way. For that I feel like giving him ample credit but upon the other hand I have heard complaints & charges prefered. As I said before perhaps some true & some false.

Thus it will always be. Now I am surely one of the last men that any person acquainted with me would think that I would speak in behalf of a Rebel, for Rebelism has cost me much trouble great anxiety at times and well nigh Broke me up.

Yet so it is his wife & little Child I am truly sorry for and had I the power as, *Vengance is not mine.*

And as there are & will be as bad men prehaps as he is going Scott free through out the Land & as he could not remain in this community but would have to Emigrate to some other Locality with his wife & child had I the power I would say sir notwithstanding your transgressions for the sake of your wife & little child go take your little family hunt you a quiete home go to work make a living for your family be a *Loyal man to your goverment* be a *good citizen* be a better *man* & *sin no more*. After mature deliberation these are my sentiments.

I may be all wrong however. Yet after all I believe it would be the best policy. They have neither wealth or influential friends to aid them, but neither weath or friends would have any undue weight with you. Your own sence of justice & wright would govern you in the premises.

Should you conclude to be lenient for the sake of the innocent, *family* it would meet with the approbation of at least some few of your friends who have always been loyal citizens. Others would complain for it will be ever thus. I hope you may be Enabled to do what is right in the case as I know, you will.[5]

Ever Truly Your friend
James. W. Harold

ALS, DNA-RG94, Amnesty Papers (M1003, Roll 50), Tenn., John T. Reynolds.

1. Many years earlier, both Harold and Johnson had served on the Greeneville city council.

2. Emma (b. *c*1845), daughter of William P. and Mary Jane Wright Cozart, married John T. Reynolds in August 1861. 1860 Census, Tenn., Knox, 1st Dist., Knoxville, 9; Burgner, *Greene County Marriages*, 141, 256.

3. Emily Wright (1820–1872) married James W. Harold in 1837. Reynolds, *Greene County Cemeteries*, 279; Burgner, *Greene County Marriages*, 112.

4. Reynolds (b. *c*1841), a painter from Norfolk County, Va., was sergeant major, 29th Tenn. Inf., CSA, and captain, 64th N.C. Inf., CSA. Captured while acting as enrolling officer of Greene County, he was imprisoned at Knoxville and tried by a military commission. Because of irregularities, his case was reviewed and he was turned over to civil authorities to be tried for treason. CSR, RG109, NA; Reynolds to Johnson, July 28, 1865, Amnesty Papers (M1003, Roll 50), Tenn., John T. Reynolds, RG94, NA; *OR*, Ser. 2, Vol. 7: 561.

5. Johnson pardoned Reynolds on November 13, 1865. *House Ex. Docs.*, 39 Cong., 2 Sess., No. 116, p. 48 (Ser. 1293).

From Hugh Kennedy

City Hall, New Orleans,
July 29th 1865

Andrew Johnson Pres. United States
Sir,

Herewith I have the honor to enclose you copies of three letters which I addressed to Major General Canby,[1] Comdg. Dept of La and Texas, explanatory & defensive of my official conduct which has been grossly misrepresented to him by Revd: Mr. Conway, Commissioner of Bureau Freed Men & in regard to the imprisonment of a negro, and to the disturbance of negroes in their places of worship.[2]

I have already had occasion to represent the conduct of Mr. Conway as calculated, if not deliberately intended, to create disturbance, and particularly designed to keep alive the agitation of the negro question at the North.

The negroes imprisoned in the Workhouse of this City have always been at Mr Conway's disposal; I implored their removal as they accumulate, yet he would make it appear that I was wantonly keeping the man Martin confined contrary to just remonstrance.

Genl Canby's interference was unnecessary, and if it had any effect it was to create the belief that the civil power in civil affairs was at his discretion.

> I have the honor to be, President,
> with great respect Your obdt svt
> Hu. Kennedy Mayor

ALS, DLC-JP.
1. On July 22 Kennedy complained to Canby about the general's "severe censure" following Conway's reports that Kennedy used city police to disrupt black churches, claiming that he was innocent of such charges. In a second letter that same day, the mayor outlined his plan to reduce crowding in the city workhouse by placing black inmates on government-controlled plantations, noting, furthermore, that whites had volunteered to take them in as "house servants." Thomas W. Conway to Kennedy, July 17, 1865, Kennedy to Canby, July 22 (2), 1865, Johnson Papers, LC.
2. Kennedy lodged another complaint with Canby on July 25, this time assailing Conway, who had protested the arrest of John Martin and had threatened to enlist the general's aid in securing Martin's release from the workhouse. The mayor accused Conway of provoking an incident that would reflect adversely on the President's policy. Kennedy to Canby, July 25, 1865, and Conway to Kennedy, July 13, 1865, Johnson Papers, LC; Wells to Johnson, July 31, 1865, Records of the Commr., Lets. Recd. (M752, Roll 16), RG105, NA.

From John Lyon

July 29, 1865, Washington, D.C.; ALS, DNA-RG60, Office of Atty. Gen., Lets. Recd., President.

A Petersburg, Va., attorney assures Johnson that the local election on July 18 "terminated without a trace of the old Sectional feeling. Original Union men and original Secessionists fraternised upon the common ground of earnest loyalty to the Union. . . . There are not one hundred men in Petersburg, whose hearts are not as your Excellency would wish them." He asks early review of pardon petitions from Petersburg residents to forestall confiscation of property and to "strengthen the hearts of patriots, and silence malcontents, by evidence that the President will exercise mercy magnanimously & wisely."

From William I. Nicholls

Washington July 29th 1865

His Excellency
The President of the United States

I called to-day with friends to see you and through my friend Mr Rohrer[1] was promised an interview, but the elements (in the shape of water prevented).

The paper of this morning announced my removal as Assistant Appraiser at the Port of Baltimore.

I could not understand how the President of the United States could remove one of the men, who labored with Mr. [illegible], and others, industriously & successfully for his nomination at Baltimore for Vice-President to make place for a man[2] who unjustly and from improper motives, worked to defeat him.

I believe the President has not seen my papers, reccommending me not only for retention in my present position, but for promotion.[3]

If you have on reflection after acquainting yourself with the facts in the case, determined to remove me I am content, and shall stand by you and the Union, whatever may be the result of your decision.

I enclose a letter from your friend Jno. M. Frazier,[4] Speaker of the Maryland House of Delegates for your consideration.

I will not annoy you with unnecessary writing. I only ask that further action, may be delayed in regard to my case, until I can be heard. I refer you to the Hon Preston King for my record.

Your friend Wm. I. Nicholls

ALS, DNA-RG56, Appts., Customs Service, Appraiser, Baltimore, William I. Nicholls.
    1. William H. Rohrer, Senate clerk.
    2. Probably Ephraim F. Anderson (c1839–fl1872), Hagerstown lawyer and Union army veteran, who replaced Nicholls as Baltimore appraiser (1865–c70). CSR, RG94, NA; Pension Records, Ephraim F. Anderson, RG15, NA; Appt. Bk. 4: 106, Ser. 6B, Johnson Papers, LC; U.S. Off. Reg. (1865–69).
    3. See Letter from William Smith Reese, July 21, 1865.
    4. The day before, Frazier had recommended Nicholls to Treasury Secretary McCulloch, and on August 2 he recommended Hooper C. Hicks, the brother of Maryland's recently deceased governor, for the other appraiser's position. Appts., Customs Service, Appraiser, Baltimore, William I. Nicholls, RG56, NA.

From Alexander H. Stephens

Fort Warren Boston Harbor Mass
29th July 1865

His Excellency Andrew Johnson
President United States
Dear Sir

Allow me to return to you my sincere thanks and grateful acknowledgement for the order releasing me from that close confinement to
which I have heretofore been subjected.[1] "Out of the abundance of the
heart the mouth speaketh."[2] As utterance in this case can not be by the
mouth I adopt this as the only channel through which that abundance
can be manifested and made known to you.

Yours most Respectfully Alexander Stephens

ALS, DLC-JP.

1. Confined to his underground cell since late May, Stephens had recently been permitted visitors, letters from home, and the freedom to walk the grounds of the fort.
Thomas E. Schott, *Alexander Stephens of Georgia* (Baton Rouge, 1988), 452.

2. Matt. 12: 34.

From Thaddeus Stevens

Bedford Springs July 29, 1865

His Excellency Andrew Johnson

My friend C. S. Eyster[1] Esqr of Chambersburg Pa. is willing to
accept a Judgeship in one of the territories. He is a gentleman in the
vigor of life, a well read Lawyer and has had a large practice. His integrity arguments, and urbane manners fit him admirably for the Bench.
He was among the sufferers at the burning of Chambersburg and prefers a Judgeship to refurnishing an office and resuming practice & I
should be much gratified at his appointment.

Thaddeus Stevens

ALS, DNA-RG60, Appt. Files for Judicial Dists., N.M., C. S. Eyster.

1. Christian S. Eyster (c1815–fl1881), native Pennsylvania lawyer and legislator,
was appointed by Johnson on March 1, 1867, as associate judge of the supreme court of
Colorado Territory and made his home thereafter in Denver. 1870 Census, Colo., Arapa-
hoe, Denver, 39; Pittsburgh directories (1857–59); George Bergner to Johnson, Aug.
1, 1865, Appt. Files for Judicial Dists., N.M., C. S. Eyster, RG60, NA; *Senate Ex.
Journal* (1866–67), Vol. 15, Pt. 1: 280–81; Denver directories (1870–81).

From J. Madison Wells

State of Louisiana, Executive Department,
New Orleans, July 29th 1865.

His Excellency Andrew Johnson
President of the United States.
Dear Sir.

You are so thoroughly cognizant of the condition of the Southern States growing out of the emancipation of the slaves, that I need hardly inform you that the question of labor for the future in connection therewith, is the great problem to be solved and with our people over-rides all other consideration. So far as Louisiana is involved, I feel authorized to say that 9/10ths of her citizens accept the abolition of slavery as a fixed and irrevocable fact and acquiesce in the result as inevitable. They have no wish or desire to revive it, neither are they disposed to find fault with and condemn the policy of the Government in the system it has adopted to regulate and make available this new and large element of free labor, for the mutual benefit of the black and the white man. They are willing to give it a fair trial by a strict compliance with all its regulations, and have done so. So long as the order requiring the negroes to remain and work on the plantations under the rules and regulations prescribed, remained in force the system was working as well as could be expected.

This has been changed however by a recent order promulgated by the Deputy Superintendent here, the Revd. Mr T. W. Conway, allowing the negroes to go where they please and to work for whom they please.[1] The effect of this order will be to utterly demoralize the negroes, besides the ruin brought on the planters in withdrawing the labor necessary to the gathering of their crops now in the ground, to say nothing of the dangerous and revengeful spirit that idleness, and want may engender in the breasts of the negroes toward the whites. Already the people in the country Parishes are in a state of alarm for their personal safety, in view of the lawless conduct of the negroes. Most of them have fire-arms, which they use in shooting down stock. Thefts and burglaries are of every days occurrence and murders have been committed on defenceless women and children. This lawless spirit will increase by the relaxation of all restraint on the negro by the order referred to, for your knowledge of the race Mr President must convince you that if left to themselves, they will not work. I tremble for the consequence if they are allowed to congregate in large bodies in a state of idleness, which they will surely do if they have the liberty.

In this connection I feel constrained, acting under a sense of my duty to the state as well as the National Government in this matter, to express to you my opinion that the Rev'd Mr T W Conway, who holds the office of Deputy Superintendent of the Freedman Bureau of this Dep't is not a fit and proper person to occupy that position. He is a radical negro suffrage man—thinks the black better than the white man and is an active political speaker and agitator for negro suffrage and equality. Inoculated as he is with these ideas, he cannot perform the part of an impartial agent in representing the General Government and particularly under the conservative policy of your administration Mr President, who while securing to the black man his rights as a freeman, have emphatically told him, "that freedom meant work."[2]

I make these remarks in no spirit of unkindness or feelings of prejudice towards Mr Conway, who leaving out his ultra radicalism on the subject of the rights of the negro, may be a very worthy and estimable man. All I suggest is, that a more practical and impartial man be appointed, who is biassed neither on the side of the negro or the white man—who will not dabble in politics—but will devote his whole time to his duties and decide as impartially as the Judge on the bench, or as that functionary is supposed to do. There is no difficulty in finding such men. I would prefer that he be not selected, from the South, unless meeting your full concurrence.[3]

Commending these observations to the consideration of the President

> I remain Very truly Your obt servant
> J Madison Wells
> Governor of Louisiana.

LS, DLC-JP.

1. On July 14, 1865, Conway had issued Circulars Nos. 1 and 2. The first showed the organization of the Freedmen's Bureau in Louisiana, listed its officers, and instructed its various clerks and assistants. The second sought to guarantee the liberty of former slaves. Freedmen were "enjoined to work" and to enter into contracts with employers, but in "no case" would they "be forced to work for employers who are obnoxious to them." Furthermore, they were "entirely free to work where and for whom they please." *New Orleans Tribune*, July 18, 1865.

2. Two days later, Wells enclosed to the President a synopsis of Conway's speech before the National Republican Association of New Orleans, which illustrated Conway's "bias in favor of the negro." Wells to Johnson, July 31, 1865, Records of the Commr., Lets. Recd. (M752, Roll 16), RG105, NA.

3. Conway had an "officious manner" which brought him into conflict with southern whites, civil authorities, and even some military officers. Recognizing that Conway had irritated Johnson by his support of universal black suffrage and by being out of step with the President's Reconstruction policy, Bureau Chief O. O. Howard replaced Conway in September 1865. Howard A. White, *The Freedmen's Bureau in Louisiana* (Baton Rouge, 1970), 19–21; William S. McFeely, *Yankee Stepfather: General O. O. Howard and the Freedmen* (New York, 1968), 174–76.

From John W. Forney

Office of the "Press," Philada.
July 30, 1865.

My Dear Mr. President—

I am not a complaining man, and if I were not night and day laboring to support and popularize your noble policy, I might be a bore, and ask you for office for my friends.

I beg to forward you a copy of a letter just sent to Mr. McCulloch, Secretary of the Treasury, which explains itself.[1] My cousin, D. C. Forney, will hand it to you.

With great respect, J. W. Forney

To the President.

LS, DNA-RG56, Appts., Internal Revenue Service, Assessor, Pa., 1st Dist., A. B. Sloanaker.

1. In protesting the appointment of Albert B. Sloanaker as assessor, Forney called it a "*grievous mistake*" and insisted that "the many prominent and unselfish friends of the President in the District should have had a chance to present a name that would have reflected credit upon him and upon them." A year later, Johnson appointed Sloanaker as collector for the second district of Pennsylvania. Forney to McCulloch, July 30, 1865, Appts., Internal Revenue Service, Assessor, Pa., 1st Dist., A. B. Sloanaker, RG56, NA; *House Ex. Docs.*, 39 Cong., 2 Sess., No. 67, p. 6 (Ser. 1292).

From William Cornell Jewett[1]

Clifton House Clifton, Niagara
July 30th 1865

President Johnson,

Having no desire to openly connect myself, at this time, with public matters, I under an impulse of duty, convey to you my judgment, from *late*-personal observation in Europe & here—as to the necessity of a *universal amnesty & recognition of Maximilian*. 1st to secure the active & hearty cooperation of the Southern leaders & people, in sustaining your government & strengthening & perpetuating the American Republic. 2d preventing a war with Europe—for—without a universal Amnesty—Southern influence, will of necessity secretly plot to distroy the general government, while under a non-recognition of Maximilian foreign powers will seek a justification, for a war, to distroy our Republic & secure to the South, coveted independence. My information is from means not within the reach of our Republican representatives—who will therefore convey information to the contrary.

God give you wisdom—for a magnanimous constitutional & independent policy.

Your friend Wm. Cornell Jewett

ALS, DLC-JP.
   1. Pamphleteer and "adventurer," Jewett had participated in the abortive Confederate peace mission in July 1864 at Niagara Falls.

From John B. Steele

July 30, 1865, Kingston, N.Y.; ALS, DLC-JP.

Steele, New York Democratic congressman, thanking Johnson for reappointing the Catskill postmaster, assures him that "We all, at least to some extent, appreciate the difficulties of your position" but feel that "your firmness, your ability & your determination to do right, will with the help of God, carry you safely through." As for federal officeholders in his district, he will not endeavor "to have any one of them removed so long as they discharge the duties of their office faithfully and are true to their President his administration & Policy."

From J. Hubley Ashton

July 31, 1865, Washington, D.C.; LBcopy, DNA-RG60, Office of Atty. Gen., Lets. Sent, Vol. E (M699, Roll 10).

In answer to Johnson's query of the 22nd requesting an opinion in the cases of 36 western Pennsylvanians indicted "for conspiracy to resist the draft," the acting attorney general suggests that—on the advice of the district attorney involved in the prosecution, and on the fact that indictments were dismissed against fourteen—all but six of the remaining should also be dropped. The defendants "seem to have been poor and ignorant men who were guilty of no overt act whatever, but whose guilt consists simply in membership of an unlawful association into which they were drawn by political and designing leaders." Of the six to be prosecuted, "four are deserters and desperadoes," while two "are very bad men"; one "a rebel emissary, and the latter a man of large influence, exerted in a most mischievous direction." [All the indictments were dismissed.]

From Green T. Henderson [1]

                                            Murfreesboro, Tennessee.
                                            July the 31st. 1865—
To his Ex-. Andrew Johnson, Prest. of the United States.
Dear Sir.
   The House of worship in this City—and the parsonage, (preacher's house) belonging to the Methodist Episcopal Church South, are at present in the hands of the military. The Church has for years past been used as a hospital. There are at present but very few patients in it, and the congregation, among whom you have many friends, are very anxious to obtain the house to use it as in past years as a house of worship; and by the solicitation of many of them, and of the trustees, I address you, as commander in chief, and solicit with confidence any assistance you can properly extend to us in obtaining the use and control of our

house of worship at the earliest period—or as soon as it is convenient for the military to abandon it as a hospital.

I doubt not, Bvt. Maj. Gen. R. W. Johnson,[2] now in command here, will readily comply with any suggestion you may make on this subject.[3]

I subscribe myself, as in the past, your friend.

G. T. Henderson

ALS, DNA-RG107, Lets. Recd., EB12 President 2520 (1865).

1. Henderson (1803–1888), a Methodist minister, edited the *Murfreesboro News*, which was suspended during the war. Jill K. Garrett and Iris H. McClain, comps., *Some Rutherford County, Tennessee, Cemetery Records* (Columbia, Tenn., 1971), 5; Carlton C. Sims, ed., *A History of Rutherford County* (n.p., 1947), 111, 113.

2. Richard W. Johnson.

3. To the contrary, the general maintained that the church belonged to the "loyal" Methodists and that the parsonage property, though belonging to the southern church, had "been taken possession of as abandoned property" and assigned to the "Chief C.S. Dist. Mid. Tenn." He recommended, therefore, that neither should revert to Henderson, the "editor of a vile rebel sheet" and preacher of the church in question. There is no evidence that the President took action. Aug. 22, 1865, endorsement to Henderson's letter.

From Reverdy Johnson

Balt. 31st July 1865

My Dear Sir:

As I wrote you in reply to your kind note of the 28th,[1] I was perfectly satisfied with the appointments that you advised me of, and I still am. But, my friend Dr. Carroll[2] finds himself unable to accept, I understand, the appraisementship because of the many dependent on him. Besides his own family he has his father's to take care of. This he cannot do if he brings them to this City, as he must if he takes that office. But the assessorship for the First Congressional District the one in which he resides, is worth about the same, and its duties he could perform without breaking up his home, and there too he can be of much greater service to your Administration than he could be here. The incumbent a Mr George Russum[3] of Caroline County and who is said to be willing to resign in Dr. Carroll's favor is also stated to be incompetent to its duties. You will therefore *greatly oblige me* by giving that appointment to Dr. Carroll, and if you do may I then recommend to fill the appraisers office Mr. Columbus Hicks[4] of Dorchester County, and who has had cast upon him the almost entire support of the family of his deceased brother, Gov. Hicks,[5] who, I regret to say, left no property behind him. How he served Maryland, and, in doing so, served the whole Country you know as well as I do. An early reply will greatly oblige me.[6]

Yours with sincere regard Reverdy Johnson

The President

LS, DNA-RG56, Appts., Customs Service, Appraiser, Baltimore, Hooper C. Hicks.
1. The Chief Executive's missive of the 28th read: "I have at length concluded to make the appointments named in the enclosed paper. I wish they will prove satisfactory to you." Earlier in the month the President had asked the Maryland senators, Johnson and John A.J. Cresswell, for suggestions concerning the Baltimore appointments. A. Johnson to R. Johnson, July 10, 28, 1865, Ser. 3A, Johnson Papers, LC; Johnson to Creswell, July 10, 1865, Tels. Sent, President, Vol. 2 (1865), RG107, NA.
2. Thomas K. Carroll.
3. Russum (c1834–fl1897), a Caroline County, Md., attorney, had been appointed assessor by Lincoln. F. Edward Wright, comp., *Caroline County 1860 Census* (Puerto Rico, 1973), 13; *U.S. Off. Reg.* (1863), 39.
4. Former Whig Hooper Columbus Hicks (1819–fl1893) received one of the two appraiser posts (1865–69). *Men of Maryland and District of Columbia*, 407; *U.S. Off. Reg.* (1865–67); Baltimore directories (1880–93).
5. Thomas H. Hicks.
6. Johnson did appoint Carroll as assessor. *U.S. Off. Reg.* (1865), 55.

To Robert Johnson

Executive Office, Washington, D.C.
July 31st 1865.

To Col Robert Johnson,
Greeneville, Tenn.

Why did you not come with the rest of the family.[1] I desire that you should come.[2]

Andrew Johnson.

Tel, DNA-RG107, Tels. Sent, President, Vol. 2 (1865).
1. Eliza, Frank, Martha and her children had arrived on June 19. *Philadelphia Press*, June 21, 1865.
2. On the same day the President telegraphed David T. Patterson in Nashville to inquire of Robert's whereabouts. Johnson to Patterson, July 31, 1865, Tels. Sent, President, Vol. 2 (1865), RG107, NA.

From John C. McConnell[1]

No 56. Saratoga St. Baltimore Md
July 31st 65

To his excellency
The President of the U. States,

As a Tennessean & a personal friend. I take the liberty of placing this communication before you, & feel assured that you will do all in your power to promote the interest of one who had rendered such valuable service to the Government during the recent rebellion.

I had the honor of raising the 1st 2nd & 3rd Maryland Regiments & in doing so, I almost exhausted my entire means, & now in my almost destitute condition I have the honor to request that you will appoint me, (as an evidence that my services have been duly appreciated) Marshal of the State of Maryland as I have just been informed that the appointment has not yet been made.

If it is not in your power to award that position to me, please do me kindness to give me some other *good* position.[2] I respectfully refer you to the Hon W. G. Brownlow Gov. of Tennessee.

I have the honor to be Very Resply
Your obt. Sert Jno. C. McConnell

Please address No 56 Saratoga st Baltimore Md.

ALS, DNA-RG60, Appt. Files for Judicial Dists., Md., John C. McConnell.

1. McConnell, a "property agent" in Baltimore before the war, had opened a recruiting office in May 1861. Baltimore directories (1856–60); J. Thomas Scharf, *The Chronicles of Baltimore* (Baltimore, 1874), 636.

2. There is no evidence that Johnson acceded to McConnell's request.

From Benjamin F. Perry and Christopher W. Dudley[1]

Greenville S.C. July 31st 1865.

His Excellency, President Johnson.

My Dear Sir

I take the liberty of writing to you, in favour of my personal & political friend, Col. C W Dudley, of Marlborough District, So Ca, whom I have known intimately, for the last thirty years. In 1836, we took our seats for the first time, in the Legislature of this State, & sat two years together at the same desk, in that Body. Our political sympathies were the same, & a strong personal friendship sprung up between us, which has remained unbroken till the present time. He is a gentleman of high honour, & sterling integrity of character—none more so. Like myself, he had the sagacity to perceive that the leading politicians were plunging the state into revolution & ruin—but, like myself also, he was unable to check them in their mad career. We had to look on, & patiently await the misery & ruin which we saw approaching. More than once, whilst the rebellion was raging fiercest, the Colonel proposed that some effort should be made, to stop the war by negotiation. I knew this was hopeless, whilst the Southern army remained in the field, & said it was fruitless to make such a movement.

Col Dudley is a lawyer of distinction at our Bar, & was once our State Reporter. He has served for many years, in both branches of our State Legislature, & was at all times, a most wise & efficient legislator—politically devoted to the best interests of the State & the Union. For several years past, he has retired from politics & the Bar—but I am happy to know, that there is a prospect of his talents & his services being once more devoted to his country, in a more extended field. It would be well for the State, if we could send to Congress, a representation composed entirely of such men as Colonel Dudley.

I know that he is devoted to the reconstruction of the Union, & harmonizing the two sections of our common country. I do not know that it will be necessary for Col. Dudley to apply for a pardon, as he held no civil or military appointments, under the so-called Confederate States, & never bore arms against the United States. But, his *charities may have made him amenable to the Confiscation Act.[2] If so, by pardoning him, your Excellency will restore to the Union, as true a spirit & as firm a patriot as ever breathed the breathe of life.

I am, with great respect & admiration,

Yours truly, (Signed) B. F. Perry

*I do not know precisely, to what Col Perry alludes unless it be to the duty I have been trying to discharge, in feeding the wives & children of the absent soldiers, as a member of a Board appointed by the State. I have not applied for a pardon, because I never yet felt myself to be a criminal—never having "*voluntarily*" lifted a finger to aid in this unholy war—& was glad enough to escape with my life, from the fury of our own people, who threatened it more than once, because I was not as great a madman, as those who commenced it without a cause, & carried it on, without brains.

C.W.D.

Copy and ALS (C. W. Dudley), DLC-JP.

1. Dudley (1808–1881), an attorney, served as a delegate to the 1865 South Carolina constitutional convention. N. Louise Bailey et al., eds., *Biographical Directory of the South Carolina Senate, 1776–1985* (3 vols., Columbia, 1986), 1: 430–31.

2. No other pardon application from Dudley has been found. Before the war his combined worth, estimated at $116,736, consisted mostly of slaves. By 1870 his assessed real property value stood at $57,660. Ibid., 430.

To William Prescott Smith[1]

Executive Office, Washington, D.C.,

July 31st 1865.

To Mr W. P. Smith Master of Transportation
Balto and Ohio Rail Road Baltimore Md

Judge Patterson will leave Cincinnati on the evening of the third (3) Thursday for Washington. Will you please have a car for himself and suite? Answer.

(sigd) Andrew Johnson

Tel, DNA-RG107, Tels. Sent, President, Vol. 2 (1865).

1. Smith (c1822–1872) had been associated with the Baltimore and Ohio since 1850. Briefly postwar collector of Internal Revenue in Baltimore, he returned to railroading, managing the New York and Washington "through line." *New York Times*, Oct. 2, 1872.

From Martin J. Spalding[1]

Baltimore July 31. 1865

To His Excellency, the President of the United States
Your Excellency:

On the 13th of June, I applied to the Secretary of State for a pardon in behalf of Bishop Lynch[2] of Charleston, under your Amnesty Proclamation. The Secretary answered me under date June 16th, that "the answer of the Department had always been that the person wishing a special pardon under the President's late Amnesty Proclamation must himself apply therefor to the President."

In accordance with this instruction, I have the honor to send herewith to your Excellency, by the hands of my Secretary, Rev. Thomas Foley,[3] an application from the Bishop himself stating his own case.[4] Your Excellency may fully rely on the statements of the Bishop, and upon his pledge to confine himself strictly to his spiritual ministrations. I will add, as I already stated to Mr Seward, that an extension of the Amnesty to Bishop Lynch according to my firm conviction, would not only be attended with no possible danger to the government, but, on the contrary, would strongly tend to conciliate, & thus to facilitate your plan for reconstruction. From what I have learned of your kind action in similar cases, I cannot doubt the favorable consideration with which you will receive this petition of Yr. Excellency's humble servant.[5]

M. J. Spalding, Archbp Baltimore

To His Excellency, Andrew Johnson
Presidt. U.S.

ALS, DNA-RG94, Amnesty Papers (M1003, Roll 46), S.C., P. N. Lynch.
1. Spalding (1810–1872), a Kentucky-born Catholic leader, editor, and author, became archbishop of Baltimore in 1864. *DAB*.
2. Irish-born Patrick N. Lynch (1817–1882), bishop at Charleston since 1858, had hand carried a letter from Jefferson Davis to the Pope expressing a desire for peace. Ibid.
3. Foley (1823–1879), Maryland native, was chancellor and vicar-general of the Baltimore archdiocese, and afterwards became coadjutor-bishop of Chicago. *Appleton's Cyclopaedia*.
4. Apparently, Spalding forwarded to Seward Bishop Lynch's June 24, 1865, application from Rome asking permission to return to Charleston. Amnesty Papers (M1003, Roll 46), S.C., P. N. Lynch, RG94, NA.
5. Spalding's plea proved successful. Lynch was pardoned August 4, 1865. Ibid.

White House Household Expenses for July 1865

Washington July 31st 1865

Presidents House

		To Bills Rendered	Dr
A S Chamberlins	Grocer Bill		252.29
Jas. H. Hazels	Butcher "		317.80

Geo. S. Krafft	Baker "	26.11
Alfred Jones	Feed	21.40
T. A. Ball[1]	Butter	79.00
Pay Roll For Servants		66.00
Thos. Stackpole	Bill of	130.60
	Incidentals	
		$893.20

Received Payment
Thos Stackpole

D, DLC-JP10.
1. Hazel (*c*1834–*c*1881), Krafft (b. *c*1830), Jones (b. *c*1816), and Turner A. Ball were businessmen in Washington's First Ward, west of the White House. The postwar wealth of Jones, a black or mulatto, was listed at $40,000. Ball apparently remained in town only from about 1862 to 1869. 1860 Census, D.C., Washington, 1st Ward, 128, 188, 202; (1870), 367; Washington, D.C., directories (1858–82).

White House Payroll, July 1865
Pay Roll for Presidents House for July 1865.[1]

July 31, 1865

Names[2]	Position	Time	Rate	Amt	Receipts
Eliza Mitchell	Cook	1 mo	20.	20.	Eliza **X** Mitchell
Kate Fletcher	Asst Cook	1 "	12.	12.	Kate Fletcher
Charlotte Howard	Chambermaid	1 "	10.	10	Charlotte Howard
Maria Meredith	Laundress	1 "	12.	12	Maria **X** Meredith
Margaret Gertrele	do	1 "	12.	12.	Margaret **X** Gertrule
				$66.00	

D, DLC-JP10.
1. This is the first full month of Johnson's occupancy of the White House.
2. Of these servants, only Charlotte Howard has been identified. See *Johnson Papers*, 7: 502*n*.

From Truman Woodruff
Confidential

Saint Louis Mo. July 31st 1865.

Hon. Andrew Johnson
Sir

How could you have re-appointed Richard J. Howard—collector of customs at this port, is certainly very strange. What has he ever done for the union party to entitle him to be thus favored? *Sir* he is just as popular with the Rebels as he is with conservatives; has no popularity with the radicals who elected Lincoln and Yourself.

I understand he has sent a petition to you[1] numerously signed soliciting his re-appointment. I will venture a considerable that a greate portion of the signers on said paper are *Rebels*—such are his warmest friends where he is known. It makes good Union Men feel, little sour to be thus treated.

Why should Mr. Howard be thus particularly favored, with a position which he has not the least claim too? And our best men thus cast aside, who have spent their time and money to sustain the good cause and to promote your election? Is this right? Now Mr. Howard would stand just as far with the copper heads if they were successful—as he does with the conservatives *now* but he is detested in the extreem with the Radicals. He could not be elected here to the most low contemptable office. Then, I inquir why thus inflict such a curse upon us? I understand that Peter L. Foy[2]—is asking to be re-appointed Post Master. He is of the same stamp as Howard. For Gods sake deliv us from such men, being plased over us as Howard and Foy.[3] I say again, not either of them could be elected to the most minor office in the gift of the people: the people have [illegible] them, then, why should we be thus cursed with them?

From Your Truly Truman Woodruff

ALS, DNA-RG56, Appts., Customs Service, Surveyor, St. Louis, Richard J. Howard.

1. Probably the undated petition, signed by 101 individuals and companies, which is found in Howard's application file.

2. Peter L. Foy (*fl*1881), associate editor of the *Missouri Democrat* (St. Louis), was subsequently editor of the *St. Louis Daily Dispatch* and president of a ferry company. St. Louis directories (1859–81).

3. Both incumbents remained in office. Ibid. (1864–67).

From D. M. Woolley

July 31, 1865, Keokuk, Iowa; ALS, DLC-JP.

A former Union soldier and an "old line democrat" admonishes that "the ship of state with her precious cargo of equl rights" must steer clear of the "shoals and quicksands that beset her," especially the "rebel hosts" who, though defeated, still cherish the idea of "an independent government for the South with slavery as its corner-stone." Suggests that "every civil and military leader in this rebellion" be disfranchised and, in turn, that "the negros the only really loyal population that can be fully relied upon in the extreme Southern States" be enfranchised. Without the black vote, "we shall find ourselves in a hopeless minority in those states," and the freedmen will have no more rights than when "they were recognized as slaves by the National government."

From Southern Merchants and Planters

[ca. August 1865][1]

Andrew Johnson, President of the United States:
Sir—

We, the undersigned, desire to represent to you, on behalf of merchants, business men and planters, from the States of Texas, Mississippi and Louisiana, that in view of the great frauds, abuses and acts of oppression and flagrant injustice daily perpetrated by the Treasury agents and the military authorities, with few exceptions, in their collection of property known as Confederate cotton; and taking into consideration, which they do not do, that most of the planters west of the Mississippi, having never received one dollar in money or bonds for this cotton that has been by force taken from them by the rebel Government, still consider it their own property, and changing both the coverings and marks, dispose of it to the merchant, who has no way to distinguish these marks, but who buys it in good faith; and also, taking in view the fact that the planter who sold it to the merchant has been misled by the Treasury agents, and even by the letter of the Secretary himself, as well as by most of the military officials, who, taking their cue from the Secretary's own orders, have, in most cases, told the people that their cotton was not to be forcibly collected, through the hands of the purchasing agent, paying to the Government (and this has been done willingly) the twenty-five per cent. The planters brought in their cotton, in good faith, on these representations of the highest officials they could see, and were disposed to sell or ship it here to the purchasing agent; but almost at once swarms of dishonest and corrupt Treasury aids and agents, like bees, swarm the South, no two of whom agree as to authority or policy, and seize everything in the shape of cotton, whether private or otherwise, thus destroying trade and commerce, and throwing over the whole South, that was just recovering from the war in some measure, a blight that cannot be remedied except by yourself.

Already the seizure of all the cotton of the South, in order to find a few bales of cotton that may have belonged to the so-called Confederate States Government, has made nearly all capitalists here timid, has almost entirely stopped trade, and will throughout the whole South, unless these acts of the Treasury agents, hardly two of which bear the same appointment, are declared illegal and done without authority is the one of all others that we wish now to avoid, that the Government is not dealing with them in good faith.

We believe that a tax of ten or fifteen per cent. on the market value in New York, to be collected by the collectors of customs at the different Southern ports, or by any other officers your Excellency or the Secretary of the Treasury may deem proper to appoint, will yield a larger revenue than would be derived from the sale of all the Confederate cotton, even were every bale faithfully delivered to the Government.

We beg leave, further, to represent that the present system of harassing merchants and planters, by seizing all the cotton, discourages the growth of loyalty and returning affection for the old Union.

Many planters who have never had a bale of Confederate cotton in their possession, and who, depending upon the sale of their small stock to obtain money to resume planting under the free labor system, have had their cotton seized and thus deprived of the power to comply with the labor regulations. We want relief, and we respectfully ask it from you; we have already laid our case before Major Gen. Sheridan,[2] through whom we forward this to you, who has, as far as lays in his power, promised to aid us and to correct the abuses of which we complain, and hoping that this, the first petition of the merchants of New Orleans and the planters of the States mentioned, may meet with the response we feel to be our right, and that you, we are sure, will be disposed to accord to us, we are, as ever,[3]

Your obedient servants.

New Orleans Daily Picayune, August 27, 1865.

1. This document first appeared in the *Washington Republican* on August 16, 1865.

2. Philip H. Sheridan (1831–1888), former chief of cavalry for the Army of the Potomac and now commander of the Military Division of the Gulf, which included Louisiana, Texas, and Mississippi. Warner, *Blue*; Dawson, *Army Generals and Reconstruction*, Apps. I and II.

3. The Captured Property Act continued to be enforced despite many protests such as this. By May 1868 gross sales amounted to about thirty million dollars, over 95 percent of which was from cotton that had belonged to both the Confederate government and individuals. Randall, *Constitutional Problems*, 326.

From Wilmington Officials

[ca. August 1865], Wilmington, N.C.; Pet, DLC-JP.

Professing their loyalty, their acceptance of freeing the slaves, and their "desire to live in peace and harmony with them while they remain among us," twenty town commissioners observe that "the presence of *colored troops* in our midst is not calculated to allay public anxiety and to produce that harmony and cheerful submission to the laws which your Excellency . . . is so anxious to preserve." They graphically detail incidents in which the soldiers have encouraged "the most extravagant pretensions of the colored inhabitants," have fostered "the spirit of animosity towards former slaveholders, to such an extent . . . as to keep up a well-grounded fear of a general outbreak and massacre," or themselves have committed "outrage" on the population. "We do not ask that *no* troops may be stationed here. We would prefer to have a small force to keep order until the civil government is established, but we desire that they should be *white troops*, for the reasons herein contained."

From Benjamin W. Berry

August 1, 1865, Wilmington, N.C.; LS, DNA-RG94, Amnesty Papers (M1003, Roll 37), N.C., Benjamin W. Berry.

A shipwright, aged forty-six, who for twenty days in 1861 was captain of a Confederate privateer which captured one vessel, "a Small skooner laden with fruit," seeks a pardon under the May 29 proclamation. For the remainder of the war his shipyard was taken over by the Confederates, his compensation being "fifty cents on each hand employed in the said yard"—the limit of his participation in the rebellion. Far from profiting from the war, he has suffered serious loss, since upon the arrival of the Federals the Confederate agents "destroyed by fire all of my buildings and marine railway." [Apparently falling under the 11th exception, Berry was not pardoned until June 15, 1867.]

From Francis P. Blair, Sr.

Silver Spring Augt. 1. 1865

My dear Mr. President

Having been in some degree associated with the leading men who have shaped the course of the liberal party during the last half century, & indulged in conferring with them in the measures proposed to advance its cause, I venture to express my views to you, now its champion, on a most important epoch, involving the fate of Republican Institutions throughout this continent and possibly beyond it.

Observe what vast questions already emerge from the rebellion. First—The policy of grafting the black race on the white race in the administration of the Government founded by the latter for its own behoof, involving in its result that of making it a hybrid Government to suit a motley hybrid race. Next—The policy of violating the rights of the States guarantied by the constitution, securing to them the regulation of the suffrage to provide for their municipal legislation as States, as well as for that of the nation, through the election of the President & Congress of the United States. And third—The policy of permitting the potentates of Europe to plant a monarchy in the midst of our Continent, thus to hold the key of the Isthmus—to open or shut the gate of the Oceans between our Atlantic & Pacific possessions and to array a great military Power on both flanks of our Republic wielded by a despot, prompt at any moment to strike it on the east or west of the Rocky mountains, to divide it or dissolve it entirely & partition it like Poland.

Now you have taken your stand on all the issues which have arisen from the rebellion, or rather which originated it, as they were all lurking in the Slavery which European monarchs imposed on our country & which their policy instigated Southern masters to employ to destroy our Government. The rebellion is crushed and with it the Slavery that animated it, but like the Hydra it puts out new heads—from the vines of the old trunk. It sprouts out with the bold front of negro equality. Negro suffrage shouts out on one side with a political aspect and on the other we have the social aspect to emerge in the shape of amalgamation. What can come of this adulturation of our Anglo-Saxon race and Anglo-Saxon Government by Africanization, but the degradation of the free spirit & lofty aspirations which our race inherited from their ancestry and brought to this continent; and turn that whole portion of it engaged as manual Operatives into that class of mongrels which cannot but spring from the unnatural blending of the blacks & whites in one common class of laborers and giving to both an assimilation through that color, which has unhappily marked servitude during all generations from the days of Ham. The result would inevitably be to make a distinction in caste and put a brand on all our race associated in employment with people of color & crisped hair. It would not create equality between those thus associated and those engaged in professional & political pursuits. It would hasten the creation of a lower order—a serfdom—a foundation for an Aristocracy crowned with Royalty.

This is the real scope of all the enemies of our Government at home and abroad. To avoid such results our fathers constituted a Government in which the white race alone were invested with all the rights it conferred. That race have hitherto held it exclusively as their heritage. They were its sole Freeholders. It was the property of its creators and none can claim rights in it without their consent. It was for this reason that the popular Sovereignty exerted through the suffrages of the people was committed by the national constitution to the guardianship & control of the State Governments which are nearest to the people. But now that paramount power which was given to the states of the South as well as the North, the partizans of the negro race in the latter, insist must be stript from the former & in effect the rights of Government in the south conferred on the freedmen. This state of things would introduce the San Domingo problem[1] in all the States of the South and the question of mastery between the races would be decided by the States of the North in declaring how many of the white race should remain under its ban of disfranchisement to subject it to the black race, all of which is enfranchised.

From the tenor of the Faneuil Hall appeal[2] which comes to this issue, it would seem to be the purpose of those speaking for the party in New England, who look upon the result of the war as giving them the South as a conquest, that Congress is to vote out every representative who presents himself from a State which does not resign its constitutional right to regulate the suffrage of its people. This is simply an attempt at revolution, a breach of the Union by a vote of Congress.

The idea that suffrage will produce equality between the two races at the South is illusory. The black freedmen will find the prejudices of caste increased among the mass of white laborers by the new priviledge. They will become competitors with the superior race in that which touches their pride and it will be found more than was necessary to get under the wing of the master who hires them, for protection. They will be obliged to have white leaders at the polls as they had in the camps of both armies & those who hire them will control their ballot more absolutely than has ever been done by persons occupying similar relations because their safety will depend upon their employers in the exercise of their priviledge in the service of an increased prejudice & more powerful caste. It is absurd to suppose that the rich, educated, intelligent men will not command the suffrages of their negro hirelings if they venture to bring them to the polls to assert equality with the whites. The Indians although always a free race in this country & accustomed to Government, never could attain in the States in which they were embodied, the equality which a fraction of the North insist on giving the negroes in the south against the will of the mass of the whites in those States. The Indians melted away under that process of civilization now contemplated for the blacks. The result of the contact of races marked by nature to be distinct has induced all the great statesmen of our country to look to colonization & segregation as the means of saving the colored race & giving to them a Government of their own & with it the equality and independence they desire & deserve. The party who oppose this scheme, (yours as well as your predecessors), have no expectation of maintaining equality for the emancipated by suffrage. They assert it for them, some with a view to drive the whites from the Gulf States—others with the design of keeping those States out of the Union. To vote their members of congress out because those States refuse to obey the behests of other States as to the regulation of the right of suffrage, committed to them by the constitution, is to vote a dissolution of the Union—a subversion of the constitution. The pretense of establishing negro equality in a country which is compelled by the fist of the central Government to submit its suffrage to its control, makes the idea of equality with the arbitrary power asserting this superiority, absolutely absurd. If the Representatives of a state in one section are expelled because it does not surrender its constitutional rights, may not a state in another section be expelled because it will not surrender some of its rights at the dictation of a majority in congress? Why not expell the representatives from California & Oregon for refusing the suffrage to the Chinese & the whole group of the North eastern States for refusing it to free negroes? This movement against the south has its motive in the ambition which prompted Mr. Chase to say at the beginning of the rebellion, "Let the Seceding States go, they are not worth fighting for."

This issue to deny equality to the Southern States on the pretense of giving Equality to the negroes, is renewed by the Faneuil Hall programme—an Essex Junto[3] of modern date, who have improved on the consolidation schemes of their prototypes. It was first made at the last session of congress against your predecessor by those calling themselves his friends. They carried a bill through congress to defeat his plan of giving the States the rights of which they were deprived by usurpation.[4] He crushed the attempt by withholding his consent. They appealed to the people & sought to defeat his re-election[5] but they were defeated and now in disregard of the verdict pronounced by the people they have renewed their efforts to compass their object. At the last congress the Democratic party sustained Mr. Lincoln, while opposed by his so called political friends. The people north & south who are at heart in favor of popular Sovereignty & of States rights to maintain it, will sustain you in your effort to accomplish the design of your predecessor, as they sustained him against the intriguers in his own cabinet[6] and their abetters in congress.

Can you not lend your aid—at least give your countenance to those fighting your battle for the fundamental principles of our federal system, against those in high places, who profess party allegiance to you when in fact they are destroying that party & intending to destroy you? Your position enables you to help those struggling for the Country's cause by simply adjusting the weights in the high stations around you, so as to manifest your inclinations. Mr. Lincoln did not do this & the weight of the members of his administration were found in the scale against him. The men in congress most active in carrying the vital measure against him were in the closest confidence with the highest cabinet officers and they used their official patronage & commanding personal influence to thwart the Presidents great scheme of adjusting the Union.[7] Would it be well now when a new epoch has arrived casting the whole burden of reorganizing our disjointed fabric on your hands, to work with the same instruments, that marred the wise patriotic designs of your predecessor? Assistants that worked *con amore* with the professing friends in Congress, ever ready to betray him, not only voting against his leading measures openly, but secretly intriguing to defeat his re-election. The principal men to whom I here point are still in congress. They are still in cooperation with those wielding your Departments and they are still more inimical to your measures & to your re-election than they were to Mr. Lincolns. Is it safe in such a boisterous time to embark on a new voyage keeping them at the helm, to steer your vessel through the currents of the approaching elections & the coming Congress? If your administration is committed by the same heads of Departments to the same hands in congressional committees—if they are to shape all movements of the body & apply the influence controlled by the Secretaries to array the rank and file under such leaders, will not your fate be worse than Mr. Lincoln's, the accumulation of your burden being greater & the preparation of your opponents to break you down, being vastly increased; You can do nothing to appease the ambition of these aspiring men. They look beyond you & rely on their measures to defeat you as the means of compassing their own ends. You must appeal to the people and rely upon the power of your principles to accomplish the general work you & they have at heart, to make you victorious. To do this you have only to say "out upon this half-faced fellowship"—to have your Assistants in the great executive trust you wield, like yourself outspoken—thorough—uncompromising in the maintenance of the constitutional cause now at stake & ready to hazard all in its defense. I have never doubted your purpose to take this stand. I think you intimated as much to me some months since & I write only to say that I think this is the accepted time. The motions of the coming elections are felt already in the great States of New York Ohio & Pennsylvania. The Democracy which gave such immense votes against Lincoln during a war that commanded even their approval at heart, are now in favor of all the objects you design to accomplish by it. You indeed make it their war by the consequences you bring from it, and those men who now seek to pervert those consequences into a defeat of the restoration of the Union, with equality among the States, deserve to forfeit the favor they gained by giving the war their countenance. The Democrats will nominate candidates pledged to support all your leading policy. Their opponents are already out in Massachusetts and other states with manifestos not only at war with your avowed policy but abhorent to the constitution & tending to make Congress a revolutionary club—a convention of northern representatives bent on subjecting the south to their will and using negro enfranchisement as the means of the disfranchisement of our white brethren of that section, of their equality as citizens and states in the Union.

This issue was broadly made by the action of Mr. Lincolns enemies in the last congress & is now vehemently pressed by the same leaders who still seek to defeat the policy which you & he inaugurated to preserve the Republic. This makes the new epoch which is to take direction from your hand. Can you give it the impulse you desire with the forces in your Cabinet every way complicated, if not absolutely combined with the hostile elements against you in & out of congress? Your Cabinet have no strength or weight in the country except among those who are inimical to your policy and they have neither the desire or power to draw them to its aid, and is there no danger that the retention of these men who are without the confidence of the great body of the liberal Republicans and Democrats, who united alone support your policy, will lose you the confidence of the only men in the nation upon whom you can rely?

It appears to me that the change you contemplate[8] ought to be made at once, as new combinations of parties are forming throughout the country looking to coming elections, which will certainly produce new combinations in the already elected congress at its next Session. If you are to have a control in these combinations, it must come from the influence you exert over public opinion by the administration you propose & the men you select to make it manifest to the people & *give it the executive stamp*. If the present cabinet remain your attitude to the next congress will be much the same with that of Mr. Lincoln to the last, with the majority of those calling themselves his party friends hostile to his measures and to his succession and poisoning the feelings of the masses of the people, solicitous for the success of the cause for which he labored, by lack of confidence as to the means employed. By the selection of a new cabinet you not only get rid of the odium incurred by the Rump left to you, but you may constitute it of men who will bring to you an accession of strength from all parties who concur in your views of the re-organization which the late conflicts have made necessary. You will of course turn [out] no man who has not distinguished himself from first to last against all the principles at the bottom of the rebellion—& who has not given his whole strength in bringing out the glorious reform that has banished slavery from the continent. Conspicuous men of this kind may be found of Democratic antecedents—of Republican antecedents—of Whig antecedents, blending both—such you may draw into your administration able & honorable men of these original types ready to merge all minor differences of by gone parties in the great *Democratic Republican* ideas of Mr. Jefferson of the Union of States combined by the popular will under a national Executive & Legislature giving full life to the constitution.

This is your mission at this moment on entering the new Era of our history and let me entreat you to open the process of the new elections and of the creation of new parties in the approaching Congress with a new Cabinet strongly imbued with your opinions, entirely worthy of your confidence and of a caste calculated to win the confidence of men of all parties, who are willing to embrace the scheme of restoration to which you commit your administration in the nomination of the heads of its Departments.

The Democracy, I learn, north and South will make its nominations for National & State Representatives & for other functionaries of men of the type to which I have Just referred. The Republicans will be divided in their nominations, a portion going for the scheme of the Faneuil Hall manifesto derived from the movement which took the shape of the bill passed & presented to the President at the last congress to defeat his plan of re-Union. If you declare your design to the nation by the creation of a new cabinet to express & to execute it distinctly & patently, the party opposed to it who would go to the people & come into congress as the friends of the administration, but really to defeat its policy, will I believe be reduced to a faction. But if you allow them to proceed under the shadow of a great party name, & under prestige already acquired by them of swaying the Cabinet they will command in Congress as at the last session & through it may command the country unless overthrown by the Democracy which will take a stand against it and the Rump Cabinet.

Let me explain my view by supposing a practical illustration. We know that the States of New York & Pennsylvania were canvassed by the Republicans & Democrats in the last Presidential election under the disadvantage to the latter of an anti-war and anti-administration platform. The Democrats lost the election by some eight or ten thousand, where many hundred thousand votes were cast—the returning soldiers carrying it for the Republicans.[9] The Democrats will present themselves at the approaching election on your programme. The candidates who will poll as Republicans on the programme presented in the bill of last Session to Mr. Lincoln to defeat his & your policy & which is now proclaimed at Faneuil Hall as the party test, will claim your support & that of Messrs Seward & Stanton, who as Cabinet ministers represent those states in your administration—suppose confidence in you personally and devotion to the plan of reconstruction you promise them should induce liberal Democrats and Republicans to coalesce so as to give the triumph to the tickets nominated in contravention of your policy, simply because they were called administration candidates. You would then have an appearance of an administration success but it would not be your success. It would be that of the Rump Parliament & Cabinet. It would establish the Faneuil Hall doctrine & defeat your policy. It would accomplish the objects of Messrs Seward & co. so far as their personal & party aims are concerned, but your power at this moment of vital interest would be paralized and your future put in "cold obstruction." If however you were at once to make a new Cabinet drawn from the different sections of the country and representing the various parties in it, yet agreeing to support your plan of reconstruction, on an issue so essential, it would be no matter what party organization returned members, men who gave in this adhesion would become identified with the administration. Their election would be your success and in this epoch of reconstruction would create a new party, embracing the whole Union, adverse to that of Faneuil Hall limited to a northern latitude and exulting in a revolutionary creed. If the old Cabinet be continued while this formation of parties is in progress it is to be apprehended that the organization which approved the existing Cabinet on the ground of its Bastile arrests—incarcerations without accusation and release upon payments of such money as the prisoner possessed or could command on the ground also of its leanings to France giving countenance to the invasion of our continent—on the ground of its demonstrations of hostility to England calculated to Justify the aristocracy there in acceding to the invitations of Napoleon to Join him in recognizing the confederacy & defy the feelings of the British commonalty in favor of our Government, will gain such strength as to induce it to look to the attainment of the control of the Government independently of the Executive head whose policy it adopts.[10]

The vote of the south will be drawn almost as an unit to the side of that party which it finds in opposition to a ministry known to be hostile to its dearest rights in the Union & confederated with the scheme promulgated at Faneuil Hall, which would deprive its *States* of equality *as States*, would create a war of caste & a war of Sections a war of factions breaking up the ancient foundations of the constitution.

Nor is it to be supposed that France will withdraw from Mexico as long as a Minister is retained who has already conceded to her the right to remain there. Nor can it be hoped that men of character can be found in our Country who will risk themselves to raise a force to expel Maximilian from Mexico without involving the country in a foreign war, so long as France & her Puppet have a steadfast friend in the Secretary of State, whose appointee and instrument is still retained in the War Department.[11] So long as they are retained the country may be pardoned even for distrusting your disposition to maintain the inviolability of our continent from the invasion of European Powers.

Yo mo af fd F P. Blair

P.S. The appointment of a new cabinet with a firm aspect looking towards mexico, might, without giving offence to France, manifest a determination that would induce a Surrender of the Scheme of giving "the ascendancy to the latin race in the South american Continent."

LS, DLC-JP. [The postscript is in Blair's hand.]

1. A reference to the interracial strife and bloodshed which plagued the island of Haiti during the early nineteenth century. Ludwell L. Montague, *Haiti and the United States, 1714–1938* (New York, 1966), 3–28.

2. On June 21 Republicans met at Faneuil Hall and endorsed black suffrage. Benedict, *Compromise of Principle*, 110–11.

3. The "Essex Junto" was a small clique of New England Federalists representing commercial interests who opposed the War of 1812 and advocated separation from the Union. Howard L. Hurwitz, *An Encyclopedic Dictionary of American History* (New York, 1970), 240.

4. Blair refers here to the Wade-Davis bill, cosponsored by Benjamin F. Wade and Henry Winter Davis. It empowered the President to appoint military governors in Confederate states under Union control, emancipated slaves in such states, and outlined a reconstruction process requiring a majority of white male citizens to proclaim their loyalty to the United States prior to the calling of a constitutional convention. Lincoln, who correctly perceived the bill as a challenge to his "Ten Percent Plan," announced the previous December, chose to pocket veto the measure. Allan G. Bogue, *The Earnest Men: Republicans of the Civil War Senate* (Ithaca, N.Y., 1981), 240–47.

5. Furious with Lincoln's refusal to sign the Wade-Davis bill, and enraged at the President's July 8, 1864, proclamation which reasserted his authority over Reconstruction, Wade and Davis issued a "manifesto" denouncing Lincoln's decision as a "rash and fatal act." Republicans, however, quickly disassociated themselves from the manifesto. *American Annual Cyclopaedia* (1864), 307–10.

6. A reference to Salmon P. Chase, Edwin M. Stanton, and probably William H. Seward. Although Seward was quite conservative on Reconstruction, Blair and his son Montgomery still harbored an intense dislike for him. Smith, *Blair*, 392.

7. Probably a reference to the successful effort of Charles Sumner in February 1865 to block Lincoln's attempt to secure congressional recognition of his unionist government in Louisiana. Benedict, *Compromise of Principle*, 94–97.

8. Blair here assumes a decision to make cabinet changes for which there is no specific evidence in the Johnson canon.

9. Lincoln carried New York by 6,749 votes and Pennsylvania by 20,075 votes. Blair's assertion about the soldiers' vote was incorrect in the case of Pennsylvania; there is no breakdown of the New York vote. *American Annual Cyclopaedia* (1864), 508, 650.

10. References to Stanton's and Seward's arrests of civilians under the suspension of *habeas corpus* and Seward's stance concerning the French in Mexico.

11. In early 1862 Seward had supported the appointment of Stanton as secretary of war. Van Deusen, *Seward*, 324.

From Benjamin R. Curtis [1]

Pittsfield Masstts. August 1st 1865.

Andrew Johnson
President of the United States
Sir;

I address you respecting Mr. John A. Campbell [2] with whom I sat on the Bench of the Supreme Court, and who is now a Prisoner in Fort Pulaski.

Though my intercourse with Judge Campbell ceased with my retirement from the Bench, I have retained a strong regard for him, founded on his purity and strength of character, his intellectual power, his great attainments, and his humane, and genial nature.

That such a man should be in any way connected with assassination is as near an impossibility, as the frailty of humanity will allow us to consider anything, respecting any man.

If I had not an entire conviction that he was incapable of entertaining the thought of such a crime, and that his apparent connection with the subject, through the "Alston letter" [3] has been satisfactorily explained to yourself, I should not address you.

Judge Campbell as you I believe know was not only clear of all connection with the conspiracy to destroy the Government, but incurred great odium in the South and especially in his own State, by his opposition to it and by his views of the power and intentions of the Government and the fallacy of the ideas upon which the attempted revolution was based.

In 1863 he was induced to take a subordinate office, under circumstances and for reasons which I suppose have been explained to you. That he used his position and influence when and as he could to put an end to the War, and restore the Southern country to the Union I have no doubt.

I can conceive that reasons may exist apart from the merits of his own case, why he should not receive a pardon at the present time, and as that subject has recently been under your consideration, I desire to say nothing concerning it, but I venture respectfully to ask your attention to the question whether his release on Parole with such limitations as you may think needful, would not promote the public interest. From his former position, his opposition to Councils which have proved so disastrous, his known devotion to the interests of the Southern people, his ability and his weight of character, he can undoubtedly exert an important influence over Southern opinion; and if, as I am convinced, that influence will be used to promote the pacification of the Country, and the conciliation of Southern opinion to the necessities of their condition, and the just demands of the Union, it cannot fail to be useful in an important degree. At present his influence for good is paralyzed and his imprisonment is in effect a continual and conspicuous representation to the people of the South that he is hostile to the Government, and desires to obstruct its measures. I believe this is unjust to him, and unfavorable to the prevalence of those feelings and opinions which you desire to promote.

At the same time I am sensible that no one can have so good means of forming an opinion on this matter as yourself. And that mine can be of no other importance, than possibly to afford some reason for your consideration of the subject. It belongs to Mr. Campbell himself and to him alone, to satisfy you what his opinions are, and actions would be; I can only express my belief that if allowed an opportunity, he would satisfy you, and my hope that such opportunity may be granted to him.[4]

With great respect I am, Mr President,
Your obt. Svt. B. R. Curtis.

LS, DNA-RG94, Amnesty Papers (M1003, Roll 2), Ala., John A. Campbell.
1. Curtis (1809–1874) had served on the U.S. Supreme Court (1851–57), resigning over dissension in the Dred Scott case. Later he became Johnson's chief counsel during the impeachment trial. *DAB*.
2. Associate justice of the U.S. Supreme Court (1853–61).
3. A letter from Confederate Lt. W. Alston—written just after Lincoln's reelection—had offered to dispose of some of the South's "deadliest enemies." When found by Federal authorities, it was immediately linked to Lincoln's assassination. In referring the missive to the Confederate War Department, Campbell, then serving as assistant secretary of war, had endorsed it: "for attention." Richard H. Leach, "John Archibald Campbell and the Alston Letter," *AR*, 11 (1958): 64–75; *OR*, Ser. 2, Vol. 8: 838–39.
4. Although Campbell's wife and his sister later appealed on his behalf to Johnson, he was not released until mid-October, when he was paroled by a special proclamation which included the proviso that he remain in Alabama until the President pardoned him. Johnson did so on April 16, 1867. Anne Campbell to Johnson, Sept. 2, 1865, Johnson Papers, LC; Rebecca A. Butler to Johnson, Sept. 9, 1865, Andrew Johnson Papers, New-York Historical Society; Richardson, *Messages*, 6: 352; Amnesty Papers (M1003, Roll 2), Ala., John A. Campbell, RG94, NA.

From Ladies of Holly Springs

August 1, 1865, Holly Springs, Miss.; Pet, DNA-RG94, Amnesty Papers, Jefferson Davis, Pets. to A. Johnson.

The petitioners ask executive clemency for Jefferson Davis, pleading that "Mr. Davis was but the representative of the defeated party . . . called . . . by the almost united voice of the southern people to preside over their councils, and guide them through the terrible storm of war, he was but doing their bidding in armed conflict, as he had before represented their views in times of peace." Now that southerners "have again become loyal citizens to the government of the United States," they "submit" that the "fraternal feeling which should exist between citizens of the same government can be more effectually restored by mildness and clemency, than by the punishment of those who . . . are, and must ever be dear to every true southerner."

To John M. Palmer

Executive Office, Washington, D.C.,
Aug 1st 1865.

Major General Palmer
Louisville Ky

I have received the following dispatch from Lexington Ky[1] of this date and wish to put you in possession of the fact. I hope you will see that the law is faithfully executed.

Andrew Johnson
Prest U S

To the President

We respectfully call your attention to Gen Palmers proclamation of July 26."[2] We consider it a palpable and intentional violation of the Act of Congress approved Feby 25" 1865,[3] to prevent Military Officers interfering in state elections in the following particulars.

First. The proclamation prescribes the qualifications of voters in Kentucky which is expressly forbidden by the Act.

Secondly. Those qualifications exclude citizens who by the laws of Kentucky are entitled to vote.

Thirdly. It threatens with arrest and military trial all who are disqualified according to that proclamation and who shall appeal to the constituted authorities to decide upon their rights of suffrage or who shall even appear at the election or ask a citizen to vote in a particular manner.

We ask for such action in regard to this proclamation as the Act of Congress requires.[4]

Tel, DNA-RG107, Tels. Recd., President, Vol. 4 (1865–66).

1. The senders were S.M.C. Johnson, Thomas H. Shelby, Sr., H. T. Duncan, Isaac W. Scott, Leslie Combs, David A. Sagne, John B. Huston, R. A. Buckner, and D. L. Price. Three hours earlier, Johnson had received a wire from Charles Egerton, James J. Miller, and D. S. Goodloe of the Union Executive Committee, supporting Palmer's election order. Tels. Recd., President, Vol. 4 (1865–66), RG107, NA.

2. Palmer's General Orders No. 51 declared that martial law still prevailed and that Confederate civil servants and anyone who "voluntarily submitted" to the Confederacy could not vote. Any who appeared at the polls would be subject to arrest and a military trial. *American Annual Cyclopaedia* (1865), 464.

3. "An Act to prevent Officers of the Army and Navy . . . from interfering in Elections in the States" expressly forbade an army officer "to fix, or attempt to prescribe or fix, by proclamation, order, or otherwise," voter qualifications under penalty of a fine up to $5,000 and five years' imprisonment. Military interference was sanctioned only if it became necessary "to repel the armed enemies of the United States, or to keep the peace at the polls." *U.S. Statutes*, 13: 437.

4. Palmer did not rescind his order. On election day, Governor Thomas E. Bramlette, who had urged Palmer to intervene, issued a statement declaring that the balloting should be free from military dictation or menace. The conservatives won a narrow victory. George T. Palmer, *A Conscientious Turncoat: The Story of John M. Palmer, 1817–1900* (New Haven, 1941), 181–83.

To Francis H. Peirpoint

Executive Office, Washington, D.C.
Aug't 1 1865

Governor F H Pierpont
Richmond Va.

Does the interference by the Military to the extent of declaring null and void the recent Richmond municipal election[1] meet your approbation.

Please advise me of the true condition of the matter.[2]

Andrew Johnson
President U.S.

Tel, DNA-RG107, Tels. Sent, President, Vol. 2 (1865).

1. Following the exclusion of about a dozen voters who had "lost their residence by reason of their absence as soldiers in the United States Army" and the election of many who had been "prominent and conspicuous for inaugurating and sustaining the rebellion," Richmond commander Gen. John W. Turner voided the July 25 elections and forbade the organization of the city council. *New York Times*, Aug. 1, 1865; Chesson, *Richmond*, 93.

2. On August 5 the governor wired that he could not give a "Categorical answer," but he promised to write "in a few days." This letter has not been found. In October, Turner allowed most of those elected on July 25 to take office. Peirpoint to Johnson, Aug. 5, 1865, Tels. Recd., President, Vol. 4 (1865–66), RG107, NA; Chesson, *Richmond*, 93.

From James Williams[1]

London August 1st 1865

To the President:
Sir

I have been residing for some time past in Germany with my family and I came to London a few days ago with the intention of proceeding to America for the transaction of private business. I have however received information which leads me to apprehend that it would not be safe for me to venture within the jurisdiction of the United States unless first authorised by you to do so. My arrest would be disastrous to the interests of my family, who are the sharers of my exile and I have therefore decided not to leave Europe until I can feel assured of my safety.

I deem it my duty however in asking this privilige to inform you that in the late war I espoused the cause of the South with all my heart, and devoted to its support all my humble abilities. Altho I was in Europe at the time the ordinance of secession was passed by Tennessee, yet believing that my allegiance was primarily due to my state I acted upon that conviction and was faithful to my principles. I could not if I would and I would not if I could plead in extenuation any pressure or coercion, for after the secession of Tennessee I espoused the cause of the south, of my own free will, and in obedience to my long cherished convictions of right, and with a full knowledge of the fact that whatever might be the result I would lose both fortune and political position.

Whether I was right or wrong the result of the war has decided that the rights I thought we possessed shall not in the future exist. If I should ever resume my citizenship I for one would expect to conform faithfully to the constitution and the laws, as interpreted by the result of the war. But I do not ask to be granted the rights of citizenship, for I must frankly say that if I were to swear a thousand times that I had changed my convictions, I would be a thousand times perjured.

For myself my career is nearly closed. I have nothing to hope from the smiles of men and but little left to lose by their frowns. I do not think Mr President that you believe I acted from dishonest motives, nor do I believe that there lives one man who will say that I ever wilfully did him a wrong, and I will not at this late period of my life compromise my own self respect by expressing a contrition which I do not feel. I know that this is not the language usually addressed by men in my position to those in power, but it is the language of honesty and truth.

I am ready to submit to my fate cheerfully whatever it may be, even though I should never again be permitted to revisit my native land. But it would be a great personal advantage to me to be allowed to return to the United states, and to remain there for a period of about three months, at the end of which time I would come back again to Europe. I need hardly say that I would do no act during the period of my stay to which the Government of the United States could take exception.

If this request should be deemed worthy of a response, I would suggest that the answer be directed to the care of the American Legation at London. I am known to Mr. Alward[2] the Asst. Secy. of Legation, with whom I will leave my address.[3]

I am Very respectfully Your Obedt Servt
James Williams

LS, DNA-RG59, Misc. Lets., 1789–1906 (M179, Roll 227).

1. Williams (c1814–1869), Tennessee-born editor, legislator, and businessman, served as minister at Constantinople during Buchanan's administration. Resigning in 1861, he moved to London, where he sold Confederate bonds and published articles on behalf of the southern cause. For this activity he was indicted for treason. Although pardoned on June 27, 1866, he remained in Europe. *BDTA*, 1: 793–94; Amnesty Papers (M1003, Roll 51), Tenn., James Williams, RG94, NA.

2. Dennis R. Alward (*fl*1886), Pennsylvania native, was appointed from New York. *NUC*; *U.S. Off. Reg.* (1865–67).

3. From Austria in September, after receiving a response from Secretary of State Seward, Williams wrote of his surprise upon learning he was charged "with 'offences committed in violation of a public trust'" and stated his desire to return to Washington for a visit to clear any "misapprehension of the facts." He returned in 1866, renewing his pardon application, at which time he had an interview with the President. Williams to Johnson, Sept. 25, 1865, Johnson Papers, LC; Williams to Johnson, May 8, 1866, Williams to Edmund Cooper, May 8, 1866, Amnesty Papers (M1003, Roll 51), Tenn., James Williams, RG94, NA.

From Alpheus Baker

August 2, 1865, Eufaula, Ala.; ALS, DNA-RG94, Amnesty Papers (M1003, Roll 1), Ala., Alpheus Baker.

Lawyer and Confederate brigadier seeks amnesty under the first exception, explaining that he voted for secession in the Alabama convention of 1861 because he believed "the Union was a revocable compact, & Secession a constitutional right," and he "vainly hoped it would put a peaceful termination to the 'Conflict' then raging in the union," which he was convinced "would overthrow Slavery, & bring thereby ruin upon the country." In sum, "I believed . . . that the two sections which lived together only in strife, would live apart, in amity and prosperity." He submits "with resignation to the inevitable result . . . and . . . would oppose all effort to disturb the verdict." [Pardoned July 11, 1866.]

From Jonathan M. Foltz[1]

Philadelphia 2nd August 1865

Sir,

Medical experience as to the Sanitary condition of the Presidents house at Washington from the years 1834 to 1851 induces me to write to you.

During the months of August and September the house is always sickly, and I have known every inmate to be sick in the same season.

A change of residence to the Soldiers home[2] or to the hills beyond Georgetown until October will restore and preserve your health, which I learn from the newspapers is impaired. Your life is so important to the life of the nation that I fear to think of the consequences should you be called away; there would be but one life (Mr. Fosters)[3] between us and chaos! and this must be my apology for addressing you.

I am with the greatest respect & esteem

Your obedient Servant. J. M. Foltz
Surgeon U.S. Navy

Andrew Johnson President of the United States.

ALS, DLC-JP.

1. A graduate of the Jefferson Medical College, Foltz (1810–1877) had been commissioned assistant surgeon in the U.S. Navy in 1831. Fleet surgeon during the Civil War, he was assigned to the Medical Board of Examiners while stationed at the Naval Asylum in Philadelphia (1864–67). *NCAB*, 5: 150.

2. Presidents Buchanan and Lincoln had spent summers at the Soldiers' Home, located three miles from the White House, and Johnson's family stayed there after their arrival in Washington, but Secretary of the Interior Harlan wrote Public Buildings Commissioner French on August 5, 1865, directing him to construct a summer home for the President on "Georgetown Heights." Informed of the project, Johnson canceled the order, saying he preferred to live closer to the Executive Office and that the Soldiers' Home could be used if necessary. *National Intelligencer*, Aug. 7, 1865; *Cincinnati Enquirer*, Aug. 15, 1865; Paul R. Goode, *The United States Soldiers' Home: A History of Its First Hundred Years* (Richmond, 1957), 62, 75–76.

3. As acting president of the Senate, Connecticut Senator Lafayette S. Foster was next in line for the presidency. *DAB*.

From M. D. Herndon[1]

Washington, D.C. Aug 2. 1865.

To the President of the United States.

The undersigned removed to the Republic of Liberia in 1854 from Kentucky—being emancipated for the purpose—and settled among the Bassas,[2] a large and powerful tribe residing on the soil and within the jurisdiction of the Republic. I have labored earnestly and, I trust, successfully among this people in making known the elevating power of civilization and the Gospel.

When about to leave for this Country the King of the Bassas Knor-Gou or "Saltwater", charged me to tender his respects and regards to Your Excellency, and to ask you to present him with a "rain Coat" or gum Coat.[3]

In preferring this request I beg leave to add that I think such a gift would tend to cement the friendship of the King and his tribe to the Government of the United States, and tend to perpetuate peace with the growing Republic of Liberia.[4]

With great respect and esteem,

Your Obedient Servant, M. D. Herndon

LS, DNA-RG59, Misc. Lets., 1789–1906 (M179, Roll 227).

1 Possibly a freed slave formerly belonging to the Herndon family of Kentucky. Tradition has it that Traverse D. Herndon (1810–1854), a Columbian College graduate and a Baptist minister, emancipated $30,000 worth of slaves and had them transported to Liberia. James B. Taylor, *Virginia Baptist Ministers*, Ser. 2 (Philadelphia, 1859), 451–61; George Braxton Taylor, *Virginia Baptist Ministers*, Ser. 3 (Lynchburg, 1912), 280–87; 1850 Census, Slave Schedule, Ky., Ohio, Dist. No. 2, p. 5.

2. A coastal, seafaring tribe in Liberia. Tom W. Shich, *The Promised Land* (Baltimore, 1977), 28–29.

3. An Americanism for a coat made wholly or in part out of rubber. Mitford M. Mathews, ed., *A Dictionary of Americanisms on Historical Principles* (2 vols., Chicago, 1951), 1: 757.

4. In an appended endorsement G. W. Samson, president of Columbian College, Abraham D. Gillette, pastor of Washington's First Baptist Church, and William Coppinger, corresponding secretary, American Colonization Society, commend for favorable consideration both Herndon and the King's request. A note written in Coppinger's hand follows: "Rev Mr. Herndon expects to leave for Africa in the Course of a few weeks. Should a favorable response be made, the Coat may be sent to his address at Colonization Rooms, Cor: 4 1/2 and Penna. Avenue, Washington City."

From Jane Johnson [1]

Raleigh N.C. Aug 2. 1865.

To Andrew Johnson
President of the United States.

The undersigned is the widow of Jesse Johnson, your uncle, who has been dead seven years. I have three children, a girl 14 years old, a boy 10 years old, and a girl 8 years old: they are all rather feeble and incapable of assisting me. I am very poor, have no home of my own and no means of support. Dr. Fabius Haywood [2] of this city, has been very kind to me and my children, and has done us much service; he gave me permission to use his house at an old tan-yard as long as I chose; but even this has been seized and by the military authority turned over to Messrs Keim, Kline & Grausman. [3] I am now ordered to leave the premises. I cannot procure an other house, and I see no way but to go into the Street. Your friends here thought if the case was presented to you, that you would assist me in some way. I hope you can in some way aid me and my children, so that at least we can have a home. [4]

I am yours very respectfully
Jane Johnson

LS, DLC-JP.

1. Johnson (b. 1820) was the second wife of Jesse (1776–1858), who, a modern genealogist has speculated, was the brother of Jacob Johnson, Andrew's father. This assertion is supported by a contemporary Raleigh diarist who recalled Johnson's living with his uncle Jesse. Hugh B. Johnston, Jr., "The 'Missing' Ancestry of President Andrew Johnson" (typescript, n.d., Andrew Johnson Project Files), 5–7; Beth G. Crabtree and James W. Patton, eds., *"Journal of a Secesh Lady": The Diary of Catherine Ann Devereux Edmondston* (Raleigh, 1979), 140, 716.

2. Haywood (1803–1880), North Carolina-born physician, applied to Johnson for amnesty in July 1865 and was pardoned January 5, 1866. *NUC*; Amnesty Papers (M1003, Roll 39), N.C., Fabius J. Haywood, RG94, NA.

3. Probably Henry Keim, A. Kline, and Moses Grausman, all German-born merchants in Raleigh. 1860 Census, N.C., Wake, Raleigh, 2, 3, 11.

4. Her pastor, B. Craven, who wrote the letter for Jane, testified as to the veracity of her statement, writing: "I think she is in every way worthy of help. She has been a consistent member of my church, and seems to be doing the best she can." A notation in Johnson's hand "Attended to" gives no clue as to his disposition of the request.

From Hugh Kennedy

New Orleans, City Hall
2nd day of Augst: 1865

Sir,

On the 31st July, Monday last, agreeably to your verbal order, an election was held here for Directors in the New Orleans & Jackson Rail

Road Co. I enclose you herewith the certified return[1] and respectfully ask for it your favorable consideration.

The new Board so far as the representatives from Mississippi upon [it] are concerned, remains as before neither Govr. Wells for the State of Louisiana, nor myself, as Mayor, for the City of New Orleans, voting for or against them, in the absence of all knowledge of their past loyalty.

Some of the old Board are now making much disturbance because this election has been had, declaring it high-handed, arbitrary and contrary to right & law, going so far as to threaten legal proceedings to determine your right, through me, to order an election, which the charter had not provided for. No objection is made in any quarter to the loyalty, or character or fitness of any of the elected so far as I can hear, and the only demand upon the stockholders by Govr. Wells and myself was that they would comply with your wish and elect loyal & proper persons.

No objection was made by any of the old directors to an election, provided I would accept a ticket they furnished; this I declined to do; as I was not prepared to vindicate to you the propriety of placing in power men of their selection.

Of the old Louisiana members elected by the State, City & individual stockholders, consisting of twelve in number, the following is their present classification:

Five are here now

Three are dead

Three are absent

One is a foreigner and owns no stock.

I would prefer, President, in every case to be able to accommodate matters amicably, and without the necessity of trespassing with your valuable time in their consideration. In this case, with every disposition to do this I could not succeed.

The old Directors have had irresponsible control of this Company and its enormous traffic within the rebel lines for four years past; have rendered all the assistance in their power to the rebel authorities, and have, it is stated, made over one million of dollars. What has become of the money so earned, whether it was lent to the Confederate government, invested in some way or another, or squandered by unfaithful servants, is unknown. Perhaps unwillingness to make the exhibit underlies the present opposition to the new direction.

Some stress is being laid upon the fact that I had no written authority from you to order the elections that have taken place for Directors for the New Orleans & Opelousas[2] and the New Orleans & Jackson rail road companies; as if mere forms should be cavilled at by honest men, when nothing is required that is unreasonable, inconvenient and unjust.

I have done my duty in this whole matter in strict conformity with your desire & command, and impartially and disinterestedly; and I now most respectfully submit the whole matter for such further action as you may please to order.

I have the honor to be President, with sincere respect your obdt. servt.

Hu Kennedy Mayor

Andrew Johnson President of the United States
Washington

ALS, DLC-JP.

1. The enclosed statement named the eighteen newly elected directors. Both the state and the city of New Orleans owned stock in the road, which was inoperable after the war until restored under president P.G.T. Beauregard. Taylor, *La. Reconstructed*, 189, 191.

2. The New Orleans and Opelousas, also a state stock road, had been maintained by the Union army and was in a good state of repair. Ibid., 6, 189, 318.

From Thomas and Bridget O'Hearn [1]

Boston Mass. August 2nd 1865.

To Hon. Andrew Johnson.
President of the United States of America.

Your petitioners *Thomas O'Hearn and his wife Bridget* respectfully and earnestly ask pardon for their son *Michael O'Hearn*.[2] He is now their only son having lost the eldest in the "Army of the Potomac" before Richmond Sergt Pat'k O'Hearn[3] Co. J. Mass. 24th. Reg.

Michl. O'Hearn is 15 years old enlisted for two years on Steamer "Shamrock". When the Shamrock Came into port to be laid up at the end of the war he Michl. heard of his brothers death and left the steamer without permission for three days to ascertain about his brother—*it was desertion*. He was sentenced to 10 years imprisonment in Weathersfield Prison Conn. for same. We ask his Pardon on account of his youth and previous good character & being aged parents with no children.

his
Thomas   **X**   O'Hearn
mark
her
Bridget   **X**   O'Hearn
mark

We the undersigned[4] testify to the good standing and well behavior of Mr. O'Hearn & Family and reccommend him to your clemency.[5]

LS(X), DNA-RG45, Subj. File N, Subsec., NO, Courts-Martial, Box 313, Michael O'Heron.

1. Probably either Thomas O'Hern, laborer, or Thomas O'Hearn, waiter, found in Boston directories (1864–66).

2. Michael O'Hearn (b. c1847), was court-martialed in July 1865. His parents' petition was recommended by Massachusetts Governor John A. Andrew, who called attention to the case as being "a hard one . . . commended to your favorable consideration."

Two other supporting letters accompanied Andrew's endorsement. Subj. File N, Subsec. NO, Courts-Martial, Box 313, Michael O'Heron, RG45, NA.

3. Irish-born Patrick O'Hearn (b. c1840), a mason, enrolled October 21, 1861, as a private and was killed at Deep Run, Va., August 16, 1864. CSR, RG94, NA.

4. Signatories were W. A. Blankenship, pastor; C. C. Loring; Reuben Y. Jenkins; Benjamin James; Alpheus M. Stetson; John S. H. Fogg, M.D.; Freeborne Adams, Jr.; Joseph H. Clinch, chaplain; Harrison Loring.

5. The President forwarded this letter on August 7 to the secretary of the navy directing that "the sentence in the within case will be so mitigated as to release from confinement and dishonorably discharge from the service—Michael O'Heron upon the expiration of his term of service—May 23d 1866." When it was referred to Johnson again in September, secretary Wright Rives returned the case with "The President declines to take any further action."

From Three McIntosh County, Georgia, Citizens

United States of America
State of Georgia.
August 2nd 1865.

To His Excellency Andrew Johnson
President of the United States.

The petition of Alexander McIntosh, John Cannon and John T. Wallace,[1] respectfully showeth, That they are and have been during all their lives, residents of the County of McIntosh in said State of Georgia, and that at the dates of the events hereinafter mentioned, were residing peacefully at their homes, obeying the laws of the United States, and fully recognizing their allegiance to the Government thereof. And your petitioners shew, that on or about the Ninth day of June, Eighteen hundred & Sixty five, Five negroes arived with muskets & guns, invested with no legal authority whatsoever & claiming none, came in a boat from Sapelo island, on the coast of Georgia, to the residence of one, M. C. Mints,[2] in the neighborhood of your petitioners homes, and demanded of the wife, of the said M. C. Mints, where her husband was, and on being told by her, that he was absent from home they the said negroes declared in a violent manner, that they would have him the said Mints, and another man, whose name they did not mention, dead or alive.

The said negroes then plundered the house of the said Mints, and proceeded with their booty towards their boat. And your petitioners further shew, that the said band of negroes had on divers occasions preceeding the one in question, plundered and harrassed the residents of McIntosh County, subjecting them to greivous insult and loss, and this they did with impunity, there being no troops of the United States, at any point, nearer than Darien, which was distant eighteen miles from the scene of this outrage whose protection the people could invoke. And your petitioners further shew, that they with other neighbors of the said Mints, assembled together and arming themselves pursued the said band of marauders and plunderers, in order to recover the stolen property and to arrest the negroes and hand them over to the authorities of the United States. And your petitioners further shew, that having overtaken the said negroes, they summoned said negroes to surrender themselves, but that the said negroes refusing to do so, fired upon your petitioners and those with them, who thereupon returned the fire, thereby killing three of the said negroes, *to wit*: Primus, Glascow and Jim. And your petitioners further shew, that they are to be tried therefor before a military Court, to be convened in McIntosh County aforesaid on the fifteenth of August instant.

And your petitioners shew, that they are true and loyal citizens of the United States, having taken the oath of allegiance thereto, before their arrest, that the Country is at peace and that not holding any position in the army or navy of the said United States or being connected thereto in any manner whatsoever, but being strictly civilians, that they are not subject to be tried under the Act of Congress specifying rules and regulations for the Government of the Army & Navy of the United States, and they humbly submit their claim to your Excellency, that the Sheild of the Constitution extends over them, and that they should be tried under the terms of said constitution, guaranteeing to every citizen the right of trial by Jury.

Wherefore your petitioners pray that your Excellency will take such action and pass such order as shall insure to them the right as vouchsafed by the organic law of the Country, and that they be detained in confinement or under bail, until a Civil Court be established competent to try them as aforesaid; and your petitioners will ever pray &c &c.[3]

Alexander McIntosh
John Cannon
Jno. T. Wallace

Pet, DNA-RG59, Misc. Lets., 1789–1906 (M179, Roll 227).

1. Alexander D. McIntosh (b. *c*1828), a wheelwright; John H. Cannon (b. *c*1842), a farmer; and possibly John Wallace (b. *c*1835), whom the 1850 Census listed as a "planter." 1850 Census, Ga., McIntosh, 22nd Dist., 413, 416; (1860), South Newport, 20, 27, and City of Darien, 4.

2. M. C. Mintz (b. *c*1825) was a North Carolina-born farmer. His wife Leonora (b. *c*1835) was a Georgia native. 1860 Census, Ga., McIntosh, 22nd Dist., South Newport, 23.

3. Despite this appeal, the petitioners were arraigned before a military commission on September 11, 1865. When the key witness repudiated his earlier testimony—which had implicated the trio in the shooting death of Jim Spaulding, a black man—the case was dismissed. Court-Martial Records, MM-3585, RG153, NA.

From John D. Ashmore

August 3, 1864[1865], Greenville C.H., S.C.; ALS, DNA-RG94, Amnesty Papers (M1003, Roll 44), S.C., John D. Ashmore.

Former congressman, who resigned his seat upon the secession of his state and subsequently for two years held an office in the Confederate post office, seeks pardon. "In Extenuation . . . he had ever been a Conservative Democrat" and as such "for many years had lived under the ban of the Charleston Mercury & State Politicians of the more violent School, as a 'Submissionist,' 'ally of the abolitionists of the North' & many other equally opprobrious Epithets." Resisting secession, he went along with it, "believing, that . . . a National Convention would be assembled to settle all questions at issue between the two Sections." He "opposed the inauguration of the war . . . & used his influence with the ruling authorities of the State not to commence it by the attack on Fort Sumter, but to no purpose." He accepted his civil office "to avoid conscription & forced military service" and refused to bear arms against the United States. "What he done after the contest began, he done in conformity to the laws then existing, & not from choice." [He was pardoned December 28, 1865.]

From William T. Moore[1]

Vicksburg August 3rd 1865

To His Excelency Andrew Johnson
President of the United States
Sir

At this time—at this place, there are wrongs perpetrated of which it is believed you are ignorant and ougt to be informed. It is at variance with your policy, your proclamation, and your believed views of justice, that acts such as are here perpetrated should be permitted.

The Military officials and Freemens Bureau have in their possession and continue to hold nearly half the property of this place. Our citizens have returned, have taken your amnesty oath, have in all things complied with the laws and constitution, and are still with-held their property upon pretences the most frivolous and sometimes contradictory. Without property or other means persons who have always been Union men, are left to wander about the streets like paupers and vagabonds, men respectable for their patriotism and character. It is naturally asked—what was the meaning of your amnesty proclamation? Was it made in good faith? Does it not give us our civil and political rights? These questions are asked. I am happy to inform you that the answer generally is that the President is ignorant of the condition of things here existing that the officials are corrupt, that they hold and rent the property for their own convenience and emoluments and account for little of the proceeds to the Government.

This is that you be informed of the facts, that knowing they may be remedied. Col Saml Thomas[2] is Chief of the Freedmens Bureau, holding much of its property, the remainder by the military. Your attention to the above will relieve many of your friends and fellow citizens.[3]

With this, I am
Your Obedient Servant
(S'd.) William T Moore

Copy, DNA-RG105, Records of the Commr., Lets. Recd. (M752, Roll 22).

1. Not identified. Col. Samuel Thomas' endorsement to General Howard on September 26, 1865, stated that "no such person now lives or ever has lived" in Vicksburg, and surmised that the President had been "imposed upon by some scoundrel." He added that he knew of "no honorable motive" for a citizen of the town to make such accusations "hiding his identity under an assumed name."

2. Thomas (1840–1903) had been brevetted a brigadier general for his recruitment of black troops and work with the freedmen in Mississippi during the war. In November 1866 he left the Bureau, subsequently amassing a substantial fortune through his successes in mining, smelting, railroads, steamships, and banking. *NCAB*, 25: 31–32.

3. Johnson forwarded this letter to Howard on August 15, 1865, endorsing it as an example of "many earnest remonstrances" received by him "against the further toleration of the gross abuses committed under the pretended sanction of law and the authority of the Government by its corrupt agents." The President directed that a "thorough investigation" be made "and all such abuses corrected as far as possible."

From Nathaniel B. Baker[1]

Clinton Iowa August 4th. 1865.

To His Excellency Andrew Johnson.
President of the United States of America
Washington D C.
Dear Sir.

Allow a citizen of Iowa, to Express his opinion to the Chief magistrate of the nation—that the pardoning power is being too freely exercised by him and—that the haste in reconstruction is not resulting in the greatest speed.

The suggestions may not be worthy of your consideration, but they come from your friend and well wisher.

With great respect I have the honor to be,
Truly Yours N B Baker

LS, DLC-JP.

1. Baker (1818–1876), former governor of New Hampshire, was adjutant general of Iowa from 1861 until his death. Johnson Brigham, *Iowa: Its History and Its Foremost Citizens* (3 vols., Chicago, 1915), 1: 322–26.

From Citizens of Louisiana[1]

New Orleans August 4th 1865.

To The Honorable Andrew Johnson
President of the U.S.

The undersigned, citizens of Louisiana, respectfully request your Excellency to pardon Thomas O. Moore,[2] who falls within the exceptions set forth in your Amnesty Proclamation.

Mr. Moore was Governor of this State from January 1860 to 1864. He is a plain planter, of great integrity of character, and thorough honesty of purpose. There can be no doubt that he was conscientious in his action in the inception of the late war, and believed he was carrying out the will of the majority of the people of the State, when he advised, and assisted in the secession of Louisiana.

If you are prompted to suggest that punishment should be visited on the authors of the war, and that ex-Governor Moore was one of the most conspicuous of them, we answer that individually and personally he is already punished to an extent more than sufficient to gratify those most clamorous for that policy. In 1861 he was worth over half a million of dollars. Now he is penniless. He has the land that constituted formerly two valuable plantations, but every house, and structure of every description that once beautified and utilized them, has been burned by the U.S. army. The whole of his property, with that exception, is swallowed—has been engulfed in the war, and from an income of a hundred thousand Dols. he is now reduced to no income whatever. The whole of his property was the fruit of a long life of toil.

He is now past sixty years of age. On the surrender of this Military Department, he apprehended that he would be arrested and imprisoned. Governors Vance of N.C. and Brown of Ga. and others, it was understood had been thus treated. Those best acquainted with his physical condition, and mental depression, advised him to leave the country *temporarily*, believing that confinement, under the apprehension of trial, would produce the worst effects on him. He is now, it is supposed, in Cuba. It is not too much to say that separation from his family is more intolerable to a man constituted like him, than to the most of those who have played conspicuous parts in the past four years. His sole occupation and his only joys are the cultivation of his fields, and the society of his wife, his only child, and his infant grandchildren.

The undersigned respectfully ask your Excellency to restore him to these enjoyments.[3] It will be a great boon to him, it will be an earnest, and the manifestation, of that wise policy of conciliation, by means of which your Excellency is attempting to heal the wounds of the country, in the further prosecution of which the undersigned humbly and ardently wish you God Speed!

Pet, DNA-RG94, Amnesty Papers (M1003, Roll 28), La., Thomas O. Moore.

1. This document was signed by eleven petitioners, including New Orleans attorney Christian Roselius.

2. Moore (1804–1876) was a sugar planter from Rapides Parish. As governor, he called the secession convention in 1861 and then removed the seat of government to Shreveport after the fall of New Orleans. Wakelyn, *BDC*.

3. Although by 1866 Moore had returned from Havana to Louisiana, he was not pardoned until January 15, 1867. Amnesty Papers (M1003, Roll 28), La., Thomas O. Moore, RG94, NA.

From John P. Kennedy[1]

Ellicotts Mills Maryland
August 4. 1865

My dear Sir

My brother, Mr. Anthony Kennedy,[2] is about to visit Washington, in the hope of being able to say a word to you in favor of either a temporary or a full release of Robt. M. T. Hunter.

Poor Hunter!—in addition to that constant misfortune of his which has hunted him through life—of always getting on the wrong side or into the wrong place—he has been pursued throughout this mad rebellion by a troop of personal afflictions which, however poignant to him, have brought tenfold anguish to his good wife[3]—one of the gentlest and most estimable of women. They have lost their eldest son during the war, and, very lately, a lovely daughter just grown to womanhood; and now, within a day or two, we have tidings of the death of the youngest boy by drowning. The mother, as you may imagine, is inconsolable, and, as we are told, dangerously ill.

Not knowing, my dear Mr. President, your purposes in regard to these prisoners, but having the most implicit confidence in your management of the public affairs, I feel great reluctance against taking up your time with even a suggestion that might look like advice. In this case, however, I am sure I am but speaking in accord with your own kind feelings when I beg you to take some early moment to determine the course to be pursued in reference to the gentleman in whose behalf I write, and to some others Standing in the same category, and, if you think the public interest will allow it, to grant him the privilege of at least visiting his family on parole.

I have much reason to believe that the administration will gain strength and influence towards the restoration of harmony and confidence in the Country by a prompt and judicious extension of the amnesty to Stephens, Hunter and Campbell[4] and some others in the South who have the reputation of being early penitents for the folly, if not the crime, of the Rebellion.[5]

With kindest regard and sincere good wishes for eminent success in your administration I am,

my dear Sir, Very truly yours
John P. Kennedy

The Hon. Andrew Johnson
President of the U.S.

ALS, DNA-RG94, Amnesty Papers (M1003, Roll 63), Va., R.M.T. Hunter.
1. Baltimore native and author, Kennedy (1795–1870) served as a Whig in Congress and afterwards as Fillmore's secretary of the navy. *DAB*.
2. Anthony Kennedy (1810–1892), lawyer and farmer, served in both the Virginia and Maryland legislatures before his election as a Unionist to the U.S. Senate (1857–63). *BDAC*.
3. Mary E. Dandridge (1817–1893) of Berkeley County, Va., whom Hunter married in 1836. Chisolm, "The Garnetts of Essex County and Their Homes," 259.
4. Alexander H. Stephens, John A. Campbell, and Hunter had been the Confederate commissioners to the Hampton Roads Peace Conference.
5. Mrs. Hunter also made a plea to Johnson; her husband received a parole in September. Henry H. Simms, *The Life of Robert M.T. Hunter* (Richmond, 1935), 206; Paroles of Sept. 6, Oct. 21, 1865, Ser. 3A, Johnson Papers, LC.

From Peter M. Dox[1]

Huntsville Ala. Aug. 5, 1865.

His Excellency Andrew Johnson Prest—

Many citizens wish to take the amnesty oath, but there is no officer military or civil in this District who feels authorized to administer it. If this state of things continues our vote will necessarily be a small one at the Election of Delegates on the 31st inst. Cannot Gen. Granger[2] be ordered by telegraph directly from the Secretary of war to administer the oath?

Respy—P. M. Dix[*sic*]

Tel, DNA-RG107, Tels. Recd., President, Vol. 4 (1865–66).
1. New York native and Huntsville lawyer, whose name the telegraphers apparently garbled in transmission, Dox (1813–1891) remained neutral during the war. He was a member of the 1865 state constitutional convention and later served in Congress as a Union Democrat. *BDAC*; Poore, *Political Register*, 374.
2. Robert S. Granger.

From Joseph E. Brown

Macon Ga Aug 7 1865.

His Ex Prest Johnson

I think it important that I have an interview with you about officers[1] here. If my health will permit I should like to start to Washn in about ten days. Please send me passport to this place by telegraph. No telegraph office at Milligeville.[2]

Jos E. Brown

Tel, DLC-JP.
1. In Brown's draft, dated July 30, this word is "affairs." Felix Hargrett Col., Joseph E. Brown Papers, University of Georgia.
2. Doubting that his earlier dispatch had ever reached the President, Brown while in Augusta on August 4 followed up with another wire requesting permission to visit Washington. Within two hours after receiving Brown's follow-up telegram on August 6, John-

son granted the ex-governor's request. Apparently Brown had not seen Johnson's authorization prior to transmitting his August 7 wire. Brown to Johnson, August 4, 1865, Tels. Recd., President, Vol. 4 (1865–66), RG107, NA; Johnson to Brown, August 6, 1865, Tels. Sent, President, Vol. 2 (1865), RG107, NA.

From William G. Brownlow

State of Tennessee, Executive Department,
Nashville, August 7 1865.

Hon Andrew Johnson President U.S.A.
Sir

The enclosed letter from Hon. Fielding Hurst[1] Judge of the 12" circuit of this state calls attention to one of the unfairest and most unjust results of the late war.

During the first years of the war, and in upper East Tennessee and West Tennessee during the *entire war* the property of loyal citizens was considered fair prey by the rebel military authorities and seized by them to the total impoverishment of the sufferers. Now it seems they have no remedy. The guilty thieves who took the property were perhaps unknown at the time or have left for parts unknown and a civil action is impossible. The Goverment, Judge Hurst informs us, and fact is known to be so, practically pays rebels for property taken from them by the national forces. Your Excellency's attention is respectfully called to this great injustice and the hope expressed that some relief may be had.

Very Respectfully, &c, W. G. Brownlow
Governor, &c.

LS, DLC-JP.
1. Hurst, a former Union colonel, complained that while "*Secesh*," whose property had been taken under federal authority, were collecting their claims, unionists had not been able to get compensation. Hurst to Brownlow, July 26, 1865, Johnson Papers, LC.

To William W. Holden

Executive Office, Washington, D.C.,
Aug't 7 1865.

To Governor W. W. Holden. Raleigh, N.C.

Your Proclamation[1] has just been read and is fully approved. It would have received earlier attention but for my indisposition. I would suggest the importance of organizing at the earliest practicable date.

Andrew Johnson President U.S.

Tel, DNA-RG107, Tels. Sent, President, Vol. 2 (1865).
1. A draft Holden had submitted for the President's endorsement. See Letter from Holden, July 24, 1865.

Order to Lafayette C. Baker

Executive Office, Washington, D.C.
August 7th, 1865

Brig. Gen. L. C. Baker, Special Provost Marshal, is directed to proceed, with the utmost dispatch, to Huntsville, Alabama, and seize, take possession of, and bring to Washington all correspondence, papers, and documents belonging to Clement C. Clay that may be found at that place or elsewhere in the Southern States. On arriving at Nashville, Genl. Baker will report to Major Genl. Thomas, commanding the military Division of the Tennessee, and submit to him, confidentially, this order. Genl. Thomas is directed to furnish to Genl. Baker all aid and assistance that he may require in the discharge of this duty, and also to give instructions to the Commanders of the Departments of Alabama and Georgia to aid Genl. Baker, and to render him such assistance as may be needed for the execution of this order. This order will be regarded as strictly confidential, and the utmost diligence will be employed to obtain possession of the correspondence, papers, and documents of the said Clay.[1]

Andrew Johnson

LBcopy, DLC-E. M. Stanton Papers.
1. Finding nothing at the Clay family home in Huntsville, Baker hurried to Macon, where he searched trunks belonging to Mrs. Clay. He retrieved what papers he could find but missed the notebook containing copies of Clay's Canadian dispatches. The next year Johnson ordered the release of Clay's real estate and personal property. Nuermberger, *Clays*, 271, 302–3; Johnson Order, Nov. 25, 1866, copy in Asst. Commr., Ala., Registered Lets. Recd., File E-9-1865, RG105, NA.

Order re *Interviews and Applications* [1]

Washington, August 7, 1865.

An impression seems to prevail that the interests of persons having business with the executive government require that they should have personal interviews with the President or heads of Departments. As this impression is believed to be entirely unfounded, it is expected that applications relating to such business will hereafter be made in writing to the head of that Department to which the business may have been assigned by law. Those applications will in their order be considered and disposed of by heads of Departments, subject to the approval of the President. This order is made necessary by the unusual numbers of persons visiting the seat of Government. It is impracticable to grant personal interviews to all of them, and desirable that there should be no invidious distinction in this respect. Similar business of persons who can not conveniently leave their homes must be neglected if the time of the executive officers here is engrossed by personal interviews with others.[2]

Andrew Johnson.

Richardson, *Messages*, 6: 348–49.

1. Because the only draft of this proposal that we have found is in Seward's hand, he is presumed to be its originator. See Misc. Lets., 1789–1906 (M179, Roll 227), RG59, NA.

2. Although reports that an "Executive Bureau" would be created appeared in the *Washington Chronicle*, August 24, 28, 1865, no evidence of Congressional appropriation for such an agency has been found.

From John P. Slough

August 7, 1865, Denver City, Colo. Terr.; ALS, DNA-RG59, Lets. of Appl. and Recomm., 1861–69 (M650, Roll 45), John P. Slough.

Army officer who, along with the Territorial delegate, had visited Johnson in June, urges removal of Colorado Governor John Evans, who is both unpopular and "a constant subject of ridicule," "for want of executive ability, yea, for imbecility." Slough claims that "The State movement here is induced principally by reason of the character of Federal officials here," i.e., "the want of an efficient Governor and Judiciary." Even if statehood is achieved, it will be some months before a government can be established. In the meantime he asks Johnson to appoint "some energetic man of tested executive ability" and "Remove Governor Evans." [Apparently Slough was unaware that Governor Evans, at Secretary Seward's request, had submitted his resignation on August 1. On October 31 Alexander Cummings became the next governor of the territory.]

From William H. Smith

August 7, 1865, Macon, Miss.; ALS, DNA-RG56, Misc. Div., Claims for Cotton and Captured and Abandoned Property.

As trustee of his "hopelessly deranged" wife, he asks Johnson "to interpose" in their behalf, so that they may keep the forty bales of cotton which he sold to the Confederate government in January 1864, "from the fear of its being burned by the troops of the Contending parties & for no other reason" and which the military authorities are demanding that he turn over to them. An "old line Henry Clay Whig," who did all he could to prevent secession, held no Confederate office and in no way supported the Confederacy, he petitions the President to save him from a "gloomy & cheerless" existence during "the few days allotted us yet to live." [Signing the endorsement, Johnson referred this letter to the secretary of the treasury, "whose special attention is called to the within."]

From Henry B.S. Williams [1]
Private.

Hickory Springs, Fayette Co' Tennessee.
Aug't 7th 1865.

Your Excellency, Andrew Johnson.
Pres'd't of the United States Washington City.

Urged by the warmest wishes for your personal happiness—sympathising sincerely (as every citizen should) with you, in the difficult duties, & heavy responsibilities apon you; & most heartily desiring the complete success of your administration,—*believing*, you will justly settle our troubles adjust the irregularities, & happily, restore the Goverment back to its peaceful operation, & constitutional vigor—to the lasting, & increased attachments of the people, I write to give you information, which may be of advantage to you.

It is, that you cannot *rely* upon, as friends, your *old party & political enimies*, who have, & are at work, gathering into their own hands, the whole power of the State—to the control of its *politics*, as well as policy—by holding closed the mouths of the people, & the sacred ballot-box, knowing full well, you are the favorite, & if allowed vent, the popular voice, would shake to pieces, the baseless fabric of their schemes of power.

I know, what I am talking about. The *old-line*-Whigs, or the *leaders*, are your bitter enimies—most determined, & implacable in their opposition; & will, so soon as their feet are firmly planted, raise the standard against your administration, & re election.

The organization is in progress; & dates to the election—*in teste*—*to the election* of Govnr. Brownlow, whom I implicate no further, than that, his official appointments are in confirmation of the fact. Most palpable preferences over true & capable *Union*-Democrats have told too plainly of this thing. There is a hatred to every thing, that is Democracy.

I have applied for nothing myself, but I keep myself on the watch, & speak what I know. The truth is, there are *Cliques* of these *old-liners*, thru' whose hands, all must pass. I know, it is so, in this, & Shelby counties, & believe, the arrangement extends all over the state.

Now, in support of what I say, let me give a few facts. Here is a resolution copied literally—which was *voted out* by a committee composed of a *majority* of these men—at a late public meeting in Somerville, called by themselves at which *Ex-Judge John C Humphreys* [2] presided; & who *appointed* the committee, at *the head* of which, was the Hon'ble Geo' W. Reeves, [3] *your own, appointee*, while acting Govnr.

3dly Resolved that we abidingly trust in the justice & magnimity of the Goverment; & with confidence not unmixed with pride of Tennesseeans, in the President of the United States, Andrew Johnson.

Your old fast friend Gen P B. Glenn[4] & our former representative (Democrat) Wm. Maris,[5] with your humble Svt. were of that committee. The said resolution bing voted out—it was of course, not reported to the meeting. So, you can judge for yourself, as to the *intention* & *direction* of things. I hate to disclose such matters, as it looks like telling tales out of School; but as I have no evil, or mischieveous intent, I satisfy myself, I have done nothing wrong.

Further, I must add the most striking of all the developments of the spirit of these men.

The low, dirty, & buffoonly letter of *Emmerson Etheridge*,[6] is bing made use of—doubtless to your prejudice. I mean the letter, lately addressed to you by the aforesaid *Emmerson*, at Columbus Ky. The country is flooded with it. The *Metropollitan*—the only paper that I have seen or heard—containing it—is mysteriously abroad—but I traced some of them to *these men*. Let me assure your honour, that, that letter meets with general disgust & contempt, as would the author, were he to come among us. He is no stranger here to these people. *The Pet* of Horace Greely in 1860, he clamors for *slavery* now, that Horaces' "battle has been fought & won". Run off by Secessionists, he returns to be *carried off* by Union-men. Poor *Ishmael*, supplanted in the hopes of the line of his father, Abraham, he wanders back to the Country of his mother—the land of the *slave*, to fulfil the promise "that he was to be a wildman; his hand against evry man, & evry mans' hand, against him."[7]

I would like to give you the state of the country, but as I shall be in Washington about the 1st proximo on my way to New Jersey with my children—to enter them to School, I will inflict no further lines upon you.

Our Condition & Situation are bad indeed. But, "*hope*—springs eternal in the human breast";[8] & our hearts beat yet trustingly in you. I know you would shed tears over our ruins. "Such tears as patriots shed, over dying laws."

I am truly your ob't Sv't

H.B.S. Williams

ALS, DLC-JP.

1. Williams (b. c1814) was an affluent Fayette County planter who ultimately moved to Memphis to practice law. In earlier correspondence with Johnson, Williams claimed that he had visited Johnson in Washington in 1860 to tell him that he was the "first choice" of the Tennessee delegation for the presidential nomination at the Charleston convention. 1860 Census, Tenn., Fayette, 7th Dist., 97; (1870), Shelby, 8th Dist., 43; Williams to Johnson, May 15, 1865, Johnson Papers, LC.

2. Humphreys (b. c1814) was a Fayette County lawyer and judge. 1860 Census, Tenn., Fayette, 1st Dist., 31; Goodspeed's *Fayette*, 802.

3. George W. Reeves.

4. Philip B. Glenn (b. c1813), Tipton County lawyer, served in the antebellum legislature. *BDTA*, 1: 289. See also *Johnson Papers*, 1: 427n.

5. Maris (c1819–fl1881) was a Fayette County farmer who had served in the legislature and later would become superintendent of public instruction (1873–81). *BDTA*, 1: 496.

6. See Letter from Etheridge, July 13, 1865.

7. Gen. 16:12.

8. Alexander Pope, *Essay on Man* (London, 1760), Epistle 1, line 95.

From Ella B. Washington [1]

Clairvaux
near Emmittsburg Frederick Co Md
August 8th [1865]

To His Excellency
The President of the U.S.

Having understood that Genl. Hancock [2] had prepared to forward to you the papers relative to transactions in regard to my property in Jefferson Co Va., permit me to ask your personal attention may be given them at the earliest time convenient.

Genl. Hancock expresses the opinion that no government Agent was authorised to make arrangements in regard to the property; as by referring to the affidavit of John Earnest [3] the present occupant (formerly Agent and manager for Mr. Washington) [4] it is proved that said property was never abandoned or unoccupied therefore the transaction was informal.

In my recent interview with you at the White House I was encouraged and cheered by your kind promise to see my husband and myself re instated in our rights, since he has obtained the Warrant of pardon under your hand and seal.

The delay caused by the necessary official investigation, has finally been concluded; and the papers forwarded with Genl. Hancocks recommendation that authority should be given Genl. Emory [5] (commanding in that district) to take military possession of the place and its belongings to be placed again in our hands. Allow me to beg that this may be *speedily* done; for I have been compelled to be a dependant on the family of my friends for so long, it has been a great trial and sorrow to me.

I have no foolish pride, but only the honest pride, of wishing to be independant once more in a home of my own, however poor or plain, only let it be mine.

Few can know the bitterness of being dependant on others, and though I know my future must be one of exertion and sacrifice, that will be new to one who has been shielded by luxury and affection from trouble or want.

I do not shrink from *any honest exertion*, but only wish to do my duty; and "act well my part," though sometimes it may be hard, I *long* to be at work, with a spirit to endure, and a heart for any fate.

Allow me to recall your promise to present me your carte de visite; and autograph.

I shall highly value the likeness, not only because it is the President, but that *the President is my friend.*

Respectfully &c Ella B. Washington

ALS, DLC-JP.

1. Ella Basset (d. 1898), wife of Lewis Washington, was mistress of "Beall Air," a plantation in Jefferson County, Va., which had been confiscated by treasury agent Maj. B. H. Morse. She became a Washington favorite during protracted attempts to recover her property and, as a pardon broker, found life in the capital city quite lucrative. James O. Hall, ed., "An Army of Devils: The Diary of Ella Washington," *CWTI*, 16 (Feb., 1978): 18–25; WPA, *West Virginia: A Guide to the Mountain State* (n.p., 1941), 314; L. C. Baker, *History of the Secret Service* (Philadelphia, 1867), 606.

2. On August 31 Thomas T. Eckert, acting assistant secretary of war, sent to Johnson the papers "referred by your order on the 12th of June last to Maj. Genl. [Winfield S.] Hancock for investigation and recommendation." Lets. Sent, Mil. Bks., Executive, 56-C, RG107, NA.

3. Earnest (b. *c*1801) was a Virginia-born blacksmith. 1860 Census, Va., Jefferson, Halltown, 118.

4. Lewis W. Washington (b. *c*1814), a prosperous farmer on the eve of the war, had been pardoned July 17, 1865, by order of the President. Ibid.; *House Ex. Docs.*, 40 Cong., 2 Sess., No. 16, p. 99 (Ser. 1330).

5. William H. Emory (1811–1887), who served mainly in the eastern campaigns during the Civil War, was commanding the Department of West Virginia in 1865. Warner, *Blue.*

From Montgomery Blair

Washn. Aug 9, 1865

My dear Mr. President

I recommend the pardon of Dr Reddell whose papers I transmit herewith.[1] I believe he was a true union man & did only what the mass of our union people at the South did & were justified in doing by the course of the Govt. under Buchanan & even for a long time after Lincoln was inaugurated. Mr. Chase the secy of the Treasury openly advocated letting the South go.[2] Mr. Seward advised the Surrender of Fort Sumpter & indeed agreed with the Rebel commr. to surrender it.[3] Genl. Scott advised that Fort Pickens should be given up also.[4] [erasure] No call was made [erasure] for troops to defend the country for more than 6 weeks after Lincoln was inaugurated altho the Rebels were seizing our forts & had a great army organized & threatened to take Washington itself. Is it surprising that citizens in the Southern States should submit to this rebellion under circumstances which gave them evry reason to believe that the Govt. did not mean to resist it? I confess that I was of that opinion myself, expected Fort Sumpter to be Surrendered, & had prepared my resignation to be handed in in that event at the Cabinet meeting at which the President decided contrary to the opinions of all the other members of the Cabinet[5] as he himself has publicly declared not to Surrender that Fort. Naturally enough the class of men who were then most yielding to the rebellion are now most savage on the rebels. I hope sir that you will not yield to their [illegible]. It is the offspring of their former subserving & cowardice. A brave man yourself you can not be vindictive. Do not allow yourself to be persuaded any good can result from adding to the miseries of our people. They have suffered & been deeply humiliated & they deserved to be. But the Union has triumphed & I can not see the wisdom or humanity of aggravating the misfortunes of any of these people & especially of that class of them to which Dr. Reddell belonged whose feelings were with the union but who were compelled to submit to the Rebellion by the failure of the Genl. Govt. to assert its authority.

I feel bound to speak for these men because I plead for them from the first. I urged active & energetic actions upon this Administration to encourage them to stand out. I felt in common with our whole people that we were wanting in our duty & foresaw that the neglect of the administration to assert the national authority was consolidating the South & evoking a terrible war. Excuses may be argued for this failure which others may deem sufficient to exculpate our authorities. I shall not contest their sufficiency here. It is enough for my present purpose that the failure existed. The result in consolidating the South was inevitable & no man of union proclivities at the South can therefore rightfully be punished for yeilding submission for the time to the rebellion.

I am Sir very respect fully your obt svt

M Blair

ALS draft, DLC-F. P. Blair Family Papers.

1. John Leonard Riddell (1807–1865), chemistry professor, botanist, and inventor, was U.S. postmaster at New Orleans who briefly served the Confederacy. Pardoned August 14, he died within two months. This letter is not in Riddell's amnesty file, which includes copies of May 1861 Riddell-Blair correspondence regarding the Confederate postal takeover and Riddell's July 5, 1865, letter to Blair asking for a recommendation. *DAB*; Amnesty Papers (M1003, Roll 29), La., John Leonard Riddell, RG94, NA.

2. Early in 1861 Chase thought that "it would be better to allow the seven States which had formed the so-called Confederate Government to try the experiment of a separate existence, rather than incur the evils of a bloody war and a vast debt." By the end of March, however, he had come to support Lincoln's decision to hold Fort Sumter regardless of the consequences. Jacob W. Schuckers, *The Life and Public Services of Salmon Portland Chase* (New York, 1874), 380; Chase to Lincoln, March 29, 1861, Lincoln Papers, LC.

3. Seward advocated that the federal government abandon Sumter while reinforcing Fort Pickens in Florida, and a trio of Confederate commissioners (in Washington to negotiate a peaceful settlement) were made aware of the secretary's preference. Van Deusen, *Seward*, 277–79.

4. In late March 1861, Scott recommended that the government evacuate both Pickens and Sumter, a position rejected out of hand. Charles W. Elliott, *Winfield Scott: The Soldier and the Man* (New York, 1937), 703–4.

5. Although Blair had prepared a letter of resignation, his recollection of the March cabinet meetings is somewhat self-serving. Francis P. Blair, Sr., later reported that Lincoln had told him that only Montgomery favored holding on to Sumter, but an exami-

nation of the written opinions submitted by cabinet members on March 29 reveals that Chase, Gideon Welles, and Simon Cameron also supported Lincoln. William E. Smith, *The Francis Preston Blair Family in Politics* (2 vols., New York, 1933), 2: 9; Richard N. Current, *Lincoln and the First Shot* (New York, 1963), 65–68.

From Walter A. Burleigh[1]
(Special)

Washington August 9th 1865.

To the President;

As I am unable to see you personally, before leaving to attend the Pennsylvania State Convention,[2] to be held at Harrisburgh, on the 17th inst. I desire to call your attention to the following.

As one of your friends and supporters, and as the chosen Representative of your political friends in Dakota, I desire to know if you will recognize the right of our Citizens to be heard in the selection of the Federal Officers to fill the various positions in our Territory; or whether the right to make these appointments from *his own personal friends*, is by your authority, vested in any member of your Cabinet.

I feel confident, that this course is now being pursued, by at least one member of your Cabinet, (who claims the right to do so,) to an extent, that is very unjust to your friends, and can not fail to rob your administration, of much of its legitimate political strength.

Much depends upon the solution of this question, whether the friends of your Administration shall fill the Federal Offices of the Country, and thereby give you the benefit of the political power which necessarily attaches to them; or the personal friends of individuals, through which appointments, if permitted to be made, the elements of your own political strength will be diverted to the purpose of building up those whose official positions are held at your will and pleasure.

While we are perfectly willing to do all in our power to support your Administration, we are not willing to pledge our support to any Member of your Cabinet who differs materially with you, upon the great questions now before the Country;—or who is willing to sacrifice your interests and friends in our Territory, and elsewhere, for the sake of his own interest, and his own personal friends, who do not, and never have lived with our people.

I most respectfully ask, that no more appointments be made for Dakota Territory, until your friends there, can be heard from.[3]

I am Sir, as ever, Your true Friend,

W A Burleigh.

Delegate to Congress from Dakota Ty.

LS, DLC-JP.

1. Burleigh (1820–1896), Pennsylvania resident, had been Indian agent in the Dakota Territory (1861–65) when elected as a delegate to Congress (1865–69) from that territory. *BDAC*.

2. The National Union party convention, which met to nominate candidates for state office, passed resolutions commending Johnson's actions, but declared that the final decision regarding Reconstruction should be handled by Congress. *Philadelphia Evening Bulletin*, Aug. 18, 1865.

3. Although Burleigh complains here, he ultimately became the patronage dispenser for Dakota Territory. Herbert S. Schell, *History of South Dakota* (Lincoln, Neb., 1975), 106.

From Richard Busteed[1]

Huntsville, Ala. August 9th 1865

To the President Of the United States,

My dear sir

I have been here now some four or five days, in company with Mr Smith[2] the U S. Dist. Attorney. Today I appointed a clerk (recommended by Col. Jos. C. Bradley & Mr Smith) of the district Court for this district, and also a U.S. Commissioner,[3] so as to afford greater facilities in taking the amnesty oath &c.

It gives me great pleasure to state that the best people in Huntsville profess great desire to rehabilitate Alabama at once in the vestments of the Constitution and the Laws; and almost without exception of note, I find their confidence in yourself and your administration to be ungrudging and sincere.

Very great difficulties of a practical character are arising out of the laws of Congress of July 2 1862 (prescribing an additional oath) and January /65 (in respect to the oath to be taken by Attorneys, &c practising in the Federal Courts.)[4] These difficulties I cannot explain, or suggest cures for, by letter, but I hope to see you this winter in Washington.

Accompanying this is an original Amnesty oath taken by Judge D. C. Humphreys[5] of this place, who, you may recollect, was spoken of for Provisional Governor. I find Mr Humphreys to be a highly respected and influential Citizen. Some days ago the Judge enclosed to the Secretary of State, an application for pardon under the 13th Section of your proclamation of 29th May 1865 hoping in this way, to get it to your early notice. He has since ascertained that Mr Seward is absent from Washington, and, in my opinion, it is desirable that his case should meet prompt attention, as it is thought best, by loyal men here, he should go as Delegate to the Convention of the 10th of September. I am also of the opinion, from what I have learned on the spot, that your Excellency will be conferring Executive clemency upon a deserving man, in favorably considering his application and I beg to add to it my own recommendation.

I am with esteem, Your Obedient Servant Richard Busteed
U.S. District Judge for Alabama.

ALS, DLC-JP.

1. Busteed (1822–1898), an Irish-born New York lawyer, was a brigadier in the Union army at the time of his resignation in March 1863. Appointed U.S. District judge of Alabama in 1864, he arrived in the state the following year. After an attempted impeachment for bribery, brought by disgruntled Alabamians, failed in 1867, he remained on the bench, but resigned seven years later to return to New York City. Owen, *History of Ala.*, 3: 272; Wiggins, *Scalawag in Ala.*, 90.

2. James Q. Smith.

3. The positions of clerk and commissioner were held by John H. King, before whom oaths were being executed in 1865. He is probably the John H. King (c1841–1866) who had been a clerk in Huntsville before the war. 1860 Census, Ala., Madison, Huntsville, 37; Dorothy S. Johnson, *Cemeteries of Madison County, Alabama* (2 vols., Huntsville, 1978), 2: 276; Joseph C. Bradley et al. to Johnson, Nov. 30, 1865, Court-Martial Records, M1326, RG153, NA.

4. The January 24, 1865, act added attorneys practicing in federal courts to the provisions of the July 2, 1862, act, which prescribed a loyalty oath for federal officeholders. However, the loyalty oath was similar to the amnesty oath of Lincoln's proclamation of December 8, 1863, as modified by Johnson's of May 29, and the two were used interchangeably by some authorities. Hyman, *Oath*, 158–59, 173n.

5. David C. Humphreys, whose oath subscribed on this day was enclosed.

From Perrin H. Cardwell[1]

Knoxville Tenn. August 9th 1865.

To His Excellency Andrew Johnson
President of the United States of America.

Your petitioner humble complaining showeth unto Your Excellency, that on the 16 day of June 1865 at a public sale held at Knoxville Tenn under decree of the Chancery Court for the   Dist of Tenn to satisfy an attachment levied by a loyal creditor for debts made before the war, he purchased a house and lot known as the "Boyd House"[2] and for the consideration of $4100.00—lawfull and good title was vested in him by the Chancery court. (A certificate of purchase is enclosed and marked "A.") Your petitioner went to the house so purchased to take possession but found it occupied by one or more persons employed as Clerks in the Quarter masters Dept at this place, who refused to deliver it to him. An application to Capt Colburn[3] A QMstr, who employes the Clerks referred to, and also one to Major Genl. Stoneman, Comdg Dept of Tenn, was of no avail. Your petitioner is advised that the Government owns at this place several buildings (erected during the war for sundry purposes but owing to the establishment of peace rendered useless for the purpose first intended) that might be assigned as Quarters for Govt. employees.

Petitioner would farther state that he now occupies together with a large family—a house rented only for a specified term and as the time has expired, a suit of detainer is now entered against him in the courts of this place, which renders him liable to heavy damages. Owing to the crowded condition of this town houses for rent are very scarce and he has not been able to find a building so as to return the one, which he now occupies contrary to law, to its proper owner.

In view of these facts, justice not being rendered by the military authorities, and as no appeal from the Department Commander lies to any person, within the knowledge of your petitioner, excepting your Excellency, these statements are respectfully laid before you for such action as may be deemed just & proper.

Your petitioner has always been a loyal citizen and earnest supporter of the United States of America.[4]

Your petitioner will always pray &c &c

P. H. Cardwell.

Pet, DNA-RG107, Lets. Recd., EB12 President 2406 1/2 (1865).

1. Cardwell (c1819–c1883) was a Knoxville dentist. Knoxville directories (1859–85); 1860 Census, Tenn., Knox, 1st Dist., 101.

2. Located at the corner of Church and State streets, the home of Samuel B. Boyd (b. c1806), Knoxville merchant dealing in "Staple and Fancy Dry Goods," was ordered sold at the January term of the court in the case of R. M. Bruce and others v. Samuel B. Boyd. On August 8 Knox County clerk David A. Deadrick certified "Doctor" Cardwell's purchase. Ibid., 73; Knoxville Whig and Rebel Ventilator, June 7, 1865.

3. Webster J. Colburn (1840–1918) was breveted major in the artillery of the Army of the Cumberland when assigned at Knoxville in July 1865. In November he went to Memphis as chief quartermaster, where he resigned the following year. In 1867 he settled in Chattanooga, where he established an insurance company. Chattanooga Times, Dec. 14, 1918.

4. With Johnson's intercession, "the within named property was turned over to P. H. Cardwell on Wednesday, September 13th 1865." Endorsements: Johnson to Stoneman, Sept. 8; W. A. Wainwright to Stoneman, Sept. 16, 1865, Lets. Recd., EB12 President 2406 1/2 (1865), RG107, NA.

From William W. Holden

August 9, 1865, Raleigh, N.C.; ALS, DNA-RG94, Amnesty Papers (M1003, Roll 39), N.C., John A. Gilmer.

Although the governor believes it "will go on the shelf for the present," he forwards the pardon application of Confederate congressman John A. Gilmer. The latter had once been "ultra right" but "went far astray under the Vance despotism." Now "much depressed" and "sincerely penitent," he still enjoys strong popular support, "especially among the old line Whigs." Holden bows to the "great" pressure exerted by them, but recommends that this petition be held in abeyance, as well as that of Vance and William A. Graham. Before a final resolution of these and others which he has asked to be suspended, he requests that they all be returned to him for review. "These suspensions are having an excellent effect in enabling us to reorganize the government, and I expect during the next month or two to add considerably to the list." [Gilmer was pardoned October 14, 1865.]

From Horace Maynard
Unofficial

Knoxville August 9, 1865—

Dr Sir—

The election-lottery is over & I have drawn the elephant.[1] My majority over Gen. Cooper[2] the next man will be nearly four thousand. In the upper district I hear that Taylor[3] is elected, & below, Stokes, Col. Cooper & Campbell.[4] The others I do not know. You may rely, I think, upon the support of three, possibly four of those elected, & possibly more than that number.

The question now is of admission to their seats. Will any opposition be made? Or will the election be silently accepted & the state allowed quietly to resume her old place?

The election in this part of the state so far as I observed, & so far as I can hear, passed off quietly; the voters were duly registered & the law executed in good faith. I speak alone of our part of the state. How it was in middle & West Tennessee I cannot say. The telegraphic report is that Etheridge[5] is elected, whether legally or not I cannot say.

A good many resignations occurred in the Legislature at the close of the Session.[6] These places have been filled at the late election, & I suspect by a class of men who may give a different complexion to that body, especially so in Middle & West Tennessee.

There is apparent among the people a feeling of great satisfaction that the old-time machinery of elections has been restored to them. They accept it as an indication that the rebellion is over & peace restored to our Land.

I am very Respectfully your obt. Servt.

Horace Maynard

His Excy, The President,

ALS, DLC-JP.

1. A reference to his election to Congress. "To draw an elephant" means to succeed at a difficult task; having lost the senatorial election in April, Maynard must have especially welcomed victory in August. Mathews, *Americanisms*, 1: 550.

2. Joseph A. Cooper.

3. Defeated for the U.S. Senate by Johnson's son-in-law Patterson, Nathaniel G. Taylor was elected to Congress.

4. William B. Stokes, Edmund Cooper, and William B. Campbell.

5. Isaac R. Hawkins, nominated after Emerson Etheridge's arrest, was elected. Alexander, *Reconstruction*, 88–89.

6. There were six resignations from the house and four from the senate, as well as vacancies in two seats which were never filled. White, *Messages of Govs.*, 5: 432–36.

From Samuel T. Bond

August 10, 1865, Edenton, N.C.; ALS, DLC-JP.

A justice of the peace for Chowan County, enclosing a petition for relief from the town's citizens, reports that Governor Holden, although willing, "is unable to do anything for us." Bond complains that "when the Union element is trying to produce in the minds of the people the necessity of respecting the Union, and the Union of the States, and to love the flag of our fathers as they once loved it . . . the Troops we have among us insult our Citizens, tear down our houses, and we fear will produce an insurrection among our people." He requests that the President "lay this matter before the Secretary of War, with such advice as you may feel disposed to give in the premises."

From John Bratton

August 10, 1865, Winnsboro, S.C.; ALS, DNA-RG94, Amnesty Papers (M1003, Roll 44), S.C., John Bratton.

Former Confederate brigadier, who "fought for the right of secession as the keystone to the Citadel of republicanism," having laid down his arms and submitted to the Union forces, conceives "it to be the duty of each and all . . . to give faithful and cordial support to the Authorities that be" in reconstructing the Union. [He was pardoned September 22, 1865.]

To Salmon P. Chase

Executive Office, Washington, D.C.
August 10th 1865.

Chief Justice Chase,
Providence R.I.

I would be pleased to have a conference with you in reference to the time place and manner of trial of Jefferson Davis, at your earliest convenience.[1]

Andrew Johnson.
President U.S.

Tel, DNA-RG107, Tels. Sent, President, Vol. 2 (1865).
1. Chase replied by telegraph two days later, fixing his arrival at Washington on the 17th. Three days after the meeting, he told Charles Sumner that Johnson "was less cordial than before I went South." The President wished to discuss trying Jefferson Davis for treason, but Chase demurred and wrote Sumner that "this did not seem to me a proper subject of conference between the President and chief justice," leaving Johnson to make "some general observations . . . about the necessity of doing something in the matter soon." Chase to Johnson, Aug. 12, 1865, Tels. Recd., President, Vol. 4 (1865–66), RG107, NA; Chase to Sumner, Aug. 20, 1865, Chase Papers, LC.

Mother and Son: Eliza and Robert Johnson
Courtesy Margaret Johnson Patterson Bartlett

From William W. Holden

State of North Carolina, Executive Department,
Raleigh N.C., August 10th, 1865.
His Excellency The President of the United States.
Sir.

I most respectfully forward for your consideration, the Petition of the Mayor and other citizens of the town of Wilmington.[1]

I am well acquainted with the signers, and know them to be reliable and influential men, and among the best citizens of the state. I know that any statement made by them can be fully relied on, and from abundant information derived from other sources, I am sure that their troubles are not too strongly stated.

I am glad to be able to add, that the citizens of Wilmington, once furious secessionists, are now quiet and orderly. I believe they are truly loyal to the National Government, and may confidently be relied on as such.

I know no difference between National Troops, whether white or black, but existing facts compel me to state, that the presence of Colored Troops, in Wilmington and other places, has greatly increased the jealousy and unkind feeling, between the white and colored citizens.

If these troops could be removed to the forts, or kept entirely away from the towns, it would greatly add to the quiet and content of both the white and the black inhabitants.

I most respectfully desire your Excellency's kind consideration of this matter, and sincerely desire that such relief may be given to the Petitioners as your judgment approves.

I am Most Respectfully
Your Obedient Servant.
W. W. Holden.

LS, DLC-JP.
1. See Petition from Wilmington Officials, August 1865.

From Cave Johnson

August 10, 1865, Clarksville, Tenn.; ALS, DNA-RG94, Amnesty Papers (M1003, Roll 49), Tenn., Cave Johnson.

Postmaster general under Polk, a unionist until the state's secession who, although he had "acquiesced in the course adopted . . . at no time took any part in the war" and had taken the non combatant's oath of allegiance in 1863, seeks special pardon. Although considering that the Constitution was the "best ever adopted by man & the Union created by it as the next in point of importance" to it, he nonetheless believed that "the interests of both sections . . . would have been best promoted by a separation & an alliance upon firm principles which would have given both sections the advantage of Union agt. foreign nations & the freedom of trade between the States." [Pardoned August 19, 1865.]

From Absalom A. Kyle[1]

Nashville, Tenn., 10th Augt 1865

Andrew Johnson Prest. of the United States
My Dear Sir,

I left home[2] on friday last, reached this place, Sabbath evening & on Monday, commenced *a search for Banks* under the Commission You so generously gave me; but up to the present, have found no B'k that will submit to Supervision.

The Union & Planters Banks, say they have made an assignment & claim exemption.[3]

The Free Banks, deny my right, to supervise & say my predecessors have never examined them. I can find no officers of the State Bank, & of course can make no examination.

I shall go from here to Memphis in a few days in search of other Banks; in a word, will do all in my power, to comply, with the official requirements of the law, but am fearful that my labors, will be of but little service to the State.[4]

Allow me to say, that I am peculiarly gratified, with the almost universal satisfaction your administration is giving, not only to the strictly loyal, but to all parties & shades of party.

I am afraid you & all of us, still have much trouble ahead of us, in the great work of reorganizing the States, in restoring them to life & a Republican form of Govt. We have troublesome neighbors North of us, who ought *now*, to content themselves, & let us shape matters to suit ourselves. The great trouble, seems to be, to fix the status of the Negro. I would say, let him bide his time, & as soon as may be give him a country of *his own* & let him go to it; this I think, will be for the good of both races. I dont think the negro, can ever be greatly elevated whilst mixed up with our race & hence he ought to desire a home & a country elsewhere. How would Mexico do for them? But I fear I am boring you.

My Son Hugh,[5] in his 16th year, now at school in Burlington N. Jersey, will visit you this month. 'Tis vacation with him & desires a little recreation.

You will see from the papers, how our Tenn' elections have gone. Things are quieting down, in E Tenn.

I would be much pleased to receive a letter from you, at any time.

I am, your friend A. A. Kyle

ALS, DLC-JP.

1. Rogersville attorney whom Johnson had appointed as supervisor of state banks and would name on August 15 as one of Tennessee's tax commissioners. William A. Browning to Kyle, Aug. 15, 1865, Ser. 3A, Johnson Papers, LC.

2. Kyle practiced law in Knoxville at this time.
3. Union and Planters banks had placed their assets in the hands of a receiver. "Report of Supervisor of Banks," *Tenn. Senate Journal, 1865–66, Appendix.*
4. In his undated report to the legislature in the fall of 1865, Kyle detailed his difficulties, including the refusal of all state banks (except Memphis Commercial) to allow him to examine their books. Ibid.
5. Hugh G. Kyle (1849–1927) graduated from Princeton in 1870, practiced law in Rogersville, and served as chancellor, second division. William S. Speer, *Sketches of Prominent Tennesseans* (Nashville, 1888), 433; *Who's Who in Tennessee* (Memphis, 1911), 498; Genealogical file, Kyle family, McClung Collection, Lawson McGhee Library, Knoxville.

From Benjamin F. Perry

Greenville S C August 10th 1865

His Excellency President Johnson
Mr President

When I had the honor of taking leave of you two weeks since you were kind enough to ask me to write you occasionally, & let you know how I was getting on in organizing a Provisional Goverment in South Carolina.

I take the liberty of enclosing to you a speech which I made, on my return home,[1] in order to prevent having to report so often the very pleasant interview I had with you & your cabinet.

I find the people very anxious to take the oath prescribed in your Proclamation & return once more to their allegiance to the Federal Goverment. The State Constitution will be changed as you desired when the Convention meets 13th September.

The only dissatisfaction is on account of colored troops garrisoning the country villages & towns. It is very desirous that white garrisons should be substituted for them as the black troops are a great nuisance & do great mischief amongst the Freed men.

I hear too that the Military authorities in South Carolina are displeased at my Proclamation appointing civil officers in the State.[2] They think that I have transcended my authority. But the Governors of Mississippi, Alabama & North Carolina have made similar appointments. My object was to get the state back in the Union or under the laws of the United States as soon as possible.

I think I may assure your Excellency that South Carolina will be the very first State in rebellion, to resume her position in the Union, & rally around your administration. From having been the most rebellious she will become the most loyal.

Truly & sincerely yours B. F. Perry

ALS, DLC-JP.
1. The enclosure could not be found in the Johnson Papers. Perry had several interviews with Johnson, beginning July 19, before returning to South Carolina at the end of the month. On August 1 he addressed a crowd in Greenville, detailing his visits with

Johnson; this speech was undoubtedly represented in the missing enclosure. Kibler, *Perry*, 385–89, 392–93.

2. On July 20 Perry issued a proclamation setting September 4 as the date for the election of delegates to a constitutional convention and restoring all state officeholders to their posts if they had subscribed to Johnson's amnesty oath. Simkins and Woody, *South Carolina*, 34–35.

From James L. Pugh

[ca. August 10, 1865, Montgomery, Ala.]; ALS, DNA-RG94, Amnesty Papers (M1003, Roll 9), Ala., James L. Pugh.

Former U.S. and Confederate congressman, who "regarded the institution of slavery as the great conservator of free government, and as indispensable to the continued growth and prosperity of the southern states" and "considered the right of secession clear, its exercise necessary and the remedy peaceful," now accepts the result of war and applies for pardon. Explaining that he owned "about sixty slaves only about twenty of whom were producers," who "remained with me during the war and labored faithfully . . . while neighboring plantations were abandoned by the slaves and stript of mules," he concludes that "I expect my former slaves to remain with me next year if I am allowed to keep what I have to employ and support them." [He was pardoned September 30, 1865.]

From John Rice

129- South 7th Street
Philadelphia August 10th 1865.

His Excellency Andrew Johnson
President U.S.A.
Dear Sir.

At the request of General Mussey,[1] I have purchased for you from Wood Brothers, New York, a carriage including slip linings and Stable cover, for the sum of $1550—(the original price was $2000.) and have ordered them to ship it, by the most convenient and safe route, and requested them to transmit Bill of lading &c direct to you.[2]

Messrs Beckhaus & Allgaier, to whom you gave the order to build a carriage, claim that they will be damaged at least $100—by countermanding the Order. As the price of the one bought in New York is as much below the price they ask, you will loose nothing by the transaction.[3]

Hopeing it will please you, and the use of it assist in relieving the cares of your official duties—

I remain Your Obedient Servt.
John Rice

LS, DLC-JP.

1. See Letter from John Rice, July 28, 1865; see also Mussey to Rice, July 29, 1865, Ser. 3A, Johnson Papers, LC.

2. Two weeks later, Johnson sent a check to Charles B. and Frederick R. Wood, New

York City carriage makers, for the coach at its discounted price. Johnson to Wood Brothers, Aug. 24, 1865, Ser. 3A, Johnson Papers, LC.

3. The President chose to honor his prior arrangements with Philadelphia carriage makers Joseph Beckhaus (c1812–fl1889) and John Allgaier (c1823–c1884) and therefore to forward them a $1,700 check in October 1865 for an ornate coach. 1870 Census, Pa., Philadelphia, Philadelphia, 18th Ward, 33; (1860), S.W. Div., 18th Ward, 38; Philadelphia directories (1857–90); Johnson to Beckhaus and Allgaier, Oct. 26, 1865, Ser. 3A, Johnson Papers, LC; *Cincinnati Gazette*, Oct. 27, 1865.

To Matthew Simpson

Executive Office, Washington, D.C.,
August 10 1865.

To Reverend Mr. Simpson,
Bishop of Methodist Episcopal Church Philadelphia

I have been waiting sometime for reply in reference to the McKendree Church at Nashville. The delay has already been too great.[1]

Andrew Johnson President U.S.

Tel, DNA-RG107, Tels. Sent, President, Vol. 2 (1865).

1. In response, Simpson, the Methodist bishop in charge of overseeing the southern churches, wired from Philadelphia: "Tried to see you three times but failed. Delayed to & from Nashville. Will conform to your wishes." Simpson to Johnson, Aug. 16, 1865, Johnson Papers, LC.

From J. Watson Webb[1]

Legation of the United States
Petropolis [Brazil], August 10th 1865.[2]

To His Excellency The President.

Although an Employee of the Government, it does not in my judgement, exempt me from the performance of evy duty, which as a Citizen, I owe to my Country. From the age of Seventeen, I have been in Public life. At Eighteen I was in command of a separate Post on Lake Huron; and after leaving the army, thirty four years of practical Public life, as Editor of the Courier & Enquirer, has at least given me the advantages of experiance.

I need not tell President *Johnson*, that as Editor of the Courier & Enquirer, I was always in open hostility to abolitionism, and the avowed advocate of the South in support of the Institution of Slavery, to the full extent that the Constitution protected and supported it.[3] I was however, always opposed to the *extension* of Slavery into the Free Territory of the Union; and when in defense of the right to extend their Institution, the South Rebelled, I advocated the Proclamation to emancipate the Slave, in order to save the Constitution, and the union it was intended to preserve.

See my Despatch on this subject in 1862.[4]

But the Union has been saved, and Slavery has been legitimately and constitutionally abolished, *to save the Union*. And now comes the question of Reconstruction. Upon this question there must of necessity, be very great diversity of opinion; and he is indeed a bold man, who has no doubts even in regard to his own judgement in the Premises. On the President devolves the responsibility of *acting*; and he is entitled to the suggestions of all who have reflected upon the subject, and whose experience may possibly, enable them to perceive all the difficulties of the crisis which is upon us.

In presuming therefore, to offer the following suggestions, I am entitled to be exonerated from the sin of *presumption*; and most assuredly, my *motives* cannot be misapprehended.

In the first place, then, I would deprecate all hasty action. *Time*, in such a contingency, is frequently the best teacher; & renders clear what in the present, is obscure.

First, therefore, I would recommend for adoption, a course, which in itself, secures *time* for reflection and justifies the avoidance of hasty action. However clear to the mind of the President, may be the course, he deems it wise to adopt, the postponement of immediate action, if there be good cause for it, will not render his course less clear.

In my poor judgement, Re-construction to be permanent, and to yield the fruits we all desire, must be based on *Universal* suffrage, and the absolute equality of *all* before the Law. I have all my life, opposed *un-restricted* suffrage; and I shall die in hostility to it. But the *basis* of Republican Institutions, is, and of right should be, *Universal suffrage*. Hence we of New York and other Northern States, and the soundest writers on Republicanism, recognise the fact, that in electing members of a convention *to frame* a Government, evy man to be governed, of legal age, whether alien, Negro, or Indian, is of right, entitled to vote for the members of such convention. Apply this rule to the Rebel States. Let the Negro vote for the members of the Convention; Exclude from voting the late Rebel; and take care that the parties elected, will permit no distinction in color before the Law. Make all equal under the Constitutions to be adopted; but at the same time, take care to provide in the constitution itself, that no person shall be permitted to vote, who cannot *read* and *write*. This of course will exclude a majority of the Negro & the "poor white"; but it would be *just*. Such a restriction on suffrage, having its origin in the presumed intelligence of the People, so directly addresses itself to the *pride* & self-respect of all, that tens of thousands who now demand *unrestricted* suffrage, would cheerfully acquiesce in it.

To me this appears one mode, and under the admitted Power of the Executive, an easy one, to arrive at a satisfactory result. And yet I think there is a still better one; which, it is true, would require more *time* but as I have heretofore said, the more *time* that can be with justice and propriety consumed in the settlement of this vexed question, the better will it be settled.

In the course of its settlement, the basis of representation must be altered; and that requires a *change* in the constitution. Such change is a matter of necessity, now that the Negro is free. Why not therefore, as the saying is, "Kill two Birds with one stone?" I propose therefore, to take from the states the right of fixing the qualifications of voters by altering the first and third Paragraphs of the 2d section of the 1st article of the Constitution as follows.

Article 1

"*Section 2.* (to read) The House of Representatives shall be composed of members chosen evy second year by the People of the several states; and all male citizens of the respective States, Indians not paying Taxes excepted, of the age of twenty one years and upwards, who can read and write, and who have not forfeited their right to vote by reason of crime perpetrated against any State or the United States, shall be deemed Electors and qualified to exercise the right of suffrage for Representatives, and for all offices made elective by this constitution or the Laws of the United States, or the Constitutions and Laws of the several states; and no state shall have authority to extend or restrict the qualifications for Electors herein provided for. All native born persons, and all aliens who have been naturalized under the Laws of Congress, and none others, are hereby declared to be Citizens of the United States."

(*Leave paragraph 2 untouched; the 3d Para. to be changed thus.*)

"3 Representatives shall be aportioned among the Several States, which may be included within this Union, according to their respective numbers, excluding Indians not taxed; and the actual enumeration in all states within which the Institution of Slavery was tolerated in 1861, shall be made without any unnecessary delay, and as at present, in all the states of the Union, within evy term of ten years, as Congress shall by Law direct."

1st. These slight changes of very few words in the 1st & 3rd paragraphs of the 2nd Section Art. 1. of the Constitution, would secure forever, to the People of all the States, universal suffrage, restricted only by the necessary and popular qualification of a certain amount of *intelligence.*

2nd. They would place all men on an equality before the Law.

3rd. They would define Citizenship, and guard against any further Dred Scott decisions.

4th. They would fix forever the basis of Representation, and get rid of the three fifth anomaly.

5th. They would deprive the States of the possibility of making persons, Citizens of a State who are *not* Citizens of the United States.

6th. They would get rid of the stumbling block in the way of direct Taxation.

Are, or are not, these changes very desirable under the existing state of things? Would they not make Smooth the path of the President in his great and arduous task of Reconstruction?

Could they be carried?

I have but little doubt that they could. Most assuredly, the Governmnt *can* carry them through Congress by the necessary 2/3rd vote; and very probably, through the necessary State Legislatures.

But suppose you fail. What then? The Executive will legitimately have gained all the *time* he desires, to watch over, ponder upon, and finally determine, the greatest question which has evr been submitted to the judgement & determination of the Chief Magistrate of any civilized Country in ancient or modern days. And because it will secure to President *Johnson* this necessary *time*, with the approval of the people, and for a legitimate purpose, I transmit these hastily written, but maturely considered reflections, without even permitting them to be copied.[5] If worthy of consideration they will doubtless be considered; while if deemed unworthy of a second thought, they will promptly find their way into the Waste-Basket. I have only to claim your indulgence Mr. President, in thus discharging a very humble duty; not doubting from my knowledge of your character, but you will appreciate my *motive* in writing; and at the same time, believe me with profound respect & admiration

Yours Very faithfully J. Watson Webb.

P.S. I need not say, that this letter is written in the full conviction, that a large and rapidly increasing servile & disfranchised Race in our midst, would be dangerous to our country. The only possible remedy for such an evil and its legitimate consequences, is to grant the *Negro* equal suffrage with the *Whites*. This in my judgement, is not a matter of choice or a temporary political expedient, in regard to which Statesmen may consult their feelings or indulge their tastes and prejudices; but a very grave and imperative *necessity*. Its justice therefore, need not be discussed, because of its necessity to the future safety and well-being of the Republic. &. &.

To His Excellency Andrew Johnson
President of the United States. &c. &c. &c.

Webb.

ALS, DLC-JP.

1. Webb (1802–1884), New York newspaperman and diplomat. Shifting from Democratic to Whig ranks in the 1830s, he became a Republican in the 1850s and was rewarded with the post of minister to Brazil (1861–69). James L. Crouthamel, *James Watson Webb: A Biography* (Middletown, Conn., 1969).

2. This letter, enclosed in William H. Seward to Johnson, November 2, 1865, probably arrived by diplomatic pouch. According to Webb's note dated May 20, 1867, on a copy found in the Benjamin Wade Papers, LC, this letter was written "*within sixty days*

after hearing of the fate of Lincoln; and after reading Mr. *Johnson*'s declaration that *Treason* was to be made *odious*, by *punishing* it as a heinous and disgraceful *crime*."

3. This sentence was omitted in the Wade Papers version.

4. Despatch No. 24, Webb to William H. Seward, Sept. 22, 1862, in Despatches from U.S. Ministers to Brazil, 1809–1906 (M121, Roll 30), RG59, NA.

5. In addition to the copy to Wade, a draft is found in the Webb Papers, Yale University Library.

From William G. Wyly

Shreveport La Aug 10th/65

Mr. President:

I returned thus far a few days since and am en route to my home at Floyd Carroll Parish Louisiana.

In New Orleans I saw Gov Wells & told him you remarked to me that Mr. Covode had been making unfavorable reports of his administration.[1]

I saw a great many loyal men in New Orleans who had come there from different parishes of this state.

I have met & conversed with a great many here & on the River, and from all the information I can get Gov. Wells is giving the greatest satisfaction.

The bone & sinew of the country who opposed this war, have the greatest confidence in Gov. Wells & will elect him to the same office, although he has not announced himself as a candidate.

There was a large majority in Louisiana who opposed this fight & particularly in the country parishes.

New Orleans was the hot-bed of secession, & the intrigues of John Slidell & J P Benjamin forced the state out by fraudulent voters, over the wishes of the majority of honest voters.[2]

I learn that a memorial has been gotten up by the Radical party in New Orleans,[3] composed chiefly of transient persons, the negro element and desperate political tricksters, to have Gov Wells removed & Genl Banks or Genl Butler appointed in his stead.

It was always very easy in New Orleans to get a few thousand persons to endorse any proposition, however absurd.

William Walker & Lopez[4] could always get wreckless floaters about New Orleans to join in their fillibustering schemes.

But how many memorialist did the Radicals get from the honest loyal voters of the country? How many who were loyal voters in 1861?

We have understood the policy of your Excellency to be, to let the large conservative element who opposed the war, take up the government which had been overthrown in this state by the Rebels.

That voters must be legal voters according to the laws in 1861, and must take the amnesty of your Excellency.

We who have been uniformly loyal in Louisiana, have suffered already too much by the "*fire eaters*" and it would now be too unhappy for us to be placed under the administration of Radical adventurers from the North.

Southern extremist have bankrupted & thrown the union men of this country into the same ruins as themselves, and it would now be deplorable to fall into the hands of northern extremist.

No doubt Gov. Wells has filled some of the offices from the Rebel army, but they were persons conscripted & forced there & such as received the amnesty from your Excellency. Gov. Sharkey of Missi has filled the county offices with the old officers as a general thing—& gov. Wells has done likewise. The county Records were in charge of those persons & they had taken the amnesty & were most servicable in restoring order to society.

The feeling of the people is becoming strong for the old flag & the present administration.

They are delighted with your appointments & also the policy you have adopted for the restoration of our state to its proper relations with the Federal Government. I have had a long interview with Judge Weems,[5] the Dist Judge here & other leading citizens, & they will hold a large mass meeting here next Friday endorsing the Administration of Your excellency & approving the appointment of Gov. Wells.

All the country will sustain Wells & the policy of states rights which you have adopted on the suffrage question.

Gov. Wells told me he had sent a suggestion of John Ray[6] for the office of United States Judge for Western District of Louisiana—the office being vacant, & he not knowing that I had filed my application for that appointment & you had been kind enough to endorse the same.[7]

Mr Ray lives in the Ouchita & had not solicited the office, nor does the governor know that he would accept it, but no one applying for it the Governor said he thought it ought to be filled & that Ray was a good man & therefore he sent forward his name.

There will be no contest between Ray & myself for the office—the Governor will probably write you withdrawing the name of Mr. Ray & urging my appointment as early as it suits your convenience.

I showed you the highest endorsement from Gov. Wells, Genl Sheridan & others, but when I left N.O. I did not expect to apply for office. I have the honor to be very Respectfully yrs

W G Wyly

ALS, DLC-JP.
    1. See Letter from Wells, July 3, 1865, and Letter from Cottman, July 20, 1865.
    2. John Slidell and Judah P. Benjamin, Louisiana's senators, had wired the secession convention, assembled January 23, 1861, to support immediate secession, an action subsequently endorsed by that body, 73–47. Because the ordinance was never submitted to a popular vote, unionists then and after the war frequently maintained that the public will had been subverted. Willie M. Caskey, *Secession and Restoration of Louisiana* (University, La., 1938), 29–41 passim.

3. Actually two memorials circulated, a conservative one in favor of Wells, and a radical one supporting the appointment of a military governor, with the abolition of civil government. Lowry, "Wells," 1045.

4. Walker (1824–1860), Tennessee-born adventurer who twice established a dictatorship in Nicaragua in the 1850s, only to face a firing squad; and Gen. Narcisso Lopez (c1798–1851), a Venezuelan who, before he was captured and shot in Havana, had attempted to subjugate Cuba and annex the country, with the help of an expeditionary force of southerners. *DAB*; *Webster's Biographical Dictionary*, 917, 1536.

5. James I. Weems (b. c1800), Shreveport lawyer, had been appointed judge of the 10th judicial district in June. 1860 Census, La., Caddo, Shreveport, 85; *New Orleans Picayune*, June 24, 1865.

6. Ray (1816–1888), Missouri-born unionist, practiced law in Monroe, La., served in the state legislature, was elected to the U.S. House in 1865, and subsequently to the Senate (1873) but was not seated either time. *Appleton's Cyclopaedia*.

7. See Letter from Wyly, July 15, 1865.

From William A. Austin[1]

Stevenson Ala. August 11th 1865

To his Exelcy Andrew Johnson
Sir

I beg leave to call your attention to the slip Inclosed cut from the Huntsville Advocate from which you will see that every person that takes your Amnesty Oath of May last has to pay a fee of $1.10/100 to enable them to vote for Delegates the 31st Int to the Convention at Montgomery.[2] I can assure you there is hundreds of Families in this County that has not One Dollars worth of Meat in their House for their Families to subsist on, and no Money to buy with, and if each voter has to pay $1.10/100 for the privilege to get to vote I can assure you their will be a verry small vote given in the state. A large portion of the people of North Alabama is Loyal to the united states and wishes to carry out the views of the Goverment and I am in hopes you will immediately have this order revoked at[and] let every poor loyal citizen take the Oath without charge and vote.[3]

I am verry Respectfully, Wm. A. Austin

ALS, DNA-RG60, Office of Atty. Gen., Lets. Recd., President.

1. Austin (1812–1875), Alabama unionist who had served in the antebellum state senate, was recently appointed a commissioner for administering the oath. Tombstone Inscription, Austin Family Cemetery, Jackson Co., Ala.; Garrett, *Reminiscences*, 753; *Montgomery Advertiser*, Aug. 22, 1865.

2. Reference to the forthcoming September constitutional convention.

3. His letter, forwarded by Mussey on order of the President, was apparently filed.

From Joseph A.L. Lee[1]

Muscogee County Georgia [ca. August 11, 1865][2]

To his Excellency Andrew Johnson
President of the United States

The petition of Joseph A L Lee of said State and County respectfully sheweth— That he is now in his fifty seventh year—that he has resided in said State and County twenty nine years—that he has been engaged in planting for fifteen years. In Politics he was a whig having supported and voted for Harrison Clay Taylor Scott Fillmore & Bell. He was violently opposed to Secession using every argument at his command against that heresy—and never gave his adhesion to the heresy of Secession until the appearance of President Lincolns proclamation (if I recollect right) of December 1863—declaring the negroes free and ruining me in all my property of every kind and nature—leaving me no place to escape but to go with the Rebellion.

Your petitioner had a large family consisting of a wife and seven children (five daughters and two sons). His Estate consisted of Land & Slaves was all situated in said State and County (in the very heart of the Rebellion). The Confederacy had laws confiscating disloyal subjects property. Your petitioner was between two Governments—the one at that time could not protect the loyal citizen or his property, the other had the power to strip him of every thing for disloyalty. Interest if not inclination drove him in to the support of the Confederacy. He has paid to that Confederacy all tythes and taxes that were required of him— and said many things in favor of the Confederacy to other citizens after that time.

Your Petitioner has never been under arrest? No proceedings have been instituted against him under the Confiscation act? He has had nothing to do with vigilance committees? He has never taken up arms during the Rebellion? He has endeavoured to be a quiet good citizen.

The act that he asks pardon for so as to enable him to become a citizen of the United States comes under exception Number one (1) of your Excellency proclamation of Amnesty & Pardon and consists in this.

Sometime during the year 1863 your Petitioner met with the Honl. E. G. Cabaniss[3] (an old friend) who had been appointed State Tax Collector for the Confederacy. He asked your petitioner who had been an old Tax Collector in Muscogee County. Your petitioner told him John W Edwards[4] had been such an officer for the State some years before. In a short time he appointed Mr Edwards Confederate Tax Collector for said County or rather for District No 41. Mr Edwards commenced the discharge of the duties of said office and in a short time afterwards it was reported to the State Collector that Edwards had commenced drinking and gamboling and had squandered a considerable amount of money. Judge Cabaniss immediately wrote to your petitioner requesting him to at once take charge of the office the papers and money and to endeavour to save him Judge Cabaniss and the Confederacy from loss. Edwards' Securities four of my neighbours also begged me to take hold of the matter and to save them from ruin. So to accomodate all the parties interested I took hold of it with the express understanding that I was to be relieved as soon as I accomplished the settlement with Edwards. This occurred in November 1863. About that time the Georgia Legislature was in session and they passed an act by which all persons between the ages of 16 and 60 were placed in the Malitia of the State. At that time Gov. Brown was very belligerent. He was for war—War not only against the United States but against Jeff Davis—the Confederacy and I believe the ballance of mankind. Being averse to taking up arms against any power and especially in favor of Joseph E Brown I discharged the duties of the office as a protection from serving in the State Malitia until the 15 of April 1865 when I packed up papers money and every thing belonging to the Confederacy in my hands and sent them to the Honl. E. G. Cabaniss by Express.

It is proper that your petitioner should say that he never received or held a commission from the Southern Confederacy.

It is also proper that your petitioner should add that he has always been a supporter of the constitution of the United States that he desires alway to do so that he has been heretofore a peaceful citizen that he hopes to remain so throughout life.

And your petitioner now prays your Honer to grant him a pardon for the offence as herein stated and as in duty bound your Petitioner will ever pray &c.[5]

J. A. L. Lee.
Pro Pers[?]

Pet, DNA-RG94, Amnesty Papers (M1003, Roll 20), Ga., Joseph A.L. Lee.

1. Lee (b. c1813), a planter and antebellum legislator, returned to the legislature in 1870. 1850 Census, Ga., Muscogee, Columbus, 591; (1860), 10th Dist., 79; Avery, *Georgia*, 251, 436, 506.

2. The petition was witnessed on this date.

3. Elbridge G. Cabiniss (1802–1872), Macon attorney, was clerk and judge of the Superior Court, a member of the legislature and the secession convention, and a congressman-elect (1865), who was not seated. During the war he was the Confederate tax collector for Georgia, for which he was pardoned on October 6, 1865. Avery, *Georgia*, 108; Northen, *Men in Ga.*, 3: 65; *NCAB*, 2: 137.

4. Edwards (b. c1815) was a farmer. 1850 Census, Ga., Muscogee, Upatoie Dist., 726; (1860), 10th Dist., 78.

5. Recommended by Governor Johnson, Lee was pardoned on September 16, 1865. *House Ex. Docs.*, 40 Cong., 2 Sess., No. 16, p. 127 (Ser. 1330).

From J. Madison Wells

August 11, 1865, New Orleans, La.; LS, DNA-RG56, Appts., Customs Service, Surveyor, New Orleans, A. T. Stone.

Wells demands removal of James Tucker, surveyor of the port of New Orleans and a northerner who "does not affiliate with the people here, and is diametrically opposd to the policy of the Administration." He recommends the appointment of native Louisianian Andrew T. Stone, "a young gentleman of great ability and rapidly rising in political importance," who "suffered much pecuniarily and otherwise" during the war. [On August 20, Johnson ordered Treasury Secretary McCulloch to make the appointment, which Stone held only briefly before resigning.]

From Pierre G.T. Beauregard

New Orleans La. August 12th 1865

To his Excellency President Andrew Johnson.
Washington, D.C.
Sir,

I have the honor to enclose you herewith, copies of two letters of the 8th ulto.,[1] addressed respectively to the Hon. Edwin M. Stanton Secy. of War & Maj. Genl. W. T. Sherman, relative to the seizure of my private baggage & papers near Athens-Geo.[2]—about the beginning of May last, in direct violation of the Military Convention entered into April 26th 1865, near Durham-Station N.C. between Genls. Sherman & Johnston.

Article IV of said convention & article V of the Supplemental terms thereto—read as follows:

IV. The side arms of officers & their private horses & baggage to be retained by them.
V. The horses & other private property of Officers & men to be retained by them.

The baggage & property seized had been sent by me to Macon, Geo. for safe Keeping, several months preceding their capture—which was made within the limits of Genl. Sherman's Command *after* the date of said Military Convention.

Having awaited in vain over one month for an answer from the Hon. Secy. of War & from Genl. Sherman—I have the honor now to appeal to your Excellency, to have restored to me the property referred to.

Feeling no longer protected by the terms of that Military Agreement, which have been thus violated once with impunity & which may be again violated likewise by the same party—I have the honor to ask for authority to leave the United States, for the purpose of transferring my home to some other Country.

Your Exys. (Signed)

Will your Excellency return under cover the letter of Genrl. Sherman accompanied by your Excellecies answer to Genrl. Beauregards letter, addressed to

Mrs. Octavia W. LeVert[3] 5th Avenue Hotel New York

Copy, NHi-Andrew Johnson Papers.
1. Not found.
2. Beauregard's papers, along with those of other prominent Confederates, were seized by federal authorities and transported to Washington to be examined for evidence, in the event treason charges were initiated. Beauregard had interviews with both Johnson and Grant. His baggage and books were subsequently returned to him. T. Harry Williams, *P.G.T. Beauregard: Napoleon in Gray* (Baton Rouge, 1955), 259; E. D. Townsend to E. L. Molineaux, June 15, 1865, Lets. Sent (Main Ser.), Vol. 40 (M565, Roll 27), RG94, NA.
3. LeVert (1811–1877), sometime author and social leader of Mobile, had moved to New York City in 1865 because of animosity toward her for entertaining Yankee officers. James, *Notable American Women*, 2: 394–95.

From Joseph P. Everitt

August 12, 1865, Hickory Flats, Va.; ALS, DNA-RG94, Amnesty Papers (M1003, Roll 60), Va., J. P. Everitt.

Trusting that Johnson is the "same accessible man you was many years ago, when I lived in Kingsport Ten, and saw you often," a Confederate postmaster applies for pardon. Appointed before the war, he refused to report to Confederate authorities and, when ordered to do so in the summer of 1862, fled north with his son. Returning before the war ended to see his family, Everitt was arrested and tried for disloyalty. To escape punishment, he took an oath of loyalty to the Confederacy and reopened the post office under their authority. He assures the President that "I did all in my power to prevent the secession of the state—have always defended the Union cause, when it was safe to do so—have never given aid or comfort to the rebellion—have never given a vote in the confederacy." [Everitt was pardoned September 11, 1865.]

From Robert H. Glass[1]

"Republican Office,"
Lynchburg, Virginia.
[ca. August 12, 1865][2]

To His Excellency And. Johnson, Prt. U.S.
Sir

I have reason to believe that from some cause or other,[3] your mind is prejudiced against me & my paper, the "*Republican*" & though I well know your time & attention are crowded with great public affairs I hope nevertheless, you will hear me a few words to relieve myself from any unjust & unfounded imputations prejudicial to my interests.

I am a frank man & shall state frankly my position past & present. When the military took possession of this city, I applyed in person to Major Gen Gregg,[4] commanding, to know what liberties would be allowed the Press. He told me that if I had taken the amnesty oath, no restrictions were upon me, except to conform to the existing state of things, & that I was at liberty to discuss all general politics as theretofore. I have labored zealously to comply with this demand, nor has Gen. Gregg had the slightest occasion to intimate to me that I was not. I have advised the people to accept the results of the war as a finality, to take & obey the amnesty oath, to recognize all laws & proclamations concerning slavery, & to respect all requirements of the military, whether harsh or mild, just or unjust. I have refused to publish several articles from the New York News, handed me by enthusiastic friends, & I refused to publish a series of letters addressed to yourself by Major James Garland[5] of this city, & recently published in another city paper, not because I dissented from their general views, but simply because I could see no good to come of such discussions now. In short, I have been a law abiding editor, & have advised everybody to be a law abiding citizen. Not a word have I uttered in favor of disloyalty, or against the Union, or against the goverment or its agents.

As to my feelings towards you personally & politically, I leave you to infer from the two articles enclosed, one of which appeared early in June last.[6] For 15 years preceding the war, I was a warm supporter of yourself in all your Tennessee campaigns, as my columns will show. We split only on the question of Secession. I was a Douglas democrat in the Baltimore Convention, refused to enter the Breckridge Convention but voted for the latter, & when Lincoln was selected & secession became a fixed fact I went for it, believing it to be right & the only mode of making peace between the sections.

As to myself *personally*, I desire to say that the information communicated to you by some malicious person, that I was a party to the indignity offered your person in this city in 1861, is infamously false, & a complete refutation of it I have just forwarded to the Attorney Generals office, Washington.[7] I was not here, knew nothing in the world of it, & united with all good citizens in condeming it. There is not a person in the world who knows me, that would suspect me of being guilty of any improper conduct knowingly.

With this statement of facts, I hope it will be your pleasure to grant me the pardon which I have asked, & that I will be permitted to earn a support for myself & family by the Press which I conduct, & which is all I have left me of my earthly goods. And you may rest assured that, though I can never be as hypocritical & cycophantic as some editors who were ranting secessionists before the surrender of Lee, I will not be the less peacable or useful citizen.[8]

I have the honor to be Very respectfully
Your obet sert R. H. Glass.

LS, DNA-RG94, Amnesty Papers (M1003, Roll 61), Va., Robert H. Glass.
1. Glass (1822–1896), proprietor of the *Lynchburg Republican*, had served as both U.S. and Confederate postmaster for the city and briefly as a staff officer for Gen.

John B. Floyd. Tyler, *Va. Biography*, 5: 619; Amnesty Papers (M1003, Roll 61), Va., Robert H. Glass, RG94, NA.

2. Glass's undated document is marked "Filed August 12, 1865."

3. Glass's pardon application had been approved on June 26, but was "suspended before delivery" after Johnson received an unsigned letter marked "private." The inform-ant not only alleged that Glass and his accomplices (the Hardwickes) had incited a Lynchburg mob to threaten and attack Senator Johnson while he was enroute to Greene-ville in the spring of 1861, but also claimed that a series of "inflamatory and denunciatory articles" criticizing Governor Peirpoint had recently appeared in Glass's *Republican*, an "original secessionist paper." Glass to Johnson, June 20, 1865; Anonymous to Johnson, June 30, 1865, Amnesty Papers (M1003, Roll 61), Va., Robert H. Glass, RG94, NA. See also Letter from William C. Ballagh, October 3, 1864, *Johnson Papers*, 7: 206–7; Edwin T. Hardison, "In the Toils of War: Andrew Johnson and the Federal Occupation of Tennessee, 1862–1865" (Ph.D. dissertation, University of Tennessee, Knoxville, 1981), 49.

4. Bvt. Maj. Gen. John I. Gregg (1826–1892), a former ironworker and Mexican War veteran, commanded a Pennsylvania cavalry brigade at Lynchburg from April to August 1865. Afterwards he served briefly as "inspector-general of freedmen" in Loui-siana. Powell, *Army List*, 342; Dyer, *Compendium*, 1566; *Appleton's Cyclopaedia*.

5. Garland (1791–1885), a former Democratic congressman (1835–41), was more recently commonwealth attorney for Lynchburg and corporation court judge. His seven articles, which appeared in the *Daily Virginian* in scattered issues during the summer of 1865, upheld states' rights and secession, lambasted Lincoln's Emancipation Proclama-tion, test oaths, and Radical Republicans, and strongly urged Johnson to restore to south-erners their constitutional rights. *BDAC*; *Lynchburg Daily Virginian*, July 7, 1865.

6. Not found.

7. His "refutation" consisted of at least two letters, and a petition signed by thirteen Lynchburg residents, vindicating Glass on both counts. Glass to C. L. Mosby, July 20, 1865, H. J. Cox to Johnson, July 27, 1865, Amnesty Papers (M1003, Roll 61), Va., Robert H. Glass, RG94, NA.

8. About a month later, after learning that his appeal had been found "unsatisfactory," Glass vowed to explain the whole matter "to President Johnson himself," which he did shortly, but with no apparent success. Glass to M. F. Pleasants, Sept. 18, 1865, Glass to Johnson, Sept. 20, 1865, ibid.

From Louisiana Citizens [1]

New Orleans, Aug. 12, 1865.

To Andrew Johnson,
President of the United States:

Sir:

The undersigned, loyal citizens of the State of Louisiana, would re-spectfully represent, that they are proprietors of plantations; that since the occupation of the State by the National troops, they have willingly complied with all the orders regarding the working of plantations, and management of colored laborers, which the Government deemed it nec-essary to prescribe.

That in compliance with military orders, they cultivated their places, in many cases at a loss, and in some instances at great loss. In pursuance of the same orders, they kept one-quarter of their cane for seed, when their individual interest would have led them to grind the whole, to save all they could. They also promptly paid the freedmen the wages demanded by the Government.

For the proof of these allegations, they confidently appeal to Chaplain Conway,[2] Assistant Superintendent of Freedmen for this State.

The undersigned are men of comparatively small means. They undertook planting to improve their condition and that of their families, by their energy and industry. They purchased plantations and slaves, investing all their means in making the cash payment of one-fifth, one-quarter or more of the value of the property, giving obligations, with mortgage on the land and slaves, payable in one to ten years, as the case might be; becoming, as it were, the agents or overseers of the sellers, until the property was fully paid for; the title, in fact, remaining in the holders of the mortgages.

Again: they purchased slaves from slave dealers, who made it a business to bring them from other States, and took in payment part cash and part notes, bearing mortgage on the slaves, and in many cases on the real estate of the purchaser. These obligations they sold at a heavy discount, to go on and renew the same transactions, making large fortunes from the profits of the trade, always repugnant, however, to the feelings of the community.

The failure of the guarantee contained in those sales, (all contain the guarantee that the slaves are slaves for life,) should, it is true, be legally sufficient to defeat the enforcement of these claims, under the present state of things; but lawyers and judges are proverbially attached to old customs and usages, and their opinions are divided on the question; many can not or will not see that the freeing of the slaves was only a legal exercise of powers always recognized, and often exercised by the States themselves, and also vested in Congress, by a change provided in the Constitution itself; and that therefore the sellers, if they wished to protect themselves from such a possibility, should have provided against it in their acts of sale, instead of giving a full guarantee. They considered the danger so slight, that they deemed it useless to mention it, well knowing that it would have greatly diminished the value of the object sold. They guaranteed—ran the risk, it seemed so small. What seemed small has become of the greatest importance; that is their misfortune; they ran the risk, they made the gain, they must now abide the consequences. This seems very clear, and is certainly very just; but neither judges nor lawyers can be depended upon in deciding such cases, arising under and through a power many of them only recognize under compulsion and against their prejudices.

The evidence of the truth of this proposition is, that the largest number of cases now pending before the several Courts here are for the foreclosure of mortgages, or the collection of debts of which slaves were the consideration, in whole or in part. The holders press them to collection, fearing that they will not be permitted to continue to collect them and nullify the Proclamations of the President and laws of Congress they have sworn to observe and obey.

The undersigned respectfully submit, that in allowing writs of seizure to issue on account of such mortgages and debts, the Courts virtually recognize a right to that kind of property, in fact, ignore the proclamations and laws of Congress declaring slaves free and no longer property. These proclamations and laws have swept the property upon which the mortgages were predicated, and when seizure of real estate is made by the Courts to satisfy mortgages in whole or in part on slave property, the Courts certainly recognize slavery.

If the payment of these obligations, so unjustly pressed, is enforced, the interest on which alone, since the war, is a severe loss, the undersigned, the working men of the South, the poor men, who work for the capitalists, who really own the soil; the men who are carrying out loyally the views of the Government, who pay the taxes, raise crops, and who alone can bring back prosperity to the country, will be scattered and destroyed, reduced to bankruptcy and ruin.

To benefit a class, which has generally stood aloof from the Government, the rich and the usurers, the men so well described by you, Mr. President, in your answer to the Richmond delegation, as those who brought on the war, to satisfy their desire for power, for an aristocracy; and who now seek, through old laws, and old codes, to strip the working men of their property, sell them out, become the owners of numerous plantations, of vast tracts of country, and succeed, by their money, in becoming what they sought by the war, the aristocracy of the land, the lords of the soil.

These men have already been benefitted by the cash payments they received, and from the subsequent instalments which have been paid; they form but a small portion of the people; should circumstances compel them now to submit to a loss, they would still realize large sums from what they have already received; they would scarcely feel it, but as a comparatively slight inconvenience.

Deprived of their slaves by the action of the Government, the undersigned bow to its decree, but respectfully submit, that the same result should extend to all claims by which that kind of property is recognized, so that the man who had a mortgage covering such property, and who is in fact the owner under the old code, should be at a loss at least to the extent of his unpaid claim, just as well as the other; that he should not be permitted to use the judicial branch of the Government to enforce payment for what the executive branch has destroyed, a proposition, the statement of which shows its injustice. And that, as in case of gambling, or usury, or of any other claim founded against law, all obligations having slaves for a basis, in whole or in part, shall be declared void, so far at least as the payment of the slaves is concerned; that the like consequences shall apply in whatever hands the obligations may be found, the present holders before purchasing them, having certainly examined the mortgages upon which they were predicated and being well aware of the character of the security.

The undersigned respectfully ask that the President may give them such relief as in his wisdom he may deem most appropriate. They beg to suggest that orders might be issued to Provisional Governors, and Military Commanders, requesting them to see that justice should be done where obligations of this character, predicated on a system now abolished, are sought to be enforced by the present tribunals, who owe their own existence to the powers which destroyed the property. That Conventions and Legislatures be advised and directed to place in their new constitutions and laws such clauses as will prevent results so disastrous to the working and loyal community, to the general prosperity of the country, and so much at variance with the presidential proclamations and laws.

The undersigned would further respectfully represent, that the organization of all the Courts in Louisiana is now complete: there are regular Circuit and District Courts of the United States; regular State, District and Supreme Courts. But there is in addition a United States Provisional Court for the State of Louisiana, consisting of one Judge, the Honorable Chas. A Peabody.[3] Whatever might have been the legality or necessity of such a tribunal before the organization of the regular United States and civil Courts is not now necessary to discuss.

That Court exercises criminal and civil jurisdiction in all cases, for all amounts, and over every portion of the State, and decides in the last resort, without appeal.

The Judge himself is a gentleman of unimpeached character and integrity, but is a common law lawyer, whilst the system of law here is, under the civil law, a grave difference.

The undersigned respectfully submit, whether it is Republican, whether it is just and proper under any form of government that any one human being should exercise such uncontrolled powers over the lives and fortunes of the people of a whole State, or any portion of them. It seems repugnant to every feeling of a free or even reasonable being, and they, the undersigned, think it is only necessary to call your attention to the subject to have a prompt remedy applied, and to have a Court, for which there is no possible use, abolished.

It is now only the means of enriching lawyers, and a source of vexation and trouble, dragging citizens in a summary manner from the most distant parts of the State to attend its sessions, in cases wherein, under the State laws, trial by a jury of vicinity is secured by law.

Relying on your well known desire to protect and guide loyal men, all over the country, to return to their former state of happiness and prosperity, the undersigned hope and trust you will extend your powerful and protecting hand over them and the people of the State, who are willing and desirous to return to the folds of our common country, and once more share and enjoy its fortunes and glory.[4]

PLS, DNA-RG107, Lets. Recd., EB12 President 3006 (1865).

1. This petition was signed by 45 people, several of whom gave their residence as Mississippi.

2. Conway had forwarded a letter ten days earlier to Maj. Wickham Hoffman, assistant adjutant general of the Department of Louisiana and Texas, protesting in a similar fashion against the enforcement of mortgages formerly secured by slave property. Lets. Recd., EB12 President 3006 (1865), RG107, NA.

3. Peabody (1814–1901), a New York attorney appointed by Lincoln in 1862 to administer a provisional court system in Louisiana, served concurrently as chief justice of the state supreme court (1863–65). Declining an appointment as attorney for Louisiana's eastern district, he returned to his law practice in New York. Brown, *Am. Biographies*, 6: 178.

4. Johnson referred this matter to the War Department for an opinion. On October 12, 1865, Judge Advocate General Holt denied the assertions of the petitioners and upheld the claims of the mortgage holders. Because the "military authorities can neither legally nor with any justice or propriety afford any remedy," he recommended no further action be taken. Lets. Recd., EB12 President 3006 (1865), RG107, NA.

From George Pfeuffer

[ca. August 12, 1865], Comal County, Tex.; ALS, DNA-RG94, Amnesty Papers (M1003, Roll 54), Tex., George Pfeuffer.

A Bavarian native, who emigrated to Texas in 1845 and opposed secession, applies for pardon. To avoid conscription, he served as a state agent to purchase gunpowder in Mexico. In December 1863 Pfeuffer was arrested by the Federals in Brownsville, when he attempted to get cotton for this purpose across the Rio Grande. As a prisoner he took an oath of loyalty on December 15, 1863, "and believing that Texas was to be permanently occupied he intended religiously to keep and observe it." Others intervened with "malicious accusations against him," and two days later he was exiled to Mexico "without investigation or trial." He remained there six months; then, having been informed that property left in his care would be confiscated in exchange for the cotton he had been given, he forwarded the gunpowder he had acquired in Mexico and returned home. He insists that he does not fall under the fourteenth exception to Johnson's May 29 proclamation, because the oath he took in Brownsville was not that prescribed by Lincoln on December 8, 1863, and because he had not knowingly aided the rebellion; he understood the powder he delivered was to be used for frontier defense only. [He was pardoned on September 20, 1865.]

From John E. Smith [1]

Hd: Qrs. Dist. of West Tennessee
Memphis Tenn Aug. 12" 1865

His Excellency Andrew Johnson
Prest. of the U.S.
Sir

Hon Wm. Wallace Atty. Genl. of this judicial Dist. leaves for Washington this P.M. who will as he informs me call upon you and at his suggestion I have the honor to address you in relation to some of the subjects of his proposed interview with you.

Considering the present condition of the people of the South brought about by the late Rebelion we have reason to be gratified at results in the Dist. of West Tenn. although these are not altogether such as could be desired yet a large majority of the people manifest a disposition to return to their allegiance to the Govt. of the U.S. Civil law is gradually resuming its authority in most of the Counties and the recent elections were quietly conducted no disturbance having been reported to these Hd. Qrs. The vote was necessarily light oweing to the restrictions of the franchise law enacted at the last session of the State Ligislature[2] and in a few Counties no election was held the people not having had an opportunity of being registered in pursuance of that Law.

The Freedmens Dept. under the energetic management of the Asst. Comr. Brig. Genl. D. Tillson[3] is being rapidly systemized and I have no doubt if Genl. Tillson is continued in charge here (which I would recommend) he will have it so perfected in the course of a few months that it will work harmoniously and to the mutual advantage of the Planters and Freedmen. Most of the Planters apparently submit to the new relations resulting from the War but it will take time to eradicate the prejudices of Education and association.

In the absence of special instructions I infer that it is not the intention of the Govt. to deal harshly with the masses of the people of the South. The people can not be held responsible for the Rebelion. At its inception a large minorty of them vainly opposed the increasing tide of public opinion until overwhelming all their interests and social relations it resistlessly swept them into the political vortex that engulphed these great communities.

Genl. Order No. 110. C.S. A.G.O. War Dept.[4] operates with undue severity in some cases. No discretion is left to Mil. Comdrs. to return property that has been taken or ordered to be vacated in obedience to Mil. necessity and not abandoned or confiscated. In making a Genl. Order this was perhaps unavoidable.

I have the honor to be Sir Very Respectfully
Your Obt. Servt. Jno E Smith
Bvt. Maj. Genl.

LBcopyS; DNA-RG393, Dept. of Tennessee, Lets. Sent, Vol. 1.

1. Smith (1816–1897), Galena, Ill., jeweler, became a brigadier in 1862 and served with distinction in Tennessee and Georgia. Promoted to major general in 1865, he commanded the District of West Tennessee, before being mustered out in 1866. Warner, *Blue*.

2. With suffrage restricted so that only Union men of proven loyalty could vote, the mass of otherwise qualified voters was effectively disfranchised. Alexander, *Reconstruction*, 74–75.

3. Davis Tillson was superintendent for the subdistrict of Memphis (July–Sept., 1865). *Preliminary Inventory . . . Field Offices of the Bureau of Refugees, Freedmen, and Abandoned Lands*, Pt. 3, p. 440, RG105, NA.

4. Gen. Orders No. 110, current series, dated June 7, 1865, carried out Johnson's
June 2 order, which authorized all U.S. officers to turn over to the Freedmen's Bureau
all abandoned lands and funds collected for the benefit of freedmen or refugees. Third
Special Agency, Lets. Recd., RG366, NA.

From James T. Soutter

August 12, 1865, Washington, D.C.; ALS, DNA-RG94, Amnesty Papers
(M1003, Roll 73), Misc. Northern and Western States, John T. Soutter.

A Virginia native living in New York in 1861, who left after the outbreak of
war and remained in Europe until 1865, asks for pardon under the thirteenth
exception to Johnson's May 29 proclamation, because he has $20,000 in tax-
able property and gave the Confederacy "his entire sympathy and moral influence, though he gave it no material support." For more than a year he worked
for an English mercantile firm involved in blockade running. Although he himself had no direct connection with any such enterprise, he remained "on terms
of friendly intercourse" with agents of the Confederate government in Europe,
entertained them at his home, and even carried a letter to the "Roman Gov-
ernt." from James M. Mason. Whether these acts "constitute voluntary participation in the *legal* sense he does not care to enquire. He feels that they do in a
moral sense," and it is for this reason that he asks for a pardon. [His request
was granted on August 14, 1865.]

From James A. Stewart

                                                 Rome, Ga., August 12th, 1865.
His Excellency Andrew Johnson,
Washington, D.C.
Dear Sir

My term of seeking refuge from the oppression of reckless rebellion
and intolerances has closed, and I am again in possession of what remains of my home in Georgia; and it is gratifying to be able to state to
you that even here, in this once turbulent and dangerous section of
Georgia, we have peace, order, and every indication of a return of substantial prosperity. There will no more war go up from the South. An
acquiescence in the new order of things, under your administration, is
clearly manifested by the masses of our people. The terms of re-admis-
sion into the Union, embraced in your proclamation will meet with no
opposition entitled to consideration. In fact, there is no record in history
of an erring people manifesting so earnestly a willingness to retrace
their steps, and help to repair the wrongs they have committed. They
have emerged from a mesmeric spell thrown over them by years of
inflamatory political harangues, and are now in their sober senses,
ready and willing to do right, and it is earnestly to be hoped that you
will have it in your power to protect us against any renewal of the
agitation in reference to the negro element. Shield us, if possible,
against negro suffrage, negro equality, or whatever tends to the rekin-
dling of sectional animosities. The people south are willing to give up

slavery; but they are not yet willing to place themselves on terms of political and social equality with the African race.

But it was my purpose, in this communication, to again address you in reference to Hon. A. Stephens. Having a thorough knowledge of Mr Stephens's position, prior to and during the whole progress of rebellion, I can say, confidently, that rebellion never met his sanction except, (through the force of circumstances) as a horrible and painful necessity, and that his imprisonment, under the circumstances, in the view of every reasonable man south, is without sufficient cause and not justifiable.

Mr Stephens, as you will perceive from the enclosed copy of a recent letter from him,[1] is rejoiced at the prospect of returning peace, and would not hesitate to encourage a speedy and full acquiescence in the terms proposed.

Release him, if in your power to do so. Release him without delay. Let me urge you as your friend, and a friend to the best interests of our country, to release him on parole, and let him return to the bosom of his friends and the comforts of home, where his delicate health and frail body may gather new strength, & where his voice of counsel may again be heard. Every body asks, "Why is Stephens held in prison, whilst Howell Cobb, R. Toombs, Gov. Brown, B. H. Hill, and others, are permitted to go at large?"

I have no prominent position to back up my solicitations in Mr. Stephens's behalf, nor can I calculate much on your very limited personal acquaintance with me; but I am an honest man and a true lover of my country, and am actuated in this appeal by no selfish or mercenary motives; and feel assured that I am addressing one equally honest and patriotic—one who will not turn a deaf ear to the pleadings, of an honest and reasonable appeal in behalf of a good man, who has committed only an error, but no willful sin.

Yours most respectfully J. A. Stewart.

ALS, DLC-JP.
1. Stephens' letter to Stewart of July 21, written from Fort Warren, can be found in Johnson Papers, LC.

From Mary C. Stokely[1]

Lexington Oglethorpe Co, Ga
Aug 12th 1865

His Excellency, Andrew Johnson
President of the United States;
Most Respected Sir:

I approach the august presence of the chief magistrate of this, the most powerful nation on the globe, with much diffidence, and yet, with a consciousness of right, and a firm confidence, in your well known,

and proudly acknowledged nobility of soul, your generosity and magnanimity to those erring ones, asking pardon at your hands.

Do not be startled that I beg, entreat this pardon, so magnanimously
granted others, for the distinguished prisoner, now in your power, Mr
Jefferson Davis!

In vain, have I listened for interceeding voices, from the magnates of
our land, North & South, for the man, who at the unanimous voice of
his people, endeavored to steer them through the breakers, which politicians North and South had entered; and which, like a fearful, writhing, seething maalstrom, engulphed us. No kindly voice is heard. No
petition for leniency is urged, entreated, and Mr Davis, is forsaken, in
his direst extremity. Though thousands of great hearts throb and ache,
to ask your Excellency's favor for him. Yet, as a very prominent gentleman said to me, "They dare not"!!

The wish, the earnest longing, to pray your mercy for him, has so
burnt into my inmost soul, that I thus dare, address you this humble
petition.

Will you not deal leniently with your prostrate foe? Can you not do
something to alleviate the privations to which he is subjected? He is
feeble. His life hangs by a thread; Like an expiring lamp it flickers,
flashes and wanes, almost extinguished. O! let me address you as a
private individual; as a Southron, in whose veins, no drop of vengeful
blood e'er flowed, As a christian, in whose heart every kindly emotion
finds a home; As an American brother to the brave Davis. O! listen to
the voice of mercy; deal kindly generously. Pardon the shipwrecked,
but noble, gallant Davis. But, you exclaim, that you must do your *whole*
duty to your *whole* country, as the President of *the people*, and not permit, "*Mercy*," to thrust aside, "*Justice*."

O! let Justice and mercy, go hand & hand. Let all the extenuating
circumstances of Mr Davis' crime, be kept in view. Your Excellency
knows his history better than I. He was merely the instrument in the
hands of the people, and not one *jot* or *tittle* more *criminal than the entire South*. The discussion of Politics the intrigues of Tricksters, the
schemes of ambition, which Napoleon like, would deluge the land for
self aggrandizement, these, come not in womans sphere. "Whom the
Gods would destroy, they first make mad." Surely madness ruled
the hour, when the North & South separated. But now, thank God, the
thundering of battle has ceased; and now O! let the wooing voice of
Holy writ, be heard; "*Blessed are the merciful, for they shall obtain
mercy*."

Would you have your name revered & cherished by nations yet un-
born? Would you have the admiration of the *world*; Would you have
the blessings of the South? the commendations of the North? the plau-
dits of the universe? Pardon Mr Davis!

Hundreds of brave hearts, now writhing at thought of defeat & subjugation, would bless you, and feel that there was yet, a bright future for them. Hundreds once living in luxury & ease, now wandering homeless penniless, would forget their own privations, & feel a joyous throb, that they were once more enfolded in the arms of a Union, where the voice of faction, prejudice & fanaticism was stilled, and Justice, Mercy & moderation, meted out to all.

Pardon me for tresspassig on your valuable time. Pardon for the loved fallen one, I entreat in the name of the ladies of Ga.

I write this on my own responsibility, with no thought, but for the unfortunate one & the good of my Country. If I presume too much I crave pardon, my extreme solicitude for your prisoner urges me on.

Should your Excellency deighn a reply, the prayers of a heart ever grateful will be thine.

> With most profound Respect
> Yours Mary C. Stokely
> Lexington Ga.

ALS, DNA-RG94, Amnesty Papers, Jefferson Davis, Pets. to A. Johnson.

1. Possibly the wife (b. *c*1834) of Steven H. Stokely, a "Country Merchant." 1870 Census, Ga., Oglethorpe, 290.

From Carl Schurz

August 13, 1865, Macon, Ga.; ALS, DLC-JP. See *Advice*, 89–99.

Having visited Savannah, Augusta, Atlanta, and Milledgeville, he avers: "Almost all I have said with regard to South Carolina, the spirit and temper of the people, their intentions and aspirations, the relations between freedmen and planters etc. will, with equal force, apply to the people of Georgia." Denies the accuracy of recent newspaper reports of enthusiastic Union meetings in Georgia. He found the plight of freedmen and Union men in the region around Atlanta "most unsatisfactory," with armed bands and planters committing "outrages . . . upon negroes." In most places the garrisons are too weak to do more than the necessary guard duty. Cites "evidence of a bad spirit on the part of the inhabitants" and says that Northern businessmen settled in the state "are quite generally complaining of the demonstrations of unfriendly feeling with which they are received." Schurz concedes that many planters condemn the outrages upon blacks and are willing to try to make the free labor movement succeed; but even these have not "succeeded in separating in their minds the idea of compulsion from negro labor." He again warns the President to move slowly in the restoration of civil government and lauds Gov. James Johnson as "the boldest and most earnest man in the State." Urging a more efficient organization of the Freedmen's Bureau in Georgia, Schurz reports critical assessments of Gen. Edward A. Wild's behavior, as well as his own generally favorable impression of the general. Suggests the need for more Bureau agents, especially with the prospect of serious disturbances around Christmas, when many blacks "firmly believe that the Government will divide among them the lands belonging to their former masters." He stresses the need for "proper mail arrangements" and asks that cases between blacks and whites and cases in which the U.S. government is concerned be excluded from the newly reorganized state courts.

To George H. Thomas

Executive Office, Washington, D.C.
August 13 1865

Major General George H. Thomas,
Nashville, Tenn.

I have been advised that innumerable frauds are being practiced by persons assuming to be Treasury agents in various portions of Alabama in the collection of cotton pretended to belong to the Confederate Government. I also understand that they are connected with the Commandant of Post at Montgomery.[1] I hope you will appoint some efficient officer under your command to proceed and examine and ascertain the facts and if any parties shall be found whether connected with the Treasury or the Military that you will deal with them in the most summary manner and report the names of persons engaged in such transactions and each case.

Mr. Dillon[2] Treasury Agent will be in Nashville in a few days and will confer with you upon this subject. I wish you would direct the attention of the Military under your Command to this subject, and especially General Hatch[3] at Montgomery.[4]

Andrew Johnson
President U.S.

Tel, DNA-RG107, Tels. Sent, President, Vol. 2 (1865).

1. Probably Lyman M. Ward (b. c1834), colonel of the 14th Wis. Inf., who assumed command at Montgomery July 19, 1865. He was mustered out in October. CSR, RG94, NA.

2. Joseph R. Dillin.

3. Edward Hatch, commander of the Northern District of Alabama. Generals' Reports of Service (M1098, Roll 5), RG94, NA.

4. Two weeks later Thomas responded: "I have caused the Charges of fraud in the cotton speculation in Ala. to be thoroughly investigated & General [Charles R.] Woods reports to me that no such transactions are now carried on & he is satisfied that proper precautions have been taken by the Military & treasury authorities to prevent further frauds." Thomas to Johnson, Aug. 29, 1865, Johnson Papers, LC. Despite these optimistic reports, more charges and investigations emerged in the fall of 1865.

From Anthony W. Dillard[1]

Confidential

Livingston Ala August 14/65

Hon A Johnson Pres &c
Sir:

I am an original Union man and am now a candidate for the Convention, in favor of returning to the Union, on the terms offered by you. The secessionists are very strong here, & are still disposed to run over the Union men, and are recieving all the offices from the federal officers,

& the Provisionial Governor. They make their boasts, that so soon as the Federal Soldiers leave, they will Kill the Union men. We ask for protection. Ex Gov. Jno A Winston,[2] now an applicant for pardon, was a secessionist. He ran for the convention & was beaten on that question, in 1861. He is now a candidate for the convention in Sept—and is opposed to emancipation.

The secessionists wish to elect him in order to make him their leader in the convention for slavery. I hope & request you will with hold his pardon until after 10 Sept 1865—the day the convention meets. The secessionists are as rebellious as ever, & the only hope of safety, is to put Known Union men in office. Parsons has not done this.

I am Respectfully Yours
A W Dillard

Refer to Wm Garett[3]
Jos C Bradley

ALS, DNA-RG94, Amnesty Papers (M1003, Roll 12), Ala., A. W. Dillard.
    1. Dillard (1827–fl1880), a former probate judge, later served as chancellor of the western district of Alabama (1868–80). Owen, *History of Ala.*, 3: 491–92.
    2. Although not pardoned until September 12, 1865, Winston (1812–1871), prewar governor and former colonel of the 8th Ala. Inf., CSA, defeated Dillard in the election and attended the Alabama constitutional convention of 1865. Ibid.; Winston's pardon in Asst. Commr., Ark., Lets. Recd., RG105, NA.
    3. Garrett (1809–fl1875), longtime Alabama secretary of state, was elected in October to the state senate. Owen, *History of Ala.*, 3: 638–39.

From James Johnson

Milledgeville Ga August 14th 1865

His Excellency Andrew Johnson Pres U.S.
Dr Sir

The aspect of affairs in Georgia is much more flattering than was anticipated and the present promise is that the condition will continue to improve. There are however many difficulties yet to be surmounted and serious dangers to be apprehended.

In the work of reconstruction I have the promise of most of the leading men of the State to aid me. Governor Brown—since his return has cooperated with me and given to the Government his influence & support. His efforts have materially benefited the cause and no doubt he will every where continue to prosecute the good work. He deserves commendation & amnesty.

Your respectfully J. Johnson

ALS, DNA-RG94, Amnesty Papers (M1003, Roll 16), Ga., Joseph E. Brown.

Pardon of Robert H. Short[1]

Copy:

Executive Office Washington D.C.

August 14. 1865.

R. H. Short of New Orleans La., having been excepted under the Amnesty Proclamation of May 29. 1865, has this day been pardoned specially, and he is thereby restored to all his rights of property, except as to Slaves, just the same as though he had been entitled to the benefits of said amnesty.[2]

Andrew Johnson

Prest.

Copy, DNA-RG56, Misc. Div., Claims for Cotton and Captured and Abandoned Property.

1. Short (c1820–fl1890) was a New Orleans cotton factor and commission merchant. Having fled the Crescent City when it fell to Federal forces in 1862, and subsequently residing in Mississippi, he applied for special pardon under exception 13. 1870 Census, La., Orleans, 3rd Subdiv., New Orleans, 3rd Ward, 11; Amnesty Papers (M1003, Roll 29), La., R. H. Short, RG94, NA; New Orleans directories (1861–91).

2. Short was pardoned on July 29, 1865, but General Howard, apparently believing that such action brought "immunity from arrest and punishment for crime only," refused to order General Banks to vacate Short's New Orleans home. Upon a second petition by Short, Johnson issued this special declaration making it clear that the property of persons whom he pardoned was to be returned. A clerk's endorsement indicates that orders were sent directly to treasury agent Benjamin F. Flanders to release the home on August 15; Banks subsequently abandoned the premises. *Montgomery Advertiser*, Oct. 8, 1865; *Augusta Constitutionalist*, Oct. 19, 1865.

From John S. Richards

August 14, 1865, Reading, Pa.; LS, DNA-RG56, Appts., Internal Revenue Service, Assessor, Pa., 8th Dist., Alexander P. Tutton.

Anticipating that an effort will be made by the political opponents of Assessor Alexander P. Tutton to have him removed from office, Richards writes to the President, asking him not to do so. An "eminently attentive faithful and efficient officer," Tutton has the "entire confidence of the Department"; the "warmest, oldest, and most reliable friends of the administration, here" earnestly trust that he will not be replaced. The effort to have George W. Alexander appointed in his place is led by a man whom Tutton compelled to pay a substantial penalty for submitting a fraudulent return, and the adherents to his scheme are all "enemies of the Administration." [Alexander was appointed on February 9, 1867, after Tutton was removed.]

To George H. Thomas

Executive Office, Washington, D.C.
Aug't 14 1865

Major General Thomas,
Nashville, Tenn.

From information lodged here the Freedmens Bureau at Nashville and Pulaski are assuming and exercising powers in taking charge of property and other jurisdiction which is incompatible with the law creating the Bureau and the design of its creation.[1] I hope you will give it some attention, and if you deem it best some suitable and efficient agent will be at once appointed to investigate its proceedings. I fear the operations of Treasury Agents and the Freedmens Bureau are creating great prejudice to the Government and their abuses must be corrected.[2]

Andrew Johnson
President U.S.

Tel, DNA-RG107, Tels. Sent, President, Vol. 2 (1865).

1. Thomas replied he knew of "no instance in which the officers of the Freedmens Bureau have exercised illegal authority in taking charge of property either here or at Pulaski." In two or three cases "Genl Fisk has restored to owners property, which had been in charge of the Treasury Agent, he being convinced after investigation that the property was not abandoned"; otherwise, "Fisk is doing all he can to settle all difficulty arising in his Bureau justly and fairly, under the law creating the Bureau." Thomas to Johnson, Aug. 16, 1865, Johnson Papers, LC.

2. On August 19, 1865, Lt. Col. Joseph S. Fullerton, writing on behalf of Gen. O. O. Howard, asked Fisk to investigate Johnson's allegations. According to Fullerton, the President had received reports that the Freedmen's Bureau agent at Pulaski had not only been confiscating private property, but also had been "keeping or sleeping with mulatto women." After conducting his own investigation, Fisk concluded that the agent in question, Lt. Lorenzo D. Barnes, was "not guilty nor has he been of either the offences alleged against him." Fullerton to Fisk, Aug. 19, 1865, Records of the Commr., Lets. Sent (M742, Roll 1), RG105, NA; Fisk to Howard, Sept. 1, 1865, Records of the Commr., Lets. Recd. (M752, Roll 14), RG105, NA. For additional information about the Pulaski matter, see Fanny M. Jackson to Johnson, Sept. 2, 1865, Johnson Papers, LC.

From Henry Wilson

Natick, Mass. Aug. 14th 1865.

To The President,
Dear Sir,

I spent two hours to-day with A. H. Stephens. He was quite sick. He is in one of the Lower rooms, and it is very damp—so much so that a fire was burning to keep it comfortable. He said when he arrived they had no better rooms empty, now they had several and he desired to have one of them. I spoke to one of the officers, and he said it ought to be done, but he thought he had no authority to do it. I hope an order will be sent at once giving him a good room.[1]

He says he is the only man in Georgia in prison—that all the men who deceived the people and carried them into rebellion are free while he who was ever opposed to it is shut up. He does not complain,—says he rather be *hung* in America than *live* in any other country,—and wants to go home. He will give bonds or go on parole. He think he could exert a good influen for the Union if he were at home.[2]

Yours truly H. Wilson

ALS, DLC-JP.
 1. See Telegram to Commanding Officer, Fort Warren, August 18, 1865.
 2. Johnson endorsed this letter: "Attended to. On private file."

From William A. Babcock[1]

Phila Aug 15, 1865

Hon. Andrew Johnson
President of the U.S.
Dear Sir

I take the liberty of thus addressing you, and perhaps when I tell you that I'm but a humble private citizen of this glorious Union. That, with the exception of some fifteen months as a Clerk in the Philadelphia Post Office I never held nor have I ever been an applicant for a public position. You may be induced to pass it lightly by as the idiosyncrasies of an over-zealous individual and not worthy of notice. But when I tell you that for over twelve years, I have been closely identified with our State, National and local politics, when I say to you that I was among the original founders of the republican party in our State and that I have the confidence of and an intimate acquaintance, with the prominent political leaders of our State, my words may have some weight. You may be induced to read it patiently and that at least you will think kindly of it. During a part of last week, I was travelling about in the interior of our Pennsylvania and met with many prominent men, leaders in our political circles, and found them as well as the majority of the friends of the administration, in a largely excited state. There were murmurings and mutterings that betoken a storm, while all among them expressed a doubt of the success of your friends, at our approaching Fall election.

And Why? perhaps you will ask, is all this excitement, these doubts and misgivings. Simply, My Dear Sir, because you persist in adhering to and following the advice of one our State long since, said "Good Bye" to, the Hon Simon Cameron[2] I mean, and at the same time disregard the advice of those who are your sincere friends and who are and will be your earnest supporters no matter what may be your policy or your actions. These latter are among the Curtins, Forneys and our City Congressmen.[3] Then why not for once be guided by them.

I enclose you slips from our City Papers, which will better explain the motives for my thus writing, and will tell you how and why the above discribed agitate state of feeling is apparent and how it originated.

After you had appointed to the position of Postmaster of our City, C. A. Walborn,[4] those who were opposing him quietly submitted to your decision and without a murmur. Hurriedly a serenade was gotten up and at which Mr. Walborn made a speech. The slip marked A is a fair report of it,[5] and in it He designates the Congressmen as *interested creatures*. No attention was paid to this speech, as the source from which I [it] came all knew and none respected. Then another serenade was arranged, when Mr. Cameron made a speech: the slip marked B is a copy of it.[6] So pointed was this latter speech, the one for whom it was especially intended to hit, could not fail in Justice to himself to reply. The slip marked, C, in [is] a fair report.[7] The other Congressmen will doubtless follow with their defence neither can any one blame them for so doing, especially when so attacked.

Even now there is some hesitation in re-appointing to a minor position, Erastus Poulson,[8] Esq. of our City as Pension Agent. Mr P. has well and faithfully fulfilled his duties during the past four years. Is recommended by the entire Department with which he is connected and by prominent men from all parts of our State, and it can but be hoped Sir, that you will carry out in *practice*, what Mr Cameron in his speech *preaches*. That of retaining Officers, were they have well and faithfully fulfilled their duties, and so re-appoint Mr Poulson.

I do not write this to advocate Mr Poulsons claims or with any intention of influencing you in his favor, but cite it as an instance and ask you to study the matter before making a change.

Trusting Sir, that it will not be deemed presuming in me to so address you, and hoping you will take it in the same kind and frank manner as written, and that you will believe me when I say that it is written with a kindly motive and with good intentions, I am as I should be

Your advocate and warm friend Wm. A Babcock
974 No 6" St Phila

ALS, DLC-JP.

1. Babcock (*fl*1867) was a bookkeeper and postal clerk (1864–65). Philadelphia directories (1861–67).

2. Upon the former secretary of war's endorsement, Johnson reappointed most of the incumbents holding federal offices in Philadelphia. *Philadelphia Bulletin*, Aug. 11, 1865; Bradley, *Cameron*, 258.

3. A reference to supporters of Governor Andrew Curtin and newspaper publisher and secretary of the Senate, John W. Forney, along with Congressmen Samuel J. Randall, Charles O'Neill, Leonard Myers, and William D. Kelley, all anti-Cameron men. Forney had been trying to obtain the customs collectorship for his son and Curtin campaigned vigorously against Postmaster Walborn. Ibid., 256–58.

4. Cornelius A. Walborn (*fl*1885), a Philadelphia merchant appointed by Lincoln in 1861, had used his "official power" in opposing "Pig Iron" Kelley's reelection to Congress. Reappointed by Johnson, he served until September 1866. Basler, *Works of Lincoln*, 4: 342; 7: 402; Philadelphia directories (1865–85).

5. Not found. Both Forney's *Press* and the *Evening Bulletin* reported the serenade and Walborn's August 1 remarks the next day.

6. Not found. Again, the *Press* and *Bulletin* reported the serenade. More likely this "slip" is from the Democratic *Philadelphia Age*. The feud between "Pig Iron" Kelley and Cameron, having its origins earlier, was exacerbated during the congressional race of 1864 and reached its height during the summer of 1865. Bradley, *Cameron*, 257; Ira V. Brown, "William D. Kelley and Radical Reconstruction," *PMHB*, 85 (1961): 318.

7. Probably the report from the *Press*.

8. Poulson (*c*1820–*fl*1900) was a lawyer, and variously a pension and claims agent. 1860 Census, Pa., Philadelphia, 3rd Ward W. of 5th St., 164; Philadelphia directories (1861–1900).

From Robert Bates

Marion Alabama Aug [15]/65 [1]

To His Excellency Andrew Johnson
President of the United States.

Your petitioner Robert Bates an applicant for special pardon under your Excellency's Amnesty proclamation of May 29th 1865 begs leave to submit the following statement of facts; on which he bases an application for Executive clemency.

1st   Your petitioner is a resident of Perry County Ala. where he has resided for many years. He was born in Barnwell County state of South Carolina in the year 1807 and he is therefore fifty eight years of age. He has been a plain farmer all his life never having engaged in any other pursuit. He was never a politician in any respect whatever, never having sought or held any office. He begun life a very poor man, and by industry, economy and attention to his farm he had acquired an ample competency previous to the war, but more than half of his estate has been swept away from him by the results of secession without any agency on his part, as he opposed secession from its inception, and fought it in all its forms by his votes and influence. The emancipation of his slaves has greatly reduced his estate, but the remainder may be worth twenty thousand dollars hence this application for special pardon as he is in no other respect denied the benefits of your Excellency's Amnesty proclamation of May 29th 1865.

2nd   Your petitioner was opposed to the so-called ordinance of secession at the time it was passed on the 11th January 1861, and was devotedly attached to the Union of the States, and to the old Government of the United States: He voted in the presidential election of 1860 for "Bell & Everett," hoping thereby that secession might be averted, and the integrity of the Union preserved.

3rd   He never was in the Confederate Army, not having volunteered, nor being subject to conscription; he never in any manner bore arms against the United States Government, nor did he ever take the oath of allegiance to the so-called Confederate States, nor did he ever hold any office or agency of any kind either under so-called Confederate

Government, or under the state of Alabama or any other state during the rebellion, or before or since. He never contributed of his means to the support of the so-called Confederate states—he only paid the taxes demanded of him, and gave of his means to aid the helpless, indigent and suffering families of soldiers in his neighborhood which was demanded by the cause of humanity.

4th   He has recognized the emancipation of slaves by employing at liberal compensation those he formerly owned; taking care of the aged helpless & infirm.

5th   It is his purpose and desire to be a peaceable, faithful, loyal citizen of the United States Government during the remainder of his life.

Your petitioner would further submit the following answer to interrogatories propounded by his Excellency L. E. Parsons Provisional Governor of Alabama.[2]

1st   I am not under arrest.

2nd   I did not order the taking of Fort Morgan, or Mt. Vernon Arsenal[3] nor aid in, nor advise the taking of either of them.

3rd   I never served on any "vigilance committee" during the war before which any person charged with disloyalty to the Confederate states were examined or tried.

4th   No person has been shot or hung by my order for real or supposed disloyalty to the Confederate States.

5th   I have not shot or hung nor aided in shooting or hanging any person for real or supposed disloyalty to the Confederate States.

6th   I have not ordered, nor engaged in hunting with dogs any one who was disloyal to the Confederate States or supposed to be.

7th   I was not in favor of the so-called ordinance of secession when it passed Jany 11th, 1861.

8th   I will be a peaceable & loyal citizen in the future.

9th   No proceedings have been instituted against my property under the Confiscation act.

10th   None of my property is in possession of the United States Government as abandoned property or otherwise.

In consideration of the foregoing statement of facts your petitioner humbly begs that your Excellency Andrew Johnson President of the United States grant him special pardon & amnesty and restore him to all the rights & privileges of a loyal citizen, which he is, and as in duty bound he will ever pray &c.[4]

Robt. Bates

LS, DNA-RG94, Amnesty Papers (M1003, Roll 1), Ala., Robert Bates.

1. This was the date on which Bates's letter was "Sworn to and subscribed" before the local probate judge.

2. To his proclamation of July 30, inaugurating the state's provisional government, Governor Parsons had appended a list of questions by which those excepted from the benefits of the President's amnesty proclamation could be judged as candidates for special pardon. Fleming, *Alabama*, 353–54.

3. On January 4 and 5, 1861, state troops seized the arsenal and fort. Everette B. Long, *The Civil War Day by Day: An Almanac, 1861–1865* (Garden City, N.Y., 1971), 21–22.

4. Bates was pardoned September 29, 1865. *House Ex. Docs.*, 40 Cong., 2 Sess., No. 16, p. 5 (Ser. 1330).

From Thomas Bragg[1]

Raleigh Aug. 15th 1865.

To his Excellency Andrew Johnson President of the United States of America.

The petition of Thomas Bragg of the City of Raleigh, State of North Carolina, aged nearly fifty five years, and by profession a lawyer, respectfully shews to your Excellency that, he is one of those made liable by the laws of the United States, to certain pains and penalties. Your petitioner, now an applicant for executive clemency, deems it due to himself and to your Excellency to make a full, true and candid Statement, as to how far and in what respect, as it seems to him, he is thus amenable.

In and by the Proclamation of your Excellency of the 29th of May last, certain classes of persons are specially excluded from the amnesty therein granted. Two of these exceptions may be supposed to apply to your petitioner. The *fourth*—"All who left seats in the Congress of the United States to aid the rebellion"—and the *first*—"All who are, or shall have been, pretended civil or diplomatic officers, or otherwise domestic or foreign agents of the pretended Confederate government". In the fourth exception your petitioner does not consider himself embraced. In the first, he is embraced.

At the time of the attempted withdrawal of the State of North Carolina from the Union, your petitioner was one of hér Senators in the Senate of the United States, having taken his seat therein on the 4th of March 1859. He remained in the Senate during the regular Session of 1860–61—was present at the inauguration of Mr. Lincoln, and also attended the extra Session of the Senate called immediately thereafter; remaining some days and taking part in the proceedings thereof, and intending to remain until its close; but was called home by a dispatch informing him of the extreme illness of his wife. For the course of your petitioner in the Senate during the time he was a member thereof, he can safely appeal to the records of that body, and to all those acquainted with his conduct therein. It was always that of moderation upon the distracting questions of the day, for your petitioner was extremely solicitous to allay & not to increase the excitement, and to bring about some amicable adjustment of the matters then at issue between the North and the South.

Your petitioner was not then, nor had he been in favor of a rupture of the Union. He supported the election of Mr. Breckinridge to the

Presidency, and in the summer and fall preceding the presidential election, he was called upon to address the people of North Carolina, and did address large assemblages of them at various points in the State. The question, whether the Southern States ought to withdraw from the Union in the event of the Election of Mr. Lincoln, was then freely discussed in every southern State. It was, on every occasion that your petitioner spoke, discussed by him, and he uniformly advised against and opposed it with whatever power he possessed. During the Session of Congress which preceded the rupture, and in the midst of the excitement, your petitioner was called from Washington to Raleigh.

The Legislature of North Carolina was then in Session and he was invited to address the members and did so. He might appeal to all who then heard him and to the press of the day, in which an abstract of his speech was published, for the moderation of his views and the anxiety manifested for an amicable adjustment. The state of Virginia had then recommended a meeting of what was known as the peace Conference.[2] Many of your petitioner's political friends in the Legislature were opposed to it, but your petitioner strongly urged the sending delegates to the proposed Conference.

The opinion was then almost universal at the South, that some additional guantees to slave property ought to be granted. Your petitioner honestly thought so and so stated in the said speech, but he then advised the acceptance of what was known as the "Crittenden proposition",[3] and was sincerely desirous that it or some similar proposition should be adopted, in the hope that peace & harmony might be restored. Your Excellency well knows how all failed and with what result.

Your petitioner hopes that these details may not be deemed inappropriate, though it is possible, that with some, his motives may be questioned for now giving them. He desires to stand truly upon the ground occupied by him, whatever it may have been at any time. And the more so, because he believes that his former position owing, perhaps, to subsequent occurrences, has been lost sight or overlooked by not a few.

Your petitioner returned to North Carolina from the extra Session of the Senate, as he has stated, but not with the intent to "aid the rebellion." True it is that, from the best information he could obtain before he left Washington he entertained little doubt of a coming rupture between the North and the South. He further believed and so expressed himself, that North Carolina, in such an event, would be compelled from her situation to take sides either with the one or the other. Several of the Southern states had already declared their withdrawal from the union and their delegations had withdrawn from Congress. All propositions for settlement had failed before Congress, and it was believed that some of the other States soon would follow those that had withdrawn. He admits that his feelings and sympathies were with the South, and that in the contingency stated he thought and said that

North Carolina should unite with her Southern Sisters. He honestly and sincerely believed that the state had a right to withdraw from the union under the circumstances likely to be presented, and that the Government of the United States had not the right to co-erce a state thus withdrawing. In common with many in the South, he had long entertained these opinions, and indeed was educated in that belief—and hence he hoped that if separation did take place, it would be peaceable and without any conflict of arms. In this he was greatly mistaken. The rupture came and with it the terrible contest through which we have passed.

Your petitioner has admitted that he was obnoxious to the charge of having held office under the so called Confederate government. While what was called the provisional government thereof was in force, he accepted the Office of Attorney General under the Laws, in the month of November 1861, and continued to act in that capacity for a little more than four months, when he voluntarily retired from the same and returned to private life.

In the month of February 1864, an act was passed by the Confederate Congress suspending, in certain Cases, the privilege of the writ of Habeas Corpus. In the month of May following a further act was passed requiring the appointment, by the Secretary of War, of Commissioners in each of the states, to examine the cases of all such persons as might be placed under arrest by Executive authority, or the military acting under its orders, with power to discharge them when no probable ground was found for such arrests, and to detain or bail such persons for trial before the civil courts, where such cause was found to exist; and the same power was conferred upon such Commissioners, by the said act, as had ordinarily been exercised by such officers when appointed by the Judges of the United States. The appointment for North Carolina was offered to your petitioner, was accepted by him, and he acted as such, until the expiration of the act, suspending the privilege of the writ of Habeas Corpus, by its own limitations, early in the month of August 1864. Your petitioner deems it due to himself to explain how he came to accept the said office, and also his conduct therein, because in the exciting time during which he held the same, he was visited with a good deal of obloquy, and he has reason to believe that his conduct and motives were greatly misapprehended. For this he has not & does not now complain. Under the circumstances it was, perhaps, to have been expected. Your petitioner neither sought or wanted such an office. There was nothing in it either of dignity or emolument that could have induced him to accept it. But the truth is this—Mr. Seddon then acting as Secretary of War wrote to your petitioner to the effect, that the Habeas Corpus Act would, in many instances, operate harshly—that it was not his desire to use it oppressively—and that his purpose was, if possible, to appoint such commissioners, as would use the power confided to them, temperately and discreetly—that he believed your petitioner would do so—and that though the office was an inconsiderable one, he hoped your petitioner would consent to serve in it. For such reasons and none other your petitioner consented to do so and by such motives was he governed while he held it. During such time not more than seven or eight arrests of civilians, all by military authority, save one, were made in this state, so far as your petitioner is aware. All of the arrests were made at Kinston, save one in this County, charged with harbouring a deserter. Those at Kinston were for passing persons through the military lines or upon charges of a like character. The cases when reported to your petitioner were examined by him publicly, the parties having the benefit of such counsel as they desired, and every opportunity given for a full and fair hearing. In every instance they were unconditionally discharged save one. In that, the party was discharged on bail to appear before a civil tribunal. These were the only offices civil or military held by your petitioner nor was he ever in the military service.

Your petitioner nevertheless desires in all candor to admit that he adhered to the southern cause, at least by his countenance if not by his acts, until it fell by the superior power of the United States. When Genl. Lee surrendered, he, however, urged, so far as he could do so, a similar course on the part of Genl. Johnston, then with his army in this vicinity, satisfied that all further resistance was futile and could only result in a further useless effusion of blood and devastation of the Country. He determined to submit himself to the authority of the Government, and advised others to do so, and in all things has since endeavored to manifest his obedience to its laws and requirements.

True it is your petitioner has not hitherto filed his petition praying for a pardon, and it has been suggested to him by some in whose judgment he greatly relies, that he erred in not doing so promptly. If so, it was from no spirit of opposition to the Authorities in any sense or particular. He simply deemed it more prudent & becoming to leave to others less involved than himself the duty and privilege of aiding in the restoration of civil government in this state, doubting whether an early application for the exercise of Executive Clemency in his case would be favorably received or entertained. But the annexed certificate will shew that in the month of May he took the Oath of Amnesty and allegiance, and his intention not only was to observe it, but in due season to apply to your excellency for a pardon—and this will also appear from the Oath hereto appended taken and subscribed by him on the 20th of July last.

Your petitioners Estate is small, much less than twenty thousand dollars now and on the 29th of May last. Besides a residence in the city of Raleigh, heretofore assessed of from five to six thousand dollars, and some domestic servants, it consisted mainly of Bank and other stocks and North Carolina Bonds issued since the attempted withdrawal of the state from the Union. These stocks, bonds &c are now considered of little or no value, so that your petitioner finds himself advanced in years & reduced in circumstances, with a large family, a wife and eight children all dependent, for the present upon his personal exertions, and five of his children, some of them of very tender years, yet to be educated. Duty, inclination and necessity all prompt him to an early resumption of the professional labors of his early life, in the hope that he may be able thereby to provide for his family & educate his children. This is his greatest, chiefest desire, and this is his intention, should it please your Excellency to extend to him a pardon, which he now respectfully asks.[4]

Ths. Bragg.

ALS, DNA-RG94, Amnesty Papers (M1003, Roll 37), N.C., Thomas Bragg.

1. Bragg (1810–1872), prewar governor and older brother of the Confederate general. William S. Powell, ed., *Dictionary of North Carolina Biography* (3 vols., Chapel Hill, 1979–   ) 1: 209.

2. The Peace Convention was held in Washington, D.C., in February 1861, with representatives from border and some northern states, as well as southern, and was presided over by ex-President John Tyler.

3. The proposal, introduced by Kentucky Senator John Crittenden as a compromise during the crisis of December 1860, would have permitted slavery south of 36°30′.

4. Recommended by Governor Holden, Bragg was pardoned October 6, 1865. *House Ex. Docs.*, 40 Cong., 1 Sess., No. 32, p. 3 (Ser. 1289).

From Elias G. Bright

[ca. August 15, 1865], Beaufort County, N.C.; LS, DNA-RG94, Amnesty Papers (M1003, Roll 37), N.C., Elias G. Bright.

A forty-three year old "poor man" with a large family, residing six miles from[1] Washington, N.C., asks for special amnesty under the 14th exception. During the Union occupation, on a visit to the town for supplies, he had been required to take the U.S. oath of allegiance. In May 1864, Washington was evacuated, and Confederate draft laws were enforced. The following August, "To avoid conscription," he volunteered in Colonel Whitford's local defense regiment, but after "only two weeks" obtained a furlough and returned home. [Bright was pardoned October 6, 1865.]

From C. Clara Cole[1]

Washington City—August 15th 1865.

To his Excellency—Andrew Johnson,—
President of the United States—

I have the honor to represent that General Fisk commanding Freedmens Bureau at Nashville Tennessee—So interprets the pardon which your Excellency granted to my nephew B. B. Leake[2]—as to justify him in retaining possession of his property. I beg your Excellency therefore to grant an order directing General Fisk to deliver the property at once to B. B. Leake—as he has no pecuniary means whatever & his health is I fear permantly injured by his long imprisonment & I have not Sufficient to support me in comfort much less both of us. By granting this request—your Excellency will much relieve & confer a lasting favor on your truly grateful friend.[3]

C. Clara Cole

ALS, DNA-RG105, Land Div., Lets. Recd.

1. The author of *Clara's Poems* was an early Johnson acquaintance in Nashville.

2. Berryman B. Leake (1838–1914), Tennessee native who was captured on Morgan's Raid near Salineville, Ohio, in July 1863 and remained in prison until the war's end. Johnson pardoned him on July 27, 1865. B. B. Leake File, Tennessee Confederate Soldiers' Home Applications, TSLA; *Interments in Nashville Cemetery*, 47; Amnesty Papers (M1003, Roll 47), Tenn., B. B. Leake, RG94, NA.

3. The next day the President forwarded Cole's letter to the Bureau for an immediate report, causing William Fowler, Howard's deputy in charge of the land division, to wire Fisk immediately. Returning the Cole letter to Johnson, Fowler noted that General Fisk had telegraphed that "he will send a full statement in a few days but cannot recommend any especial favor in this case." Johnson, refusing to let the matter pass, returned Cole's letter for further action. Fisk returned the property, writing to Commissioner Howard on the 26th that before he had received word of Leake's pardon and having no formal applications for return of the property, he had acted under the Bureau's Circular 13 in refusing to restore the property. Fisk to Howard, Aug. 26, 1865, Records of the Commr., Lets. Recd. (M752, Roll 14), RG105, NA. See also Endorsement *re* Property of Berryman B. Leake, August 16, 1865.

From John W. Duncan

Atlanta Georgia August 15th 1865

His Excellency Andrew Johnson
President United States
Dear Sir

My friend Judge Lochrane[1] being about to visit Washington, among other purposes, to intercede with you in behalf of the Hon Lucius J. Gartrell[2] of Atlanta, for the exercise of Executive clemency, I beg to write you a line on the same subject, & to ask your kind consideration of the case.

I am satisfied that could Mr Gartrell see you in person & explain his views & intentions in the future, you would feel a complete assurance, that he would maintain a true & faithful allegiance to the Government of the Union & be useful in the restoration of law & order & government to the sorely distracted community in the State of Georgia.

I am happy to assure you Mr President that since my return home from my interview with you in Washington—the condition of affairs has been slowly but surely advancing, & I have no doubt, under a benign policy such as you have inaugurated, we shall again have a return to many of the blessings we enjoyed before the war. Still there is much to be done to reconcile conflicts & clashings arising out of our new condition. There could hardly be so great a change, as has been made by the setting free of such a large body of the population of these States

596 AUGUST 1865

without some rough demonstrations, but we ought all to be grateful, that there has been so little violence or difficulty as yet & if wise counsels can secure the quiet application of the Negro to the various departments of labor, we shall pass through the trying ordeal, with more satisfaction & safety than could have been expected.

Allow me to assure you of my earnest co-operation in sustaining you & the policy of your administration, & my readiness at all times to promote the views you expressed to us in our interview in June last, & to be the medium here of such other views as from time to time you may think proper to communicate to me in accordance therewith.

Gen Carl Schurz paid us a visit last week, & I endeavored to afford him all information in my power, but was sorry his stay at each point in his trip was so short & hurried, as to afford but little opportunity for making a full & satisfactory investigation into the condition & progress of affairs here. He could scarcely gain a very correct knowledge from so rapid a tour. Judge Lochrane can give you in person the fullest account of the state of things in Georgia.

I am with high regard very respectfully
Your Excellency's obedt. servt John W. Duncan

ALS, DNA-RG94, Amnesty Papers (M1003, Roll 18), Ga., Lucius J. Gartrell.
1. Osborne A. Lochrane.
2. Gartrell (1821–1892), who studied law in the office of Robert Toombs, was a states' rights Whig when first elected to Congress and a Democrat during his second term. Serving in both the Confederate army and Congress, he resumed his law practice after his pardon of October 13, 1865. Warner, *Gray*; *House Ex. Docs.*, 39 Cong., 2 Sess., No. 31, p. 9 (Ser. 1289).

From Sanford Elliott[1]

Gainesville Ala, Aug. 15 1865

To the President of the U.S.
Hon Sir,

As commander of this Post and having been in the country for some time and have observed things as closely as one could under all the circumstances, causes me to address you this communication, having the wellfare of our hole country at heart and desiring to see our once united and beloved country a gain in that happy flurishing condition that it was before the war commenced, brings the case at once up and causes me to ask what will be the policy of the Goverment and what can it do to reinstate or ever do to get this Southern portion to be a member of the old family again. I am certain over one half of those who I have administered the oath to are careless in regarding it. They say they care not ever to vote again. Some say they intend winding up there buisness and getting out of the Country. A delegation has left this place for Brazil.[2]

Well this war has ended and in our favor and the union I hope will be preserved, but I am fully satisfied the south is ruined for years to come if ever restored to her once Greatness again. Unless some cistem is fixed up and Cotton Growing can be carried on better than at present, the united States will have to import cotton and Sugar in less than five years or Stop her cistem of manufactories. Much more I might mention but this letter is much lengther than I anticipated when I commenced to write.

I am your most Obt Sevt &c S. Elliott
Com' of the Post and of the 93d Ind. Inf.

P.S. We have about 1200 Negros in this Camp and not one in fifty will try to do any thing for themselves or when they get a home they will not stay but come back to Camp in two or three days to frolick and play & I am tired seeing it.

The Goverment will of corse Judge best but my honest opinion is from evry day observation that the longer the Goverment keep up those Camps and feed the negro the worse the negro will be demoralised, and the more careless he will become in regard to his future wellfare. Infact I fear this winter will be a hard and destructive time on this race of people, thrown out of there homes and crowded in to little camps will be certainly the cause of disease and death on all sides, for they are dying by dozens now, and it must be much worse when cold wet rainy season commences. The Negro seems to be so constituted in this part of the country but very few will do any thing for themselves or any one else except when compelled, and since the whites of this section has given up all hope of the negro being of any more benefit to them, they care nothing for them and rather seem anctious to get them out of the Country. If the planters carry out what I understand to be there intention *To wit* after the present crop is housed send them all to camp or away from there present home.

I cant see what will become of them this winter unless the Goverment will go to a Great expens in takeing care of them—and if this is the case this winter it will be then to continue unless some other prepperation is made. There will be not more than a support made in the country and the white man will not let the negro have any thing only for the money and the amt they get of the Growing Crop will not feed them very long from the fact the crops has been very badly cultivated &c. From what I see and can learn the amount of cotton planted this year in the south is much smaller than any year since the war commenced. Infact in this section of country a good cotton growing section, there is almost none planted and it has been so badly cultivated, it will not do to count at all, and the planters here seem with the lights before them to talk as they never intend planting any more. And from the very best information I can learn, the most of these men ware union men even after the war commenced. There excuse is the south as well as them selves are ruined & to ever mend up in this country is impossible.

Infact the old men go with there heads bowed down while the young men seem to be demoralised and ruinned.

As to the negro question I have some considerable expreince with them. They are also demoralised very badly and dont seem to understand the position he at present occupies. They come to this post with all kind of Stories, and not a few come threw idle cureosity—and worst of all those who come and get in camp and have nothing to do but eat & Sleep seem very hard to get out of Camp to do any thing. Very frequently they hire themselves out for a reasonable price, and in afew days return to camp. Ask them why they returned so Very soon, and the answer is very generally that they are so very lonesome, out of camp. In camp they pat, sing, & dance and this is about all they think of outside of sleeping & eating.

ALS, DNA-RG105, Records of the Commr., Lets. Recd. from Executive Mansion.

1. Elliott (b. c1834) of Nebraska, Ind., enlisted in the 93rd Ind. Inf. in October 1862 and was mustered out in November 1865. *Off. Army Reg.: Vols.*, 6: 149; CSR, RG94, NA.

2. Planter Robert L. Brown of Sumter County, Ala., joined the expedition led by William W.W. Wood of Mississippi, which departed in August 1865 for Brazil. Brown was one of 19 agents representing 11,000 southern families interested in migrating. Amnesty Papers (M1003, Roll 2), Ala., Robert L. Brown, RG94, NA; Eugene C. Harter, *The Lost Colony of the Confederacy* (Jackson, Miss., 1985), 33; Blanche H.C. Weaver, "Confederate Emigration to Brazil," *JSH*, 27 (1961): 37.

From John W. Forney

Washington
Aug. 15, 1865.

To the President
My Dear Sir:

I venture to present the name of Col. Thos. C. McDowell[1] of Pennsylvania for the vaccancy occasioned by the resignation of Mr. Holloway as Commissioner of Patents. His testimonials speak for themselves. Altho' no recommendation of mine has as yet secured a single federal appointment in Pennsylvania, tho' I have specially presented several names for your consideration, I am in hopes that this appeal in favor of my friend McDowell will be more fortunate.[2]

Yours' Very Truly
J. W. Forney

P.S. Col. McDowell prepared the Law under which the present organization of the Patent office was perfected.

ALS, DNA-RG48, Appts. Div., Misc. Lets. Recd.

1. MacDowell (c1814–*fl*1882), Harrisburg, Pa., lawyer and newspaper editor, had been a consul in Brazil under Polk, and lieutenant colonel, 84th Pa. Inf. (1861–62). 1880 Census, Pa., Dauphin, Harrisburg, 87th Enum. Dist., 1; Harrisburg directories (1867–82); MacDowell to Johnson, June 12, 1865, Appt. Files for Judicial Dists., Pa., Thomas C. McDowell, RG60, NA.

2. MacDowell did not get the appointment.

From Robert A. Hill

August 15, 1865, Jackson, Miss.; ALS, DNA-RG60, Appt. Files for Judicial
Dists., Miss., Robert A. Hill.

Having written before for an appointment as a district judge in Mississippi,
then abandoning his attempt when he read in a newspaper that Ephraim S.
Fisher had been appointed, Hill renews his application upon discovering that
the office is still vacant. About Fisher he writes, "I know nothing to urge
against his appointment, only that I am somewhat selfish, and would prefer
obtaining it myself." The appointment of loyal Mississippi citizens, such as
himself, "would greatly facilitate the rapid progress now being made in the
restoration of the state." For references, he asks Johnson to inquire of generals
Dodge, Thomas, Spencer, and Jeff C. Davis, "with all of whom I have the
pleasure of a personal acquaintance," and Grant, "who I presume learned my
standing whilst in command in this state." [Johnson appointed Hill judge of
the Northern District of Mississippi on April 16, 1866.]

From Preston King

New York City Aug 15, 1865

To The President

I arrived here this evening by the through Train all safe and intend
to complete my papers to morrow or next day and go home for a few
days and shall If I can get back so as to come and see you for a single
day before I settle here on the 1st day of Septr.[1]

very Respectfully & Truly Yours Preston King

ALS, DLC-JP.
   1. Having developed a close relationship with Johnson by the time of the latter's
nomination as vice president, King had received the appointment as collector at New
York, a post he held until his suicide later in the year.

To William L. Sharkey

Executive Office, Washington, D.C.
August 15, 1865.

Governor William L. Sharkey,
Jackson, Miss.

I am gratified to see that you have organized your Convention without difficulty. I hope that without delay your Convention will amend
your State Constitution abolishing slavery, and denying to all future
legislatures the power to legislate that there is property in man—Also
that they will adopt the Amendment to the Constitution of the United
States abolishing slavery.

If you could extend the elective franchise to all persons of color who
can read the constitution of the United States in English and write their
names, and to all persons of color who own real estate valued at not less

than two-hundred and fifty dollars and pay taxes thereon, you would completely disarm the adversary and set an example the other States will follow.

This you can do with perfect safety, and you thus place the Southern States, in reference to free persons of color, upon the same basis with the Free States. I hope and trust your convention will do this, and as a consequence the Radicals, who are wild upon negro franchise, will be completely foiled in their attempts to keep the Southern States from renewing their relations to the Union by not accepting their Senators and Representatives.

Andrew Johnson
President U.S.

Tel, DNA-RG107, Tels. Sent, President, Vol. 2 (1865).

From James B. Steedman
Personal

Head-Quarters Department of Georgia,
Augusta, Ga., Aug 15, 1865.

Andrew Johnson Prest U States,
Dear Sir—

Knowing, the anxiety you must have about the success of your plan for the restoration of the revolted States to their Constitutional relations with the Government, I take the liberty of writing you, privately, as to the Condition of things in Georgia.

In my opinion, everything is moving satisfactorily towards the complete restoration of this State upon a basis that will be perfectly satisfactory to you and the Country, as well as a triumphant indication of the wisdom of your policy. The Convention, I think, without doubt, will adopt the *"Wilmot Proviso"*[1] and make such other provisions as are necessary to secure and protect the liberty of the Freedmen. The sensible men of the State—the men who will control the action of the Convention—all concede that the blacks must be clothed with authority to sue and be sued—to plead and be impleaded—and to testify in all the Courts. The whites are unanimously opposed to extending suffrage to them. On the question of suffrage there will be no debate in Georgia. With the exception of a few isolated cases of outrage upon them—and these cases would have been as likely to occur under the same circumstances in Ohio or N. York, as in Georgia—the Freedmen have been kindly treated, and, have conducted themselves well. A couple of weak, fanatical men—Bvt. Brig Genl. Wild and Capt Bryant[2]—sent here by Genl. Saxton, of the Freedmans' Bureau, have caused some trouble, and occasioned a good deal of alarm in the minds of the people, by inciting a turbulent spirit among the blacks;

but I have corrected some of their abuses, and everything is moving quietly now.

The Assistant Special Agents of the Treasury Department, are all over the State, and I think are oppressing and wronging the people. It is almost impossible for a citizen to move a bale of cotton, without being interfered with by an Agent of the Treasury Department. In the present impoverished condition of the State—requiring that every thing that will bring money should go as speedily as possible to market, this annoyance is very depressing. Every Agent appears to have a legion of Deputies—each one of whom assumes to have all the powers of the Secretary of the Treasury. They are almost as notorious—some of them—as the Army Police of Genl. Rosecrans.[3]

Carl Shutz, has been here, and made thorough and impartial enquiry as to the condition of affairs in the State. I could see very plainly, however, that he is opposed to your policy, and regards your effort to restore the revolted states as premature, if not an absolute blunder.

Mrs Jeff Davis, is here and desires to go North. I inclose a copy of her letter to me.[4] Unless you have determined conclusively not to permit her to visit the North, I would respectfully suggest that she be permitted to go either to one of the places she names in the north, or to Canada. I think her own sense of propriety would prevent her from making any display whatever, and if the privilege were granted her, it would deprive your enemies of a considerable capital. The ladies of this city, attempted to hold a meeting to express sympathy for Jeff Davis, but I prevented it, by telling a gentleman who called on me to get my consent, that I could not permit such a meeting to be held.

I think it would do good if you were to pardon as rapidly as you can consistently, citizens excluded by the 13th exception[5]—especially business men—many of whom would join earnestly and sincerely in the work of restoration and in sustaining your policy, were they released from the ban which exclusion places them under.

I believe that the release of Mr. Stevens—even on parole—if you can consistently do it—would gladden the heart of almost every man, woman and child in Georgia. The people—the masses—are very strongly attached to him.[6]

I inclose for you, two of my orders,[7]—the most important I have issued, which I hope will meet your approval.

I am afraid Gov. Johnson has gone a little too far, in restoring all the civil authorities at this time; but I will avoid collision, if in my power to do so, and I think with the remedies given before my Pro. Marshals to Freedmen, there need be none.[8]

With esteem Your friend & Obt. St.
James B. Steedman.
Maj Genl. U.S Vols

ALS, DLC-JP.

1. Steedman's allusion is unclear, but perhaps he equates the Wilmot Proviso, which sought to ban slavery in the territories gained by conquest from Mexico, with the 13th Amendment, which would prohibit slavery in the "conquered provinces" of the South.

2. Edward A. Wild (1825–1891) helped raise black regiments in Massachusetts and commanded a brigade of black troops along the Carolina coast. Appointed subassistant commissioner in August, he was removed in September following an investigation into his harassment of citizens. John E. Bryant (1836–1900), a Maine native, aided in the organization of black troops at Port Royal under Gen. Rufus Saxton, who appointed him to be general superintendent of the Bureau in Augusta. Bryant, too, was relieved of duty by the end of the year. Samuel Barnette to E. P. Alexander, Aug. 2, 1865, Capt. G. M. Brayton to Col. S. B. Moe, Aug. 4, 1865, Alexander to Howard, Aug. 10, 1865, Saxton to Howard, Sept. 12, 1865, Records of the Commr., Lets. Recd. (M752, Roll 20), RG105, NA; *Advice*, 97–98, 205; Ruth Cussie-McDaniel, *Carpetbagger of Conscience: A Biography of John Emory Bryant* (Athens, Ga., 1987), 4–56.

3. Organized at Nashville in December 1862, by civilian William Truesdail under Rosecrans' authority, this organization was intended to maintain order, detect violations of trade regulations, and institute a counter-espionage system. Its multifarious activities, its secrecy, and its interference with civilian affairs aroused both fear and hostility. Johnson was a sharp critic of Truesdail and his detectives. *Johnson Papers*, 6: 114.

4. Varina Howell Davis' letter to Steedman, August 6, 1865, is in the Johnson Papers, LC.

5. See Amnesty Proclamation, May 29, 1865.

6. The next day Steedman again suggested a parole for Alexander H. Stephens, insisting that "his presence in Georgia, at this time, will do good." Steedman to Johnson, Aug. 16, 1865, Johnson Papers, LC.

7. Not found.

8. See Telegram to Steedman, August 23, 1865.

From William B. Stipe[1]

Lewisville N.C. Aug 15" 1865

His Excellency Andrew Johnson
President of the United States of America
Dear Sir

You are probably not aware that the subject of repudiation is assuming a very high standard in North Carolina.[2]

Repudiationists call the debt of N.C. the "*War debt*" and in consequence are driving it on the people that it must be *repudiated* as a necessary condition of our being recieved back in the union and inculcating the doctrine that the President's Proclamation so declares it; which I have been unable so far to so construe. If you please I would request you by your self or some other person to give me some light on the subject so that I may be able to enlighten such of my neighbors and freinds as call on me for light on the subject as I expect to in a short time to address the people of my county in a canvass and wish to state nothing but facts & as I am a Union friend Elected on the Holden ticket to the Legislature of N.C. in 1864 from Forsyth County.[3]

very truly & Fraternally yours—W. B. Stipe

ALS, DNA-RG60, Office of Atty. Gen., Lets. Recd., President.

1. Stipe (1824–1901) was a former blacksmith. Donald W. Stanley et al., eds., *For-*

syth County, N.C. Cemetery Records (5 vols., Winston-Salem, 1976–78), 4: 939; 1850 Census, N.C., Forsyth, 501.

2. A reference to the repudiation of the state's Confederate war debt by the 1865 constitutional convention. Some North Carolinians, in their enthusiasm to repudiate all debts, tried to place a broad interpretation on the term "war debt." Stipe had a personal interest at stake; he still held prewar state bonds, and was unsure of their value. Dan T. Carter, *When the War Was Over: The Failure of Self-Reconstruction in the South, 1865– 1867* (Baton Rouge, 1985), 102.

3. The President's staff referred the letter without comment to the attorney general's office. See also Holden to Johnson, Oct. 17, 20, 1865, Tels. Recd., President, Vol. 4 (1865–66), RG107, NA; Johnson to Holden, Oct. 18, 1865, Tels. Sent, President, Vol. 2 (1865), RG107, NA.

From Albert Case

August 16, 1865, Boston, Mass.; ALS, DNA-RG56, Appts., Customs Service, Collector, Boston, Albert Case.

Boston businessman calls on Johnson to ignore political factions boosting various candidates for the position of collector of the port by passing over the nominees and selecting Richard S.S. Andros, former first deputy collector, who "has more practical knowledge of the duties connected with the collection of the Revenue than any other man." This would not only "'Settle the Matter,'" but "would silence all clamor for the office and satisfy this Community, mercantile & all." [Johnson later appointed Hannibal Hamlin to the position.]

Endorsement re *Berryman B. Leake*

Executive Office August. 16. 1865.

Respectfully returned to the Commissioner of Bureau of Freedmen Refugees &c. The records of this office show that B. B. Leake was specially pardoned by the President on the 27th ult'o, and was thereby restored to all his rights of property except as to slaves.

Notwithstanding this, it is understood that the possession of his property is withheld from him. I have therefore to direct that General Fisk, Ass't Comm'r at Nashville, Tenn, be instructed by the Chief Commr. of Bureau of Freedmen &c to relinquish possession of the property of Mr. Leake, held by him as Ass't Comm'r &c, and that the same be immediately restored to the said Leake.

The same action will be had in all similar cases.[1]

Andrew Johnson
President U.S.

ES, DLC-JP (Letter from C. Clara Cole, August 15, 1865).

1. This case, and others like it, precipitated the President's confrontation with the Freedmen's Bureau over the redistribution of abandoned lands and culminated in General Howard's Circular No. 15 on September 12. Issued with Johnson's approval, the circular specified that the Bureau had control over only those lands already condemned and sold by court decree, making other "abandoned" property, including that condemned but not yet sold, subject to restoration to its pardoned owners. George R. Bentley, *A History of the Freedmen's Bureau* (Philadelphia, 1955), 95; Nieman, *Law in Motion,*

51–53. See Letter from William T. Moore, August 3, 1865, Pardon of Robert H. Short, August 14, 1865, and Letter to O. O. Howard, August 24, 1865.

From Hugh McCulloch

August 16th 1865

Sir:

I have the honor to transmit herewith for your consideration a copy of a letter from Theodore Cook[1] Esq. to the Chairman of the Chamber of Commerce of Cincinnati Ohio, relating to the propriety of employing certain freedmen, collected at various points on the Mississippi river—now without occupation, and supported by the Government in repairing the broken Levees, on the Lower Mississippi—and suggesting a plan for a return of the outlay, by a tax on the land benefitted thereby—Also a copy of a letter from the Secretary of the Chamber of Commerce,[2] covering Mr Cook's communication.

With great respect, H McCullogh
Secretary of the Treasury.

The President

LBcopy, DNA-RG56, Lets. Sent to President (Letterpress Copies).
    1. The copy has not been found. Cook (1823–1894), a Cincinnati businessman, was the owner of a steamboat enterprise. A War Democrat and later a Republican, he had actively worked for unionist causes. *History of Cincinnati and Hamilton County, Ohio* (Cincinnati, 1894), 878; Bonadio, *North of Reconstruction*, 66, 172.
    2. Not found.

From Hugh McCulloch

Treasury Department August 16th 1865.

The President.

Sir:

Representations are being frequently made to this Department, that powder and shot are very much needed in the States lately in insurrection to be used for shooting game and other legitimate purposes. These articles still remain contraband of war and cannot be carried into any of the Southern States except Tennessee, in relation to which state, the same having been declared not in insurrection by the proclamation of June 13th 1865, I issued the order, a copy of which is enclosed, allowing shippments of such articles upon proper permit approved by the General Commanding the military Department.[1]

If, as seems probable the condition of the Southern States has become such as to render unobjectionable, the importation therein of articles hitherto contraband of war I would respectfully suggest that it may be expedient to issue an Executive Order allowing the same in reasonable quantities, and for proper purposes.[2]

> I have the honor to be Very respectfully Yours.
> H. McCulloch Secy of the Treas.

LBcopy, DNA-RG56, Lets. Sent *re* Restricted Commercial Intercourse (BE Ser.), Vol. 10.

1. See Letter from McCulloch, July 10, 1865.
2. Perhaps reflecting the procedure instituted in Tennessee, a draft proclamation, written on August 21, provided for the issue of permits for the import of munitions, gray cloth, and railroad and telegraph equipment into the South. The proclamation as promulgated on August 29, however, stated simply that trade in "contraband of war" henceforth would be "subject only to such regulations as the Secretary of the Treasury may prescribe." Yet, on the following day Johnson expressed some misgivings to McCulloch about the shipment of weapons into the South. Lets. Recd., EB12 President 3006 (1865), RG107, NA; Richardson, *Messages*, 6: 331. See Letter to McCulloch, August 30, 1865.

From Matthew Simpson

Phila. Aug 16. 65

His Excellency President A. Johnson.
Hon & Dear Sir,

Genl. Mussey forwarded a copy of a despatch from Mr. Baldwin of Nashville, saying that McKendree Church had not been given up &c &c.[1]

Immediately on the receipt of your despatch last week[2] I telegraphed to Rev Mr. Gee to give possession of the church to the South and to procure a Hall.[3] And the same evening I wrote a letter giving more full directions. The despatch may have failed to reach its destination as is sometimes the case, or it is possible Rev Mr. Gee was absent from the city, and if so there might be a delay. But I have no reason to doubt that the Church will be given up.

Lest Mr. Gee may be absent I write tonight to Gov Brownlow who will see that the message is given to our friends.

I regret that there shd. be any unnecessary delay.

> Yours respectfly M. Simpson.

ALS, DLC-JP.
1. Mussey had sent the Rev. Samuel D. Baldwin's response to Johnson's query of the 15th. In his reply, Baldwin had asserted that McKendree Church had not been returned to its trustees. Mussey to Simpson, Aug. 16, 1865, Tels. Sent, President, Vol. 2 (1865), RG107, NA; Baldwin to Johnson, Aug. 16, 1865, Johnson Papers, LC.
2. See Telegram to Matthew Simpson, August 10, 1865.
3. See Letter from Allen A. Gee, August 23, 1865.

From Alexander H. Stephens

Fort Warren Boston Harbor Mass
16 August 1865

His Excellency Andrew Johnson
President United States Washington D.C
Mr. President
Dear Sir

With profound acknowledgement for the relaxation of the order for my close confinement I am induced to make an other appeal to you. I am exceedingly anxious to have a personal interview and conference with you. I am not without Strong convictions that if I could have such an interview that I could easily Satisfy you that my request for a release on parole or bail Should be granted no less on private than public considerations. Will you be pleased to grant such interview? If you should and I should be released so far as to go to Washington I need not assure you I trust that in case the further release on parole to go to my home should not be granted after the interview I Should promptly return to this place. My conduct and well known position before my first arrest and since I feel assured is a sufficient guaranty that in no possible contingency would I attempt an escape.

My petition is earnestly though briefly submitted. Act upon it as you think best.[1]

Yours most respectfully Alexander H Stephens

ALS, DLC-JP.

1. Despite the pleas by others, as well as a subsequent petition by Stephens, Johnson allowed the Georgian to remain in prison until mid-October. See James B. Steedman to Johnson, Aug. 16, 1865, Felix Watson to Johnson, Aug. 17, 1865, James T. Pratt to Johnson, Aug. 23, 1865, B. H. Bingham to Johnson, Sept. 14, 1865, and Alexander H. Stephens to Johnson, Sept. 16, 1865, Johnson Papers, LC; Richardson, *Messages*, 6: 352.

From George G. Garrison

[ca. August 17, 1865], Princess Anne County, Va.; ALS, DNA-RG94, Amnesty Papers (M1003, Roll 61), Va., George G. Garrison.

A Virginia native, who served as a staff officer in the Army of Northern Virginia, seeks a presidential pardon. Five days after he returned home on parole, confiscation proceedings were initiated in the U.S. District Court against his interest in a lot and house left to his wife by her father. Although he took Lincoln's amnesty oath on April 29, 1865, and the one required by Johnson on August 17, he is excluded from amnesty because of the suit against him, and the court has not yet met. "Your petitioner cannot suppose that your Excellency intended so unequal an operation of Executive clemency, or would allow its application to be affected by circumstances so purely accidental." [Johnson granted Garrison's pardon on September 4, 1865.]

To George H. Thomas

Executive Mansion Washington D.C.
Augt. 17th 1865

General:

The Methodist Episcopal Church in the City of Nashville, Tenn. known as the "McKendree Church" was taken possession of under an order of the Secretary of War issued November 30th 1863 and as I am reliably informed, is held at this date in pursuance of said order by other parties than the rightful claimants.

There being some controversy about the right of such parties to retain possession of the property in question, the President of the United States was applied to for redress, and he, under date of Augt. 31st 1864 endorsed upon the application of John S. Brien, of counsel for the McKendree congregation, as follows. This case is submitted to the discretion of Governor Johnson: (Signed) A. Lincoln.[1]

Acting under this authority I, as Military Governor of Tennessee, investigated the case, and made a report thereon,[2] but final action has not yet been had.

I now enclose herewith a Copy of the determination then arrived at by me, and respectfully call your attention to the endorsement and order thereon.[3]

Very Respectfully &c &c
(Sgd) Andrew Johnson
President of the U S.

Major General Geo. H. Thomas[4]
Comd'g Mil. Div. Tenn Nashville, Tenn.

Copy, DNA-RG109, Union Provost Marshal's File of Papers Relating to Two or More Civilians (M416, Roll 69).

1. See Petition from McKendree Church Trustees, December 31, 1864, *Johnson Papers*, 7: 370n.

2. See Decision in McKendree Church Case, January 23, 1865, ibid., 426–27.

3. Attached to this letter is Johnson's order affirming his earlier decision that the property be returned to the Methodist Church South congregation and directing that "the action indicated in said report be immediately had, and further, that all moneys received, as rent for said property, since the date of said report, to wit: the 23d January 1863 [1865] be at the same time turned over to the parties restored to the possession of the premises." Three days later he wired to correct the date. Tels. Sent, President, Vol. 2 (1865), RG107, NA.

4. See Letter from Allen A. Gee, August 23, 1865. See also Thomas to Johnson, Aug. 26, 1865, Johnson Papers, LC.

To Commanding Officer, Fort Warren, Mass.[1]

Executive Office, Washington, D.C.,
Aug't 18 1865.

To Commanding Officer, Fort Warren, Mass.

You are hereby authorized and directed to furnish to Alexander H. Stephens the most comfortable quarters at your disposal.[2] You are also requested to inform Mr. Stephens that I have received his letter of the 16th and that it will be answered.

Andrew Johnson President U.S.

Tel, DNA-RG107, Tels. Sent, President, Vol. 2 (1865).
    1. Charles F. Livermore (c1830–fl1892), who recently had been promoted to major, 1st Btn. Mass. Heavy Arty. CSR, RG94, NA; Pension File, C. F. Livermore, RG94, NA; OR, Ser. 2, Vol. 8: 1034.
    2. Two days later Stephens would be moved to a suite of three rooms which he considered "more comfortable [than] any hotel in Boston or New York." Myrta L. Avery, ed., Recollections of Alexander H. Stephens: His Diary Kept When a Prisoner at Fort Warren, Boston Harbour, 1865 . . . (New York, 1910), 476; Schott, Stephens, 452.

From Cox[1]

Washington, Aug. 18, 1865.

To the President:

I desire to present for your *personal* consideration, the facts which, *by outside influences*, operate to *prevent* the obtainment of a pardon by my brother, Richd. S. Cox,[2] of Georgetown, D.C.

At the outbreak of the Rebellion, seduced by the delusions of the hour, and more especially by the persuasions of his wife,—a native of Virginia,—he was induced to leave his home in Georgetown and join the Confederates. He left his house in possession of his sister and his three children. Shortly after he left, *She was dispossessed by order of the War Department*, and left without a home, and his furnished residence and the adjoining grounds were appropriated as a Home for colored women and children; and it has been occupied as such for nearly three years.[3]

After the capture of Richmond and the close of the war my brother took the oath of allegiance and applied for a pardon &c. His application was well endorsed, and among others, by Genl. Carrington,[4] the U.S. District Attorney for this District.

The application at first was *favorably considered by* the Attorney General, and his name put in the list of those for whom pardons were to be made out by the Dept. of State and submitted to Your Excellency. Before that list, however, left his office, Judge Underwood,[5] of Alexandria, accidentally called at the Attorney General's office, and upon looking at the list, said, that my brother's name should be stricken out, or suspended for further consideration.

On learning that fact, I saw Judge Underwood on the subject, and he said, that he would oppose his obtaining a pardon unless he would *make a contribution* to the colored Home, now occupying his property. This was in June. On his behalf, I offered that they might remain until Sept.; that all crops in the ground might be removed &c. This offer was made to the Atty. Genl. and to Genl. Howard. But this offer was not deemed sufficient. I then offered the sum of $1,000—but the officers of the Home, have refused this amount and have solemnly resolved that my brother shall not have his pardon, nor a restoration of his property, unless he makes a *forced* contribution of $10,000—, as will appear by accompanying papers:[6] and threats of *Confiscation* are vaguely hinted, if he does not comply with their demand.

The only reasons, it seems, why my brother as contradistinguished from other applicants for pardon should be subjected to this *black-mail*, are the facts, that he has been so unfortunate as to have his property occupied during his absence by the Colored Home, instead of his Sister; and that they having been so fortunate as to occupy it So long, without compensation, are now determined *to extort* from him that sum of money, *as the price of his pardon*.

I cannot for a moment believe, that such a proceeding *has*, or *can have, your sanction*; and hence, I have determined to lay the case before you for your individual and direct action.

If you should be disposed to Sanction their demand, then the only question would be, how much he ought to pay. My brother has nothing but his homestead in Georgetown—a wife and six children. From my knowledge of his affairs, he could not pay $10,000. The demand for that sum rests upon an exaggerated and false estimate of his means.

By the accompanying papers, Your Excellency will see, that Genl. Howard recommends my brother's pardon, and is willing to leave the questions of property to be settled by the courts of law. He also respectfully asks the interposition of the President in the case.

I join him in that request, and will cheerfully acquiesce in whatever conclusion your sense of justice and fair dealing may dictate, as proper under the circumstances, suggesting at the same time—that a place much more suitable than my brother's residence can be found in some one of the numerous abandoned hospitals in the neighborhood of the city of Washington, built and owned by the Government.[7]

With great respect, I have the honor to be, your Obedient Servant,
[Cox]

L, NRU-William H. Seward Papers.
1. Probably either Walter S. (1826–*fl*1891), a lawyer and subsequent member of the District of Columbia supreme court, or his brother Thomas C. Cox (1829–*c*1882), a State Department clerk who, during the war, went "on a special mission to France" and later was variously a District of Columbia realtor, clerk for the board of audit, and water

registrar. *NCAB*; *Men of Maryland and District of Columbia*, 99–100; Washington, D.C., directories (1858–91).

2. Cox (*c*1825–*fl*1890), former clerk in the paymaster's office, accepted a commission as major in the Virginia forces (1861), ultimately serving as quartermaster in the Confederate "Pay Bureau." 1850 Census, D.C., Georgetown, 475; *Staff Officers*, 37; Washington, D.C., directories (1883–90); Amnesty Papers (M1003, Roll 73), D.C., Richard S. Cox, RG94, NA.

3. Cox's mansion in Georgetown Heights had served since 1863 as a home for black orphans under the auspices of the National Association for the Relief of Destitute Colored Women and Children, an organization promoted by prominent Washington matrons, many of whom were congressional wives. Ibid.; James H. Whyte, "Divided Loyalties in Washington during the Civil War," *Records CHS*, 60–62 (1962): 117.

4. Edward C. Carrington (b. *c*1825), a Virginia native and lawyer, was U.S. district attorney (1865–70). 1860 Census, D.C., Washington, 3rd Ward, 201; *U.S. Off. Reg.* (1865–71); Washington, D.C., directories (1869–70).

5. John C. Underwood.

6. Not found. However, documents supporting these statements are in Amnesty Papers (M1003, Roll 73), D.C., Richard S. Cox, RG94, NA.

7. Although the case did not fall under the Freedmen's Bureau jurisdiction, General Howard in 1866 was requested to find other suitable quarters for the destitute women and children. With the President's intercession, Cox received his pardon in May 1866, but his property was not restored until 1868. Howard to James Speed, July 7, 1865, Records of the Commr., Lets. Sent (M742, Roll 1), RG105, NA; Eliza Heacock to Stanton, Aug. 16, 1866, Records of the Commr., Lets. Recd. (M752, Roll 35), RG105, NA; *House Ex. Docs.*, 39 Cong., 2 Sess., No. 31, p. 15 (Ser. 1289); Constance M. Green, *Washington: Village and Capital* (2 vols., Princeton, 1962–63), 1: 294.

From Melvin M. Sams [1]

Beaufort, So. Ca. Augt. 18, 1865

To Andrew Johnson, President of the
United States of North America
Dear Sir

In behalf of myself and family I most respectfully solicit your kind consideration of this petition which I will endeavour to make as brief as possible. In November 1861 we were ordered by the Military Authority then existing to evacuate the town of Beaufort So. Ca. and our plantations. The said authorities we were compelled to obey, nor were we allowed to return, though I am informed that frequent proclamations inviting us to do so, had been published, none of which was ever seen by your petitioner.[2]

What I request of your Excellency, is the restitution of my residence in the town of Beaufort So. Ca., which residence has always been appropriated by the Government, as a hospital, and now, there being no war, and but few patients in hospital, I hope it will not be necessary to refuse me the use of the same. My family are at this moment houseless and penniless, neither home or means of support, unless your Excellency will order restitution of my home to us. I have never borne arms against our common country, or has any of my sons, one old enough to bear arms being in Penn during the whole time of the war, the others, *minors*. I have had no part in this rebellion, but most sincerely regret, that those who should have instructed the people more wisely, should have acted so foolishly and criminally.

I will likewise petition for a return to me of an Island, called *Lemon Island*, situated on Broad River, St. Lukes Parish, Beaufort District. Said Island I am informed was sold for taxes, though Brevt Maj Genl. Saxton told me he was not certain it was so, and could not give me any positive information as the commissioners had returned North; taking it for granted, that, that disposition has been made of it, I apply to your Excellency for restitution, as it was not by my voluntary act, that the Island was abandoned, but by the orders of my Superiors, I being help-less in the matter. And until the armistice between Genls. Sherman and Johnston, was not allowed to return, to claim any property of mine. Your Excellency will perceive how many of us, always loyal citizens—were obliged to fold our hands, and submit to utter ruin. To you and you alone Mr. President are our eyes turned, to pity our sufferings and redress as far as able our grievances.[3] And that you may live to enjoy the heartfelt thanks of your now suffering fellow citizens—is the prayer of your

Most obt Servt M. M. Sams

ALS, DNA-RG60, Office of Atty. Gen., Lets. Recd., President.

1. Sams (1815–1900) was a Beaufort physician. Marie H. Heywood and Alice R. H. Smith, "Inscriptions from St. Helena Churchyard, Beaufort, South Carolina," *SCHM*, 32 (1931): 227.

2. On November 8, 1861, Gen. Thomas W. Sherman ordered residents to abandon resistance and accept the fact of Union occupation, promising not to interfere with "social and local institutions." Three days later he rebuked his troops for committing "gross depredations" upon private property. However, many planters fled of their own accord. *OR*, Ser. 1, Vol. 6: 4–5, 187–88; Willie Lee Rose, *Rehearsal for Reconstruction: The Port Royal Experiment* (Indianapolis, 1964), 15–16.

3. Referred to the attorney general's office.

From William L. Sharkey

Executive Office, Jackson, Miss.,
August 18th 1865.

His Excellency Andrew Johnson
President of the United States
Dear Sir

I take great pleasure in introducing to your acquaintance, my friend Judge E S Fisher,[1] formerly a member of the Supreme Court of our State. I may say to you that Judge Fisher has never flinched on the great question of the Union, having been always bold in his denuncia-tion of secession, even to such an extent as to put his safety at hazard.

You may remember that Judge Fisher is the gentleman whose name we left with you as a suitable person to fill the office of District Judge in this State.[2]

The Judge will visit Washington on business and desires very much to make your acquaintance.

I have the honor to be Your Obedient Servant

W. L. Sharkey

LS, DNA-RG60, Appt. Files for Judicial Dists., Miss., E. S. Fisher.

1. Ephraim S. Fisher (1815–1876), a Coffeeville, Miss., attorney, was later a circuit judge. Irene S. and Norman E. Gillis, comps., *Abstract of Goodspeed's Mississippi* (Baton Rouge, 1962), 195.

2. During the summer of 1865 Sharkey supported Fisher for the district judgeship, but the following October he signed a petition endorsing Robert A. Hill, the eventual recipient of the position. Sharkey and Edward M. Yerger to Johnson, June 13, 1865, Johnson Papers, LC; Sharkey to James Speed, Aug. 5, 1865, and Sharkey et al. to Johnson, Oct. 19, 1865, Appt. Files for Judicial Dists., Miss., Robert A. Hill, RG60, NA.

From David J. Baldwin[1]

Houston Texas Saturday
19 August 1865

To His Excellency Andrew Johnson
President of The United States.
President:

In June last Gov. Hamilton of this state did me the honor to recommend me to be appointed attorney for the United States for the Eastern District of Texas; and though I have never yet received the commission, have had my eye, as a good citizen upon the interests of this nation as if actually in commission.[2] I have been home but Eleven days while the Governor has been here near a month at the Capitol at Austin. He was at once beset by prominent rebels for special pardon, and has been misled into recommending one John S. Sydnor[3] of this city for special pardon. The Gov. has been absent three years from the State. I was here in prison because I was a union man, and for no other cause.

He had never had opportunity to know the facts. Sydnor was the most bitter rebel and incited mobs to murder Union men, and Federal prisoners of war; and if such as he are to be readily pardoned the whole scheme of pardons is a most ridiculous mockery and farce. Sydnor, one of the most infamous is reported to have been recommended for pardon and brags that he has the Governors signature.

As an american citizen, who have lived here and suffered all the most infernal fire of rebel persecution and know whereof I speak, I do most solemnly protest against Mr Sydnors pardon, unless the whole scheme is to be abandoned.

I inclose this to the Attorney General; and remain your friend and obdt. sevt.

D. J. Baldwin

Another rebel recommended by the Governor for pardon *Wm. P. Ballinger*[4] was Receiver under the rebel govt concern at this place and Galveston and was swift to accept office under it, which he held up to the very last moment; and the community very justly think that if such men are pardoned, there is little room left on which to base that respect which is necessary to the existence of all good government. The Governor has been misled into these things I feel assured; but unless the pardon is to be universal, it is unjust that the most infamous and mischievous should be first pardoned.

B.

ALS, DNA-RG94, Amnesty Papers (M1003, Roll 55), Tex., John S. Sydnor.

1. Baldwin (b. *c*1818–*fl*1877), was a New Jersey-born attorney. 1860 Census, Tex., Harris, Houston, 3rd Ward, 140; *U.S. Off. Reg.* (1867–73, 1877).

2. The Senate approved Baldwin's appointment in April 1866. Appt. Bk. 4: 211, Ser. 6B, Johnson Papers, LC.

3. Sydnor (1812–1869), a former slave trader, had served briefly as a Confederate colonel. In 1866 he moved to New York City and became a broker. Webb and Carroll, eds., *Handbook of Texas*, 2: 700.

4. Ballinger (1825–1888) was formerly U.S. attorney for Texas (1850–54). Ibid., 1: 104.

From John M. Botts

Willards Hotel Augt. 19th 65

To his Excellency Andrew Johnson Prest U S

Dear Sir

This letter will be handed you by an old friend[1] who desires to be introduced to you & to ask pardon for his past offenses. He was an original Union man but drifted into the whirlpool with the rest of the State which he now found to have been a great error—& has since deeply regretted.

He is one of those who have been informed indirectly that for $900 a pardon will be guaranteed for himself, & his two sons[2]—which I have urgently advised him not to countenance, but to make his appeal at once to the proper authorities.

Prompt action is most desirable in his case as his property is more or less disturbed every day by parties who have a pecuniary interest in libelling all property for confiscation.

I recommend his case for your favorable consideration[3] and am

most respectfully your obdt svt

Jno M Botts

P.S. Mr Alexr. Dudleys[4] Post office is Richmond.

ALS, DNA-RG94, Amnesty Papers (M1003, Roll 57), Va., Thomas Branch.

1. Thomas Branch (1802–1888), a Petersburg, Va., merchant and former mayor, had been a unionist member of the secession convention but had voted for separation. After the war he moved to Richmond, where he was a founder of the Merchants' National Bank. Tyler, *Va. Biography*, 5: 1056.

2. Both James R. (*c*1828–*fl*1869) and John P. Branch (1830–1915), business partners with their father, served as officers in the Confederate army. Ibid., 4: 412–13; 1860 Census, Va., Dinwiddie, Petersburg, Centre Ward, 297; Richmond directories (1866–1901); Amnesty Papers (M1003, Roll 57), Va., James R. Branch, John P. Branch, RG94, NA.

3. Following Governor Peirpoint's recommendation, presidential pardons had been granted on July 18 for James R., and on August 1 for John P. and Thomas Branch. *House Ex. Docs.*, 40 Cong., 2 Sess., No. 16, pp. 43, 45, 47 (Ser. 1330).

4. Dudley (1820–1869), Richmond attorney and president of the Richmond and York River Railroad, had been Confederate purchasing agent at Yorktown. Amnesty Papers (M1003, Roll 59), Va., Alexander Dudley, RG94, NA; *Richmond Dispatch*, Sept. 14, 1869.

From Daniel S. Dickinson [1]

Binghamton Aug 19 1865

My Dear Sir

The first serious illness of my life has just left me.[2] I say *left*, for the *disease* has passed away, though I have not yet gained my customary strength or steading of nerve. Both are however returning to me. I expect to go to Coopertown the coming week,—the residence of Judge Nelson[3] of the U.S. Supreme Court, to meet my first assistant & unite in the argument of an important *revenue* question, in the celebrated "Banker & Broker Case".[4] This will be the first business of consequence, since my attack. I anticipate returning to the City about 1st proxo. when the courts are to open & Judges & lawyers generally return. My physicians advise me not to go before, as the heat is violent,—the air bad, & my system susceptible in its present state. They say that my fever was the fruit of years of over tasking body and brain in popular efforts,—having developement in that hard and sleepless journey I took to Washington, when I had the pleasure of greeting you.[5] But they encourage me with the opinion, that when my strength returns, my system will be renovated, and I will be better than for years. So much for what is very personal to myself and interesting to one who has *recovered* from *such* a malignant fever.

I have some time desired to give you my somewhat crude views of public affairs, and where matters are drifting, for I know you cannot but feel anxiety under such crushing responsibilities as bear upon you: And it is my belief, the newspapers have come to be about the last sources of truth & intelligence that can be relied on. The public appetite has, by the rebellion & its incidents, been whetted to extreme excitement, and the public palate seems to demand, at any rate the public *taste to* devour, every thing *sensational*, and the ambition & rivalry of the press, furnish the supply. But their sage speculations about *parties* & *divisions* and *cliques* and *"radicals"* are nine tenths the merest *bosh*, and were I a stranger to New York politics, I should not get the faintest idea of the real state of things from what they say. I can scarcey command my nerves to write, even as *well* as *usual*, but will do as well as I can, and promise, by saying what none will dispute, that our state is a *large one*,—the patronage Federal, State & Metropolitan tremendous, and you know just what *such* a state of things produces.

Present state of *parties.*

For all practical political purposes, in the *next national* campaign, the *present* organizations are of little consequence. They will, or rather the popular elements of which they are composed will, be disintegrated and *reformed.* There will be an effort to keep on foot, and give control, to the Republican party. But *it* died in the election of Mr Lincoln in 1860, and nothing preserved & perpetuated its elements or the fragments of them but the rebellion. It took, in that contest, the Union side, and Union democrats, under the *name* of *Union*, went along, as you & I did, to put down rebellion and save the government; without putting on *their* uniform, or adopting their general creed, if they had one. That portion, who will try to keep this defunct organization at the head of the Union organization, & call it "Republican", will *generaly* come from the old whig ranks,—the old democrats who joined the Republicans for a single purpose, will look for a new healthy organization, of democratic tendencies, and the democrats (*war* democrats I mean who opposed Mr Lincoln in 1860, but supported his administration to put down rebellion[)], will of course assist their own *independent* creed. It is, as you percieve, *my theory*, that the Republican party has no real effective party existence,—that the *Union party*, having conquered the rebellion,—*its* mission, has been discharged, & it must go to pieces by reason of *overgrowth*, with no mission before it, and from incongruous elements. The Union party then, will fall from *strength*, and no object whereon to exhourt it, for *reconstruction* and *restoration* are new questions. Now as to that suicidal faction, who borrowed the name of the Democratic party under which to commit self destruction, it will court oblivion, and fall from inherent weakness,—a vicious organization and principles which would have broken down the hero of the Hermitage in the heyday of his popular eclat. The leaders thought, that by force of *party drill*, compact organization and an honored name, they could stem & resist a great popular current, wherein was flowing the best life blood of the nation. They *now* believe that they,—these same leaders, can rally around *their* disgraced organization the masses of the party because they have called it democratic, but, the memories of the last four years are too vivid, & it cannot and will not be done; but, they must all ground arms & fall into the ranks, to be *re-mustered* under her issues, and her leadership. Now we have got all parties disbanded, except in *name*, & for mere *temporary* & local *purposes*, & you enquire what is to be done with this numberless mass of men? I answer "reconstruct", around a new standard bearer, with a creed so *truly democratic*, so catholic & comprehensive, that every true patriot can come in. This is what should be, what must be to ensure soundness & success, and what I think *will be*. What shall be that new name? It may be called Democratic or Democratic Republican, as it character should be, or union as should be its leading purpose, or perchance, as in the case of Jackson, for more complete designation, it may assume *temporarily*, the name of its chosen leader. But who shall he be? He must be before the people now, & well & widely known, & enjoy the popular confidence. In *your own person*, you hold these essential requisits, & *fine* success in your administration, will give you the future as you have the present. The question of "reconstruction" is a delicate & difficult one. It will require wisdom, patience & self reliance; and it will be as hazardous to "swap horses" in 1868, (if we have a good one) as it was in 1864. The popular judgment is with you, clearly & decidedly thus far. They approve of your policy distinctly, and are prepared to sustain you in all rallying in the same direction. The masses want a *man representing* great *truths* & *principles*, to rally around, & hence *you* have the vantage ground. The days of *mere party* leadership, and *blind following* is over. We have entered upon a new era, and should take heed accordingly. Your views on the negro suffrage will, I am persuaded, obtain in every old free state except perhaps Massachusetts. Undoubtedly it is preferd, that they should be given the ballot, when they have learned self reliance, preservation and how to think & act, but all see that it must & ought to be left to the States. No issue can be raised on it *here*, & I presume none will be proposed generally. As to "radicals" the only trouble *I* apprehend from them, in this state is, the creation of a sickly sentimentality against punishing treason & murder when lawfully convicted.

Since I have sketched the out line of my favorite movement,—the one or such an one as I contend will command success, you will perhaps enquire what is to be the nature of the *opposition*, & whence is it to come? My predictions are, that while there will be some, say two or perhaps three candidates of *some class*, the *real* contest will be with *Epouletts*! from which *I say*, good Lord deliver us! If you look only to a successful administration of the Government, the *present term*, it is proper you should be advised by your friends, how matters stand, & with what you have to deal. If you have future ambitions, as it is right & *natural* & proper you should have, it is doubly so, for present success will secure future triumph. I have watched the popular elements long & carefully,—have analized them minutely and contemplated them philisophicaly, and am pretty certain I understand them. The future is to give us less manipulation of leaders,—successful manipulation I mean, and more of an earnest popular struggle. Pardon this long and rambling epistle. It is extended far beyond my intentions when I took up my pen. If at any time you should be spared a moment, it would be a great gratification to receive a note, however brief, expressive of your views or wishes.

I am glad to hear of your improved health, but this reminds me, that a friend in the City has just written me, condemning the White House for unhealthiness, & saying you ought not to be there in the warm season.

I have the honor to be, & Sincly Yours D. S. Dickinson
His Excelly Andrew Johnson Prest &c

ALS, DLC-JP.

1. Appointed by Lincoln in April 1865 as U.S. attorney for the southern district of New York, Dickinson served until his death the next year.

2. Dickinson was recovering from a bout with typhoid fever. John R. Dickinson, ed., *Speeches, Correspondence, etc. of the Late Daniel S. Dickinson* (2 vols., New York, 1867), 2: 672.

3. Nominated by Tyler to the U.S. Supreme Court, Samuel Nelson (1792–1873) took his seat in 1845. His knowledge of international and maritime law caused Grant to appoint him to the Joint High Commission to settle the *Alabama* claims (1871). The following year he resigned his seat. *DAB.*

4. Probably *Van Allen v. The Assessors*, 3 Wallace 573 (1866) in which Nelson delivered the majority opinion upholding a New York law allowing the state to tax bank shareholders, even when part of the bank's capital was invested in U.S. securities. Fairman, *Reconstruction and Reunion*, 46–47.

5. Reports of this visit have not been found.

From James A.L. McColloch[1]

Cane Hill, Washington Co, Arks
August 19th 1865—

To the Hon. Andrew Johnson, President of the U.S.
Sir.

On the 12th of February 1864, I took and subscribed, an oath of allegiance to the government of the U.S. before the Provost Marshall at the Post of Van Buren, Arks. In the early part of November following I went to the State of Texas. I remained within the lines of the Southern armies until their forces were surrendered by Genl E. K. Smith, when I at once, returned to my home. When I took the oath abovementioned, it was done in good faith, and punctually observed, until it became necessary to preserve my life, that I should leave home.[2] That it was necessary for self preservation that I should leave home is evident from the fact that nearly all the citizens of my neighborhood who remained at home, were either hanged or shot, and the country burned up and devastated, by a portion of the men who pursued Genl Price[3] from Missouri in November last. I removed no negroes, and only took sufficient transportation for my personal Comfort. The only representative of money which I possessed, was of a character which would be useful to me only in a southern state. I was originally a Union man, voting for that ticket, at the inception of our troubles, when the state Convention was organized.

Having read your proclamation of the 29th May last, and seeing that those who have once taken the oath and afterwards gone south, are excepted from the amnesty therein contained, and may apply to the President of the U.S. for restoration of rights &c, I hereby respectfully ask that the disability which I have unwittingly incurred be removed, and that *pardon* and *amnesty* be granted me.[4]

I have the honor to be Very Resp'f'ly Your Ob't sv't
James A. L. McColloch

Address J. A L. McColloch
Care of D. C. Williams[5] Van Buren Arks

ALS, DNA-RG94, Amnesty Papers (M1003, Roll 14), Ark., James A. L. McColloch.
1. McColloch (b. *c*1820) was a Tennessee-born tailor. 1850 Census, Ark., Washington, Cane Hill Twp., 836.
2. The pardon application of fellow townsman Lewis W. Gates, bearing the same date and in McColloch's hand, also indicated that exiling oneself was necessary because of "the violence of men who hanged and shot citizens regardless of age or political proclivity." Amnesty Papers (M1003, Roll 14), Ark., Lewis W. Gates, RG94, NA.
3. Sterling Price.
4. McColloch, falling under the 10th and 14th exceptions to Johnson's proclamation, was granted a pardon on September 13, 1865. Amnesty Papers (M1003, Roll 14), Ark., James A. L. McColloch, RG94, NA.
5. Williams (1815–*fl*1881) was a New Orleans-born wholesale merchant, who had migrated to Arkansas. William S. Speer and John H. Brown, eds., *The Encyclopedia of the New West* (Marshall, Tex., 1881), "Arkansas," 223.

From Charleston Methodist Episcopal Laymen[1]

Charleston S C Aug 20th 1865.

To His Excellency Andrew Johnson
President of the United States

The undersigned your petitioners respectfully ask a revocation of the order by which the Churches in the City of Charleston known as *Trinity, Spring St* & *Old Bethel* with the *Parsonage*, the property of the Methodist Episcopal Church (South) have been put into the possession of the Methodist Episcopal Church (North).

Your petitioners respectfully show that none of this property could be properly termed "abandoned."

Trinity church was under the shells & after being repeatedly struck was closed up as untenable.

Spring St was impressed by the Military authority then in power in the City for medical purposes.

Old Bethel was regularly poss[ess]ed and occupied up to the time of the capture of the City by the United States Armies.

The Parsonage—in consequence of the ill health of the pastor who had been sent away months previously by his physicians—was in charge of two respectable colored people Samuel & Mary Logan.

Your petitioners respectfully represent that their church buildings are entirely occupied by the blacks[2]—many or most of whom are not members of our church communion—to the exclusion of those who built & occupied them; still your petitioners in asking to be repossesed of their church buildings have no desire to restrict any of the opportunities or privileges of worship hitherto cheerfully accorded to the colored people, but pledge themselves to extend to them the same accommodations which they have always afforded them in their churches, in former years which was always ample. The occupation of our Parsonage and church buildings by the Rev Mr. Lewis[3] under an order of the Secretary of war—at a meeting of the official members of the church in the City at that time—was acquiesced in as a necessity of war immediately upon the capture of the City by the United States Armies when his authority was exhibited. But while Mr. Lewis has proven himself a laborious and diligent minister, it is not unnatural that with the return of quiet and good order & our Pastors having taken the oath of Amnesty we earnestly desire to return immediately to our former Pastors & wrship.

And your petitioners will ever pray.[4]

Pet, DNA-RG107, Lets. Recd., EB12 President 3010 (1865).
1. Sixteen signatures from stewards, trustees, and an elder were appended.
2. According to an endorsement, only two churches had been reassigned by the military for blacks' use.
3. T. Willard Lewis, serving as a Methodist missionary in reorganizing black churches in Charleston, is not otherwise identified. *Charleston Courier*, June 1, 1865.
4. Referred to the War Department by the President's office, the petition was forwarded to the commanding officer at Charleston, William T. Bennett, who endorsed restoration "to their former trustees in case they are willing to assist in providing places of worship for the Colored population."

To Commandant of Post, Richmond, Va.[1]

Executive Office August 20. 1865
Commandant of Post, Richmond, Va.

Mr. Alexander Dudley, President of some Railroad in Va., and now in Richmond, obtained a pardon from this office on Thursday last.[2]

I hope you will without delay if Mr. Dudley is in Richmond have him found and request to deliver the Pardon to you which you will transmit to this office by mail. Explanation will be made to Mr. Dudley for recalling this Pardon when he applies to this office.

I hope this will be attended to promptly.[3]

Andrew Johnson President U.S.

Tel, DNA-RG107, Tels. Sent, President, Vol. 2 (1865).
1. Orris S. Ferry (1823–1875), a Norwalk, Conn., attorney who served in Congress as a Republican (1859–61), rose to brevet major general in 1865, after four years of

service in Virginia. Afterwards he was elected to the U.S. Senate. *BDAC*; Warner, *Blue*.

2. Dudley's pardon was dated July 6, but he evidently did not receive it until he personally appeared in Washington in mid-August. Amnesty Papers (M1003, Roll 59), Va., Alexander Dudley, RG94, NA; *House Ex. Docs.*, 40 Cong., 2 Sess., No. 16, p. 55 (Ser. 1330).

3. The next day the President dispatched another wire to Ferry saying if Dudley "does not immediately deliver to you the pardon he obtained here, you will cause his arrest, and have him sent here." Johnson to Commandant of Post (Ferry), Aug. 21, 1865, Tels. Sent, President, Vol. 2 (1865), RG107, NA.

From James Fitzpatrick

August 20, 1865, Macon, Ga.; ALS, DNA-RG94, Amnesty Papers (M1003, Roll 23), Ga., M. S. Thomson.

A former refugee, never "Stained with perjury or treason," who has lived in New Haven, Conn., since the fall of 1863, protests against the pardoning of Methven S. Thomson, Confederate mayor of Macon, until "the whereabouts of James Melcher & Mr Bowman are ascertained." Thomson had made examples of these Union men, who were sentenced to leave the state, and since that time "have not been herd from." Fitzpatrick also laments that "the Same city officials that on divers occasions in 62 & 63 would countenance and encourage mob law and Lynch law" against Union citizens still occupy the same positions. [Thomson, claiming that as mayor he had helped "rescue several parties from popular violence," was pardoned September 20, 1865.]

From W. H. Griffin [1]

Cahaba Dallas Co. Ala. Aug 20th 1865

Hon A. Johnson President U.S.A.

Dear, & Honoured Sir.

Many, many long years have passed away, Since Our Acquaintance, commenced, & which was of Short duration, & no doubt, I have never been thought of by you Since. About the time the Short Acquantance Commenced, in the year 1828[*sic*] At Laurence [Laurens] Court House South Carolina, whilst you worked with Mr. Denton.[2] You may possably remember me, as the Village School Master at that time, & possably may remember my Marriage to the Daughter of Mr. Allen Barksdale[3] of the Vicinity of Laurensville. And possably may remember that you were the maker of my Wedding Coat, a beautiful mixed homespun. Many & various have been the Scenes which we have both passed through Since that day. I having in the revolve of time only arose to an humble Legislator of this my State, & Judge of A. County Court. Whilst you have far outstriped me, in filling Some of the highest positions belonging to the United States, & now filling the most exalted position that it has ever falen to the lot of man to fill, "that of President of the United States of America." While God in his Providence has Seen fit to exault you to the pinicle of fame, I am left far behind an humble planter, & In that position I come before you as an humble petitioner in behalf of One who for Twenty five years, I have been Politically opposed to, & one whose later Acts have not pleased me, & one whose Sins I trust are not of So deep a dye as to prevent them being forgiven. I Allude to Jefferson Davis Late President of the Confederate States.

Our Saviour Asked that his Vile persecutors & murderers Should be forgiven. He also forgave the thief on the Cross. And cannot man, be induced to forgive a poor erring man? Jeff. Davis was the Representative President of the mass of the people of the Confederate States, & expected by them to carry Out their principles, the Same as it is expected of you to carry out the principles of the United States. The people who Elected him were the real offenders, he being only one of the people. But he has been overpowered the Confederacy Subdued, Our Banner furled, & the whole come to an end. Why not now forgive the offenders? Pardon him, & he can never again cause a rebellion in the Land. His worst enemies here are Anxious for his being pardoned, & let me beg of you, to extend clemency towards him, & let him go free. He can never again cause an outbreak in this Government. I will further ask your clemency towards a perticular friend (Personally) of mine, but a Strong Political enemy, in the Person of George W. Gayle[4] of Cahaba, Alabama, who wrote in one of his Sprees, offering a reward to have Mr. Lincon put to death. No one here Attached any importance to the Advertizement knowing that he was utterly unable to advance money or cause any move towards having the thing Accomplished. Socially he is an excellent man, & an Able Lawyer, & has one of the most interesting Families in the State. I will State that I was Always opposed to Secession. I wrote against it, I Spoke against it, telling in what it would result. It is true after the State Seceded, I was with my State, but we have been overpowered & Subdued, & ruined. Have we not Suffered enough? I think we have, & trust in God that you in the exercise of the great powers entrusted to your hands, will come to the Same conclusion, & extend mercy to all offenders. Trusting in the great Ruler of nations, & men that in the future we may all live in Amity, & friendship. Trusting that you may give due Consideration to the Above, I Remain honoured Sir your most obedient, & humble

Servant. W. H. Griffin

P.S. Should you remember me, I will State that Mr Denton died long Since That my Father in law Mr. Allen Barksdale & wife[5] are Still living So is John Garlington[6] Clerk of the Court & that I moved to this State in 1832 & Am living within a few miles of Cahaba Ala.

Yours W.H.G—

ALS, DLC-JP.
1. Griffin (b. c1801) was a farmer. 1860 Census, Ala., Dallas, Cahaba, 78.
2. Not found. Tradition has it that Johnson spent a brief—possibly a year—sojourn in Laurens, S.C. Griffin is clearly wrong about the year, for it should be 1824 or '25.
3. Barksdale (1783–1870) was a South Carolina farmer. 1860 Census, S.C., Lau-

rens, Laurens Court House, 139; James L. and Margaret E. Bolt, comps., *Family Cemeteries Laurens County, S.C.* (2 vols., Greenville, S.C., 1983), 2: 7.

4. Gayle (1807–1875), former district attorney and legislator, had advertised in December 1864 for "cash or good securities" worth one million dollars with which he would "cause the lives of Abraham Lincoln, William H. Seward and Andrew Johnson to be taken by the 1st of March next." Arrested after Lincoln's assassination, he was released the following December, without trial, and was pardoned by Johnson on April 24, 1867. Willis Brewer, *Alabama: Her History, Resources, War Record, and Public Men* (Montgomery, 1872), 219; Gandrud, *Early Alabama Newspapers*, 128; John W. DuBose, *Alabama's Tragic Decade* (Birmingham, 1940), 257; *Bangor Whig and Courier*, Dec. 19, 1865; Amnesty Record, Vol. 3, Ser. 8C, Johnson Papers, LC.

5. Nancy Barksdale (1787–1866). Bolt, *Cemeteries*, 2: 7.

6. John Garlington (1784–1866), former county clerk having over $100,000 of real and personal property on the eve of the war, took the oath on August 19 and was pardoned by Johnson, September 27, 1865. Horace E. Hayden, *Virginia Genealogies: A Genealogy of the Glassell Family of Scotland and Virginia* (Baltimore, 1959[1891]), 259; 1860 Census, S.C., Laurens, Laurens Court House, 4; Amnesty Papers (M1003, Roll 45), Va., John Garlington, RG94, NA.

From Landon C. Haynes [1]

Statesville N.C. August 20 1865.

To his Excellency Andrew Johnson. P.U.S.

Sir:

I address your Excellency this note respectfully to request your permission to go to and return from Washington City at such time as may suit your convenience together with the privilege of a personal interview with you. Surrounded by serious embarresments greatly effecting the comfort of my family, who are here with me, and conscious that your Excellency alone can afford me any relief; I am anxious to have a personal interview, in the hope, that I may be able to satisfy your Excellency that your magnanimity and clemency will not be misdirected, in granting my application for pardon and amnesty under your proclamation of the 29th of May 1865 this day forwarded.

Will your Excellency be so kind, as to signify to me through Col. N. Boyden [2] the bearer of this note, or by telegram at Salisbury N.C., whether you are pleased to grant me this privilege? [3]

Respectfully your Obt Svt.

Landon C. Haynes

ALS, DNA-RG94, Amnesty Papers (M1003, Roll 39), N.C., Landon C. Haynes.

1. Fellow East Tennessee Democrat and frequent antagonist, Haynes had been Confederate sequestration receiver when Johnson's property was seized and was later a Confederate senator. Although living in Statesville at war's end, Haynes eventually resettled in Memphis. *BDTA*, 1: 348; see *Johnson Papers*, 5: 37, 105–8.

2. Nathaniel Boyden (1796–1873), North Carolina lawyer, served as a Whig congressman before the war, and afterwards as a Republican (1868–69). *BDAC*.

3. Johnson issued a pardon for Haynes on June 11, 1866. Amnesty Papers (M1003, Roll 39), N.C., Landon C. Haynes, RG94, NA.

From Sam Milligan

Nashville Ten August 20, 1865

To/ His Excellency Andrew Johnson
President of the U.S.
Sir:

Since I saw you I have had the pleasure of meeting Gov. Brown and Judge Stephens[1] of Georgia. With the former you are personally acquainted, and the latter is a brother of the Hon. Alexander Stephens, and formerly one of the Judges of the Supreme Court of Georgia. They are both on their way to Washington, to ask Executive Clemency for themselves.[2] Today I had an unreserved and highly gratifying interview with them. I do not doubt their sincerity, and certainly their political views do not materially differ with what I conceive to be the policy of your administration. At least, I am thoroughly satisfied it is to the interest of the Country that their applications should be promptly granted. I am aware of the great embarrassments you labor under, and the caution necessary to be observed in such cases, but it does seem to me, that the high character these gentlemen sustain at home, and the great influence they can, and I doubt not, will exert in the state, make it a matter of policy as well as justice, to grant their pardons without delay.

Excuse the freedom I have taken on this note, and beleve me

Your friend truly Sam Milligan

ALS, DNA-RG94, Amnesty Papers (M1003, Roll 16), Ga., Joseph E. Brown.

1. Linton Stephens (1823–1872), Alexander H. Stephens' half-brother, was a lawyer, Confederate field officer, and state legislator. Wakelyn, *BDC*.

2. Although they tried to see the President, in Brown's case at least four times, apparently neither Brown nor Stephens made their way through the White House throng. Both, however, acquired their pardons: Stephens on September 2 and Brown four days later. Amnesty Papers (M1003, Roll 23), Ga., Linton Stephens, RG94, NA; *New York World*, Sept. 5, 1865; *Washington Evening Star*, Sept. 4, 7, 1865.

From George V. Moody [1]

Port Gibson Mississippi
August 20" 1865.

To His Excellency, Andrew Johnson,
President of the United States of America.

The petition of George V. Moody of the county of Claiborne, state of Mississippi, Respectfully shows that he is a native of the city of Portland in the state of Maine, whence, during the first year of his life, his father & family became domiciled in & residents of the state of Maryland, where your petitioner continued to reside until the spring of 1837 when he came to Port Gibson Mississippi & has resided here ever since.

He is now forty-nine years of age, has been a straight out whig voter ever since his majority, until the American Party arose. During its existence he voted & acted as a native american & since its decease, he has acted & voted with the whig & union parties. Your petitioner never held & does not now beleive the doctrine of secession. From 1848 until 1860 your petitioner combated the same & supported the union party, but when the state seceeded, he, as a revolutionist, went into the army of the Confederacy as captain of artillery & served as such until 5" December 1863, when he was captured near Knoxville, Tenn & was held as a prisoner of war until 18" March 1865, when he was sent to Richmond, Va., on parole, to be exchanged, which parole he has kept inviolate, ever since. Afterward he was informed of his promotion to a colonelcy of Artillery but has not recd. official notice of the fact. After the fall of Richmond he went to Greensboro North Carolina, & there heard of the surrender of Genl. R. E. Lee. Being then on parole he received verbal orders to go to his home & across the Mississippi & there await his exchange & orders. In obedience thereto, he started on the journey & at Washington Georgia on first of May last, met with Mrs Davis, wife of Mr Jefferson Davis. She was there with her family of four young children & a young sister & desired your petitioner to travel with them as a friend & protector. Believing that Mr J. Davis was at that time going through to the Trans-Mississippi Dept. via northern Georgia & Alabama, & Mrs Davis believing the same & intending to go south from Washington, your petitioner agreed so to travel with her party, & on 1st May did so, going south. On the 2nd or 3rd May last to the surprise of the whole party, Mr Jefferson Davis joined their party, remained a few hours & resumed his line of travel westward; Mrs D & party going south. Shortly after this your petitioner was informed that Mrs D. desired to go to Florida & thence to Europe. Your petitioner being requested to continue to travel with this party consented so to do until she should reach Florida & be in some safety & comfort. To his surprise, on the morning of the 8" May last, Mr J Davis again joined Mrs. Ds. party aforesaid, stating he had made a forced march of 60 miles out of his course, to protect her from confederate deserters & paroled soldiers, who were then taking, by force, all the horses & mules they saw anywhere from anyone. Your petitioner was then informed & beleives that Mr Davis then intended to leave Mrs Davis' party as soon as his animals could be ridden again & beleives Mr. Davis would have so left Mrs Davis' party & pursue his westerly course, on the morning of the tenth of May last, but for his capture at daybreak of that day. Your petitioner was then sent to Fort McHenry Md. as prisoner of war where he was held until 14" July last, when, by the order of your Excellency he was released on parole to report to the Secretary of War when required &c. Your petitioner has never been a candidate for, nor has he held any civil office under the

state, Federal, or Confederate Government. He beleives his property is
not, & was not on the 29" May last, worth $20,000. in cash, neither
would it sell for so much but not knowing who may, hereafter, estimate
its value, fears he cannot safely rely of the effect of taking the amnesty
oath, without a special pardon. He further shows that no proceedings
have been instituted against him, or his property by the United States,
nor have they seized, or taken possession of any part thereof. Your petitioner sincerely desires and intends to be a truly loyal citizen of the
United States & has taken the amnesty oath, a copy of which is herewith filed & made part hereof. Thereupon your [petitioner] prays for a
special pardon in the premises & as in duty bound will ever pray &c.[2]

George V. Moody

ALS, DNA-RG94, Amnesty Papers (M1003, Roll 34), Miss., George V. Moody.

1. Moody (c1816–1866), a lawyer, was murdered after the war. Haskell M. Monroe,
Jr. et al., eds., *The Papers of Jefferson Davis* (6 vols., Baton Rouge, 1971-), 4: 125;
Sylvester Weeks, ed., *A Life's Retrospect: Autobiography of Rev. Granville Moody, D.D.*
(Cincinnati, 1890), 362.

2. Recommended by Governor Sharkey, his brother Granville Moody, and others,
Moody was pardoned September 20, 1865. Amnesty Papers (M1003, Roll 34), Miss.,
George V. Moody, RG94, NA.

From Benjamin F. Perry

Greenville So. Ca. August 20th 1865

His Excellency President Johnson

When I issued my Proclamation[1] there were no garrisons in the upper part of the State, and consequently no one to administer the Oath
of Allegiance. I therefore ordered that civil magistrates who were appointed by me, and who had taken the Oath might administer it to
others. This was done so as to qualify the voters to vote at the election
for members of the Convention. There are several Districts, in which
there are yet, no military officers to administer the oath, and the election
will take place in two weeks. The military authorities have issued an
order prohibiting the magistrates administering the Oath under my
Proclamation.[2] I see the Provisional Governors of Mississippi, Alabama
and North Carolina, have done what I did and I suppose for the same
purpose, to enable the people to vote at the election.

The military authorities in some portions of the State refused to let
the civil officers act, at all, in their official capacity, under my Proclamation. The Governor of Mississippi has organized his Provisional
Government in the same way that I did, and the Governor of Alabama
likewise in a great measure. I made known to your Excellency whilst I
was in Washington the plan I had adopted and I thought it met your
sanction.

It seems to me that it would be much better to let the civil authorities
act in concert with the military and take cognizance of certain classes

of cases which ought to be decided according to law. The Provost Marshalls decide the *same* cases differently in almost every District. They have no general rule for their decisions. This is productive of great dissatisfaction.

I am disposed to harmonize with the military authorities, and all I desire is to preserve order and peace in the State and get her back into the Union as speedily as possible. I hope your Excellency will make known to me your views and wishes in relation to these matters.[3] I am with great respect and consideration, yours truly &c.

B. F. Perry

LS, DLC-JP.
    1. See Letter from Perry, August 10, 1865.
    2. Gen. Q. A. Gillmore countermanded Perry's order, insisting that only provost marshals under his authority would administer the oath. James E. Sefton, *The United States Army and Reconstruction* (Baton Rouge, 1967), 29; Kibler, *Perry*, 402–3.
    3. See Telegram to Perry, August 29, 1865.

From Benjamin F. Perry

Greenville S. C August 20th 1865

His Excellency President Johnson
My dear Sir

Ex-Governor F. W. Pickens[1] has taken the oath of allegiance and applied for pardon under your amnesty Proclamation. I have approved his application & forwarded it on to you. In the mean time, & until your Excellency considers his application, he has requested me to ask for him of your Excellency, a Parole to prevent his being arrested or disturbed.

The Ex Governor is heartily with us in reforming the constitution, abolishing slavery, electing Governor and Presidential Electors by the People, & also in destroying the Parish representation. He is a candidate for the convention & I hope you will send a pardon for him,[2] when you send for Col. Orr, Generals McGowen, Bratton & Hampton,[3] so that he too make [may] be able to take his seat in the convention. Colonel Orr informs me that you requested him to forward you a list of such applicants for pardon as will be in the convention & assist in carry out the changes necessary to be made. James P Boyce & Wm. W. Boyce & James Conner[4] are also to be members of the convention. But my present purpose in writing you was to obtain a parole for Ex Governor Pickens, who wishes to visit Georgia & fears that he may be arrested once there.

Every thing is going on well in South Carolina, & all are willing to give up slavery forever. Governor Pickens told me last night that if his three hundred & twenty five negroes were tendered back to him he would not accept them as slaves. All are anxious to get back into the Union, & I believe sincere in their penitence.

I am with great respect & esteem
yours truly & very sincerely B. F. Perry

ALS, DNA-RG94, Amnesty Papers, S.C., Francis W. Pickens.

1. Francis W. Pickens (1805–1869), lawyer, planter and secessionist governor, had taken refuge at his home in Edgefield, S.C. John B. Edmunds, Jr., *Francis W. Pickens and the Politics of Destruction* (Chapel Hill, 1986), 175.

2. A special parole for Pickens has not been found. Although he later served as a delegate to the South Carolina constitutional convention, Pickens failed to receive a pardon from Johnson, despite subsequent pleas by himself and other endorsements by Perry. Ibid., 175–80; see Pickens to Johnson, Sept. 29, 1865, Perry to Johnson, Sept. 25, Oct. 29, 1865, Johnson Papers, LC; Pickens to Johnson, Nov. 30, 1865, Appt. Files for Judicial Dists., S.C., F. W. Pickens, RG60, NA.

3. James L. Orr, Samuel McGowan (1819–1897), John Bratton (1831–1898), and Wade Hampton (1818–1902), all postwar South Carolina politicians, were pardoned on August 9, September 27, September 22, and November 13, 1865, respectively. All served as convention delegates except Hampton, who, though elected, failed to attend. Warner, *Gray*; *House Ex. Docs.*, 39 Cong., 2 Sess., No. 31, p. 4 (Ser. 1289); Amnesty Papers (M1003, Roll 45), S.C., Wade Hampton, RG94, NA; *House Ex. Docs.*, 40 Cong., 1 Sess., No. 32, p. 46 (Ser. 1311); *Senate Ex. Docs.*, 39 Cong., 1 Sess., No. 26, pp. 153, 174–75 (Ser. 1237); Amnesty Record, Vol. 1, Ser. 8C, Johnson Papers, LC.

4. A first cousin to William W. Boyce, James Pettigru Boyce (1827–1888) was a Baptist theologian and South Carolina unionist. Conner (1829–1883) was a lawyer and Confederate general. *Encyclopedia of Southern Baptists* (4 vols., Nashville, 1958–82), 1: 183–84; Kibler, *Perry*, 343; James P. Boyce to Johnson, Sept. 19, 1865, Johnson Papers, LC; Henry M. Cox, "Notes on the Boyce Family of Laurens and Newberry," *SCHM*, 61 (1960): 82.

From William L. Sharkey
In Cypher

Jackson Miss Aug 20th 1865

His Excellency Andrew Johnson
Washington.

Your dispatch received. The following amendment to our constitution will pass by a large majority[1]—that neither Slavery nor involuntary servitude otherwise than in the punishment of crime whereof the party shall have been duly convicted shall hereafter exist in this State and the Legislature at its next session and thereafter as the public welfare may require shall provide by law for the protection and security of the persons & property of the Freedmen of this State and guard them and the State from any Evils that may arise from their sudden emancipation.

Many are in favor of giving them the right to testify but probably this and the right of suffrage may be left to the Legislature. The amendment to the constitution of the United States is referred by Congress to the Legislatures. Can we not now get rid of martial law and have the habeas corpus restored? The Dept having charge of the negroes I fear is badly managed here.[2] The negroes are bold in their threats and the people are afraid. I have called for volunteer companies of militia in each county to suppress crime[3] which is becoming alarming. Cannot the State arms be turned over to me. It may be done with perfect safety. Perhaps I may think it necessary to organize the whole of the militia. These measures, I ask, would have a good effect in the other States and certainly here.

W. L. Sharkey
Prov Govr of Miss

Tel, DLC-JP.

1. This reference is to a vote in the Mississippi constitutional convention, then meeting in Jackson. An amended version of this clause passed 87–11. Harris, *Presidential Reconstruction*, 53–54.

2. Col. Samuel Thomas headed the Freedmen's Bureau. Several white planters, including Joseph Davis, brother of the Confederate president, resented the Bureau's intervention to protect black laborers. Ibid., 93–97.

3. A reference to Sharkey's August 19 proclamation calling on each county to raise two militia companies to serve as a police force. The proclamation ignited a serious controversy over civil versus military authority under Johnson's plan for Reconstruction.

From Jesse F. Bunker

August 21, 1865, Bunker's Hill, Knox County, Tenn.; ALS, DNA-RG105, Records of the Commr., Lets. Recd. from Executive Mansion.

After observing the "popular indignation of many Citizens in this State . . . against the Black man, and indeed throughout the South . . . if we may credit the Correspondence of Southern papers," this "Adopted Citizen of Tennessee" believes that "our Govt., by all means, at the earliest opportunity, should transport these people beyond the limits of this Hemisphere." He approves Governor Wells's reconstruction in Louisiana, and warns that "Negro suffrage must not be tolerated in this nation as a general principle . . . for the people, who are sovereign . . . are already chafed to exasperation upon this subject." Bunker reminds Johnson of Lincoln's promise of compensation to loyal slaveholders who relinquished their slaves for Union military service.

From Lewis D. Campbell

Hamilton O. August 21st, 1865.

My Dear Sir—

When I returned from my hasty visit to Washington in April last it was my design to go back and see you again after the overwhelming melancholy excitement which then prevailed should subside. On my return home I wrote you a letter[1] according to promise touching the policy which my feeble judgment dictated as proper under the peculiarly embarrassing circumstances which surrounded you. That letter I presume you received, and you must permit me now to express my satisfaction that the line of policy you have thus far pursued has so fully coincided with my own views. I have oftentimes felt a strong desire to see and talk with you and express in person this satisfaction; but since my return I have been so constantly engaged in driving my farming business that I have not been absent from home for a single day or as far away from my fields of labor as Cincinnati. You may conclude from this, perhaps, that I have either put myself on my good behavior or am confined to the *jail limits*, (as was the case when Gen. Buell's Capt. Greene put me under arrest when, as Provost Marshal of Nashville I peremptorily refused to turn the Military Governor of Tennessee out of possession of a Rebel Colonel house and instal therein his theiving and dissolute Quarter Master.[)][2] Let me assure you however, that I am about as great a sinner as ever, and that the last time I have been in *duress vile* was on that interesting occasion of my cutting the troublesome knot of military authority and rank which that *skissicks* Greene and you got up for me. But as my crops are now all made I shall be entirely at leisure, and think of running on to Washington between this and the meeting of Congress to have another free and frank talk with you about the men and measures of the day. On receiving your dispatch of the 19th[3] I was half inclined to gather up Kate (whose health is still rather delicate) and make a flying trip to the metropolis—the great centre of political iniquity. Having spent ten years of the better part of my life in trying to "get the hang of that School house" and studying its ways, I think that I might at my present advanced stage of life spend a few days there without having my morals entirely corrupted. But I could scarcely expect (unless from the fact that I have neither power nor place nor money to contribute to the vultures that hover around the capitol) to escape the abuse and misrepresentation of the hired *penny-a-liners*[4] to manufacture sensational items and minister them to the morbid *maw* of an inquisitive public.

But of this enough! My chief purpose in writing to you is accomplished in expressing my satisfaction with your general course, and especially in your disposition of the Negro suffrage question. Sensible people generally are satisfied. When your North Carolina proclamation was issued the howl of a certain class of politicians of the Chase-Sumner-Wilson brand, was loud and ferocious. They swore that they would either ignore or repudiate the Johnson policy at the Ohio Union State Convention; but through an active outward pressure and a large Soldiers' delegation (which was a *unit*) we *hived* the swarm of radicals and your policy was triumphantly approved. I hope you found some comfort in that result.

But the Chase men were bound not to give it up so. Oberlin is their head quarters. Its population think that when Oberlin takes snuff the whole world must sneeze![5] It was, before the rebellion, the strong hold of Northern Secessionists and disunionists, and the *terminus* of all the *underground rail-roads* that were used to run to Canada the Slaves of the South. Father Giddings[6] was all-potent there, and there it was that

they got up meetings and resolved to resist forcibly the execution of the
fugitive slave law, denouncing judges and officers appointed to execute
it. There talent was concentrated, measures concocted and feelings intensified with a view "to fire the Southern heart" and provoke a collision which your southern people were fools enough at last to inaugurate
and which has resulted in so much wretchedness and woe! I might call
them the "ice eaters of the north" co-operating with the "Fire eaters of
the South" for the destruction of the Union. Well, it was at Oberlin that
the "Chase guard" got up the letter on Negro suffrage addressed to
Gen. Cox,[7] with a hope that he would put himself in a position of *antagonism to your administration*. In this they again failed as you will
have seen by Gen Cox's manly reply.[8]

Whatever may be the professions the Chase and Beecher men make
to you personally, *I know* that they are preparing to make war on your
administration, and you may expect it. But the great mass of the Union
party and nearly the whole of those who have been in the Army will
stand by you if you remain firm in your adherence to your present
policy. For every Chase radical who leaves you at least ten fair minded
Democrats will flock to your standard. Mixing as I do with the common people daily I think I am in position to know whereof I write.
Bitter as have been the Butternuts[9] here, the most intelligent of them
declare their purpose to sustain your administration if it moves on as it
has commenced.

Do not permit Chase (Chief Justice though he be) and his co-labor-
ers to deceive you. I have known him intimately for more than thirty
years. He is cold and selfish and cares for no friendships that cannot be
used for his own aggrandizement. His ambition is vaulting and he
means to be President. He is now sitting himself up as the "representative man" of the antagonistic element of your administration. He is a
shrewd man, and I know that he has already an organization in Ohio
who believe in "taking time by the forelock."[10] You can depend on it
the representatives of this class will make war on you in the next Congress and you had as well begin to *fortify*! A few breast works would
do no harm. Although you do not pretend to be much of a military
man, you know that in time of danger *it is not wise to harbor many of
the enemy in your own camp.*

I have already written too much perhaps, and with such freedom
about a prominent man that you may suspect that I am either *crazy* or
drunk. But I assure you that my mind was never clearer nor my convictions better grounded, and I know that in four months I have drank
nothing stronger than *lager*—not even as *medicine*.

There are divers other points both as to *men* and *measures* on which
I should like to say something; but I must postpone them until a better
opportunity is afforded for free expression. Before concluding however,

pardon me for suggesting just one matter for your earnest consideration. The people now want *"retrenchment & Reform."* Take up your
bugle and strike that keynote and its reverberations through the length
and breadth of the Nation will awaken a thrill of joy. Direct all officers
not in actual service to be relieved and every unnecessary avenue to the
vaults of the Treasury to be cut off. It is thought that this is especially
necessary in the War Department. As the privates are mustered out and
the fighting is over, the excess of Major Generals, Brigadiers and Colonels might also be able to *bear* the suggestion to betake themselves to
the pleasant paths of peace. If you will send a few of them (clever fellers)
to me I will give them an equal partnership in raising corn, pork, horses
&c &c *for the next war*. Besides, in the event of another war you will
find it much easier to get *officers* into the service than *privates*. Such at
least was my little experience in raising the "Johnson Guard" in
1861—the 69th Ohio. I could recruit plenty of officers, but the rank &
file came slowly; and then I hadn't got nearer the front than Nashville
until every officer from Lieut Col. *Cassilly* [11] down to the 8th Corporal
of Company K. thought he was fit for Colonel and ought to have command of the Regiment *immediately* and *sooner if possible*.

Very truly Yours &c
Lewis D Campbell

His Excellency Andrew Johnson
President Washgton.
P.S. After writing this I am satisfied that any one who would write so
long a letter is a fit subject for trial before a Military Commission.
L.D.C.

ALS, DLC-JP.
    1. See Letter from Lewis D. Campbell, May 8, 1865.
    2. For Johnson's difficulties with Capt. Oliver D. Greene, see *Johnson Papers*, 5:
544–56 passim.
    3. On August 18 Johnson telegraphed Campbell, "Will you be in Washington soon?"
The next day Campbell replied, "I thought of visiting Washington in about a month.
Can go any time without inconvenience if you desire it." Tels. Sent, President, Vol. 2
(1865), RG107, NA; Tels. Recd., President, Vol. 4 (1865–66), RG107, NA.
    4. A derogatory reference to newspaper reporters paid by the line. Eric Partridge, *A
Dictionary of Historical Slang* (Harmondsworth, Middlesex, England, 1972), 678–79.
    5. A reference to Oberlin College's dissemination of radical reform ideas. Roseboom,
Civil War Era, 190.
    6. Congressman Joshua R. Giddings.
    7. Jacob D. Cox, Republican candidate for governor of Ohio in 1865. Samuel Plumb,
mayor of Oberlin and Republican candidate for the state legislature that year, wrote Cox
in July bluntly asking for his position on the black suffrage issue. Bonadio, *North of
Reconstruction*, 47–48, 86–87.
    8. Cox replied to Plumb that, since racial prejudice argued strongly against racial
harmony, attempts to promote equality between the races were futile and offered as his
alternative the colonization of blacks in South Carolina, Florida, Alabama, and Georgia,
accompanied by an exodus of whites from those states. Ibid., 86–87.
    9. Confederate sympathizers.
    10. Take time by the forelock—Thales of Miletus. John Bartlett, comp., *Familiar
Quotations* (Boston, 1948), 26n.

11. Lt. Col. William B. Cassilly, who succeeded Campbell as colonel of the 69th Ohio, and, if overly ambitious, paid for it in an inglorious dismissal from service. *Johnson Papers*, 5: 188n.

From Enoch T. Carson

Cincinnati August 21, 1865

Dear Sir,

On the 26th of July I took the liberty of addressing you a *confidential private note* in relation to the removal of Capt. Smith as pension agent in this city.[1] I am Surprised to learn that my note is now in this city in the possession of the Editor of the Cincinnati Gazette.[2] I was induced to write this friendly note to you, presuming that I had the honor to be recognised as a personal friend. So far as I was personally concerned I had no interest in the matter further than my friendship for yourself, and a real desire for the most complete Success of your administration.

Of all the government officers at this place I (feel warranted in saying) I was about the only one who was a warm personal friend and admirer of yourself and this friendship dated long *anterior* to your advancement to the high and honorable position you now hold.

For reasons no doubt satisfactory to yourself I was superseded in my office, although I did not expect this from you, yet I did not murmur or find fault. I said you was my personal friend, and that my Supersedure was pressed by an outside influence, that would have been embarrassing to you to contend with, and therefore I was content. I am now a private citizen have nothing to ask for myself or anybody else, therefore care nothing for the consequences that might result to me from the making public of my note. I am ready to stand up to what I said. As a friend of yours and real well wisher for the Success of your Administration I did think that I might occasionally venture to address you confidentially. I fear I have presumed too much.

Truly Yours E. T. Carson,

Hon. A. Johnson President

ALS, DLC-JP.

1. Carson had protested the dismissal of Robert S. Smith (*fl*1881), whose "removal has been gotten up by a *dirty clique* of *one horse politicians*." Smith had resigned from the army in January 1865 and had been appointed pension agent the following March. He later moved to Columbus, Ohio, where he became treasurer of the Columbus and Xenia Railroad. Carson to Johnson, July 26, 1865, Johnson Papers, LC; Powell, *Army List*, 597; *Williams' Cincinnati Directory* (1866), 387, 414; Columbus directories (1867–81). See *Johnson Papers*, 6: 600n.

2. Richard Smith (1823–1898), an Irish immigrant who was longtime editor of the *Gazette*, a Radical Republican organ. Greve, *Cincinnati and Citizens*, 2: 602.

From Charles Casey

August 21, 1865, Lancaster, Ky.; ALS, DLC-JP.

Hearing that Henry C. Burnett, former U.S. and Confederate congressman, "has been released and that his property also is restored," the writer hopes that the "case will be re-considered, and steps taken to prove to Burnett that 'Treason is something more than a political difference.'" Burnett and Breckinridge "both remained at Washington in their Congressional seats acting the spy all through the summer of 1861 . . . and then *went home, and persuaded their neighbors to go with them to Richmond.*" The guilty leaders ought to be punished; "the good of the nation calls for it, the dead from their bloody graves call for it, true policy calls for it."

Interview with Pardon Seekers [1]

August 21, 1865

Some fifty persons were present, most of them seeking pardons. A Mr. KEITT,[2] of South Carolina, (not LAWRENCE M., he having been killed by a loyal bullet at Fort Wagner,)[3] approached the President, and informed him that he desired a pardon. "What have you done?" asked Mr. JOHNSON. "I opposed secession until my State decided to go out of the Union, and then I determined to go with it. I never joined the army. I did nothing to bring on the rebellion," was the reply. "You," rejoined the President, "are like all the rest; you did nothing. Now," he added, "my experience is, that the men who didn't join the rebel army, but who acquiesced in rebellion, were the most mischievous and dangerous men we had. I cannot pardon you, Sir." Mr. KEITT made several other efforts. Among other things he reminded the President that he had come all the way from South Carolina and had been in Washington some time; that hotel living here was very high, and that altogether his daily expenses were extravagantly large, and that he would like to get away as soon as he could go. The President responded that the hardships of which he complained were the direct results of the rebellion; that he did not bring on, or contribute to bring on the rebellion; that he was not responsible for and could not extricate Mr. KEITT from the difficulties he complained of, nor hasten his pardon on account of them. The President was firm. His answer was a finalty. Exit KEITT. A Mr. BIRCH,[4] member of the late rebel Legislature of Virginia, next approached the President and applied for a pardon. Similar questions were put to him by the President as were asked Mr. KEITT. From the answers it appeared that BIRCH did nothing, only, as a member of the Virginia Legislature in obedience to instructions, he voted that Virginia should secede from the Union of the United States. That is all he did that was—"nothing." The President refused to pardon him. <Exit

BIRCH.> Next came a rebel clergyman[5] who asked the President to grant him a pardon. "What great sin have you committed that you come here in clerical robes and crave Executive pardon?" "I was a rebel," was the answer, "and I desire your Excellency to pardon me that I may be restored to citizenship and be able to support and live under the government of the United States." "You rebel preachers," responded the President, "have done the government a great deal of harm. You have proclaimed devilish doctrines and misled the people. You forgot that it was your duty to yield obedience to the powers that be. You must rest awhile upon the stool of repentance. I decline to grant you pardon at present." Exit reb. clergyman.

The President then remarked, addressing the entire crowd in the room, that it was a little singular that most of the non-combatants who had come here from the South for pardon assert that they did nothing, were opposed to the rebellion at the beginning, only acquiesced, and thought the rebel government ought to have surrendered earlier and stopped bloodshed; yet not one of them took advantage of the amnesty proclamation offered by Mr. LINCOLN, an act which would have shown sincerity on their part, and contributed so much toward saving the enormous expenditure of life and treasure. "I will grant no more pardons for the present," was the emphatic conclusion of the President, and turning to Col. BROWNING, he directed him to issue the order to the Attorney-General.

New York Times, August 23, 1865.

1. Although pardon applications by this time were usually sent from the White House to the attorney general's office for examination and recommendation before presidential action thereon, the President was continuously besieged by applicants. *Philadelphia Evening Bulletin*, Aug. 14, 1865.

2. Possibly well-to-do Orangeburg farmer Jacob G. Keitt (b. *c*1818). 1860 Census, S.C., Orangeburg, Orangeburg Dist., 24.

3. Lawrence M. Keitt actually died in June 1864 as a result of wounds received at Cold Harbor. *Johnson Papers*, 4: 50n.

4. Probably Edward C. Burks (b. *c*1821), an attorney and farmer. Amnesty Papers (M1003, Roll 57), Va., Edward C. Burks, RG94, NA.

5. Not identified.

From Carl Schurz

August 21, 1865, Montgomery, Ala.; ALS, DLC-JP. See *Advice*, 99–105.

Recommends that the Freedmen's Bureau not depend on the assignment of military officers as agents but rather on men sent from Washington, thereby providing a necessary continuity. Schurz doubts that "Alabama juries at the present time are prepared to find a white man who killed a negro, guilty of murder, or another, who whipped a negro, guilty of assault and battery." Citing instances of violence toward blacks, he asserts that most of these outrages could be easily prevented if troops were not concentrated at certain points but were distributed so as to be within reach of every county in the state. Describes large amount of stealing which is going on; steps must be taken "to repress the lawless spirit of numerous classes of people." He reports Governor Lewis Parsons' optimism concerning the general acceptance of the new order, anticipating a liberal-minded state convention, which will adopt the constitutional amendment, permit blacks to give testimony in the courts, and perhaps refer the matter of black franchise to the legislature. Schurz does not share the governor's "expectations." He believes the new system of labor would be more successful if blacks were transferred from the plantations where they had been slaves to other locations, "where they could at once enter into their new relation with their employer as free laborers." Schurz recommends procedures to monitor judicial proceedings involving freedmen so that the authorities may "form a clear opinion of the working of the system adopted by Gen. Swayne." Shocked by the incidence of murder and mayhem inflicted by whites on blacks, he concludes by advising Johnson not to pardon Dr. James T. Andrew, sentenced to ten years' imprisonment for killing a black. "Unless the severest punishments . . . be visited upon white men killing negroes the Southern States will soon be a vast slaughter pen for the black race." [Johnson ordered Andrew's release on October 26, 1865.]

To William L. Sharkey

Executive Mansion. Washington D.C.
Aug't 21 1865.[1]

Governor Wm. L. Sharkey
Jackson, Miss.

Your dispatch received. I am much gratified to hear of your proceedings being so favorable. If you need military force to preserve order and enforce the law you will call upon the Commandant of the Department, General Slocum,[2] who will furnish whatever force is needed.

I would not organize the militia until farther advances are made in the restoration of State Authority. The Military Authority and the suspension of the writ of Habeas Corpus will be withdrawn at the earliest moment it is deemed safe to do so. Your Convention can adopt the Amendment to the Constitution of the United States or recommend its adoption by the Legislature. You no doubt see the turn that is being given to the attempts in the South to restore State Governments by the extreme men in the North—hence the importance of being prompt and circumspect in all that is being done. The proceedings in Mississippi will exert a powerful influence on the other States which are to act afterwards.

God grant you a complete success and that your doings will set an example that will be followed by all the other States.

Andrew Johnson
President U.S.

Tel, DNA-RG107, Tels. Sent, President, Vol. 2 (1865).

1. Although Johnson drafted this wire on the 21st, Sharkey did not receive it until the 24th. Because of telegrapher's errors, the copy sent, rather than the recipient's, is used. See Johnson to Sharkey, Aug. 24, 1865, Governors' Papers, Ser. E, RG27, Mississippi State Archives.

2. Henry W. Slocum (1827–1894), West Point graduate, served in nearly every major campaign in the East, before being transferred west in the fall of 1863. Subsequently he was with Sherman in the Carolinas. After the war he practiced law in Brooklyn, N.Y., and was thrice elected to Congress. *DAB*.

From N. G. Smith [1]

Jackson Tenn August 21 1865
Hon Andew Johnson Prst of the U.S.

Dr. Sir

Knowing your time to be precious I Shall proceed to lay before your honor the object of this communication without a lengthy introduction or preamble.

In the first place I would like if I could bring before your view a true picture of the condition of our country. The matter however I wish to brng before you is the condition of the negroes and what is likely to be the State of affairs about Christmas. Many of the negroes of this county are Still with there former owners and disposed to remain untill Christmas nearley all of them haveing crops of their own upon the plantations where they are liveing. Those that are at home however are douing no good for their employers nor themselves. The *great trouble* is to get them to *work*. We are perfectly willing and anxious to give them up and let them go but they have been made to believe by Some meddlesome person that the lands now belonging to their owners will be taken from them and given to them at Christmas. We are disposed and willing to hire them or work them for a part of the crop and give them Such a chance that they could do well if they work. Believing as they do that the whites will be turned out of their homes and they put in their places makes them almost intolerable and if the thing is Suffered to go on as it is now I fear it will lead to very bad results. I am just from a trip to your City on my return from Va & N C and I found in both of those States the Same feeling existing and that in Va & N C they had Suppressed an insurrection that was planed and the one in S.C. proved to be a very curious matter before it could be Stoped. The Same-thing will take place here if the negro is encouraged in his belief that he is to be made the Superior of the white man. I Should like to See the negro either removed from our midst or Some arrangement entered into So that we could get along in peace & get them to work for a liveing. It is the wish of all here to give them employment and acknowledge them free and employ them as freemen but it requires Some cystem to get the theory to work and I think there is a plan if addopted would secur this most desirable object and that is to place in each County a goverment agent Selected from among the citizens of the County. Get a man that is familiar with the habits of the negro & one that would take an interest in the matter one that would give the matter his entire attention one to whom both negro and white man could apply for redress one that would impartially arrange the contracts between the negro and the white man by having an agent live and to remain here during the next year. Now we could in that time get everything to work So that after next year there would be no trouble upon this Subject & the entire South could moove on in the culture of cotton and in a few years we would produce an astonishing amount of cotton. There must be Something done to get this labor Started in the right direction and the people of the South look to you as the President and friend and feel that you are the only one we have to look too & you will find in the course of time that the people of the South & North West are your true friends; time will prove this to you. You have perhaps forgotten me. I have had the pleasure [of] being numbered among your friends in times that have passed and gone & I feel now that I am Still your friend and hope Some day to have an opportunity of proving it to you. For the correctness of what I have written I can refer you to your old frnd T P Scurlock Saml McClannahan[2] and any one else of your old frinds of madison. We have a Small force here under the Command of Maj Smith.[3] I have not heard of their doing any thing which could give offense to the citizens. They are courtieous gentleman and polite. It is not them that we complain of but it is a low trifling Set of white men that are alwas ready to disturb the quiet of the county. I do not wish to tax your time any farther. You have the matter now before you. I hope you may give it a fair Consideration and if in your judgmut you think my views right you will act promptly and let the matter take Some Shape before Christmas. I called at the White House to See you but finding a large no of person and cards ahead of me and being Short of funds I could not wait. Hopeing you will pardon me for intruding upon your time I reman

yous Truly, N. G. Smith

P.S. If it Suits your Convenience I Should like to hear from you.[4]

N. G. Smith

ALS, DNA-RG105, Records of the Commr., Lets. Recd. (M752, Roll 16).

1. Not identified.

2. Scurlock (b. c1812) and McClanahan, neighbors in Jackson, Tenn., were lawyers. The latter had received a presidential pardon on August 19. 1860 Census, Tenn., Madison, Jackson, 33; Amnesty Papers (M1003, Roll 50), Tenn., Samuel McClanahan, RG94, NA.

3. Possibly Emil Smith (c1826–fl1870) of Dayton, Ohio, formerly a lieutenant, 8th Indpt. Bty. Ohio Lgt. Arty., and now major, 3rd U.S. colored Hvy. Arty., whose command was scattered through the District of West Tennessee. CSR, RG94, NA; Dayton directories (1868–70); Dyer, *Compendium*, 1721.

4. The endorsement to O. O. Howard reads: "The writer is known to me as a person of veracity and intelligence. Andrew Johnson Prest U.S."

From Edwin M. Stanton

August 21st 1865.

Mr. President:

I have the honor to acknowledge your note of last evening, with the accompanying newspaper slip.[1] Since our conversation on Friday, I have given careful consideration to the condition of things in South Carolina. The following observations occur to me:

1st. That in Genl. Thomas' command,[2] and wherever there is any loyal sentiment, there appears to be no difficulty in regard to the presence of colored troops—complaint being confined chiefly to the most rebellious States—South Carolina and Mississippi.

2nd. That there may, notwithstanding, be some ground for complaint or apprehension of collision in South Carolina; and it is the duty of the Government to guard against such evil.

3rd. That, to ascertain the real condition of things and provide a proper remedy, Genl. Meade, commander of the Division, should be ordered to go to South Carolina, and make investigation and report.[3]

If you approve, I will issue the order to him.

Your obedient Servant, Edwin M. Stanton,
Secretary of War.

LBcopy, DLC-E. M. Stanton Papers.
    1. Not found.
    2. Military Division of the Tennessee, with headquarters in Nashville.
    3. George G. Meade (1815–1872), former commander of the Army of the Potomac (1863–65), subsequently in charge of the Third Military District (1867–68), did travel south, meeting with the provisional governors of Virginia and the Carolinas, where he was favorably impressed with the relationship between military and civil authorities. Warner, *Blue*; George Meade, ed., *Life and Letters of George Gordon Meade* (2 vols., New York, 1913), 2: 283–84.

From Walter H.S. Taylor

August 21, 1865, Richmond, Va.; ALS, DNA-RG94, Amnesty Papers (M1003, Roll 69), Va., W.H.S. Taylor.

Second auditor of the Confederate treasury until February 1865, when he resigned, "utterly disgusted and dissatisfied," applies for amnesty. Living as a private citizen in Richmond upon its occupation by Union forces, he was arrested and "confined closely for between seven and eight days," during which time all he had was taken, "leaving me nothing but the clothes I had on." Now "nearly 59 years of age, and . . . exceedingly anxious to find something to support myself and a large family," he reminds Johnson that "for more than twenty four years" he was a military accountant in the Third Auditor's Office of the United States and "had a slight personal acquaintance with your Excellency." [No pardon for Taylor has been found. In late November 1865, his application was being "held over, under the 10th clause of the President's proclamation."]

From Michael Burns

August 22, 1865, Nashville, Tenn.; ALS, DLC-JP.

As president of the Nashville and Chattanooga Railroad, Burns submits a list of those elected as directors and reports that 4,187 stockholders voted in the election. After praising the presidential order for the military to return all railroads to civilian control, he expresses concern about "a disposition on the part of Some in official station to retard and evade the order." He specifically exempts General Thomas from his complaint but indicates that it is urgent that he relinquish the Nashville and Northwestern, of which Burns also serves as president, by August 28, because the latter has "made a contract with a line of steamers from St Louis to connect with Johnsonville." He adds that "these boats are waiting patiently," expecting Johnson's order to be implemented. While the "turning over of the Chattanooga road is Somewhat more indefinite," Burns has "faith in Genl Thomas that he will have it turned over as Soon as practible." [In response to the presidential directive on August 8, Thomas returned the Northwestern on September 1, 1865, and the Chattanooga road on September 15.]

Circular to Provisional Governors [1]

War Dept. Washington D C.
August 22d, 1865.

Gov. Wm. W Holden Raleigh.

Information comes to me that reports are freely circulated in influential quarters and where without contradiction they are calculated to do harm—to the effect that in appointments to Office and in the recommendations for appointments the true Union men are totally ignored and the Provisional Governors are giving a decided preference to those who have participated in the Rebellion. The object of such representations is to embarrass the Government in its reconstruction Policy, & while I place no reliance in such statements I feel it due to you to advise you of the extended circulation they have gained and to impress upon you the importance of encouraging & strengthening to the fullest extent the men of your State who have never faltered in their Allegiance to the Government. Every opportunity should be made available to have this known & understood as your Policy & determination.

Acknowledge receipt of this Telegram.[2]

Andrew Johnson President U.S.

Tel, Nc-Ar, Governor's Papers.

1. Although here addressed to Holden, the circular was sent to other provisional governors.

2. In responding, Holden disclaimed giving any preference to ex-Confederates. "Doubtless some have been appointed . . . but, upon the whole, only loyal Union men have been appointed and recommended at Washington." Holden to Johnson, Aug. 26, 1865, Johnson Papers, LC. For answers from others receiving this circular, see Telegrams from Lewis E. Parsons, August 24, and William L. Sharkey, August 25, and Letter from Benjamin F. Perry, August 29. See also James Johnson to Johnson, Sept. 1, and Andrew J. Hamilton to Johnson, Sept. 23, 1865, Johnson Papers, LC. Governor William Marvin of Florida either did not respond or his answer has been lost.

From William Hick[1]

Atwater, Portage Co. Ohio.
Aug. 22nd 1865

Andrew Johnson
Sir

Can it be possible that in the turmoil of Political labor which now oppresses you, a fugitive moment could be snatched from your hurry to listen to the word of an old Radical, who, nearly twenty years ago, ranked you with pleasure and pointed to you with hope, as the only man in the South endorcing our Land Reform doctrines. I have watched your course with joy from that day to this; and now it is something grand to boast of, by me, that one of my own band of brave pioneers in human progress should be so honorably, though unexpectedly filling the office of President of these United States,—sitting on the highest pinnacle of usefulness and power in the Government of the strongest nation under the heavens.

Since then, a great work has been accomplished. What upheavals! What overturnings! The retrospect is astounding! We have fought the good fight! We have kept the faith!

You have been favored with continuous work in the field.

When the Freesoil Party was organized, which finally merged into the *Republican* Party—our thunder being stolen—we, the old original Freesoilers were broken up. Chafing and pouting and jealous of our Radicalism, we could not heartily work with the *meceginated* amalgamated mass of old Whigs and doubtful disappointed democrats; the most we could find to do was to keep up a little skirmishing and bushwacking which finally settled down into the belief that our work was done; some of us rather gloomily retired to the companionship of books to rust away in unburied forgetfulness and "*moral solitude*." For my own part, although my Editorial labors were apparently ended, though my Lecturing, plodding and pecuniary sacrifices for the cause of Land Reform might be considered past, I could not remain idle in the cause of humanity but have kept on Preaching, on my own hook, the Democracy of Christianity as opportunity served. Since the commencement of this war, I have Lectured some on "*What shall be done with the Slaves?*" and other kindred themes, endeavoring to the best of my ability to strengthen the Government—wrestling in the breech against the Goths, Vandals and Vagabond Politicians of the Vallandigham[2] and Copperhead school.

Since you became President I have been longing to take a hand in "*Reconstruction*." The work I desire is this. Give me Five to Ten thousand Acres of Confiscated Land and Five hundred to One thousand families of negroes making in all 5,000 to 10,000 persons. Give me the

barest kind of means—rations, work tools, cabins or even Tents—
means for one year only,—I will go to work, organize into proper departmental form for useful labor—educate them Preach to them on
Sundays and train them in all useful science, virtue and Religion—and
present you with a Community of *Equal* and United Christians in a few
Years, such as the world never saw before; and return back to the Government whatever may be advanced to commence with.

You promised to be Moses,[3]—the God of Heaven now sends you an
Aaron, skilled in the work and in all useful necessary labor—"*apt
to teach*,"—one of your own school of Pioneers. I refer you to the
Honl.Geo. W. Julian[4] with whom I have occasionaly corresponded;
and from my own neighborhood, through Gen. Garfield, Judge Luther
Day[5] and a host of good men and true, you shall be satisfied that any
Confidence you may place in me in this direction will not be misplaced.

Without trespassing further upon your time and waiting your reply
I shall still remain the same old Radical pioneer in human redemption.[6]

Very Respectfully your Obedient Servant
William Hick

ALS, DNA-RG105, Records of the Commr., Lets. Recd. (M752, Roll 16).
1. Hick (*c*1811–*fl*1870), a painter and local temperance leader. 1870 Census, Ohio,
Portage, Atwater, 12; Hick to James A. Garfield, June 1, 1868, Garfield Papers, LC.
2. Clement L. Vallandigham.
3. For this reference, see Johnson's "The Moses of the Colored Men" Speech, *Johnson Papers*, 7: 251–53.
4. Julian (1817–1899), Indiana lawyer and a Free Soiler in Congress before the war,
was a Republican congressman (1861–71). *BDAC*.
5. James A. Garfield and Luther Day. The latter (1813–1885) was an Ohio jurist,
first on the court of common pleas and subsequently as justice of the state's highest court.
DAB.
6. The September 14 response from the Freedmen's Bureau, to whom Hick's letter
was referred, indicated that his plan was not practical because the acreage desired could
be acquired only through purchase or congressional appropriation. Furthermore, abandoned lands held by the Bureau were subject to the presidential restoration policy and
were being "rapidly restored to their former owners." Records of the Commr., Lets. Sent
(M742, Roll 1), RG105, NA.

From Evelyn H. King

August 22, 1865, Selma, Ala; LS, DNA-RG94, Amnesty Papers (M1003,
Roll 6), Ala., Mrs. Evelyn H. King.

The widow of Capt. William T. King with "two little daughters to bring up,"
applies for a "full pardon and amnesty" under the thirteenth exception. She
aided the rebellion by sympathizing with her husband, encouraging men to
fight, and by contributing to hospitals and indigent soldiers' families. After the
capture of Selma, Gen. James H. Wilson's forces took or destroyed, "without
any military necessity," about twenty thousand dollars of her property, including "some valuable plate presented by the uncle of her husband,—the late
Honl. Wm. R. King, vice president of the United States, on which his name
was marked." [Mrs. King's pardon became effective September 12, 1865.]

From Sam Milligan

Nashville Ten. August 22, 1865

Confidential

His Excellency Andrew Johnson
President of the U.S.
Dear Sir:

Since I reached this place I have found the Rail Road men of Tennessee, and I may say, the citizens generally delighted with the Secretary of War's order, directing the Rail Roads of the State to be turned over to the companies.[1] It is regarded as a stroke of wise policy, and perfectly just both to the Government and the companies. Genl Thomas is vigorously acting under it, and will I doubt not turn every road over by the first of September next. I feel sure the order will seriously interfere with many a well devised scheme of profits by some who have charge of the roads. But that is all the better for the reputation both of yourself and the Secretary of War.

But what I desire to say is in relation to the Government Rolling Mill, and Machine Shops at Chattanooga. You will see by Genl McCallum's advertisement,[2] that these extensive erections are to be sold early in Sept., and the mode of sale is by *sealed proposals made to him* &c. I am thoroughly satisfied from facts of which I was not apprised when I saw you, that there is a manifest fraud contemplated on the Government in this sale. Many recent developments go to establish the fact, that this Mill was originally built with a view of its passing into certain hands as their private property at the close of the war. Under the mode of sale adopted by Genl McCallum this scheme can easily be accomplished, and one of the finest Rolling Mills in the U.S. pass at less than one third its original cost into the hands of speculators.

This Mill with the Machine shops attached, I understand, cost $290,000. It was just finished when the war closed, and is as good as new, and ought not to be sacrificed.

The whole sheme could be averted by changing the mode of sale. Why not adopt the wise & just rule prescribed in your order to General Thomas directing him to turn over the R. Road property &c? Let the Rolling Mill be appraised by disinterested & competent men, and the sale directed at public auction, with instructions that it shall not be struck off to any one below its appraised value? In this way you secure the Government against fraud and loss, and let in a class of bidders who, I am sure, will not now attempt to purchase it at all.

This machinery ought to be purchased by the Tennessee Rail Road Companies, and I am fully satisfied if they are convinced they can have a fair chance at the sale, they will give more for it, by thousands, than any one else.

This Mill I doubt not cost more than it could have been erected for by private enterprise, yet it is one of the finest in all the Southern States, and will be of incalculable advantage to the country, if controlled, by the proper hands.

I believe it would be wise to sell it on time with the purchase money well secured.

I hope you will excuse these suggestions, for they are made from an earnest desire to shield your administration against an imputation to which it will be obnoxious if things are carried out as they are now begun, and which I know is averse to your vey nature, and could not under any circumstances meet your approval.[3]

I am your friend Sam Milligan

ALS, DLC-JP.

1. On August 8, 1865, Stanton, at Johnson's request, had ordered Gen. George H. Thomas to arrange for the transfer of Tennessee railroads to civilian control. *House Reports*, 39 Cong., 2 Sess., No. 34, pp. 459–60 (Ser. 1306).

2. Although the copy sent by Milligan has not been found, Gen. D. C. McCallum's notice, dated July 31 and appearing in the *Nashville Press and Times*, August 22, 1865, advertised that bid proposals would be received on September 13, in his office as director and general manager of the military railroads. Milligan had reason to be concerned about McCallum's motives, for, along with Abram S. Hewitt, northern industrialist, the general was one of the purchasers of the mill and equipment, built by the government in 1864. Charles D. McGuffey, ed., *Standard History of Chattanooga, Tennessee* (Knoxville, 1911), 175.

3. Johnson scrawled across the envelope: "To be Shown to the Secretary of War" and "Attended to."

From George R. Powel[1]

Wards Station Ga
August 22nd 1865

President Andrew Johnson

On yesterday I took the Amnesty Oath and as [I] belong to one of the Excepted classes have made an application by Petition to you for special pardon. My application will be forwarded by the proper Officer on to day.

If it be a fault to have been a Rebel I have been grieviously at fault. No man [knows] better than yourself when I take sides how ardent are my feelings. I took sides from the conviction that I was right. War the great arbiter of Nations has decided against me, and I submit.

This war has I hope caused no bitterness between us. We were once good friends. I have done you many acts of kindness when you needed friends, some in years gone by, others which you know not of—of a more recent date. Doubtless you have done me many acts of kindness.

I am now in distress, greatly distressed; when the war broke out I was worth from 60 to 70 thousand—dollars. Now I am almost a beggar. In fact I do not know how I am to live.[2] I am getting as you know smartly in years. I have a large & helpless family.[3] My poor wife is in delicate health. My health is not good. I look forward to the future with but little hope. I am here in Georgia and have no means to take me to Tennessee. I will be able to do so this fall, by selling some property which I will need. Will you do me the favour to act upon my petition promptly and send me the papers as soon as possible?[4] It is of vital importance to my family to have the rent of my lands for their actual Subsistence. They have no other means of living. Can you spare the time to drop me a line? Your career has been the most extraordinary one upon record. You are now the first man on the Continent of America. Deal kindly with the South and commit no errors & at the end of four years you will be the first man in the world.

                                                    Very Respectfully Geo R Powel

ALS, DNA-RG94, Amnesty Papers (M1003, Roll 22), Ga., George R. Powel.

1. Powel was an old political friend of Johnson, who fell under the 13th exception and who believed himself indicted for treason. Powel to Johnson, ca. Aug. 21, 1865, Amnesty Papers (M1003, Roll 22), Ga., George R. Powel, RG94, NA.

2. His application, attached to this letter, indicates that Powel's Hawkins County, Tenn., farm had been leased out by the Knoxville treasury agent.

3. In 1860 the Powels had ten children ranging in age from four to twenty-one. Eliza Ruth Fain (1815–1872) had married Powel in 1836. 1860 Census, Tenn., Hawkins, 10th Dist., 11; Hawkins County Genealogical Society, *Cemeteries of Hawkins County* (2 vols., Rogersville, Tenn., 1985–86), 2: 209; Prentiss Price, *Hawkins County Tennessee: Marriages 1789–1865* (Knoxville, 1958), 117.

4. He was pardoned July 5, 1866. *House Ex. Docs.*, 40 Cong., 2 Sess., No. 16, p. 135 (Ser. 1330).

From Returned Confederate Soldiers

August 22, 1865, Luney's Creek, W. Va.; Pet, DNA-RG60, Office of Atty. Gen., Lets. Recd., President.

Forty-one Confederate privates who were in service until the surrender of General Lee, many of whom have taken the amnesty oath, complain to the President about writs being issued against them by the West Virginia government since their return home. Union men claim "the most exorbitant damages" for property often not taken, or taken by some of them under orders of their commanding officers. They returned home "with [the] conviction that we were fairly beaten" and determined "to be true to the United States" but find themselves "weighed down by unjust and oppressive suits," to be tried sixty miles away and instituted by men "whose Military Career consisted in hiding in the fastnesses of the Mountains and making inroads upon and plundering the defenceless." On the grounds that they were regular paroled soldiers, recognized as belligerents who, "by the express terms of the surrender" were allowed to return home and remain "*unmolested*," they entreat Johnson's interposition by September 14, the trial date, so "that the vanquished shall not be oppressed and trampled in the dust." Desiring to support the Chief Magistrate's administration, and believing that they "are *now* truer Union men than the men who, under the form of law, seek to plunder and oppress us," they ask "fair play" and that the suits be stopped. [Johnson apparently took no action, except to forward the petition to the attorney general.]

To Volunteer Refreshment Saloon Committee

Aug 22nd [1865][1]

Robert R. Carson[2]   Cor. Secy. Joint Committee,
Volunteer Refreshment Saloon Philadelphia.
Sir,

I have the honor to acknowledge the receipt of the invitation you extended in behalf of the Joint Committee, Volunteer Refreshment Saloon of your city to attend their closing ceremonies on the 28th instant.[3] I desire to thank the Committee for the compliment thus tendered me and to express my sincere regret that circumstances prevent my compliance with their invitation. I avail myself of this occasion to assure them of my high appreciation of the great and good work in which they have been engaged during the past four years, by which they have gained the gratitude both of the brave soldiers to whose wants they have so efficiently ministered and of their friends throughout the union.

I am Very Respectfully
Your obedient servant

LBcopy, DLC-JP3A.
1. This letter appears in the August 1865 sequence in Johnson's letterbook.
2. Carson (1831–1904), one of the founders of the Saloon, was a coal merchant who became active in various reform movements. *DAB*.
3. Opened in Philadelphia in May 1861, and one of only two such organizations, the Saloon sought to provide writing materials, envelopes and stamps, as well as refreshments, to northern volunteer regiments en route to the front. Russell F. Weigley et al., eds., *Philadelphia: A 300-Year History* (New York, 1982), 398–99.

From Allen A. Gee

Nashville Tenn Aug 23, 1865

Prest U.S. Honored Sir

Perhaps it may not be out of place to inform you that as Pastor of M'Kendree M.E. Church which we have been for some time holding under an Order from Sect'y Stanton I received on the night of the 12th inst a telegram from Bp Simpson to turn said property over to the former occupants, with which I proceeded at once to comply—and completing the necessary arrangements I this morning placed the keys in the hands of Genl Thomas private Sec'y.

Having received it through the Military power I know of no way to return it but by the same channel. I explained the object of surrendering the keys and stated that it was in compliance with your wish that it (the church) should be returned to its former occupants.

I also informed one of the trustees that the keys were at "Head Quarters" and I presume he has them now.

I was very much surprised on learning from Bp Simpson this morning that Mr Baldwin had telegraphed to you as follows.

M'Kendree Church Property has not been given up to me and the holders say they will *not give it up from any order from you.*[1]

On the contrary I proceeded at once to make the necessary arrangements to comply with Bp Simpson's instructions and never thought of any thing else but compliance nor was any thing else talked of by any of our people.

Feeling it due to ourselves that the misstatement be corrected is my only apology for this note.

With the most profound respect

Your obt Servt A A Gee

ALS, DLC-JP.
1. See Letter from Matthew Simpson, August 16, 1865.

To James B. Steedman

Executive Mansion. Washington, D.C.
Aug't 23 1865

Maj Gen Steedman,
Augusta, Georgia.

I thank you for your letter.[1] Your course in reference to the Freedmens Bureau as far as understood is approved. I hope that Bureau will move clearly in the limits prescribed by law. There seems to much apprehension on the part of many citizens of Georgia that the negro population is being incited to insurrection by the colored troops and some few white emissaries. I hope you will keep a vigilant watch upon this subject and at once suppress any and all moves of an insurrectionary character.

Andrew Johnson President U.S.

Tel, DNA-RG107, Tels. Sent, President, Vol. 2 (1865).
1. Letter from Steedman, August 15, 1865.

From John H. Taggart

August 23, 1865, Washington, D.C.; ALS, DNA-RG56, Appts., Internal Revenue Service, Assessor, Pa., 1st Dist., John H. Taggart.

The Washington correspondent of the *Philadelphia Inquirer* and of the *Chicago Republican*, and a former newspaper editor, seeks a position as Internal Revenue assessor. Having raised a volunteer company and served as colonel of the 12th Pa. Reserves on active duty in 1861–62, he cites other war-related service, such as having been chosen by "'The Philadelphia Surpervisory Committee for Recruiting Colored Troops,' as the Chief Preceptor of 'The Free Military School for Applicants for the Command of Colored Troops'"—an institution which "graduated more than five hundred (500) commissioned officers for Colored Troops." [Although his name does not appear in the *U.S. Off. Reg.*, Taggart apparently worked as collector of Pennsylvania's 1st district for a short time.]

From James Dixon
Private & Confidential

Hartford Aug 24, 1865

My Dear Sir,

The public mind has now had time to consider, and come to a conclusion upon your plan of reconstruction. You cannot be blind to the fact that the radical portion of the Republican party denounce your policy in language restrained only by their fears. That they bitterly oppose it in their hearts is certain. On the other hand, the masses—the thinking, calm honest unselfish masses, most earnestly approve your policy & support it with zeal and energy. I see proofs of this daily. In the shops, in the factories on the farms—every where the first remark is "Mr Johnson is doing right." Such is the almost universal feeling. I know not whether it reaches you—for the truth seldom enters the White House—but so it is.

Looking calmly upon the situation, it is to me evident that you will be sustained by the people in your present liberal policy, in such a manner as has never been witnessed, except perhaps in the case of Washington. It looks as if honest men of all parties, were coming to your standard. If you persevere in your present course, this result is certain.

I should be very glad to hear from you & know from yourself what are the prospects of reconstruction. Anything you may say to me will be strictly confidential.

I am my Dear Sir with great respect
Truly your friend James Dixon

The Honble. Andrew Johnson
President of the U.S.

ALS, DLC-JP.

From William H. Hidell

August 24, 1865, Memphis, Tenn.; ALS, DNA-RG94, Amnesty Papers (M1003, Roll 19), Ga., William H. Hidell.

A Georgia citizen, not sure whether his position was "contemplated by the terms 'civil officers' " in the May 29th proclamation, "But in order to set at rest any and all doubts upon the subject," requests a special pardon. At the time of secession he attended college in Virginia, and when the southern capital was moved to Richmond, he became Vice President Stephens' private secretary, "until the collapse of the Confederacy." In October 1862 the Confederate Congress made his position a government office. [Hidell's pardon was granted September 20, 1865.]

To Oliver O. Howard

Executive Mansion Washington, D.C.
August 24 1865.

Maj Genl. O. O. Howard
Commr. Bureau R., F. & A.L.
General,

I desire an early conversation with you on matters connected with the administration of the affairs of your Bureau in Mississippi.

Reliable information has been received here, that the officers of your Bureau are converting to the use of the Bureau, in that State, the property of all men worth over $20,000.[1]

I am General Very Truly Yours
Andrew Johnson
Prest U.S.

LS, DNA-RG105, Records of the Commr., Lets. Recd. (M752, Roll 16).

1. Bureau agents, directed by Col. Samuel Thomas, assistant commissioner, were seizing property of all not yet pardoned, an action which resulted in confusion and conflict. The day after this inquiry, Howard's office wired Thomas to refrain from seizing personal property and to maintain control only over those lands already confiscated by the U.S. courts or defined as abandoned in earlier orders. Harris, *Presidential Reconstruction*, 88; J. S. Fullerton to Samuel Thomas, Aug. 25, 1865, Records of the Commr., Lets. Sent (M742, Roll 1), RG105, NA.

From Lewis E. Parsons

Montgomery Ala Aug 24 1865.

His Excy Andrew Johnson
Sir

Your telegram of the 22d is just recd. In reply I have the honor to say in cases of special appointments union men have received preference in every instance, where one resonably qualified would accept the office. When such could not be obtained those least objectionable have been appointed. In no instance has a union man been neglected or set aside for Secessionists. All County officers from Justice of the Peace down were re-appointed by my proclamation, but reserving the right to remove for disloyalty or other good cause. All the higher officers of the County & State were specially appointed. A very few cases only of removal under the general appointments have occured.

Lewis E Parsons Prov Govr

Tel, DLC-JP.

From James M. Baird

August 25, 1865, Washington Co., Miss.; ALS, DNA-RG94, Amnesty Papers (M1003, Roll 31), Miss., J. M. Baird.

Mississippi physician, who opposed secession but acquiesced in Confederate rule "under the pressure of . . . laws and public opinion," seeks amnesty under the $20,000 exception. Educated at Greeneville College in Tennessee, he "recollects with much satisfaction how he & other students viz: the Vances, Seviers & Wylies used to congregate on saturdays around your Tailor Shop & listen with delight to your anecdotes as well as your bold & manly sentiments of encouragement to young men." [He was pardoned October 20, 1865.]

From William H. Echols [1]

[Huntsville, Ala., August 25, 1865] [2]

To His Excellency, Andrew Johnson,
President of the United States of America.

The undersigned respectfully states that he is a citizen of Huntsville, County of Madison and State of Alabama, and was born in said town on the eleventh day of March 1834.

That he was graduated at the military academy at West Point in the class of 1858, and continued in the military service of the United States until the month of March 1861, when, learning that Alabama had, in a convention of her people, severed her connection with the United States and believing it to be his duty to obey the commands of his native State, he resigned his commission in the United States army and subsequently, (recieving the acceptance of his resignation) entered the service of the Confederate States.

The undersigned, by reason of the foregoing facts, finds himself excluded from the benefits of your amnesty proclamation, although willing to renew, in good faith, his allegiance to the United States and to accept as a fact the overthrow of the Confederate States with the attendant consequence of the abolition of slavery. He is not excepted under any other clause of your proclamation.

The undersigned, therefore, having taken the oath, as appended hereto and answered the interrogatories of the Governor of Alabama, respectfully solicits a special pardon to be extended to him, pledging himself to be a peaceable and loyal citizen of the United States. [3]

Wm. H. Echols

LS, DNA-RG94, Amnesty Papers (M1003, Roll 3), Ala., William H. Echols.

1. Echols (1834–1909), a Confederate major of engineers, was a cotton farmer and banker after the war. Marks, *Alabama*, 59.

2. On this date John H. King, the U.S. commissioner for northern Alabama, headquartered in Huntsville, certified Echols' appearance and testimony.

3. Months later Echols visited Johnson, who on November 22 endorsed his petition, writing to Attorney General James Speed that "If there are no objections on file in your office, in the case of William H. Echols of Alabama, for Pardon under the Proclamation

of 29th May 1865, you will issue a warrant for his conditional Pardon." The pardon, which was granted on November 24, 1865, was reportedly the first issued to a West Point graduate in Confederate service. Amnesty Papers (M1003, Roll 3), Ala., William H. Echols, RG94, NA; *Lynchburg Virginian*, Nov. 29, 1865.

To Oliver O. Howard

Aug. 25th [186]5

Mrs. A. S. Flash[1] petitions for the return of her property—a lot and house with furniture—in New Orleans now held by the U.S. Military authorities—and for remuneration for that portion destroyed while in possession of the military.

In support of this petition she states—

1st—That at the breaking out of the rebellion her husband was, and for sometime prior, had been a confirmed invalid and never in any manner aided the rebellion.

2d—That she then resided in a dwelling house No. 45 Rampart St. New Orleans said house being her own property, and not that of her husband—in proof of which she submits certified copy of an "Act of Sale" dated in 1857, vesting her with the property in her own name and title, this house being the one applied for.

3rd. In February 1862 upon the opinion of his physician that to stay in N.O. would shorten his life, her husband went to Bladon Springs Ala. and that she accompanyed him and returned to N.O. May 1865, the health of her husband not having been restored and that in May 1865 her husband died.

4th. That she is, and always has been a loyal woman—in proof of which she submits what purports to be a copy of an oath taken before the Provost Marshals swearing allegiance to the Gov't. that she has never held any office civil or military under the Rebel Gov't. that she has never borne arms against the U.S. and that she has never in money property or other article of value contributed to the support of the Rebellion.

5th—She has applied unsuccessfully to the military authorities at N.O. They however promised the return of her property.

6th. That she has taken the amnesty oath and is willing to take any oath that may be required.

Letter of Mrs. Cutler[2] accompanying—states that the property is now in the hands of the "Freedmens Bureau."

Respectfully referred to Major Genl. O. O. Howard, Freedmen's Bureau. If the facts as herein stated are true, I desire that Mrs. A. S. Flash, the petitioner, be put in immediate and full possession of the property herein described.

Andrew Johnson
President United States.

LBcopyS, DLC-JP3A.

1. Mrs. Alexander Flash, Jr. (b. c1840), whose given name was omitted by the census taker, by the beginning of the war was the mother of three. She resided at 45 Rampart Street as late as 1868. 1860 Census, La., Orleans, New Orleans, 4th Ward, 143; New Orleans directories (1857–68).

2. Possibly the wife of either Wyatt C. or R. King Cutler, both born in Louisiana about 1830. 1860 Census, La., Jefferson, Jefferson City, 51, 109; New Orleans directories (1861–73).

From Benjamin F. Perry

Greenville S C August 25th 1865

His Excellency President Johnson
My Dear Sir

I take the liberty of enclosing to your Excellency three papers[1] with reference to the colored troops & freedmen in different parts of South Carolina.

The condition of affairs in reference to the Colored troops & freed men is becoming allarming. The colored troops ought to be removed.[2] They are demoralizing the freedmen & we have serious cause to apprehend an insurrection.

We have a parcel of them in this place & last night they knocked down a gentleman walking with a lady, and another man peacibly returning home. They like wise robbed a wagoner last night in this place. The freedmen are encouraged by them to be unmanageable & idle.

The cause of these outrages was that one of the colored troops was shot by a white scoundrel near the village and wounded in the leg. He ought to be punished, but innocent citizens ought not to suffer for it. They have threatened to burn our Village. I fear the officer in command can not control them.

The people are generally quiet & cheerfully taking the oath. They are *all* anxious to resume their allegiance to the U States & truly sorry for their past Rebellion. They will act in good faith hereafter. The Convention meets the 13th of September. The election is next week. The Constitution will abolish slavery & carry out the other views we discussed.

I am with great respect yours truly &c
B. F. Perry

ALS, DNA-RG105, Asst. Commr., S.C., Unregistered Lets. Recd.

1. Not found.

2. By mid-September General Gillmore had ordered the withdrawal of black troops to the coast. Simkins and Woody, *South Carolina*, 36; Thomas J. Rawls to Johnson, Sept. 12, 1865, Johnson Papers, LC.

From Richmond Citizens [1]

Richmond, August 25, 1865

To His Excellency Andrew Johnson,
President of the United States
Sir:

We have been deputed by the Citizens of Richmond to invite you to visit Richmond, and to tender to you the hospitality of the City.

We obey the wishes and express the feelings of our people, when we say that this is no unmeaning formality. It is the hearty tender of cordial hospitality by a frank and generous people.

The rude blast of War has just swept over Virginia leaving her fields desolate, and her homesteads in ruins. Of our once thriving and beautiful City, the most valuable portion has been consumed by fire and now lies an appalling mass of smouldering ruins.

The fate of battle has been against us. We have been conquered.

But "grim visaged War has smoothed his wrinkled front,"[2] and with a full knowledge of our condition we have accepted it, and with it the amnesty which was tendered to us by your predecessor, as well as by yourself, pledging ourselves by the highest tie which can bind honorable men, to support and defend the Constitution of the United States, and the Union created by it. We made that pledge in good faith, and in good faith we intend to keep it.

But we have been maligned, in false representations which have been made to you. You have been told that our people are not honorable, and do not intend to keep the faith which they have pledged. They confide however in your justice, ability and patriotism. They have been much gratified by the stand which you have taken in behalf of the Constitutional rights of the Southern people, who stand upon the ground occupied by the citizens of all other parts of our Country; all being citizens of one Country, protected by one Constitution, and bound by one obligation, and they do not doubt that it is your purpose to administer your great office, faithfully, according to the Constitution, and with justice to all. Our people invite you therefore to come among them and partake of their hospitality, and judge for yourself of their purposes towards the Government by the reception which they give you its chief executive officer.[3]

With high respect. We have the honor to be Your Obdt. Servts:

LS, DLC-JP.

1. Signed by sixty-four designated committee members, this invitation was enclosed in James B. Jameson to Johnson, Sept. 6, 1865, Johnson Papers, LC.
2. Shakespeare's *King Richard the Third*, Act I, sc. 1, line 19.
3. Although Johnson had indicated to his cabinet a desire to visit Richmond and

Raleigh in early October, he did not go. Beale, *Welles Diary*, 2: 375; James Speed, *James Speed: A Personality* (Louisville, 1914), 67–68.

From William L. Sharkey

Jackson Miss Aug 25 1865.

A Johnson President

Your two dispatches are recd.[1] I have endeavored to avoid the appointment or recommendation of Secessionists both from inclination & duty. It has been an indispensible requisite that parties applying should be free from this objection. Perhaps in a few unimportant instances parties objectionable in this respect may have been accidentally appointed, but never from disign. I was diceived in one instance by recommendation good as I thought, after having charged the parties that appointees must be unobjectionable in this particular, but it was for a temporary office. I am sure the Union men are satisfied. I notice what you say about the Militia. They will leave us in a helpless condition. Genl Slocum has no cavalry & has not force enough to protect us. His Negro troops do more harm than good when scattered through the Country.

W L Sharkey

Tel, DLC-JP.
1. See Telegram to Sharkey, August 21, 1865, and Circular to Provisional Governors, August 22, 1865.

To William L. Sharkey

Executive Office, Washington, D.C.
August 25 1865

Governor W. L Sharkey
Jackson Miss

Your dispatch of this date has been received. The prompt and efficient action taken by your Convention will Exert a decided influence upon the public mind. I trust and hope that your example will be followed by the other Southern States. If so the day is not distant when the Union will be restored and with it that feeling of friendship and amity which has characterized the whole people of the United States from the dawn of the Government. As the feud subsides the people will feel more cordial towards each other than ever before and rejoice that Peace, Happiness and Prosperity have been restored to a suffering and bleeding country.

In regard to the Troops now stationed in Mississippi which seems to be producing dissatisfaction to a great extent the Government does not intend to irritate or humiliate the People of the South but will be mag-

nanimous and remove the cause of your complaint at the earliest period
it is practicable to do so.[1]

Please telegraph me a synopsis of the amendments adopted.[2]

Andrew Johnson
Prest U.S.

Tel, DNA-RG107, Tels. Sent, President, Vol. 2 (1865).
1. In November 1865, after complaints from Sharkey's successor, Johnson was still
giving assurances of the removal of troops whenever peace and order and civil authority were restored. Johnson to B. G. Humphreys, Nov. 17, 1865, Ser. 3A, Johnson Papers, LC.
2. See Telegrams from Sharkey, August 20, 28, 1865.

From J. Madison Wells

State of Louisiana, Executive Department.
New Orleans, August 25/1865.

His Excellency Andrew Johnson
President of the United States.
Dear Sir

On the 16th inst in reply to a private telegram of the 12th[1] from
Washington informing me that before appointing me Provisional Governor you required that I should so desire, I telegraphed at once directly
to you such wish on my part, stating that it was the wish of almost all
influential parties here likewise.

On the 21st the following telegram was sent me from the Military
telegraph office. I do not exactly comprehend it.

"Dept of the Gulf
U.S. Military Telegraph Office
New Orleans, Aug 20th 1865
Washington Aug 12th 6.30 P.M.

Cipher
Gov J M Wells
care of Major Smith N.O.[2] Does Gov. Wells desire the appointment of a
Provisional Governor for Louisiana or had you better proceed as you have commenced? What number of persons who are active and prominent desire the
appointment of Provisional Governor? Answer what shall be done in the premises? Dr. Cottman is still here.

A Johnson. Pres't U.S.
The above has been delayed for correction operator."

Had this dispatch came to hand in time I should have put my own
meaning on it and telegraphed back more fully. As it is, I will here state
that I am in favor of the appointment of a provisional Governor for
Louisiana beleiving it to be the true interests of the State and as the
only constitutional mode of restoring her natural relations to the Federal government.

Standing as I do at this moment, it is doubtful whether I have any
power save as I may have it doled out on urgent solicitation by the

Military power, which in its turn claims to exercise and does exercise in many objectionable ways the right to interfere in the civil concerns of citizens and to control them. I had hoped that on my return from Washington, as I understood was your determination, an end would have been put to this interference which is both vexatious to citizens and humiliating to the civil authorities.[3]

I have the honor to be Your Very Obt Servant

J. Madison Wells

Governor of Louisiana.

ALS, DLC-JP.

1. To Johnson's telegram of the 12th, Wells had responded: "I deem it the interest of Louisiana that I should be appointed Provisional Governor." Wells to Johnson, Aug. 16, 1865, Tels. Recd., President, Vol. 4 (1865–66), RG107, NA.

2. Not identified.

3. For Johnson's response, see his dispatch to Wells, Sept. 18, 1865, Tels. Sent, President, Vol. 2 (1865), RG107, NA.

From J. Madison Wells

State of Louisiana, Executive Department.

New Orleans, August 25th 1865.

Andrew Johnson

President of the United States.

President

I have the honor to enclose copies of correspondence which has passed between Major Gen'l Canby Commd'g Dept here and the Hon'l Hu Kennedy Mayor of the City of New Orleans.[1]

The continued interference of the Commanding Gen'l with many important civil matters not conceivably connected with his military duties so contrary to what I know is your wish, I sincerely regret and in the present instance, I cannot but greatly feel aggrieved as the pretentions he sets up would denude not only all civil officers of the power you wish them to exercise, but the people individually and collectively of all control of the property they consider their own.

The Mayors letter[2] fully explains the immediate question in controversy: and as I consider he is both capable of reorganizing the City government and restoring it to its proper place both of loyalty and prosperity, I would with the most respectful earnestness ask for it your attention. Mr. Kennedy has encountered he informs me great obstructions to his reformatory measures in these wayward, eccentric and abitrary proceedings, but desires that Brevet Major Genl W T Sherman[3] should be officially commended by me as one officer who has upon all occasions kindly sympathized with him in his endeavours to restore the City to its former substantial prosperity and to a greatly improved police.

I hope President this considerate friendship of a brave soldier to a City greatly needing support and in his instance all the more honorable from being spontaneously rendered, may entitle him to your consideration.

I have the honor to be with great respect
Your obt Servant J Madison Wells
Governor of Louisiana

LS, DLC-JP.

1. On August 23, Canby, through a subordinate, notified Mayor Kennedy that certain "levee and wharf space" had been "selected and reserved for military purposes," which would prevent the leasing of the same by the city. All titles to the wharves belonged to the U.S. government as captured property, and any contemplated use by city officials should be reported to Canby's headquarters or to the "proper authorities at Washington." The mayor's reply to Canby has not been found. George L. Andrews to Kennedy, Aug. 23, 1865, Johnson Papers, LC.

2. On the 24th, Kennedy had enclosed the Canby correspondence in a covering letter to Wells. He did "not forsee the interference herein revealed" and noted that "no portion of the wharves included in what was leased was then or is now in use by any department of the national government." General Canby's claim was particularly embarrassing, considering the "deplorable condition of our city finances." Kennedy to Wells, Aug. 24, 1865, Johnson Papers, LC.

3. The Sherman here referred to is actually Thomas W. (1813–1879), a West Point graduate, who had served in the Department of the Gulf since 1862. Warner, *Blue.*

From James Gordon Bennett[1]

Fort Washington 26th Augt 1865

His Excellency President Johnson
My Dear Sir

A very old friend of mine, Mr. H. Wikoff,[2] going to Washgton on some business of his own, I have requested him to state to you the political situation of things here and in the North generally as regards the restoration of the South. We are preparing to get up a demonstration in opposition to the Boston agitators which I think will be successful at all hazards. Let me say a few words more. You occupy a position in this country only equaled by that of the first President after the revolution of 1776, but with a future far beyond the past in breadth and volume. I suppose you have but little time to devote to foreign affairs but for the first time in the history of the U.S. our foreign relations loom as high and important as those of home matters. The U.S. came out of the recent war as one of the great powers of the world and her foreign policy is equally as important. It seems to me that we ought to settle our foreign questions with Europe without war, and the best means to do so would be in a Congress of all the great powers. If I had any idea what your government thought on that subject, I could in my own way aid and assist your administration with more efficiency. I have given Mr. W. my ideas on that and other subjects which he will be glad

President Andrew Johnson, 1865, by Mathew Brady
Courtesy National Archives

to detail to you if you desire him. If they are advisable I should be most happy to proceed in that course.

I am Dear Sir Yours most truly
James G. Bennett

ALS, DLC-JP.
  1. Conservative Republican editor of the *New York Herald*.
  2. Henry Wikoff (1813–1884) was an adventurer and minor diplomat who acted as liaison between the editor and the President. *DAB*; Cox, *Politics, Principles, and Prejudice*, 90.

From Celia A. Grove[1]

August the 26 1865
Washington City D.C.

To His Excellency
The President of the U States
Dir Sir

   Though a stranger to you, I feel authorised to appeal to your heart for Justice—which I do know I would most asshuredly get could you only know my Sufferings. Now in my old Age I am with out where to lay my head. I have had all the welth I could desire. From crueltyes from this cruel war am left puneless. I never Aided this unholy Rebellion, God knows all, and I have every proof of my resistance to it as strong as man can give. I have allways stood firm and desided for my Country, have Saccrifyced my dearest ties I have on Earth on that account. I have Received letters from Rebble lines to keepe my self out of ther lines for thay would handle me roughfly. I was orderde from my home by three Rebble Genls & Ex Govenor Moore of Louisiana on the account of my principles. I was called upon for Subscriptions for building Gun Boats. I refused to give it. Thay then burned one hundred & thirty one Bales of my Cotton. I had hid one hundred & four Bales of Cotton that I got a friend to claim as his own, and since Genl Lees surrender that has bin taken from me, so I am left with out any thing but Sorrow. I have bin Scoffed at, laft at, abused in Every way, & asked how I liken my good Union that has protected me. Four years ago I was in my quiet home when all my Neighbours had fled, from the Army of the U S troops. I [s]tood firmly at my post, and when ordered to leave that once happy home I refused to go. Thay then said we will not protect your property. I told them I ask not your protection for with my Goverment I stand, & with my government I fall. Now my Goverment stands whilst I have fallen, a marter. Now will my Country see me a begger, which I am. I was remooved from my once happy home when my only and darling Child was dying. She with her uplifted hands begged let me die in my mothers house; we had to go, put on a Boat. She died too years a go, las February and as yet She lies uncoffined: and when Genl Lee surrendred his Army I received a message to remoove the remains of my dear Child. She was in Louisiana and I in Vicksburg, in a house that was assined me by order of Millitary, but now I have to give up the house and go out of doors. I was remooved from my own *home by Genl Sherman.*[2] H*e occupied my House. When he left it some one* burned it and Every building, and not a vestage left me on Earth. My Cotton that was there My Corn Cattle Horses Mules Stock of Ever kind and sort gone, and I but thirty minuts to go a way, and my Child dying. I could not attend to any thing. Consiquently, I lost all I had. My heart was broken. I could not do any thing. Fifty hours I had not one morsel to put in my lips. Now president Jonson, I had a promised interview, with president Lincon, last Spring, a year ago, but I did not have one dollar to come on hare. Consiquently I could not come. There are thousands of U S officers say, if you knew my Case you would make a special Case for me. I ask nothing but what I am wholy entitled. I have no Vouchers for any thing yet I have proof from the Millitary suffient to satisfy any predied [prejudiced] mind of the wrongs done me, and will not my Goverment stand by me as I have by it. I have proofs where I have saved the life of Solgiers & officers. My Loyalty has never bin douted. My Acts are two well known. *I want now pay, for forty Bales of Cotton, that was taken at the time I was remooved from my home three years a go.* My Child was then dying. I did not get Vouchers nor did I know who took it, but officers of the U.S. Army gives proof that it was taken for Hospital purposes. Can I *get that your* influence is all. I would ten thousand times rather be shot than return South a beggar. My pride forbids. President Jonson God sees all. He will reward you for Justice to me.

I am not a Criminal, nor have never bin. I only as[k] a little of the mutch taken. My Clooths & those of my dead Childs were taken from me & *the Men* that took them are now here waiting favours. All I have the proof with me.

Now president Jonson I am left desolate in this Cold Cold world. I have not a Rellation on Earth to assist me in any way. Must I perish. Oh could I but see you. Do not deny me this. Do not turn a deaf Ear to my pleadings. If I can see you, you will not doubt one word I have said. Hear me now or I must perish.[3] If you have any message for me send it to the care of Govenor *Stanton*,[4] near your own Residence.

very respectfully Mrs. C. A. Grove

P S My home was in Louisiana Near Vicksburg.

ALS, DNA-RG107, Lets. Recd., EB12 President 2355 (1865).

1. Grove (b. *c*1814), wife of George W., had a plantation in Madison Parish. Her house was "Burnt a total loss $8,000.00" and 100 horses and mules, about 300 head of cattle, and 100 hogs, along with other animals, fodder, and equipment, had been appropriated by Union soldiers. In all, "not a building or fence" was left standing on her

plantation. Grove's undated petition and affidavit of Tobias Smith, March 23, 1864, Lets. Recd., EB12 President 2355 (1865), RG107, NA; 1850 Census, Miss., Warren, Vicksburg, 378.

2. Thomas W. Sherman.

3. Johnson forwarded this plea to the secretary of war for a "thorough investigation." Mrs. Grove's claim for damages by Union troops had been reviewed a year earlier by a military board in Vicksburg which had recommended reimbursement; ultimately, however, her claim was ruled upon adversely by the Southern Claims Commission as her "loyalty not established." J. B. Holloway, comp., *Digest of Claims Referred by Congress to the Court of Claims from the 48th to the 51st Congress* . . . (Washington, D.C., 1891), 17.

4. Probably Frederick P. Stanton, former Tennessee congressman and acting governor of Kansas Territory, now residing in Washington, D.C., at 224 F Street north. *DAB*; *Boyd's Washington and Georgetown Directory* (1865), 334.

From William W. Holden

Raleigh Aug 26 1865.

The President

Sir

In reply to your dispatch of the 22d August I have the honor to state in No instance in making appointment to office or in recommending for appointment have I shown any preference for persons who have participated in the Rebellion. On the contrary I have been very careful to prefer and to appoint persons who were original union men & persons who were in favor of restoring the authority of the Federal Govt. Doubtless in many appointments (some four thousand) some have been appointed who ought not to have been & in some cases even friends have misled to some slight extent by their recommendations but upon the whole, only loyal union men have been appointed & recommended at Washington. It is my purpose & wish to encourage & strengthen those who have never at heart faltered in their allegiance to the federal Govt. I have proceeded deliberately and carefully in the work of reorganizing & thus far I am sure there are no grounds for apprehending that North Carolina will not present an acceptable Constitution. The great body of her people are loyal & submissive to National authority. I know there are malcontents, radicals, & not good men who are engaged in misrepresenting facts & fermenting strife for certain purposes, but none of these things move me in the performance of duty. Thanking you heartily for the Confidence you have heretofore reposed in me & for the honor you have done me in making me Prov'l Govr of this Noble state.

I am sir &c W. W Holden
Prov Govr

Tel, DLC-JP.

From Hugh Kennedy

State of Louisiana, Mayoralty of New Orleans,
City Hall 26 day of Aug. 1865

Andrew Johnson
President of the United States
President.

In all things I have endeavored since my resumption of Mayoralty duties on the 1st July last, to conform with vigorous exactitude to the views you did me the honor to express in regard to Louisiana affairs, when I was in Washington.

I have found, however, President, that there is an under current of opposition to all measures having for their object the tranquillization of the country, and the early crystallization of all its elements into support of your administration. I have taken the liberty hitherto of reporting to you upon this subject. You will, perhaps, recollect that when Govr. Wells and Dr. Cottman, in May last, expressed confidence in Genr'l Canby, you asked me what I thought; I replied that I had no confidence in such people, unless they were specifically instructed; which I explained at your request to mean, unless they were restricted to military matters exclusively. I regret that such specific instructions were not given, as I am sure you intended they should be; for if they had, I cannot suppose the difficulties of civil administration I have experienced could have been near so serious.

Genr'l Canby has made it be understood that all the railroads and the city corporation property has been confiscated as captured property; and by countenancing these and other disorganizing ideas, so contrary to your assurances to me, he has very seriously disturbed the public mind.

Nothing President shall be allowed to swerve me from the direct and straight course you indicated for me, and all that I ask is that you will uphold me in what is just and right for people and government.[1]

I have the honor to be, President,
with very great respect Your humble servant
Hu. Kennedy Mayor

LS, DNA-RG107, Lets. Recd., EB12 President 2573 (1865).
1. Kennedy's letter was referred to the War Department.

From Albert R. Lamar

[ca. August 26, 1865, Columbus, Ga.]; ALS, DNA-RG94, Amnesty Papers (M1003, Roll 20), Ga., A. R. Lamar.

Columbus lawyer "obnoxious to the first clause" of the May 29 proclamation, by virtue of service as clerk in the Confederate Congress, seeks a pardon. Believing in states' rights and convinced the rise "to power of a sectional party of open and avowed hostility to the peculiar institution of the South . . . demanded the practical exercise of the right peaceably if practicable forcibly if necessary," Lamar "spared no means or effort moral or material to promote the welfare and success" of the Confederacy. Yet with the "failure of the South to maintain this right," he accepts the results, intending to be a loyal citizen and to counsel "others to do likewise." [Lamar's pardon was granted October 28, 1865.]

From Lavinia C. Vaughan

August 26, 1865, Washington, D.C.; ALS, DNA-RG94, Amnesty Papers (M1003, Roll 70), Va., Lavinia C. Vaughan.

Widowed mother of seven and citizen of Elizabeth City County, Va., a resident in part of her own house, asks that the remainder, "occupied for a colored school and place of worship may be restored to her now,—and that she be authorized to collect rent . . . for her land." During the war, although "utterly opposed to Secession," she lived with her husband in Petersburg and Farmville until his death in February 1863, after which she "endeavored in vain to obtain permission to pass into the Federal lines." Her land "was confiscated after her husband's death, but not sold." [Evidently falling under the 12th exception, Mrs. Vaughan was pardoned August 29, 1865.]

To William W. Holden

Executive Mansion, Washington, D.C.
Augt 27 1865.

Gov W. W. Holden, Raleigh N.C.

My telegram[1] was merely intended to call your attention to the impression being made by those who are opposed to the Southern States resuming their former relations with the Federal Government, and in making appointments to guard against it as far as practicable, and thereby deprive them of all excuse for opposing a restoration of State Governments. It is not certain that I will visit Richmond but if I determine to do so I will include Raleigh.[2] Mississippi has acted promptly and well. God grant that the Southern people would see their true interest and the welfare of the whole country and act accordingly.

Andrew Johnson President U.S.

Tel, DNA-RG107, Tels. Sent, President, Vol. 2 (1865).
    1. See Circular to Provisional Governors, August 22, 1865.
    2. Johnson was responding to Holden's invitation of the day before: "It is stated in

the Papers that you Contemplate soon making a visit to Richmond. I would be pleased if you would extend your visit to Raleigh." Johnson did not make the trip. Holden to Johnson, Aug. 26, 1865, Johnson Papers, LC.

From John Erskine

New York. Aug. 28. 1865.

His Excellency, Andrew Johnson,
President of the U. States. &c. &c.
Sir,

As Ex-Gov Joseph E. Brown of Georgia is a solicitant for amnesty and pardon, I respectfully beg leave to present to your Excellency a few facts in his behalf;—flattering myself that you will not deem me presumptuous.

Until the breaking out of the rebellion, Gov. Brown and I had been political and personal friends. That event necessarily ended our political associations. Continuing nonetheless, our friendly personal relations, gave me frequent opportunities of talking freely with him; and my conclusions were, and still are, that he was opposed to the rebellion in its inception. And if I am right in saying that he was opposed to it, still it was beyond his power to prevent it, for the large slave owners, and their dissolute dependents, threatened the people that the Union must be disrupted, or they must accept the horrid alternative of civil and internecine war among themselves. War was inaugurated;—The result is before the world.

Shortly after it began, the quick sense of Brown perceived that constitutional liberty was already submerged and a central despotism had risen in its place. The most tyrannical acts were committed; sequestration, and other confiscatory laws, were passed. These Acts met the instant condemnation of Brown; and he said to me, in the hearing of several persons: that even common honesty had fled their councils. On the promulgation of the various conscription, and impressment laws, Brown boldly remonstrated with Davis, and his sec. of war. Several of Gov. Brown's dispatches, on these subjects, I myself read; and in my humble opinion, they showed intelectual capacity of the highest order. Finding his remonstrances vain, he inhibited the impressing officers from taking the provisions and cattle of the poor till just compensation was first made. And when *his* orders were violated, he seized and imprisoned, in the county jails, several of these *Ghouls* till the people were paid for their goods. No threats could intimidate him.

Brown is endowed with that rare attribute, proper respect for the conscientious influences that control others. This noble trait of character was often made manifest, and of this I am one of the many witnesses: Being within the conscription age I was daily and nightly harrassed by the conscribing officers. I at last sought Gov. Brown, and frankly told him, that I never would bear arms against the United States; and mentioned the names of many others who were of like determination. His reply was, in substance, this: I have given this subject much thought and reflection, and have come to the conclusion that success cannot follow where men are compelled to fight in a cause when their moral convictions are against it. As for you, he continued, knowing you as I do, I will protect you at all hazzards. And all others like yourself—not the weak-spirited, remember—who are conscientiously opposed to going into the army, bring them or properly recommend them to me, and I'll protect them here, if I can, or give them passes, so far as is my power, to leave the country; and one or the other of these kindnesses he did in many, many cases. I could enumerate many other acts in his favor, but I fear, sir, that I have already trespassed. Permit me another word: If Gov. Brown's petition for pardon meets your approval, you will never have cause to regret your clemency. There is not one among the poor, the industrious farmer, or the mechanic, or the kind-hearted, in Georgia who will not rejoice to know that Brown is pardoned. The legal oblivion you bestow on him, will knit his heart to the Government of the United States. He will then return home untrammelled, and effect great good in Georgia,—greater, perhaps than any other man. He is a man of truth—he never equivocates—and his heart is full of gratitude. Every Georgian, whom I meet here, hopes that he will be pardoned, and the people of this City express the same wish.[1]

You, sir, may trust him: his friends will never have cause to blush for him. What I have written is intended to express my personal feelings for Gov. Brown, and, as I said, to communicate to your Excellency a few facts.

With, profound respect, I remain, your Excellency's Obt Servt.
John Erskine of Georgia.

ALS, DNA-RG94, Amnesty Papers (M1003, Roll 16), Ga., Joseph E. Brown.

1. Isaac Scott, endorsing Erskine's appeal for Brown's pardon, attested to the accuracy of the "principal facts stated," as he was "congnizant of their truth."

From George J. Knight

August 28, 1865, Brownville, N.Y.; ALS, DLC-JP.

In a long discourse, "an old man" who has "lost two brave sons in this cruel war" speaks the sentiments "of thousands and perhaps of millions," when he suggests that "Evil will result from too freely pardoning those who have for years done all in their power to destroy our Constitution and wise system of government." He thinks that "designing politicians and prime movers of the rebellion" should be kept "in suspense as hostages for their own and others good behaviour," until the reconstruction of the Union has been "amicably arranged."

From Sebastian Kraft[1]

Union Dist S.C Agst 28. 1865

To his Excelency Andrew Johnston.
President of the United States of America.

Your Excelency will no doubt be much surpriced and Consider this letter a great pice of impudence, comming as it dose, from an humble Citizen, with whom your Excelency, has neither a social, or political aquaintance. But I hope when Your Excelency perceives the motive—that actuated me, a ready pardon will be granted for the liberty, I am about to take.

Your Excelency is well aware, of the contition of Sou Carolina before this rebellion, and need not to be informed, that but few, men were, and remaind true, to the Old Union, and it is also known to your Excilency, that those few, were in danger of their lives, & property, during the war, saying nothing of the abuse dayly heaped upon them, being as it where, in the Enemys country, without means of Escape. But all that we should willingly forgit If the future would only promise *Protiction* and *Peace*. But now the Government has indirectly turned loos, an Element up on us, which threatens, an Extermination of all, (*Union*, or *rebells*,) the white race. It will be out of the power of the Government in a short time, to controle the Negroes, as they have no other Idia, of self Government & freedom; there Liberty, means, to Eat, Drink, & be Idle, the result of which is, robbery, murder, and a perfect war bethween the Black & white raaces in a short time.

Your Excelency will however not understand that we here, plead, for the future Existance of slavery, or the nonpunishment, of those rebells, who hatched the secession parricide, which nearly destroyed, our once happy Country. To the contrairy, I believe, it necessary to good order, and future Peace, that some, should be capitally punished.

But at the same time, Your Excelency should remember Lot, and not destroy us, with the guilty, when we, as Union men, have sufferd the reproaches of the rebells, for several years, saying nothing, of the danger, of our lives, & property. Our lot is hard indeed; leiving here, without means of excape, or protection. Exposed to the Lawlessness of the negroes, who, unless put to work right off, will steal, and destroy every thing we got. If they dont massacre the white Race, it is not because the desire dont exist.

Negroes feel disapointed, and dont beleive the Union agents, and say they will have Horses, Land, &C and that without work. Good men who are able, will all leave the Country, (unless protection be speedy), which will leave the Country a wilderness.

We therefore thinke it a duty, Your Excelency ows us (if it be the intention of the Government, to destroy Carolina) to give notice to some of us, in order, that we may at least safe our wifes, & Childern, from the fury of a race, who through the instrumentality of a savage people, have become worse than Devels.[2]

Trusting in God and the Country.
I remain your Excelencys most humble Citizen
Sebastian Kraft.

P.S. Your Excelency will find many from this state Sueing for pardon, of which non deserves more punishment then Wm. H. Gist,[3] as one of the prime leaders in the rebellion.

S. K.

ALS, DNA-RG105, Asst. Commr., S.C., Registered Lets. Recd., File K-23-1865.
1. Kraft (b. c1815) was a German-born farmer. 1860 Census, S.C., Union, Goshen Hill, 8.
2. Johnson's secretary referred this to General Howard, whose office in turn forwarded Kraft's letter to Gen. Rufus Saxton, assistant commissioner, for "such action as the interest of the Bureau may require."
3. A leader of the ultras and Governor of South Carolina who called the legislature into session in November and signed the secession ordinance in December 1860.

From William L. Sharkey

Jackson August 28 [1865][1]

His Excellency Andrew Johnson
President of the United States
Sir

Our convention has concluded its labors, the chief amendment to the constition being the same as telegraphed to you.[2] I shall forward a perfect copy to the Department of State. The negro is protected in his rights of person and property, and the legislature is charged with the duty of carrying out this injunction. How it will do this I cannot say. Possibly it may allow the negro to testify, as such was the desire of a cons[id]erable number of the convention, but this was thought to be an appropriate legislative duty. Such a desire I think is growing. The right of suffrage I do not think will be extended to them; indeed there is an inclination to limit the right of suffrage with the white man.[3] In regard to the amendment to the Constitution of the United States prohibiting slavery I do not think the State ever will adopt the second article or provision of the amendment.[4] I took the liberty of having your despatch on the subject read to the convention,[5] and it gave satisfaction.

In one of your despatches you seem to disapprove of the plan of organizing the militia of our state.[6] I could give several good reasons for having done so. In the first place the forces in the State are wholly insufficient to protect the people. There is no cavalry here, and without it, crime cannot be checked. In the next place the presence of negro soldiers is not always a protection, and as proof of this I beg you to read a letter, a copy of which is enclosed,[7] and similar events are daily reaching me. One has come in whilst I am wrting. But there is also a wide spread opinion amongst the people and it is justified by threats, that about christmas they intend a general uprising for the purpose of taking the property, as they say they have not yet got all their rights. It was to satisfy the people, and begin the preparation for such an emmergency, and to suppress crime, that I ordered the organization of the Militia. The negroes congregate around the negro garrisons in great numbers, and are idle and guilty of many petty crimes. We have at this place a General[8] who is anxious to do his duty, but I fear this is not the case with many of the Post Commanders. I fear the department of the government having control of that people here, is badly managed. If the negro is ever to be useful to himself or to the Country, he ought not to be encouraged in idleness in the beginning, or he will expect it hereafter. A gentleman of high intelligence now sitting by me says the freedmens beareau here is a curse and generally so regarded. I give you this as public opinion. The people think that they are now entitled to be relieved of martial law and to have the habeas corpus restored, and to have also the negro garrisons removed. If we must have soldiers, we would like to have white ones, who would not draw to them congregations of idle negroes. There is much complaint and distrust on the part of the people towards the government, on account of these restrictions, and under these circumstances I am agreeably surprised that the convention did so well. There is an opinion here, but too prevalent I fear, that the north will be content with nothing but the humiliation & degradation of the south, which arises I think to some extent from the management of the freed mens beareau here. I think the people of Mississippi are now entitled to the consideration of the Government, and to be treated as though the rebellion had ended. I write to you Sir, in a spirit of frankness, and in a spirit of friendship, & hope you will excuse the liberty I take.

Your Obt Servt W L Sharkey
Provisional Govr of Miss

ALS, DLC-JP.

1. The letter's internal evidence makes 1865 the obvious date.
2. See Telegram from Sharkey, August 20, 1865.
3. This is Sharkey's response to Johnson's suggestion of August 15. The convention felt the suffrage question to be beyond the purview of its deliberations, preferring to leave the matter to the legislature when that body was organized. In addition, old-line Whigs in the convention found the idea of Negro suffrage a repugnant concept, no doubt reflecting Sharkey's sense of the general populace's attitude. Harris, *Presidential Reconstruction*, 59–60.
4. The second section of the 13th Amendment gave Congress the "power to enforce the provisions of this article."
5. See Telegram to Sharkey, August 15, 1865.
6. See Telegram to Sharkey, August 21, 1865.
7. J. W. Wade to Sharkey, Aug. 23, 1865, Johnson Papers, LC.
8. Peter J. Osterhaus (1823–1917), who emigrated from Prussia and settled in Illinois, subsequently moved to St. Louis. In the Union army he became a brigadier in 1862 and took part in several major western and southern campaigns. On August 21 Oster-

haus, objecting to the raising of militia, had assured the governor of all necessary military assistance. Harris, *Presidential Reconstruction*, 73; Warner, *Blue*; Boatner, *CWD*.

From John V. Wright[1]

Eutaw Greene Co Ala
Aug 28th 1865.

Hon Andrew Johnson
President. U S.
Dear Sir;

I have forwarded through the usual channels my application for Amnesty and Pardon, with the necessary oaths attached.

I am not included, in any of the excepted Classes of your, proclamation, unless I am included in the 1st Class, by reason of having accepted and held the office of a Representative in the so called Confederate Congress from the state of Tennessee.

For the part which I acted there I can only refer you to the printed records, and to your and my friend Hon Geo W Jones.

I can not, by any construction be classed as a *leader* either in the origination or prosecution of the Secession idea. I belonged to the same school, of politics, with your Excellency, having voted for you, and sustained you in every political contest in which you were engaged from the period of my manhood up to 1860. I have sustained your course as President of the U S. from the period of your inauguration and expect to continue to do so believing that your course is the only one which will lead to the peace & prosperity of the country.

My property which was small, not exceeding in value, more than 8 or 10 thousand dollars by the chances of war, has been pretty well destroyed.

My wife had a seperate estate which has also been nearly ruined & rendered nearly valueless.

I am very anxious to go to some kind of business, by which I can make a support for my family and I can do nothing until I obtain your pardon.

Could you not, in case my papers do not reach you, by the time this letter does, on your own knowledge of my case, & the statements herein contained, Send me a pardon by the bearer of this, Col Tyree,[2] or some other safe hand?

I would have come to you in person, but for the scarcity of funds & the broken up and deranged state of Rail Roads &c, & the additional fact, that I did not desire to trouble you by adding to the throng now in Washington.

Hoping to receive a favorable hearing at your hands[3] I am

truly & sincerely yr. Obedient Servt &c
Jno V. Wright

ALS, DNA-RG94, Amnesty Papers (M1003, Roll 12), Ala., John V. Wright.

1. An antebellum congressman, formerly of McNairy County, Tenn.
2. Thomas T. Tyree (1808–1886), a Mobile cotton factor and Greene County, Ala., planter. Helen A. Thompson, comp. and ed., *Magnolia Cemetery* (New Orleans, 1974), 386; 1860 Census, Ala., Mobile, Mobile, 1st Ward, 34; Greene, Knoxville Precinct, 78; Amnesty Papers (M1003, Roll 11), Ala., Thomas T. Tyree, RG94, NA.
3. Wright, who was under indictment for treason, was pardoned at Johnson's direction on October 27, 1865. *House Ex. Docs.*, 39 Cong., 2 Sess., No. 116, p. 53 (Ser. 1293).

To Andrew J. Martin[1]

Executive Mansion, Washington, D.C.
Aug't 29 1865.

A. J. Martin, Nashville, Tenn.

You will please call on General Fisk and request him to state upon what grounds Mrs Margaret Donalson's property is held by the Freedmen's Bureau.[2] I have been advised that she has strictly complied with all the regulations which would entitle her and orphan children to their home. The reason for refusal to give up the property you will please communicate to me. You are authorized to show this to Gen Fisk.[3]

Andrew Johnson
President U.S.

Tel, DNA-RG107, Tels. Sent, President, Vol. 2 (1865).

1. Martin (1832–*fl*1896), an attorney, later moved to Memphis, where he also dealt in real estate. Goodspeed's *Shelby*, 1005–6; Nashville directories (1866–69); Memphis directories (1876–96).
2. The President had just received Margaret Donelson's wire: "I had thought my farm released but have learned that it is not. Will you please order the release. I have no home. Telegraph care of A J Martin." Donelson to Johnson, Aug. 29, 1865, Tels. Recd., President, Vol. 4 (1865–66), RG107, NA.
3. Despite Johnson's intervention, this dispute continued for several months. See Fisk to Johnson, Sept. 1, Oct. 3, 1865, Donelson to Johnson, Sept. 29, 1865, Johnson Papers, LC.

From Benjamin F. Perry

Greenville So Ca August 29th 1865

His Excellency President Johnson
My dear Sir

I had the honor of receiving your telegraphic Dispatch of the 23rd[1] Inst. yesterday evening, informing me that reports are freely in circulation in influential quarters that, in appointments to office, the true Union men are totally ignored and the Provisional Governors are giving a decided preference to those who have participated in the rebellion. I immediately telegraphed your Excellency[2] that such reports were not only untrue, but without the shadow of foundation, so far as the Provisional Governor of South Carolina was concerned. That all of my sympathies were naturally and necessarily with the "true Union men," who had firmly maintained their principles, but that I felt no partiality for those *pretended* Union men whose latent unionism, was only brought to light and made known by the hope of office. I stated further that there were not a dozen prominently active and decided union men in the whole State, and none of them had applied for office. That the great mass of the people of South Carolina were now true and loyal, having voluntarily taken the oath of Allegiance, and would as readily defend the Union, as they had attempted to depart from it. In all of my appointments I had solely regarded the integrity, capacity and fitness as well as loyalty of the applicants. If in any instance I had disregarded the claims of a pretended union man, it was because I had either doubted his fitness or his unionism.

I now beg leave to further explain to your Excellency, that in organizing a Provisional Government, in South Carolina, I knew it was impossible to fill the appointments with union men. In a large portion of the State there were no union men, none who had ever made their weight and influence felt, when the Union was imperilled. I thought it wisest and best to restore to office those who had been chosen by the people, were familliar with their official duties, had taken the oath of Allegiance, and were pardoned. I had confidence in their honor and plighted fidelity and loyalty. This put in operation, at once, the machinery of civil government perfected and complete, which the necessities of the State imperiously demanded. It was calculated to sooth and harmonize the people in their pledged loyalty to the Union. The Provisional Governors of Mississippi Alabama and Georgia have pursued the same course. I informed your Excellency of the plan I had adopted and the reasons which impelled me to it.[3]

In selecting my appointments from those who were equally guilty in their rebellion, I did think, and still think, that they who had the courage and manhood, to imperil their lives in battle, and were maimed and helpless, were more deserving, than their compeers, who had meanly skulked from danger and kept out of the war. In other States the Provisional Governors may have had a sufficient union material to fill their appointments, but I assure your Excellency this was not the case in South Carolina. This assurance I gave your Excellency before my Proclamation was issued. And I never will appoint any man to office on account of political principles in whose honor and integrity I have no confidence. My observation in life has proved that a man without honor and integrity has no political principles.

Let me assure your Excellency that it is my purpose, as it is my duty to aid the Government in its policy of re-construction.[4]

I am with great respect and esteem yours truly &c

B. F. Perry

LS, DLC-JP.
1. See Circular to Provisional Governors, August 22, 1865. The telegram to Perry found in the Alabama Department of Archives and History is dated August 23.
2. See Perry to Johnson, Aug. 28, 1865, Johnson Papers, LC.
3. See Letter from Perry, August 10, 1865.
4. Johnson responded on September 2, encouraging Perry to "proceed with the work of restoration as rapidly as possible and upon such principles as will disarm those who are opposed to the States resuming their former relations with the federal government. This is all important." Tels. Sent, President, Vol. 2 (1865), RG107, NA.

To Benjamin F. Perry

Washington Aug 29 1865

To Gov B. F Perry
Greenville SC

Your letter of the 20th has just been received. For information in regard to who shall administer the oaths your attention is directed to the circular of the sect'y of State dated 29th of May last and appended to my proclamation of that date which states expressly that any civil or military officer in the service of the U.S. or of a state who by the laws thereof may be qualified for administering oaths &c.[1]

Andrew Johnson Presdt U.S.

Tel, A-Ar, B. F. Perry Papers.
1. By mid-September Perry and Gillmore had reached an agreement allowing civil authorities to administer the oaths. Kibler, *Perry*, 404; Perry to Johnson, Sept. 23, 1865, Johnson Papers, LC.

From Carl Schurz

August 29, 1865, Vicksburg, Miss.; ALS, DLC-JP. See *Advice*, 106–17.

Additional visits in Alabama, at Selma and Demopolis, confirm Schurz's opinion "that the civil authorities . . . are entirely incapable of restoring anything like public order and security." He observes that "theft and robbery as well as negro-whipping . . . prevail . . . all over the State" and warns that it "is unsafe to deplete these States too rapidly. We may need more troops three months hence than we do now." The Mississippi convention's rejection of the secession doctrine and its abolition of slavery in the state came only because they thought such actions "were indispensable to secure readmission." Only two or three among the members of the convention were "thorough going Union men." "If the people succeed in securing a true representation [in the forthcoming legislature], we must look for bad results." There is far less disorder in Mississippi than in Alabama, as a result of its being "more perfectly garrisoned than any of those [states] that I have visited." Believes that Governor Sharkey, in his effort to organize the state militia, is being influenced "by a set of old secessionists" who surround him. Thus Schurz commends General Slocum's order setting aside the governor's militia proclamation and taking steps to use Federal troops to preserve order; he further suggests that Slocum's policy "would have a most excellent effect" if applied to Alabama and Georgia. Johnson's intention that Union men take over the state governments "has been most completely disregarded in Mississippi." In fact, "a Union man was virtually removed from office to make room for one of the most active and odious disloyalists." Schurz cites a number of instances to prove that "if any discrimination is made, it is made in favor of men of rebel antecedents." Without questioning Sharkey's loyalty, Schurz does not see him "as the right man in the right place." He strongly advises the President to approve General Slocum's order openly, and also to resist pressure to remove black troops from the state. "There is nothing that will make it [black freedom] more evident than the bodily presence of a negro with a musket on his shoulder." Schurz urges that William Porterfield, "one of the most disreputable characters in this part of the country in every respect" and currently an applicant for a most lucrative mail contract, receive no favors at the hands of the government.

From Joseph E. Brown

August 30, 1865, Washington, D.C.; ALS, DNA-RG94, Amnesty Papers (M1003, Roll 16), Ga., Joseph E. Brown.

The former governor of Georgia and the possessor of property "worth over $20,000" applies for amnesty and pardon. Avowing that he has no Federal or Confederate property "in his hands or possession or under his control"; that he has never had charge of nor cruelly treated prisoners of war; and that no indictment for treason is pending against him, he "accepts the results of the late unfortunate struggle as a settlement of the issues involved" and "will support the entire abolition of slavery." Believing that his activities and policies during the war are well enough known, he does not think it proper to lengthen his petition by a statement of the facts.

From Varina Davis

Mill Wood, Near Augusta Ga
Aug 30th 1865.

His Excellency, Presdt Johnson,
Sir,

As I see by a recent paper my Husband has been permitted to correspond with Mr Gillet,[1] who is said to be one of the counsel employed for his defence, I am led to hope that I will now be permitted at least to send open letters through the proper channels. My anxiety about his health is intense, and I am seperated from all my children[2] because I had a faint hope that in diminishing my family so much you might perhaps consent to let me go to Mr Davis. I would bear any privations, imprisonment, or restrictions, take and keep any parole, to be with him, even if only for an hour each day. His health is always frail, and I have been used to ministering to him at such times as he has been suffering, and consider it the chief priviledge of my life. Before you refuse me pray remember how very long I have been seperated from him and how much I have suffered.

With the hope that you may answer my petition favorably[3] I am Sir
Very respectfully Your obt sert—
Varina Davis.

ALS, DLC-JP.
1. Ransom H. Gillet (1800–1876), New York lawyer, former congressman, and an official in the Polk administration. *BDAC*.
2. With Davis' capture, Varina, her children, and her mother, were closely confined to Savannah and environs. In late July she sent the two oldest, Margaret (Maggie) (1855–1909) and Jefferson, Jr. (1857–1878) to Canada, accompanied by their grandmother. When Varina was allowed to move in late summer, she had the younger children—William (1861–1872) and Varina (Winnie) (1864–1898)—with her. Monroe et al., *Davis Papers*, 1: 523–24; Ishbell Ross, *First Lady of the South* (New York, 1958), 257, 265–67.
3. Johnson did not answer, though a discussion of the selection of the government's prosecuting team and a possible trial date in the case against Davis had been topics in the cabinet session the day before this letter. Beale, *Welles Diary*, 2: 367–68.

From Alexander Dudley

Washington City D C Augt 30th 1865

To His Excellency Andrew Johnson Prest U S.

Sir

In reply to your inquiry[1] as to whether I had said, while applying at your office for a pardon, that I had been informed by some one in your secretarys office, that I Could obtain a pardon by paying five hundred dollars or any other sum for it, I have to say, that I have never made any such statement.

I further state, that no one in or about your office, has at any time stated to me that I could obtain a pardon by paying for it.

I have said repeatedly, that a proposition had been made to me, by parties applying for pardons to unite with them in employing a pardon Broker, which I had declined to do.

Any statement inconsistent with the above is either a misunderstanding or misrepresentation of me.[2]

I am Very Respectfully
Your obt Svt Alex Dudley

ALS, DLC-JP.
1. Two days earlier Johnson had notified Dudley that a "personal explanation is necessary in connection with your pardon, and I hope that without delay you will be in Washington, where the nature of the explanation will be made known." Johnson to Dudley, Aug. 28, 1865, Tels. Sent, President, Vol. 2 (1865), RG107, NA.
2. Dudley's pardon was restored within a few days. *Cincinnati Enquirer*, Sept. 5, 1865.

From Four Texans

August 30, 1865, Austin, Tex.; Pet, DLC-JP.

James H. Bell, Thomas H. Duval, Elisha M. Pease, and Francis M. White, all unionists, address the President on the "political condition" of Texas. Governor Pendleton Murrah had "issued a call for a Convention, and a proclamation convening the legislature," but eventually he and others fled. Then, "many leading Secessionists" schemed to elect a governor who was well known for his

devotion to the United States, but who "could be induced to accept" secessionist support. This failed, as did also the suggestion that the people hold meetings
in the respective counties and elect delegates to a convention to amend the old
constitution or adopt a new one and reestablish regular state government.
Meanwhile, the people had been told that the "Emancipation Proclamation was
a violation of the Constitutional rights of the Slave States, would be so declared
by the Courts, and that slavery would yet be rescued," or that the U.S. government would "be forced to make compensation to owners." Many were "reluctant to take the oath of amnesty," believing that by doing so they could not
claim such compensation. During the war the press and politicians had tried,
with "a very great degree" of success, to prejudice the people against Andrew
J. Hamilton, the current provisional governor. The "immense geographical
extent" of the state and the "want of mail facilities" make it difficult to dissemi-
nate "intelligence amongst the people." The press of Texas, with a few exceptions, has been disposed "to keep alive, in the minds of the people, a feeling of
discontent with the policy of the general government." Therefore, "the true
friends of the Union," upon Governor Hamilton's arrival, advised him "to take
his measures with great caution, and to allow time for the public mind to become tranquilized" before he called a convention. It was important to organize
a provisional government so that the civil arm might aid the military in the
"suppression of disorder, the protection of property, and above all, for supplying the means of ascertaining the loyal men of the State, to whom the right of
suffrage may safely be extended." The quartet with "great pleasure" expresses
to Johnson their "conviction that Gov. Hamilton had adopted a wise policy,"
and asks for "firm and unwavering support" of the governor "in the arduous
work that lies before him."

From Andrew J. Hamilton

Executive Office Austin Texas
30th Augst 1865

Mr President

It is now more than a month since I wrote to you from Galveston [1]
upon my arrival at that Port: and about a month since my arrival here,
the Capitol of the State. I found the great mass of the people awaiting
with anxiety and some impatience my arrival. They had been for nearly
two months not only without Government but singularly ignorant it
seems as to the designs and purposes of the Government.

This can scarcely excite surprise when it is remembered that the
people of Texas have been since the beginning of the War systemati-
cally excluded from all truthful information in regard to public affairs,
and who were imposed to some extent by the most absurd stories told
them by their late leaders prior to their flight to Mexico—(whither
most of them have gone)—to escape the consequences of their manifold
crimes. [2]

Immediately upon my arrival in the State at Galveston, I issued a
Proclamation a copy of which I herewith enclose,[3] which, I am happy
to say, had as I have abundant reason to believe, the most happy effect
in allaying the fears and anxiety of the public mind and producing in
their stead a hopeful and cheerful temper. My invitation in said Proclamation to the loyal men from different Sections of the State to meet

me at this place and confer with me upon the present and future interests of the State has been responded to with unexpected alacrity; so
much so that I have great Satisfaction in announcing that the work of
reorganizing the Provisional State Government has proceeded with a
rapidity highly Satisfactory. Notwithstanding the immense territory
over which our people are scattered and the entire absence of mail facilities I have been visited by deputations of loyal men from more than
eighty Counties, riding on horse-back in many instances four hundred
miles, who furnished the names of tried and loyal men for county Officers, delighted with the prospect of something like civil Government,
to supercede the long and terrible Military despotism under which they
have suffered so cruelly. They bring me generally a good account of the
feelings and wishes of the people. The masses wish to do right and will
in the end, but they have scarcely had time to break the fetters which
have so long Shackled their minds. They have not yet had opportunity
to learn the extent to which they have been made the dupes of the men
whose lead they followed in the late rebellion. But this information is
being rapidly disseminated even in the absence of mails; and although
the mal-contents—late Slave-ow[n]ers as a class and leading Secession
politicians are exerting a desperate energy to retain their hold upon the
people, it only wants a little time to insure their final emancipation.
The work is now going on most hopefully, but would be greatly accel-
erated by the aid of appliances to which I will call Your Excellency's
attention presently.

It was the concurrent and unanimous opinion of all the Union men
in the State, without an exception so far as I have heard, that it would
not do to hazzard calling a convention at as early a day as has been done
in most of the other States lately in rebellion. There were many reasons
for this. In the first place it will necessarily require two or three months
to enable the people to avail themselves of the oath of amnesty to qualify
them to vote as prescribed in your Proclamation. We are without mail
facilities to enable the people at once to be put in possession of correct
information touching the policy of the Government and its wisdom and
propriety. We have but few Newspapers and they are with two or three
exceptions the organs and instruments of the late military Despots and
still full of the virus of treason, restrained in language by wholesome
fears, but covertly attempting to engender in the public mind distrust
of the Government and its friends. There are so far no U.S. Courts in
operation here and consequently no proceedings instituted against even
the most flagrant sinner, to inspire a proper sense of the crime of treason
in the public mind, and impose a prudent restraint upon the conduct
and language of the evil disposed, especially those who are excluded
from general amnesty.

Thus situated, and being Sustained in my judgment by the United
Voice of the Union men of the State, I have deemed it necessary to

organize a more formal Provisional Government than would under other circumstances have been necessary. The actual condition of the Country seemed to demand the organization of tribunals of justice both civil and criminal.

Crime is rife and private property and individual rights in a great measure disregarded.

This condition of things could only be remedied by military authority or by the enforcement of law.

The Military power would in most cases where it is present be able to correct the most glaring evils, but in a very large majority of the Counties no military force is present. Besides it is most grateful to the people to be permitted once more to look to the laws of the State for protection from wrong and for remedies for rights long denied them: and nothing in my judgment is better calculated to win them back to a full appreciation of the maternal kindness and justice of the Government.

It was indispensibly necessary to create officers of some sort to administer the oath of amnesty to the citizens and make a Register of loyal men authorized to vote for Delegates to a convention—and assessors and collectors of Taxes to raise a revenue to meet current expenses and provide the means to defray the expenses of a convention when called. It involved but little more trouble to provide officers for the administration of justice and this the people every where desired and are more than willing to be taxed to defray the expenses.

Actuated by these considerations I have so organized the Provisional Government of the State, I beleive to the satisfaction of every good man in the State, and without one dollar of expense to the Government of the United States. Even the Secretary of State[4] will not look to the U.S. for his Salary unless for political reasons it should be deemed proper that he should be thus paid. I trust the course thus far pursued will meet your Excellency's approval, as it does that of the loyal people of this State.

I can not say at what time it will be prudent to call a convention, but hope for early indications of correct public sentiment that will justify it. Be assured that no unnecessary delay will happen. But to facilitate such a State of public feeling, I most respectfully, but earnestly urge the importance of setting in motion the Federal Courts in this State. This was directed to be done by your Proclamation of the 17th of June last,[5] but so far no appointments have been made of Marshals and District Attorneys. We have Judges for the two Districts of Texas,—Judge Watrous[6] for the Eastern District and Judge Duval[7] for the Western District, both of whom have remained loyal to the Government of the United States. Judge Watrous has not been in Texas or in the South since the rebellion occurred, but has resided during the whole time I believe in the State of New York.

Judge Duval remained in Texas for a time after the rebellion commenced but was finally driven from the State and from his family on account of his loyalty and was an exile until the war terminated. His loyalty and integrity are well known to the Hon. Joseph Holt, Judge Advocate Gen'l of the U.S. I say unhesitatingly that no better or truer man lives in the Union than Judge D. There can be no objection to him. It is true I heard when I was in Washington in June last, that certain parties were representing that he had held office under the Confederate Government. This is unqualifiedly false. For a short time before he was forced to leave his home in Texas, he was compelled (being poor and destitute of any means of supporting a numerous family) to write as a Clerk in the Land Office of the State of Texas, in order to procure bread for his family, being for the time-being cut off from his Salary as Judge. Said Clerkship is not and never was an office under the State and of course wholly disconnected with the confederate Government. There is not *one loyal* man in Texas who will not in all things endorse Judge Duval.

As to Judge Watrous, he has for many years had a very strong party arrayed against him in Texas and who have sought by memorials to Congress for his impeachments to dismiss him from the Bench;—and I have reason to know that some of those who are hostile to him deprecate the idea of his assuming again his functions as Judge of the Eastern District of this State.

I have no possible interest (personal) or concern in the quarrel between Judge Watrous and his accusers[8] and without personal knowledge of the facts leave the matter to be disposed of in the future in a legitimate way. I confess I cannot see how Judge Watrous can be disposed of otherwise than by successful impeachment or congressional legislation abolishing his District.

In the mean time I cannot concur with those who—however honest in their views—prefer no organization of the Federal Judiciary in our State than that Judge Watrous should be permitted to resume his duties. Parties who are not now in Texas and who have not been here since the rebellion occurred are hardly in a condition to appreciate, as those of us who are engaged in the work of re-organization, the needs of the hour.

I deem it of vital importance that these courts should be set in motion at once. No more potent machinery can be invoked to restrain and punish the only persons from whom serious opposition is to be anticipated. In fact it is the only really effective Agency to humble incorrigible traitors even those who have fled to Mexico leaving property behind will have opportunity through friends to convert personal property and effects.

Besides, although it may not be the policy to proceed to prosecute and confiscate generally the property of those who are excluded from general amnesty, yet it is easy to understand how very different the conduct and influence of that class may be when they are not only liable to such proceedings but courts ready to act and vigilant officers watching their movements.

A movement towards the confiscation of the property of *a few* of the leading rebels—although never consumated—would have a tremendous effect upon the entire class. I feel all this much more strongly than I can express and pray your excellency to appoint the proper officers and direct the immediate organization of the Courts.

I beg also most respectfully to call your Excellency's attention to the condition of the Freedmen in this State and the great necessity existing for official means to prevent the many wrongs and cruelties being perpetrated upon them.

It gives me pleasure to say that some of the late owners are pursuing a humane and wise policy; admitting their freedom and hireing their labour for fair compensation,—but it is also true that many of the late owners—I fear a majority, pursue a very different course.

They seem to be disposed to vent upon the poor negro, all the bitterness which they feel towards the Government, for making him free; and in districts remote from military forces openly deny the negroes freedom—insist that the President's Proclamation of emancipation is but a military order which has spent its force, and the laws of Congress upon the Subject unconstitutional and void &c. &c. and exercising the most rigorous restraints upon the freedom of the negroes. It is undoubtedly true that many Freedmen have been killed by their late master's and very many more greatly abused. If the Freedman's Bureau is to be a permanent thing then it is most important to the interests of the Freedmen and to the well being of Society that proper officers be at once sent to take charge of the matters pertaining to it in Texas.

I must also call your Excellency's attention to the fact that we are entirely without mail facilities. I am aware that we cannot expect much in that way until an appropriation by Congress shall have been made;—but a few lines of greatest importance being established would be a great releif and I trust that the Hon. Post Master General will be able to do this much for our releif.

I beg also to call your Excellency's attention to the matter of recommending applications for special pardon. I have probably recommended thirty out of one hundred and fifty and may when satisfactory evidence is presented me, act favourably on others which I have so far refused. My rule is to recommend in every case where I am well satisfied that the party was never a willing rebel (and, as you know, there are many such cases) or has sorely repented and wishes and intends in perfect good faith to help repairs the wrongs inflicted upon the country. But in cases where I have serious doubts as to the future action of the applicant or when his sins have been enormous I have promptly refused. These men of course will make their representations at Washington, and many of them by the aid of money will be able to present very respectable endorsements and recommendations.

I trust however that they will at least be postponed until the final establishment of civil Government in our State, to the end that they may not be relieved and enfranchised to become active opposers of the Government and its friends at a time when we can least afford it.

I cannot close this communication without doing myself the pleasure of bearing testimony to the uniform kindness courtesy and friendly assistance of the military officers of the Government since my arrival in Texas.

Indeed on reaching New Orleans on my way to Texas, I was placed under many obligations by the kindness and assistance of Major Genl Sheridan.[9] He promptly furnished me transportation to Galveston and issued orders to Major Genl Granger[10] then in Galveston to furnish me transportation and an escort to this place—all of which was done by Genl Granger in the most prompt and obliging manner. I have received assurances from Major Genl Wright[11] now commanding the Department of Texas, and from his Subordinate Generals assurances of their readiness to aid me in every possible way compatible with their duty, in re-establishing order and civil Government in Texas.

In conclusion I will say to your Excellency, that no one knows better than yourself how impossible it is for any one occupying my position to escape malice, hate envy and opposition even from quarters whence it should not come. I feel confident in the support of the loyal men of Texas and the generous support which my humble efforts may deserve at your hands.

Wishing you health to sustain you in your great labours

I have the honor to be
Your Excellency's Obdt Servant. A J Hamilton
Provl. Govr. of Texas

His Excellency Andrew Johnson
President U S Washington

LS, DLC-JP.
1. See Letter from Hamilton, July 24, 1865.
2. Confederate governor Pendleton Murrah and Gens. E. Kirby Smith and John B. Magruder joined the flight to Mexico with Gen. Joseph O. Shelby in June 1865. Charles W. Ramsdell, *Reconstruction in Texas* (New York, 1910), 29–30; Carl Coke Rister, "Carlota, A Confederate Colony in Mexico," *JSH*, 11 (1945): 36–38.
3. A copy of Hamilton's proclamation has not been found in the Johnson Papers, LC. For another opinion on its reception, see Letter from Christopher C. Andrews, July 28, 1865.
4. James H. Bell (1825–1892), a former associate justice of the Texas Supreme Court (1858–64), was appointed secretary of state by Hamilton and served for a little more than a year. Webb and Carroll, *Handbook of Texas*, 1: 141. See also Hamilton to Johnson, Oct. 21, 1865, Johnson Papers, LC.
5. Johnson's proclamation appointing Hamilton provisional governor and setting forth provisions for reorganizing the state.

6. John C. Watrous (1806–1874) had been attorney general of the Republic of Texas (1838–40). Appointed a federal judge before the war, he resumed the bench (1865–69), but subsequently moved to Baltimore. Webb and Carroll, *Handbook of Texas*, 2: 869.

7. Thomas H. Duval (1813–1880), former secretary of the Territory of Florida (1843), secretary of state for Texas (1851), and federal judge for the Western District of Texas (1857–61), had fled the state following secession. Resuming his seat on the bench in 1865, he served until his death. Ibid., 1: 529; *U.S. Off. Reg.* (1867–79).

8. Watrous had been embroiled in controversy during much of his prewar tenure as a federal judge. Actually, Hamilton had been involved as a congressman in 1861 by presenting memorials against him. Webb and Carroll, *Handbook of Texas*, 2: 870.

9. Philip H. Sheridan.

10. Gordon Granger.

11. Horatio G. Wright (1820–1899), a regular army officer, was a division commander at Gettysburg and served in the Virginia campaigns as corps commander under Sheridan. At war's end he was chief of the Department of Texas, returning ultimately to the corps of engineers. Warner, *Blue*.

From Rutherford B. Hayes

Cincinnati Ohio
30th August 1865

Sir

I have the honor to request a pardon for Guy M Bryan,[1] a Secessionist of Texas.

I know Mr Bryan intimately. He is an upright and truthful man. He will hereafter be a loyal and valuable citizen of the United States. He has made the proper application and taken the prescribed oath. He will keep it faithfully and in the right spirit. He served as a major and Colonel in the Rebel service but never persecuted or oppressed Union people; on the contrary he protected them from persecution.

I shall regard as a great personal favor the granting of Mr Bryan's application.[2]

Respectfully R. B. Hayes
M C 2d Dist of Ohio

To President Andrew Johnson Washington D C

ALS, DNA-RG94, Amnesty Papers (M1003, Roll 52), Tex., Guy M. Bryan.

1. Bryan (1821–1901), a Mexican War veteran, planter, state legislator, and congressman, had been a Confederate staff officer and organizer of the Texas Cotton Bureau. *BDAC*.

2. He was pardoned on September 14, 1865. *House Ex. Docs.*, 39 Cong., 2 Sess., No. 116, p. 54 (Ser. 1293).

To William W. Holden

Executive Office, Washington, D.C.,
Aug't 30 1865.

To Gov W. W. Holden, Raleigh, N.C.

Maj Gen Meade has been sent South for the purpose of inspecting all the troops with power to assign them as the interest of the country seems to demand. I hope you will see Gen Meade and confer with him freely as to the disposition of the forces in North Carolina. I have no doubt all will be arranged satisfactorily to the people. I hope all is going on right.

Andrew Johnson President U.S.

Tel, DNA-RG107, Tels. Sent, President, Vol. 2 (1865).

To Hugh McCulloch

Executive Mansion, Washington, D.C.
Aug't 30 1865.

Sir:

You will please not authorize the shipment of any shot guns South, until I see you on the subject. There is one reason for making this request.[1]

Very Respectfully, Andrew Johnson

To the Secretary of the Treasury.

LS, DNA-RG56, Misc. Div., Claims for Cotton and Captured and Abandoned Property.
   1. An endorsement on Johnson's request read: "Covered by Circular of Septem 1." On that date, McCulloch, as a precautionary measure, required anyone desiring to transport "guns, pistols and ammunition" into the former Confederacy, to submit a written application to the Treasury Department for approval. By late October 1865, McCulloch modified his order to include "blasting powder and fuses for mining purposes," and directed that customs collectors would henceforth grant permits. Circulars of Sept. 1, 15, Oct. 23, 1865, Circular Lets. Sent (T Ser.), RG56, NA.

From Rachel Parker[1]

Lake Village N.H.
August 30. 1865.

To President Johnson
Dear sir

I was sold from Charleston S.C. 17 years ago away from my Parents, 3 Brothers and one sister. Was sold to a man in New Orleans whre I was kept a slave until Gen Butler took possession of the city. I then escaped from bondage and took refuge in Federal lines. I remained at Camp Pprupt [Parapet] until I had an opportunity to come North. I came here with the 15th N H V.[2] During the 17 years I had not heard from one of my relitives. This springe I sent a letter to the Christian Commision,[3] requesting them to search for my relitives. The did so and found my Father & 2 Brothers & sister. What joy it brought to this lone heart but my poor Mother they write me was sold to Savannah. They have not heard from her for 8 years. My Father is very desireous for me to go Charleston that he may se me before he dies. I do want to go and see my Father, Brothers & sister.

My object in writing to you is to ask you to grant me and my little girl a free pass to Charleston. Will you please be so kind.[4]

I will enclose to you my picture so you may not doubt me. You can do with it as you please.

Yours with respect Rachel Parker
Lake Vill. N H

L, DNA-RG105, Records of the Commr., Lets. Recd. (M752, Roll 16).

1. Not identified.

2. The 15th New Hampshire Volunteers served in several posts around New Orleans—including Camp Parapet, La.—and in the Port Hudson campaign before returning home and being mustered out on August 13, 1863. Dyer, *Compendium*, 1352.

3. Initially organized under the aegis of the Young Men's Christian Association for the benefit of soldiers, this organization later focused on aiding black refugees. McFeely, *Yankee Stepfather*, 24; McPherson, *Ordeal By Fire*, 386.

4. Although John Aldrich, a former major in the 15th N.H. Vols. from Lake Village, endorsed Parker as a "respectable woman & well worthy any favor you may see fit to grant," her request for transportation was denied.

From Lewis E. Parsons

Montgomery, Ala., August 30, 1865.

His Excellency the President:

Sir:

There are parts of this State in which civil authority is insufficient without aid from the military arm to enforce law and protect the people, white and black, from violence. Some gangs of desperadoes can only be found by hunting them down. The State is divided into four military districts, and Major General Woods[1] commands the whole, his headquarters at Mobile. This renders prompt action in some cases impossible. Brigadier General Swayne,[2] assistant commissioner Freedmen's Bureau, whose headquarters are here, applied some time since to have the second Maine cavalry, now at Barrancas, Florida, report to him for the purpose of taking immediate action in all cases requiring it, and that he may be able to prevent crimes, stationing them at proper points in the State. I am acting in concert with the general to secure these objects, and therefore respectfully and earnestly urge that this or a similar force may be ordered to report to him at once.[3]

Respectfully, Lewis E. Parsons,
Provisional Governor.

Senate Ex. Docs., 39 Cong., 1 Sess. No. 26, pp. 244–45 (Ser. 1237).
    1. Charles R. Woods (1827–1885), a West Point graduate, had been a division commander under W. T. Sherman. Warner, *Blue*.
    2. Wager Swayne (1834–1902), a Columbus, Ohio, lawyer, was promoted major general of volunteers in 1866. Ibid.
    3. Johnson's answer of September 1 reassured the governor that "All that can be will be done." In a separate telegram of the same date Johnson suggested to Parsons the formation of "an armed mounted *posse comitatus*" in each county. Tels. Sent, President, Vol. 2 (1865), RG107, NA; Johnson Papers, LC.

To Carl Schurz

Executive Office, Washington, D.C.,
Aug't 30 1865.

To Maj Gen Carl Schurz,
Vicksburg, Miss

I presume Gen Slocum will issue no order interfering with Governor Sharkey in restoring the functions of the State Government without first consulting the Government, giving the reasons for such proposed interference. It is believed there can be organized in each County a force of citizens or Militia to suppress crime, preserve order, and enforce the Civil authority of the State and of the United States, which would enable the Federal Government to reduce the Army, and withdraw to a great extent the forces from the States, thereby reducing the enormous expenses of the Government. If there was any danger from an organization of the citizens for the purposes indicated, the Military are there to detect and suppress on the first appearance any move insurrectionary in its character. One great object is to induce the people to come forward in the defense of the State and Federal Government. General Washington declared that the people or the Militia was the Army of the Constitution or the Army of the United States, and as soon as it is practicable, the original design of the Government must be resumed and the Government administered upon the principles of the Great Chart of Freedom handed down to the people by the founders of the Republic. The people must be trusted with their Government, and if trusted my opinion is they will act in good faith and restore their former Constitutional relations with all the States composing the Union. The main object of Major General Carl Schurz's mission to the South was to aid as far as practicable in carrying out the policy adopted by the Government for restoring the States to their former relations with the Federal Government. It is hoped such aid has been given. The proclamation authorizing restoration of State Governments requires the Military to aid the Provisional Governor in the performance of his duties as prescribed in the proclamation and in no manner to interfere or throw impediments in the way of consumating the object of his appointment, at least without advising the Government of the intended interference.

Andrew Johnson
President U.S.

Tel, DNA-RG107, Tels. Sent, President, Vol. 2 (1865).

From William L. Sharkey

Executive Office, Jackson, Miss.,
August 30th 1865.

His Excellency Andrew Johnson President &C
Sir

I take the liberty of introducing to you my friend & relation, Genl. W R Peck,[1] who is a son of Judge Peck[2] of east Tennessee, who is probably an old acquaintance of yours. Genl. Peck desires very much to have an interview with you, and will himself explain his object. I will take the liberty of saying however that he is desirous of being a loyal citizen, and fully acquesces in the changed condition of affairs. He feels the more solicitude in accomplishing his purpose on account of his Father and mother who are now old and destitute, and depend upon him for a support, as they have no other son who can aid them. Some time since I presented his case to Mr. Speed, but received no reply. I hope it may be in your power to aid him consistently with your sense of duty.[3]

General Peck has shown me a letter from East Tennessee which represents a terrible State of things there.

Very respectfully Your Obt Servt.
W. L. Sharkey
Provisional Govr of Miss

ALS, DNA-RG94, Amnesty Papers (M1003, Roll 29), La., William Raine Peck.

1. William R. Peck (1818–1871), a planter in Louisiana since the early 1840s, rose from private to brigadier general in the Confederate army. He claimed to have known Johnson "well in my early youth when a student at the College of Dr Coffin near Greenville Tenn." Warner, *Gray*; Peck to Johnson, June 6, 1865, Amnesty Papers (M1003, Roll 29), La., William Raine Peck, RG94, NA.

2. Jacob Peck (1779–1869), a lawyer and state senator, was a member of the Tennessee supreme court (1822–34) and publisher of a volume of the court's decisions. *BDTA*, 1: 577.

3. During the succeeding weeks, General Peck tried at least twice to see the President regarding his pardon. Finally, on October 13, 1865, his pardon was issued. *Washington Morning Chronicle*, Sept. 28, Oct. 12, 1865; Amnesty Papers (M1003, Roll 29), La., William Raine Peck, RG94, NA.

From William L. Sharkey

Jackson Miss Aug 30 1865.

A Johnson President

In our last interview you distinctly stated to me that I could organize the militia to suppress crime if necessary, Deeming it necessary I issued a proclamation on the 19th inst calling on two companies one of Cavalry to organize in each Co for the detection of criminals the prevention of crime & the preservation of order, not called into actual service. Gen Slocum has thought proper to issue an order to prevent any such organization & to arrest those who attempt it. His chief reasons seem to be because I did not consult him. Here is a collision that must be settled & it rests with you to do it. I wish to be able to vindicate myself when trouble comes as we apprehend it will. Copies will be forwarded.[1]

W. L. Sharkey

Tel, DLC-JP.

1. Johnson's telegram to Schurz was sent before Sharkey's wire was received. See Telegram from Sharkey, August 31, 1865.

From Robert S.S. Tharin[1]

White House, Aug. 30, 1865.

Your Excellency

Having intimated that I should search the record of the vacancies in my state at a general reception on Saturday last and having last night appointed a special time—today—when you would see and hear me, I most respectfully inform you that the U.S. District Judgeships for South Carolina are vacant and I hereby apply for that in which the city of Charleston is included. The accompanying papers I have the honor to submit to prove my sufferings on account of my pronounced Unionism where Unionism was most unpopular,[2] and beg to subscribe myself

Yours with reverence and respect, R. S. Tharin, of Charleston, S.C.

To His Excellency President Johnson.

ALS, DNA-RG60, Appt. Files for Judicial Dists., S.C., R. S. Tharin.

1. Tharin (1830–fl1891), Wetumpka, Ala., lawyer, served briefly as a Union soldier before publishing *Arbitrary Arrests in the South* (1863). For many years after the war he resided in Charleston, before becoming a clerk in the Sixth Auditor's Office at Washington, D.C. *Appleton's Cyclopaedia; NUC; U.S. Off. Reg.* (1889–91).

2. In an accompanying affidavit, Tharin was described as the "champion of the middle, or non-slaveowning class," who was "brutally treated . . . by a mob of politically inflamed men, in 1861" and finally forced to seek Federal protection. "His Unionism is considered the most pronounced and his course the most fearless and consistent of any Unionist" in Alabama. Nevertheless, he failed to obtain the office he was seeking. Affi-

davit of Alexander W. Tharin, July 21, 1865, Appt. Files for Judicial Dists., S.C., R. S. Tharin, RG60, NA.

From William G. Brownlow

Knoxville, August 31st, 1865.

President Johnson:

Before leaving for Nashville, I desire to write you a line. I have been as high up as Watauga River and I find all quiet and prosperous. The Franchise Act[1] was observed in East Tennessee.

But we have a bad state of things here. Our 8th, 9th & 13th Regiments are here to be mustered out, and there is a bad state of feeling between them and the *colored troops*. The negroes are too ready to shoot and use their bayonets,[2] and we are threatened with serious consequences. To be candid with you, we need no troops of any color in East Tennessee, and especially ought colored troops to be removed. Let them go to the rebellious portions of Tennessee, or to the Cotton States, where the spirit of the Rebellion is kept up. East Tennessee can now take care of herself, and will do better without troops than with them, I am confident. And I know I speak the sentiments of the Union men, from Taylorsville to Chattanooga.[3]

Wishing you health and success, I have the honor to be,

Very truly, &c. W. G. Brownlow

Governor &c, &c.

ALS, DLC-JP.

1. The 1865 franchise bill limited suffrage to unconditional Union men. The August congressional elections were the first test of the law. Alexander, *Reconstruction*, 77–78.

2. The previous day Brownlow's newspaper had reported several local incidents involving black volunteers. One soldier had "shot and killed" a veteran of the 8th Tenn. Cav. at the Loudon depot. Another had stabbed a member of the 9th Tenn. Cav. on Gay Street in Knoxville. The editor decried both murders, objecting "to the freedom with which" black troops wielded "their bayonets and level[ed] their muskets at white men." *Knoxville Whig and Rebel Ventilator*, Aug. 30, 1865.

3. On September 6, 1865, Johnson telegraphed that he "had just anticipated the subject referred to in your letter by dispatching to General Thomas to relieve East Tennessee of the difficulty." The President added that he had "received various accounts from East Tennessee all confirming and recommending the suggestions made" by Brownlow. Tels. Sent, President, Vol. 2 (1865), RG107, NA.

From Edward H. East

Nashville Aug 31/65

Dear Sir

I herewith enclose to you at the request of the assessor's and collectors, a division of the state creating the different District for Internal Revenue Assessor's and collectors.[1] I have made 8 divisions the same number as of Congressional District, but did not adopt the Congressional District, because of the fact, that some of them extend across the entire state and are too difficult of access. The Divisions made, look to the means of transportation from one point in the District to the other, by Railroads, Rivers, and other roads and facilities of Subordinates to report to the principals of the District. Also it is about as fair a distribution, with relation to the poeple territory and amount of Taxes to be collected as can well be made. I have also taken the liberty of writing names for the different positions in that connection. I do not know that all these Gentlemen will accept or desire the positions, except Messrs Gibbs Ralston and Ramsey[2] and these Gentlemen desire the appointment and will make good officers I doubt not. I have omitted to name any one, for the two East Tennessee Districts and the Montgomery District. The latter because I did not know any one who desired it, and who could be properly recommended. And the former because I thought you knew, better than any other.

I am Resp Edward H East

To The President of United States

ALS, DLC-JP.
1. Not found.
2. Theodore H. Gibbs (1806–1886), a "Machinist" or "Wool Carder," who had been a Lincoln elector; possibly Robert S. Raulston (1806–1867), a Marion County farmer-lawyer, currently in the state house; and Shelbyville resident Joseph Ramsey, who in March 1867 became collector for the 4th District. Irene M. Alexander and Carrie H. Gresham, comps., *At Rest: Cemetery Records of Lawrence County, Tennessee* (Lawrenceburg, Tenn., 1968), 39; 1850 Census, Tenn., Lewis, 8th Dist., 808; (1860), Wayne, 14th Dist., 190; *Nashville Times and True Union*, Nov. 28, 1864; W. G. Brownlow et al., to Johnson, Sept. 2, 1865, Appts., Internal Revenue Service, Assessor, Tenn., 5th Dist., T. H. Gibbs, RG56, NA; *BDTA*, 1: 607–8; Appt. Bk. 4: 228, Ser. 6B, Johnson Papers, LC.

From William A. Hill

August 31, 1865, Fort Smith, Ark.; LS(X), DNA-RG94, Amnesty Papers (M1003, Roll 13), Ark., William A. Hill.

Fifty-five-year-old "unconditional union man," who "opposed by my vote and influence the Cesssion" of Arkansas and took the oath on December 8, 1863, but "went south for the purpose of preserving my personal property . . . principaly in horses" which "were constantly being stolen," has returned home, and, falling under the 14th exception of the Amnesty Proclamation, prays for pardon. [Pardoned November 10, 1865.]

To George G. Meade

Executive Office, Washington, D.C.,
August 31st 1865.

To Major General Meade U.S.A.
Hilton Head S.C.

Governor Perry will not be interfered with in his work of Restoration by the Military Authorities without orders from me upon presentation of the facts in the case and nature of interference proposed.

Andrew Johnson Prest U.S.

Tel, DNA-RG107, Tels. Sent, President, Vol. 2 (1865).

From Armistead T.M. Rust[1]

Washington, Aug 31, 1865—
To His Excellency President Andrew Johnson,

Your Excellency kindly instructed me yesterday to leave my name with a statement of my case.

My property has been confiscated in Judge Underwood's[2] court to be sold by the marshal on twenty days notice.

Genl. Howard has just issued an order to his assistant commissioner to take immediate possession of my property for the use of freedmen &c.

This will turn my wife and five children out of doors without shelter or means of subsistence.

My situation is so distressing and case so urgent that I pray your Excellency's prompt and effective interposition.

I most respectfully refer to my petition and papers on file in the Attorney General's office for further particulars.

My sincere desire is to do every thing in my power to support your Excellency's public policy as becomes a good citizen. I have the honor to be with the highest respect your Excellency's obedient servant[3]

A. T. M. Rust—
Near Leesburg, Loudoun County, Virginia—

ALS, DNA-RG94 Amnesty Papers (M1003, Roll 68), Va., A.T.M. Rust.

1. Rust (c1819–1887), a West Point graduate who resigned twenty years earlier, had been a militia commander and colonel in the Confederate judge advocate's office. *West Point Register* (1970), 234; Amnesty Papers (M1003, Roll 68), Va., A.T.M. Rust, RG94, NA.

2. John C. Underwood.

3. On September 2, 1865, Johnson signed an endorsement referring Rust's letter to the attorney general, "with the request that a warrant for pardon issue in this case if the circumstances thereof justify favorable action." Four days later the pardon was granted. Amnesty Papers (M1003, Roll 68), Va., A.T.M. Rust, RG94, NA; *House Ex. Docs.*, 40 Cong., 2 Sess., No. 16, p. 86 (Ser. 1330).

From William L. Sharkey

Jackson Miss Aug 31, 1865

His Excellency A. Johnson

May I publish your dispatch of yesterday to Genl Schurz, a copy of which has been furnished me? It will do great good. It will soothe a troubled public mind. It will give implicit Confidence in you.[1]

W. L. Sharkey
Prov Govr

Tel, DNA-RG107, Tels. Recd., President, Vol. 4 (1865–66).

1. Two days later, the President telegraphed: "My dispatch was not intended for publication but you can make such use of it as you deem best." In a second transmission on September 2, Johnson ordered Gen. Henry W. Slocum to revoke any order that countermanded Sharkey's August 19 proclamation regarding militia companies. Johnson to Sharkey, Sept. 2, 1865, and Reuben D. Mussey to Slocum, Sept. 2, 1865, Ser. 3B, Johnson Papers, LC.

From Mark R. Watkinson[1]

[ca. August 31, 1865][2]

Andrew Johnson, Pres't U.S.

Honored Sir.

Permit a few words from a disinterested observer. A native of the North, but having resided South, let me say that New England would sooner reach the judgment of common sense touching re-construction, if 100,000 colored troops could be a few months quartered in the principal towns of Maine, Massachusetts, and Vermont. Or if 500,000 of the helpless old blacks of the South could be indiscriminately scattered through those six New England States. "A hint to the wise is sufficient."

Unquestionably such men as James Redpath,[3] the English Radical, at Charleston, South Carolina, are using our National troops to breed incessant mischiefs. Better far withdraw every soldier from the South, if re-construction is desired.

There is conservatism in the South, but the bayonet is in its way.

Yours, with purest motive, M. R. Watkinson
Minister of the Gospel,
A loser by rebel confiscation at Portsmouth,
Virginia, but now of Camden, N.J.

ALS, DLC-JP.

1. Watkinson (b. 1824), a New Jersey native, had been a Baptist minister in Portsmouth, Va. His proposal of a motto for U.S. coins led to Congress' adoption of "In God We Trust." 1860 Census, Va., Norfolk, Portsmouth, Jackson Ward, 183; *Philadelphia Sunday Bulletin*, "Suburban West" section, Apr. 12, 1964.

2. The presidential stamp indicates that Johnson's office received this letter on this date. The provenance of the letter is uncertain.

3. Scottish-born abolitionist who became superintendent of freedmen's schools in Florida, Georgia, and South Carolina.

Appendix I

[Adapted from Robert Sobel, ed., *Biographical Directory of the United States Executive Branch, 1874–1971* (Westport, Conn., 1971).]

Office	Name
Secretary of State, 1865–69	William H. Seward
Secretary of the Treasury, 1865–69	Hugh McCulloch
Secretary of War, 1865–68	Edwin M. Stanton
Secretary of War ad interim, 1867–68	Ulysses S. Grant
Secretary of War, 1868–69	John M. Schofield
Attorney General, 1865–66	James Speed
Attorney General, 1866–68	Henry Stanbery
Attorney General ad interim, 1868*	Orville H. Browning
Attorney General, 1868–69	William M. Evarts
Postmaster General, 1865–66	William Dennison
Postmaster General, 1866–69	Alexander W. Randall
Secretary of the Navy, 1865–69	Gideon Welles
Secretary of the Interior, 1865	John P. Usher
Secretary of the Interior, 1865–66	James Harlan
Secretary of the Interior, 1866–69	Orville H. Browning

*from March 13, 1868, when Stanbery resigned, until July 20, 1868, when Evarts assumed office, Browning discharged the duties of attorney general in addition to his functions as head of the Interior Department.

Appendix II

PROCLAMATIONS AND EXECUTIVE ORDERS (MAY–AUGUST 1865)

[Asterisks indicate items printed in this volume; all are printed in James D. Richardson, comp., *A Compilation of the Messages and Papers of the Presidents* (10 vols., Washington, D.C., 1896–99), Volume 6.]

Date	Proclamation	Richardson, *Messages*
May 2	* Proclamation of Rewards for Arrest of Sundry Confederates	307–8
May 10	Proclamation *re* Insurgent Cruisers	308–9
May 22	Proclamation Opening Certain Ports	309–10
May 29	* Amnesty Proclamation	310–12
May 29	* Proclamation Establishing Government for North Carolina	312–14
June 13	Proclamation Establishing Government for Mississippi	314–16
June 13	Proclamation Removing Trade Restrictions East of the Mississippi	317–18
June 17	Proclamation Establishing Government for Georgia	318–20
June 17	Proclamation Establishing Government for Texas	321–23
June 21	Proclamation Establishing Government for Alabama	323–25
June 23	Proclamation Removing Blockade of All Ports	325
June 24	Proclamation Removing Trans-Mississippi Trade Restrictions	326
June 30	Proclamation Establishing Government for South Carolina	326–28
July 13	Proclamation Establishing Government for Florida	329–31
Aug. 29	Proclamation Removing All Trade Restrictions	331

Executive Order

Date		Richardson, *Messages*
May 1	* Order for Military Trial of Presidential Assassins	334–35
May 4	* Order *re* Closing for Lincoln Funeral	335
May 9	* Order Restoring Virginia	337–38
May 31	* Order *re* Closing Federal Offices	339

Appendix III

PRESIDENTIAL RECONSTRUCTION
UNDER JOHNSON'S PLAN, 1865

Provisional Governor Appointed	Convention Delegates Election	Convention Dates	Governor/ Legislature Election	Legislature Convened	Governor Inaugurated/ Took Office
ALABAMA					
Lewis E. Parsons (June 21)	Aug. 31	Sept. 12–30	Nov. 6	Nov. 20	Robert M. Patton (Dec. 13/20)
FLORIDA					
William Marvin (July 13)	Oct. 10	Oct. 25– Nov. 8	Nov. 29	Dec. 20	David S. Walker (Dec. 20)
GEORGIA					
James Johnson (June 17)	Oct. 4	Oct. 25– Nov. 8	Nov. 15	Dec. 4	Charles J. Jenkins (Dec. 14/19)
MISSISSIPPI					
William L. Sharkey (June 13)	Aug. 7	Aug. 14–24	Oct. 2	Oct. 16	Benjamin G. Humphreys (Oct. 16/ Dec. 25)
NORTH CAROLINA					
William W. Holden (May 29)	Sept. 21	Oct. 2–20	Nov. 9	Nov. 27	Jonathan Worth (Dec. 15/28)
SOUTH CAROLINA					
Benjamin F. Perry (June 30)	Sept. 4	Sept. 13–27	Oct. 18	Oct. 25	James L. Orr (Nov. 29/ Dec. 21)
TEXAS					
Andrew J. Hamilton (June 17)	Jan. 8, 1866	Feb. 7– April 2, 1866	June 25, 1866	Aug. 6, 1866	James W. Throckmorton (Aug. 9, 1866)

Appendix IV

SAMPLE PAROLES

Parole for William W. Boyce

Executive Office
Washington D C
June 8, 1865

William Boyce

Permission is hereby granted to *William W. Boyce* of South Carolina to return to his home upon his Parole of Honor that he will faithfully observe and obey the Laws of the United States and that he will endeavor to cultivate and diffuse a Loyal Sentiment among the people of his State and that he will aid to the extent of his ability in the restoration of South Carolina to her legitimate relations to the other States and to the Federal Government and that he report to me weekly his whereabouts and what progress he is making.

The Quartermaster's Department will furnish him transportation to his home.

Andrew Johnson
President U.S.

LBcopyS, DLC-JP3A.

Parole for Fayette McMullen

August 17th [186]5

Fayette McMullen of Virginia is hereby permitted to pass through and remain in the United States upon the condition that he takes the oath of allegiance, and gives his parole of honor to conduct himself as a loyal citizen and that he reports monthly by letter to me. While complying with these conditions he will not be molested or interfered with by the Military or Civil authorities of the United States.

Andrew Johnson
President U.S.

LBcopyS, DLC-JP3A.

Parole for John Overton

August 19th [186]5

John Overton of Tennessee is hereby paroled upon condition that he will deport himself as a loyal citizen of the United States and, while so conducting himself he shall not be molested nor interfered with by the Military or Civil authorities of the United States.

President U.S.

LBcopy, DLC-JP3A.

Index

Primary identification of a person is indicated by an italic *n* following the page reference. Identifications found in earlier volumes of the *Johnson Papers* are shown by providing volume and page numbers, within parentheses, immediately after the name of the individual. In Volume 8 the only footnotes which have been indexed are those that constitute identification notes.

"A Plebian": from, 147
Abbey, Richard, 420, 421*n*
Abell, Edmund, 6, 8*n*, 269
Able, Barton, 299*n*; from, 298–99
Adams, Charles Francis (1: 147*n*), 88
Adams, John Quincy, 396
Agawam, USS, 106
Aiken, William, 25, 25*n*, 283, 348
Alabama: appointments in, 75, 158, 648; attitudes in, 297, 322–23, 635; conditions in, 278, 312–13, 597; convention in, 583; cotton in, 158, 582; elections in, 566; provisional government in, 120–21; provisional governor for, 45, 103, 170, 172, 183–84, 207, 216, 313, 323; railroads in, 425; restoration in, 182–83, 183–84; unionists in, 145, 207, 239, 582–83
Alabama, CSS, 86–87
Albright, Charles: from, 368
Alexander, A.J. (or B.S. or B.), 28
Alexander, George W., 584
Allen, Nimrod B., 274
Allen, William W.: from, 476
Allgaier, John, 495, 559, 560*n*
Allis, H. B.: from, 490
Allison, Abraham K., 101, 101*n*
Allison, Richard T.: from, 164
Alston, W., 524
Alward, Dennis R., 528, 528*n*
Ames, Edward, 391
Amnesty: northern opinion on, 185, 196–97; payment for, 613; proposed, 127; revocation of, 92–93, 619, 673; universal urged, 505
  applications, 578; from Alabama, 142–45, 166, 199, 337, 425, 440, 457–58, 476, 529, 550, 559, 588–89, 641, 649, 668; from Arkansas, 202, 287, 288, 300, 332, 337, 408, 617–18, 687; from D.C., 608–9, 662; from Florida, 268–69, 287; from Georgia, 164, 171–72, 202–3, 237–38, 319, 357–60, 466, 497, 567–68, 595–96, 643–44, 647, 662, 663–64, 672; from Kentucky, 362, 426–28; from Louisiana, 214–15, 299, 423, 547–48, 684; from Maryland, 167, 267, 320, 372, 430; from

Mississippi, 348, 623–25, 649; from North Carolina, 223, 249, 303–4, 368, 372, 480, 515, 552, 590–94, 594, 622; from South Carolina, 193–94, 264, 348, 434, 509–10, 536, 554, 626–27; from Tennessee, 109, 155, 158–59, 161, 178–79, 188–90, 191, 206–7, 277, 279–80, 316–17, 331, 334–35, 363, 365–66, 391, 483–84, 494–95, 498–99, 556–57; from Texas, 244, 324–25, 351–52, 431–32, 435, 576, 680; from Virginia, 45, 156, 164, 164–65, 232, 254, 256, 262–63, 269, 271, 271–72, 302, 335, 382–83, 492, 539, 570, 570–71, 606, 613, 638
  recommendations: from Arkansas, 314, 356, 490; from Georgia, 424, 620, 623; from Louisiana, 538; from North Carolina, 463–64; from South Carolina, 511; from Tennessee, 386, 456, 485; from Texas, 459–61, 612–13; from Virginia, 354–55, 369–70, 387, 449
Amnesty oath, 129, 137; administration of, 39–40, 44, 78, 107, 293, 356, 409, 441, 457, 467, 540, 671, 676
Amnesty Proclamation, 128–30; interpretation of exceptions, 374–75; reaction to, 201, 322, 371–72, 461–62
Anderson, Ephraim F., 501, 501*n*
Anderson, Larz (4: 485*n*), 169
Anderson, Robert (4: 113*n*), 362
Andrew, James T., 635
Andrew, John A. (7: 415*n*), 333; from, 278
Andrews, Christopher C. (6: 435*n*): from, 59, 278, 491
Andros, Richard S.S., 603
Appointments: diplomatic, 65, 387, 475; interior, 86–88, 265–66, 598; judicial, 19, 32–33, 34, 38, 54, 58–59, 75, 100, 113, 170–71, 179–80, 198, 243, 246, 262, 268, 307, 310–11, 336, 388, 391, 412, 448, 450, 451, 481, 494, 502, 508–9, 599, 611–12, 685; military, 108; post office, 116, 122–23, 270, 276, 354, 378, 379, 391, 424–25, 439, 450, 506, 512–13; treasury, 32, 50, 79, 89,